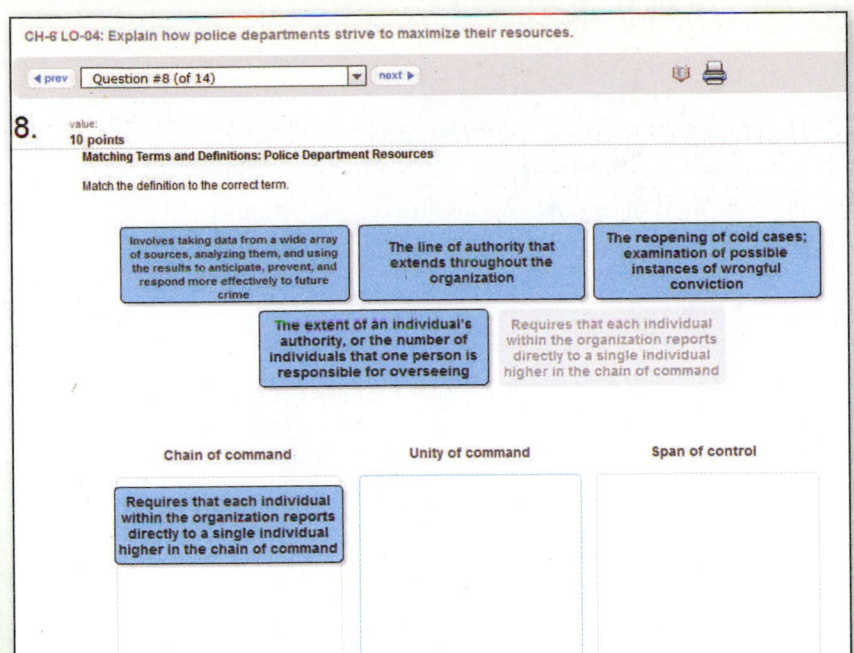

CH-6 LO-04: Explain how police departments strive to maximize their resources.

◀ prev   Question #8 (of 14) ▼   next ▶

8. value:
10 points

Matching Terms and Definitions: Police Department Resources

Match the definition to the correct term.

Involves taking data from a wide array of sources, analyzing them, and using the results to anticipate, prevent, and respond more effectively to future crime	The line of authority that extends throughout the organization	The reopening of cold cases; examination of possible instances of wrongful conviction
The extent of an individual's authority, or the number of individuals that one person is responsible for overseeing	Requires that each individual within the organization reports directly to a single individual higher in the chain of command	

Chain of command	Unity of command	Span of control
Requires that each individual within the organization reports directly to a single individual higher in the chain of command		

Criminal Justice—ranging from multiple-choice questions, to drag-and-drop exercises, to critical thinking questions based on current events— directly correspond with the textbook via the chapter-opening learning objectives presented in *Criminal Justice*, First Edition. Students' results are reported directly to the instructor's gradebook.

LearnSmart

This groundbreaking adaptive learning system, tied directly to the textbook, helps students know what they know while guiding them to experience and learn important concepts that they need to know for success—both in their course and in the future.

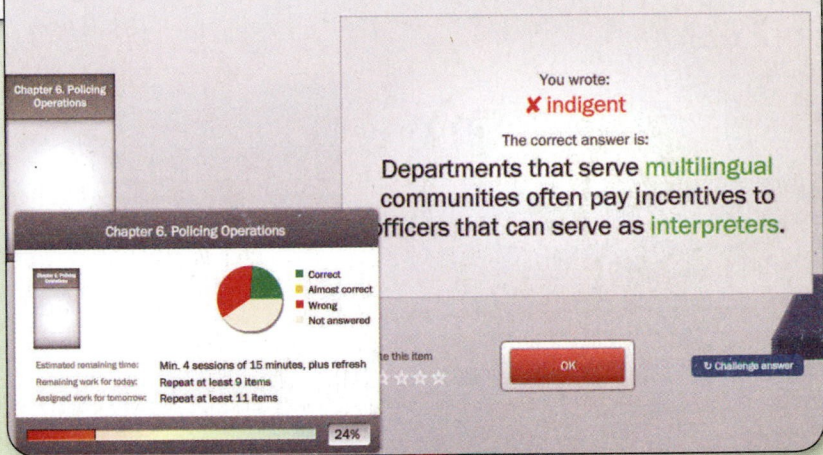

Video Program from CNN News

Connect Criminal Justice includes a suite of new videos from CNN. Videos are tied directly to chapter learning objectives and include supporting pedagogy so they can be assigned within Connect. Results are uploaded directly to the instructor's gradebook.

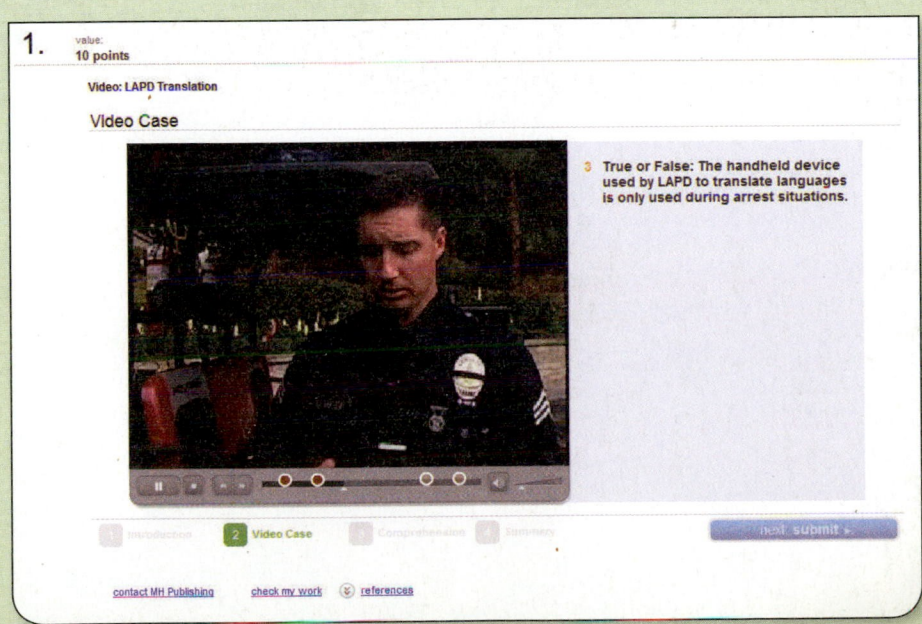

EXPERIENCE CRIMINAL JUSTICE

NICOLE HENDRIX

Radford University

McGraw Hill

Connect
Learn
Succeed™

The McGraw·Hill Companies

EXPERIENCE CRIMINAL JUSTICE, FIRST EDITION

ISBN   978-0-07-814090-7
MHID   0-07-814090-0

Senior Vice President, Products & Markets: *Kurt L. Strand*
Vice President, General Manager: *Michael Ryan*
Vice President, Content Production & Technology Services:
  Kimberly Meriwether David
Managing Director: *Gina Boedeker*
Brand Manager: *Bill Minick*
Director of Development: *Dawn Groundwater*
Content Development Editor: *Susan Messer*
Editorial Coordinator: *Fiso Takirambudde*
Digital Product Analyst: *John Brady*
Digital Development Editor: *Meghan Campbell*
Marketing Manager: *Caroline McGillen*
Marketing Coordinator: *Marcus Opsal*

Director, Content Production: *Terri Schiesl*
Project Manager: *Anne Fuzellier*
Buyer: *Nicole Baumgartner*
Designer: *Debra Kubiak*
Cover/Interior Designers: *Jane Hambleton,*
  Cuttriss & Hambleton/Debra Kubiak
Content Licensing Specialist: *Jeremy Chesareck*
Photo Researcher: *Ira Roberts*
Media Project Manager: *Katie Klochan*
Typeface: *10/12 Minion Pro Regular*
Compositor: *Thompson Type*
Printer: *R.R. Donnelley Willard*

Cover images: ©iStockphoto.com/ThePokerMan, ©iStockphoto.com/NickS, ©iStockphoto.com/Djgunner, ©iStockphoto.com/Syldavia, ©iStockphoto.com/VladimirCetinski, ©iStockphoto.com, HadelProductions

All credits appearing on page 391 are considered to be an extension of the copyright page.

Library of Congress Cataloging-in-Publication Data
Hendrix, Nicole.
  Experience criminal justice / Nicole Hendrix. — 1st ed.
      p. cm.
  Includes bibliographical references and index.
  ISBN 978-0-07-814090-7
  1. Criminal justice, Administration of—United States.   I. Title.
  HV9950.H466   2013
  364.973—dc23

2012038222

CONTENTS IN BRIEF

CONTENTS

PART THREE   THE COURTS   197

PART FOUR   CORRECTIONS   289

A NOTE FROM THE AUTHOR

Each semester, like many faculty members around the country, I begin by telling my students that we are all going to introduce ourselves, to share something about ourselves, and finally, to tell why we became interested in criminal justice. I go first. I usually say that I have always been interested in the machinery of the criminal justice system, fascinated by news and media depictions of crime and justice, and intrigued by the perception that some parts of the process work and others do not seem to work at all. It was an introductory course, much like the ones I teach, that opened the world of criminal justice to me and inspired as much as frustrated me about the criminal justice process.

This introductory book stems from my own experiences—both as a student and as a teacher. When I was a student, the core introductory material gave me a foundation for examining complex and critical issues in criminal justice. Now, as an instructor, I rely on this material as groundwork for our class explorations into more challenging topics. As a reinvention of the classic *Criminal Justice* by James Inciardi, this new text is meant to bridge those goals for both students and faculty. It is my intention to include only the most essential material in this core text and to use every inch of space to further students' understanding of criminal justice. Thus, this edition marks a return to the core of introductory criminal justice material—police, courts, and corrections—so that students are able to identify the key elements, issues, and challenges currently facing professionals in the field, often in the students' own communities. It is my hope that this more streamlined core material will enable a deeper analysis and critique of the machinery of justice.

Success IN YOUR CRIMINAL JUSTICE COURSE

To help students focus on the most important concepts, *Experience Criminal Justice* is streamlined in both content and design: The book has 13 manageable chapters with a limited number of feature boxes, no marginalia, and a clear, straightforward photo and graphics program. *Experience Criminal Justice* provides the foundation necessary for all students studying criminal justice—those who want to enter the field as professionals as well as those who come merely to satisfy their curiosity.

PART FOUR **CORRECTIONS**

11 The Structure and Function of American Corrections

LEARNING OBJECTIVES

- Identify the key themes in the history of punishment, including the contributions of the classical school of criminology.
- Describe the structure of corrections in the United States.
- Compare and contrast the types of correctional institutions operating in modern America.
- Describe the typical administrative features of correctional institutions.
- List and describe the types of programs that commonly operate in correctional facilities.

■ **Students study more effectively with Connect Criminal Justice** Connect Criminal Justice is an assignable and assessable learning platform that contains a wealth of videos, interactivities, and simulations, giving students hands-on tools to experience criminal justice. Detailed reporting helps students and instructors gauge comprehension and retention—without adding administrative load. All the activities in Connect Criminal Justice are written directly to textbook **learning objectives** and automatically graded, so students can master core content. **LearnSmart** uses adaptive technology that continuously changes the content each student receives, focusing students' learning on their areas of weakness.

You wrote:
✗ indigent

The correct answer is:
Departments that serve multilingual communities often pay incentives to officers that can serve as interpreters.

Role of Discretion

IN THE CRIMINAL JUSTICE SYSTEM

Understanding discretion comes from using discretion. With *You Make the Call: Discretion in Criminal Justice*, students take on the roles of law enforcement professionals and are challenged to make

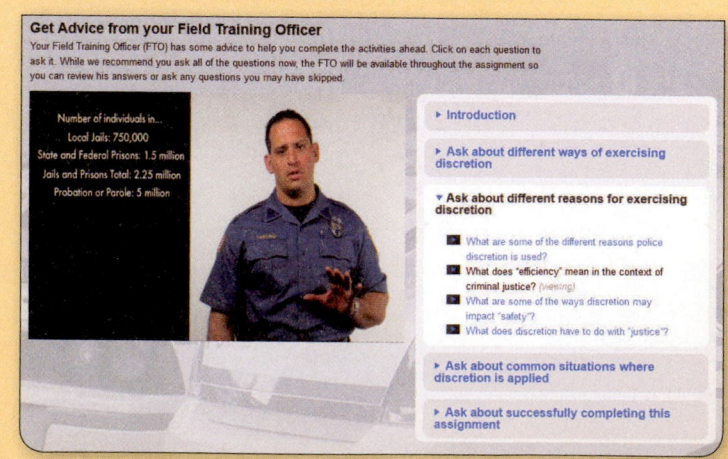

Get Advice from your Field Training Officer

Your Field Training Officer (FTO) has some advice to help you complete the activities ahead. Click on each question to ask it. While we recommend you ask all of the questions now, the FTO will be available throughout the assignment so you can review his answers or ask any questions you may have skipped.

Number of individuals in...
Local Jails: 750,000
State and Federal Prisons: 1.5 million
Jails and Prisons Total: 2.25 million
Probation or Parole: 5 million

▸ Introduction
▸ Ask about different ways of exercising discretion
▾ Ask about different reasons for exercising discretion
- What are some of the different reasons police discretion is used?
- What does "efficiency" mean in the context of criminal justice? (viewing)
- What are some of the ways discretion may impact "safety"?
- What does discretion have to do with "justice"?
▸ Ask about common situations where discretion is applied
▸ Ask about successfully completing this assignment

and justify discretion-related decisions that occur every day in the world of criminal justice—specifically related to a traffic stop, the pretrial process, and probation.

- Throughout *Experience Criminal Justice*, **Discretion Matters questions** highlight the role discretion plays in the decision making of criminal justice professionals. Instructors can use these questions to call students' attention to the potential impact on particular cases.

CONNECT TO THE
Stories
OF CRIMINAL JUSTICE

Each chapter of *Experience Criminal Justice* begins with the story behind a classic Supreme Court case, featured in all its gritty detail. The purpose is to focus students' attention on the chapter topic as well as the decision-making of various actors within the criminal justice process.

- Videos and news articles within Connect Criminal Justice bring the stories of criminal justice to life for students. New videos from **CNN News** were vetted by criminal justice faculty and selected because of their relevance to textbook learning objectives. Connect Criminal Justice also includes **more than 40 news articles**, written specifically to align with course learning objectives, and accompanied by comprehension and critical thinking questions.

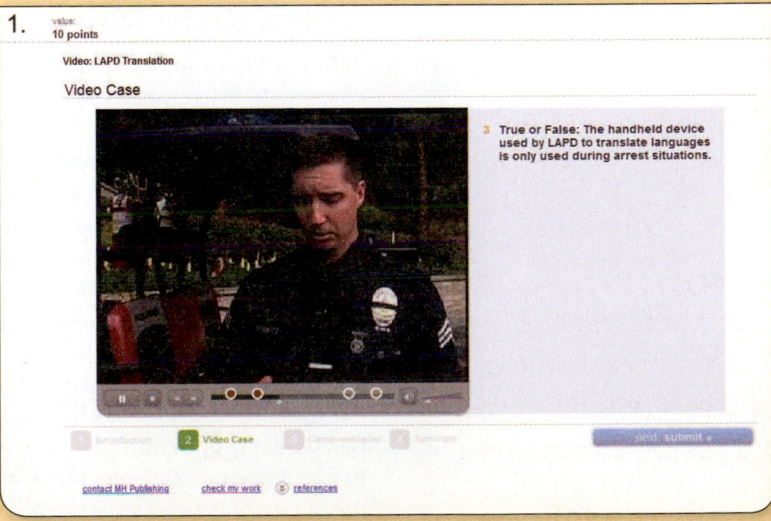

AUTHORS

Nicole Hendrix is an Associate Professor in the Department of Criminal Justice at Radford University, where she teaches a number of courses, including introduction to criminal justice. Dr. Hendrix completed her undergraduate and master's degrees at the University of North Carolina at Charlotte, where her love of exploring crime and justice grew from several projects that emphasized academic and applied research. She researched the use of force by police officers at the Charlotte-Mecklenburg Police Department, studied the application of the death penalty in North Carolina, and interviewed individuals who had recently been arrested and incarcerated at the Charlotte-Mecklenburg County Jail. Dr. Hendrix went on to receive her PhD in Criminal Justice from the University at Albany–SUNY, where she worked on numerous research projects, including the Rochester Youth Development Study. Upon completing her doctoral work, Dr. Hendrix began her current teaching position. Her most recent research focuses on the sale of firearms in Virginia and the national temporal trends of firearms sales. Much of her work reflects her belief that building bridges between academia and professional criminal justice results in the best outcomes for communities.

James A. Inciardi (1939–2009) was director of the Center for Drug and Alcohol Studies at the University of Delaware, a professor in the Department of Sociology and Criminal Justice at the University of Delaware, an adjunct professor in the Department of Epidemiology and Public Health at the University of Miami Miller School of Medicine, and a guest professor in the Department of Psychiatry at the Federal University of Rio Grande do Sul in Porto Alegre, Brazil.

Dr. Inciardi received his PhD in Criminology and Medical Sociology at New York University and had a background in law enforcement, corrections, drug-abuse treatment, and research. He began his career with the New York State Division of Parole, first as an institutional parole officer at New York's Green Haven Prison, then as an investigative and undercover parole officer with the New York State Division of Parole's Bureau of Special Services, and finally as a field parole officer in a special narcotics project. After leaving the New York State Division of Parole, he conducted street research in many cities across the United States.

As director of his university's Center for Drug and Alcohol Studies, Dr. Inciardi oversaw a multinational research center with field offices in Delaware, Florida, the U.S. Virgin Islands, and Porto Alegre, Brazil. Dr. Inciardi authored more than 450 articles, chapters, and books in a variety of areas pertaining to criminal justice and criminology, including substance abuse, history, folklore, public policy, AIDS, medicine, and law.

CONTRIBUTORS

William Flynn and David F. Owens served as special consultants on the policing chapters to help ensure the accuracy and balance of these materials.

William Flynn teaches criminal justice classes at Raritan Valley Community College in New Jersey. Before he began teaching, he worked in law enforcement for 31 years, holding multiple positions with the New Brunswick Police Department in New Jersey. He has also taught at Rutgers University, the College of New Jersey, and many police academies. He has a BS in the Administration of Justice from Rutgers and an MA in Forensic Psychology from John Jay College of Criminal Justice.

David F. Owens is a professor of Criminal Justice at Onondaga Community College in Syracuse, New York. He has served as president of the Criminal Justice Educators Association of New York State (CJEANYS) and the Northeastern Association of Criminal Justice Sciences (NEACJS). He has also served as the Region One Trustee of the Academy of Criminal Justice Sciences (ACJS) and is currently the ACJS Treasurer. Before entering academia, Professor Owens served for 20 years as a police officer for the Syracuse Police Department.

CRIMINAL JUSTICE TOOLS FOR *TODAY'S* INSTRUCTORS AND STUDENTS

Connect Criminal Justice gives students access to a wealth of online interactive activities and assignments, including LearnSmart, *You Make the Call: Discretion in Criminal Justice,* CNN videos, more than 40 news articles from the McClatchy-Tribune Newspaper Group, an optional e-book, and more.

LearnSmart, an unparalleled adaptive testing program, diagnoses students' knowledge of a subject and then creates an individualized learning path to help them master criminal justice concepts. No two students are alike. McGraw-Hill LearnSmart™ is an intelligent learning system that uses a series of probing questions to pinpoint each student's knowledge gaps. LearnSmart then provides an optimal learning path for each student, so that they spend less time in areas they already know and more time in areas needed. The result: students retain more knowledge, learn faster, and study more efficiently.

INSTRUCTOR SUPPLEMENTS

Find materials you need to get your course up and running on **www.mhhe.com /hendrixcj1e.** There, you will find:

- **Test Bank** – The test bank for *Experience Criminal Justice* includes 50 multiple choice, 15 true/false, and 10 fill-in-the-blanks questions for every chapter. Each question is tagged with Bloom's Taxonomy learning domains and page references from the textbook/e-book. McGraw-Hill's computerized **EZ Test** allows instructors to create customized exams using these test items or instructors' own questions. A version of the test bank is also provided in Microsoft Word files for instructors who prefer that format.
- **PowerPoints** – PowerPoint presentations for each chapter of *Experience Criminal Justice* can be used as-is or modified to meet the needs of individual instructors. On average each PPT deck has 20–25 slides per chapter, including key graphics and images.
- **Instructor Manual** – For every chapter of *Experience Criminal Justice* the instructor's manual includes learning objectives, a chapter summary, chapter outline, topics of interest, key terms and concepts, supplementary lecture materials, and class projects and discussion topics.

McGraw Hill create Design your own ideal course materials with McGraw-Hill's **Create™, http://www.mcgrawhillcreate.com.** Rearrange or omit chapters, combine material from other sources, upload your syllabus or any other content you have written to make the perfect resource for your students. You can also search thousands of leading McGraw-Hill textbooks to find the best content for your students; then arrange it to fit your teaching style. When you order a Create book, you receive a complimentary review copy. Get a printed copy in 3 to 5 business days or an electronic copy (e-Comp) via e-mail in about an hour. Register today at **http://www.mcgrawhillcreate.com,** and craft your course resources to match the way you teach.

McGraw-Hill Campus™ is a new one-stop teaching and learning experience available to users of any learning management system. This institutional service allows faculty and students to enjoy single sign-on (SSO) access to all McGraw-Hill Higher Education materials, including the award-winning McGraw-Hill Connect® platform, from directly within the institution's website. McGraw-Hill Campus provides faculty with instant access to all McGraw-Hill Higher Education teaching materials (e.g., eTextbooks, test banks, PowerPoint slides, animations and learning objects), allowing them to browse, search, and use any instructor ancillary content in our vast library at no additional cost to instructor or students.

Tegrity Campus is a service that makes class time available around the clock. It automatically captures every lecture in a searchable format for students to review when they study and complete assignments. With a simple one-click start-and-stop process, you capture all computer screens and corresponding audio. Students replay any part of any class with easy-to-use browser-based viewing on a PC or Mac. To learn more about Tegrity, watch a two-minute Flash demo at **http://tegritycampus.mhhe.com.**

REVIEWERS

More than forty professors influenced the development of this first edition, and we would like to thank them for their thoughtful feedback and guidance.

CONTENT REVIEWERS

Sabina Burton, University of Wisconsin–Platteville
Robert Cacciatore, Orange County Community College
Jennifer Capps, Metropolitan State College of Denver
David Celeste, Montgomery College–Rockville
Charles Chastain, University of Arkansas–Little Rock
Allison Cotton, Metropolitan State College of Denver
Elmer Criswell, Harrisburg Area Community College
Randall Davis, Santa Ana College
Patricia DeAngelis, Hudson Valley Community College
Bertram Delmage, Nassau Community College
Charles Dreveskracht, Northeastern State University
Janine Ferraro, Nassau Community College
Richard Finn, Western Nevada College
Tracey Friedman Woodard, University of North Florida
Adam Garcia, Truckee Meadows Community College
Kelly Gould, Sacramento City College
Patrick Hauser, East Los Angeles College
John Hill, Salt Lake Community College
Steven Hougland, Southwest Georgia Technical College
Linda Keena, University of Mississippi
David Keys, New Mexico State University–Las Cruces
Michael Kwan, Salt Lake Community College
Jodi Levit, William Rainey Harper College
Patricia Marek O'Neill, Hudson Valley Community College
Kathy Oborn, Los Angeles Pierce College
Ross Olmos, William Rainey Harper College
Angie Ondrus, Owens Community College
Wayne Posner, East Los Angeles College
Tom Powell, Maricopa Community College
Cara Rabe-Hemp, Illinois State University
Amy Ramson, Hostos Community College
Debra Ross, Grand Valley State University
Steven Ruffatto, Harrisburg Area Community College
Diane Sjuts, Metropolitan Community College
Ronald Sopenoff, Brookdale Community College
Terry St. Clair, Lindenwood University
Rita Turcotte, Community College of Rhode Island–Warwick
Robert Vaughn, Cedarville University
Jeff Walker, University of Arkansas–Little Rock

ACKNOWLEDGMENTS

This book is the result of an extraordinary amount of work and effort by teams of people, many of whom helped and supported me along the way. I am very lucky to be surrounded by so many amazing people—family, friends, and colleagues.

A few special people deserve very specific acknowledgement:

- Thank you to James Inciardi for his work in the field of criminal justice and for the foundation he laid for this book;
- To Alan Lizotte, my mentor and friend, who continues to counsel me in all things academic, even though I don't call home often enough;
- To Beth Bjerregaard, who demonstrated that research could be interesting and fun—but most of all useful;
- To Melissa Fenwick, my coconspirator and collaborator;
- To Susan Messer, who helped convey my vision of this book;
- To Bill Minick, for his willingness to see what could be;
- And, most of all, to my husband, Ryan, and my daughters, Isabel and Emma. Without their love and unwavering support, this project would not have been possible.

EXPERIENCE

CRIMINAL JUSTICE

1

Criminal Justice in America

LEARNING OBJECTIVES

- Compare and contrast the meaning of the terms *criminal justice, criminology, criminal law,* and *criminal procedure.*

- Summarize the models of criminal justice, including the due process, crime control, wedding cake, and funnel models.

- Describe the development of criminal justice as a professional and academic field.

- Identify and explain the major themes in modern criminal justice.

- Acquire tools for critically analyzing information you encounter about the criminal justice system and process.

Criminal justice entails a broad spectrum of activities, actors, and outcomes. In a narrow view, criminal justice is the application of law to individuals within our society, including the detection, apprehension, prosecution, and punishment of those who break its laws. Each of these activities depends to some extent on decision-making by professionals in the field. Many of these individuals work with a great deal of autonomy and utilize a significant amount of discretion as they respond to offenses and process cases and offenders. For the purposes of this book, the term *discretion* refers to the ability of criminal justice personnel to choose from an array of options or outcomes based on their judgment and experiences, their department policies, and the laws of our community. In criminal justice, professional discretion can result in a range of outcomes for offenders, the system of justice, and the community. How, why, and when criminal justice professionals use their discretion are keys to understanding the nature of criminal justice in America. This is a central theme in this text. In each chapter, we will use classic cases, like the one discussed next, to highlight the challenges professionals face in responding to crime.

DISCRETION MATTERS

Think about your own experiences with criminal justice. Can you identify instances when criminal justice professionals might use their discretion to affect outcomes in the justice system?

SEARCHING FOR CRIME AND JUSTICE

The complex relationship between discretion and justice is no clearer than in the experience of being approached by a police officer. An officer's decision to approach a citizen is fraught with discretion. For many, this interaction results in nothing more than a pleasant conversation; however, for those who have committed a crime or who arouse suspicion in any way, this encounter can result in the ultimate loss of liberty.

On October 13, 1995, someone contacted the Miami-Dade Police Department about a young black male at a bus stop in the city. The caller, who did not leave a name with his recorded message, said that the youth was wearing a plaid shirt and carrying a gun.[1] A short time later, two officers went to the bus stop and saw three young black men. One wore a plaid shirt. An officer approached him, told him to put his hands up, and patted him down. The officer found a gun in one of his pockets. The other officer searched the other two individuals but found nothing. The youth wearing the plaid shirt was ten days away from his sixteenth birthday and was charged with violating state law—specifically, carrying a concealed firearm without a license and possessing a firearm while under the age of 18.[2]

This incident led to the landmark Supreme Court case of *Florida v. J.L.* In this case, the court was asked whether unsubstantiated and anonymous information given to police could be used to support the search of an individual, even when the report alleged the presence of a particular threat, like that of a firearm. The court recognized the safety issues but stated that the Constitution requires more than an anonymous tip as evidence of a crime.[3] The concern was that without more substantial support or a police investigation, the determination of whom to approach and/or search could be based on factors that are not legally valid. Because the officers in this case had only an anonymous tip as evidence, the system protected the individual rights of the youth in striking down the conviction.

For anyone interested in criminal justice, part of a basic education in the field should include occasional visits to local jails, prisons, or courts. Observations of

Media images often depict glamorized criminal justice professionals and their work. The actors on the popular show *CSI: Crime Scene Investigation* are very different in background, training, and experience from the officers of any real-life police department.

police activities, including ride-alongs, usually available to citizens, are also very enlightening. Individuals often come away with the impression that the criminal justice process is like a machine, grinding along through its many phases: police investigating crimes and apprehending suspected offenders; courts separating the guilty from the not guilty and applying sanctions within the boundaries of constitutional law and established criminal procedure; and correctional organizations warehousing, supervising, and sometimes even educating and rehabilitating offenders convicted and sentenced by the courts. To many observers, the machinery of justice in the United States appears comparable to a factory assembly line, with participants moving from one stage to the next.

That, however, is an inaccurate and unbalanced view of our criminal justice system. Criminal justice entails more than just the police, the courts, and the correctional organizations—and it is far more complex than any television drama. The system of justice has many moving pieces, and numerous actors are involved in those processes. Moreover, the overwhelming majority of criminal cases are handled in a way that is nothing like what we see on TV. Media-fed images and preconceptions—whether from the nightly news, amateur footage of "real cops," or the latest Hollywood crime thriller—show little about how our society responds to crime and criminals.

One goal of this book is to carry you beyond these preconceptions and limitations. Whether you aspire to become a criminal justice professional, enter a field that interacts with some part of the criminal justice system, or simply remain a private citizen, this book will help you develop an accurate understanding of how our system works—and how it can fail—with a special focus on the impact of professional discretion all along the way. It will also assist you in critically examining the issues that drive the system today and into the future.

To begin our exploration of the criminal justice system and process, this chapter first defines the key terms students of criminal justice should know and use in discussing the field. In addition, this chapter puts the development of criminal justice within a larger historical context; we return to the 1960s and to what we think of as the roots of the contemporary criminal justice system. We then examine the important contemporary themes and issues and conclude with a section about critical thinking and its importance in the field of criminal justice.

UNDERSTANDING CRIMINAL JUSTICE IN AMERICA

To begin our discussion of criminal justice, let us first define some key terms. The term **criminal justice** refers to the structure, functions, and processes of those agencies that deal with the management of crime—the police, the courts, and corrections. The content of criminal justice studies comes from a variety of disciplines, including criminology, criminal law, criminal procedure, and constitutional law. To fully understand the process and system of criminal justice, we must also define these terms and place them within the larger context of the field.

Criminology is the scientific study of the nature and causes of crime, the rates of crime, the punishment and rehabilitation of offenders, and the prevention of crime. The great majority of courses and textbooks in criminology provide an overview of the criminal justice system, but the structure and processes of the system are not the major focus of a criminology course.

Criminal law is the branch of modern jurisprudence that deals with offenses committed against the safety and order of the state. Many aspects of criminal law are addressed in criminal justice studies, including definitions and elements of crime, criminal intent, justifications, and defenses against crime.

Criminal procedure encompasses the series of orderly steps and actions—authorized by law or the courts—used to determine whether a person accused of a crime is guilty or not guilty. Although much of the field of criminal procedure is addressed in law courses, many of its basic components are also covered in criminal justice courses.

Constitutional law focuses on the legal rules and principles that define the nature and limits of governmental power and the duties and rights of individuals in relation to the state. The parts of constitutional law that are examined in criminal justice courses are those associated with criminal procedure and the behavior of criminal justice practitioners.

Although criminology is more than a century old, and legal studies have been in existence for millennia, it was not until the end of the 1960s that criminal justice was established as an academic discipline. The field developed as an outgrowth of the many calls for "law and order" that emerged during the presidency of Lyndon B. Johnson in the 1960s.

The Emergence of Criminal Justice as a Field of Study

During the 1960s, crime rates increased in both urban and rural areas (Exhibit 1.1). Riots occurred in many of the nation's cities, brought on in part by racism and the deterioration of inner-city neighborhoods. Turbulent demonstrations took place on campuses and in the streets in opposition to the war in Vietnam. And at least four important political figures were assassinated—President John F. Kennedy in 1963, Nation of Islam leader Malcolm X in 1965, and civil rights leader Dr. Martin Luther King Jr. and Senator Robert F. Kennedy in 1968.[4]

Emotionally charged appeals for **law and order** began circulating early in the decade. Those appeals, in part, reflected the temperament of grassroots America, which sought a return to what citizens thought of as the morality of previous decades. The call for law and order came as well from citizens who despised not only crime in general but also the anarchy that appeared to be taking over the streets.[5]

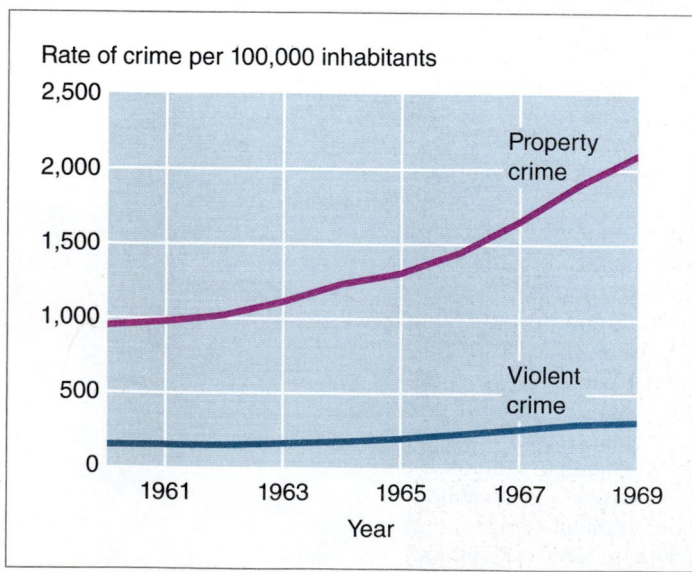

Rate of crime per 100,000 inhabitants

EXHIBIT 1.1   **U.S. Crime Rates, 1960–1969**
Source: FBI, Uniform Crime Reports

Also visible at this time was a trend toward the "nationalization" of the Bill of Rights. The framers of the U.S. Constitution intended for the Bill of Rights to apply at the national level—that is, at the level of the federal government—not at the state level. Thus, defendants in state criminal trials were not accorded many of the constitutional protections that were routinely given to those tried in the federal courts. In the 1930s, the U.S. Supreme Court began extending these rights to state defendants. It was not until the 1960s that significant gains were made. By 1969, nearly all the provisions of the Bill of Rights relating to criminal violations were binding on the states, including the prohibitions against compulsory self-incrimination, illegal search and seizure, and cruel and unusual punishment, as well as the rights to counsel, a speedy trial, and confrontation of hostile witnesses.[6] Several of these decisions came early in the 1960s, and many interpreted them as attempts to "handcuff" police and "coddle" criminals.

More than 50,000 people formed the funeral cortege for assassinated civil rights leader Dr. Martin Luther King Jr. in 1968. As violence escalated during the decade, so did the outcry for "law and order."

On July 25, 1965, in response to growing fears of crime and disorder, President Lyndon Johnson's "war on crime" was officially launched with the establishment of the **President's Commission on Law Enforcement and Administration of Justice.**[7] Unknown to Americans at the time and even to Johnson himself, the commission would initiate a new era for criminal justice in the United States. This commission, commonly referred to as the President's Crime Commission, appointed several task forces to study the crime problem and the structure of criminal justice administration and to make recommendations for action. The commission, made up of 19 commissioners, 63 staff members, 175 consultants, and hundreds of advisers, studied most aspects of the crime problem and the machinery of criminal justice.[8]

Police officers used dogs on protestors during the civil rights era of the 1960s.

The most serious criminal offenses occur in the poorest areas of cities. This housing project in the Bronx is an example of a lower-socioeconomic area.

After hundreds of meetings, tens of thousands of interviews, and numerous national surveys, the President's Crime Commission released a series of reports on the police, courts, corrections, juvenile delinquency, organized crime, science and technology, drunkenness, narcotics and drugs, and the assessment of crime—all of which were summarized in its general report, *The Challenge of Crime in a Free Society*.[9] This summary report targeted seven specific objectives, which in many ways shaped the direction of criminal justice for years to come:

1. Society must seek to prevent crime before it happens by assuring all Americans a stake in the benefits and responsibilities of American life, by strengthening law enforcement, and by reducing criminal opportunities.
2. The aim of reducing crime would be better served if the system of criminal justice developed a far broader range of techniques with which to deal with individual offenders.
3. The system of criminal justice must eliminate existing injustices if it is to achieve its ideals and win the respect and cooperation of all citizens.
4. The system of criminal justice must attract more and better people—police, prosecutors, judges, defense attorneys, probation and parole officers, and corrections officials with more knowledge, expertise, initiative, and integrity.
5. There must be much more operational and basic research on the problems of crime and criminal administration by researchers both within and outside the system of criminal justice.
6. The police, courts, and correctional agencies must be given increased funding if they are to improve their ability to control crime.
7. Individual citizens, civic and business organizations, religious institutions, and all levels of government must take responsibility for planning and implementing the changes that must be made in the criminal justice system if crime is to be reduced.[10]

In addition to these major objectives, the commission's reports made more than 200 specific recommendations. Many of these focused on poverty as a root cause of crime. For example, the commission stated that "warring on poverty, inadequate housing, and unemployment is warring on crime"; that "a civil rights law is a law against crime"; and that "money for schools is money against crime."[11] However, some saw these conclusions as naive. The relationship between crime and poverty had been studied at length for many generations, with the inescapable conclusion that the root causes of crime could not be found in any simplistic equation involving only the disadvantaged segments of society.

Poverty and segregation clearly perpetuate crime, the noted criminologist Edwin H. Sutherland had argued, but "poverty as such is not an important cause of crime."[12] Political scientist James Q. Wilson also targeted the peculiarity of the poverty-crime nexus by describing the paradox of the sixties as "Crime amidst plenty."[13] Wilson was referring to the fact that at the beginning of the 1960s, the United States entered its longest sustained period of prosperity since World War II. During this time, the economy as a whole grew stronger, many people's incomes increased, and the educational attainments of the young rose sharply. Yet, at the same time, crime increased at an alarming rate, along with youth unemployment, drug abuse, and welfare. Thus the suggestion of the President's Crime Commission that the war on crime should focus on poverty alone caused acute disappointment among those who had spent their lives studying the problem.

Criminal Justice as a System

In contrast, the President's Crime Commission's analyses of the *processes* of criminal justice had a great impact. They awakened a consciousness of criminal justice as an integrated "system"—an orderly flow of managerial decision-making that begins with the investigation of a criminal offense and ends with the offender's reintegration into the free community:

> The criminal justice system has three separately organized parts—the police, the courts, and corrections—and each has distinct tasks. However, these parts are by no means independent of each other. What each one does and how it does it has a direct effect on the work of the others. The courts must deal, and can only deal, with those whom the police arrest; the business of corrections is with those delivered to it by the courts. How successfully corrections reforms convicts determines whether they will once again become police business and influences the sentences the judges pass; police activities are subject to court scrutiny and are often determined by court decisions.[14]

The President's Crime Commission, however, was not altogether unaware of the shortcomings of what it called the "system" of criminal justice, and it called for extensive research and an upgrading of criminal justice personnel and practices. In these areas, the commission had its most visible impact on criminal justice in America.

DISCRETION MATTERS

How might attempts to improve criminal justice personnel and practices affect the role of discretion in the field?

The Omnibus Crime Control and Safe Streets Act of 1968

The year 1968 has a unique significance in the history of criminal justice in America. As noted earlier, it was a year of riots, protests, and assassinations. It was also a year of increasingly visible street crime. Among the 4.5 million known major crimes that occurred in that year, there were almost 13,000 homicides, 31,000 forcible rapes, 262,000 robberies, 283,000 serious assaults, 778,000 auto thefts, 1.3 million larcenies, and 1.8 million burglaries. At least 1 out of every 45 Americans was the victim of a serious crime.[15]

The use of heroin and other illegal drugs had also reached significant proportions by 1968, having expanded from inner-city areas to suburbia during the early part of the decade.[16] Associated with drug abuse was street crime—burglaries, robberies, and muggings. It was in this setting that the President's Crime Commission was established. Noting the growing fear in the United States, the commission wrote that the purpose of its report was to recommend a broad and comprehensive attack on the "root causes" of crime.[17]

Nevertheless, the recommendations of the commission did not culminate in the type of war on crime it envisioned. To launch a comprehensive attack on the root causes of crime was unrealistic, for, as noted earlier, those causes have never been fully understood. The search for the causes of crime has been going on for generations, as you will learn in Chapter 2, with only minimal results. In fact, numerous researchers have concluded that a search for causes is a "lost cause" in criminology.[18]

President Johnson's proposals for the war on crime resulted in the passage of the Omnibus Crime Control and Safe Streets Act of 1968, a piece of legislation that generated heated controversy. Rather than being a reform bill, the act appeared to some to be a political maneuver aimed at allaying fears about crime, calming agitation over inner-city riots, and reducing anger over Supreme Court decisions that allegedly tied the hands of the police. Title II of the act attempted to overturn numerous Supreme Court decisions by stating that all voluntary confessions and eyewitness identifications—regardless of whether a defendant had been informed of his or her rights—could be admitted in federal trials.[19] Title III of the act empowered state and local law enforcement agencies to tap telephones and engage in other forms of eavesdropping for brief periods

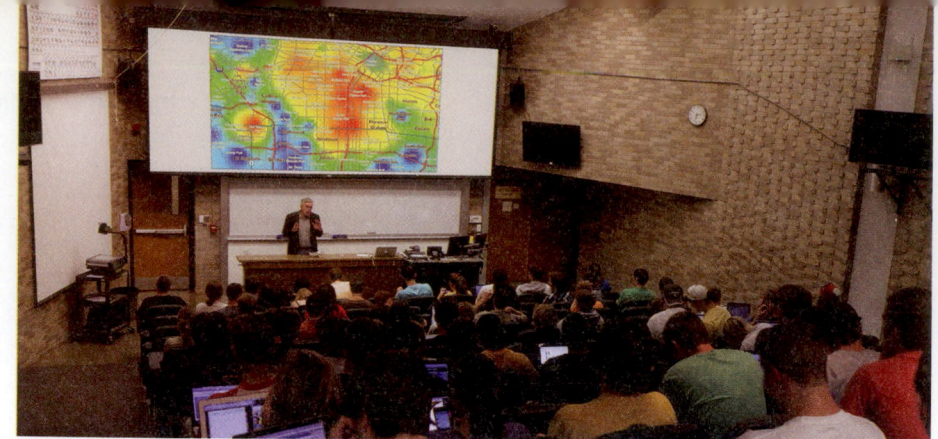

By the 1970s, the country had 729 academic programs educating more than 100,000 criminal justice majors in colleges and universities.

even without a court order. Primarily because of these two provisions, a number of liberal and reform-minded observers looked upon the Omnibus Crime Control and Safe Streets Act as a bad law, one that constituted a significant move toward the establishment of a police state.

The Law Enforcement Assistance Administration

The primary provision of the Omnibus Crime Control and Safe Streets Act was Title I, which created the **Law Enforcement Assistance Administration.** More commonly known as LEAA, it was organized within the Department of Justice to develop new devices, techniques, and approaches in law enforcement; to award discretionary grants for special programs in the field of criminal justice; and to supply states and municipalities with funds for improving their criminal justice systems and for training and educating criminal justice personnel.[20]

During its early years, the LEAA was criticized for overemphasizing the funding of a "technological" war on crime and for providing grants for purposes beyond its original mission.[21] However, not all LEAA funds were misdirected or misused, nor were all funds channeled for the development of technological tools for a war on crime.

A significant proportion of LEAA expenditures were also targeted for social programs and research, court reform, and correctional programs. Moreover, throughout the 1970s LEAA provided more than $40 million per year for the Law Enforcement Education Program (LEEP), charged with the education of some 100,000 persons employed in or preparing for a career in criminal justice. The report of the Twentieth Century Fund Task Force, which examined the operation of LEAA, maintained that the education program was among the agency's most constructive and successful efforts. As such, it was LEEP that initiated the first academic programs in criminal justice. Since then, criminal justice education has become a dominant course of study in community colleges and universities throughout the United States, helping to establish criminal justice as an academic field as well as beginning the systematic analysis of the processes of justice. These foundational studies and analyses have since shaped policy and procedures in law enforcement agencies, courts, and corrections agencies across the country.

Models of Criminal Justice

The procedures for crime control, the processing of criminal defendants, and the sentencing, punishment, and management of convicted offenders are closely linked to the guarantees and prohibitions found in the Bill of Rights and to interpretations of those provisions by the Supreme Court. Interestingly, the major criminology and criminal justice textbooks used during the first half of the twentieth century made no mention of either the Bill of Rights or the U.S. Supreme Court.[22] Not until the 1960 publication of *Crime, Justice, and Correction* by lawyer-sociologist Paul W. Tappan did Supreme Court decisions creep into discussions of criminal justice processing and the machinery of justice.[23] Actually, this should *not* be surprising. As will become apparent throughout this book, concerted Supreme Court activity in matters of criminal justice did not begin until the early 1960s. Since then the court has been extremely active.

The court's decisions and subsequent impact on the American justice system is best understood within the context of two competing models: the *due process model* and the *crime control model.* Since these models underlie much of the discussion in later chapters, we will look at them closely here. Although no single model can describe the reality of the criminal justice system in a completely satisfactory manner, each concept lends important insight into the philosophies on which the American criminal justice system is based.

The Due Process Model Herbert Packer's classic book *The Limits of the Criminal Sanction* elaborates on the fundamental ideas of the **due process model.**[24] This model stresses the possibility of error in the stages leading up to a trial. It therefore emphasizes the need to protect procedural rights even if this prevents the legal system from operating with maximum efficiency. Essentially, the model assumes that justice is better served if everyone gets his or her fair day in court, even if a few guilty people go free as a result. The avoidance of locking up an innocent person takes precedence. Remember the chapter-opening case. Rather than focusing on the positive of punishing an individual for carrying an illegal gun, the due process model focuses on protecting the rights of the person.

In the 1960s, the **Warren Court**—the Supreme Court under the leadership of Chief Justice Earl Warren from 1953 into 1969—announced a large number of decisions that were in accordance with the due process model.[25] This Court applied a relatively strict version of the due process model to criminal justice. Beginning in the 1930s and extending into the 1960s, the states increasingly were required to grant criminal defendants many of the constitutional safeguards that were already routinely accorded to those accused of federal crimes.

The Crime Control Model In contrast to the due process model, the **crime control model** emphasizes efficiency and is based on the view that the most important function of the criminal justice process is the repression of criminal conduct. Proponents of this model put a premium on speed and finality, and they cannot understand why obviously guilty defendants should go free simply because of errors by police or court personnel. The model assumes that it is acceptable to suspend individual rights or perhaps overlook technicalities in procedure in the interest of protecting society from criminal behavior.

> **DISCRETION MATTERS**
>
> Under a due process model of criminal justice, how would professionals be most likely to use discretion as they carry out their duties?

The Supreme Court under the leadership of Chief Justice Earl Warren: (*seated, from left*) John M. Harlan, Hugo L. Black, Earl Warren, William O. Douglas, and William J. Brennan Jr.; (*standing, from left*) Abe Fortas, Potter Stewart, Byron R. White, and Thurgood Marshall.

DISCRETION MATTERS

Under a crime control model of criminal justice, how would professionals be most likely to use discretion as they carry out their duties?

The **Burger Court**—the Supreme Court under the leadership of Chief Justice Warren Burger from 1969 into 1986—appeared attuned to the crime control model in its decisions.[26] A legislative enactment of this model includes the "three-strikes" laws, a concept that parallels the sport of baseball. In baseball, it's three strikes and you're out, while under this legislation, the conviction of three crimes means you're imprisoned; in both scenarios, it's futile to argue your way out of the system no matter how controversial the call. Further legislative examples and major Supreme Court rulings based on both the due process and the crime control models are examined throughout the remaining chapters of the text.

Other Models of Criminal Justice   The crime control and due process models help identify the competing goals of the justice system. However, two additional models assist in examining the system's process and caseload. These are the *wedding cake model* and the *funnel model*. Unlike the models described above or the Crime Commission's model of the criminal justice process, these two emphasize the often disconnected aspects of the process and the challenges of processing the wide variety of offenders and cases under a single model.

The **wedding cake model** was developed by Lawrence Friedman and Robert V. Percival but is most often attributed to Samuel Walker. Depicted in Exhibit 1.2, the concept is that very few of the cases that pass through the criminal justice system look like the celebrated ones portrayed in the media. The bottom layer of the cake encompasses lower-level misdemeanors that receive very little attention within the system, even though they constitute the vast majority of the caseload in most jurisdictions. The next two layers comprise felonies, with the less serious felonies on the lower of the two layers and the more serious on the upper layer. Criminal justice personnel give these

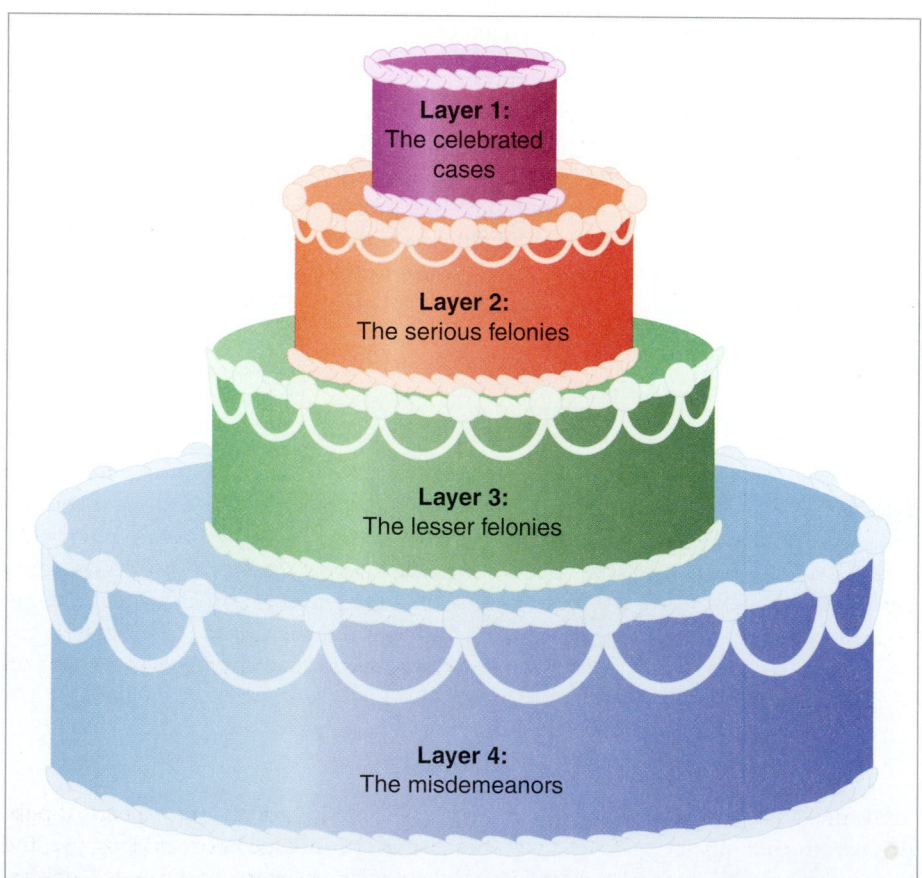

EXHIBIT 1.2   The Wedding Cake Model of Criminal Justice

cases much more attention than they do the misdemeanors, and offenders convicted of these offenses are often given serious punishments. The top layer consists of the celebrated cases—the offenders and offenses that we hear so much about in the media.[27]

Despite findings from the President's Crime Commission that many offenses were reported to the police, few offenders were or continue to be ultimately incarcerated, which is the basis for the **funnel model** of criminal justice. More specifically, the commission's data collection found that of the approximately 2.8 million serious criminal cases reported to police, only 63,000 offenders went to prison.[28] However, many cases are dropped out of the process of justice for very good reasons, including a lack of evidence or the diversion of offenders to more effective means of responding to criminal behaviors. For example, as you can see in Exhibit 1.3, most juvenile offenders are removed and handled through the juvenile court system. These "funneling" decisions, then, ensure that cases are handled in the most efficient and effective manner possible.

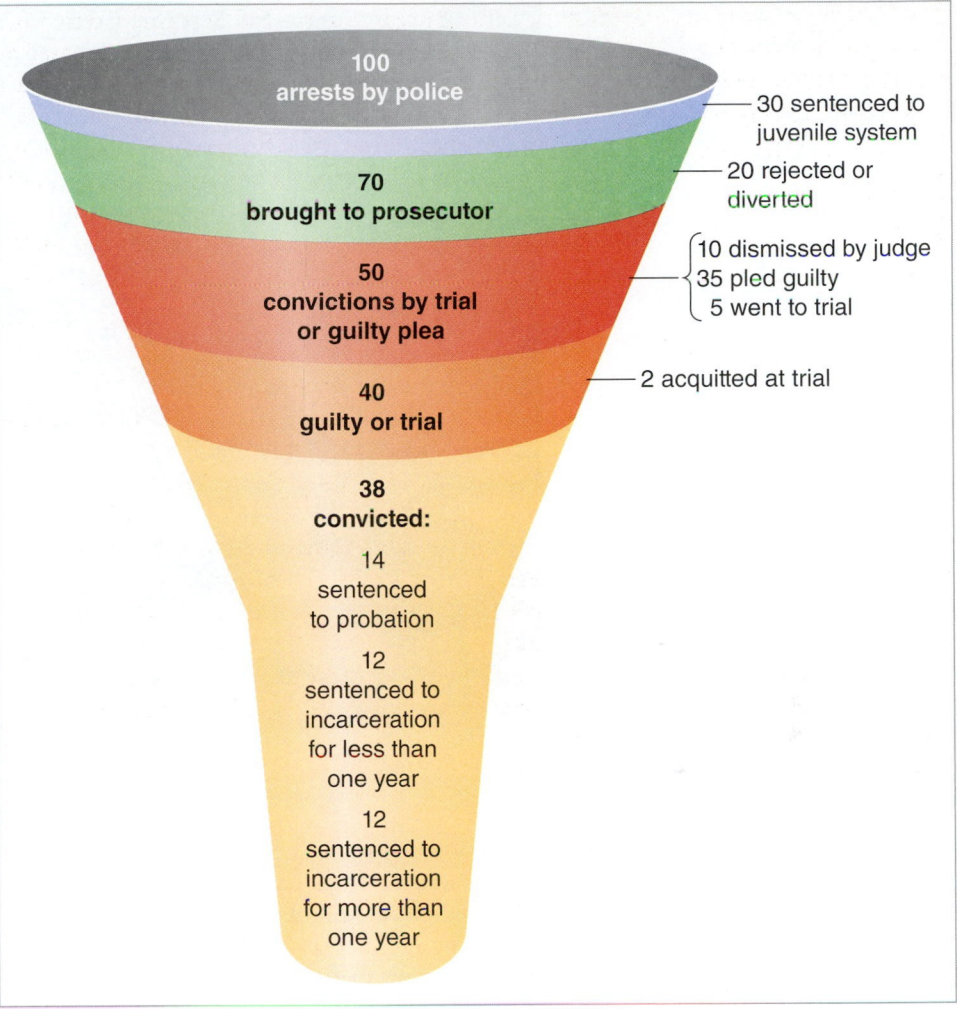

EXHIBIT 1.3   The Funnel Model of Criminal Justice
Source: President's Commission on Law Enforcement and Administration of Justice, 1967

MAJOR THEMES IN MODERN CRIMINAL JUSTICE

In addition to being familiar with the terminology and major models of criminal justice, students of crime and justice in America need to be familiar with the impact of six important trends on contemporary criminal justice procedures and policies. Those trends are the continued war on drugs, the increasing rate of criminality among women, the ways in which the so-called system of criminal justice is sometimes a "nonsystem," the importance of involving crime victims in the process of justice, the influence of the media on the justice process, and, most recently, the impact of global terrorism on all aspects of the criminal justice system.

The War on Drugs

Since the late 1960s, the nation's "war on drugs" has shaped various aspects of public and criminal justice policy. In fact, because of the linkage between drug use and crime, the policy agenda of almost every U.S. president over the past five decades has addressed the drug problem in one way or another.

The war on drugs has resulted in numerous challenges to the criminal justice process with little success in terms of outcomes, deterrence, rehabilitation, or reduced recidivism.

The war on drugs has engendered a criminal justice process that appears to be "drug driven" in almost every respect. New laws have been passed to deter drug involvement and increase penalties for drug-related crime. Street-level drug-enforcement initiatives have been expanded, and these, in turn, have increased the number of drug-related arrests. In the judicial sector, the increase in drug-related cases has resulted in crowded dockets and courtrooms, as well as the creation of new drug courts, special dispositional alternatives for drug-involved offenders, and higher conviction and incarceration rates. In the correctional sector, the higher incarceration rates have caused further crowding of already overpopulated jails and penitentiaries, the establishment of liberal release policies, and experimentation with new prison-based drug-treatment programs.

The focus on drugs has also impacted state finances. In a report released by the National Center on Addiction and Substance Abuse at Columbia University, it was estimated that states dedicated 13 percent of their budgets to dealing with drug abuse but allocated only four cents out of every dollar spent for treatment and prevention.[29] At the same time, however, both federal and state court systems rely heavily on the substance-abuse treatment system. In 2006, for example, the criminal justice system was the principal referral source for almost 40 percent of all substance-abuse treatment admissions.[30] These trends have continued as federal, state, and local communities have struggled to respond to the increasing numbers of offenders who are addicted or abusing illegal substances. Adding to this challenge are concerns about prison overcrowding due to harsh penalties for drug crimes. Many jurisdictions are moving to more rehabilitative models to alleviate pressure on correctional systems.

Gender, Crime, and Criminal Justice

Another important trend in the United States today is the increasing visibility of women in the criminal justice system. The system has traditionally been male-dominated, and there are a variety of reasons for this. Historically, the great majority of offenders

Since the 1970s, the number of female law enforcement officers has increased.

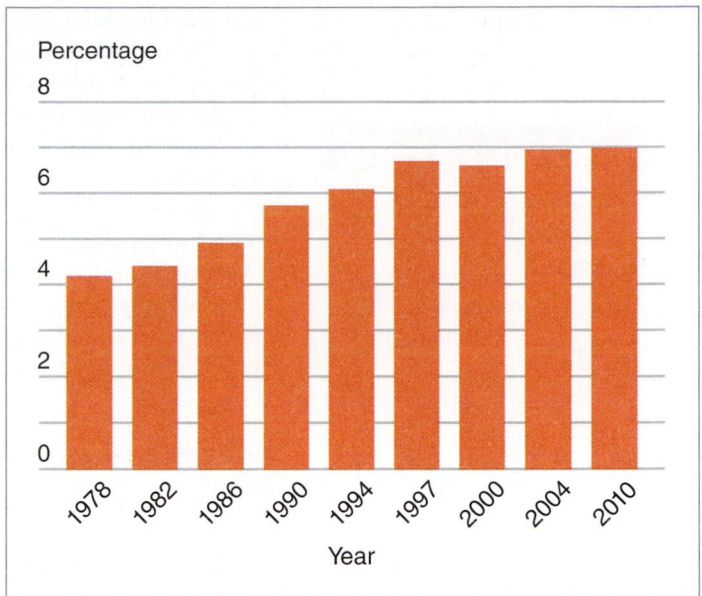

EXHIBIT 1.4 **Proportion of Female Inmates in State and Federal Correctional Institutions**
Source: Bureau of Justice Statistics

have been men, and correctional institutions and programs have been designed for men, by men. Moreover, many of the female offenders who have come to the attention of police, courts, and prisons have received shorter and less severe sentences than men.[31] This discrepancy was not due to leniency on the part of police officers and judges; rather, women typically participated in less serious offenses and played less significant roles in criminal activity.[32]

Over the past decades, this situation has changed. Since the early 1970s, the number of female offenders has risen, and their roles in criminal activity have increasingly paralleled those of men. This trend is most evident in prison statistics. In 1970, only 2.9 percent of state and federal prisoners were women, yet by 2006, this proportion had increased to 7.2 percent and has remained fairly consistent since that time, even though prison populations are decreasing slightly.[33] Moreover, since 1995, the total number of male prisoners has grown by 38 percent, whereas the number of female prisoners has increased by 64 percent (Exhibit 1.4). At the same time, the proportions of female police officers, judges, attorneys, corrections officers, and other criminal justice personnel have also increased.[34]

The Criminal Justice "Nonsystem"

As mentioned earlier, the notion of criminal justice operating as a well-oiled machine may not be entirely accurate. Scholars have proposed two competing perspectives of the organization of the criminal justice system: the *consensus model* and the *conflict model*. Likely more of an ideal than a reality, the consensus, or *systems,* model argues that the organizations that make up the criminal justice system work cooperatively to produce justice. In this model, agencies share information and coordinate their efforts, thereby moving offenders seamlessly through the justice process.

In contrast, the conflict model, also known as the *nonsystem* perspective, posits that the branches of justice work competitively rather than cooperatively, as parts of an integrated whole. As such, the interrelationships among police, the courts, and corrections are often beset with both inefficiency and failure. Because of this lack of coordination and failure of purpose, as long ago as the 1960s the American Bar Association referred to criminal justice as a "nonsystem."[35]

DISCRETION MATTERS

How do criminal justice professionals use their discretion to make the process work more or less like a system?

In most jurisdictions, the courts and correctional systems serve as holding pens for convicted offenders, and the community—under the protection and patrol of the police—is the reentry point for those released from jails and prisons. Rarely does each segment of the criminal justice process operate with full awareness of the long-term cyclical implications of its activities. Moreover, according to the conflict model, some individuals who work in the justice process are tainted by personal interests such as fame, promotions, raises, and notoriety, which create conflicts with the larger system. Criminologist Jerome Skolnick argues that *clearance rates* (the rate of solving crimes) serve as an example of conflict in the system, as police are sometimes more focused on appearing to solve crimes than on actually solving crimes. He cites an incident in which police coerced a man into confessing to over 400 burglaries just so that they would appear to have a high clearance rate.[36]

Victims and Justice

Historically, crime victims and their families have been forgotten in the processing of criminal offenders. Although police contact victims for information that might initiate an arrest, victims generally have had little opportunity to participate in the judicial and correctional processes. This circumstance exists for at least three reasons:

- Historically, in the legal tradition of many cultures, it is the state, not the individual, that is officially the victim of crime.
- A dominant perspective in criminal justice has been that most victims will "get in the way" during police investigations and judicial proceedings.
- Another dominant concern has been that victims are both partial and impatient, and hence are incapable of making an objective contribution to the process of justice.

Recognition of the importance of involving crime victims in the justice process began during the late 1960s; the most significant changes were implemented in the 1980s and have broadened in scope since then. The criminal justice system has also established victims' advocacy programs and restorative justice programs, which offer alternatives to incarceration. The wider roles of victims are discussed in later chapters as they relate to specific areas of criminal processing.

Criminal Justice and the Media

Of all the murders, muggings, and rapes reported to the police, less than 5 percent receive public attention beyond a brief mention from local media. In perhaps 1 percent of cases, a crime attracts sustained state or local attention primarily because it is unusual. And on very rare occasions a criminal case galvanizes broad national attention.

There are few outward similarities between such famous cases as the assassination of John F. Kennedy in 1963, the murders of Nicole Brown Simpson and Ronald Goldman in 1994, the accusations of child molestation against Michael Jackson in 2003, the incarceration of Paris Hilton for various traffic and legal violations in 2007, and the sentencing of Lindsay Lohan for jewelry theft in 2011. But although the details of these cases are very different, each has become an object of continuous investigation, speculation, and analysis. Why? What has driven our fascination with these cases? There are two answers.

One answer lies in the details of each case. The Michael Jackson accusations, for example, involved the King of Pop, one of the most celebrated and talked about entertainers of our time. John F. Kennedy was the president of the United States. The Nicole Brown Simpson and Ronald Goldman murders implicated O. J. Simpson, widely known as a football superstar and celebrity. Both Paris Hilton and Lindsay Lohan were young pop-culture icons featured in numerous entertainment and news media stories. The sheer visibility of the players in these cases guaranteed attention.

Another answer is curiosity. The drama of these stories and the celebrities behind them take people away from the boredom of everyday life. People are also morbidly fascinated by certain unspeakable criminal acts, and they want to convince themselves that they are immune from similar fates or are incapable of such wickedness. And finally, the American public has a stake in whether justice is being done, because we all desire a just society.

Terrorism, Criminal Justice, and the Constitution

Modern criminal justice agencies and officials face the challenges associated with the "war on terrorism" that began after the 9/11 attacks. The impact of the war on terrorism in the criminal justice domain is broad and complex. Unlike responses to more common street offenses, criminal justice responses to acts that fall under the definition of terrorism often involve numerous levels of government law enforcement and, at times, the cooperation of international and foreign entities. Terrorism, the focus of these complex efforts, is the systematic use or threat of extreme violence directed against actual and symbolic victims; it is typically performed for psychological rather than material effects, with the goal of coercing individuals, groups, communities, or governments into making political or tactical concessions. More concisely, United States law defines terrorism as "premeditated, politically motivated violence perpetrated against noncombatant targets by subnational groups or clandestine agents."[37] The terrorist attacks on September 11, 2001, had a chilling effect across the United States and around the world, and they marked a quantum leap in the deadliness and audacity of modern terrorism. In addition, they revealed a vulnerability that many Americans had never before realized or appreciated, sparking a fundamental debate about the tension between liberty and security in the United States.[38] These attacks raised a question that is crucial to criminal justice: How can the government keep Americans secure without sacrificing due process of law and other hard-won freedoms?

This question is not easily answered. Because the 9/11 attacks involved airplanes, airport security has became a central focus of the debate. Increased scrutiny of both passengers and flights, along with an intense focus on multiple arenas of homeland security, has altered the everyday lives of Americans. We are all familiar with the extensive screening methods of the Transportation Security Administration, and the reasons for them, but some say that the newly implemented and controversial measures have not made us any more secure.

Unquestionably, the 9/11 attacks introduced a new era in U.S. criminal justice. Every sector of the system has been affected. New laws have been passed to protect citizens, and new procedures have been implemented for ensuring national security and the processing of those suspected of terrorist activity. These changes affect law and due process, as well as the operations of the police, the courts, and correctional systems.

As you can see, the study of criminal justice often forces students to examine controversial issues and their implications for individuals, groups, communities, and countries. This text will help you maintain a critical perspective as you embark on this journey. In the next sections, we highlight concepts to keep in mind as you undertake this process.

STUDYING AND WORKING IN CRIMINAL JUSTICE[39]

The portrayal of the criminal justice field on television or in movies is generally far more exciting than the one that exists in true life. In part because of these media portrayals, students come to study criminal justice with preconceived ideas about what it is like to work in the field. One purpose of academic criminal justice programs is to educate students about the realities of criminal justice and to expose them to knowledge and information that will help them become better professionals and citizen consumers of criminal justice policy.

DISCRETION MATTERS

What impact might media portrayals of celebrity crime have on the application of law and responses to crime in your community?

DISCRETION MATTERS

How might community fear of certain types of crime—for example, terrorism—affect the criminal justice professional's use of discretion?

The behavior depicted in crime dramas (left) is often a far cry from the reality of police activity (right).

As an academic field, criminal justice is the study of the agencies and procedures set up to manage both crime and the persons accused of violating the law. Criminal justice has become one of the most popular undergraduate majors in the United States, due in part to the obsession of American culture with dramatic depictions of crime and justice. Academic programs offer students the opportunity to pursue their interest in this field through studies leading to law school, graduate school, or careers in the administration of justice. Degree programs are generally structured around a core of criminal justice courses on such topics as law enforcement, the judicial process, juvenile justice, corrections, criminology, and criminal law and procedure. Other courses provide in-depth examinations of such areas as juvenile delinquency, criminal violence, the jury, alcohol and drug abuse, criminal evidence, criminal justice policy and administration, and prisoners' rights. Since the criminal justice process in any jurisdiction does not exist in isolation but naturally reflects the structure, ideas, and concerns of the community and society in which it operates, criminal justice programs draw from a wide variety of academic disciplines: political science, psychology, history, sociology, and even anthropology.

An integral component of degree programs in criminal justice is field experience—a directed practicum with a criminal justice agency that gives students the opportunity to bridge the gap between the theory and applications learned in the classroom and the practice of criminal justice in the real world. In field-experience courses, students work on a first-hand basis in agency situations—police departments, law offices, and correctional settings. Such hands-on experience prepares students for the unique nature of work in the justice system.

James Inciardi, who built the foundation for the text you are reading, taught courses in criminal justice at the University of Delaware for many years, and he taught the introductory course in criminal justice to well over 10,000 students. He was intrigued by the popularity of the course and regularly asked his students, "Why are you here?" He kept a tally of the answers over the years, and they turn out to be quite interesting.

First of all, a little over a third were nonmajors or undeclared students. They chose the course as an elective because they heard it was interesting and had a number of "real-world applications," as they put it. The remaining were criminal justice majors, half of whom wanted to pursue traditional career paths, including law enforcement, corrections, and the legal profession; the other half had not yet made any definitive career decisions but simply felt that criminal justice was a "good," "safe," and "practical" choice.

For 15 years of his tenure at the University of Delaware, Inciardi was director of its undergraduate criminal justice program, and on more than one occasion he conducted follow-up studies of the program's graduates. The findings were fascinating. Most of those who had specific career plans at the outset of their undergraduate studies ultimately secured those positions. Many of them had moved up in the ranks in

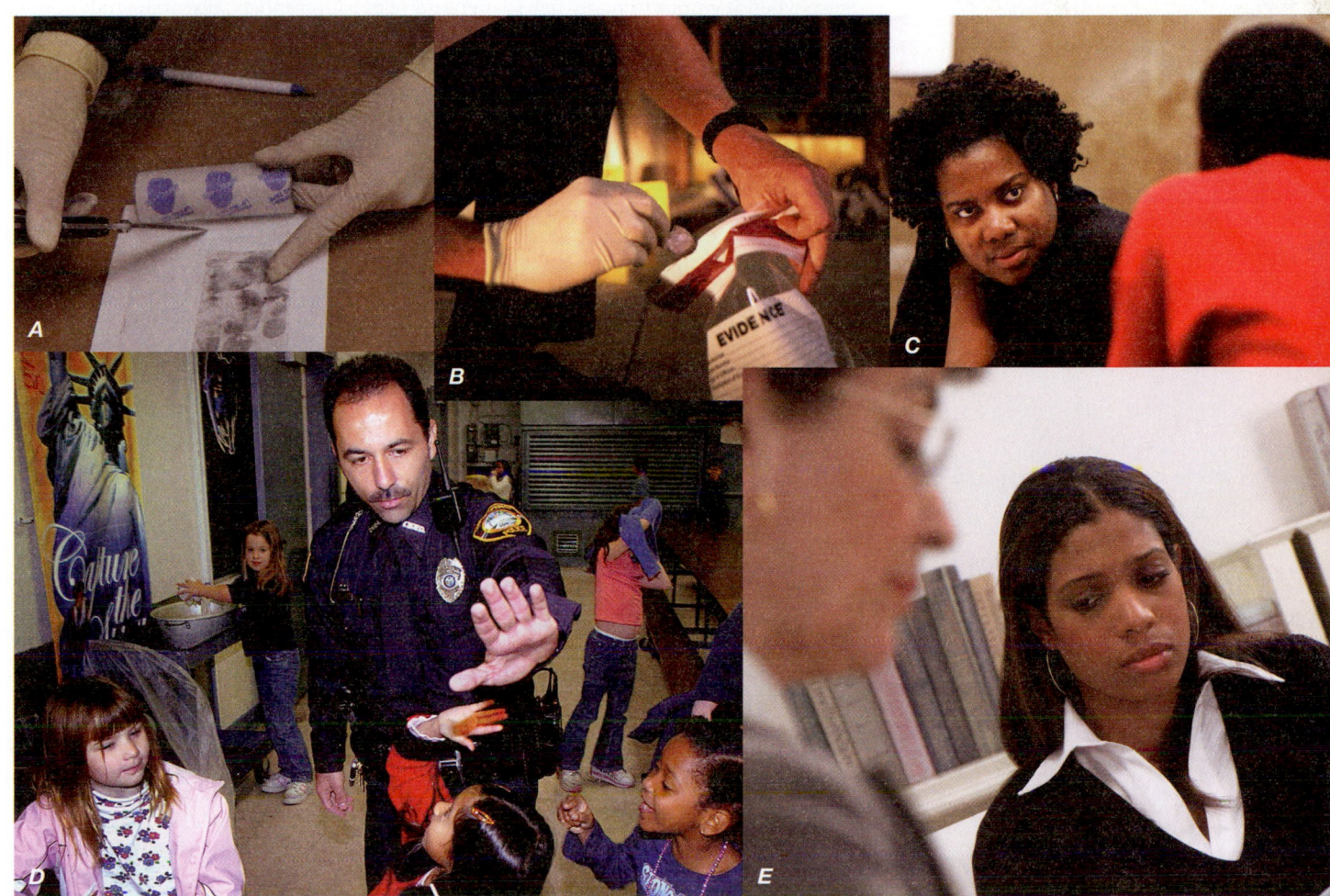

Criminal justice education prepares you for a variety of jobs, including the following sworn, staff, and ancillary criminal justice positions: (A) crime-lab technician, (B) police officer collecting evidence, (C) counselor working with urban youth, (D) school resource police officer, (E) counselor with a domestic violence victim.

their chosen occupations or had shifted into other areas of criminal justice work. Of those who had no specific career plans when they entered college, about a third were working in the criminal justice field, while the balance seemed to be working everywhere from hotel management to advertising and sales.

Former students who pursued work in the criminal justice field repeatedly emphasized that after taking entry-level positions in law enforcement, the courts, or corrections, they began to hear about the many less-visible occupations in the field. Scores of graduates shifted into these areas. In fact, in addition to working in the more traditional roles, former majors were employed in well over 100 types of criminal justice professions, including such jobs as crime-lab technician, polygraph operator, police photographer, youth-gang street worker, school safety officer, and witness-protection agent. Descriptions of specific positions in the criminal justice field appear on this book's McGraw-Hill Connect Web Site. Understanding the reality of criminal justice careers when compared to the televised fantasy is important for students interested in entering the field.

DISCRETION MATTERS

How can criminal justice education help future professionals develop the skills they need to exercise their discretion appropriately?

CONCLUSIONS

There is the old saying that "things aren't always as they appear." This is certainly the case when it comes to many newspaper and television reports, research studies, and other materials in the area of criminal justice. The media, for example, often selectively report information or distort the facts to lure readers and viewers for the sake of sales and ratings. And even in scientific research papers, mistakes and biases are commonplace. Accordingly, consumers of crime and justice reporting and research must think critically. Thinking critically does not mean criticizing the material or its authors. Rather, critical thinking means looking below the surface for potential bias, analyzing different perspectives, examining one's own biases, and judging the value of content from an analytical perspective rather than an emotional one. Below are some guidelines to help you develop critical-thinking skills.[40]

1. *Examine how terms are defined and how concepts are measured.* Suppose, for example, that you see this newspaper headline: "Fear of Crime Greater in Southern States." As you read the article, you find that the study compared people from all over the country who called in to radio talk shows concerning their fears about neighborhood crime. The first thing to consider is the fact that the story relied on self-reports (which are often either over- or understated), rather than on more objective measures of fear—such as people's use of home and auto security systems, the number of locks on their doors, or their habits of going out at night alone, or not at all. The point here is that conclusions may change when the definitions of terms are adjusted and the methods of collecting data are considered.

2. *Inspect the evidence.* Suppose the same newspaper article reported that the fear of crime was especially high among women, particularly older women. This conclusion immediately raises a few questions. First, how many men called in to the talk show? How many younger versus older women called in? How large were the differences between genders and between older women and younger women? Were tests of statistical significance conducted?

3. *Look for potential biases.* Returning to the newspaper article examining the research on fear of crime one more time, can you think of anything that may have biased the information? The fact that the conclusions were based on call-ins to talk shows is an automatic bias, because it doesn't include people who don't call in to talk shows. Another bias is that systematic studies have demonstrated that older people view themselves as more vulnerable to crime and hence are more fearful of it. Moreover, many retired people prefer warmer climates, and there

are higher proportions of older people in some parts of the South than in the North; in addition, because they are retired, they are more likely to be listening to a daytime talk show than younger working people. Perhaps most important, virtually all surveys and polls—regarding the fear of crime, attitudes toward the police, opinions about the death penalty, or any other issue—are biased because of a person's self-selection to participate, whether by calling in to a talk show or responding to an Internet, magazine, or telephone survey.

4. *Ask whether the conclusions have been oversimplified.* As you likely suspect already, criminal justice operations are complex. Consequently, you should be very suspicious whenever a report seems to oversimplify a relationship, trying to argue that something very complex can be distilled into a single important answer or catchy slogan. For example, some years ago radical sociologist Paul Takagi commented on the police use of deadly force: "police have one trigger finger for blacks and another for whites."[41] This is an oversimplification, and a particularly inflammatory one.

5. *Ask whether the conclusions have been overgeneralized.* Often, politicians, officials, and even citizens attribute changes in crime patterns or trends to changes in policy or politics. When you see news reports about increasing or declining crime rates or the deterrent effects of particular policies, think critically about the issues, and examine the nature of the claims being made. What other factors might be at play?

6. *Consider other possible interpretations.* Healthy skepticism is one of the trademarks of critical thinking, and critical thinkers enjoy pursuing alternative explanations to common conclusions. Proponents of California's "three strikes and you're out" law initially claimed that the legislation was effectively deterring violent crime, citing the more than 42,000 offenders currently incarcerated under the rule. Looking to California's success, other states and the federal government followed its lead and enacted similar legislative efforts. However, recent concerns about the economic costs of incarceration have led many to question the utility of this legislation. Struggling with the economic challenges posed by the three-strikes legislation, California is reconsidering this "successful" policy with a proposed ballot measure in 2012 that would limit the three-strikes sentence to violent or serious offenders and allow a small group of those already sentenced to apply for a reduced sentence.[42] Do the sheer numbers of individuals locked up under a particular law demonstrate its success, particularly given the potential negative effects of this legislation on communities and local economies? What types of crimes are people "striking out" on? Is the number of people incarcerated evidence of crime deterrence? Finally, what might be the implications of such a policy for those who are incarcerated?

7. *Consider who is offering the explanation.* If a report is released praising the effect of a particular criminal justice approach, be skeptical. Determine who did the evaluation. Was the report based on a self-evaluation or on the findings of an independent research group? If the latter was the case, did this group have an agenda of its own?

8. *Think through the topic.* In analyzing information you encounter in the news or elsewhere, draw on what you are learning from this textbook. Combine that information with what you know from experience and logic. For example, questions are raised in later chapters about the effectiveness of boot camps as a rehabilitative approach, about Internet-based sex-offender registries, and a number of other topics. When thinking critically about these issues, draw on what you know, and think about what kinds of additional information you might need to arrive at an educated opinion.

An introductory course in criminal justice is not simply a collection of definitions and court cases linked together by case studies and anecdotal commentary. Rather, the material is organized in a manner that facilitates students' understanding of the basic foundations, structure, and components of the justice process. Throughout this text, you will find multiple issues that require critical thinking. Specifically, the text highlights the role of individual discretion within the criminal justice process and asks you to examine your own reactions and thoughts about how the system responds to crime and criminal offenders. As you sharpen your critical-thinking skills, you will become increasingly adept at examining the challenging issues facing not only those who work in the criminal justice system specifically but also our society more generally.

SUMMARY AND REVIEW

- **Compare and contrast the meaning of the terms** *criminal justice, criminology, criminal law,* **and** *criminal procedure.*

  - Criminal justice refers to the structure, functions, and processes of those agencies that deal with the management of crime—the police, the courts, and corrections.
  - Criminology is the scientific study of the causes of crime, rates of crime, the punishment and rehabilitation of offenders, and the prevention of crime.
  - Criminal law is the branch of modern jurisprudence that deals with offenses committed against the safety and order of the state.
  - Criminal procedure is the series of orderly steps and actions, authorized by law or the courts, used to determine whether a person accused of a crime is guilty or not guilty.

- **Summarize the models of criminal justice, including the due process, crime control, wedding cake, and funnel models.**

  - Herbert Packer's classic book *The Limits of the Criminal Sanction* contains an analysis and description of two models of the criminal justice process. The crime control model is focused on efficient processing of cases in order to control crime and keep society safe from criminals. The due process model emphasizes the potential for error in the processing of cases.
  - The wedding cake model depicts the cases processed by the criminal justice system arranged in four layers. The bottom layer encompasses lower-level misdemeanors that receive very little attention from the system. The next two layers contain felonies, with the less serious felonies on the lower of the two layers and the more serious on the upper layer. These cases receive much more attention from criminal justice personnel, and offenders convicted of these offenses are often given serious punishments. The

top layer represents the celebrated cases, offenders, and offenses that receive so much media attention.
  - The funnel model depicts the diminishing number of cases that are processed by the criminal justice system as cases are removed from the system for such reasons as diversion to juvenile court and dismissal for lack of evidence.

- **Describe the development of criminal justice as a professional and academic field.**

  - The field began developing in the 1960s. Rising crime rates and social unrest related to racism and the civil rights movement contributed to concerns about "law and order" in our society. The nationalization of the Bill of Rights and growing concerns about civil liberties helped fuel the national discussion about crime and criminal justice.
  - Recommendations by the President's Commission on Law Enforcement and Administration of Justice altered the future of criminal justice in the United States.

- **Identify and explain the major themes in modern criminal justice.**

  - War on Drugs
  - Gender, Crime, and Criminal Justice
  - The Criminal Justice "Nonsystem"
  - Victims and Justice
  - Criminal Justice and the Media
  - Terrorism, Criminal Justice, and the Constitution

- **Acquire tools for critically analyzing information you encounter about the criminal justice system and process.**

  - Examine the definition of terms, the evidence used to support assertions, and the methods of collecting that evidence.
  - Be wary of bias, oversimplification, and overgeneralization.
  - Consider alternative interpretations and the source of explanations.

KEY TERMS

Burger Court (p. 12)
constitutional law (p. 6)
crime control model (p. 11)
criminal justice (p. 6)
criminal law (p. 6)
criminal procedure (p. 6)

criminology (p. 6)
due process model (p. 11)
funnel model (p. 13)
law and order (p. 6)
Law Enforcement Assistance
    Administration (LEAA) (p. 10)

President's Commission on Law
    Enforcement and Administration
    of Justice (p. 7)
Warren Court (p. 11)
wedding cake model (p. 12)

ISSUES FOR CRITICAL THINKING AND DISCUSSION

1. What roles do you think citizens and politicians play in the development of criminal justice policies?
2. How does the Omnibus Crime Control and Safe Streets Act of 1968 resemble recent legislative efforts to combat terrorism in the United States?
3. How does the existing social climate affect the policies that are being implemented? How has the social climate shaped criminal justice policies in the past?
4. To what extent do you think criminal justice in America is a "system" or "nonsystem"?
5. How might studying criminal justice help citizens become better consumers of criminal justice policy?
6. In your opinion, how significant a role does discretion play in criminal justice decision-making? How significant a role should it play?

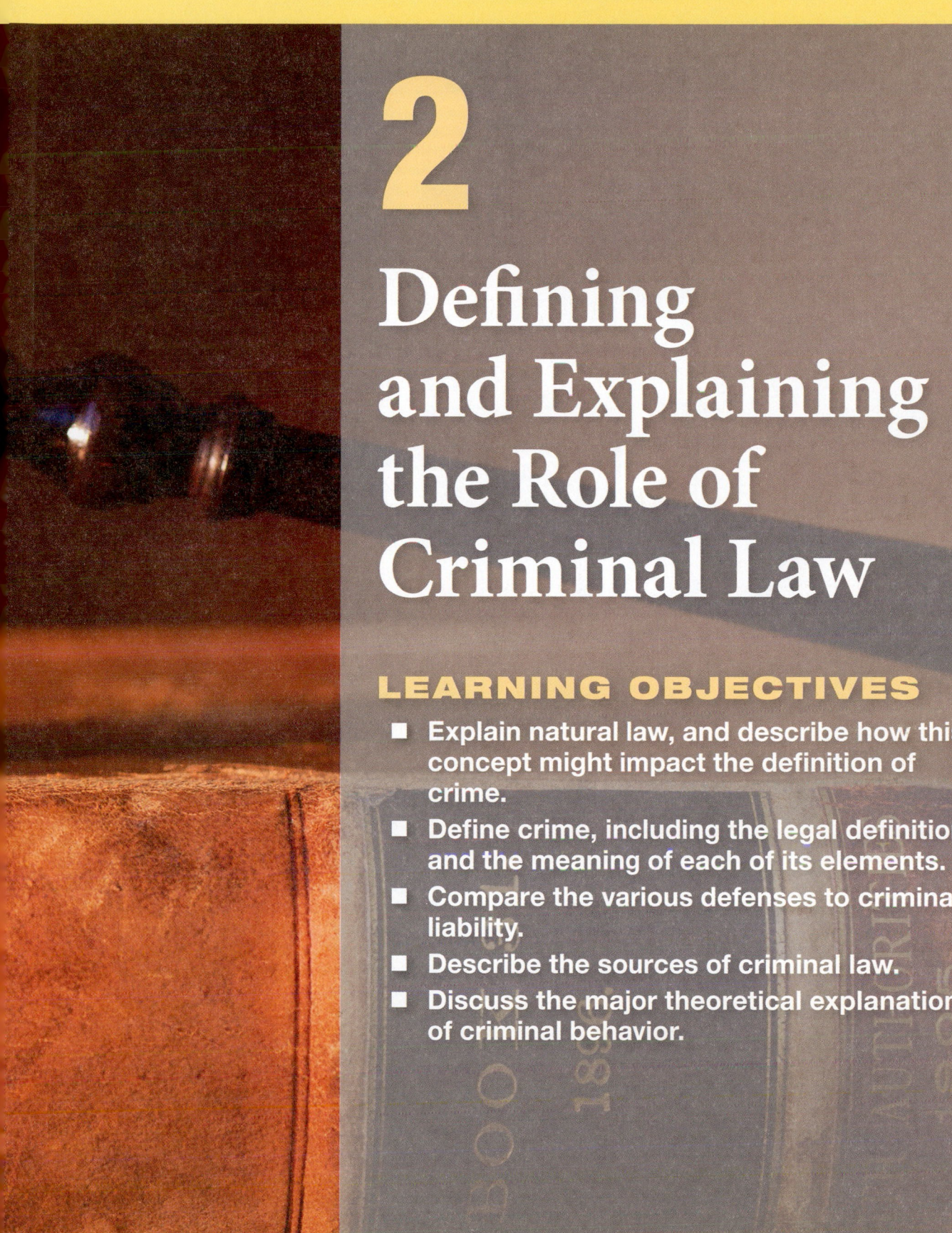

2

Defining and Explaining the Role of Criminal Law

LEARNING OBJECTIVES

- Explain natural law, and describe how this concept might impact the definition of crime.

- Define crime, including the legal definition and the meaning of each of its elements.

- Compare the various defenses to criminal liability.

- Describe the sources of criminal law.

- Discuss the major theoretical explanations of criminal behavior.

CRIMINAL BEHAVIOR, NOT CRIMINAL SELF

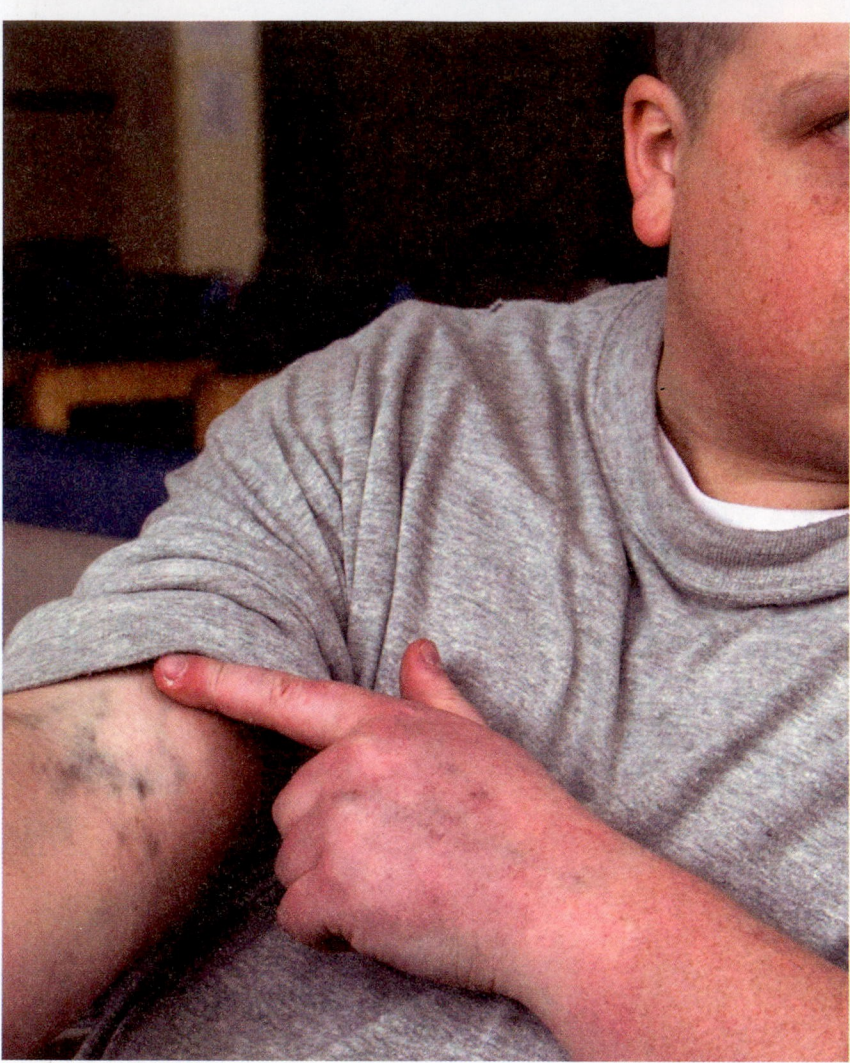

The *Robinson* case examined the ability of states to criminalize drug addiction as a status.

A police officer stopped Lawrence Robinson on a Los Angeles city street. The officer observed scabs and what he believed to be needle marks on the inside of Robinson's arm, and he arrested Robinson under a California law that made it illegal to "be addicted to the use of narcotics."[1] The following morning, while Robinson was being held in the Los Angeles Central Jail, his arms were again examined and photographed for evidence of his addiction. Here the story becomes a bit less clear. Officers testified that Robinson admitted to using narcotics in the past, while Robinson contended that the conversation never happened and that the marks were the result of an

allergic condition contracted during his military service. The testimony of two witnesses supported this assertion.[2]

Interestingly, the Supreme Court did not care about this contradiction in the record in *Robinson v. California.* In this landmark case, the justices found that California's statute outlawing a condition or status, particularly that of addiction, was inconsistent with constitutional protections. Because the law relied on a condition rather than any action, the court reasoned, a person who used narcotics might never be free from prosecution. Merely having been an addict could put the individual in jeopardy of criminal prosecution.[3] In addition, the justices were concerned that such laws could make other statuses—mental or physical illness, for example—illegal. Defining a condition rather than behavior as criminal was an issue of serious concern.

How our law defines criminal behavior is an important issue for students of criminal justice. Distorted media images have left many Americans with inaccurate conceptions about what crime is, who defines something as a crime, and how such definitions come to be. Some see crime as intrinsically evil and as a pattern of behavior that threatens individual rights, civil liberties, and perhaps the very foundations of society. In response, they seek to protect themselves by installing expensive security systems and avoiding places and situations they have come to perceive as dangerous. They think of crime as something that exists outside organized society. As the Robinson case reveals, determining what constitutes a crime is at times far more complex than media depictions suggest.

In actuality, crime goes well beyond the prostitution, street crime, violence, and theft portrayed in the popular media. Moreover, the volume and rates of crime differ considerably from what conventional wisdom suggests. Although assault and theft may appear to be the most typical forms of lawbreaking, thousands of offenses can be labeled as crimes, and the majority of them rarely come to our attention unless they are propelled into national consciousness through some media event. White-collar crime, for example, is a term that describes the illegal activities of individuals conducting business. It involves billions of dollars annually in price-fixing, embezzlement, restraint of trade, stock manipulation, misrepresentation, bribery, false advertising, and consumer fraud (Exhibit 2.1). The economic toll from white-collar crime well exceeds the dollar losses from all known robberies, burglaries, and other thefts—yet it is rarely included in the average person's conception of "crime."

Also important is the fact that many activities are considered crimes in some jurisdictions but not in others and in some nations but not in others. Some previously criminal activities are now legal, and some behaviors that many people consider normal and common are nevertheless defined as criminal under the law.

What, then, is crime? In this chapter we answer this question through an analysis of how behaviors come to be defined as crime and the relation of these crimes to law. To begin this discussion, we look at the development of crime from the concept of natural law. We then explore the ways in which society constructs definitions of crime, moving from there to the modern codified criminal statutes. Last, we examine attempts to explain criminal behavior. These explanations help us see how criminal behavior fits in other psychological, social, and environmental contexts.

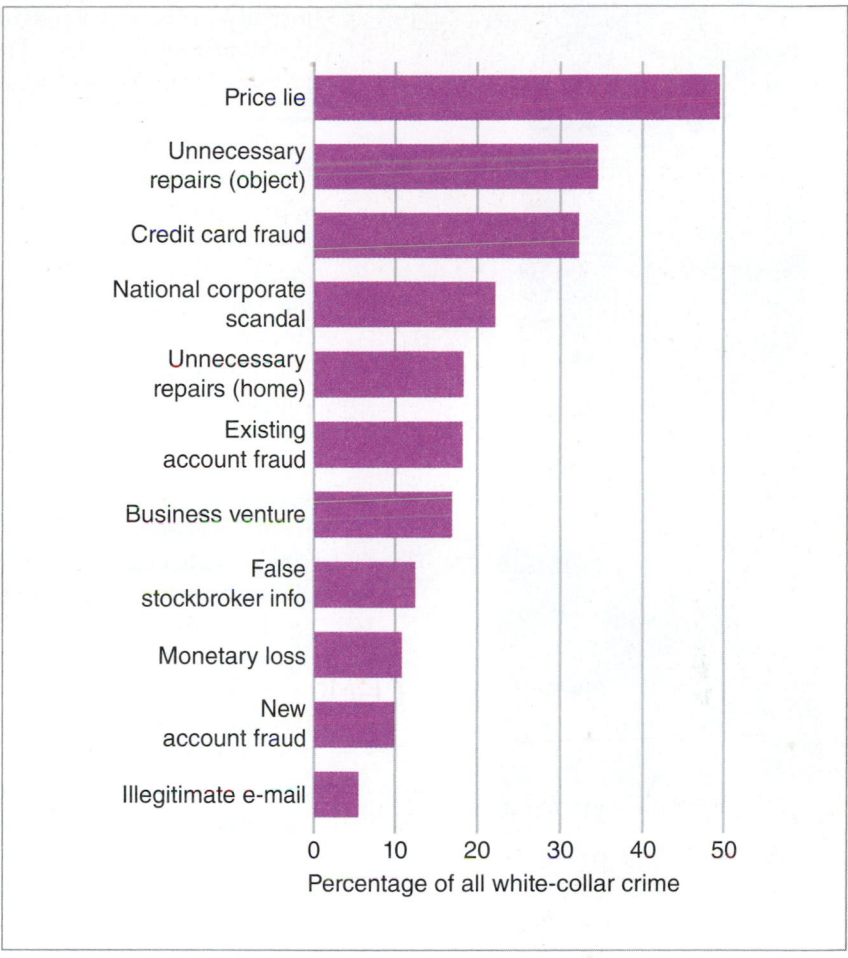

EXHIBIT 2.1   As the graph shows, white-collar crime includes numerous types of offenses that affect the daily lives of many Americans.
Source: Bureau of Justice Statistics

THE NATURE AND DEFINITION OF CRIME

In its broadest sense, **crime** is the violation of a generally accepted set of rules that are backed by the power and authority of the state. Nevertheless, this definition of crime evolved from historical images of right and wrong and the precepts of natural law. Understanding these earlier concepts will help you see why defining crime is a continually evolving and complex matter.

Natural Law

The concept of **natural law** has been a fundamental attribute of human societies for over 20 centuries. It refers to a body of principles and rules imposed on individuals by some extra-human power and is therefore considered to be uniquely fitting for and binding on any community of rational beings. Since natural law has generally determined what is right and wrong, it follows that its precepts should be eternal, universal, and unchangeable. However, an examination of natural law from the time of the ancient Greeks to the present suggests that there is no single and unchanging view of the concept. To Roman jurists, for example, *jus naturale*, or natural law, meant a body of ideal principles that people could understand rationally and that

DISCRETION MATTERS

Why do criminal justice agencies focus on some types of crime while giving less attention or resources to others?

The Code of Hammurabi is a large stone pillar that was displayed in public areas so all could see the laws governing the community. This one, from 1754 BC, contains both images and words, though in some cases these are difficult to decipher.

included the perfect standards of right conduct and justice.[4] Throughout the Middle Ages, the law of nature was identified with the Bible, with the laws and traditions of the Catholic Church, and with the teachings of the church fathers.

The power of natural law suggests that certain acts—for example, killing or stealing—would be considered criminal by rational persons everywhere. However, research has failed to yield examples of activities that have been universally prohibited. For example, many people believe that incest is a universal crime or taboo, because rules forbid such behavior in one form or another in every known society. However, societies and cultures vary considerably in their view as to what exactly constitutes incest. While in virtually all settings incest refers to sexual relations between parents and children and between siblings, in some royal marriages and sacred rituals, the incest taboo has been lifted. As another example, even the act of murder is not universally viewed as criminal, and in some contexts, such as war and state use of the death penalty, it is legally permitted. In traditional Comanche society, for example, if a husband killed his wife—with or without good cause—the act was not viewed as criminal; it was an absolute privilege and right that not even the family of the victim could challenge. In fact, the only crime in the Comanche legal system was excessive sorcery, for it was considered a threat to the tribe as a whole.[5]

In sum, there has been a persistent conviction throughout history that some higher law exists, the violation of which constitutes crime. These differing conceptions of what laws are have resulted in conflicting and confusing understandings and definitions of crime. Natural law is significant, however, in both the evolution of criminal laws and modern conceptions of natural crimes. Elements of the natural law concept were incorporated into the Code of Hammurabi, the first-known written legal document, which dates back to about 1700 BC.[6] This idea also played a key role in the formulation of Greco-Roman law, and it is a cornerstone of a portion of contemporary Anglo-American law.

Crime as a Social Construct

As noted, the ideas of natural law and natural crime lack both clarity and precision. Conceptions of crime as amoral behavior are even more confusing when one considers that there is no moral code to which all people subscribe, even within a single society or community. A number of social scientists, therefore, have come to describe crime as a human construction.[7] By this they mean that the definition of behavior as deviant or criminal comes from individuals and social groups and involves a complex social and political process that extends over time. Hence, this idea suggests, people and groups create crime by making rules. Exhibit 2.2 illustrates how people in the United States rank the problems of crime versus poverty. Notice how this distribution, particularly the changing importance of crime, varies over time. How do you think current events or splashy, high-profile offenses or offenders might impact these statistics?

This sociological view of crime rejects the notion that the rightness or wrongness of actions has a divine origin. Instead, it examines how certain behaviors come to be seen as criminal. This perspective focuses specifically on **deviance**—a concept that is considerably broader than crime. It assumes that people and societies create rules in response to behavior that they perceive to be harmful to the larger group. Thus, as sociologist Kai T. Erikson wrote, "The term *deviance* refers to conduct which the people of a group consider so dangerous or embarrassing or irritating that they bring special sanctions to bear against the persons who exhibit it."[8]

Crime and Moral Crusades The mechanisms through which society comes to view behavior as deviant were described by sociologist Howard S. Becker as a process undertaken by "crusading reformers," "rule creators," and "moral entrepreneurs."[9] According to this view, the reformer or crusader views certain elements in society as unconditionally evil and feels that rules must be made to correct and remove such wickedness. The crusader's role, then, involves bringing the deviant behavior to the attention of the public, society's opinion makers, and ultimately the designated rule creators and enforcers. Note that although the deviance perspective suggests a process by which some definitions of deviance and crime come into being, it fails to explain how or why many long-standing definitions of crimes against person and property initially came into being.

Crime and Deviance Not all deviant behavior is criminal—and conversely, not all criminal behavior is deviant. Numerous kinds of activities receive social disapproval and may even be deemed blatantly antisocial, but they are not necessarily crimes. To many Americans, picking one's nose in public, espousing Nazism, or being an alcoholic deviant are not criminal activities and are not treated as such. The behaviors might even be strongly disapproved of, with the deviants being subject to severe ostracism by their peers—but criminal sanctions would not be brought to bear against them.

By contrast, numerous other behaviors are indeed criminal, but the participants are not necessarily considered deviant. Wagering money with friends on the outcome of the World Series or the Super Bowl may violate the criminal law in some jurisdictions, yet to society at large the practice is hardly deviant. Similarly, certain intimate sexual activities may violate state and local criminal laws, but within the context of a consenting adult relationship, those activities are considered normal by some individuals in our society.

Finally, although the deviance perspective does not offer a basis for a working definition of crime, it does explain how some definitions of crime come into being and, in that sense, how crime can be socially constructed and defined. More important, however, this perspective illustrates how people come to be labeled as deviant or criminal, how society may react to them, and how the process of labeling them as outsiders might affect their behavior. Society may react to this behavior in a variety of ways—with disgust, anger, hate, gossip, isolation, physical punishment, incarceration, or even execution.

Crime as a Legal Construct

Because definitions of crime as violations of natural law or as deviance lack precision, we need to look directly at law for a formal definition. This need was best stated nearly seven decades ago by Jerome Michael and Mortimer J. Adler:

> The most precise and least ambiguous definition of crime is that which defines it as behavior which is prohibited by the criminal code. The criminal law describes many kinds of behavior, gives them names such as murder and arson and rape and burglary, and proscribes them. If crime is defined in legal terms, the only source of confusion is such ambiguity as may inhere in the legal definitions of specific crimes. It is sometimes difficult to

EXHIBIT 2.2
Proportions of U.S. Population Reporting Crime or Poverty as the Most Important Problem Facing the Nation (percentages)

Year	Crime	Poverty
1990	2	11
1993	9	15
1996	23	5
2000	13	3
2004	1	1
2008	1	3
2011	1	2

Source: The Gallup Organization

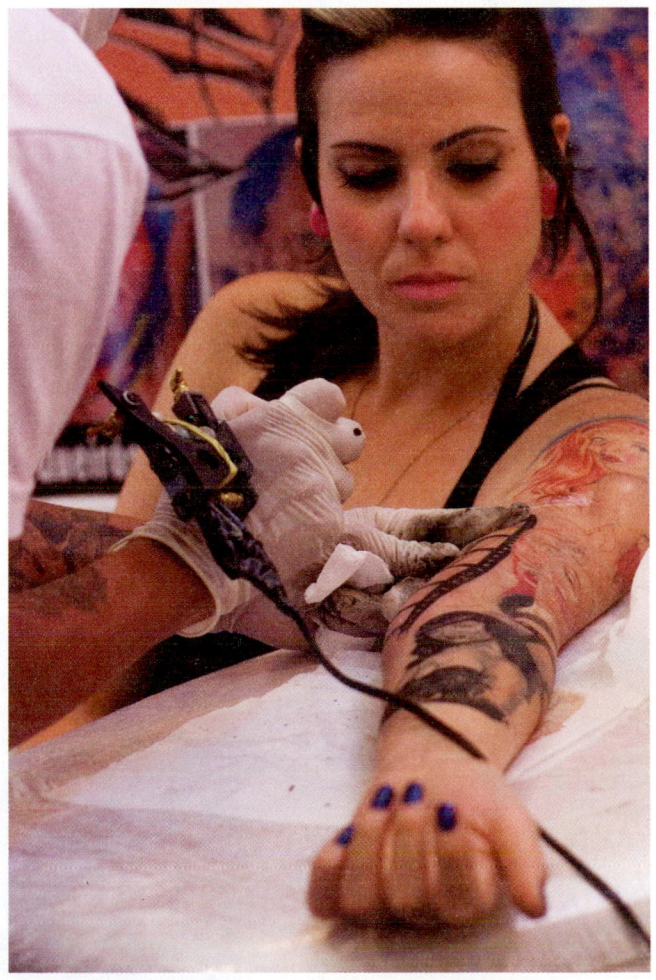

Tattoos were once considered markers of participation in deviant subcultures. Research by the Pew Center indicates that more than 45 million Americans have tattoos today, including about 36 percent of 18- to 25-year-olds.[10]

tell whether specific conduct falls within the legal definition, whether, for example, a specific homicide is murder or what degree of murder, as that offense is defined by law. But even so, the legal rules are infinitely more precise than moral judgments or judgments with regard to the antisocial character of conduct. Moreover, there is no surer way of ascertaining what kinds of behavior are generally regarded as immoral or antisocial by the people of a community than by reference to their criminal code, for in theory, at least, the criminal code embodies social judgments with respect to behavior and, perhaps more often than not, fact conforms to theory.[11]

The word *crime* has its roots in the Latin *crimen,* meaning judgment, accusation, or offense. Numerous social scientists and legal scholars have offered definitions of crime within this legal perspective. Edwin H. Sutherland, perhaps the most renowned American criminologist of the mid-twentieth century, wrote that "the essential characteristic of crime is that it is behavior which is prohibited by the State and against which the State may react."[12] *Black's Law Dictionary* defines crime as "a positive or negative act in violation of the penal law; an offense against the state."[13] In contrast, in the field of criminal justice, crime is defined simply as "an act or omission prohibited by law."[14] Yet these definitions, while correct, lack the precision necessary to fully understand the term. Lawyer and sociologist Paul W. Tappan has offered a definition of crime that marks its major boundaries:

> Crime is an intentional act or omission in violation of criminal law (statutory and case law), committed without defense or justification, and sanctioned by the state as a felony or misdemeanor.[15]

Tappan's definition is the one used throughout this text. Each element of this definition is analyzed in detail in the following sections of this chapter.

Act or Omission Central to the American system of law is the philosophy that a person cannot be punished for his or her thoughts. Thus, for there to be a crime, there must be the commission of an act that is legally forbidden or the **omission** of an act that is legally required. A person may wish to commit a crime or think about committing a crime, but the crime does not typically occur until the act takes place. If that person were to consider murdering someone, for example, there would be no crime of murder until the killing, or an attempt to kill, occurred. Moreover, the person could conceivably plan for a long time to commit a crime, but again, the crime of

DISCRETION MATTERS

Why does the law define only some, not all, harmful actions or behaviors as crimes?

The elaborate plan of Nathan Leopold and Richard Loeb to murder a 14-year-old boy demonstrates the complexity of the crime of conspiracy.

murder would not come into being until the act took place. This person may be found guilty of conspiracy to commit murder, but not murder without the actual act.

In certain circumstances, planning to commit a crime is a criminal act in and of itself. **Conspiracy** is concert (collaboration) in criminal purpose, and it must involve two or more people. Perhaps the best-known case of conspiracy was related to the Leopold and Loeb killing of 14-year-old Robert Franks in 1924. Nathan F. Leopold Jr. was a graduate of the University of Chicago and the son of a multimillionaire shipping magnate; Richard A. Loeb was a University of Michigan graduate and the son of Sears Roebuck and Company's vice president, Albert A. Loeb. Leopold and Loeb had structured what they felt would be the perfect crime—the kidnapping, ransoming, and killing of an innocent youth. Their planning extended over many weeks and involved renting a car; opening a bank account for the ransom money; riding trains to the tentative ransom site; purchasing rope, a chisel, and hydrochloric acid with which they would garrote, stab, and mutilate their victim; gathering rags with which they would bind and gag the victim; selecting wading boots to be worn in the swamp where they would leave the victim's body; preparing a ransom note; and discussing potential victims. Because of these actions, Leopold and Loeb were guilty of conspiracy to commit a crime. Their agreement to murder, combined with their extensive preparations, constituted a criminal act. When they selected Robert Franks as their victim and then abducted and murdered him, their crimes advanced from conspiracy to include kidnapping and homicide.[16]

In a related context, people become parties to crime when they assist, aid and abet (help), incite, or otherwise encourage others to commit crimes. More specifically, an **abettor** is one who, with the requisite criminal intent, encourages, promotes, instigates, or stands by to assist the perpetrator of a crime. An **accessory before the fact** is an individual who abets a crime but is not present when the crime is committed. By contrast, an **accessory after the fact** is one who, knowing that a felony has been committed, receives, relieves, comforts, or assists the perpetrator to hinder apprehension or conviction.

Failure to act in a particular case can also be a crime if there is some legal duty to act. To illustrate, let us consider the case of *People v. Beardsley,*[17] in which a legal duty

The legal duty to act is often established through some contractual obligation or relationship. For example, colleges and universities are often expected to protect the students living in the dormitories on their campuses. If that relationship is violated or if students are harmed because a university did not uphold that obligation, the university may be criminally or legally liable.

to act was absent. This case involved a man who spent a weekend with his mistress. After a serious argument, the woman took an overdose of narcotics, but the man made no attempt to obtain medical help to save her life. His failure to assist her did not constitute a crime. Although he may have had a moral obligation to help her, he had no legal duty to do so. The two had no contractual relationship such as might exist between parents and a day care center or between a patient and a hospital; the two had no status relationship that imposed a legal duty, such as that between husband and wife; and there was no legal statute imposing a legal duty on the man.

DISCRETION MATTERS

How do you think a particular offender's intent affects the decision-making of criminal justice personnel?

Criminal Intent   For an act or omission to be a crime, the law requires the presence of a blameworthy mind, or *mens rea*—from the Latin for "guilty mind." The concept of mens rea is based on the assumption that people have the capacity to control their behavior and to choose between alternative courses of conduct. Thus, the notion of **criminal intent** suggests that the person is aware of what is right and wrong under the law and intends to violate the law, as contrasted with a person who is too young or is mentally retarded or mentally ill and may not be capable of full use of reason.

Most legal commentaries divide criminal intent into two basic types of intent: specific and general. Specific intent is present when the circumstances of the crime show that the offender must have consciously desired the prohibited result. For example, the crime of burglary reflects the notion of specific intent. Burglary involves two broad elements: entry into the dwelling of another and the intention to commit a crime (usually theft) therein. The burglar manifests specific intent because he or she consciously desires the prohibited result—theft.

By contrast, consider the case of a man outraged by his neighbor's barking dog. He expresses his disapproval by warning the neighbor that if the dog is not quieted, he will shoot the animal. When the threat is ignored and the dog continues to bark, the angry man fires three shots through his neighbor's window, intending to kill the dog. Instead, one of the bullets kills his neighbor. Although specific intent is not present in this case, general intent is. General intent refers to conscious wrongdoing from which a prohibited result follows, even in the absence of a desire for that particular result. In other words, general criminal intent involves the conscious and intentional commission of a crime when the specific result of that crime was not necessarily intended.

Although criminal intent, whether specific or general, is necessary for an act to be considered a crime, there are some exceptions to this rule of law. Under the doctrine of **vicarious liability** (referred to in some jurisdictions as *respondent superior*), liability can be imposed on an employer for certain illegal acts committed by employees during the course and scope of their employment. This doctrine is generally directed at the protection of the public health.[18]

Violation of Criminal Law   For an act or its omission to be a crime, not only must there be criminal intent, but the behavior must violate the criminal law. **Criminal law**—as opposed to noncriminal, or civil, law—is the branch of jurisprudence that deals with offenses committed against the safety and order of the state. As such, criminal law relates to

The sale of cigarettes to minors by a clerk in a drugstore or convenience store is an example of vicarious liability and can result in criminal fines for the store's manager and/or owner.

actions that are considered so dangerous, or potentially so, that they threaten the welfare of society as a whole. This is why in criminal cases, it is the government that brings the action against the accused. **Civil law,** by contrast, is the body of principles that determines private rights and liabilities. In civil law cases, one individual or organization brings an action against another—a plaintiff versus a defendant—as opposed to the government bringing an action against an accused person. More specifically, civil law is structured to regulate the balance of rights between individuals or organizations; it involves such areas as divorce, child support, contracts, and property rights. Civil law also includes torts, which are civil wrongs for which the law provides redress.

There are three basic types of criminal law: statutory law, case law, and common law. **Statutory law** consists of laws or statutes enacted by legislatures. Each state has a statutory criminal code, as does the federal government. The laws that define the boundaries of such offenses as homicide, rape, burglary, robbery, and larceny are generally statutory. By contrast, **case law** is law that results from court interpretations of statutory law or from court decisions in cases in which rules have not been fully codified or have been found to be vague or in error.

Classic examples of case law are the Supreme Court decisions used at the beginning of each chapter, including *Robinson v. California,*[19] the one you read about in this chapter that overturned Robinson's conviction as a narcotics addict under a section of the California Health and Safety Code. The Supreme Court's ruling in *Robinson v. California*[20] represents case law in that it defined narcotics addiction as a status that was no longer punishable under the law. Many of the cases you will read about in this book are presented precisely because they prompted changes in the case law regarding criminal justice and procedure.

Common law refers to customs, traditions, judicial decisions, and other materials that guide courts in decision-making but that have not been enacted by legislatures or are embodied in the Constitution. Among the more familiar aspects of common law are the rights set forth in the Declaration of Independence and other doctrines protecting life, liberty, and property. We will return to this topic later in the chapter.

Defense or Justification   For an act (or the omission thereof) to be a crime, it must not only be intentional and in violation of the criminal law but also be committed without defense or justification. **Defense** is a broad term that can refer to any number of situations that would mitigate legal guilt in a criminal offense. The most common defenses are insanity, mistake of fact, mistake of law, duress, consent of the victim, entrapment, and justification.

Insanity.   The term **insanity** refers to any unsoundness of mind, madness, mental alienation, or want of reason, memory, and intelligence that prevents an individual from comprehending the nature and consequences of his or her acts or from distinguishing between right and wrong conduct. Insanity is a legal concept rather than a medical one, but it is a very complex issue. A few jurisdictions recognize that some defendants can be partially insane with respect to the circumstances surrounding the commission of a crime but sane as to other matters.

The definition of insanity varies across the United States. The cornerstone of the insanity defense and one of the major definitions of insanity emerged from the 1843 case of Daniel M'Naghten, who had killed the secretary to Sir Robert Peel. At his trial, heard before the British House of Lords, he claimed that at the time he committed the act he had not been of a sound state of mind. From this came the **M'Naghten Rule**—the "right-or-wrong" test of criminal responsibility:

> If the accused was possessed of sufficient understanding when he committed the criminal act to know what he was doing and to know that it was wrong, he is responsible therefore, but if he did not know the nature and quality of the act or did know what he was doing but did not know that it was wrong, he is not responsible.[21]

The M'Naghten test was severely criticized on the grounds that it is arbitrary and applies to only a small percentage of people who are mentally ill. In 1954, the U.S. Court of Appeals for the District of Columbia broadened the M'Naghten Rule, creating what has become known as the **Durham Rule.** In *Durham v. United States,*[22] the court held that an accused person is not criminally responsible if he or she suffers from a diseased or defective mental condition at the time the unlawful act is committed. This rule has also been criticized and was overturned at the federal level in 1972 by *U.S. v. Brawner.*[23] Critics claim that the Durham rule is far too broad and places too much power in the hands of psychiatrists and juries in determining the presence or absence of insanity. The insanity defense is recognized in most U.S. states with the exception of Montana, Kansas, Idaho, and Utah. Many state jurisdictions do not use the M'Naghten Rule but develop complex tests and rules for use of the insanity defense. However, the impact of the M'Naghten and Durham Rules has not diminished.

Conventional wisdom suggests that the use of the insanity defense is widespread and that many clever and willful murderers have avoided death sentences through pleas of guilty by reason of insanity. Despite this public perception, an eight-state study in the 1990s found that the insanity defense, while used in less than 1 percent of the cases, was successful only in a quarter of those.[24]

Mistake of Fact. A mistake of fact is any erroneous understanding of fact or circumstance resulting in some act that would not otherwise have been undertaken. Mistake of fact becomes a defense when an individual commits a prohibited act in good faith and with a reasonable belief that certain facts are correct, which, if they were indeed accurate, would have made the act innocent. Further, the mistake must be an honest one and not the result of negligence or poor deliberation.

For example, if Smith walks away with Jones's suitcase thinking that it is his own, Smith's defense would be that he was operating under a mistake of fact because both parties had identical luggage. Such a mistake precludes Smith from having criminal intent. As a result, he has a defense against a conviction for larceny.

Mistake of fact has been used as a defense in cases of statutory rape—that is, sexual intercourse with a person below the age (usually 16 or 18) required to give legal consent. Although a defendant may claim that his or her underage sexual partner "looked older," the courts are decidedly mixed in their acceptance of this defense.

Mistake of Law. A mistake of law is any lack of knowledge or acquaintance with the laws of the land insofar as they apply to the act, relation, duty, or matter under consideration. The old cliché that "ignorance of the law is no excuse" suggests that mistake of law is no defense against prosecution. Indeed, simple ignorance of forbidden behavior is not usually an acceptable defense; all persons are assumed to have knowledge of the law. This is true for both citizens and foreign nationals. For example, if a British woman were to drive on the left side of the road when visiting the United States, because that is the law in her native land, her ignorance would not serve as a defense against a U.S. traffic violation. Similarly, in many jurisdictions it is a crime to fail to come to the aid of a police officer when so ordered if the request is not hazardous to the citizen. This law is not well known to most citizens. Nevertheless, should an individual fail to comply with such an order on the basis of ignorance, his or her lack of knowledge of the law would not be an adequate defense against the crime. In contrast, however, as the Supreme Court ruled in *Lambert v. California,*[25] ignorance of the law may be a defense against crime if the law in question has not been made reasonably well known.[26] In that case, the Supreme Court overturned Lambert's conviction for failing to register as a felon with the city of Los Angeles; Lambert had not been aware that the city required registration of felons who remained within Los Angeles for more than five days. The court decided that knowledge or probability of knowledge of a statute is required to convict someone of a notice offense. So Lambert's mistake or ignorance did in fact excuse her criminal behavior.

Duress and Consent. The concept of **duress** and consent refers to any unlawful constraints exercised on an individual that force him or her to consent to committing some act that he or she would not otherwise have done. A typical example of duress and consent is often portrayed on television and in movies. The local bank official is forced to aid the thieves in a bank robbery while his family members are held captive by a second group of criminals. If the banker fails to cooperate, his family will be harmed. In this case duress and consent is a legal defense against crime, since the bank official had no criminal intent and since the rule includes injuries, threats, and restraints exercised not only against the individual but against his family as well. However, such threats or restraints must be against a person (as opposed to property), and they must be immediate (not future). Had the bank official been threatened with the slaying of his family at some future date, there would be no immediate and imposing threat. Similarly, if the threat had been to destroy his house, the notion of duress would be a poor defense. Duress is typically a defense only to crimes against property, not persons.

Consent of the Victim. Consent of the victim is any voluntary yielding of will causing the victim to agree to the act of the offending party. This defense has several elements. First, the victim must be capable of giving consent. Thus, this rule excludes any consent offered by individuals who are mentally ill, mentally retarded, or below the age of reason. Second, the offense must be a "consentable" crime. Murder is considered to be a nonconsentable crime, as is statutory rape—that is, the victims cannot consent to such crimes. Moreover, there are offenses, such as disorderly conduct, for which no victim can generally consent. Third, the consent cannot be obtained by fraud. For example, should an auto mechanic suggest to a customer that the car's transmission must be fully replaced when in fact only a small bolt requires tightening, the prosecuted mechanic cannot raise the victim's consent as a legal defense. Fourth, the person giving consent must have the authority to do so. Although one party may have the right to give consent to have his or her property taken, such authority cannot be applied to the property of another party.

Entrapment. **Entrapment** is the inducement of an individual to commit a crime that he or she did not previously contemplate, undertaken for the sole purpose of instituting a criminal prosecution against the person. Cases of entrapment occur when

In some jurisdictions, if a vice squad officer in plain clothes offers a female prostitute money in return for sexual favors and then arrests her, entrapment might be an available defense. Even though the accused is a prostitute by profession, the case could be one of entrapment since the offense for which she was arrested occurred only because of police inducement.

police officers, or civilians acting at their behest, induce a person to commit a crime that he or she would not have otherwise undertaken.

Inducement is the key word in the entrapment defense. It refers to the fact that the accused had no intention of committing the crime until persuaded to do so by the police officer. Should Officer Jones approach Smith, convince him to rob Brown, and then arrest Smith after the crime has been committed, the defense of police entrapment would be available.

In years past, the entrapment defense has been weakened by court decisions that have considered the offender's "predisposition" to commit a crime. In the 1976 case of *Hampton v. United States,*[27] the Supreme Court ruled that it was not entrapment for an undercover agent to supply illicit drugs to a suspected dealer and then for another agent to act as a buyer when the agent had reason to believe that the suspect was inclined, or "predisposed," to commit the crime anyway. What makes this case different from that of the prostitute is the legality of the behavior in question. Sexual intercourse is generally legal, regardless of whether one's partner is a prostitute. What constituted the crime was acceptance of money for the sexual act, and what constituted entrapment was the plainclothes officer's offer of money. In contrast, Hampton's dealing in illicit drugs was illegal; it was not the undercover agent's inducement that made the behavior illegal. Moreover, in contrast to the case of Officer Jones convincing Smith to rob Brown, Hampton was reputedly a drug dealer while Smith was not a robber by trade.

Justification. **Justification** is any just cause or excuse for the commission of an act that would otherwise be a crime. The notion of justification as a defense against crime typically involves the use of force or violence in protecting one's person or property or that of others, in preventing crime, or in apprehending offenders. Justifiable homicide includes cases of death resulting from legal demands—the execution of a duly condemned prisoner, the killing of a fleeing inmate by a prison guard, or the shooting of an armed robber by a police officer. Excusable homicide includes cases of death from accidents or misfortunes that may occur during some lawful act. Self-defense or the defense of some other individual can be viewed as either a justifiable or an excusable act, depending on the circumstances of the case.

Other Defenses and Justifications for Criminal Behavior. Some jurisdictions have particular statutes that may extend the boundaries of justifiable cause or excuse. Until 1974, for example, a Texas law defined as justifiable homicide a husband's shooting and killing of his wife's lover if he found them in the act of adultery. The law specified, however, that the shooting had to occur before the couple separated and that the husband must not have been a party to, or approved of, the adulterous connection. (Interestingly, this statute did not extend to women who found their husbands engaging in adultery.)

Still, many kinds of defenses are not allowed. For example, although the First Amendment to the Constitution guarantees religious freedom, religious practices that violate criminal law generally cannot be used to justify or excuse criminal conduct. Similarly, if a given law typically is not enforced, this does not justify the violation of that law. Ethnic custom is another defense that courts generally do not accept, as in the case of Lee and Neng Vue of South Dakota, who argued that the raw opium they were carrying was customarily used for medicinal purposes in their culture.[28] Finally, many people have attempted to use intoxication as a defense, claiming that while under the influence of alcohol or drugs they were not in control of their behavior and therefore were not criminally responsible. However, most jurisdictions distinguish between voluntary and involuntary intoxication. Voluntary intoxication is not a defense under most circumstances. In cases of involuntary intoxication, however, in which liquor or drugs are forced on an individual, a reasonable defense can be mounted, depending on the defendant's "degree of intoxication" at the time of the criminal act.

On occasion, medical necessity has been accepted as a defense in cases of marijuana possession. Advocates of the medical use of marijuana say that the drug is effective in combating the nausea associated with cancer chemotherapy and AIDS wasting syndrome. Thus in 2001, a California state court acquitted a man who offered the medical-necessity defense to a charge of cultivating 850 marijuana plants.[29] That same year, however, in *United States v. Oakland Cannabis Buyers' Cooperative*,[30] the Supreme Court ruled against the medical-necessity defense. The High Court's ruling was quite narrow, though, and over the next decade, more than a dozen states implemented laws that allow access to medical marijuana, including Alaska, Arizona, California, Colorado, Hawaii, Maine, Michigan, Montana, Nevada, New Jersey, New Mexico, Oregon, Rhode Island, Vermont, Virginia, Washington, and Washington, DC.

Other unusual health-related defenses, particularly relating to mental health, have also come before the courts. For example, an Illinois woman was spared from prison because of a shopping-addiction defense. Her lawyers argued that she suffered from "diminished mental capacity" and used shopping to "self-medicate" her depression. For embezzling $241,061 from her former employer to support her shopping compulsion, she was sentenced to probation and a number of other conditions; her sentence allowed her to continue psychotherapy sessions.[31]

Some health-related defenses are gender-specific, essentially defending a woman's crime on the basis of her mental state during times of hormonal fluctuation. For example, some courts have accepted the PMS defense (premenstrual-syndrome defense) for generations.[32] Perhaps the most notorious gender-specific case involved postpartum depression. In that 2001 case, Andrea Yates, a suburban Houston housewife, drowned her five children in a bathtub and then lined up their dead bodies in bed. Although Yates had a long history of psychotic postpartum depression, her husband, Rusty, insisted on having more children, even against the advice of the first psychiatrist to treat her. The Yates family's lifestyle was guided by a small fundamentalist Christian sect, and Rusty was in charge of all household decisions. The children were homeschooled, and Andrea rarely had the opportunity to interact with others in public. In the end, she was convinced that her children were possessed by the devil

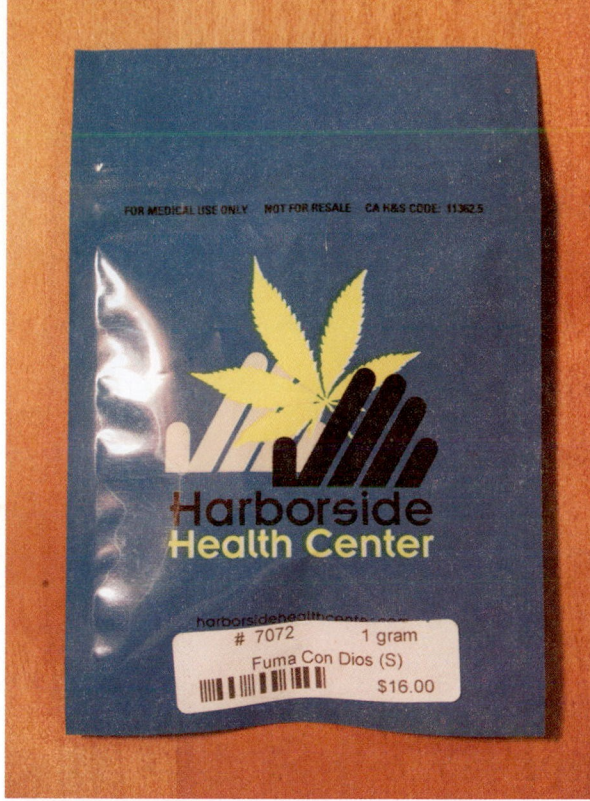

This packet from Harborside Health Center in Arch Cape, Oregon, is typical of those used to dispense medical marijuana.

DISCRETION MATTERS

How do certain defenses—for example, insanity or duress—give criminal justice professionals the ability to respond to offenders with special circumstances?

The case of Andrea Yates provides an example of gender-specific mental illness defense issues.

and that killing them would save their souls. However, the notoriously conservative Harris County jury rejected her insanity defense, instead convicting her of capital murder and sentencing her to life in prison.

In 2006, after a series of appeals, Yates was tried again and found not guilty by reason of insanity. She was committed to a Texas psychiatric facility until 2007, when she was moved to a low-security mental hospital in the state.[33] Other syndrome defenses include posttraumatic stress disorder and battered-woman syndrome. These have been used with mixed results in criminal court trials.

Law Sanctioned by the State

The maxim *nullum crimen sine poena* (no crime without punishment) dictates that a law must be written, that persons cannot be tried for acts that are not crimes in law, and that persons cannot be punished for acts for which the state provides no penalty. These principles clearly are necessary for the preservation of social order. If a legal system had no written law, on a whim, the court or the state could potentially construe any act as a crime, resulting in a situation of tyranny. Moreover, if certain types of behavior were defined as crimes but there were no penalties for engaging in them, people would have little respect for the law, and the society would be characterized by high levels of normlessness. American law, therefore, consists of written codes describing the various prohibited forms of behavior and the range of punishments that might result from their commission.

The law must be specific, however, for many acts, depending on the circumstances, may or may not be crimes. The act of sexual intercourse, for example, can occur in any number of potentially criminal situations, including adultery, fornication, forcible and statutory rape, seduction, and incest. Sexual intercourse is also a normal, lawful act between partners. However, even as a lawful act it might be referred to as obscenity, pornography, indecent exposure, or disorderly conduct, depending on the place where it occurs. Further, at one time the ethnicity of each partner might have been relevant, and it could have been called *miscegenation* (marriage involving people of different races), which was a crime. Thus, the law must be specific as to which sex acts are prohibited and between whom, where, and under what circumstances.

Also significant in American criminal law is the doctrine that only the offender can be punished. This rule has its roots in the Old Testament doctrine that "every man shall be put to death for his own sin." However, this rule may not necessarily apply in a variety of situations. Recall, for example, the doctrine of vicarious liability, which says that an employer can be held responsible for certain crimes of his employees.

LAW AND CRIME

Legal scholar Sir James Fitzjames Stephen defined law as "a system of commands addressed by the sovereign of the state to his subjects, imposing duties and enforced by punishments."[34] Many other definitions exist, however—both philosophical and pragmatic—and they generally describe all law as a body of rules for human conduct that the courts recognize and enforce. The origins of law likely date from before the beginning of recorded history. It would be safe to assume, then, that even the simplest forms of primitive social organization needed some regulation, and law quickly evolved to fill that need.

Since the beginnings of civilization a number of distinct legal systems have emerged, including the Egyptian, Mesopotamian, Chinese, Hindu, Hebrew, Greek, Roman, Celtic, Germanic, Catholic Church (canon), Japanese, Islamic, Slavic, Romanesque, and Anglican systems.[35] The earliest of these was the Egyptian, dating from about 4000 BC, followed by the Mesopotamian in 3500 BC and the Chinese in 3000 BC. U.S. law is comparatively recent; it draws from Greek, Roman, and Catholic Church law but has its major roots in the Anglican or English common law. Other sources of U.S. law include state and federal constitutions, statutory law, and the regulations of administrative agencies. We will take a closer look at each of these and their relationship to criminal law.

Common Law

The history of common law can be traced to eleventh-century England, when King Edward the Confessor declared the existing collection of rules, customs, and traditions to be the law of the land. Much of it was unwritten, "preserved mainly in the breasts and closets of the clergy, who, as a rule, were the only persons educated in the law; in the knowledge and recollection of the thanes [barons] and the landowners whose lands and whose persons were governed by it; and in the traditions handed down from fathers to sons."[36] When William the Conqueror seized the English throne in 1066, he found a system of law that was based on the customs of the people as reflected in the decisions of judges.[37]

As time passed, a process emerged whereby this largely unwritten customary law of the land was translated into specific rules. As judges reached their decisions, a body of maxims and principles developed that was derived, in theory, from customs. The result was a set of legal rules in the form of judicial decisions that provided precedents for the resolution of future disputes. This body of decisions became the common law,[38] as opposed to law created by statute. Much of common law, moreover, reflected natural law ideas of right and wrong, as well as direct statements from the Holy Scriptures.

The early criminal laws of the American colonies developed within the tradition and structure of English common law and the English charters for the founding of settlements in the New World. As the colonies became more mature, they developed their own legal systems, but these varied little from English common law.[39]

Other Sources of Criminal Law

Although English common law rests at the foundation of American criminal law, contemporary criminal codes also reflect the content of constitutional law, administrative law, and federal and state statutory laws. Let's begin with a look at constitutional law.

Constitutional Law At the apex of the American legal system is constitutional law, or law set forth in the Constitution of the United States and in the constitutions of the various states. Constitutional law is the supreme law of the land. As such, it presents the legal rules and principles that define the nature and limits of governmental power, as well as the rights and duties of individuals in relation to the state and its governing organs. These are interpreted and extended by courts exercising the power of judicial review.

The U.S. Constitution, which embodies the fundamental principles by which the affairs of the United States are conducted, was drawn up at the Constitutional Convention in Philadelphia in 1787. The Constitution was signed on September 17, 1787, and was ratified by nine states (the number required to put it into effect) by June 21, 1788. It superseded the Articles of Confederation—the original charter of the United States—which was ratified in 1781. It is concise, and includes a preamble, seven articles, and 26 amendments. Although not all of the Constitution relates to criminal law, Supreme Court and lower-court interpretations of its articles and amendments have had a direct impact on criminal law and criminal procedure, as will be evident throughout this book.

The United States Constitution provides the legal principles that limit governmental power and outline the rights of citizens.

DISCRETION MATTERS

Criminal statutes vary from state to state. Would our system be more effective if jurisdictions had less discretion as to which behaviors they chose to outlaw?

Statutory Law Next to constitutional law in order of authority are the federal statutes, which are enacted by Congress, and state statutes, which are passed by state legislatures. Federal statutes must conform to the Constitution, and state statutes must conform to both the U.S. Constitution and the constitution of the state in which they are enacted.

With 50 separate state legislatures creating laws, and an even greater number of separate court systems interpreting them, the application of statutory laws becomes exceedingly complex. Moreover, statutory laws are far from uniform. For this reason, criminal laws established by statute tend to vary from one jurisdiction to another, and what may be a violation of the criminal law in one state may not necessarily be a violation in another.

Administrative Law Finally, criminal law can descend from **administrative law,** a branch of public law that deals with the powers and duties of government agencies. More specifically, administrative law refers to the rules and regulations of administrative agencies; the thousands of decisions made by them; their orders, directives, and awards; and the court opinions dealing with appeals from the decisions and with petitions by the agencies to the courts for the law enforcement of their orders and directives.

Much of the content of administrative law is not concerned directly with criminal behavior. Nevertheless, the rules of certain agencies bear directly on violations that would be dealt with by the criminal courts. The Drug Enforcement Administration, for example, defines substances such as heroin and marijuana as illegal. This is an administrative regulation that has been translated into criminal statutes by Congress, as well as many state legislatures.

EXPLAINING CRIMINAL BEHAVIOR

The Rosetta Stone, now in the British Museum, was found in the Nile River delta by an engineer traveling with Napoleon's troops in 1799. It was a slab of volcanic rock erected in 196 BC to honor Ptolemy Epiphanes of Syria and was inscribed in three languages—Greek, demotic Egyptian, and hieroglyphic. The significance of the stone was that it furnished Egyptologists with the key by which they could decipher the meaning of Egyptian hieroglyphics, and since that time the Rosetta Stone has served as a symbol for things that may unravel the more elusive mysteries of nature and human behavior. In like manner, the fervent efforts of students, theorists, and researchers of crime often reflect a belief in some sort of criminologist's stone—one monolithic approach or theory that would ultimately account for the entire range of behaviors interpreted by one society or another to be crime.

The question "Why do people commit crime?" has challenged the brightest minds in the criminal justice field for centuries. For example, over the past hundred or so years, the following theories have been proposed:

- A biological approach has attempted to relate crime to heredity.
- Physiological and biomedical approaches have correlated crime with both normal and abnormal physiological functions and types.
- A psychological approach has analyzed motivation and diagnosed personality deviations in relation to crime.
- A geographical approach has tried to demonstrate the influences of climate, topography, natural resources, and geographical location on crime.
- An ecological approach has investigated the impact of the spatial distribution of persons and institutions on behavior patterns.
- An economic approach has looked for relationships between various economic conditions and crime.
- A social approach has considered educational, religious, recreational, occupational, and status factors as they relate to crime.
- A cultural approach has examined various institutions, social values, and patterns and their relationship to crime patterns.
- A sociological approach has concerned itself with the nature and effects of social values, attitudes, and relationships on behavior.
- A conflict, or "critical," approach has focused on crime as a consequence of the conflicts inherent in law creation.
- A multifactor approach has sought to combine any or all of these issues to explain criminal behavior.

The existence of so many theories should not suggest that the explanations proposed have been without merit. Instead, the number should illustrate what a complex preoccupation criminal behavior represents for the field of criminology and criminal justice. In the following sections, we will examine and evaluate the major biological and sociocultural theories of crime.

Biological Theories

Biological theories are grounded in the concept of biological determinism, the notion that the causes of crime are the result of some biological or physical element—that criminals may be "born," not made. Most closely associated with the biological school of thought is Cesare Lombroso (1835–1909), an Italian doctor. Often referred to as the "father of modern criminology," Lombroso conducted systematic observations and measurements of the physical attributes of criminals and identified certain atavistic, or "prehuman," traits in his subjects. These included certain "stigmata of degeneration," such as a slanting forehead, excessive dimensions of the jaw and cheekbones, ears of unusual size, peculiarities of the eyes, abnormal teeth, excessively long arms, a sparse beard, a twisted nose, woolly hair, fleshy and swollen lips, or the presence of tattoos."[40] He also noted such nonphysical abnormalities as a lack of morality, excessive vanity, and cruelty.[41] Thus, he maintained, the criminal was born a criminal—defective or degenerate in some way. The atavistic features were apparent in both male and female criminals alike.[42]

Cesare Lombroso is identified as the father of modern criminology because of his contribution to the systematic study of criminals and criminal behavior. He used photos like these to show the physical features of criminal offenders.

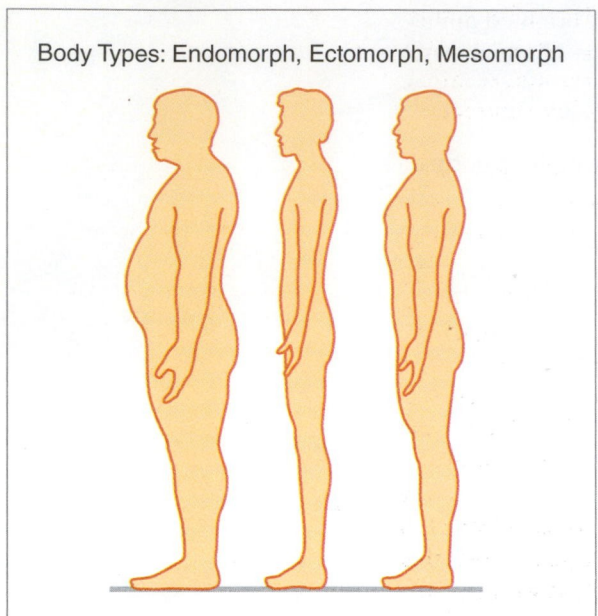

Body Types: Endomorph, Ectomorph, Mesomorph

EXHIBIT 2.3 Why might Sheldon's body types be associated with different behavioral patterns?

Source: William H. Sheldon, *The Varieties of Human Physique,* 1940

A number of other biological theorists have suggested that criminal tendencies might be inherited or innate. In 1874, Richard Dugdale traced 709 members of the Jukes family back to the year 1790 and found that 20 percent had been either habitual thieves or prostitutes or had been prosecuted for bastardy. He concluded that their criminality had been caused by "bad" heredity and that the biological transmission of feeblemindedness resulted in degeneracy.[43]

In 1939, Harvard University anthropologist Earnest A. Hooton published *Crime and the Man,* a study based on the measurements of almost 14,000 prisoners in ten states, plus a large sample of noncriminals.[44] According to Hooton, criminals belonged to a class of biological degenerates who exhibited a clear pattern of physical inferiority. Therefore, it was necessary to eliminate this "criminal stock" through sterilization, euthanasia, and cutbacks in welfare so as to breed a race disinclined toward criminal behavior.[45]

Shortly after the publication of Hooton's book, William H. Sheldon and his associates at Harvard presented a thesis for explaining criminal behavior.[46] They contended that all persons could be divided into roughly three basic body types, by which their personalities and their criminal potential could be predicted: The endomorph had a soft and round body with tapering limbs. The ectomorph had a thin, linear body with delicate bones, a small face, a sharp nose, and fine hair. The third type, the mesomorph, was a ruggedly muscular individual with a large trunk, heavy chest, and strong limbs (Exhibit 2.3). Each of the three body types had its accompanying temperament. Endomorphs were relaxed creatures of comfort who were eternal extroverts. Ectomorphs were introverts—inhibited, secretive, and restrained. Mesomorphs were assertive, aggressive, and action-oriented. Sheldon held that mesomorphs were more inclined toward criminal behavior, a conclusion he stressed again years later, subsequent to his studies of juvenile delinquents. Sheldon never denied the impact of social variables on deviance, but he held firmly that differences in body type produced differential responses to environmental pressures.

Advances in the field of molecular biology and micropathology during the second half of the twentieth century suggested a link between chromosome abnormality and criminal behavior. Chromosomes are the parts of each living cell nucleus that carry hereditary information in the form of genes. The normal chromosomal pattern that features two similar-size chromosomes is the female, or the XX, pattern. The normal male pattern, or the XY pattern, is characterized by two dissimilar chromosomes. But an XYY pattern has also been observed among some men. In the XYY pattern, the chromosomes that control the inheritance of sex-linked characteristics are abnormal. Researchers speculate that 1 in every 700 males possesses an XYY chromosomal makeup, resulting in the physical characteristics of tallness, severe acne, long arms, and other skeletal irregularities. The psychological attributes of possible mental retardation or pronounced mental illness, aggressiveness, and perhaps even social isolation, sexual deviation, and criminality were also postulated.[47]

As one might suspect, the biological theories of crime have not received widespread support. From the "atavistic man" to the "XYY man," the logical base for almost every theory has been structurally weak. To begin, proponents of biological explanations continually ignored the influences of environmental, cultural, social, and legal factors. Moreover, the study samples utilized in biological research included convicted criminals, prison inmates, and certified delinquents; rarely were nondeviant control populations introduced. In addition, many of the samples were so small that the conclusions drawn from them had little meaning. Finally, interpretations were often based on unsound reasoning, contorted logic, or blatant prejudice. Still, a number of biological theories have not been disproved by empirical studies. Moreover, the idea that there may be some biological basis for criminality continues to have some research support.

In 1985, the idea that criminals may be born, and not made, received international attention with the publication of *Crime and Human Nature,*[48] written by prominent Harvard professors James Q. Wilson (a political scientist) and Richard Herrnstein (a psychologist). The book's central thesis was that at least a portion of criminality is innate. Wilson and Herrnstein were influenced heavily by studies of IQ and constitutional inferiority, and while they rejected the idea of a specific criminal gene, they proposed the existence of a particular personality type with features that make a person more likely to value crime. These features, or "constitutional factors" as Wilson and Herrnstein referred to them, either are inborn or emerge early in life and are only minimally influenced by family. Even less influence is credited to cultural and economic factors. The authors argued, for example, that impulsiveness—the inability to contemplate the long-term consequences of one's actions—is a critical element in the criminal personality. Criminals are stunted in their ability to weigh the costs that sanctions will exact or the future benefits that discipline at school, at work, or in a career will bring. Consequently, they opt for the immediate emotional and material gratification that crime provides.

Scientific advances in our comprehension of the human genome have reinvigorated the debate over the "born criminal." At the same time, however, many biological theorists admit that although vitally important, genetics alone is insufficient to explain all criminal behavior. Perhaps the best way to encapsulate the modern compromise is to say that nature endows us with certain innate personality traits and attributes that are then nurtured, for better or for worse, through socialization processes and cultural influences.

Sociocultural Theories

Sociocultural theories examine criminality in terms of how it may relate to society and culture. The core ideas suggest that an individual's place within the social and cultural structure determines his or her tendency toward criminal behavior and that socialization processes in the family, schools, and peer groups influence and control deviant behaviors. Modern outgrowths of the sociocultural school are organized under two broad categories: (1) social and cultural structure theories and (2) social and cultural process theories. Structural theories include social disorganization theory, strain theories (anomie and general strain theory), and cultural deviance theory; process theories include social and cultural learning theory, social control theory, and labeling theory.

These sociocultural perspectives shift the focus from the individual level of the biological theories to a whole range of sociocultural questions: In which situations does crime tend to occur? Why is crime more common in certain places, within certain groups, and under certain circumstances than in others? What is the process by which some persons become criminals? Why is it that some behaviors are defined as criminal while others are not?

Social and Cultural Structure Theories   In this school of thought, criminals are not viewed as inherently evil people but rather as disadvantaged in terms of their social environment. Disorganized and decaying neighborhoods, weak social support, and a lack of economic opportunity push many individuals to seek alternate means of survival. In this view, the social structure, rather than the individual per se, is the primary cause of crime.

Social Disorganization Theory. The sociological perspective within the field of criminology in the United States originated with sociologist Robert E. Park and his colleagues at the University of Chicago. The Chicago School, as it was later called, examined the influence of social forces in specific neighborhoods on rates of crime. Park suggested that human communities were divided into "natural areas."[49] He theorized that the anthropological methods of observation and detailed description could lend insight into how neighborhoods developed over time and how areas of destitution formed. Park sent his students out to utilize these methods in studies of the natural areas of Chicago.[50]

Among Park's students were Clifford R. Shaw and Henry McKay, who found that delinquency was concentrated in the deteriorated areas of the inner city and that these areas maintained their high rates of delinquency in spite of constant population changes.[51] Through a number of case studies, Shaw and McKay promoted a social disorganization theory, directly linking high crime rates to neighborhood ecological characteristics. Their work found that youths from disadvantaged neighborhoods were participants in a subculture in which delinquency was approved behavior and that criminality was acquired in these social and cultural settings through a process of interaction.[52] Related social-cultural structure theories are anomie theory, general strain theory, and culture conflict and the cultural deviance theory—the topics we explore next.

Anomie Theory. The concept of anomie was first introduced during the latter part of the nineteenth century by the French sociologist Émile Durkheim, who described the phenomenon as a condition of normative confusion, or "normlessness," in which the existing rules and values have little impact.[53] Criminologists who have incorporated the concept of anomie into theories of criminal behavior are known as strain theorists. In general terms, strain theorists view crime as a direct result of the "strain"— frustration, anger, and hopelessness—that comes from living in disadvantaged, disorganized, and otherwise "normless" communities where legitimate opportunities for prosperity are all but unavailable. To relieve this strain and as an alternate means to reach their goals, it is theorized, people turn to deviant and criminal behavior.

Building on Durkheim's work, Robert K. Merton of Columbia University developed a general theory of criminal behavior in which two basic complementary concepts are in operation: a culture and a social structure.[54] The culture consists of a set of norms, values, and attitudes that establishes the goals that individuals should pursue and the acceptable means and behavior patterns for achieving those goals. The social structure involves the organized set of social relationships in which the members of a society play their various roles. American society, in both its culture and its social structure, places a high value on wealth, material comforts, status, and power. Moreover, the society specifies the rules for how to attain these valued goals properly— education, hard work, "smart" business practices, savings, and investments. While a high premium is placed on these goals, the possibility of achieving them is curtailed for many by reason of their position in the social structure. Crime results, Merton explains, from the strain between these aspirations and achievable goals.

Given these conditions, Merton suggested five modes of adaptation people might employ—conformity, ritualism, innovation, retreatism, and rebellion—to reconcile this conflict between cultural goals and institutionalized means. Conformity is the acceptance of cultural goals and the approved means of achieving them. Most people conform. Moreover, they do so even when the legitimate means of reaching the valued goals are out of their grasp. They play by the rules and earn a living the best way they can. And they do so because there are other society-wide cultural influences that support conformity—religious values, belief in opportunity, public education, and the absence of formal legal restrictions against upward mobility.

Ritualism is the rejection of society's goals but the acceptance of society's means of achieving those goals. Ritualists accept the means for their own sake; the goals

In Robert Merton's view, individuals living on the streets are retreating from society, rejecting both the cultural goals of attaining wealth and success and the means of attaining those goals by not participating in legitimate work.

become irrelevant and are ignored. Ritualism is thus often "mindless" behavior. The most cited example of a ritualist is the government bureaucrat who gets bound up in "red tape" and procedure and insists on strictly enforcing every petty rule.

Merton's other three adaptations relate to crime. The first, innovation, involves acceptance of cultural goals but rejection of the means a society deems proper for reaching them. The innovator selects disapproved means. Students cheating on exams, for example, and thieves, con artists, stock manipulators, drug dealers, and digital pirates attain cultural goals, such as wealth or grades, but have rejected conventional routes toward wealth and success. Innovation, however, is actually a poor term for this form of adaptation. Most criminals merely copy illegitimate means already known to them. Thus, using disapproved means is hardly the same thing as inventing or creating new ones.

Retreatism describes the rejection of both the goals a society or culture establishes and the means society prescribes for achieving these goals. The retreatists are the people living on skid row and on the streets of our central cities, as well as in rural and suburban America—the junkies, psychotics, vagrants, and vagabonds who live on the fringes of society.

Rebellion is also characterized by a rejection of the goals and the means of achieving those goals established by society. Rebels, however, characteristically aim to establish some new social order and create a new set of goals and norms governing appropriate means. The most visible examples of rebellion involve the various terrorist organizations throughout the world that resort to kidnappings, bombings, and assassinations to draw attention to their causes and to initiate change. Other rebels are the legion of adolescents who revolt in one way or another against the adult value system that has been imposed on them. Many band together into gangs, while others may live in communes.

Merton's theory of anomie is important to the study of crime and criminal justice, for it not only offers a simple paradigm for understanding the range of criminal behaviors but also suggests how and why such behaviors emerge. Merton's theory does have its limitations, however. First, while it may explain why people commit certain crimes (property crimes, for example), it fails to explain other forms of criminality, particularly violent crimes of passion. Second, Merton's approach is strongly grounded in the assumption that some sort of value consensus exists in society. This assumption ignores the process through which certain behaviors come to be defined as criminal—a process that often involves a conflict in values between those who have the power to influence public opinion and policy and those who do not. And third, Merton's theory leaves a number of questions unanswered. For example, it does not explain why an individual chooses one mode of adaptation over another or how norms begin to decay when an individual cannot achieve her or his goals. In addition, material success may not rank as high in the values of most people as Merton seems to suggest.

General Strain Theory.   Further expanding on the concept of anomie, general strain theory was developed in 1992 by sociologist Robert Agnew.[55] While Merton's theory focuses on social-class differences in criminality, Agnew's theory centers on the reasons why individuals who feel strain are more likely to commit crimes. Moreover, Agnew offers a more general explanation of crime with applicability to all segments of society, rather than restricting his analysis only to those in the lowest socioeconomic classes. General strain theory suggests that criminality is the direct result of negative affective states that are produced by negative social relationships. Specifically, strain creates negative emotions (e.g., anger and anxiety) within the individual, which in turn can create the inclination toward deviance and criminal behavior.

Going further, general strain theory outlines four general types of strain an individual might encounter: (1) the failure to achieve positively valued goals, (2) the disjunction between expectations and achievements, (3) the removal of previously attained positive achievements, and (4) exposure to negative stimuli.[56] The more sources of strain and the more vigorous the strain that individuals must contend with, the more likely the individual will turn to crime and delinquency.

Culture Conflict and the Cultural Deviance Theory.   In the 1930s, Jerome Michael and Mortimer J. Adler argued that crimes were no more than instances of behavior that are prohibited by the criminal law: "the criminal law is the formal cause of crime."[57] In other words, if there were no laws and norms, there would be no crimes.

Thorsten Sellin's *Culture Conflict and Crime* proposed the related idea that the types of conduct the rules prohibit and the nature of the sanctions attached to their violation depend directly on the interests of those individuals who influence legislation. According to Sellin, "In some states, these groups may comprise the majority, in others a minority, but the social values which receive the protection of the criminal law are ultimately those which are treasured by dominant interest groups."[58]

Crime, in this orientation, can result from a conflict between (1) the norms, values, and goal orientations of one social or cultural group and (2) the legal codes imposed by an alternative group that has the greater power to shape public policy. Yet, within this framework, the crime that emerges from group conflict can occur when the purposes, interests, and valued goals of groups become competitive with one another in other ways. A related view—Albert K. Cohen's concept of the "delinquent subculture"—focuses on working-class youths who are handicapped in attaining social and economic status.[59] Some of these youths eventually succeed, but those who do not band together into gangs, which provide them with arenas for striking back at the middle-class values they oppose and give them status as subcultural groups.

Richard Cloward and Lloyd Ohlin agreed with Cohen that delinquent subcultures are a part of society and that certain delinquent behaviors are required of its members in order to belong. Cloward and Ohlin proposed a differential opportunity theory in their 1960 book *Delinquency and Opportunity*.[60] They suggested that criminals need access to illegitimate opportunities and that different groups have access to different opportunities. Disadvantaged youths with few economic opportunities outside menial, minimum-wage employment may join gangs for the increased prestige and money that drug trafficking, burglary, larceny, robbery, and prostitution promise.

An alternative view that might be interpreted within the culture conflict mode was offered by Walter B. Miller, who contended that certain "focal concerns" within lower-class cultures could lead to antisocial conduct.[61] He defined focal concerns as areas or issues that command widespread and persistent attention and a high degree of emotional involvement. Within lower socioeconomic classes, they include a preoccupation with "toughness," a sensitivity to "smartness," excitement, autonomy, a belief in fate, and a chronic awareness of "trouble." The illegal activity often found in low-income areas represents an adolescent adaptation to the lower-class cultural concerns that are often in conflict with those of the wider society.

Social and Cultural Process Theories Social and cultural process theories posit that criminality is a function of individual socialization. Process theories focus on the interactions that individuals have with various social and cultural institutions and the processes of family socialization, peer relations, education, and employment. If the process of development and the relationships and attachments that individuals form to society are positive, then individuals should be able to succeed and live by legitimate means. On the other hand, if relationships and influences are dysfunctional, individuals may resort to criminal behavior as a way of attaining goals. Process theories, three of which we will discuss below, suggest that all individuals, regardless of gender, ethnicity, or socioeconomic position in society, have the potential to carry out criminal behavior.

According to Cloward and Ohlin, persons of middle- and high-socioeconomic status have the means to commit the less visible and rarely prosecuted white-collar offenses.

Social and Cultural Learning Theory. Social and cultural learning theorists suggest that crime is learned through the deviant norms, values, and behaviors that are linked with criminal activity. Perhaps the most prominent of these theorists was Edwin H. Sutherland, whose theory of differential association maintains that individuals learn criminal behavior in the same way they learn conformity, and they do so within the context of intimate social groups that are criminal.[62] The learning includes the techniques of committing crimes, as well as the attitudes and rationalizations that justify such behavior. What distinguishes these attitudes and rationalizations is that they involve a cultural rejection of legal and other social norms. Persons become criminal, Sutherland argued, because they encounter an excess of definitions favorable to violating the law over definitions favorable to complying with the law.[63]

In 1966, Robert L. Burgess and Ronald L. Akers reformulated Sutherland's thinking and called it differential reinforcement theory.[64] Criminal behavior is not only learned but also reinforced by an individual's social and cultural environment. This theory provided more insight into the learning process and refined the mechanism by which deviant, and for that matter conforming, behavior is produced.

These theories represented major breakthroughs for the study of crime. The theoretical conceptions attempted to "normalize" criminal behavior—"normal" in the sense that individuals learn it through the same processes that they learn other, noncriminal behaviors. Further, they suggested a chain of learning experiences that made the commission of crime understandable; they advanced a framework within which other theories of crime might be better understood; and they challenged the earlier theories that sought to explain crime in terms of head size and shape, broken homes, feeblemindedness, body structure, and other factors.

Differential association theories, however, also have limitations. First, they focus only on those kinds of criminality that are systematic, such as professional theft, organized crime, drug selling and trafficking, and certain forms of white-collar crime. They fail, however, to explain certain impulsive and irrational acts that result in crime, such as the majority of homicides, assaults, and forcible rapes. Second, many criminal behaviors are learned through contact with ideas, rather than with people. Third, many criminal behaviors—purse snatching, shoplifting, robbery, assault, and prostitution—require little, if any, training. Finally, differential association theory does not address why some persons with extensive contacts with criminals nevertheless resist crime themselves.

Social Control Theory. Travis Hirschi proposed a new theory of criminality in his 1969 work *Causes of Delinquency,* which centered not on individuals' motivations to act deviantly but on how the social structure constrains individuals.[65] Social control theory assumes that people are rational beings motivated by the desire to maximize pleasure and minimize pain. Thus, people will behave in ways that will maximize their own personal benefits, regardless of the behavior's deviance or conformity. Of interest to social control theory are the mechanisms that keep individuals from acting in deviant ways.

Hirschi proposed four elements of what he called the "social bond," or the measure of an individual's tie to conventional society. The first of these bonds is attachment—that is, how closely attached an individual is to the conventional social world, which includes parents, teachers, religious leaders, and peers. Commitment and involvement, the second and third bonds, relate to the time and energy one invests in conforming activities, such as schoolwork and extracurricular activities. Finally, beliefs are the moral standards by which an individual lives—the measure of "right" and "wrong" in the social world. These four bonds, according to Hirschi, are the key factors in a person's rational decision-making process, and they can contribute to whether one will behave in conforming or deviant ways.

Boys and Girls Clubs of America were developed to offer youth in troubled neighborhoods alternatives to criminal activity and to strengthen their bonds with conventional society. The group pictured here is revitalizing trails at Joshua Tree National Park in California.

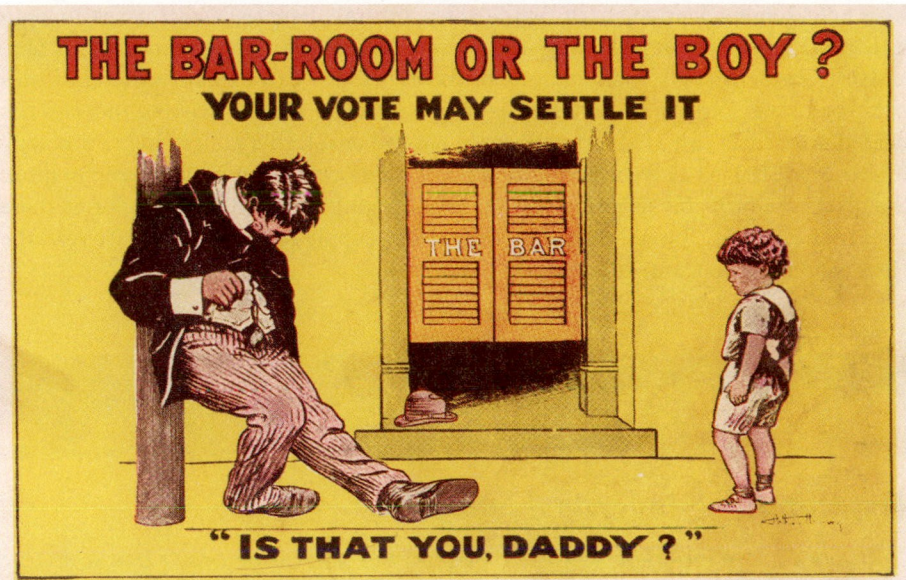

This propaganda poster was one of many used in the campaign to define the liquor trades as "evil." Such posters and the ratification of the Eighteenth (prohibition) Amendment in 1919 are clear illustrations of the labeling process.

However, Hirschi's theory leaves a few questions unanswered. How do social bonds that change over time affect delinquent behavior? For example, how does the changing relationship between parents and children as they grow up impact behavior? Furthermore, do weakened bonds lead to criminal behavior, as Hirschi contends, or does criminal behavior break down social bonds?

Labeling Theory. This theory addressed the question of why apparently similar acts are treated differently. For example, why is the possession of cocaine illegal while the possession of alcohol is not? Why is a convicted burglar more likely to end up in prison than a convicted embezzler? How does society formulate definitions of crime? In considering how the labeling process works, refer to the earlier section in this chapter "Crime as a Social Construct."

The impetus for the labeling perspective came in 1951, when sociologist Edwin M. Lemert made an important distinction between primary and secondary deviations.[66] Primary deviation is the violation of some norm (i.e., some offensive act or characteristic). Secondary deviation results from the societal reaction to the violation—the demeanor and conduct that people cultivate as the result of being labeled deviant or criminal. This distinction between primary and secondary deviation suggests that labeling can indeed have consequences, that the labeling itself adjusts people's perceptions of and reactions to criminals, and that these reactions can operationalize the "offender's" criminal role. Most, if not all, people break rules now and then, but they do not necessarily think of themselves as "criminal." However, when circumstances result in their being defined and reacted to as "criminal," they may begin to actively fulfill those roles.

Similarly, many of those labeled as criminal may be forced out of a corner of conventional society and into a situation or subculture that further stigmatizes them and makes the continuance of the criminal role inevitable. Persons labeled as cocaine addicts may lose their jobs and their friends; they are thus pushed into the drug subculture and the hustling world of the streets for companionship and financial support.

As a final note, it would be unrealistic to expect that any one theory of crime could explain all forms of criminal behavior. Certain aspects of biological theories may hold some scientific merit, while sociocultural theories—with bases in both structural and process reasoning—also contribute to our understanding. In fact, each theory or various combinations of theories likely can explain different kinds of lawbreaking. Keep in mind also that only a small portion of existing theories has been discussed in this chapter; one would have to enroll in a course in criminology to appreciate the extensive range of theories of crime causation. Finally, keep in mind that there are probably as many reasons for engaging in criminal behavior as there are kinds of crime. To see how some of these ideas apply to juveniles, please read the "Juvenile Justice in Context" feature.

JUVENILE JUSTICE IN CONTEXT

The Nature of Juvenile Justice

An adult is a person who has reached the age of majority—some "magic number" (usually 18) that indicates the individual is legally responsible for his or her actions and behavior. An adult has the right to vote, marry, hold government office, and enter into contracts. Moreover, if an adult violates the criminal law or is accused of a crime, he or she is processed through a justice system that is grounded in the due process of law guaranteed by the U.S. Constitution.

A juvenile is a person who has not reached the age of majority—and therefore is deemed to have a special status. Juveniles are held to a standard of behavior that is different from that for adults. Children are required to attend school between the ages of 6 and 16; they are expected to obey their parents; they are forbidden to purchase alcohol or cigarettes or to drive motor vehicles; they may not marry without parental permission; they cannot enter into business or

A child's experience with juvenile court can have a range of outcomes—social services, programming, educational assistance, counseling, psychiatric services, and/or detention.

financial contracts; and they are not permitted to vote, enter the military, or run away from home. Some jurisdictions place other restrictions on juveniles, such as curfews or laws against "incorrigible" or "immoral" behavior. Like adults, children can be charged with violations of the criminal law. However, because of their special status, an alternative system of justice has evolved for dealing with juvenile lawbreakers.

The juvenile justice system in the United States is based on the philosophy that the special status of children requires that they be protected and corrected, not necessarily punished. But as the system has evolved, it has failed to accord juveniles any individual rights. After all, in American society, a juvenile is essentially in the "custody" of parents, guardians, or the state.

Beyond the philosophical orientation stemming from the special status of children, one can see other differences between adult and juvenile justice systems. For adults to fall within the jurisdiction of the criminal courts, they must be charged with some violation of the criminal law. A young person, however, can come to the attention of the juvenile courts in a variety of ways. First, the juvenile may indeed be found to have violated the criminal law. Second, he or she can be charged with having committed a status offense—an act declared by statute to be a crime because it violates the behavior standards expected of children. Because of their status, only juveniles can be charged with the offenses of running away, truancy, or being incorrigible. Third, a child may fall within the jurisdiction of the court because of the behavior of an adult. That is, should a juvenile be the victim of abuse, neglect, or abandonment by a parent or guardian, the courts may intervene.

Perhaps the major difference between the adult and juvenile justice systems involves the purpose and nature of the sanctions imposed. As you will see in Chapter 10, five competing philosophies guide sentencing in adult courts—retribution, vengeance, incapacitation, deterrence, and rehabilitation. By contrast, actions taken in juvenile courts are, at least in theory, deemed to be "in the best interests of the child." The juvenile justice system, then, is based on the notions that every child is treatable and that judicial intervention will result in positive behavioral change. Modern juvenile courts struggle to maintain their focus on helping the child. In fact, growing frustration with repeat juvenile offenders and reactions to media-dramatized, serious juvenile crime have resulted in harsher juvenile sentences and the increase in juveniles transferred to adult court for the processing of their criminal cases. We examine these issues in later chapters.

DISCRETION MATTERS

Do you think professionals within the criminal justice system should have more or less discretion when responding to juvenile offenders? Why or why not?

CONCLUSIONS

As you can see from the preceding discussion, the concept of crime, and its evolution as both a social and legal concept, is complex and not well understood by most people. Many, for example, think it is illegal to be a drug addict, but this is not true, as you learned in the opening case of *Robinson v. California*. The nature or type of crime one is charged with is often related to one's reasons for committing it, and an understanding of this relationship may lead to system responses that reduce crime and increase public safety. Scholars and practitioners have developed numerous theories to explain the willingness of some in our society to violate the law and harm others. Understanding both the legal and social definitions of crime and the possible explanations for these offenses is an important pursuit for our society and system of justice. It will also be key to your study in upcoming chapters of how police, courts, and corrections respond to crime.

SUMMARY AND REVIEW

■ **Explain natural law, and describe how this concept might impact the definition of crime.**

- Natural law refers to a body of principles and rules imposed upon individuals by some power higher than man-made law and is therefore considered to be uniquely fitting for and binding on any community of rational beings.

■ **Define crime, including the legal definition and the meaning of each of its elements.**

- Most people do not understand the concept of crime. It goes well beyond the rather imprecise boundaries of "street crime" and the limited issues of violence and theft that are a major focus of mass-media news and entertainment.
- Drawing on standards of what constitutes sin, or immoral behavior, people have often defined crime as violations of natural law. However, this definition implies that all individuals define right and wrong the same way.
- Sociologists argue that people's ideas about appropriate and inappropriate behavior are culturally and historically specific. That is, social scientists choose to focus on the processes through which crime arises, and they suggest that crime is a social construction that changes over time and in different contexts.
- Scholars have argued that not all deviant behavior is criminal behavior and that not all criminal behavior is deviant behavior. Rather, criminal and deviant behaviors are defined by the culture.
- The only precise definition of crime, then, is a legalistic one. As such, crime is an intentional act or omission in violation of criminal law (statutory and case law), committed without defense or justification and sanctioned by the state as a felony or misdemeanor.
- Key elements of this legal definition include:
  - an act that is legally forbidden or the omission of an act that is legally required
  - the presence of criminal intent, or mens rea— from the Latin for "guilty mind"
  - a behavior that is in violation of the criminal law
  - lack of defense or justification for the act or omission

■ **Compare the various defenses to criminal liability.**

- Insanity is a legal concept, not a medical one, and is specified as any unsoundness of mind, madness, mental alienation, or want of reason, memory, and intelligence that prevents an individual from comprehending the nature and consequences of his or

her acts or from distinguishing between right and wrong conduct.
- Mistake of fact is any erroneous understanding of fact or circumstance resulting in some act that would not otherwise have been undertaken.
- Mistake of law is any want of knowledge or acquaintance with the laws of the land insofar as they apply to the act, relation, duty, or matter under consideration.
- Duress and consent refer to any unlawful constraints exercised on an individual forcing him or her to consent to committing some act that would not have been done otherwise.
- Consent of the victim is any voluntary yielding of the will of the victim causing him or her to agree to the act of the offending party.
- Entrapment is the inducement of an individual to commit a crime not previously contemplated by him or her, undertaken for the sole purpose of instituting a criminal prosecution against the offender.
- Justification is any just cause or excuse for the commission of an act that would otherwise be a crime. The notion of justification as a defense against crime typically involves the use of force or violence in protecting one's person or property or that of others, in preventing crime, or in apprehending offenders.

■ **Describe the sources of criminal law.**

- Common law refers to customs, traditions, judicial decisions, and other materials that guide the courts in decision-making but that have not been enacted by legislatures or are embodied in the Constitution.
- Constitutional law is derived from the U.S. Constitution and associated Supreme Court and lower-court interpretations of the document.
- Statutory law refers to both federal and state statutes outlining behavior prohibited within our society and specifying punishments associated with the violation of these statutes.
- Administrative law refers to the rules and regulations of administrative agencies.

■ **Discuss the major theoretical explanations of criminal behavior.**

- Biological theories attribute the causes of crime to some biological or physical element.
- Wilson and Herrnstein proposed the existence of a particular personality type with features that make a person more likely to value crime. These features, or "constitutional factors" as Wilson and Herrnstein referred to them, either are inborn or emerge early in life and are only minimally influenced by family.

- Sociocultural theories suggest that an individual's place within the social and cultural structure determines his or her behavior and that socialization processes in the family, schools, and peer groups influence and control deviant behaviors.
- Social and cultural structure theorists believe that crime is caused by disorganized and decaying neighborhoods, weak social support, and a lack of economic opportunity. In this view, the social structure rather than the individual is the primary cause of crime.
- Strain theorists view crime as a direct result of the "strain"—frustration, anger, and hopelessness—that comes from living in disadvantaged, disorganized, and otherwise "normless" communities where legitimate opportunities for prosperity arc all but unavailable. To relieve this strain, and as an alternate means to reach their goals, it is theorized, people turn to deviant and criminal behavior.
- General strain theory suggests that criminality is the direct result of negative affective states that are produced by negative social relationships and negative emotions that can create the inclination toward deviance and criminal behavior.
- The culture conflict perspective explains crime as the result of a conflict between the norms, values, and goal orientations of a social or cultural group and the legal codes imposed by an alternative group that has greater power to shape public policy.
- Social and cultural learning theorists suggest that crime is learned through the deviant norms, values, and behaviors linked with criminal activity.
- Social control theory assumes that people are rational beings who are motivated to maximize pleasure and minimize pain. Thus, people are presumed to behave in ways that will maximize their own personal benefits regardless of deviation or conformity.
- Labeling theory focuses on why some acts and actors are defined as criminal while others are not. Theorists working within this perspective examine the impact of being identified as an offender and reacted to by the criminal justice system.

KEY TERMS

abettor (p. 31)
accessory after the fact (p. 31)
accessory before the fact (p. 31)
administrative law (p. 40)
case law (p. 33)
civil law (p. 33)
common law (p. 33)
conspiracy (p. 31)

crime (p. 27)
criminal intent (p. 32)
criminal law (p. 32)
defense (p. 33)
deviance (p. 28)
duress (p. 35)
Durham Rule (p. 34)
entrapment (p. 35)

insanity (p. 33)
justification (p. 36)
M'Naghten Rule (p. 33)
natural law (p. 27)
omission (p. 30)
statutory law (p. 33)
vicarious liability (p. 32)

ISSUES FOR CRITICAL THINKING AND DISCUSSION

1. How do natural law conceptions of sin, sociological considerations of deviance, and legalistic definitions of crime differ?
2. In the Leopold and Loeb case, when do you think the conspiracy actually began? What elements were present?
3. Under what kinds of circumstances should the consent of the victim be an acceptable defense against crime? What are some examples?
4. Should anything be done about the insanity plea? Do you think individuals declared incompetent or insane should be treated differently by the criminal justice process? Why?
5. Do you think we can develop a single theory to explain all criminal behavior? What, if anything, might all offenders have in common that might explain their willingness to break the law?
6. How might theories explaining criminal behavior affect the responses of criminal justice professionals to criminal offending?
7. Theories of criminal behavior have numerous policy implications for criminal justice actors and agencies. Devise a policy that might help reduce crime.

3

Identifying and Measuring Crime

LEARNING OBJECTIVES

- Provide legal definitions for the major categories of criminal offenses: homicide, forcible rape, assault, robbery, arson, and burglary.
- Describe the major contexts of criminal offending.
- Identify and describe the two major sources of crime statistics.
- Compute and interpret a crime rate.

DEFINING HATE CRIME IN AMERICA

The case of aggravated assault by Todd Mitchell illustrates the difficulty of defining the complex issue of hate crime.

Late on an October evening in Kenosha, Wisconsin, a group of young African American men, including Todd Mitchell, were hanging out at someone's apartment. They were talking about a scene from the film *Mississippi Burning,* in which a white man beats a young African American boy. The discussion became heated, and the group moved outside, where witnesses stated that Mitchell said, "Do you all feel hyped up to move on some white people?"[1] A young white boy was walking toward the group on the opposite side of the street when Mitchell pointed to him and said, "There goes a white boy; go get him."[2] According to witnesses, Mitchell counted to three, and the group ran after the boy, beat him severely, and stole his tennis shoes. The boy remained in a coma for four days following the attack.[3] Mitchell was convicted of aggravated battery, which would usually result in a maximum sentence of two years' imprisonment. However, the trial jury found that Mitchell, having selected the boy because of his race, should be sentenced under Wisconsin's hate- or bias-motivated crime statute, which meant four years' imprisonment.[4]

Mitchell appealed his sentence under First Amendment grounds, arguing that punishing him for selecting a victim based on race was tantamount to punishing his offensive thoughts or beliefs rather than the act he committed. The U.S. Supreme Court ultimately heard the case and disagreed with Mitchell. The justices found the definition of hate crime to be sufficiently narrow and connected to the behavior outlawed; they decided, therefore, that the Wisconsin statute did not violate the constitutional protection afforded in the First Amendment. The court also noted that law can regulate motive as well as behavior, particularly where the impact on a victim is so devastating. Finally, the court found the longer sentence to be justified, particularly because of the infliction of emotional harm on the victim and the larger issue of community conflict and unrest.[5]

How Wisconsin and other jurisdictions respond to and process bias-motivated offenses helps illustrate some of the complex issues surrounding the identification of crime and the criminal justice response. In fact, the willingness of communities and legislators to impose harsher penalties when an offender chooses a victim due to a particular bias highlights the flexibility of criminal law and the means available to lawmakers in responding to important community issues. Concerns about the vagueness and implications for free speech have led to challenges, such as this case. Here, the motive was key in the sentencing and was the focus for the Supreme Court. Hate crimes are such an important topic in our society that we track the commission of these crimes nationwide, using data from local law enforcement agencies.

In any study of crime, one must understand not only the content of criminal codes but also the wider social contexts in which crime occurs. For example, an assault might occur within serious and specific situations, such as an act of domestic violence, a hate crime, or an act of terrorism. These categories are what we call *contexts for crime,* and the choice of context influences how the public will see it, how society will react, and how the

DISCRETION MATTERS

What characteristics of an offense would likely lead a police officer to identify it as a hate crime?

justice system will manage the crime and criminals. This chapter, therefore, begins by discussing the legal aspects of various crimes as they are described in criminal codes so that we can briefly discuss specific patterns, or contexts, of criminal behavior that receive widespread attention. The chapter's final section expands on those definitions and contexts by examining how crime is counted and what issues arise in the collection and use of data on crime.

LEGAL CATEGORIES AND DEFINITIONS OF CRIME

As noted in Chapter 2, the law prohibits thousands of acts. These prohibited acts are designated as felonies, misdemeanors, and violations of federal, state, and local criminal codes. A separate body of administrative law lists additional violations. All of these laws result in a huge catalog of crimes.

Felonies and Misdemeanors

Crimes have been classified in many ways. One distinction is between *mala in se* and *mala prohibita* offenses. Acts are considered to be *mala in se* when they are inherently evil—immoral in their nature and injurious in their consequences. Such acts include murder, rape, and theft. *Mala prohibita* crimes are those that may not necessarily be wrong in themselves but are wrong simply because they have been prohibited by statute. Moral turpitude—that is, depravity or baseness of conduct—is the basis for the distinction between these two types of crime, but since attitudes regarding moral turpitude tend to vary from one jurisdiction to the next, the distinction that is almost universally used instead is that between felonies and misdemeanors.

Historically, under common law, **felonies** were crimes that were punishable by death or forfeiture of property. They included such offenses as murder, rape, theft, arson, and robbery. Misdemeanors were considered less morally reprehensible than felonies. The current distinction between the two types of offenses is similar. In most jurisdictions, felonies are serious crimes that are punishable by death or imprisonment (usually for one year or longer) in a federal or state penitentiary. **Misdemeanors** are minor offenses that are generally punishable by no more than a $1,000 fine and/or one year of imprisonment, typically in a local jail. The felony-misdemeanor classification goes beyond the *mala in se–mala prohibita* distinction, since a number of felonies do not reflect moral turpitude. For example, the crimes of wiretapping, carrying a concealed deadly weapon, or possessing forgery instruments are felonies in some jurisdictions in spite of the perpetrator's lack of moral turpitude.

In the legal codes of most jurisdictions, felonies and misdemeanors encompass the boundaries of what is defined as crime. In a few states, however, there is a third category. This category has resulted from the redefinition of certain offenses as less serious than misdemeanors; such offenses are generally referred to as violations. In the New York State Penal Law, for example, *violation* means an offense for which a sentence to a term of imprisonment in excess of 15 days cannot be imposed.[6] Included in this category are such minor offenses as disorderly conduct, loitering, public intoxication, and patronizing a prostitute.

Of course, only a few crimes can be discussed here, so the focus is on the ones that appear most often in local criminal courts and receive the most attention from state-level criminal justice agencies. These crimes encompass more than 90 percent of the criminal law violations handled by state and local criminal justice agencies.[7] While rates of homicide and crime in general are declining (Exhibits 3.1 and 3.2), these offenses generate a great deal of fear in the public and concern from criminal justice agencies and policymakers.

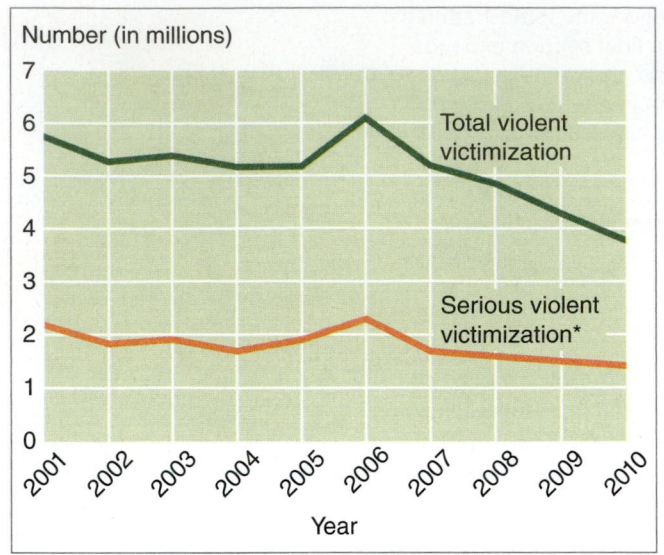

EXHIBIT 3.1　Violent Crime Rate, 2001–2010
*Includes rape, sexual assault, robbery, and aggravated assault.
Source: National Crime Victimization Survey, 1973–2010

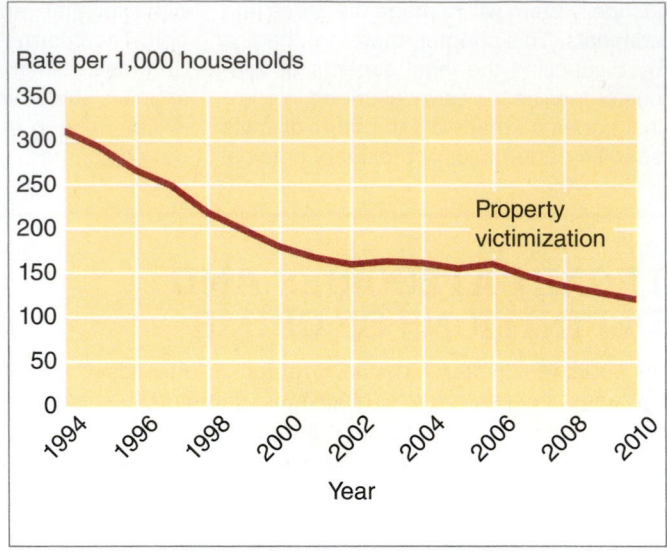

EXHIBIT 3.2　Property Crime Rate, 1994–2010
Source: National Crime Victimization Survey, 1973–2010

Criminal Homicide

The killing of one human being by another is **homicide.** If it is not excusable or justifiable (see Chapter 2), it is called *criminal homicide.* Criminal homicide is usually divided into the general categories of murder and manslaughter, each of which is typically subdivided into many degrees (e.g., murder in the first or second degree) or levels, most typically related to the level of responsibility of the offender. Here we will look more closely at these distinctions, beginning with murder.

Murder　Under common law, **murder** was defined as the felonious killing of another human being with **malice aforethought.** That last phrase implies a definite malicious intent to kill. Common law did not differentiate between murders in the first or second degree, however, and there were varying interpretations of malice aforethought.

Modern criminal codes, however, are more specific. Today, murder is generally divided into two degrees: first and second. In most jurisdictions, first-degree murder includes the notions of malice aforethought, deliberation, and premeditation. Malice aforethought refers to the intent to cause death or serious harm or to commit any felony whatsoever. **Deliberation** refers to full and conscious knowledge of the purpose of killing, suggesting that the offender has considered the motives for the act and its consequences. **Premeditation** refers to a design or plan to do something—that is, a conscious decision to commit the offense (even though such a decision may occur only moments before the final act or may be an instantaneous decision).

An excellent illustration of first-degree murder involving malice aforethought, deliberation, and premeditation is the well-known case of Timothy McVeigh, who was convicted, sentenced to death, and executed for the bombing of the Alfred P. Murrah Federal Building in Oklahoma City in 1995. Court testimony and evidence demonstrated that he had planned an act of violence against persons and property, obtained and constructed the components of a truck bomb, parked the truck bomb directly outside the federal building during regular business and day-care hours, and caused the truck bomb to explode.[8] This event was shocking both for the death and destruction resulting from it and for the apparent callousness with which McVeigh approached the planning, execution, and preparation.

In a number of jurisdictions, statutes also designate murder to be in the first degree when specific circumstances are present. In many states, for example, murder by poisoning automatically carries a first-degree charge, and in some areas a charge of "murder-one" is also mandatory if the homicide involved torture, ambush, the use of destructive devices, the killing of a law enforcement officer, or a murder for hire.

Second-degree murder refers to instances of criminal homicide committed with malice aforethought but without deliberation and premeditation. Murders of this type may be impulse killings but are primarily killings where intent is not clear or easily proven. They occur between family members or lovers, often as the outgrowth of an argument or difference of opinion. The killing is a spur-of-the-moment episode that occurs without planning or full consideration.

Currently, 33 states and the District of Columbia divide murder into two degrees. Three states, however—Florida, Minnesota, and Wisconsin—have more than two degrees of murder.[9] Although rarely seen in modern criminal statutes, third-degree murder charges are most commonly levied for homicides that involve negligence or indifference. These cases typically involve legal duty, such as that of a parent to a child.

Murder is the most serious offense committed within our society and provides unique challenges for the criminal justice system and personnel. Here, officials secure a crime scene in Brooksville, Florida, where a man with a rifle shot two people—one mortally—before fleeing the scene.

The Felony-Murder Doctrine Under common law, the **felony-murder doctrine** maintained that any death resulting from the commission of, or attempt to commit, the crimes of arson, burglary, larceny, rape, or robbery was to be considered murder. In many contemporary legal statutes, the felony-murder doctrine provides that if a death occurs during the commission of a felony, the person committing the primary offense can also be charged with murder in the first degree.[10] Thus, if an individual commits the felonious crime of arson by setting fire to his place of business and one of his employees is killed in that fire, the arsonist would be charged with first-degree murder. Forty-six states have a felony-murder rule.[11] The rule equates intent to commit the felony with intent to murder.

A great deal of confusion surrounds this doctrine. First, the felony-murder statute is unusual in that the three essential elements required of first-degree murder under the law—malice aforethought, deliberation, and premeditation—are only implied. The offender is seen to act in a deliberate manner and is therefore responsible for any natural and probable consequences. A second difficult issue is whether the felon must be the agent of the killing. For example, if a case of arson results in the death of a firefighter, can the arsonist be charged with first-degree murder under the felony-murder doctrine? This is unclear in some states.

Manslaughter **Manslaughter** is an alternative category of criminal homicide, typically charged when a killing occurs under circumstances that are not severe enough to constitute murder yet are beyond the defenses of justifiable or excusable homicide. Manslaughter is distinguished from murder in that the latter implies malice, whereas manslaughter does not. Some jurisdictions divide manslaughter into as many as four degrees, although most differentiate only between voluntary and involuntary manslaughter.

Voluntary manslaughter refers to intentional killings committed in the absence of malice and premeditated design. The essential elements include a legally adequate provocation resulting in a killing done in the heat of passion. Thus, if two people

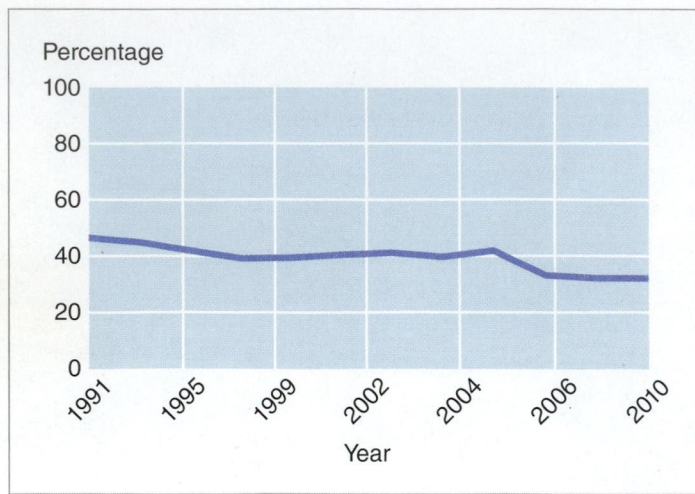

EXHIBIT 3.3   Percentage of U.S. Traffic Deaths from Drunk Driving, 1991–2010

Source: National Highway Traffic Safety Administration

become involved in a quarrel and one kills the other, the offender can be charged with voluntary manslaughter. In contrast, involuntary manslaughter exists when a death results unintentionally as the consequence of some unlawful act or through negligence. For example, if a motorist is driving while intoxicated and loses control of the vehicle, thereby killing a pedestrian, involuntary manslaughter could be charged. In this case, the killing would be unintentional, yet the motorist's intoxicated condition while driving is a violation of the law. In some jurisdictions, however, the charge might be vehicular homicide or driving while intoxicated or second-degree murder. In 1997, a court in Winston-Salem, North Carolina, set a legal precedent with a first-degree murder conviction in a drunk-driving killing. Prosecutors held that the defendant could be convicted without the intent to kill because he had been acting out of "culpable negligence," as shown by a long history of mixing alcohol with drugs and driving.[12] As you can see from Exhibit 3.3, about one-third of traffic fatalities in the United States result from drunk driving, so the legal standard with regard to culpability is relevant to a large number of people.

Assault

Contrary to popular notions, assault does not refer to the infliction of an injury on another person. In legal terms, **assault** is simply an intentional attempt or threat to physically injure another person. *Battery* is the term for the nonlethal culmination of an assault. Thus, **assault and battery** is an assault that inflicts some violence on the victim. *Aggravated assault* refers to an assault made with the intent to commit murder, rape, or robbery or to inflict serious bodily harm; simple assault is one in which the intended harm fails, or no serious harm was ever intended.

Robbery

Robbery is the felonious taking of money or goods from a victim's person, or in a victim's presence, and against his or her will, through the use or threat of force and violence. As such, it involves aspects of both theft and assault, and since the use or threat of violence is present, it is generally classified as a crime "against the person." The specific elements necessary for a robbery to take place are clear in its definition: (1) the felonious taking (with intent to steal) (2) of money or goods (3) from a person or in his or her presence (or custody, care, or control) (4) against his or her will (5) through the use or threat of force and violence. Thus, an armed bank holdup, a street mugging, and a purse snatching would all be robberies. If one or more of the five elements just listed were missing, the action would not be a robbery but rather some other crime, or perhaps no crime at all. If the use or threat of force were absent, for example, the crime would be theft.

Some jurisdictions divide robbery into degrees. Robbery in the first degree is charged when the offender

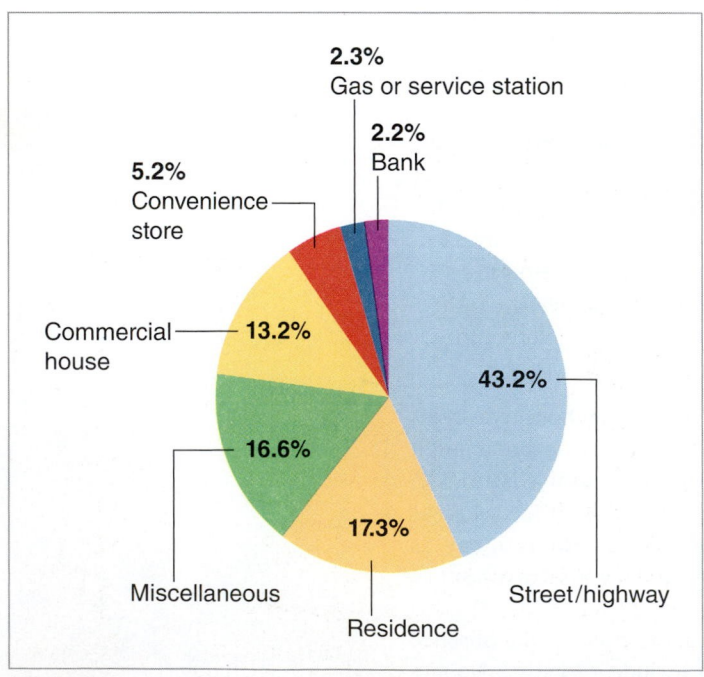

EXHIBIT 3.4   Robbery Distribution by Location, 2010

Source: FBI, *Crime in the United States, 2010*

is armed with a deadly weapon or dangerous instrument. Other jurisdictions have specific statutes that recognize unarmed robbery, armed robbery, train robbery, safe and vault robbery, and carjacking (Exhibit 3.4 illustrates the distribution of robbery by location).

Arson

Common law conceptions of **arson** referred to the malicious burning of the dwelling of another person, but modern statutes have extended the parameters of arson in a variety of ways. First, while arson originally carried the ideas of fire and burning, most jurisdictions now include the use of explosives in the definition of this crime. Second, contemporary statutes include not only dwellings but

The crime of arson costs thousands of dollars in damage each year. These torched SUVs were the result of domestic terrorism by overzealous environmentalists.

also other types of buildings, as well as the property of the arsonist (if, for instance, there is an attempt to defraud an insurer or if the building is occupied). Thus, a person is guilty of arson when he or she intentionally damages a building by starting a fire or causing an explosion.[13]

Arson is a felony in all jurisdictions. Most often it is divided into at least two degrees and sometimes three. In general, if the premises that are set afire are occupied, the charge will be first-degree arson. If they are unoccupied, the case will be one of second-degree arson. A person is guilty of arson in the third degree if the premises burned are his or her own or, if they are unoccupied, if the purpose is to defraud the insurer. From a legal perspective, the major problem in arson cases is the element of criminal agency, or intent. A conviction depends on the state's proving that an accused person had both the intent and the opportunity to commit arson, which is difficult in many cases.

Burglary

At one time, burglary was viewed as a crime against the habitation—that is, an invasion of the home—and was defined only in terms of the **breaking and entering** of a dwelling, at night, with the intent to commit a felony. In current statutes, the definition of burglary has been broadened: It includes unlawful entrance into structures other than a dwelling; it is applicable whether the illegal entry occurs during the night or day; and it can involve an intended felony or misdemeanor. As you can see from Exhibit 3.5, more than 70 percent of burglaries occur in residential locations.

The term *breaking and entering* is often used synonymously with *burglary*, but this can be misleading because both breaking and entering need not be formally present for a burglary to occur. *Breaking* suggests forcible entry, but the mere opening of a closed door is sufficient to constitute a breaking. Moreover, simply remaining in a building until after it has closed and then engaging in some criminal activity can also constitute a burglary, even though no actual breaking occurs.

EXHIBIT 3.5 Location and Time of Burglaries, 2010

	Numbers	Percentage
Residence (dwelling)	1,402,214	73.9
Night	389,910	20.5
Day	722,231	38.1
Time unknown	290,073	15.3
Nonresidence (store, office, etc.)	495,749	26.1
Night	204,605	10.8
Day	168,912	8.9
Time unknown	122,232	6.4

Source: Federal Bureau of Investigation, Crime in the United States, 2010.

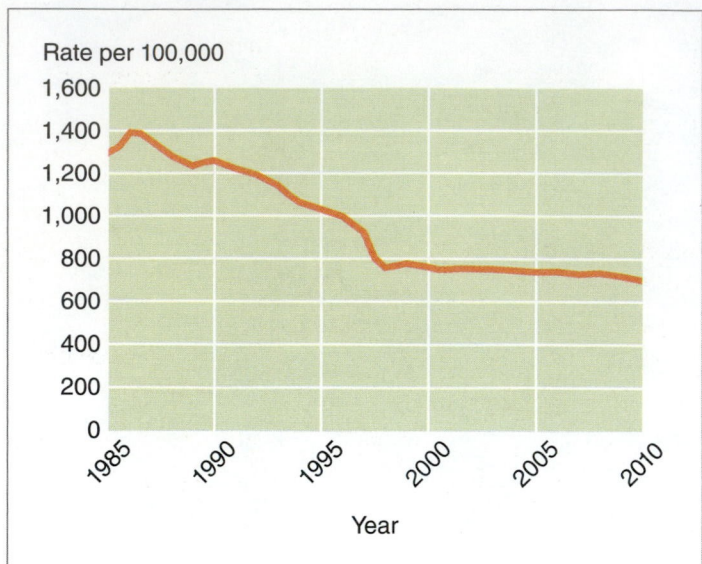

Rate per 100,000

EXHIBIT 3.6   Burglary in the United States, 1985–2010
Source: FBI, Uniform Crime Reports

Entering is the more essential element; it can be limited to the insertion of any part of the body or any instrument or weapon into the building and still be sufficient to constitute a burglary.

Burglary is another offense that appears in a large number of degrees and varieties, although its occurrence had been on a downward trend over the past 20 years (Exhibit 3.6). A person is typically guilty of burglary in the third degree when he or she knowingly enters or remains unlawfully in a building with the intent to commit a crime therein. The burglary becomes an offense in the second degree if the building happens to be a dwelling, if the offender is armed, or if any person who is not a participant in the crime is physically injured. Burglary in the first degree involves unlawful entry or remaining in a dwelling at night, combined with the offender being armed or causing physical injury.[14]

Since burglary involves a criminal intent—that is, unlawful entry for some criminal purpose—two additional points must be stressed. First, even if the purpose of the entry was to commit a minor crime, such as petty theft or some other misdemeanor, the burglary has been consummated and a felony has been committed. Further, the offender can be charged not only with burglary but with the other offense as well. Second, because of the criminal intent aspect, a number of jurisdictions have structured their laws so that attempted burglary is included in the definition of burglary.

Closely related to burglary are a number of other crimes that are generally defined in separate statutes. For example, it is illegal to possess burglar's tools, which can include many types of devices, ranging from sophisticated lock picks and explosives to simple everyday tools such as screwdrivers and chisels.

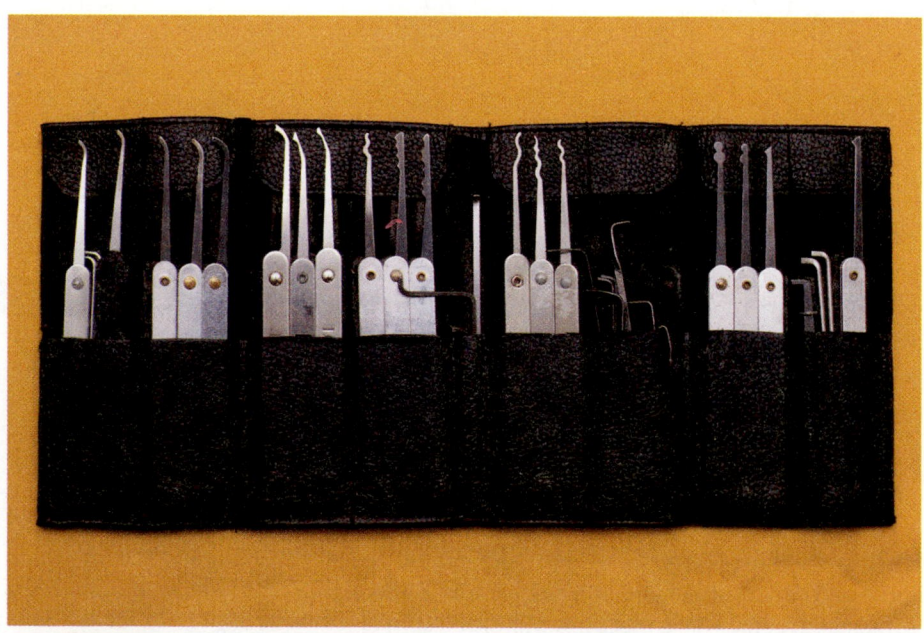

In many jurisdictions the very possession of burglar's tools, like those pictured here, can be prosecuted as a felony.

Other Property Offenses

It is difficult to describe the full range of property offenses, because jurisdictions define and categorize them in different ways. In Louisiana, for example, the technical dimensions of the **theft** statute are quite broad:

> Theft is the misappropriation or taking of anything of value that belongs to another, either without the consent of the other to the misappropriation or taking, or by means of fraudulent conduct, practices, or representations. An intent to deprive the other permanently of whatever may be the subject of the misappropriation or taking is essential.[15]

This definition covers a multitude of property crimes, including what other states may define as larceny, embezzlement, and fraud. Further, while many states may have a broad larceny statute, which refers to the taking and carrying away of the personal property of another person with the intent to deprive permanently, other states, such as Delaware, define shoplifting—a clear instance of larceny—as a separate offense.[16] In Ohio and several other jurisdictions, theft statutes include the unlawful use of a person's service.[17] In general, however, theft seems to be the broadest of terms relating to property offenses and can be loosely defined as the unlawful taking, possession, or use of another person's property without the use or threat of force and with the intent to deprive permanently. Exhibit 3.7 provides data on different types of larceny-theft. Within the boundaries of this definition, theft includes the following:

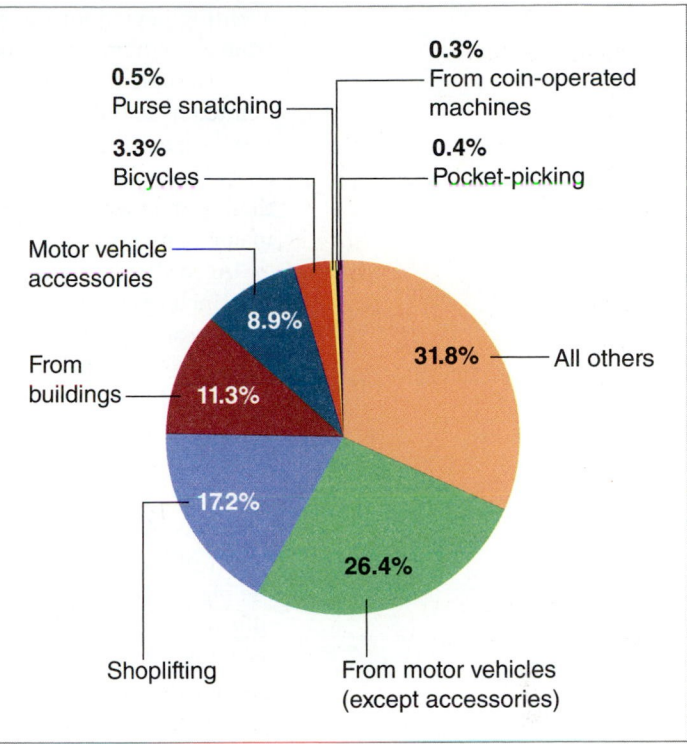

EXHIBIT 3.7 **U.S. Larceny-Theft, 2010**
Source: FBI, *Crime in the United States, 2010*

- Larceny: the taking and carrying away of the personal property of another person with the intent to deprive permanently
- Shoplifting: the theft of goods, wares, or merchandise from a store or shop
- Pickpocketing: the theft of money or articles directly from the garments of the victim
- Embezzlement: the fraudulent appropriation or conversion of money or property by an employee, trustee, or other agent to whom the possession of such money or property was entrusted
- Fraud: theft by false pretenses; the appropriation of money or property by trick or misrepresentation or by creating or reinforcing a false impression as to some present or past fact that would adversely affect the victim's judgment of a transaction
- Purchase, receipt, or possession of stolen goods: the buying, receiving, or possessing of goods known to be stolen

This list may be longer or shorter depending on how an offense is interpreted in a particular jurisdiction. In addition, there is not room here to detail all the crimes that might fall into this category. Extortion, for example, is included in the theft statutes of some states and can be defined to include not only the taking of money or property under threat of physical injury if the property is not delivered (which may also be construed as a form of robbery) but also what has been defined as blackmail. The theft of services also appears as a separate offense in some areas. This refers, for example, to a situation in which a homeowner illegally taps into another household's television cable or electric meter or alters the mechanism in his or her own meter, thus avoiding paying for the service. More recently, stealing the wireless Internet signal from a neighbor's home has been charged under this offense.

Also note that the offenses in the list are not mutually exclusive. What has been defined as counterfeiting may appear under forgery statutes; confidence games are clearly special varieties of fraud; and shoplifting and pickpocketing are forms of larceny. Here we will focus on larceny, since this classification includes many types of theft and, at least in terms of official criminal statistics, is the most common of all major crimes.

According to the legal definition provided in the preceding list, the crime of larceny includes five essential elements: (1) the taking and (2) carrying away of the (3) personal property (4) of another (5) with the intent to deprive permanently. The element of taking suggests that the offender has no legal right to possession of the property in question. In this sense, taking involves a trespass in that the possession of property has been wrongfully obtained. This point highlights the difficult distinctions among possession, custody, and control as they relate to larceny. Taking can occur even when a person has authorized custody or control of an object if his or her use or disposal of that object ultimately deprives someone else of possessory rights. The carrying-away aspect of larceny, also known as *asportation,* involves removal of the property from the place it formerly occupied. The distance of movement, however, need not be significant. The removal of a wallet from a pocket, for example, represents complete asportation. Personal property, the third element of larceny, refers to anything that can be owned, except land or things permanently affixed to it. The property must also be that of another, since larceny is a crime against possession and therefore cannot occur with what one already possesses.

The final element of larceny involves intent—intent to permanently deprive. If the intent is to deprive only temporarily, there is no larceny, although many states have structured their criminal codes to cover this kind of situation with such lesser offenses as unauthorized use of a vehicle and misappropriation of property. Whether the intent is to deprive permanently or only temporarily, however, is a question of fact on which the court must rule, and the distinction between permanent and temporary can be a matter of interpretation. The distinction between larceny as a felony and as a misdemeanor, or between "grand larceny" and "petty larceny," is statutory in nature. The dividing point ranges from as little as $50 in some jurisdictions to as much as $2,500 in others.[18] At a value below these amounts, the larceny is a misdemeanor, while anything valued at or above the statutory figure is a felony.

Sex Offenses

The scope of illegal sexual activity is quite broad in American society and often confusing for the general public. This is due to several factors, including the legacy of the early Puritan codes and impact of the Holy Scriptures, attempts to maintain standards of public decency through the legislation of morality, and efforts to protect those who are too young or are otherwise unable to make decisions as to their own sexual conduct. Although in recent years the codes regulating many sexual activities, such as contraception and miscegenation, have been eliminated or severely limited, the list of sex offenses is still long and includes the following:

- Forcible rape: having sexual intercourse with a person without his or her consent, including through the use or threat of force or fear
- **Sexual assault:** any sexual contact with another person that occurs without the consent of the victim or is offensive to the victim
- Statutory rape: having sexual intercourse with a person under a stated age (usually 16 or 18, but sometimes 14), with or without his or her consent
- Incest: sexual intercourse between parent and child, any pair of siblings, or close blood relatives

- Indecent exposure (exhibitionism): exposure of the sexual organs in a public place
- Lewdness: degenerate sexual behavior that may result in the corruption of public decency
- Obscenity: that which is offensive to morality or chastity and is calculated to corrupt the mind and morals of those exposed to it
- Pornography: literature, art, film, pictures, or other articles of a sexual nature that are considered obscene by a community's moral standards
- Bigamy: the act of marrying while a former marriage is still legally in force
- Polygamy: the practice of having several spouses
- Prostitution: the offering of sexual relations for monetary or other gain
- Child molestation: handling, fondling, or other contact of a sexual nature with a child
- Voyeurism (peeping): the surreptitious observance of an exposed body or sexual act

Although the offenses of forcible rape, incest, and child molestation appear in some form in all U.S. jurisdictions, not all sexual behaviors listed here are universally prohibited. Fornication, seduction, and pornography are disappearing from the penal codes of many state and local areas; indecent exposure, in the form of topless dancing and live sex shows, has been decriminalized in several jurisdictions; and prostitution is legal in several parts of Nevada.[19]

Forcible rape is the sex offense about which there is most concern, but rape statutes are often confusing for the public. In many jurisdictions, rape was historically defined as the unlawful "carnal knowledge" of a female without her consent and against her will.[20] However, nearly all jurisdictions have redefined the act of rape, identifying it as a gender-neutral offense in which a wide range of circumstances can characterize each individual crime.[21] The traditional definition of rape suggests that men are the only possible offenders and women the only possible victims. However, one cannot discount the many instances of sexual assault that occur between men or between women in prisons and jails.[22]

Historically, statutory rape laws included only sexual intercourse with an underage girl. In 1981, the California statutory rape law was challenged before the U.S. Supreme Court on the ground that it discriminated on the basis of gender (only men were criminally liable under the statute). The court upheld the power of the states to enact such statutes, since many were intended to prevent teenage pregnancies.[23] Nevertheless, the statutes in some jurisdictions have become more gender-neutral. A case in point was the 1997 prosecution of Mary Kay Letourneau, a sixth-grade teacher in Burien, Washington, on several counts of second-degree rape of a child. For more than a year, Letourneau had a sexual relationship with one of her students, eventually becoming pregnant and bearing his child. What was perhaps most interesting about the case was the public's reaction. While some observers called Letourneau a pedophile, others asked, "How can you rape the willing?"[24] Letourneau further complicated the historical analysis of this case when she married the father of her child following her release from prison.[25]

Although rape is considered the most serious of the sex offenses, prostitution seems to be the most common if one examines official data on these crimes. We lack confidence in the validity of these data, however, given how difficult it can be to collect information on all sex offenses. Prostitution is providing sex in return for money or some other desired commodity. It includes not only sexual intercourse but also any other form of sexual conduct with another person for a fee. Where prostitution is illegal, it is typically a misdemeanor.

The case of Mary Kay Letourneau highlighted the complex gender and consent issues in sex crime statutes.

Drug Law Violations

The federal and state statutes that regulate nonmedical use of drugs and that control the manufacture, sale, and distribution of "dangerous" drugs have evolved since the early twentieth century. The Pure Food and Drug Act of 1906 was the first piece of federal legislation that targeted the distribution of drugs that were considered dangerous.[26] The purpose of the law was to limit the uncontrolled manufacture of patent medicines and over-the-counter drugs containing cocaine and narcotics such as opium, morphine, and heroin.

Before the passage of this and numerous other federal laws, state drug laws and penalties varied greatly. For example, in at least 19 jurisdictions there was no distinction between penalties for the mere possession of one marijuana cigarette, or reefer, and those for the sale of large quantities of heroin.[27] By 1972, however, the majority of states adopted the provisions of the Controlled Substances Act, thus helping standardize drug laws in most parts of the nation. During the 1980s and 1990s, penalties for drug offenses were increased dramatically, including a glaring disparity in the sentencing of crack versus powder-cocaine offenders, with much higher sentences for offenders convicted of crack possession as compared to offenders convicted of powder-cocaine possession.[28] Reforms in 2010 reduced the sentencing disparity and mirrored changes nationwide in the penalties for drug offenses.[29]

In jurisdictions that have not adopted the federal model, drug laws vary considerably. While federal penalties for the possession of even small quantities of marijuana specify probation or a sentence of up to one year of imprisonment and/or fines of up to $5,000, penalties in some jurisdictions range from as little as a citation without arrest in New York to imprisonment for up to ten years in Georgia, Texas, and Louisiana.[30] As you can see in Exhibit 3.8, arrests for marijuana possession account for the largest number of arrests, even though cocaine production and distribution continue to garner public attention and concern.

While there tends to be consensus about the criminality of other substances, reform of laws related to marijuana use has garnered wide support.

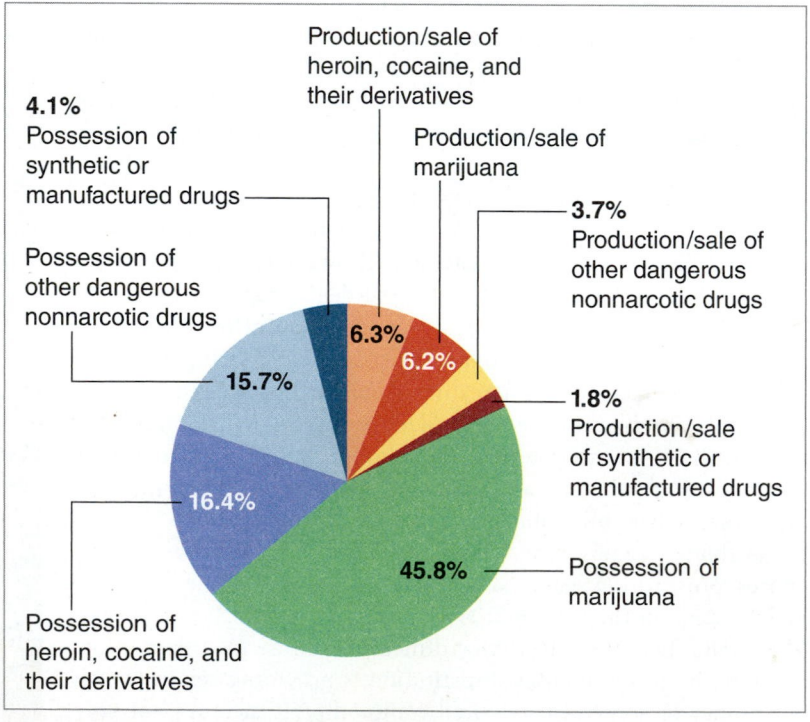

EXHIBIT 3.8   **Drug Law Arrests, 2010**
Source: FBI, *Crime in the United States, 2010*

In addition to laws that control the manufacture, transfer, distribution, sale, and possession of drugs, some jurisdictions have laws against the possession of narcotics paraphernalia such as hypodermic syringes and needles. And some states require that controlled substances, such as prescription drugs, be kept in the containers in which they were originally dispensed. Many states are altering their responses to drug offenders, particularly low-level ones, as jails and prisons have become overcrowded and criminal justice costs have escalated.

Crimes against Public Order and Safety

The final category, called **public order crimes,** tends to include a rather sweeping collection of offenses, mostly misdemeanors that disturb public order and safety. The laws in this category vary considerably from one place to another, but the following crimes appear in one form or another in most jurisdictions:

- Disorderly conduct: any act that tends to disturb the public peace, scandalize the community, or shock the public sense of morality
- Disturbing the peace: any interruption of the peace, quiet, and good order of a neighborhood or community
- Breach of the peace: the breaking of the public peace by any riotous, forcible, or unlawful proceeding
- Harassment: any act that serves to annoy or alarm another person
- Stalking: the willful, malicious, and repeated following or harassing of another person
- Drunkenness: the condition of being under the influence of alcohol to the extent that it renders one helpless
- Public intoxication: the condition of being severely under the influence of alcohol or drugs in a public place to the degree that one may endanger persons or property
- Loitering: idling or lounging on a street or other public way in a manner that serves to interfere with or annoy passersby
- Criminal nuisance: any conduct that is unreasonable and that endangers the health and safety of others
- Vagrancy: the condition of being idle and having no visible means of support
- Desecration: the defacing, damaging, or mistreatment of a public structure, monument, or place of worship or burial

DISCRETION MATTERS

Should law enforcement officials be used to control social unrest, political conflict, or public demonstration? If not, who, if anyone, should? How might law enforcement officials misuse their discretion in responding to these social conflicts?

The members of the Westboro Baptist Church in Topeka, Kansas, have become known for picketing soldiers' funerals, primarily in opposition to gay rights. The resulting controversy led to a 2011 Supreme Court decision protecting the group's right to picket under the First Amendment.

- Driving while intoxicated (DWI) or driving under the influence (DUI): operating a motor vehicle while under the influence of alcohol or illegal drugs
- Gambling: the playing or operation of any game of chance that involves money or property of any value that is prohibited by the criminal code
- Violation of privacy: any unlawful trespass, interception, observation, eavesdropping, or other surveillance that serves to infringe on the private rights of another

In recent years, the constitutionality of many criminal codes designed for the preservation of public order and safety has been challenged. Numerous cases of disorderly conduct, breach of the peace, and vagrancy have come before the U.S. Supreme Court on the grounds that they violate First Amendment protections of free speech and assembly or because they are too vague. Moreover, the use of such statutes as mechanisms for penalizing people who are viewed as political and social undesirables has been questioned as a violation of rights of due process. Nevertheless, these statutes remain in the criminal codes of most jurisdictions. Arrests for vagrancy and disorderly conduct alone may total as many as 1 million annually.[31]

CONTEXTS OF CRIMINAL OFFENDING

The preceding discussion provides a basis for understanding the major categories of crime. However, some offenses occur within larger contexts or situations that alter how we respond to or interpret them. As you saw in the opening case, Mitchell was convicted of aggravated battery, but in the context of his motives—the racial factor—his crime was classified as a hate crime, and he received a longer sentence. Criminal codes cannot explain the social and behavioral contexts in which certain crimes occur or the relationship of certain criminal acts to the wider social order. Further, the criminal law suggests nothing about differences in patterns of crime or victim-offender relationships, nor does it tell us how these differences affect the management of crime. In short, each category of crime has two important aspects: (1) its legal description as stated in the law and (2) the behavioral system that brings it into being.

Dozens of criminal behavior systems and explanations have been identified in the criminal justice and criminological literature.[32] Domestic violence, hate crime, white-collar crime, and, most recently, terrorism are examples of behavioral contexts that are often in the public and media spotlight. Organized crime is another crime context that not only persists but also continually re-creates itself. This section illustrates the way these five contexts of criminality operate.

Domestic Violence

Domestic violence is a form of violent personal crime and can be defined as activities of a physically aggressive nature occurring between members of a family, current or former spouses or lovers, and others in close relationships, as a result of conflicts in their relations. Domestic violence typically occurs in the home, but it can also take place at the house of another family member or a neighbor, at the victim's place of employment, at a commercial establishment, or even in public. The victim and offender are most often of opposite genders, although they may be of the same gender.

The scope of domestic violence is quite broad and includes a wide range of behavioral patterns and offense categories. Battering by spouses and lovers is a consistent pattern of behavior that seeks to establish dominance and control over another through the use or threat of force or violence. Abuse, which may be psychological or economic, involves ridicule, threats, and harassment. Other forms of domestic violence include marital and date rape, elderly abuse, and child neglect and abuse. These, however, are broad categories. The criminal statutes involved include murder and manslaughter, assault, rape, incest, harassment, and stalking, to name a few.

An important aspect of domestic violence is the relationship between the victim and the offender. In the case of murder, for example, many offenses occur between people who know each other. According to the FBI publication *Crime in the United States, 2010,* of the 12,996 murder victims reported during 2010, less than half (44 percent) did not know their attacker(s) (see Exhibit 3.9). Nearly 14 percent were family to the victim, while another nearly 30 percent were known friends, neighbors, or acquaintances. Of those who were known to the victim, including family, 10.2 percent were spouses or significant others (boyfriend or girlfriend).[33]

Official statistics on assault are not as complete as those on criminal homicide. However, the pattern of these offenses has garnered more attention as our society has focused on the disturbing issue of domestic violence. Random street muggings do indeed occur, but nearly two-thirds of all known aggravated assaults result from domestic arguments. Further, victim-offender relationships are typically intimate, primarily involving family members and close acquaintances.[34]

Child abuse, or domestic violence directed against children (also termed battered-child syndrome), has also received widespread attention. Studies suggest that the offenders are typically parents or guardians and that the abuse is an enduring pattern provoked by behaviors that are typical of children—persistent crying, failure to use the toilet, aggression toward siblings, breaking toys or household items, or disobedience.[35]

Another form of abuse is child molestation, which is most frequently manifested as parent-child incest, sexual fondling of a child, or persuasion or coercion of a child to engage in other kinds of sexual acts with a parent, sibling, or guardian. Contrary to popular belief, women and children are not the only victims of domestic violence, and men are not the only offenders. Although men are the offenders in most domestic violence situations, studies have found that men are at risk as well, and there is indeed a "battered-husband syndrome."[36]

Hate Crime

Hate crimes can be defined as offenses motivated by hatred against a victim because of his or her race, ethnicity, religion, sexual orientation, handicap, national origin, or tribal membership. The chapter-opening case of *Wisconsin v. Mitchell* illustrates the challenges of interpreting hate-crime statutes. Also referred to as bias-motivated crimes, hate crimes are often difficult to identify, primarily because criminal acts motivated by bias can easily be confused with forms of expression that are protected by the U.S. Constitution.

The Romans' persecution of the Christians almost two millennia ago, the Nazis' "final solution" for the Jews during World War II, the "ethnic cleansing" in Bosnia in the early to mid-1990s, the genocide in Rwanda during the 1990s, and the killings in Darfur beginning in 2003—all of these hate crimes and more have shaped and sometimes defined world history. In the United States, racial and religious biases have inspired most hate crimes. During the nation's early history, Native Americans became the targets of bias-motivated intimidation and violence. Later there were lynchings of African Americans, followed by hate crimes directed against Chinese laborers. More current examples of hate crimes include assaults on gay Americans, the painting of

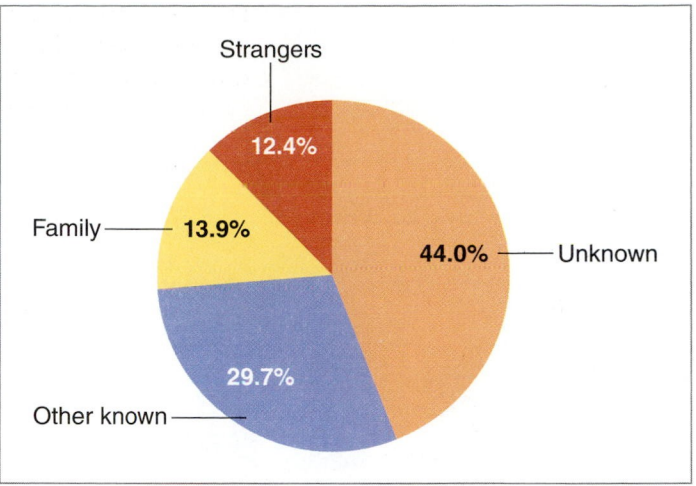

EXHIBIT 3.9 Murder Circumstances by Relationship, 2010
Source: FBI, *Crime in the United States, 2010*

Pie chart labels: Strangers 12.4%, Family 13.9%, Unknown 44.0%, Other known 29.7%

Most aggravated assault occurs between intimate partners or family members, and such cases are typically categorized as domestic violence.

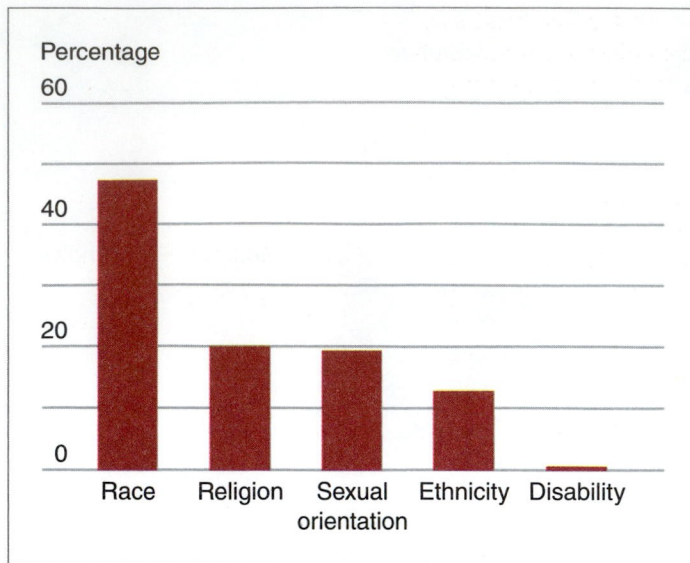

EXHIBIT 3.10   Hate Crimes by Motivating Factors, 2010
Source: Hate Crime Statistics; FBI, *Crime in the United States, 2010*

EXHIBIT 3.11   Hate Crimes by Type, 2010
Source: FBI, *Crime in the United States, 2010*

swastikas on Jewish synagogues, and post-9/11 attitudes and behaviors toward Muslim and Arab individuals.[37]

The number of hate crimes that occur in the United States is difficult to calculate and is quite small in official statistics. According to Justice Department estimates, fewer than 1 out of every 2,000 homicides and 1 out of every 8,000 reported rapes are bias-motivated, but many hate crimes likely go unreported. In 2010, 6,628 hate-crime incidents were reported by law enforcement agencies. More than 60 percent involved race or ethnic bias, with slightly less than 20 percent involving sexual-orientation bias.[38]

The victims of hate crimes in the United States are most often African Americans, followed by Jews, gays, Asian Americans, and, increasingly, Muslims. Although the Ku Klux Klan and Nazi skinhead groups are the most visible perpetrators of hate crimes, the majority of offenders are individuals rather than groups. During 2010, there were 4,824 hate-crime offenses against persons and 2,861 against property reported to the FBI. Of the suspected offenders where the race was known, 58.6 percent were white, 18.4 percent were black, and the remaining 23 percent were Native American, Asian Pacific Islander, multiracial, or of unknown race or ethnicity.[39] Exhibit 3.10 provides data on the motivation behind the incidents known to police, and Exhibit 3.11 outlines the forms such crimes take.

The idea behind hate-crime legislation is to provide special protection for members of minority groups who are frequently targeted simply because of who they are. Supporters of these laws argue that hate crime does double damage—first to the immediate victim and then to members of his or her minority group in the form of terror and intimidation. They also emphasize that the enhanced penalties have a deterrent effect.

Those opposed to the laws claim that they violate the principle of equality under the law. Why, they ask, should someone who utters a racial slur while assaulting an African American receive a more severe sentence than a person who says nothing while committing a similar assault? Why should gays get special protections? Opponents also claim that deterrence doesn't work and is not necessary in many instances.

Supporters of hate-crime legislation counter these arguments by emphasizing that painting swastika graffiti on a synagogue wall is far more than just petty vandalism, and many feel that the law should acknowledge that. Furthermore, thousands of peaceful, law-abiding Muslims in the United States live in fear of retribution for acts of terrorism they had nothing to do with.

White-Collar and Corporate Crime

White-collar crime—also known as corporate crime—can be defined as offenses committed by persons acting in their legitimate occupational roles. Generally, these crimes are committed for financial gain and rely on tactics of deception and fraud instead of physical violence. First introduced by Edwin H. Sutherland in an address to the American Sociological Society Meeting in 1939, the concept of white-collar crime can be analyzed from three broad perspectives: by the type of offender (of a high socioeconomic status or occupation), the nature of the offense (economic motivation), or the organizational structure and culture that permit such offenses.

The offenders include businesspeople, members of the professions and government employees, and other varieties of workers who, in the course of their everyday occupational activities, violate the basic trust placed in them or act in unethical ways. Crime is neither the way of life nor the chosen career of white-collar or corporate offenders but, rather, something that occurs in conjunction with their more legitimate work activities—for example:

- In the business sector: financial manipulations, unfair labor practices, rebates, misrepresentation of goods and consumer deception by false labeling, fencing of stolen goods, shortchanging, overcharging, black-marketeering
- In the corporate sector: restraint of trade, infringement of patents, monopolistic practices, environmental contamination, misuse of trademarks, manufacture of unsafe goods, false advertising, disposal of toxic wastes
- In the financial sector: embezzlement, violation of currency-control measures, stock manipulation
- In the medical sector: illegal prescription practices, fee splitting, illegal abortions, fraudulent reports to insurance companies
- In the criminal justice sector: accepting bribes, illegal arrest and detention practices, illegal correctional practices

Currently, losses from white-collar and corporate crime are conservatively estimated to be in excess of $300 billion annually.[40] However, there are also hidden costs. For example, the corruption of corporate officers undermines the public's trust in business; environmental crimes jeopardize public health; and the faulty manufacturing of products can endanger lives.

In the United States, most white-collar crime is committed for financial manipulation and gain, and it accounts for approximately 4 percent of reported crime. In 2006, fraud accounted for the majority of all white-collar crime arrests (280,693), followed by embezzlement (20,012). The total number of embezzlement arrests dropped almost 28 percent between 1997 and 2006, according to the FBI's Uniform Crime Reports. Overall, however, embezzlement accounts for only about 1 percent of the total persons arrested for federal offenses.[41]

Organized Crime

Organized crime, the fourth crime context we discuss, consists of business activities directed toward economic gain through unlawful means. Unlike white-collar criminals, who act in their legitimate occupational roles, those involved in organized crime engage in illegal activities such as gambling, loan-sharking, commercialized vice, bootlegging, trafficking in narcotics and other drugs, and disposing of stolen merchandise. Some forms of organized crime are both national and international in scope.

As a criminal pattern, organized crime is typically an occupational career. Crime organizations have a hierarchical structure that includes various levels of responsibility, knowledge of criminal activity, and gain from the criminal enterprise. People are often recruited on the basis of kinship, friendship, or neighborhood, where such activities are a means of gaining economic respectability. Individuals make a long-term commitment to the career, and their entire social organization and lifestyle revolve around crime.

Historically, discussions of organized crime have focused almost exclusively on groups like the Mafia (La Cosa Nostra), and individuals such as Al Capone. More recent analyses, however, have looked at other criminal ethnic groups—including Asians, Jamaicans, Latin Americans, and Russians, to name only a few.[42]

Terrorism

As you learned in Chapter 1, terrorism is a significant focus of modern criminal justice system. Like organized crime, terrorism often entails the use of the multiple criminal enterprises and behaviors to further the goals of groups and organizations conducting

DISCRETION MATTERS

Why do you think our society chooses not to focus on white-collar crime as much as it does street crime?

On October 18, 1931, Al Capone—probably one of America's best-known gangsters—was convicted and later sentenced to eleven years in federal prison, fined $50,000, and charged $7,692 for court costs, in addition to $215,000 plus interest due on back taxes.

Acts of terrorism around the world have altered the landscape of criminal justice in America, expanding its focus from a local one, on street crime, to a global one of potential threats to safety in the community.

terrorist operations, and multiple organizations and personnel are engaged in detecting, preventing, investigating, and prosecuting it. The National Counterterrorism Center (NCTC) gathers national and international data about terrorism and publishes an annual report on incidents of terrorism around the world. The NCTC relies on a definition of terrorism provided in U.S. statutes: "premeditated, politically motivated violence perpetrated against noncombatant targets by subnational groups or clandestine agents."[43] In accordance with this definition, in 2010, more than 11,500 terrorist attacks occurred in 72 countries. These resulted in nearly 50,000 victims, including almost 13,200 deaths .[44] As you can see from this chapter's coverage of crime patterns and contexts, how crime is measured has considerable impact on the view of crime in the United States and around the world. The attention paid to patterns and trends also affects how criminal justice resources are used and how individuals perceive the effectiveness of both the agencies and agents of justice in the community. The counting and measuring of crime incidents is the topic for our next section.

MEASURING CRIME IN THE UNITED STATES

A stark difference generally exists between public perceptions and actual crime rates, just as the legal definitions of crime often do not mesh well with the public idea of what constitutes a particular offense. Measuring crime and communicating the findings are important functions of criminal justice personnel. Such data help identify the nature and pattern of crime in the United States, guide the allocation of criminal justice resources, shape citizens' view of their government and community, and help the system formulate responses that increase safety for all.

The following sections describe the major sources of information we have about the magnitude, pattern, and temporal trends of crime. More specifically, you will learn how information is compiled, what it includes, and how it might best be applied and interpreted.

Citizens, academicians, and researchers have three broad areas of crime information at their disposal. These include official data developed, collected, and measured by personnel and agencies in the criminal justice systems around the country; victimization data derived from surveys; and self-report data, including surveys and interviews of individuals who have committed crimes or experienced crime victimizations. We begin with an examination of the best-known source of crime statistics, the Uniform Crime Reports.

The Uniform Crime Reports

Systematic official collection of crime statistics for the nation as a whole began in the 1920s. Prior to that time, little was known about the extent of crime in the United States. At the 1927 annual meeting of the International Association of Chiefs of Police, the Committee on Uniform Crime Reports was commissioned to prepare a manual on standardized crime reporting for use by local police agencies. On the basis of this committee's efforts, Congress authorized the Federal Bureau of Investigation (FBI) to collect and compile nationwide data on crime. The FBI provides standardized forms to police departments and compiles and publishes the data received in the **Uniform Crime Reports** (UCR). The UCR is presented annually in a document entitled *Crime in the United States,* which is available to the public via the FBI website.[45]

Administrators, politicians, policy makers, opinion makers, the press, criminal justice agencies, and the public rely on this volume for information about crime trends and patterns. Yet the FBI reports have their problems. They can be incomplete and structurally biased, resulting in the creation and persistence of many myths about crime in the United States. Moreover, they have been misused and misinterpreted. As a result, inaccurate and distorted representations of crime are continually being offered to both professional and lay audiences, and public pronouncements about "the crime problem" often have only limited basis in fact. The following sections explore these issues.

Structure and Content of the UCR

The FBI's Uniform Crime Reports presents a nationwide view of crime based on statistics submitted by city, county, and state law enforcement agencies.[46] As of 2010, 18,108 law enforcement agencies were contributing crime data, representing more than 93 percent of the national population.[47] The report contains a number of components that help criminal justice agencies track crime and develop strategies for responding to issues within their own communities. This report also provides the public with information about crime that they can use to assess the effectiveness of the criminal justice system.

The Crime Clock. The UCR begins with a rather alarming crime clock. As illustrated in Exhibit 3.12, it suggests that in 2010 one murder occurred every 35.6 minutes, one forcible rape every 6.2 minutes, one robbery every 1.4 minutes, and a property crime every 3.5 seconds, as well as other crimes in similarly frequent intervals. The reader is cautioned that the crime clock display should not be interpreted to mean that crime occurs at a particular tempo; it simply represents the annual ratio of crime to fixed time intervals.[48]

Collecting Data on Criminal Offenses. The UCR presents statistics in two categories: (1) crimes known or reported to the police and (2) arrests. "Crimes known to the police" include all events either reported to or observed by the police in those categories of crime that are the most serious: criminal homicide, forcible rape, robbery, aggravated assault, burglary/breaking and entering, larceny-theft (other than motor vehicle theft), motor vehicle theft, and arson. Within the data on crimes known to police, the UCR also contains information about the clearance of these offenses. Clearance refers to the offenses that are closed by arrest or exceptional means.[49] "Arrests" include compilations of arrest reports for all serious offenses combined with reports for 20 additional categories of less serious crimes. These include other assaults, forgery and counterfeiting, fraud, embezzlement, stolen property (buying, receiving, and

DISCRETION MATTERS

Why do you think the FBI and law enforcement in general focus on the most serious offenses? How might this decision affect a citizen's view of crime in America?

EXHIBIT 3.12   2010 Crime Clock Statistics

A Violent Crime occurred every	25.3 seconds
One Murder every	35.6 minutes
One Forcible Rape every	6.2 minutes
One Robbery every	1.4 minutes
One Aggravated Assault every	40. 5 seconds
A Property Crime occurred every	3.5 seconds
One Burglary every	14.6 seconds
One Larceny-theft every	5.1 seconds
One Motor Vehicle Theft every	42.8 seconds

Source: FBI, *Crime in the United States, 2010*

possessing), vandalism, weapons (carrying and possessing), prostitution and commercialized vice, sex offenses (except forcible rape, prostitution, and commercialized vice), drug abuse violations, gambling, offenses against the family and children (nonsupport, neglect, and desertion), driving under the influence (of alcohol or drugs), liquor law violations, drunkenness, disorderly conduct, vagrancy, violations of curfew and loitering laws, suspicion, and "all other."[50]

Information on the serious violent and property offenses is grouped by city, metropolitan area, state, region, and the nation as a whole to reflect an "Crime Index" for a given year. First published in 1960, the Crime Index has been under scrutiny for its consistency as a barometer of criminality. Since the Crime Index is a total that does not distinguish the seriousness of crimes, giving the same weight to larceny or theft as it does to murder or rape, critics have charged that it creates a biased overall **crime rate.** The crime rate is determined by taking the total number of crime incidents, dividing that number by the total population, and multiplying that number by 100,000 (Exhibit 3.13). This tells us how many of those offenses occurred per 100,000 individuals in our society. In addition, the FBI continues to publish a violent crime total and rate and a property crime total and rate. The crime rate calculation contains several terms that are important for reading and interpreting any crime statistics:

EXHIBIT 3.13   Crime Rate Calculation

Total Crime Incidents ÷ Population x 100,000 = Crime Rate

Total crime incidents: the sum of all violent and property offenses reported to or observed by the police (i.e., "crimes known to the police") during a given period in a particular place (in this example, during 2010 for the total United States)

- Violent crime: the sum of all violent offenses (homicide, forcible rape, robbery, and aggravated assault) known to police

- Property crime: the sum of all property offenses (burglary, larceny-theft, motor vehicle theft, and arson) known to police

- Rate per 100,000 inhabitants: the crime rate, or the number of violent and property offenses known to police that occurred in a given area for every 100,000 people living in that area

EXHIBIT 3.14   Crime in the United States, 1987/2010

	Total U.S. Population	Total Crime	Violent Crime	Property Crime
1987	242,288,918	13,508,708	1,483,999	12,024,709
Rate per 100,000 inhabitants		5,575.5	612.5	4,963.0
2010	308,745,538	10,329,135	1,246,248	9,082,887
Rate per 100,000 inhabitants		3,345.5	403.6	2,941.9

Sources: FBI, *Crime in the United States, 1987;* FBI, *Crime in the United States, 2010*

In addition to presenting rates for violent and property offenses, the UCR also breaks down arrest data for each offense by age, gender, and race of those arrested and by population area; it also provides extensive information on criminal justice employees, including the number of law enforcement officers assaulted or killed during the given year. The bulk of what the UCR provides to the police, then, is fairly standard information on crime. However, UCR data are also often used to highlight particularly important topics of interest, including hate crimes, and to produce special reports in collaboration with the Bureau of Justice Statistics on topics such as white-collar crime.

The Extent of Crime The data presented in Exhibit 3.14 provide some preliminary indicators of the extent of crime in the United States, at least in terms of those crimes known to the police. About 10 million violent and property crimes were reported during 2010, including 14,748 murders, 84,767 rapes, 367,832 robberies, 778,901 aggravated assaults, 2.1 million burglaries, 6.2 million larcenies, and 737,142 motor vehicle thefts.

As noted earlier, some less serious offenses are reported in the UCR only in terms of arrests. Therefore, we have no measure of the relative prevalence of these crimes throughout the nation. However, approximately 13,120,947 arrests occurred during 2010, of which over 11 million involved lower-level offenses.

Reliability of Estimates With the exception of the data on homicide, UCR estimates of the volume and rates of crime are considerably lower than the actual frequency of criminal acts. Homicide figures tend to be nearly complete, because most deaths and missing persons are reported and investigated in one way or another. Moreover, comparisons of homicide rates compiled by the FBI and by the Office of Vital Statistics reflect similar figures. But in all other crime categories, UCR estimates are severely deficient. Let's look at the reasons why.

Concealment and Nonreporting. Crime, by its very nature, is not easily measured. It is subject to concealment by victims and offenders and nonreporting by authorities, with the result that official crime statistics fall significantly short of the full volume and range of offenses. For example, wide areas of criminal behavior rarely find their way into official compilations. When family and other relationships are involved, criminal codes often conflict with emotions and social norms, resulting in the concealment of various crimes, such as adultery, sodomy, and statutory rape. In the legal and health professions, both practitioners and clients fail to report white-collar crimes, primarily in the areas of illegal adoption practices, fee splitting, illegal prescription- and drug-dispensing practices, falsification of claims, perjury, bribery, and conflicts of interest. Similar levels of concealment and nonreporting occur in both the private business and public sectors. Finally, many victims fail to report crimes to the police out of fear of publicity and reprisal, lack of confidence in law enforcement or other authorities, or unwillingness to get involved with crime reporting and control.[51]

Individuals have many reasons why they may not want to become involved with the police. Consider the case of a liquor-store owner whose place of business was held up at gunpoint on three separate occasions. His combined losses were more than $10,000 in money and goods, which could have been reimbursed by his insurance coverage had he reported the robberies to the authorities. He did not, however, because he was hoping to sell his business and felt that if word got out that his establishment had been targeted, its potential market value would drop significantly.

Crime statistics are also subject to manipulations by criminal justice authorities for political and public relations purposes. For example, as crime rates fell in many parts of the United States during the 1990s, police officials in a number of cities were under pressure to show similar patterns in their cities. In New York City in 2000, several police commanders were either demoted or reassigned because they had manipulated statistics in an effort to "bring down the crime rate" in their precincts.[52] Concerns about the manipulation of crime data led to audits of both reporting and data-entry systems in law enforcement departments in Nashville, Tennessee, and New Orleans.[53]

Problems in Reporting Official Crime Data. The methods used to record crimes at the local level can also affect the reliability of crime statistics. Clearly, failures to report offenses can have a significant impact on the compilation of crime statistics. A study sponsored by the Justice Department, for example, found that the FBI was not informed of approximately one in every five crimes reported by the public. Separately, an independent audit of Atlanta's police department, completed in 2004, unveiled systemic underreporting of crimes and sloppy record-keeping. Furthermore, unlike those of most cities, Atlanta's figures did not include all crimes reported by

Drug offenses, particularly those that may be widespread and difficult for law enforcement to observe, are often underreported in official data sources.

the 15 local law enforcement agencies that operated within the city. Therefore, the city's crime statistics were actually a serious underrepresentation of the true crime rate.[54]

Criminal justice agencies are not the only organizations known for underreporting crime events. Colleges, universities, and other educational institutions, for example, are notorious for failing to report crimes. Since 1990, Congress has required all U.S. colleges and universities to report all crimes so that prospective students will have some relative indication of campus safety. However, possibly out of fear of bad publicity, many colleges have regularly understated the number of campus crimes. Many colleges do not count offenses that occur on the city streets that run through their campuses; others omit on-campus rapes that are reported to local police or crisis-intervention centers rather than to campus security or police forces. Still other institutions ignore incidents that occur in sorority and fraternity houses.[55]

In addition to these problems, others arise from the UCR process itself. The FBI's *Uniform Crime Reporting Handbook* provides specific definitions of the 29 crime categories in the UCR. The FBI also provides standardized reporting forms to police agencies for compiling their data. But not all law enforcement bureaucracies follow definitions and instructions to the letter, potentially resulting in inaccurate statistics.

Evaluating the UCR. How useful, then, are the Uniform Crime Reports? Are they reliable enough to provide the researcher, administrator, and observer with baseline data on the phenomenon of crime? If we examine UCR figures from the perspective of rates and proportions, as opposed to absolute numbers, we can determine the overall growth, decline, or persistence of particular types of criminal behavior. We can also determine the extent to which the behavior is or is not being brought under control. Further, the rates and proportions can suggest the segments of the population that are most prone to a particular form of criminality, and they can indicate the changing social and economic severity of a given offense.

The most effective use of rate and proportion analysis occurs at the local level. By combining existing UCR data with statistical compilations available from local, county, and state criminal justice agencies, planners, administrators, and observers can identify crime trends in the community. In 1987, the Department of Justice began testing and implementing a new National Incident-Based Reporting System (NIBRS). The system is designed to collect and report data in 22 crime categories with regard to the following factors:

- Incident—date and time
- Offense—whether completed or attempted, type(s) of criminal activity, weapons or force involved, premises involved and method of entry (if applicable), location, whether computer equipment was used, whether the offender used alcohol or drugs during or before the crime
- Property—type of property loss, value, recovery date, type and quantity of drugs involved (if appropriate)
- Victim—type (person or business), characteristics (age, sex, race, ethnicity), circumstances if the crime was a homicide or assault (e.g., a lovers' quarrel, death in the line of duty), relationship between victim and offender
- Offender—characteristics (age, sex, race), date of arrest, arrest offense[56]

Though limited in usefulness, the Uniform Crime Report and other official crime data sources offer one image of the crime situation in the United States. The data in these reports come directly from law enforcement officials.

As of 2010, the implementation of NIBRS had been slow, with contributing police agencies representing just 25 percent of the U.S. population.[57] Since conversion to the NIBRS program requires computerization, training, technical assistance, and support at each reporting point, full implementation on a nationwide basis is not expected for some time. While limited, this data source offers a supplement to the UCR data and attempts to respond to the issues and drawbacks of that data.

Victim Survey Research

In 1965, in an effort to determine the parameters of crime that did not appear in official criminal statistics, the President's Commission on Law Enforcement and Administration of Justice initiated the first national survey of crime victimization ever conducted. During that year, the National Opinion Research Center (NORC) surveyed 10,000 households, asking whether the person questioned, or any member of his or her household, had been a victim of crime during the preceding year, whether the crime had been reported to the police, and, if not, what the reasons for not reporting were.[58] The households were selected so that they would be representative of the nation as a whole, and as is the case with political polling and election forecasting, the results were considered to be accurate within a small degree of error. The Bureau of Social Science Research, located in Washington, and the Survey Research Center at the University of Michigan conducted more-detailed surveys of medium- and high-crime areas in Washington, DC, Boston, and Chicago.

These **victimization surveys** quickly demonstrated that the actual amount of crime in the United States at that time was likely to be several times that reported in the UCR. The NORC survey suggested that during 1965, forcible rapes were almost four times the reported rate, larcenies were almost double the reported rate, and burglaries and robberies were 50 percent greater than the reported rate. Vehicle theft was lower, but by a smaller amount than the differences between other categories of crime; the homicide figure from the NORC survey was considered too small for an accurate

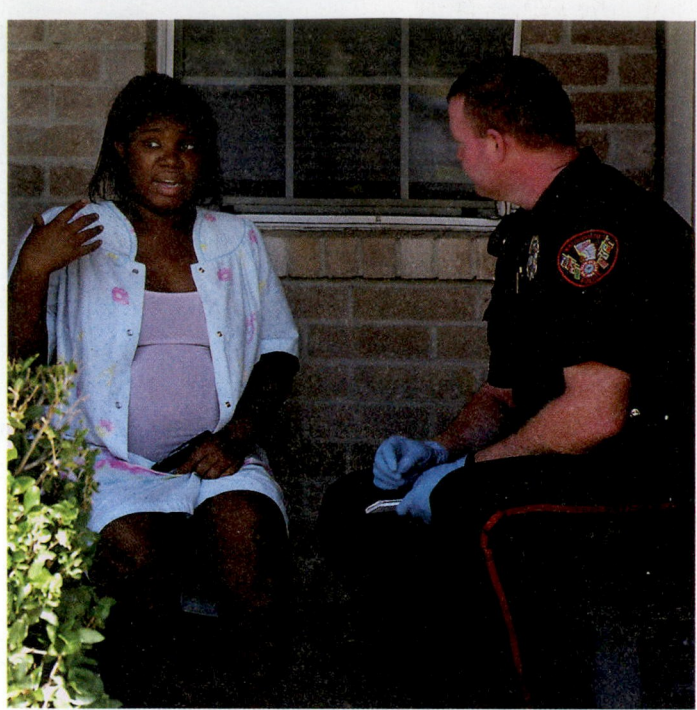

Self-report data, like that in the National Crime Victimization Survey, offer insights into the experiences of crime victims.

statistical projection. As high as the NORC rates were for violent and property crimes, they were still considered to have understated the actual amounts of crime to some degree, since the victimization rates for every member of each surveyed household were based on the responses of only one family member.

The National Crime Victimization Survey The interest and knowledge generated by this research stimulated the Law Enforcement Assistance Administration (LEAA) to continue the effort with surveys of its own. Its first survey, conducted by the U.S. Bureau of the Census in 1972, further documented the disparities between unreported crime and crimes known to the police. In some cities the ratio between the two was greater than 5 to 1.[59] This portion of crime became known as the "dark figure of crime" and represented the crime not identified nor responded to by the criminal justice system.

Since this study, victim survey research has continued. The National Crime Victimization Survey (NCVS) is conducted by the Bureau of the Census under the direction of the Department of Justice. NCVS data reflect the nature and extent of criminal victimization, characteristics of the victim, victim-offender relationships, the times and places of the crimes, the degree of weapon use, the extent of personal injury, the extent of victim self-protection, the amount of economic and work-time loss due to victimization, the extent to which crimes are reported to police, and the reasons for nonreporting. Survey findings from 2010 were based on interviews with 40,974 households and 73,283 individuals age 12 and older.[60] Although NCVS and UCR data are not fully comparable, data suggest that the 18.7 million violent and property crimes projected by the NCVS go well beyond what appeared in the UCR for the same year.

The major reason for these large discrepancies is that citizens did not report significant numbers of crimes to the police. The major reason for this high level of nonreporting was the victims' belief that the police could do nothing about the crimes or that the victimizations were simply not important enough to report. Other less frequently mentioned reasons were fear of reprisal, the feeling that reporting was too inconvenient or time-consuming, the assumption that the police would not want to be bothered, and the belief that the crime was a private and personal matter.

Although UCR and NCVS data have often been compared, the two are not fully comparable. First, the UCR bases its crime rates on the total U.S. population, while the NCVS victimization data relate only to people age 12 and older. Second, the NCVS measures crime by victimization rather than by incident. For crimes against persons, the number of victimizations is normally greater than the number of incidents, since more than one person can be involved in any given incident. Third, NCVS and UCR crime classifications are not always uniform. While purse snatching is included with robbery according to UCR definitions, it appears as theft in NCVS data. Fourth, NCVS data on homicide are considered unreliable because violence of that type is relatively rare and the unreported instances that emerge during a survey are too few to permit accurate projections to the nation as a whole.

Comparisons between NCVS and UCR crime figures and rates must therefore be viewed with caution. Neither reporting mechanism alone can offer a fully accurate picture of the extent of specific crimes. Nevertheless, such comparisons do indicate some general weaknesses of the UCR and suggest the relative large amounts of crime that go unreported.

Applications and Limitations of Victimization Surveys The focus on the victim as a more complete source of information on instances of criminal activity has been the chief contribution of victim-survey research. The material derived from such surveys helps determine the extent and distribution of crime in a community. In addition, the surveys target not only victimizations but also public conceptions of crime, characteristics of victims and offenders, and conceptions of police effectiveness, as well as other data. Therefore victim-focused studies can also be used for the following purposes:

1. To evaluate the effectiveness of specific police programs
2. To develop better insights into certain violent crimes through the analysis of victim-offender relationships
3. To structure programs for increased reporting of crimes to the police
4. To sensitize the criminal justice system to the needs of the victim
5. To develop training programs that stress police-victim and police-community relations
6. To create and implement meaningful public-information and crime-prevention programs

Despite their usefulness, however, victimization studies do have limitations. For example, researchers who conduct these surveys find that those interviewed have trouble remembering exactly when a crime occurred; in property offenses, they forget how great the losses were. But by far the major problem is the cost of such studies. Most locales simply cannot afford them.

Although some victims of serious offenses may seek help from the police, victimization surveys demonstrate that many thousands of crimes go unreported for a variety of complicated reasons, including the victim's involvement in crime and the relationship of the victim to the offender.

Self-Reported Criminal Behavior

Since the 1930s, when the FBI began publishing the Uniform Crime Reports, criminological research has produced studies that have confirmed the limitations of official crime statistics. Among the earliest of these research efforts was a rudimentary victimization survey, conducted in 1933, that found that of some 5,314 instances of shoplifting occurring in three Philadelphia department stores, fewer than 5 percent were ever reported to the police.[61]

Another primary mechanism for determining the nature and extent of this "dark figure," or unknown crime, is research into **self-reported crime.** The first major study of self-reported crime came in 1947, when two researchers obtained completed questionnaires from 1,020 men and 678 women of diverse ages and a wide range of conventional occupations regarding their involvement in 49 different offenses. Ninety-nine percent of the respondents admitted that they had committed one or more of the offenses listed. The percentages of both men and women who had engaged in many types of crime were significant.[62]

This pioneer effort demonstrated that criminal activity was considerably more widespread than police files even began to suggest. Since then, studies of self-reported criminal involvement have become more common. In addition to their use as a check on the limitations of standard crime-reporting mechanisms, they can also determine the following:

1. How much crime is committed by the typically noncriminal population
2. What kinds of crime typically remain unknown
3. How the official system of crime control selects cases to pursue
4. Whether certain categories of offenders are over- or under-selected by law enforcement officials
5. Whether explanations and theories of crime developed for officially known offenders apply to nonregistered offenders as well[63]

Studies of self-reported crime have provided numerous insights into these issues, but such research has some limitations. First, there are methodological questions of validity and reliability. *Validity* refers to how good an answer the study yields. When the respondents admit to criminal behavior, are their answers true? Do they underreport or exaggerate their criminal behavior? Are the respondents' estimates of the frequency of their crimes accurate? *Reliability* refers to the precision, or accuracy, of the instruments used to record and measure self-reported behavior. In other words, does the interview measure what it is intended to measure? Does the respondent interpret the meaning of words such as *burglary, robbery,* or some other category the same way the researcher does?

Besides these potential methodological problems, other possible sources of error include the following:

- Those who agree to answer questions may be markedly different from those who refuse, leaving in doubt the representativeness of any sample of people interviewed.
- Those who respond to such inquiries may be truthful in their answers but may choose to conceal large segments of their criminal backgrounds.
- Most studies have focused on groups of students and other juveniles, stressing the incidence of unrecorded delinquency; few studies have targeted populations of adult offenders.

In general, despite sample biases and other methodological limitations, studies of self-reported crime are important to criminological research. In addition to the advantages mentioned earlier, studies that focus on particular populations (such as drug users) can tell us more about the patterns and styles of criminal careers than can any other form of data.

Other Sources of Data on Crime and Justice

To date, a national crime statistics program has yet to emerge. The Uniform Crime Reports is voluntary and remains the primary source of data on crime, supplemented to some extent by victimization surveys and to a lesser degree by self-report studies. However, many state and federal agencies also compile data on their own particular areas of interest, and they make these data available to interested students and researchers in the *Sourcebook of Criminal Justice Statistics,* published annually by the U.S. Department of Justice in conjunction with the State University of New York at Albany.

The extent to which the use of illegal drugs has affected crime rates and criminal justice processing is seen in the fact that more than two dozen new databases have been developed on drug-use patterns, trends, and correlates. Those of particular significance from the standpoint of criminal justice are the *National Survey on Drug Use and Health* and the *Monitoring the Future* survey.

National Survey on Drug Use and Health Funded by the U.S. Substance Abuse and Mental Health Services Administration and conducted on a regular basis, the *National Survey on Drug Use and Health* estimates the use of major illicit drugs by the general household population of the United States. The estimates tend to be incomplete because they do not include the homeless or people living in jails or prisons, in other institutions, or on military bases; but the data do provide valuable information about the use of drugs and the impact of drug use on the health and well-being of citizens in our community.

Monitoring the Future Sponsored by the National Institute on Drug Abuse, the survey called *Monitoring the Future* is conducted annually with a representative sample of high school students. It explores trends in drug use, attitudes about drug and alcohol use, and lifestyle orientations of American youth. However, because it excludes high school dropouts, significant numbers of drug-using adolescents are missing from its estimates.

Of special interest to anyone interested in the drug problem and rates of substance abuse in the United States are the data reports and publications of the National Institute on Drug Abuse (NIDA). This federal agency funds almost 90 percent of the drug-abuse research that is undertaken throughout the world, and much of the information collected can be found on the NIDA Web site. To name only a few, topics covered are current trends in the drugs being abused, research on the effects of marijuana use, emerging problems with prescription-drug abuse, and approaches for the prevention and treatment of drug abuse.

CONCLUSIONS

Thousands of acts and behaviors are prohibited by law and designated as felonies or misdemeanors in federal, state, and local criminal codes across the United States. Homicide, assault, robbery, arson, burglary, sex offenses, drug law violations, and offenses against the public order and safety account for some 90 percent of the criminal law violations processed by U.S. courts. However, although crime is in part conduct prohibited by the criminal law, its dynamics include certain patterns, contexts, or circumstances, as well as systems of behavior. Understanding these fundamentals is the purpose behind counting and studying criminal behavior. Collecting crime data is often a first step in assessing and understanding the existence of crime in our society. It is crucial for students of criminal justice to be aware of the definitions of crime, as well as the methods for collecting data about it. These definitions and data, in turn, provide the foundation for policy-making decisions, and they drive public understanding of how criminal justice operates in communities around the nation.

SUMMARY AND REVIEW

- ■ **Provide legal definitions for the major categories of criminal offenses.**
  - ▪ Homicide: the killing of one human being by another
    - ▪ Murder: the felonious killing of another human being with malice aforethought, premeditation, and deliberation
    - ▪ Manslaughter: typically charged when a killing occurs under circumstances that are not severe enough to constitute murder yet are beyond the defenses of justifiable or excusable homicide; distinguished from murder in that murder implies malice whereas manslaughter does not
  - ▪ Forcible rape: having sexual intercourse with a person against his or her will and through the use or threat of force or fear
  - ▪ Assault: an intentional attempt or threat to physically injure another person
  - ▪ Robbery: the felonious taking of money or goods from a victim's person, or in a victim's presence and against his or her will, through the use or threat of force and violence
  - ▪ Arson: felonious and malicious burning of objects, structures, people, and other items
  - ▪ Burglary: the act of knowingly entering or remaining unlawfully in a building with the intent to commit a crime therein

- ■ **Describe the major contexts of criminal offending.**
  - ▪ Domestic violence is defined as activities of a physically aggressive nature occurring among members of a family, current or former spouses or lovers, and others in close relationships. Domestic violence typically occurs in the home, but it can also take place at the house of another family member or a neighbor, at the victim's place of employment, at a commercial establishment, or even in public.
  - ▪ Hate crimes are defined as offenses motivated by hatred against a victim because of his or her race, ethnicity, religion, sexual orientation, handicap, national origin, or tribal membership. Also referred to as "bias-motivated crimes," hate crimes are often difficult to identify, primarily because criminal acts motivated by bias can easily be confused with forms of expression that are protected by the U.S. Constitution.
  - ▪ White-collar crime, or corporate crime, can be defined as offenses committed by persons acting in their legitimate occupational roles. Generally, these crimes are committed for financial gain and rely on tactics of deception and fraud instead of physical violence.
  - ▪ Terrorism is defined by the National Counterterrorism Center (NCTC) and in U.S. statutes as "premeditated, politically motivated violence perpetrated against noncombatant targets by subnational groups or clandestine agents."
  - ▪ Organized crime refers to illegal activities such as gambling, loan-sharking, commercialized vice, bootlegging, trafficking in narcotics and other drugs, and disposing of stolen merchandise. Organized crime can occur in both national and international arenas and is typically an occupational career.

- ■ **Identify and describe the two major sources of crime statistics.**
  - ▪ Uniform Crime Reports
    - ▪ The FBI's Uniform Crime Reports (UCR) presents a nationwide view of crime based on statistics submitted by city, county, and state law enforcement agencies throughout the country.
    - ▪ Data are collected on crimes known to police and arrests for criminal homicide, forcible rape, robbery, aggravated assault, burglary/breaking and entering, larceny-theft (other than motor vehicle theft), motor vehicle theft, and arson. Data on a number of lesser offenses are also collected.
    - ▪ The National Incident-Based Reporting System (NIBRS) is an innovation developed by the FBI to collect more-detailed case-specific crime data. Approximately 25 percent of the nation is represented by NIBRS reporting coverage.
  - ▪ National Crime Victimization Study
    - ▪ This household survey examines the self-reported victimization experienced by citizens in both urban and suburban locations.
    - ▪ The survey contains information on the nature and extent of criminal victimization, characteristics of the victim, victim-offender relationships, the times and places of the crimes, the degree of weapon use, the extent of personal injury, the extent of victim self-protection, the amount of economic and work-time loss due to victimization, the extent to which crimes are reported to police, and the reasons for nonreporting.

- ■ **Compute and interpret a crime rate.**
  - ▪ Total Crime Incidents ÷ Population x 100,000 = Crime Rate
  - ▪ The crime rate refers to the number of offenses per 100,000 individuals in the general population.

KEY TERMS

arson (p. 61)
assault (p. 60)
assault and battery (p. 60)
breaking and entering (p. 61)
crime rate (p. 74)
deliberation (p. 58)
domestic violence (p. 68)
felony (p. 57)
felony-murder doctrine (p. 59)

hate crime (p. 69)
homicide (p. 58)
malice aforethought (p. 58)
manslaughter (p. 59)
misdemeanor (p. 57)
murder (p. 58)
organized crime (p. 71)
premeditation (p. 58)
public order crimes (p. 67)

robbery (p. 60)
self-reported crime (p. 79)
sexual assault (p. 64)
theft (p. 63)
Uniform Crime Reports (UCR) (p. 73)
victimization surveys (p. 77)
white-collar crime (p. 70)

ISSUES FOR CRITICAL THINKING AND DISCUSSION

1. In cases where the felony-murder doctrine has been invoked, the intent to commit murder has often been absent. In such circumstances, is conviction of murder in the first degree a just disposition? Why or why not?

2. Which sex offenses, if any, should be abolished from contemporary criminal codes? Why?

3. Should the thoughts or bias of the offender affect his or her punishment for a criminal act? Why or why not?

4. How might official statistics, victimization data, and self-reported crime data be collected and combined to provide a more accurate picture of crime in the United States?

5. Why is it difficult to use official statistics to make universal claims about crime trends and patterns?

6. Why do you think crime rates are down?

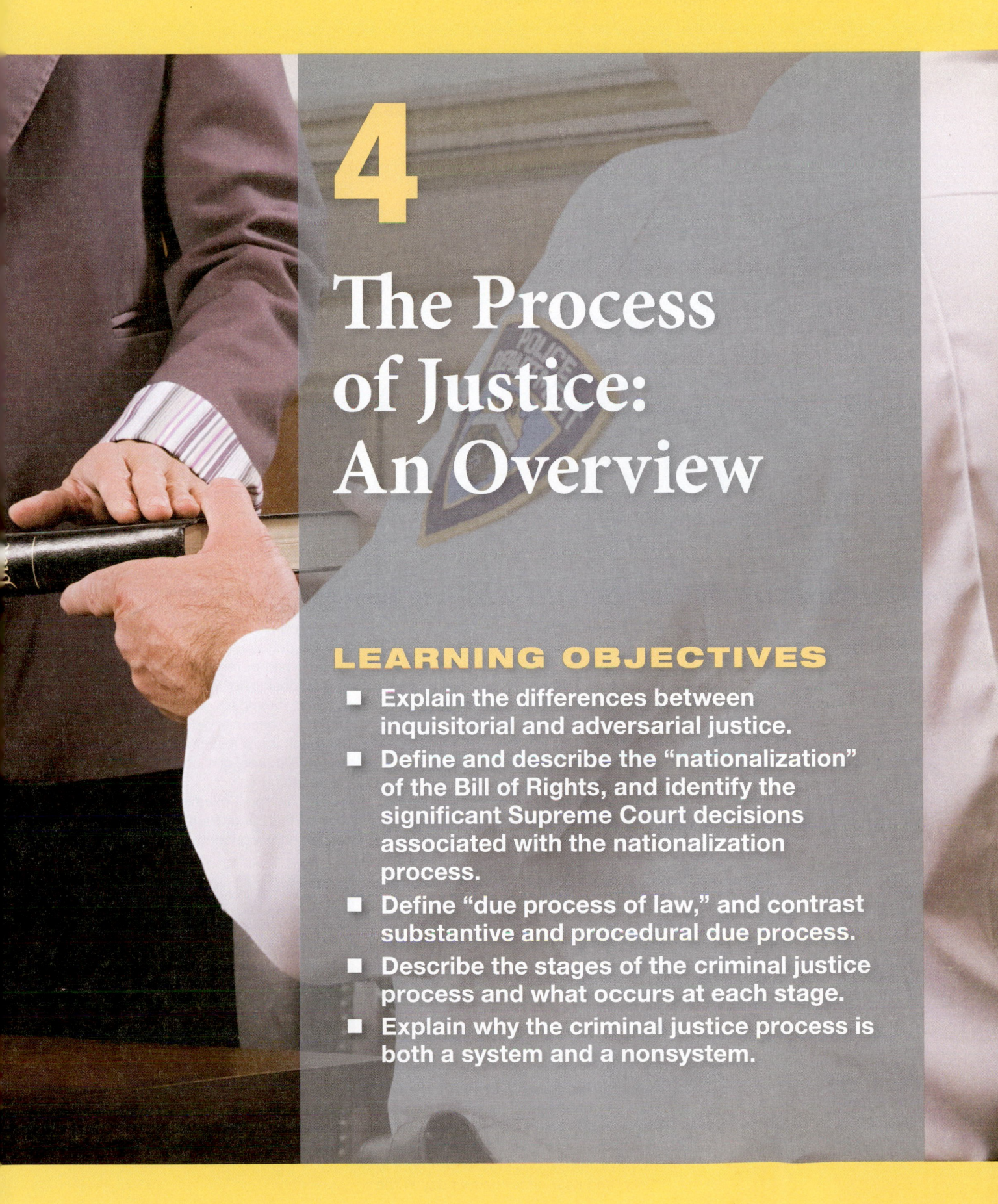

4

The Process of Justice: An Overview

LEARNING OBJECTIVES

- Explain the differences between inquisitorial and adversarial justice.

- Define and describe the "nationalization" of the Bill of Rights, and identify the significant Supreme Court decisions associated with the nationalization process.

- Define "due process of law," and contrast substantive and procedural due process.

- Describe the stages of the criminal justice process and what occurs at each stage.

- Explain why the criminal justice process is both a system and a nonsystem.

THE SUPREME COURT AND THE BILL OF RIGHTS

Dick Heller initiated the Supreme Court case challenging the ban on handguns within the District of Columbia.

Dick Heller was a special police officer at the Federal Judicial Center in Washington, DC, and was authorized to carry a handgun while on duty there. He applied for a registration certificate to keep a handgun in his home for defense purposes. However, the Washington, DC, criminal code both forbade the carrying of an unregistered firearm and prohibited the registration of handguns within the city. Heller filed suit in federal court, on Second Amendment grounds, to prevent the city from enforcing laws related to handgun ownership.

The District of Columbia laws described above were coupled with a separate provision that prohibited people from carrying unlicensed handguns but authorized the police chief to issue one-year licenses and required residents to keep lawfully owned firearms unloaded and disassembled or bound by a trigger lock or similar device. According to Heller, trigger locks prevented the effective use of the handguns for self-defense in the home. This case made its way to the highest court, and finally, on March 18, 2008, the Second Amendment right to "keep and bear arms" had its day in the

Supreme Court.[1] Five justices, a bare majority, signaled their belief that the Second Amendment gives individuals a right to have a gun for self-defense in the home.

The justices thus struck down the District of Columbia's ban on handguns—the nation's strictest gun-control law. The court's primary holding, found in the majority opinion written by Justice Scalia, stated that the "Second Amendment protects an individual right to possess a firearm unconnected with service in a militia, and to use that arm for traditionally lawful purposes, such as self-defense within the home."[2] The outcome of this case impacted numerous state and city ordinances, most notably in Chicago, Illinois.

This case brought attention to the variety of gun laws across the country and the fact that local and state jurisdictions have the ability to regulate all aspects of firearm behavior—the sale, use, carrying, and concealed-carrying—but only within certain limits. While few think of legislative action as involving individual discretion, the decisions local and state officials make to ban or regulate some behaviors while choosing not to regulate others have a significant impact on law and justice in America. These very discretionary decisions epitomize justice in our communities, legislatures, and courtrooms across the nation.

This chapter examines the implications of the Bill of Rights and the emergence and conceptualization of due

process of law in American jurisprudence. We focus on the concept of due process because it is central to the other major topic of this chapter—the stages of the criminal justice process. Like all cases adjudicated in the U.S. courts, Heller ben-efited from the rules of due process as his case made its way through the levels and procedures of the federal court system. Let's begin this discussion with the nature of due process in American criminal justice.

CRIMINAL DUE PROCESS

No person shall be . . . deprived of life, liberty, or property, without due process of law.
    —From the Fifth Amendment

Nor shall any State deprive any person of life, liberty, or property, without due process of law.
    —From the Fourteenth Amendment

Through the ages, justice processes have taken numerous and varied forms. During the early centuries of the Catholic Church, for example, trials were not considered necessary for thieves caught in the act of stealing. If they were poor and could not pay even the smallest fine, they were simply put to death with little formality. In doubtful cases, however, some degree of innocence or guilt had to be determined. One way of accomplishing this was the "ordeal by water," which was carried out by a priest.

Trial by Ordeal

A cauldron of boiling water was placed in the center of the church. Spectators, who were required to be fasting and "abstinent from their wives during the previous night," assembled in two rows on either side of the church and were blessed by the priest. While they prayed that God would "make clear the whole truth," the priest bandaged the arm of the accused person. Into the bottom of a vat of boiling water the priest dropped a small stone. The accused had to plunge his arm into the cauldron and pluck out the stone. After three days, the bandages were removed, and evidence of scalding was deemed proof of guilt.[3]

This ordeal by water, which was not formally abolished in England until 1219, could be replaced by similar tests. The accused could be ordered to walk barefoot over red-hot plowshares, place his hand in a glove of near-molten metal, or walk three paces carrying in his bare hands an iron bar reddened with heat. In these cases as well, it was believed that God would make known the truth and that if the accused was innocent, he would not be burned.

For those who had more resources, guilt or innocence could be determined by *compurgation*. Here the accused would assemble a number of his peers who would make an oath with him that he was innocent. Such oaths were accepted, although perjury must have been rampant.

In this trial by ordeal, a suspected witch was thrown into the river. If she sank, she was considered to be innocent; if she floated, she was considered guilty.

Inquisitorial versus Adversarial Justice

Trials by ordeal, or perhaps by battle, were the cornerstones of the **inquisitorial system** of justice. Under this system the accused person was considered guilty until proven innocent. Inquisitorial justice became manifest when some form of divine intervention spared the accused from pain, suffering, or death, or when the accused readily admitted his or her guilt, usually after torture or other forms of corporal punishment. This system—which now might more properly be called the **inquiry system**—still exists in a modified form (that is, without expectation of divine intervention) in most countries that did not evolve from English or American colonial rule. In the modern inquiry court, all the participants—judge, prosecutor, defense attorney, defendant, and witnesses—are obliged to cooperate with the court in its inquiry into the crime. It is believed that the truth will emerge out of this inquiry.

By contrast, American judicial process reflects the **adversarial system,** in which the accused person is presumed to be innocent, and the burden of proof is placed on the court or state. In the adversary court, the judge is an impartial arbiter, or referee, between adversaries—the prosecution and defense. The opposing sides fight within strict rules of procedure, and it is believed that the side with the truth will win. Adversary proceedings are grounded in the right of defendants to refrain from harming themselves in the context of the legal process and in the notion of **due process of law,** a concept that relates to ensuring the fundamental principles of justice and implies the administration of laws that do not violate individual rights. This definition is clarified and expanded later in the chapter.

The Law of the Land

During the Middle Ages—when championing the weak was held up as an ideal, and when valor, courtesy, generosity, and dexterity in arms were the summit of any man's attainment—inquisitorial justice was dominant. Due process meant nothing more than adhering to the law of the land, and torture was the most common method of ascertaining guilt. Periods of active torture were usually preceded by imprisonment in a foul dungeon or small cell. Defendants were ill-fed and left in an uncomfortable and half-starved condition to contemplate the infinitely worse treatment that awaited them.

Eventually, the defendant was brought to a torture room to face his or her accusers and those in charge of the gruesome ceremonies. A mechanism called the *strappado* was used in the early phases of torture. The hands of the accused were tied behind his back and then drawn up by a rope and pulley, thus wrenching the shoulders from their sockets without leaving outward marks. Later phases of torture included the application of thumbscrews, or "Spanish boots," through which pieces of wood were pressed down on thumbs or shins in such a way as to crush both flesh and bone. Also common was the German *schnure,* in which a piece of rope was sawed back and forth across the limbs of the accused until the flesh was rubbed away, exposing the bone.

If confessions could not be forced by these and numerous other exercises in horror, the final stage of torture, which typically led to death, was initiated. Devices used in this stage included spiked barrels and cradles in which the accused was rocked back and forth, a spiked chair to which the accused was tightly strapped, or the infamous iron maiden. The last implement was a hollow statue constructed of wood or iron and braced with metal strips. Long spikes were attached to the inside, and when the accused was placed inside and the vessel was closed, the spikes entered the eyes and body, producing certain death. During the Middle Ages such methods were viewed as "due process," because existing law sanctioned the use of torture for eliciting confessions.

The early-nineteenth-century British case of *Ashford v. Thornton* illustrates a less gruesome, though equally curious, reflection of an early conception of due process.[4] Ashford appeared before the king's justices, charging Thornton with murder. He swore that Thornton had raped and drowned Mary Ashford, the accuser's young sister. The sheriff found Thornton and brought him to court, and the justices ordered him to make a plea. "Not guilty," he maintained, "and I am ready to defend the same with my body."[5] He then drew off his glove and threw it onto the floor of the court, a signal that he was demanding trial by battle. It would be his life against Ashford's, and if Thornton won, he would be judged innocent. Ashford argued that the circumstances were so exceptional that Thornton should be denied the right to defend himself in battle, but the justices were not persuaded. They ruled that the established procedure for cases of this kind must be followed—that is, trial by battle. Ashford refused to fight, and due process followed its course: The judgment was that Thornton should go free.[6]

Even in the United States in the early nineteenth century, the concept of due process was vague at best. The framers of the Constitution had stated in the Fifth Amendment that persons shall not be deprived of life, liberty, or property "without due process of law." The due process guarantee was repeated when the Fourteenth Amendment was added to the Constitution in 1868. But what did they intend by these words? It is a hotly debated issue, even today.

The Bill of Rights

During the first Congress, in June 1789, two years after the signing of the Constitution, James Madison of Virginia, who would later become the fourth president of the United States, proposed a dozen amendments to the Constitution. Congress approved ten of them in September 1791, and they took effect on December 15 after having been ratified by the required number of states. These first ten amendments to the Constitution have become known as the **Bill of Rights.**

The significance of the Bill of Rights is that it restricts government rather than individuals and private groups. It was added to the Constitution at the insistence of those who feared a strong central government. More than a century and a half later, U.S. Supreme Court Chief Justice Earl Warren made this comment:

> The men of our First Congress . . . knew that whatever form it may assume, government is potentially as dangerous a thing as it is a necessary one. They knew that power must be lodged somewhere to prevent anarchy within and conquest from without, but that this power could be abused to the detriment of their liberties.[7]

Within the Bill of Rights, the First Amendment prohibits laws and practices that have the effect of establishing an official religion. It also protects freedom of speech, the press, religion, and assembly, and it guarantees the right to petition the government for redress of grievances (Exhibit 4.1). The Second Amendment, referred to in this chapter's opening case, guarantees the right to keep and bear arms as part of a well-regulated militia; the Third Amendment forbids the government to quarter soldiers in people's homes; and the Fourth Amendment protects a person's right to be secure in his or her person, house, papers, and effects against unreasonable searches and seizures.

The Fifth Amendment requires indictments for proceedings in serious criminal offenses; it forbids compelling

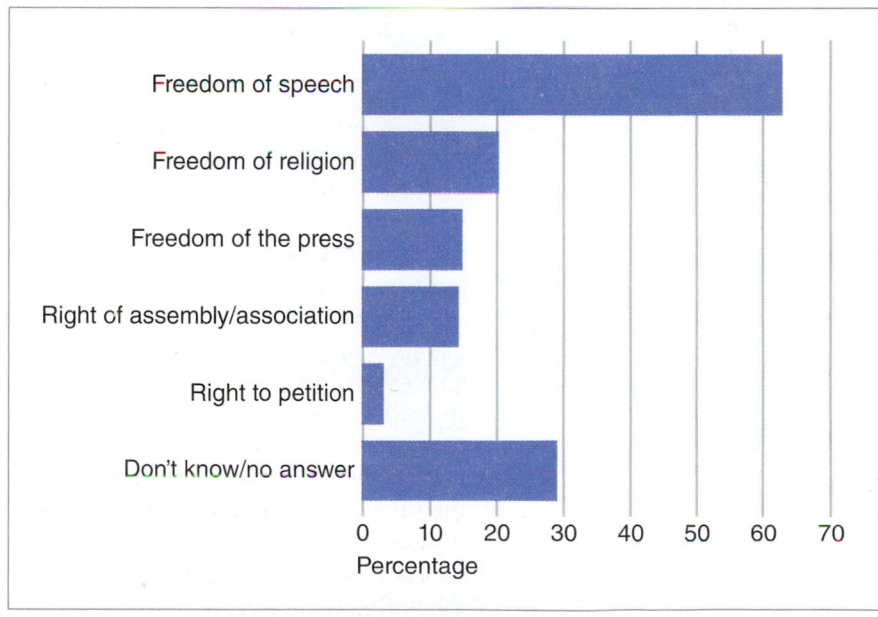

EXHIBIT 4.1 Understanding the First Amendment

When asked which rights are guaranteed by the First Amendment, most Americans think only of freedom of speech. Responses of a nationwide sample are shown here.
Source: New England Research Associates

The use of various methods of execution, including the electric chair, has been challenged under the Eighth Amendment protection against cruel and unusual punishment.

an individual to incriminate him- or herself or trying a person twice for the same offense ("double jeopardy"); it also contains the initial constitutional statement on "due process of law." The Sixth Amendment sets out certain requirements for criminal trials, including the defendant's right to counsel, notification of the charges, a speedy and public trial before an impartial jury in the jurisdiction in which the crime was allegedly committed, and the related rights to confront hostile witnesses and have compulsory processes for obtaining defense witnesses. The Seventh Amendment guarantees the right to a jury trial in common-law civil suits involving $20 or more; and the Eighth Amendment forbids excessive bail, excessive fines, and cruel and unusual punishments.

The Ninth Amendment has never been cited as the sole basis of a U.S. Supreme Court decision, and there is a long-running debate over what the nation's founders intended it to mean.[8] On its face, it states that the enumeration of specific rights elsewhere in the Constitution should not be taken to deny or disparage other rights that are not enumerated but are retained by the people. The Tenth Amendment clearly was designed to protect states' rights and guard against excessive federal power, but it, too, is subject to a variety of interpretations by judges and legal scholars.

Because no rights are absolute, and because they are subject to reasonable regulation through law, the original intent of due process was not self-evident. Madison expected the federal courts to play the major role in implementing them, and he clearly emphasized this point to his fellow members of Congress:

> Independent tribunals of justice will consider themselves . . . the guardians of those rights; they will be an impenetrable bulwark against every assumption of power in the Legislative or Executive; they will naturally be led to resist every encroachment upon rights expressly stipulated . . . by the declaration of rights.[9]

During the decades immediately following the ratification of the Bill of Rights, the Supreme Court had little occasion to apply the guarantees of due process. Slavery, for example, was viewed as a matter of property rights, not human rights; and the constitutional guarantees of civil liberties and due process placed restrictions on government only at the federal level.

Nationalization of the Bill of Rights

In 1833, the Supreme Court made it quite clear that the Bill of Rights provided no protection against state or local action, but only against federal authority. In *Barron v. Baltimore*,[10] the owner of a wharf challenged a local action that seriously impaired the value of his wharf by creating shoals and shallows around it. Barron maintained that this represented a "taking" of his property without just compensation, in violation of the Fifth Amendment. Chief Justice John Marshall ruled, however, that the Bill of Rights had been adopted to secure individual rights only against actions of the federal government.

Barron v. Baltimore[11] seemed to have closed the door on the argument that the Bill of Rights should provide protection against abuses of individual rights by state and local governments. However, with the ratification of the Fourteenth Amendment to the Constitution in 1868, it once again became possible to argue that the Bill of Rights should be understood to restrict the powers of the state and local governments as well as the federal government.

Section 1 of the amendment includes the following statement:

> No State shall make or enforce any law which shall abridge the privileges or immunities of citizens of the United States; nor shall any State deprive any person of life, liberty, or property, without due process of law; nor deny to any person within its jurisdiction the equal protection of the laws.[12]

Legal historians disagree over whether Congress intended the Fourteenth Amendment to make all the provisions of the Bill of Rights binding on the states.[13] This process is initially referred to as *incorporation*. This term identified the gradual and specific application of federal constitutional rights to the states. *Incorporation* is often differentiated from *nationalization,* which refers to the broad application of those constitutional protections of the Bill of Rights as a whole. In its first decisions after ratification of the Fourteenth Amendment, the Supreme Court rejected the notion that the due process clause ("nor shall any State deprive any person of life, liberty, or property, without due process of law") had "incorporated" the Bill of Rights, thus making all the provisions of the Bill of Rights applicable to state and local governments. Nonetheless, following the passage of the Fourteenth Amendment, nationalization was nearly completed through a series of cases examined in this chapter. In the upcoming sections, we examine a number of historical cases that illustrate the process of incorporating the Bill of Rights to apply to the states.

Hurtado v. California   In *Hurtado v. California* (1884),[14] the court declared that the states had no obligation to follow the Fifth Amendment's requirement that individuals prosecuted for a capital or "otherwise infamous crime" must first be indicted by a grand jury. The practical result of *Hurtado* was that California was permitted to use the practice of *information* (a process in which the prosecutor merely submits the charges in an affidavit of evidence, supported by sworn statements) as a substitute for the more time-consuming and difficult requirement of obtaining an indictment from a grand jury. But the most important aspect of the decision was the court's holding that the Fourteenth Amendment's due process clause did not obligate the states or localities to adhere to the specific provisions of the Bill of Rights.

Only one Supreme Court justice dissented from the court's position. Justice John Marshall Harlan, often referred to as "the great dissenter," insisted that all of the rights in the Bill of Rights are "fundamental" and that there was ample evidence that Congress had intended the Fourteenth Amendment to make each and every provision of the Bill of Rights binding on the states. In his dissents in *Hurtado* and several other notable cases,[15] Justice Harlan unsuccessfully endeavored to convince a majority of his colleagues that "no judicial tribunal has authority to say that [the Bill of Rights] may be abridged by the States."[16]

Gitlow v. New York   Justice Harlan died in 1911, not knowing that future Supreme Court decisions would largely accept arguments for "incorporating" the Bill of Rights. The first step in this direction came in 1925, in the famous case of *Gitlow v. New York.*[17] Benjamin Gitlow, a member of the Socialist Party, had been convicted of violating a New York sedition law because he had printed and distributed some 16,000 copies of the "Left Wing Manifesto." This tract called for the overthrow of the United States government by "class action of the proletariat in any form" and urged the proletariat to "organize its own state for the coercion and suppression of the bourgeoisie."

Gitlow appealed his conviction to the Supreme Court, contending that the New York statute unconstitutionally deprived him of his First Amendment right to

DISCRETION MATTERS

How do you think the grand jury can serve as a limiting force on the use of police and prosecutorial discretion?

freedom of speech. The court sustained the conviction, holding that free speech was not an absolute right and that Gitlow's manifesto fell within the category of speech that could properly be prohibited by law. Over the dissenting votes of Justices Louis Brandeis and Oliver Wendell Holmes, both of whom argued that political speech should be barred only when it created a "clear and present danger" to the security of the nation, the majority of the justices reasoned that Gitlow's tract could properly be suppressed even if it merely contained language that might have the effect of inciting violent attempts to overthrow the government (the so-called bad-tendency test).

Although Benjamin Gitlow lost his effort to overturn his conviction, he won one of his other arguments—a victory that had an enormous influence on the evolution of the American criminal justice system. To convince the justices to hear his appeal, Gitlow had asserted that the First Amendment rights of free speech and free press were enforceable against the states. If the court had not accepted this proposition, it would have lacked any legal basis for accepting the case for review and considering the merits of Gitlow's First Amendment arguments. In a seemingly casual passage in his majority opinion, Justice Edward T. Sanford made judicial history by formally accepting the principle of incorporation of the free-speech and free-press provisions of the Bill of Rights:

> For present purposes we may and do assume that freedom of speech and of the press—which are protected by the First Amendment from abridgement by Congress—are among the fundamental personal rights and "liberties" protected by the due process clause of the Fourteenth Amendment from impairment by the States.[18]

It soon became apparent that this decision was the first step in a case-by-case process that would significantly expand the Supreme Court's authority to protect individual rights against unconstitutional acts of state and local government officials. In 1927, a unanimous Supreme Court confirmed the incorporation of freedom of speech in the case of *Fiske v. Kansas.*[19] Four years later, in *Near v. Minnesota,*[20] the court again declared that freedom of the press was enforceable against the states when it struck down the so-called Minnesota Gag Law as an infringement of the freedom of the press guaranteed by the Fourteenth Amendment.

Powell v. Alabama   In 1932, the Supreme Court overturned the convictions of seven indigent, illiterate black youths who had been convicted of the rapes of two white women after a raucous trial in an Alabama courtroom in which they did not have the opportunity to consult with a defense attorney. The case was *Powell v. Alabama,*[21] the first of the notorious Scottsboro Boys cases, and the court's 7–2 holding made it obligatory for the states to provide defense counsel in capital cases (i.e., cases subject to the death penalty) in which indigent defendants faced such disadvantages as illiteracy, ignorance, and extreme community hostility. Although the *Powell* ruling affected only certain types of capital trials, it represented at least partial incorporation of the Sixth Amendment's right-to-counsel clause.

Palko v. Connecticut   The next provisions of the Bill of Rights to be incorporated were the First Amendment's guarantees of freedom of religion,[22] freedom of assembly, and freedom to petition the government for a redress of grievances.[23] By 1937, the process of incorporation was well under way. But many questions remained unanswered. Should all the provisions of the Bill of Rights be made binding on the states, as Justice Harlan had argued in 1884? Were only certain provisions worthy of incorporation? If so, what principles should the court apply in deciding which provisions to incorporate? What was needed was an opportunity to explore more fully the legal and philosophical issues involved.

That opportunity came in the historic 1937 case of *Palko v. Connecticut.*[24] The state of Connecticut had charged Frank Palko with first-degree murder for the

DISCRETION MATTERS

How does providing defense counsel in capital cases reduce or direct the use of discretion in criminal justice processing?

The case of the so-called Scottsboro Boys highlighted the racial tension across the South while also recognizing the need to provide counsel for indigent defendants in all capital cases.

shooting deaths of two policemen. However, the jury chose to convict Palko of second-degree murder—a decision that resulted in a sentence of life imprisonment but spared Palko from the death penalty that surely would have followed a conviction for murder in the first degree. Undaunted, the prosecutor, citing a Connecticut statute that permitted prosecutorial appeals based on an "error of law to the prejudice of the state," sought and won a retrial on the original first-degree charges. At the second trial, the unfortunate Palko was promptly convicted and sentenced to die in Connecticut's electric chair. After losing all his appeals in the state courts, he and his attorneys appealed to the U.S. Supreme Court on the grounds that his second trial constituted a violation of the Fifth Amendment protection against double jeopardy and that the Fifth Amendment was binding on the states as a result of the Fourteenth Amendment's due process clause. (See Chapter 9 for more discussion of double jeopardy.)

There was—and is—no question that Frank Palko's retrial and conviction had violated the double jeopardy clause. In a majority opinion written by Justice Benjamin Cardozo, however, the court ruled against his claims, and Palko was subsequently electrocuted. It would be reasonable to say that Frank Palko did not die in vain. For Justice Cardozo's majority opinion laid the foundation—a series of guidelines and principles—that eventually led to the incorporation not only of the double jeopardy clause but of nearly all the other key provisions of the Bill of Rights.

At the heart of Justice Cardozo's opinion was his rejection of the notion of total incorporation and an effort to establish what has been called the "Honor Roll of Superior Rights." Cardozo wrote eloquently of "those fundamental principles of liberty and justice which lie at the base of all our civil and political institutions."[25] He cited freedom of speech as the cardinal example of a "fundamental right," stressing that the right to speak freely "is the matrix, the indispensable condition, of nearly every other form of freedom." Justice Cardozo also cited freedom of the press and the Fifth Amendment's prohibition of governmental seizure of private property without just compensation (the so-called eminent-domain clause) as examples of fundamental rights in a democratic society.

At the other end of the continuum of rights were "formal" rights that are admirable and worthy of respect but without which "justice would not perish." As examples,

A Chicago police sergeant takes serious exception to being photographed. The tumultuous era of the 1960s resulted in numerous changes to criminal justice policy and law.

Cardozo cited the Sixth Amendment right to trial by jury and the Fifth Amendment right to be indicted by a grand jury when charged with "a capital or otherwise infamous crime."[26] "Such rights, he explained, are not of the essence of a scheme of ordered liberty. To abolish them is not to violate a principle of justice so rooted in the traditions and conscience of our people as to be ranked as fundamental."[27]

Justice Cardozo next turned to the Fifth Amendment protection against compulsory self-incrimination. This, too, was not a "fundamental" right, he asserted, because "justice would not perish if the accused were subject to a duty to respond to orderly inquiry."[28] Having set forth the standards to be applied, Cardozo finally posed the question that would determine the fate of Frank Palko: Did Connecticut's denial of Palko's Fifth Amendment protection against double jeopardy violate those "fundamental principles of liberty and justice which lie at the base of all our civil and political institutions"?

He concluded that the answer was no. The state of Connecticut wasn't trying to harass and wear down Palko by repeatedly charging him with the same crime; the authorities were merely asking that "the case against him . . . go on until there shall be a trial free from the corrosion of substantial legal error."[29] This, Cardozo asserted, was no great affront to fundamental principles of justice. Thus the double jeopardy clause failed to make the Honor Roll of Superior Rights, thereby leaving the states free to pass laws in violation of the Fifth Amendment's command that no person shall "be subject for the same offense to be twice put in the jeopardy of life or limb."[30]

Justice Cardozo's distinctions between "fundamental" rights are still in effect. The criteria set forth in *Palko* are firmly in place and unlikely ever to be modified or transformed. In fact, Justice Cardozo's Honor Roll itself changed only twice between 1937 and 1961. In 1947, the court added the First Amendment's requirement of "separation of church and state" to the list of rights that apply to the states as an element of the Fourteenth Amendment's due process clause.[31] One year later, the Sixth Amendment's guarantee of the right to a "public trial" was incorporated, thus barring the states from conducting trials and sentencing hearings in secret.[32]

The Criminal Law "Revolution"

By the early 1960s, the composition of the Supreme Court had changed, and so had the beliefs and values of the American people. Under Chief Justice Earl Warren, who was appointed by President Eisenhower in 1953, the Supreme Court made it clear that constitutional rights were not static concepts, frozen in eighteenth-century notions of justice and fairness. The protections of the Bill of Rights, according to Chief Justice Warren, "must draw [their] meaning from evolving standards of decency that mark the progress of a maturing society."[33]

The year 1961 marks the beginning of what many *legal scholars* call the *criminal law revolution*. Throughout the 1960s, the Supreme Court, applying the guiding principles set forth by Justice Cardozo in *Palko,* greatly expanded the Honor Roll of Superior Rights. By 1969, almost all the criminal-law-related provisions of the Bill of Rights had been made binding on the states as elements of Fourteenth Amendment due process.

In the historic 1961 case of *Mapp v. Ohio,*[34] the Supreme Court declared that both the Fourth Amendment's prohibition of "unreasonable searches and seizures" and the exclusionary rule (prohibiting the use of illegally seized evidence in a criminal trial) are applicable to the states (see Chapter 6 for more about *Mapp* and these issues). The Eighth Amendment's ban on cruel and unusual punishment was incorporated in 1962,[35] and the Sixth Amendment's right to counsel was imposed on the states one year later in the famous case of *Gideon v. Wainwright.*[36] In 1964, the Fifth Amendment's protection against self-incrimination was incorporated,[37] and in 1965, the Sixth Amendment right to confront hostile witnesses was given the same status.[38] In 1966, *Parker v. Gladden* incorporated the Sixth Amendment right to an impartial jury.[39] The year 1967 saw two Sixth Amendment protections added to the Honor Roll: the guarantee of a speedy trial[40] and the right to compulsory processes for obtaining defense witnesses.[41]

The process of incorporating or nationalizing the Bill of Rights reached its climax in two decisions announced shortly before the end of the Warren Court era. In 1968, the court declared that the Sixth Amendment's guarantee of trial by jury applied to state criminal trials involving serious offenses.[42] And in the 1969 case of *Benton v. Maryland,*[43] the justices finally ruled that the time had come to make the Fifth Amendment ban on double jeopardy binding on the states. The court ruled that the provision against double jeopardy is a "fundamental right that was implicit in the concept of ordered liberty."[44] This decision overruled *Palko v. Connecticut* (32 years too late for Frank Palko) and completed—for now—the process of nationalizing the Bill of Rights.

Since *Benton,* the Supreme Court has not incorporated any more provisions of the Bill of Rights. However, in 1965 in *Griswold v. Connecticut,* the court incorporated the right to "privacy"—a right that is not specifically cited in the Bill of Rights (or anywhere else in the U.S. Constitution).[45] This ruling overturned a Connecticut law that made it a crime for any person, married or single, to use any kind of contraceptive. In the majority opinion written by Justice William Douglas, the court reasoned that a right to privacy is implicit in the Constitution as a result of "zones of privacy" created by the "liberty" safeguards in the due process clauses of the Fifth and Fourteenth Amendments and by the "penumbras" (rights guaranteed by implication) surrounding the First, Third, Fourth, Fifth, and Ninth Amendments.

The question of whether it was proper for the court to find a right to privacy in the Constitution remains controversial. Certainly, the most famous application of this newly discovered right to privacy came in January 1973 with the announcement of the court's decision in *Roe v. Wade.*[46] In that decision the Supreme Court held that the right of privacy rendered unconstitutional all state laws that made it a crime or otherwise restricted a woman's right to obtain an abortion in the first three months of pregnancy. On the other hand, in 1986, in *Bowers v. Hardwick,*[47] the court held

DISCRETION MATTERS

Would nationalization of the Bill of Rights lead to more or less consistency in use of discretion by criminal justice officials across the nation?

Courts and legislatures across the country have struggled with the privacy issues related to women's reproductive-health choices. Ultimately, the Supreme Court will make a final determination of whether actions women take regarding their own bodies will be defined as crimes.

that this same right to privacy could not be used to invalidate state laws making it a crime for consenting adults to engage in homosexual sodomy in the privacy of their own homes. In 2003, however, in the case of *Lawrence v. Texas,*[48] the Supreme Court overturned the decision in *Bowers v. Hardwick.* Thus, at this point, it seems safe to say that a right to privacy has been found to be implicit in the Constitution and enforceable against the states but that the precise scope of this right will have to be decided on a case-by-case basis.

Due Process of Law in Modern America

Currently, nearly all the provisions of the Bill of Rights, as well as the right of privacy, are binding on the states as elements of the Fourteenth Amendment's due process clause. The easiest way to remember what is and is not incorporated is to list the rights that are *not* binding on the states. Of the first eight amendments (those that refer to the specific rights of individuals), these are the only provisions that have not been incorporated:

1. The Third Amendment protection against involuntary quartering of soldiers
2. The Fifth Amendment protection against being prosecuted for "a capital, or otherwise infamous crime, unless on a presentment or indictment of a grand jury"
3. The Seventh Amendment right to a jury trial in cases involving more than $20
4. The Eighth Amendment protection against excessive bail
5. The Eighth Amendment protection against excessive fines

For those studying criminal justice, it is important to understand that although the Supreme Court has not fulfilled Justice Harlan's hope for total incorporation of the Bill of Rights, it has achieved what legal scholars call **selective incorporation.** This means simply that most, but not all, of the provisions of the Bill of Rights are binding on the states. This accomplishment—the nationalization of the Bill of Rights—has radically altered the practice of criminal justice by state and local governments. None of the major court-imposed changes in criminal procedure to be discussed in this text (such as the exclusionary rule, the *Miranda* rule, and changes in death penalty laws) could have occurred in the absence of selective incorporation.

The process of selective incorporation also made the phrase *due process of law* more specific. Nevertheless, the concept of due process is still not precise. Whether a particular police practice or court rule is held to violate due process will always depend on the facts and circumstances of each case and on the court's effort to apply those facts and circumstances in the context of one or more principles of law. Thus, due process should be understood as asserting a fundamental principle of justice rather than a specific rule of law. It implies the administration of laws that do not violate the foundations of civil liberties; it requires in each case an evaluation based on a disinterested inquiry, a set of facts stated fairly and precisely, the consideration of conflicting claims, and a judgment that seeks to reconcile the needs of continuity and change in a complex society. As Daniel Webster maintained, due process is based on "law which hears before it condemns; which proceeds upon inquiry, and renders judgment only after trial."[49] Yet even these comments fail to explain the due process clause fully. A better understanding might be achieved by considering two aspects of due process: *substantive* due process and *procedural* due process.

Substantive Due Process   **Substantive due process** refers to the content or subject matter of a law. It protects people against unreasonable, arbitrary, or capricious laws or acts of government. An example is the void-for-vagueness doctrine. In accordance with this doctrine, the Supreme Court has struck down criminal statutes and local ordinances that, for example, made it unlawful to wander the streets late at night "without lawful business,"[50] to "treat contemptuously the American flag,"[51] and to willfully "obstruct public passages."[52] In all of these cases, the issue of substantive due process and the void-for-vagueness doctrine came into play because the statutes were neither definite nor certain as to the category of people they referred to or the precise conduct that was forbidden.

A landmark case involving substantive due process occurred in 1927 in the case of *Buck v. Bell*.[53] Carrie Buck was an 18-year-old "feebleminded" white woman who had been committed to the Virginia State Colony for Epileptics and the Feeble-Minded. During this time period, it was common to use this term in reference to individuals with substantial mental illness, though the term may appear shocking to contemporary readers. She was the daughter of a feebleminded mother and was the mother of an illegitimate feebleminded baby. At that time, a Virginia statute provided that in certain cases the health of the patient and the welfare of society may be promoted by the sterilization of individuals with mental defects. The superintendent of the state colony where Buck resided could make recommendations to its board of directors regarding the sterilization of residents. Buck's sterilization was ordered, and although she may have been mentally deficient, she understood what was about to happen to her and filed an appeal.

The county circuit court as well as the Virginia Supreme Court of Appeals both affirmed the sterilization decree, stating that the sterilization law was a "blessing" for "feebleminded persons" like Carrie Buck. Her lawyers then appealed to the U.S. Supreme Court on the grounds that the *substance* of the Virginia law represented a denial of due process; that the law was arbitrary, capricious, and unreasonable; and that it was a violation of the Fourteenth Amendment guarantee of equal protection. Chief Justice Oliver Wendell Holmes Jr. upheld the Virginia statute, making the following comment:

> It is better for all the world, if instead of waiting to execute degenerate offspring for crime, or to let them starve for their imbecility, society can prevent those who are manifestly unfit from continuing their kind. Three generations of imbeciles are enough.[54]

Issues related to cyber criminal offenses present unique challenges for substantive due process because of the difficulty of defining electronic, digital, and online activity.

Each criminal offense poses both substantive and procedural challenges, even a simple street mugging like the one depicted here. Substantive issues relate to how crimes are defined—for example, what if the mugger is taking something that originally belonged to him? Procedural issues focus on the responses of the criminal justice process—for example, how police gather evidence, including the video from which these shots are taken.

Carrie Buck was ultimately sterilized, but the philosophy of *Buck v. Bell* has since been subjected to heavy criticism. The case well illustrates the concept of substantive due process and its inherent challenges.

In *Skinner v. Oklahoma*,[55] which was a test of the constitutionality of Oklahoma's Habitual Criminal Sterilization Act in 1942, the Supreme Court ruled differently. Arthur Skinner was to be sterilized because he was a three-time habitual offender. (One of the felonies the prosecutor cited was the theft of three chickens.) The court struck down the sterilization law because it denied both substantive due process and equal protection, since it applied only to felony offenses likely to be committed by poor people, while not considering such felonies as embezzlement, political offenses, and other crimes likely to be committed by more-affluent defendants. In retrospect, the fact that Skinner was about to be sterilized partly because he was a chicken thief points to the unfairness and cruelty inherent in the Oklahoma statute.

Substantive due process focuses on the content of the law rather than how law is applied or crimes are processed. This is the area we turn to next as we examine procedural due process.

Procedural Due Process   Neither *Buck v. Bell* nor *Skinner v. Oklahoma* had any argument with the procedures through which the decision to sterilize had been made. Rather, they were attacking the *substance* of the laws that demanded sterilization. By contrast, **procedural due process** is concerned with the notice, hearing, and other procedures that are required before the life, liberty, or property of a person may be taken by the government. In general, procedural due process requires the following:

1. notice of the proceedings
2. a hearing

DISCRETION MATTERS

How might the protections of procedural due process reduce the potential negative impact of discretionary decision-making in the criminal justice process?

3. opportunity to present a defense
4. an impartial tribunal
5. an atmosphere of fairness

United States v. Valdovinos-Valdovinos (1984), an immigration case, represents a good historical case example involving violations of procedural due process.[56] In fact, in that case, the U.S. District Court for the Northern District of California considered the government's conduct so outrageous that the charges had to be dismissed. The issue of immigration continues to cause controversy in America. This case can help us frame the current discourse and understand how these laws developed.

In *Valdovinos-Valdovinos,* the Immigration and Naturalization Service (INS) was attempting to stem the flow of illegal immigrants from Mexico. Its major method of doing so was a "cold line," an undercover telephone operation in which agents posing as U.S. employers offered to reimburse immigrants for the expense of being smuggled into the country and ultimately give them jobs.[57] In short, the INS used the operation to advise Mexican nationals still within Mexico that it was appropriate to violate U.S. law. The district court ruled that the procedure was a violation of due process; the operation amounted to "the generation by police of new crimes merely for the sake of pressing criminal charges." As such, it constituted entrapment and fundamentally reduced the atmosphere of fairness.[58]

Since the 1960s, when questions concerning the procedural rights of criminal defendants came under closer and more frequent scrutiny by the Supreme Court, the due process clauses of the Fifth and Fourteenth Amendments have been clarified and extended. The court's decisions have had a significant impact on the processing of defendants and offenders through the criminal justice system—from arrest to trial and from sentencing through corrections. These phases of the criminal justice process are outlined and described in the remainder of this chapter.

THE CRIMINAL JUSTICE PROCESS

The purpose of criminal justice is to control and prevent crime. The **criminal justice process** involves all the agencies and procedures set up to manage both crime and those accused of violating the criminal law. The agencies of criminal justice include (1) the law enforcement agencies charged with the prevention of crime and the apprehension of criminal offenders, (2) the court bureaucracies charged with determining the innocence or guilt of accused offenders and sentencing convicted criminals, and (3) the network of correctional institutions charged with the control, custody, supervision, and treatment of individuals convicted of crime. The steps of this process can be seen in the graphic on the interior of the front cover of this textbook.

The criminal justice process includes many steps. Exhibit 4.2 broadly outlines the prearrest phase as it occurs at the federal level. Although there are some differences from one jurisdiction to the next, most state and local courts follow the general model of the federal system.

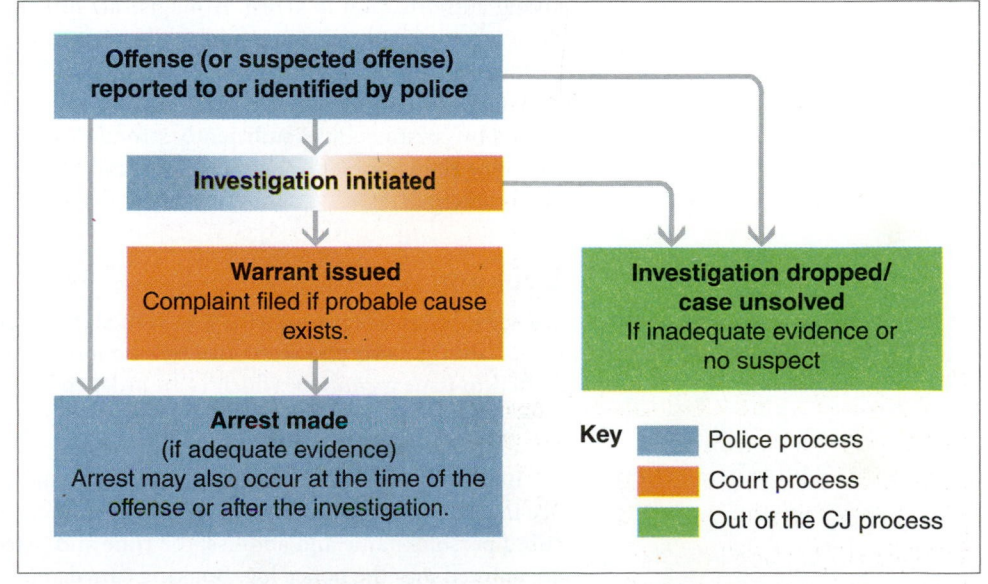

EXHIBIT 4.2 The Prearrest Phase

Prearrest Investigation

Although one might assume that the first phase of the criminal justice process is arrest, this usually occurs only when a police officer directly observes a crime. In other situations, the process begins with some level of investigation. Prearrest investigation can be initiated when police receive a complaint from a victim or witness or knowledge from informers; ongoing surveillance may also lead to an investigation. Typically, investigative activities include an examination of the scene of the crime, a search for physical evidence, interviews with victims and witnesses, and efforts to locate the offender. Data from informers or general surveillance can suggest that some suspicious activity is occurring—perhaps drug sales, prostitution, or systematic theft—at which point an officer's or a detective's "go-out-and-look" investigations take place.

Prearrest investigations can also occur in another manner, sometimes even before a crime has been committed. Law enforcement agencies at the local, state, and federal levels become involved in long-term investigations when crime is not necessarily known to have occurred but is strongly suspected or believed to be imminent. This type of investigation is most typical of federal enforcement agencies such as the Department of Homeland Security, the Federal Bureau of Investigation, the Internal Revenue Service, the Customs Service, and the Drug Enforcement Administration. Such investigations, which include the use of informers, undercover agents, surveillance, and perhaps wiretapping and other electronic eavesdropping devices, have become common in recent years in investigations of drug trafficking, international money-laundering operations, organized crime, and suspected terrorist activity, to name but a few examples.

It should be noted that in all types of prearrest investigation, investigation activities may continue beyond the point at which the evidence necessary for an arrest has been gathered.

Arrest

When an investigation finds that a crime may have been committed, or when a police officer directly observes a crime, an **arrest** is made. Although the legal definition of arrest tends to vary from one jurisdiction to another, in practice an arrest is simply the action of taking a person into custody for the purpose of charging him or her with a crime. In most jurisdictions, an *arrest warrant* is necessary in misdemeanor cases, unless a police officer has observed the crime. The warrant is a written order giving authorization to arrest. A magistrate or someone with equal authority issues the warrant. Felony arrests can be made without a warrant if the officer is reasonably certain that the person being arrested is indeed the offender. *Reasonable certainty* (or probable cause) refers to the arresting officer's "rational grounds of suspicion, supported by circumstances sufficiently strong in themselves to warrant a cautious man believing the accused to be guilty."[59] Exhibit 4.3 depicts the process of arrest through arraignment.

Booking

For some lesser offenses—as in New York State, where prostitution is a minor offense punishable in some circumstances by no more than a fine[60]—the police may be permitted to issue a *citation,* which is an order to appear before a judge at some future date. In all other circumstances, however, a physical arrest occurs when the suspect is present, and the process continues to the booking phase.

Booking refers to the administrative steps and procedures carried out by the police in order to record an arrest properly and officially. At the time of booking, the accused person's name and address, the time and place of arrest, and the arrest charge are entered into the police log. Booking can also include the fingerprinting and photographing of the suspect.

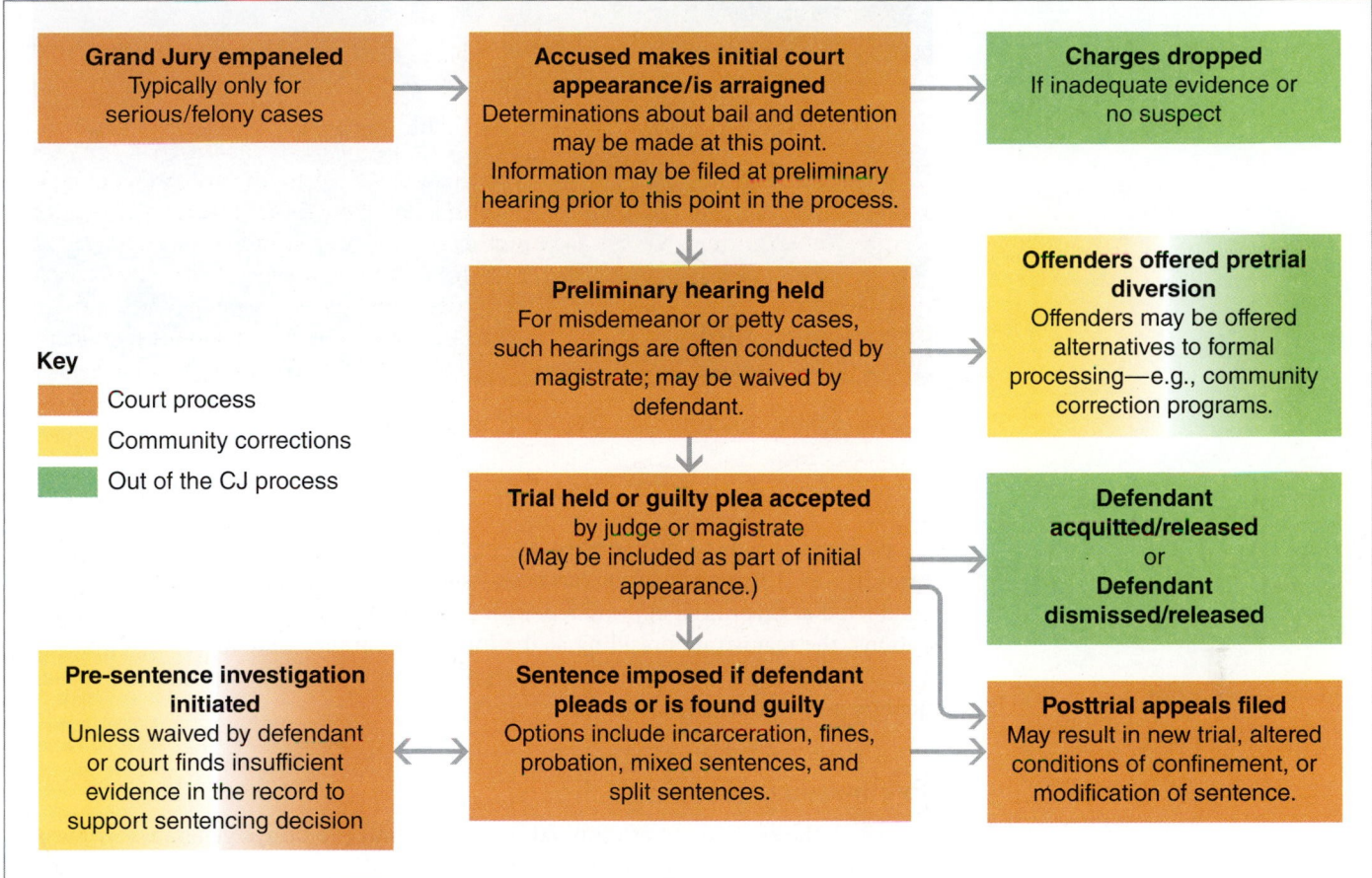

EXHIBIT 4.3 Arrest through Arraignment

The booking phase is the first point at which the accused can drop out of the criminal justice process with no further proceedings. Charges may be dropped if the suspect was arrested for a minor misdemeanor or if there was a procedural error by the police, such as lack of probable cause for arrest or illegal search and seizure. In the case of a procedural error, an assistant prosecutor or a high-ranking police officer can make the decision to drop the charges. Booking is also the first point at which some defendants can be released on bail.

Bail (from the French *baillier,* meaning "to deliver or give") is the most common form of temporary release. It involves the payment of a specified sum by the accused (or by someone else on his or her behalf), guaranteeing that he or she will appear at trial—at which point the money will be returned.

Initial Appearance

Due process requirements mandate that within a reasonable (not extreme or arbitrary) time after arrest, the accused person must be brought before a magistrate and given formal notice of the charge. Such notice occurs at the initial appearance. At this time the accused is also notified of his or her legal rights, and bail is determined for those who did not receive temporary release during the booking phase. *Release on recognizance (ROR),* a substitute for bail, can also occur, typically at the recommendation of the magistrate, when there seems to be little risk that the accused will fail to appear for trial. The accused is released on his or her own personal recognizance, or obligation.

Although they are rare, preliminary hearings can protect defendants from unwarranted prosecutions.

For some kinds of minor offenses, such as being drunk and disorderly, or in cases in which a simple citation has been issued, summary trials and sentencing are conducted at this initial appearance, with no further court processing. In other situations, the magistrate presiding at the initial appearance may determine that the available evidence is not sufficient to warrant further criminal processing and consequently may dismiss the case.

Preliminary Hearing

Owing to the complexity of criminal processing and the delays generated by overloaded court calendars, in many jurisdictions defendants have the option to bypass the initial appearance and proceed directly to the preliminary hearing.

The major purpose of the preliminary hearing is to protect defendants from unwarranted prosecutions. Thus, the presiding magistrate seeks to do the following:

- Determine whether a crime has been committed
- Determine whether the evidence is sufficient to establish probable cause to believe that the defendant committed the crime
- Determine the existence of a probable cause for which the warrant was issued for the defendant's arrest
- Inquire into the reasonableness of the arrest and search and the officer's compliance with the requirements of the warrant
- Set the appropriate bail or temporary release, if this was not already done

Preliminary hearings are rare. In some jurisdictions, the defense may waive this hearing in order to keep damaging testimony temporarily out of the official records. The defense may also hope that by the time the trial does occur, witnesses may have forgotten some things, become confused, or disappeared. However, other defense attorneys insist on this hearing as a tactic for gaining insight into the strengths and weaknesses of the prosecution's case.

Determination of Formal Charges

Whether the initial court processing does or does not include an initial appearance or preliminary hearing, the next step in the criminal justice process is the formalization of charges. One mechanism is *indictment* by a grand jury. The indictment is a formal charging document based on the grand jury's determination that there is sufficient cause for a trial. The decision must be supported by a majority of the

DISCRETION MATTERS

In your opinion, which criminal justice professional retains the most discretion during the preliminary stages of the criminal justice process?

jurors. When the jury reaches a decision, it issues a *true bill* containing the following information:

- The type and nature of the offense
- The specific statute alleged to have been violated
- The nature and elements of the offense charged
- The time and place of the crime
- The name and address of the accused or, if not known, a description sufficient to identify the accused with reasonable certainty
- The signature of the foreperson of the grand jury
- The names of all codefendants, as well as the number of criminal charges against them

Because the grand jury does not weigh the evidence presented, its finding is by no means equivalent to a conviction. It simply requires that the accused be brought to trial. If the grand jury fails to achieve the required majority vote, the accused is released; this determination is referred to as a *no bill*.

Grand juries are available in about half of the states and in the federal system, but in only a limited number of jurisdictions are they the only mechanism for sending a defendant to trial. The most common method for bringing formal charges is the *information*, a charging document drafted by a prosecutor and tested before a judge. Typically, this testing occurs at the preliminary hearing. The prosecutor presents some, or all, of the evidence in open court—usually just enough to convince the judge that the defendant should be bound over for trial. As indicated earlier, however, the preliminary hearing is sometimes waived, and in those circumstances the information document is not tested before a magistrate.

Arraignment

After the formal determination of charges through the indictment or information, the actual trial process begins. The first phase is the arraignment. The accused person is taken before a judge, the formal charges are read, and the defendant is asked to enter a plea. There are four primary pleas in most jurisdictions:

1. *Not guilty:* If the not-guilty plea is entered, the defendant is notified of his or her rights, a decision is made as to whether the defendant is competent to stand trial, counsel is appointed if the defendant is poor, and in some jurisdictions the defendant can choose between a trial by judge or a trial by jury.
2. *Guilty:* If a plea of guilty is entered, the judge must determine whether the plea was made voluntarily and the defendant understands the full consequences of such a plea. If the judge is satisfied, the defendant is scheduled for sentencing; if not, the judge can refuse the guilty plea and enter "not guilty" into the record.
3. *Nolo contendere:* This plea, not available in all jurisdictions, means "no contest," or "I will not contest it." It has the same legal effect as the guilty plea but is of different legal significance in that an admission of guilt is not present and cannot be introduced in later trials.
4. *Standing mute:* Remaining mute results in the entry of a not-guilty plea. Its advantage is that the accused does not waive his or her right to protest any irregularities that may have occurred in earlier phases of the criminal justice proceedings.

The Trial Process

The complete trial process (Exhibit 4.4) can be long and complex and will be discussed more fully in Chapter 9. It may begin with a hearing on pretrial motions entered by the defense to suppress evidence, relocate the place of the trial, discover the

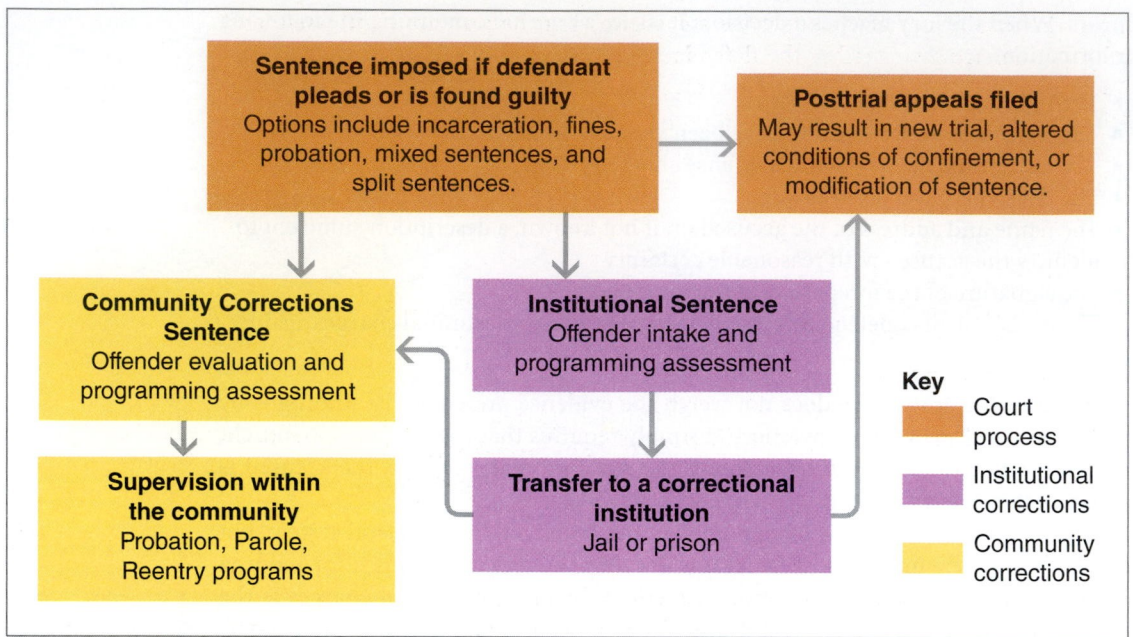

EXHIBIT 4.4 The Trial Process

nature of the state's evidence, or postpone the trial itself. After the pretrial motions (if there are any), the jury is selected and the trial proceeds as follows:

1. *Opening statements by the prosecution:* The prosecutor outlines the state's case and how the state will introduce witnesses and physical evidence to prove the guilt of the accused.

2. *Opening statements by the defense:* The defense, if it elects to do so, explains how it plans to introduce witnesses and evidence in its own behalf.

3. *Presentation of the state's case:* The state calls its witnesses to establish the elements of the crime and to introduce physical evidence; the prosecutor accomplishes this through direct examination of the witnesses. The witnesses may then be cross-examined by the defense.

4. *Presentation of the defense's case:* The defense may open with a motion for dismissal on the grounds that the state failed to prove the defendant guilty "beyond a reasonable doubt." If the judge concurs, the case is dismissed, and the accused is released; if the judge rejects the motion, the defense's case proceeds in the same manner as the state's presentation.

5. *Prosecutor's rebuttal:* The prosecutor may present new witnesses and evidence, following the format of the state's original presentation.

6. *Defense's surrebuttal:* The defense may again make a motion for dismissal; if denied, it too can introduce new evidence and witnesses.

7. *Closing statements:* In most jurisdictions, the defense attorney and then the prosecutor make closing arguments. These statements sum up their cases and the conclusions that can be drawn from the evidence and testimony.

8. *Charging the jury:* In jury trials, the judge instructs the jury as to possible verdicts and orders them to retire to the jury room to consider the facts of the case, deliberate on the testimony, and return a verdict.

9. *Return of the verdict:* After the jury has reached a decision, they return to the courtroom with a verdict, which a member of the court reads aloud. The jury may be *polled* at the request of either the defense or the prosecution; that is, each member may be asked individually whether the verdict announced is his or her individual verdict.

In the case of a trial by judge, the steps involving the jury are eliminated, and the judge determines whether the defendant is guilty or not guilty. In the majority of jurisdictions, the victim may have a role in the process, either through active participation or through legislative protection. Posttrial motions can also occur if the defendant is found guilty. The defense is given the opportunity to seek a new trial or to have the verdict of the jury set aside (*revoked*).

Sentencing

After conviction or the entry of a guilty plea, the defendant is brought before the judge for the imposition of the sentence. The sentencing process may begin with a presentence investigation, a report that summarizes the offender's family, social, employment, and criminal histories, and serves as a guide for the judge in determining the type of sentence to be imposed. Victim-impact statements may also be included as part of this process of determining the most appropriate sentences for convicted offenders (see the "Victims and Justice" feature). Depending on the nature of the offense and the sentencing guidelines established by law, a simple fine or period of probation in the community might be imposed. Sentences can also include other forms of community-based corrections, imprisonment, or even death.

> **DISCRETION MATTERS**
>
> In your opinion, during which stage in the process do criminal justice professionals exercise the most discretionary action? Why?

VICTIMS AND JUSTICE

Victim Advocacy

The victims are usually the main sources of information about crime and criminals. In fact, the majority of crimes known to the police come from reports by victims, in contrast to the one-third reported by witnesses and the even smaller proportion directly observed by the police themselves. Victims, not surprisingly, typically suffer the most as a result of crime, yet they are often left in the shadows of the criminal justice system. In the majority of cases, the justice process may revictimize the victims. They are frequently shuffled around by law enforcement and court bureaucracies, questioned insensitively by police, subpoenaed by courts, bewildered by procedures for securing restitution, kept ignorant about important court dates, and denied possession of their own property being held as evidence. On the whole, the criminal justice system is not only insensitive to the needs of victims but is also repeatedly and deliberately intimidating.

To counter the hapless treatment of victims, grassroots movements appeared at the local level during the early 1970s. More focus was given to the movement in 1982, when the President's Task Force on Victims of Crime recommended a variety of victim assistance programs. Since the beginning of the 1990s, a number of jurisdictions have instituted programs aimed at providing support services for victims, including the following:

- *Victim compensation programs,* which help victims receive reimbursement for their losses

The criminal justice process is often focused on the criminal offender. Victim advocacy increases the role of victims, such as the man in this photo, in the search for justice.

- *Victim restitution programs,* in which offenders directly compensate victims for their losses
- *Victim assistance programs,* which aid victims in making social, emotional, and economic adjustments
- *Victim-witness assistance programs,* which help to explain court procedures to victim-witnesses, make them aware of court dates, and assist them in providing better testimony in court

A second outgrowth of the victim advocacy movement has been the wider use of victim impact statements—written or oral statements by victims or survivors—to assist judges and other criminal justice officials in making sentencing decisions. Currently, all 50 states and the District of Columbia allow some form of victim impact statement either at the time of sentencing or as part of a presentence report. Such statements, however, particularly in death penalty cases, have been controversial. In fact, two such cases have come to the attention of the U.S. Supreme Court.

Booth v. Maryland[61]
John Booth was convicted of murder in the first degree in a Baltimore court. During his sentencing, a victim impact statement was read to the jury so that his sentence might be intensified. Booth was sentenced to death, but he appealed, arguing that the victim impact statement was a violation of his Eighth Amendment right against cruel and unusual punishment. The Supreme Court agreed with Booth, holding that a victim impact statement creates an unacceptable risk that a jury may impose the death penalty in an arbitrary and capricious manner.

Payne v. Tennessee[62]
Pervis Payne was convicted of murder in the deaths of a young woman and her 2-year-old daughter. Severely wounded in the incident was the woman's 3-year-old son, who witnessed the murders. At sentencing, the surviving child's grandmother testified that the boy cried daily for his dead mother and sister. Payne was sentenced to death and appealed to the U.S. Supreme Court. In an about-face from *Booth,* the High Court upheld Payne's death sentence, thus condoning the use of victim impact statements at sentencing hearings.

In recent years, these statements have come under fire for swaying judges and juries to increase the length of offenders' sentences. Legal scholars have argued against the use of these statements because they introduce a level of emotionality into the process of sentencing an offender. Others argue that victims deserve to have their voices heard in court.

THINK ABOUT THIS

1. How might victims feel about being included in the court process? How would you feel about it if you were the victim of a crime?
2. How might the fairness of the criminal justice process be impacted by the inclusion of victims?
3. Will offenders be likely to receive harsher punishments in cases where victims are highly involved in the process? Why or why not?

Sources: Paul G. Cassell, "In Defense of Victim Impact Statements," *Ohio State Criminal Law Review* 6 (2009): 611; Steven R. Donziger, ed., *The Real War on Crime: Report of the National Criminal Justice Commission* (New York: HarperPerennial, 1996); Robert C. Davis and Barbara E. Smith, "The Effects of Victim Impact Statements on Sentencing Decisions: A Test in an Urban Setting," *Justice Quarterly* 11 (September 1994): 453–69; J. V. Roberts and M. Manikis, "Victim Impact Statements at Sentencing: The Relevance of Ancillary Harm," *Canadian Criminal Law Review* 15 (2010).

Appeals and Release

After conviction and sentencing, defendants who have been found guilty may appeal their cases to a higher court. Appeals are based on claims that due process was not followed, that new evidence has become available, or that the sentence imposed was "cruel and unusual," in violation of constitutional rights.

Release from imprisonment occurs after the time specified in the sentence has been served or if the offender is released on parole—a conditional release that occurs after only a portion of the sentence has been served. Release from prison, or any type of sentence, can also occur through *pardon*—a "forgiveness" for the crime committed that bars any further criminal justice processing. Other factors that can affect a sentence are the *reprieve,* which delays the execution of a sentence, and the *commutation,* which reduces a sentence to a less severe one.

Criminal Justice as a "System"

The preceding summary of the various stages in the criminal justice process might suggest that the administration of justice occurs as an orderly flow of managerial decision-making that begins with the investigation of a criminal offense and ends with a sentence. This, as noted in Chapter 1, was the ideal fostered by the 1965 President's Commission on Law Enforcement and Administration of Justice in its commentary on criminal justice in America:

> The criminal process, the method by which the system deals with individual cases, is not a hodgepodge of random actions. It is rather a continuum—an orderly progression of events—some of which, like arrest and trial, are highly visible and some of which, though of great importance, occur out of public view. A study of the system must begin by examining it as a whole.[63]

However, the notion of criminal justice operating as an orderly system was and remains a myth. The justice "system" is composed of a series of bureaucracies operating along different and often conflicting paths.

Differences in how actors in various segments define and interpret events can make criminal procedure even more complex. Police officers, for example, interpret situations to determine whether a law has been violated. Prosecutors and defense attorneys interpret the law and the circumstances in which the offense occurred to determine which laws were violated and assess the culpability of the accused person. Juries interpret the information provided by the police and courts to determine the innocence or guilt of the defendant. Judges interpret the evidence presented and the character of the offender to determine the nature and type of sentence and to ensure that due process has been achieved. Finally, correctional personnel interpret their knowledge of the law, social science, correctional administration, and human behavior to determine the appropriate custodial, correctional, rehabilitative, and punitive treatment for each convicted criminal.[64]

The various segments—meaning police, courts, and corrections—not only lack unity of purpose and organized interrelationships, but each one also has its own interpretations of crime, law, evidence, and culpability, which creates inefficiency in every phase of the process. Criminal justice in the United States, therefore, is hardly a system. However, such flaws are counterbalanced by the fact that our democratic society has built in checks and balances at every level of the justice process so that due process can be achieved. This is true not only of the adult criminal justice system but also of the justice system that has emerged for juveniles—the topic addressed in the "Juvenile Justice in Context" feature.

Release from the criminal justice process can result from dismissal of charges, acquittal, release for community sentence, or completion of institutional sentence.

DISCRETION MATTERS

If we assume that criminal justice works as a system, will professionals have more or less discretion in individual cases?

JUVENILE JUSTICE IN CONTEXT

The Emergence of Juvenile Justice

From the early colonial period in America through much of the nineteenth century, juvenile offenders were handled in essentially the same way as adults. Children beyond the age of reason (about 7 years old) were held to adult standards of behavior. For criminal offenses, they were subject to the same sanctions, placed in the same institutions, and hanged from the same gallows.

Reformation in the treatment of juvenile offenders began during the early decades of the nineteenth century, but it was piecemeal at best and limited to only a few jurisdictions. Especially noteworthy was New York City's House of Refuge, established in 1825 as the first systematic attempt to separate juvenile offenders from adult criminals and to provide "correction" rather than punishment. In the courts, the separation of juveniles from adults in trial proceedings first occurred in Chicago in 1861. Chicago's lead was followed by Massachusetts in the early 1870s and by New York and Rhode Island in the 1890s.[65]

These changes in the processing and treatment of juvenile offenders marked the beginning of widespread reforms. During the latter part of the nineteenth century, the public became increasingly aware that the roots of crime and delinquency did not necessarily lie within individual offenders but, rather, were products of the culture and environment in which they lived. This new awareness, coupled with ongoing concern over the abuse and neglect of children both in and out of institutions, led to the emergence of a new juvenile justice philosophy based on the already established concept of *parens patriae.*

Under the common law in England at the time, the Court of Chancery had the authority to intervene in property matters to protect the rights of children. In the United States this jurisdictional focus was expanded to include the handling of "dependent and neglected" children. Court intervention was justified by the theory that such a child's natural protectors—the parents—were unable or unwilling to provide an appropriate level of care. The court took the place of the parents; hence, *parens patriae,* meaning "the state as parent."

Reformers merged the concept of *parens patriae* with the medical model of treatment to establish a system of juvenile justice designed to reform and rehabilitate young offenders. The underlying philosophy was that if a child "went astray," it was the parents who had failed. The court could take over the role of the parent, diagnose the problem, and prescribe the appropriate treatment. It did not matter what the child had done. His or her deviant behavior was merely a symptom of the problem. The duty of the court was not to blame the child or determine guilt but to identify and treat the underlying problem. Moreover, the youth's welfare was to be the central concern of the court. This would not only protect the future of the child but also permit an informal court process that considered the entire history and background of the child's difficulties, without being hampered by the limitations and requirements of official criminal procedure. Thus, juvenile processing would be a civil rather than a criminal matter.[66]

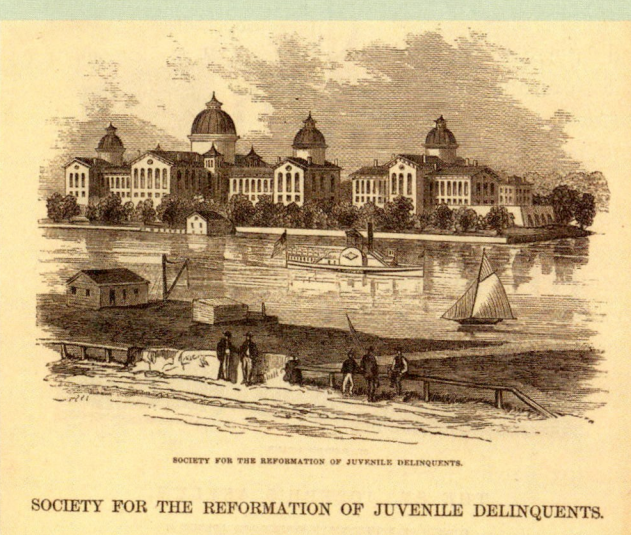

SOCIETY FOR THE REFORMATION OF JUVENILE DELINQUENTS.

SOCIETY FOR THE REFORMATION OF JUVENILE DELINQUENTS.

HOUSE OF REFUGE, RANDALL'S ISLAND.

The House of Refuge, illustrated here, accepted children who had been adjudicated for delinquent acts or who were poor, orphaned, or considered in danger of getting into trouble.

A number of penologists, philanthropists, and women's organizations, collectively known as the "child savers," heavily promoted these early juvenile justice reform efforts. The child-savers movement crystallized in 1899 with the passage of the Illinois Juvenile Court Act, which established the first statewide juvenile court system in the United States.[67]

CONCLUSIONS

Interpretations of the meaning of due process have varied throughout history. In the Middle Ages, due process merely meant adhering to the law of the land. Currently, due process of law—as guaranteed by the Fifth and Fourteenth Amendments—implies the administration of laws in a way that avoids violating civil liberties. It requires in each case an evaluation based on disinterested inquiry, a balanced order of facts exactly and fairly stated, the detached consideration of conflicting claims, and a judgment mindful of reconciling the needs of continuity and change in a complex society.

The concept of due process is anything but precise, as the chapter-opening case illustrates. The access Heller had to the court process provided resolution to conflicts in the law and perspectives. While communities and individuals may differ on the underlying issues, such as gun control, the criminal justice system must ensure due process, both substantive and procedural, in all cases. Still, the criminal justice process, from investigation and arrest through trial and sentencing, is structured to guarantee due process of law at each of its many stages. Moreover, it is designed to be a system—meaning an orderly flow of managerial decision-making that begins with the investigation of a criminal offense and ends with a correctional placement.

It can be argued, however, that the criminal justice process is anything but a system, that it lacks unity of purpose and organized interrelationships among its components. The conflicting paths within the system and the disparate goals among the various players (lawyers, judges, police officers, defendants, members of the jury, and victims) all contribute to a nonsystem of criminal justice. Moreover, the impact of discretion on decision-making at various stages and by various actors challenges popularly held beliefs that justice and due process are clear and structured. Students of criminal justice must keep the competing goals and nature of this process in mind as we begin our discussion of the three separate components of the system: police, courts, and corrections.

SUMMARY AND REVIEW

■ **Explain the differences between inquisitorial and adversarial justice.**

- Trials by ordeal, or perhaps by battle, were the cornerstone of the inquisitorial system of justice. Under this system, the accused person was considered guilty until proven innocent.
- Inquisitorial justice became manifest when some form of divine intervention spared the accused from pain, suffering, or death, or when the accused readily admitted his or her guilt, usually after torture or other forms of corporal punishment.
- The American judicial process is an adversarial system, in which the accused person is presumed to be innocent and the burden of proof is placed on the court. In the adversary court, the judge is an impartial arbiter, or referee, between adversaries—the prosecution and defense.
- The opposing sides fight within strict rules of procedure, and it is believed that the side with the truth will win.
- Adversary proceedings are grounded in the right of the defendant to refrain from hurting himself or herself and in the notion of due process of law, a concept that asserts fundamental principles of justice and implies the administration of laws that do not violate individual rights.

■ **Define and describe the "nationalization" of the Bill of Rights, and identify the significant Supreme Court decisions associated with the nationalization process.**

- In 1833, the Supreme Court made it quite clear in the *Barron v. Baltimore* case that the Bill of Rights provided no protection against state or local action, but only against federal authority.
- After the ratification of the Fourteenth Amendment to the Constitution in 1868, it once again became possible to argue that the Bill of Rights should be understood to restrict the powers of the state and local governments, as well as the federal government.
- The historical development of this process of nationalization highlighted the developing application of the Bill of Rights to the states and included the following important cases:
  - *Hurtado v. California*
  - *Gitlow v. New York*
  - *Powell v. Alabama*
  - *Palko v. Connecticut*
  - *Mapp v. Ohio*
  - *Gideon v. Wainwright*

■ **Define "due process of law," and contrast substantive and procedural due process.**

- Due process of law is a concept that asserts fundamental principles of justice and implies the administration of laws that do not violate individual rights.
- Substantive due process refers to the content or subject matter of a law. It protects people against unreasonable, arbitrary, or capricious laws or acts of government.
- Procedural due process is focused on the procedures that are required before the life, liberty, or property of a person may be taken by the government. In general, procedural due process requires the following: notice of the proceedings, a hearing, opportunity to present a defense, an impartial tribunal, and an atmosphere of fairness.

■ **Describe the stages of the criminal justice process and what occurs at each stage.**

- Prearrest investigations may begin before or after a crime has been committed and can include an examination of the scene of the crime, a search for physical evidence, interviews with victims and witnesses, and efforts to locate the offender.
- Arrest is the taking of a person into custody for the purpose of charging him or her with a crime.
- Booking refers to the administrative steps and procedures carried out by the police in order to record an arrest properly and officially.
- Initial appearance is the initial presentation of the defendant before a magistrate. At this time the accused is also notified of his or her legal rights, and bail is determined for those who did not receive temporary release during the booking phase. In addition, depending on the jurisdiction and the type of charge, summary trials and sentencing are held at this appearance.
- Defendants may bypass the initial appearance and proceed directly to the preliminary hearing, though it is a rare option in many jurisdictions. The preliminary hearing is designed to protect defendants from unwarranted prosecutions.
- Determination of formal charges is conducted at the indictment or information stage.
- Arraignment is the first phase in the actual trial stage. Defendants enter a plea at this stage of the process. The trial process continues from there forward.
- After conviction or the entry of a guilty plea, the defendant is brought before the judge for the imposition of the sentence.
- Following the sentencing, defendants who have been found guilty may appeal their case to a higher court.

■ **Explain why the criminal justice process is both a system and a nonsystem.**

- Criminal justice acts as a system because it consists of an orderly flow of managerial decision-making that begins with the investigation of a criminal offense and ends with a sentence.
- Criminal justice acts as a nonsystem in that it is composed of a series of bureaucracies operating along different and often conflicting paths.

KEY TERMS

adversarial system (p. 88)
arrest (p. 100)
Bill of Rights (p. 89)
booking (p. 100)

criminal justice process (p. 99)
due process of law (p. 88)
inquiry system (p. 88)
inquisitorial system (p. 88)

procedural due process (p. 98)
selective incorporation (p. 96)
substantive due process (p. 97)

ISSUES FOR CRITICAL THINKING AND DISCUSSION

1. What do you think the framers of the Constitution meant by due process of law?
2. How does due process of law differ from the law of the land?
3. Do you think the criminal justice process offers enough due process protections? Thinking about the steps in the criminal justice process described in this book, are there steps you might add or remove? If so, why?
4. What other rights and liberties do you think should have been incorporated into the Bill of Rights?
5. How might the lack of cooperation and presence of conflicting goals of criminal justice agencies affect the efficiency and effectiveness of the criminal justice process? Give specific examples.

5

The Structure and Function of Policing

LEARNING OBJECTIVES

- Trace the historical development of modern policing.
- Identify the differences between federal, state, and local law enforcement agencies in terms of jurisdiction and authority.
- Describe the functions of police.
- Explain the structure of police organizations.
- Discuss the status of women in American policing.
- Define police discretion and its relationship to selective law enforcement.
- Identify the components of the police subculture and personality.

POLICE DISCRETION AND THE WAR ON DRUGS

In 1984, Broward County sheriff department officers boarded a Miami-to-Atlanta bus during a stopover in Fort Lauderdale. Without any particular suspicion, the officers conversed with passenger Terrance Bostick, requesting his identification and ticket. They reviewed these documents and returned them to him. Although disputed somewhat, the facts of the case indicate that after telling Bostick that he could refuse, the officers requested consent to search his luggage. He agreed, and during their search, the officers found cocaine in his bag. Bostick was arrested and charged with drug trafficking.[1]

At Bostick's trial, his attorney argued that the seizure of the cocaine was improper because it violated the Fourth Amendment protection against unreasonable search and seizure. He also argued that Bostick did not feel he could refuse the search, given the tight quarters of the bus, the highly intimidating police interaction, and, especially, the fact that one officer was carrying a gun. Neither did he feel he could get off the bus because it was about to leave the station, and he would have been stranded without his luggage.[2] The concept of search and seizure will be explored in detail in Chapter 6, but note here that the case moved through the Florida courts and, ultimately, found its way to the U.S. Supreme Court, where the justices ruled against Bostick, holding that "bus sweeps" for drugs do not inevitably result in unreasonable "seizures."[3] The court explained that the search of Bostick's luggage was allowed because he consented and because the police were applying the same constitutional rules the court had developed for police encounters on the street and in other public places.

If police officers approached you on a bus, train, or plane, would you feel you could refuse their request to search your luggage? Putting the constitutionality of the search aside for the moment, how do you think officers decide which passengers to ask for permission to search their luggage? Clearly, each officer exercises a considerable amount of discretion as she or he makes these decisions. To help you understand the role of police, particularly the role of discretion in their behavior, this chapter examines the history of policing, the role of police in society, and the duties of police officers, as well as the larger challenges posed by contemporary criminal justice issues.

The police represent the largest and most visible segment of the criminal justice system. As organized agents of law enforcement and peacekeeping, police officers are charged with the prevention and detection of crime, the apprehension of criminal offenders, the defense of constitutional guarantees, the resolution of community conflicts, the protection of society, and the promotion and preservation of civil order. They have often been

The case of Terrance Bostick questioned the nature of consented searches by police, particularly those occurring on buses.

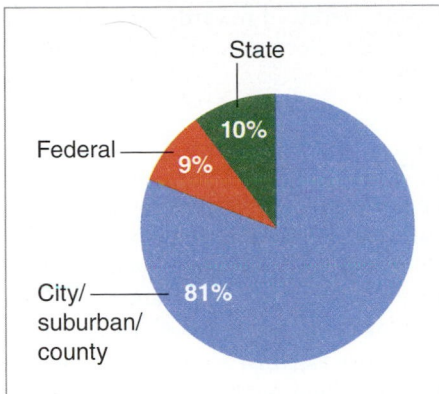

EXHIBIT 5.1 Jurisdictional Distribution of Sworn Police Officers in the United States

Source: U.S. Department of Justice

Police officers serve the communities within which they work and often must choose which goals to focus on.

referred to as a "thin blue line" between order and anarchy in modern society.

In carrying out these important functions, however, police have extensive latitude. To begin, policing in the United States is decentralized; that is, there is no national police force. The country has thousands of independent police agencies at the local, state, and federal levels, and as you can see from Exhibit 5.1, the vast majority of officers work in city, county, or suburban police forces, while the rest work for state or federal agencies. In spite of their independence from one another, though, these enforcement units are remarkably similar. This chapter presents a detailed analysis of the structures that police institutions in the United States have in common. First, however, we trace the origins of policing, beginning in medieval England.

THE EMERGENCE OF MODERN POLICING

Policing can be traced to the latter part of the ninth century, when England's Alfred the Great was structuring the defenses of his kingdom against an impending Danish invasion. Part of Alfred's strategy depended on his country's internal stability, so he instituted a system of **mutual pledge,** which organized the country around family groupings that assumed responsibility for the acts of their members. Specific geographical areas were combined to form *shires* (now called *counties*)—administrative units governed by a *shire-reeve,* or *sheriff.*[4]

By the seventeenth century, officials had duties that included enforcing the law and keeping the peace. *Magistrates* presided in courts, ordered arrests, called witnesses, and examined prisoners. *Parish constables,* carryovers from the days of Alfred the Great, had limited powers of arrest in relatively small districts. And *beadles,* constables' assistants, were paid twenty pounds a year to clear vagrants from the city streets. But most magistrates and constables were corrupt and had a minimal impact on law enforcement.

Also serving the public were the **thief-takers**—private detectives who were paid by the Crown on a piecework basis.[5] Anyone could be a thief-taker; the thief-takers had no official status as police and no more authority than private citizens. Like the bounty hunters of the American West, thief-takers received rewards for apprehending criminals. In the eighteenth century, the period we look at next, the policing system advanced considerably.

The British Roots of Modern Policing

Henry Fielding is credited with laying the foundation for the first modern police force. In 1748, Fielding was appointed magistrate in Westminster, a city adjacent to central London, and he moved into a house on Bow Street. Although Fielding could accomplish little by himself, within a year he had obtained the cooperation of several other public-spirited constables. Together they formed a small, unofficial investigative division that was the first organized force ever used against criminals in England. Fielding's constables—the Bow Street Runners—were not paid as police officers, but they were entitled to the standard thief-takers' rewards. In time, the government provided funds to support their activities.[6]

The next major step came in 1828, when Sir Robert Peel drew up the first police bill that was passed by Parliament. The result—London's new Metropolitan Police, established in 1829—was a centralized agency with responsibility for both preventing crime and apprehending offenders.[7] Eventually, advances by individuals such as Henry Fielding and Sir Robert Peel crossed the Atlantic and influenced the development of policing in America.

Law and Order in Early America

The American colonists felt themselves to be constantly threatened—on land by Native Americans and from the sea by pirates and foreign enemies. The military dealt with most of the problems of defense. The towns, however, had no protection against lawbreaking from within. In the seventeenth century, village authorities began selecting men to serve as guardians of the peace. The titles and functions of these first police officers were similar to those of the English constable and included a range of duties from enforcing the laws to maintaining the peace.[8]

Constables   Constables, or *schouts* in the Dutch settlements, appeared in all the colonies as soon as local governments were organized. They were paid for their services through fines. "Military watches," "rattle watches" composed of paid volunteers, and "bellmen" provided nighttime security. By the eighteenth century, the daytime peacekeeping of the constables and the nighttime protection of the watches were common. Unlike the situation in England, where citizens despised the notion of a paid police force, in the colonies most peacekeeping activities were supported by municipal authority.[9]

As the colonial town populations grew, the number of street riots, drunken brawls, and other types of violent behavior increased considerably. However, those charged with keeping the peace were incapable of enforcing all the laws and were often lax in their duties. By midcentury, growing levels of lawlessness, combined with corruption within the ranks of the watch, led to the organization of more-formal police forces.

The Sheriff   The *sheriff,* the first of the formal law enforcement agents to appear in the vast territories beyond the Mississippi River, was closely modeled after British counterparts. However, while the powers of the English sheriff had diminished over time, those of the American sheriff expanded. Sheriffs in the United States not only apprehended criminals but also conducted elections, collected taxes, and took custody of public funds. Moreover, American sheriffs were eventually chosen by popular election.

As western America became more populated and more lawless, the sheriff evolved into an active agent of law enforcement, but fiscal and administrative duties were quickly subordinated to the more colorful activities of rounding up cattle thieves, highwaymen, and other bandits and engaging in gunplay with serious outlaws.

View of the PUBLIC OFFICE Bow Street, with Sir John Fielding preparing a prisoner under examination.

Sir Henry Fielding presides over the examination of a prisoner at Bow Street. Fielding formed the first organized, though not official, force of thief-takers to respond to crime in England. They were commonly known as the Bow Street Runners.

Rarely did the local sheriff have a paid staff of trained deputies to call on, for example, to track fleeing outlaws. Thus, the *posse* became crucial in frontier law enforcement. The origins of the posse go back many hundreds of years. During the time of Alfred the Great, when mutual pledges bound people together, one of the peacekeeping instruments was the **posse comitatus,** Latin for the "power of the county," which consisted of all the able-bodied men in a county. This group was at the absolute disposal of a sheriff, and members were required to respond when called on to do so. The institution of posse comitatus was transferred intact to American soil.[10] Here, it became an important component of criminal justice machinery as the frontier moved westward, for it could place the entire power of a community under the leadership of the sheriff.

Territorial Agencies Also among the lawmen of the West were territorial police agencies. The Texas Rangers were the first of these organized forces. Equipped by Stephen F. Austin in 1823 to help protect settlers against the Native American tribes, the Rangers were organized as a corps of fighters when the Texas revolution against Mexico broke out in 1835. After 1870, the Rangers evolved into an effective law enforcement agency.[11] Following the lead of the Texas Rangers, the Arizona Rangers were established in 1901 and the New Mexico Mounted Police in 1905—but these were primarily border patrol forces and were abandoned within a few years.[12]

In early America, an individual armed only with a lantern, as shown in this woodcut, provided nighttime security for the community.

Federal and Town Marshals When the United States came into being with the ratification of the Constitution, the dual sovereignty of state and republic required the designation of special officers to represent the authority of the federal courts. In 1789, Congress established the position of federal marshal, but officials appointed to this rank did not come to prominence until after the Civil War. The popular image of federal marshals and their deputies maintaining law and order along the trail and in the violent mining communities has little foundation in fact. Most of the marshals' working time was spent on routine functions related to civil and criminal court activity.[13]

In addition to these federal marshals, mayors or city councils also appointed city and town marshals. These marshals served as local police. The legendary "Wild Bill" Hickok, for example, was a local marshal in the towns of Hays City and Abilene, Kansas, as was Wyatt Earp in Dodge City, Kansas.

Policing the City In 1838, Boston established the first police service. A few years later, in 1845, New York City organized a metropolitan police force that offered 24-hour, 7-day-a-week protection for the first time. In both cases, the motivator was fear of crime and social disintegration.

At the beginning of the nineteenth century, New York was no longer the homogeneous community with a common culture and a shared system of values and moral standards that it had been in colonial times. In the 55 years before the establishment of the new police force, the population of the city had increased by more than 1,000 percent—from 33,131 in 1790 to 371,223 by 1845.[14] A significant proportion of the new arrivals came from abroad, making the city a mosaic of smaller communities separated by barriers of class, culture, language, attitudes, and behavior derived from vastly different traditions. The increased population, combined with growing levels of poverty, led to an increased crime rate. The highly visible wealthy attracted criminal predators, both foreign and domestic.

During this period, the city was patrolled by a few hundred marshals, constables, and watchmen who were all unsalaried but received fees for their services. This system resulted in numerous instances of graft, corruption, laxity, and misdirected effort, as officers concentrated on duties that would earn them money rather than on bringing criminals to justice.[15]

By the outbreak of the Civil War, Chicago, New Orleans, Cincinnati, Baltimore, Newark, and a number of other large cities had followed the lead of Boston and New York.[16] The foundation of today's local police departments had been established.

STRUCTURE AND ORGANIZATION OF POLICING IN THE UNITED STATES

In a nation with a population above 300 million people—all of whom are under the authority of competing political jurisdictions at federal, state, and local levels—law enforcement in the United States today reflects a structure more complex than that found in any other country. Depending on how one defines and counts professional police agencies, there are between 23,000 and 25,000 of them in the public sector alone—each representing the enforcement arm of a specific criminal code or judicial body.[17] To these can be added numerous others in the private sphere. The duties and authority of each are in some respects vague and overlapping. For example, although enforcing the law and keeping the peace may be the responsibilities of a local police agency within a small suburban community, also active in that same community may be a county sheriff's department, a state police bureaucracy, and numerous federal enforcement bodies. This situation can be further complicated by jurisdictional disputes, agency rivalries, lack of coordination and communication, and failure to share information and other resources.

New York City reflects the nature of this complex structure. First, there is the well-known NYPD (New York City Police Department), a force of approximately 34,500 officers whose jurisdiction covers the five boroughs that make up the city as a whole. There are also New York State Police, private police, federal enforcement bodies, and an interstate agency—the New York/New Jersey Port Authority Police—whose jurisdiction and authority cross both county and state lines. In sum, most places in the United States , like New York City, have several levels of police authority, and their jurisdictions often overlap. The result is a highly complex law enforcement system. The rest of this chapter examines the various levels of law enforcement authority and describes each in detail.

Federal Law Enforcement Agencies

Federal law enforcement agencies have two unique features. First, since their primary task is to enforce the statutes contained in the United States Code, their units are highly specialized, often with distinctive resources and training. Second, since they are located in the executive branch of the U.S. government, their jurisdictional boundaries, at least in theory, are limited by congressional authority.

The major federal entities with enforcement powers are the Federal Bureau of Investigation (FBI) and the cabinet-level Department of Homeland Security (DHS). There are also the individual agencies more commonly thought of as law enforcement, including the Bureau of Alcohol, Tobacco, Firearms and Explosives (ATF), the Drug Enforcement Administration (DEA), the U.S. Marshals Service, the U.S. Customs and Border Protection, the U.S. Secret Service, the U.S. Coast Guard, the Criminal Investigation division of the Internal Revenue Service (IRS), the U.S. Postal Inspection Service, and the Federal Air Marshal Service, to name but a few. All of these agencies are now housed within the Department of Justice as part of the reorganization that occurred after the World Trade Center attacks on September 11, 2001. Let's take a closer look at the key agencies.

Federal Bureau of Investigation (FBI)   The FBI is the chief investigative body of the Justice Department, with legal jurisdiction extending to all federal crimes that are not the specific responsibility of some other federal enforcement agency.[18] The more significant crimes that fall under FBI jurisdiction are kidnapping; crimes against banks; aircraft piracy; violations of the Civil Rights Act; interstate gambling; organized crime; interstate flight to avoid prosecution, custody, or confinement; and terrorism—both domestic and international.

Bureau of Alcohol, Tobacco, Firearms and Explosives (ATF)   Originally organized to enforce prohibition, the ATF has responsibility for protecting the nation from violent criminals, criminal organizations, the illegal use and trafficking of firearms, the illegal use and storage of explosives, acts of arson and bombings, acts of terrorism, and the illegal diversion of alcohol and tobacco products.[19] It has been housed within the Department of Justice since 2002.

Drug Enforcement Administration (DEA)   The DEA was formed in 1973 as a consolidation of other drug-enforcement agencies. Its major responsibility is to control the use and distribution of narcotics and other controlled substances.[20] As with many other federal agencies, the DEA coordinates with local and international entities to enforce the nation's drug laws.

U.S. Marshals Service   Under the direct authority of the U.S. attorney general's office, the U.S. Marshals Service is the country's oldest law enforcement agency. It has the power to enforce all federal laws that are not the specific responsibility of some other federal agency, although its major activities involve administering proceedings at the federal courts.[21] U.S. marshals also protect relocated witnesses, federal and state judges, and other important governmental officials.

Department of Homeland Security (DHS)   The creation of the DHS consolidated 22 executive-level agencies into a single cabinet department in 2002 and represents the most significant transformation of the U.S. government since 1947. In the aftermath of the terrorist attacks on September 11, 2001, President George W. Bush decided that the United States needed strategic coordination between government agencies.[22] The result was the DHS, whose first priority is to protect the nation against

Even with modern technology and a modified role, U.S. Marshals continue to track down offenders who have absconded or refuse to appear in court, much as their predecessors in the Wild West did.

A U.S. border patrol agent with the U.S. Customs and Border Protection agency drives along the United States–Mexico border in Jacumba, California, as men wait on the Mexican side for sunset to attempt an illegal crossing.

further terrorist attacks. The 233,000 men and women of the DHS analyze threats and intelligence, guard our borders and airports, protect our critical infrastructure, and coordinate the response of our nation for future emergencies. The department is also dedicated to protecting the rights of American citizens and enhancing public services, such as natural-disaster assistance and citizenship services.

In terms of law enforcement, the major DHS agencies include the following:

- *U.S. Immigration and Customs Enforcement (ICE)* As the largest investigative arm of DHS, the ICE is responsible for identifying and shutting down weaknesses at the nation's borders.
- *U.S. Customs and Border Protection (CBP)* The CBP represents a unification of agencies (including the former Customs Service) responsible for administering the laws that regulate the admission, exclusion, naturalization, and deportation of aliens, as well as preventing the illegal entry of aliens and the smuggling of illegal goods.
- *U.S. Citizenship and Immigration Services (USCIS)* Replacing the former Immigration and Naturalization Service, the USCIS has inspectors and investigators whose responsibilities include the administration of laws related to the importation of foreign goods; the collection of duties, penalties, and other fees; and the prevention of smuggling.
- *U.S. Secret Service* Known primarily for its role in protecting the president of the United States, his family, and other government officials, the Secret Service also has investigative units that focus on the forgery and counterfeiting of U.S. currency, checks, bonds, and federal food stamps. In this post-9/11 era, a special emphasis of the Secret Service has been the tracking of counterfeit money used by terrorists to finance their networks.
- *U.S. Coast Guard* The Coast Guard is a special naval force with responsibilities for suppressing contraband trade and aiding vessels in distress.

Many other federal agencies also have law enforcement powers and operate like local, state, and other federal policing agencies. These include the following:

Internal Revenue Service (IRS) Housed within the Treasury Department, the IRS is responsible for the administration and enforcement of the federal tax laws.[23] Its major enforcement activities in the criminal area are to investigate possible criminal violations of the tax law.

U.S. Fish and Wildlife Service Housed within the Department of the Interior, this agency has a mission to conserve, protect and enhance fish, wildlife, and plants and their habitats for the continuing benefit of the American people. As such, the U.S. Fish and Wildlife Service enforces federal wildlife laws, protects endangered species, manages migratory birds, restores nationally significant fisheries, conserves and restores wildlife habitats such as wetlands, and helps foreign governments with their international conservation efforts.[24] Many of these duties require officers to enforce laws, arrest offenders, confiscate property, and collect evidence for the prosecution of wildlife offenders. Officers in this agency have some of the broadest law enforcement powers in the United States.

Bureau of Diplomatic Security The security and law enforcement arm of the Department of State is the Bureau of Diplomatic Security. Its focus is international investigations, including threat analysis, cyber security, counterterrorism, security technology, and protection of people, property, and information.

Other Federal Law Enforcement Agencies In addition to the preceding agencies, a variety of other federal agencies have enforcement functions. For example, the departments of Labor, Agriculture, Defense, and Interior have developed enforcement or quasi-enforcement units to deal with operations of a criminal or regulatory nature. As the law enforcement and audit arm of the U.S. Postal Service, the Postal Inspection Service has jurisdiction in all criminal matters infringing on the integrity and security of the mail and the safety of all postal valuables, property, and personnel. Independent regulatory bodies such as the U.S. Securities and Exchange Commission (SEC) and the Federal Trade Commission (FTC) also have enforcement powers. And

The U.S. Fish and Wildlife Service manages more than 520 national wildlife refuges; operates 66 national fish hatcheries, 64 fishery resource offices, and 78 ecological-services field stations; and employs over 700 officials to meet its mission of conservation, protection, and enhancement of fish, wildlife, and plants and their natural habitats.

special investigative and enforcement bodies appear from time to time, stemming directly from the executive, judicial, and legislative branches of government.[25]

The most secretive of America's law enforcement agents are the federal air marshals. The practice of placing armed federal law enforcement officials on high-risk flights was initiated by President Kennedy in 1963. The Federal Air Marshal Service is the Federal Aviation Administration's (FAA) unit of high-tech sharpshooters. Dressed in civilian clothes, they board all flights in and out of Washington, DC, and other cities at random or in response to specific threats, carrying weapons and special ammunition—hollow-point aluminum bullets that can kill without penetrating the skin of airplanes. The FAA refuses to divulge the number of marshals it has or what they look like.[26]

An international organization, Interpol, also plays a role in the federal law enforcement bureaucracy. Founded in 1923, Interpol (International Criminal Police Organization) is the largest crime-fighting organization in the world. With headquarters in Lyon, France, Interpol serves its 190 member countries as a clearinghouse and depository of information about wanted criminals. Although it is neither an investigative nor an enforcement agency, it plays active roles in crime prevention, extradition, and forensic science. In addition, Interpol works with many national police agencies.[27]

As you have seen, the list of federal agencies is extensive, and each agency plays an important role in responding to crime at the federal level. In addition, each offers support and resources to local and state law enforcement agencies as they respond to crime and offenders within our communities.

State Police Agencies

In addition to all those federal agencies, each U.S. state maintains its own law enforcement agency that enforces state law and investigates crimes. Nationwide, these agencies also provide law enforcement services in rural areas that have no local policing entities. Their roots lie in the post–Civil War era, the topic we turn to next.

Sheriffs and State Police: The Beginning
During the late 1800s and early 1900s, states began experimenting with forces similar to those of the Texas Rangers, primarily because of the basic deficiencies in existing rural police administration and practices. In the decades that followed the Civil War and Reconstruction, population growth and demographic shifts, changing economic conditions, and the complexities of a pluralistic society resulted in increased crime. The office of the sheriff, the only form of law enforcement that existed in many communities, had a variety of weaknesses that limited its effectiveness in preventing and controlling crime. The most important issue was term limits; sheriffs were elected by popular vote, often for two-year terms, making them continuously vulnerable to political influence and, in turn, to corruption. A second problem was that sheriffs were responsible for the conduct of civil processes, the administration of the county jail, and in some cases the collection of taxes as well, leaving little time for law enforcement. Also, they were historically compensated under a fee system that made civil duties more attractive than law enforcement. These difficulties also existed in communities where civil and police duties were in the hands of local constables.[28]

In these early days of policing, one municipality had no effective means of communication or cooperation with other cities and towns. The formation of state police agencies was a direct response to these issues. They were geographically unconfined, with an organizational and administrative structure, resources, training, and means of communication that could be applied to an entire state.

The Beginning of Modern State Police Administration
Modern state police administration began in 1905, with the creation of the Pennsylvania State Constabulary. This was the first professional statewide force whose superintendent

had extensive administrative powers and was responsible only to the governor. From the beginning, it operated as a uniformed force, used a system of troop headquarters and widely distributed substations as bases of operations, and patrolled the entire state, including the most remote rural areas.[29] In the years that followed, other states established police departments based on the Pennsylvania model, and by 1925 formal state police departments existed throughout most of the nation.

Currently, each state has its own police agency, and although the structures and functions vary, they all fulfill some of the regulatory and investigative roles of federal enforcement groups, as well as some of the uniformed patrol duties of local police. In general, they are organized into one of two models. In the first model, like that followed in Michigan, New York, Pennsylvania, Delaware, Vermont, and Arkansas, the state police agencies have general police powers and enforce state laws. In addition to performing routine patrol and traffic regulation, they have specialized units that investigate major crimes, intelligence units that investigate organized criminal activities and drug trafficking, juvenile units, crime laboratories, and statewide computer facilities. In the second model, the state police agencies focus primarily on enforcing laws that govern the operation of motor vehicles on public roads and highways. State highway patrols of this type operate in California, Ohio, Georgia, Florida, and the Carolinas. In some cases these agencies also investigate crimes that occur on state highways or state property or crimes that involve the use of public carriers.

State highway patrol officers respond to traffic offenses on the statewide highway system and investigate offenses when local law enforcement agencies require or request assistance.

County and Municipal Policing

Despite the existence of the large federal enforcement bureaucracies and the state police agencies, most law enforcement and peacekeeping in rural, urban, and unincorporated areas is provided by county and municipal authorities. These agencies include various city, town, and county organizations, including sheriffs in some locations.

The office of sheriff has been established by either a state constitution or statutory law in every state but Alaska. The sheriff serves as the chief law enforcement officer in his or her county and has countywide jurisdiction. The sheriff is elected in most counties. Currently, the sheriff's office has three primary responsibilities in most jurisdictions. First, it provides law enforcement services to the county. Second, it typically maintains the county jail and receives prisoners who are in various stages of the criminal justice process or awaiting transportation to a state institution. Third, it provides personnel to serve as court bailiffs, to transport defendants and prisoners, and to act in civil matters—delivering divorce papers or subpoenas and enforcing court-ordered liens, eviction notices, and forfeitures of property.

With the establishment of city, town, and other municipal police agencies during the twentieth century, a number of jurisdictional disputes emerged. Many states have given cities and towns authority to provide for their own police protection, thus limiting the sovereignty and jurisdiction of the county police or sheriff's office to rural and unincorporated areas. In other instances, agreements have been reached between county and town police departments whereby sheriffs will not enforce the criminal laws in particular municipalities, except in instances of civil strife, police corruption, or when called on to do so.

Sheriff's deputies in many jurisdictions manage the operation of local jail facilities.

Police in the Private Sector

Interest in private policing has increased in recent decades. Among the reasons for this are rising concern over street crime; dramatic increases in industrial thefts, shoplifting, and employee pilferage; incidents of employee violence in the workplace; and the desire of corporate managers to secure their places of business. But private-sector police forces are not new. Before formal public police agencies were organized during the nineteenth century, *all* policing, with the exception of the military, was private. The constables, shire-reeves, and members of the mutual-pledge groups in ninth-century England were essentially a form of private police.

Today private police provide guard, patrol, detection, protection, and alarm services, as well as armored-car transportation, crowd control, and retail and industrial security. In addition to carrying out routine private policing chores, private security employees guard and monitor public and privately owned nuclear facilities, Department of Energy sites, and the Kennedy Space Center, to name but a few major posts. Some even design, build, staff, and operate jails and prisons for local and state governments.

In addition, they may step into areas of criminal and noncriminal activity that conventional law enforcement is either ill-equipped to handle or otherwise prohibited from handling. In cases of suspected insurance fraud, for example, most public police agencies have neither the personnel nor the financial resources to undertake intensive investigations. The search for runaway children is also far too large a problem for public agencies, and surveillance of unfaithful spouses is beyond the authority and jurisdiction of any public service agency.

Nationally, we now have more than 2 million private police, far more than the total number of federal, state, and local police. Many of these private law enforcement and security officers have formal partnerships with more-traditional policing agencies.[30] Perhaps the best-known agency today is the former Wackenhut Corporation, originally a mom-and-pop private-eye shop in southern Florida that was recently purchased by G4S, a Danish security corporation. Wackenhut has employed some 42,000 individuals and has annual revenues in excess of $2.3 billion.[31] And as many budget-conscious communities trim the size of their police forces and increasingly focus on national security issues, the number of private police agents continues to grow.[32]

In contrast to public and private policing agencies, which operate under local, state, and federal laws, **vigilantes** are individuals who take the law into their own hands. From the 1760s through the beginning of the twentieth century, vigilante activity was common in America.[33] It appeared in numerous forms, ranging from spontaneously formed mobs to quasi-military groups that banded together to establish "law and order" and administer vigilante justice in areas where courts and law officers were nonexistent, corrupt, unwilling, or incapable of dealing with the problems at hand.[34] Unlike the frontier lynch mobs, some vigilante groups were highly structured. Still, like the posse comitatus, they often seized innocent people and were guilty of depriving their targets—whether innocent or guilty—of justice and constitutional rights.[35]

The incidence of vigilantism declined by the close of the nineteenth century, but it never fully disappeared. During periods of stress, fear, and intergroup tension, it periodically reemerges in rural areas.[36] In more modern times, quasi-vigilante groups have cooperated to some extent with the police. Their main activity is patrolling in order to identify, report, and discourage criminal acts against residents of their communities. One benevolent example is the Guardian Angels—a nonprofit international organization that has worked to combat crime and increase safety since its founding in 1979 in New York City.

This discussion of the major law enforcement agencies—describing their history and structure—offers only highlights of the policing component of the criminal justice system. Keep this information in mind as we discuss the day-to-day functions of police officers and the challenges of policing in modern America.

THE NATURE AND FUNCTION OF POLICE

Many of us equate police work with dramatic confrontations between police and lawbreakers. We may envision dusting for fingerprints, searching for elusive clues, and investigating, pursuing, and ultimately arresting suspects. However, police work goes well beyond controlling crime, as you will see in the following sections as we discuss the various roles of police and the types of organizations within which they operate.

The Peacekeeping Role of Police

Although police work does entail the dangerous task of apprehending criminals, officers assigned to patrol duties, even in large cities, typically confront few serious crimes. In smaller cities and towns, such crimes are even less frequent, and in rural jurisdictions they may be extremely rare. Most police work centers around a peacekeeping role. It can include intervening in situations that threaten the public order—citizens exercising their right of free speech, street-corner gatherings of people whose intentions seem questionable, belligerent drinkers who annoy or intimidate passersby. It can include enforcing civil ordinances—for example, issuing citations for parking and minor traffic offenses or even littering. Peacekeeping can also include more general areas of public service such as directing traffic and settling disputes.

Peacekeeping also includes patrol, a crime-prevention activity we cover in detail later in the chapter. Prevention and protection activities also include programs to reduce community tensions, promote safe driving, and educate the public about strategies for avoiding victimization. Finally, police sometimes must maintain extended surveillances, transport suspects, protect witnesses, write arrest and other reports, and testify in court.[37]

Even the law enforcement aspects of police work do not always involve dangerous crime. Of the millions of arrests made each year in the United States, less than 20 percent of those arrests involve the more serious Crime Index offenses (see Chapter 3)—homicide, forcible rape, robbery, aggravated assault, burglary, larceny, vehicle theft, and arson. In contrast, about 30 percent of arrests are for lesser crimes such as gambling,

DISCRETION MATTERS

Do you think police officers have more discretion in performing their peacekeeping functions than in their crime-fighting functions? Why or why not?

Much of what police officers do every day is focused on helping the community. Actions such as responding to automobile accidents or helping stranded citizens serve the community in ways that have little to do with fighting crime.

driving while intoxicated, liquor law violations, disorderly conduct, prostitution, vagrancy, and drunkenness; and another 12 percent are for drug law violations.[38]

This is not to suggest that arrest activity that is not recorded by the Crime Index is either unimportant or risk-free. More than 50,000 assaults on police officers occur in the United States each year, and many are associated with drug-related arrests; one-third occur when officers are responding to "disturbance" calls. Less than a fourth occur when police are responding to robbery or burglary calls or attempting arrests for other types of crimes.[39]

The peacekeeping role, which involves the legitimate right to use force in situations whose urgency requires it, is key in separating police functions from those of private citizens.[40] Modern democratic society severely restricts the right of private citizens to use force and urges them to use legal channels to work out their disputes. This restriction extends to virtually all situations except those involving self-defense; and even in cases of self-defense, one must show that all reasonable means of retreat were exhausted. The law does recognize, however, that at times, resort to the courts or other mechanisms of dispute settlement would take too long to prevent harm. Aside from the limited role of citizens in defending themselves, police forces have been established to handle such situations; the idea is that it is better to have a small group of people (police) with a monopoly on the legitimate use of force than to allow anyone with a weapon to respond to such immediately demanding situations. In modern democratic society, this right of the police to use force in situations that demand it justifies their role in crime control, peacekeeping, traffic control, and everything else they do. It is the essence of their peacekeeping role.

In his influential book, *Varieties of Police Behavior (1968),*[41] noted criminologist James Q. Wilson identified three distinct styles of performing the peacekeeping role:

- *Legalistic style* focuses on violations of law and the use of threats or actual arrests to solve disputes. Officers in departments organized under this style are highly productive in law enforcement components of policing. Large numbers of traffic tickets characterize this style.

- *Watchman style* focuses on informal ways of resolving conflicts and disputes in the community. Order maintenance is the primary motivation behind this style, with significant community involvement by the officers and their department. As Wilson notes, in watchman style, the police judge "the seriousness of infractions less by what the law says about them than by their immediate and personal consequences."
- *Service style* emphasizes community satisfaction as opposed to the enforcement of specific laws. This style is characterized by a focus on maintaining a good working relationship with the community and responsiveness to the needs and concerns of the community.

As you might guess, the behavior of individual police officers is closely linked to the structure and function of the department within which they work. The organizational structure of the agency provides the resources and training and thus shapes the focus, behavior, and goals of individual officers. As departments increasingly take on issues related to terrorism and national security, they are increasingly merging the legalistic style with militaristic and intelligence-led policing models in which the collection and analysis of data inform decision-making.[42]

The Police Organization

Today virtually all police organizations in the Western world are structured on a militaristic model, which means that they are built around a hierarchy of clearly defined roles and responsibilities. Rules and regulations guide police activities, and a chain of command and an administrative staff work to maintain and increase organizational efficiency. In the following sections, we describe the typical division of labor, chain and units of command, and organizational rules, regulations, and discipline of a police department. This transition to a militaristic style has resulted primarily from increased focus on issues of national security and increasing standards of professionalism. As departments strive to ensure the best possible service to their communities, departmental organization becomes more important.

Division of Labor   All large police organizations and many smaller ones have a relatively fixed and clearly defined division of labor. Exhibit 5.2 provides an example of the organization of a large, urban department. Each unit has a distinct responsibility—for example, narcotics, vice, homicide, and training—and its own divisions and sections. Only under extraordinary circumstances would the personnel assigned to one division work in the area of another. The organizational arrangements of smaller police agencies are similar, although scaled down in proportion to their size and workload.

Chain and Units of Command   In theory, orders, requests, or any other types of information should flow up or down through each level of the police hierarchy without bypassing any level of supervision or command. Referring again to Exhibit 5.2, if an officer in the narcotics unit has a request that must be acted on by the chief of police, the communication will go up through the chain of command—from the officer to the head of the narcotics unit, to the central vice control section, to the head of the investigations bureau, then upward to the investigations/administrative division and finally to the chief of police.

Within this structure, each employee has only one immediate superior. In addition, supervisors in the chain of command have complete and full authority over their subordinates, and the subordinates, in turn, are fully responsible to those immediate superiors.

Although police organization have not adopted uniform terminology for ranks, grades of authority, functional units, territorial units, and time units, military-style designations are most common. Ranks and titles include *officers, commanders, sergeants, lieutenants, captains, majors, chiefs,* and sometimes even *colonels.* Functional units include *bureaus,* which are composed of *divisions,* and these, in turn, can include

DISCRETION MATTERS

What role do you think discretion might play in the legalistic style of policing versus the watchman, service, and militaristic styles?

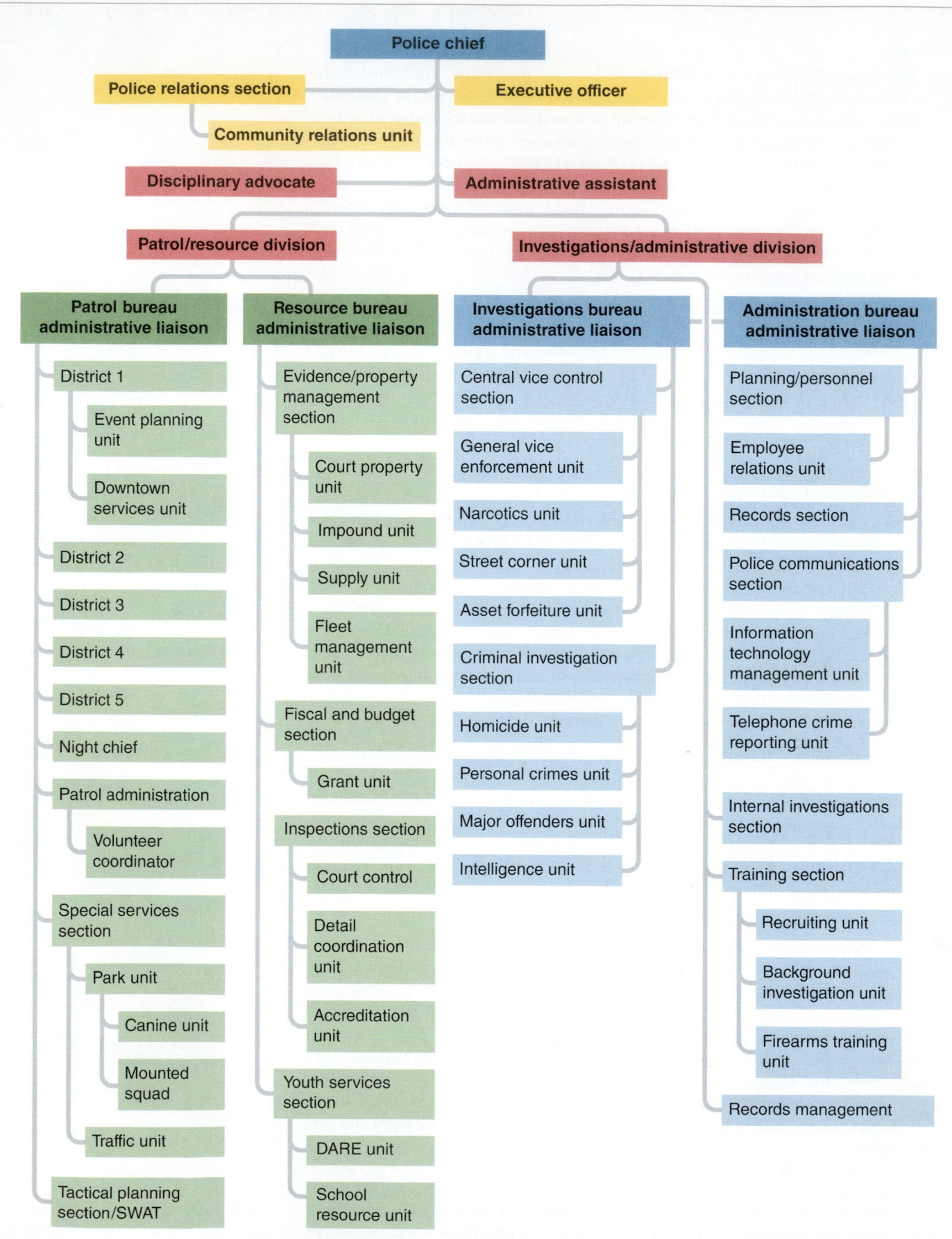

EXHIBIT 5.2 Typical Law Enforcement Agency Organization

sections, forces, or *squads.* Territorial units may be called *posts* (fixed locations to which officers are assigned for duty), *routes* or *beats* (small areas assigned for patrol purposes), *sectors* (areas containing two or more posts, routes, or beats), and *districts* and *areas* (large geographical subdivisions). Finally, time units include *watches* and *shifts,* and the officers assigned to a particular watch or shift are members of a *platoon* or *company.*[43]

Rules, Regulations, and Discipline Most police organizations have a complex system of rules and regulations designed to control and guide the actions of officers. Operations manuals and handbooks are generally lengthy, containing regulations and procedures to guide conduct in most situations. In New York City, the current rule book is almost a foot thick.[44] Officers are instructed as to when they can legitimately fire weapons (clear and present danger of injury to an officer or citizen, never as warning shots, and not from a moving car). If shots are fired, there are detailed rules and procedures for "sweeping the street" (locating spent bullets and determining whether any injury or property damage occurred). Written reports of such matters must follow certain guidelines and be prepared in a specific manner; word processing is required in nearly all jurisdictions with the advent of in-car computer units.

Elaborate regulations also deal with such varied phases of internal operations as the receipt of complaints from citizens, the keeping of records, the transportation of nonpolice personnel in official vehicles, and the care and replacement of uniforms, ammunition, and other equipment. Policies and rules also guide the manner in which an officer makes an arrest, deals with medical emergencies, inspects the residence of a vacationing citizen, or takes a stray dog into custody. In some jurisdictions, rules historically governed even mundane and personal activities, including how and when an on-duty officer could take bathroom breaks.[45] While having so many rules may seem absurd at first glance, in an organization where members can use deadly force, rules must be carefully articulated. Over time, as circumstances change or become more complex, the number of rules grows.

The police process demands compliance with departmental regulations as well as vigorous law enforcement and peacekeeping activities. These demands sometimes conflict, and when they do, proper conduct can take a backseat to the desirability of making an arrest. Moreover, although some procedures seem explicit and comprehensive, in practice they cannot possibly cover all contingencies, so much is left to the discretion of individual officers, as you saw in the chapter-opening story of the Bostick case. For a discussion of the role discretion can play when officers handle domestic violence cases, read the "Victims and Justice" feature.

DISCRETION MATTERS

Should departments increase the number and complexity of policies to limit line officers' use of discretion? Why or why not?

VICTIMS AND JUSTICE

Interpersonal Violence and Police Discretion

Current data indicate that more than 1,000 women are killed each year by their husbands, ex-husbands, or boyfriends. In addition, some 2 million women annually, or an average of one every 16 seconds, are assaulted.[46] Research has found that about 25 percent of women will experience interpersonal violence in their lifetime, with 40 percent of those sustaining physical injuries as a result these assaults.[47] In fact, the Centers for Disease Control have listed abuse by husbands and partners as a leading cause of injury to women between the ages of 15 and 44.[48] Many of these women will not report their assaults to police, particularly because of concerns that law enforcement is

Domestic violence situations can be chaotic, complex, and particularly challenging for police officers.

unwilling or unable to help them. Agencies around the country have taken steps to alter this image—for example, by providing additional training and creating specialized units to respond to victims of interpersonal violence.

Nevertheless, a number of factors appear to influence police discretion in responding to domestic abuse situations. The most notable of these factors are the often ambiguous nature of domestic abuse circumstances and the historic legality of domestic abuse. For example, some argue that the phrase *rule of thumb* dates back to English common law, which held that a man could strike his wife with a stick if it was no wider than his thumb.[49] The legality of wife beating was formally established in an 1824 Mississippi Supreme Court decision that codified a version of the rule of thumb from English common law.[50] Since then, police, legislators, judges, prosecutors, offenders, and even victims have been reluctant to view such behavior as illegal.

Police attitudes about interpersonal violence are complex, and many officers believe that counseling would be a more appropriate response than arrest and criminal prosecution.[51] In addition, formal police action has often been inhibited by victims, many of whom are unwilling to initiate formal charges against their abusers for a variety of reasons—feelings of shame, confusion, or fear of retaliation. Moreover, police may be reluctant to respond to interpersonal violence calls when they have reason to believe that an arrest will bring further harm to the victim. In these cases, police may refer the victim to a battered-women's shelter so that she can escape the situation without risking additional harm.

Finally, police risk physical harm when they intervene in these situations. A number of studies support a correlation between response to domestic disturbance calls and assaults on officers.[52] As you can see, then, many factors, including historical grounds and societal attitudes, determine how the criminal justice system and its agents respond, particularly to incidents involving intimate interactions and relationships.

THINK ABOUT THIS

1. What would you consider to be an ideal response to domestic violence situations and victims?
2. What factors complicate the response of police to such victims?
3. How might the age, race, gender, sexuality, or social class of the parties involved impact an officer's reaction to both the victim and the situation?

Categories of Policing Activities

Most police activities fall into three general categories: line services, administrative services, and auxiliary services. *Line services* include such activities as patrol, criminal investigation, and traffic control. Depending on the size of the agency, line services might also have specific divisions or units that focus on vice, organized crime, intelligence, and juvenile crime, as you saw in Exhibit 5.2. *Administrative services* back up the efforts of the line staff. These include such areas as training, personnel management, planning and research, legal matters, community relations, and internal investigation. *Auxiliary services* assist the line staff in carrying out the basic police functions, with specialized units assigned to communications, record-keeping, data processing, temporary detention, laboratory studies, and supply and maintenance. Line services—specifically patrol, criminal investigation, and certain specialized services—are the focus of the following sections, because they reflect the primary and most visible aspects of policing.

Patrol For generations, the "cop on the beat" has been the mainstay of policing. In fact, to most people, policing is embodied in the omnipresent force of officers dispersed throughout a community, in uniform, armed, and on call 24 hours a day. Whether officers are on foot, in cars, or on bicycles, **patrol** remains basic to police work.

Patrolling city streets entails a variety of tasks, from administering first aid, to breaking up family fights, pursuing a fleeing felon, directing traffic, investigating a crime scene, calming a lost child, or writing a parking ticket. Whatever the tasks, the patrol force is the foundation of the police department and its largest operating unit.

Police patrols have five specific functions: to (1) protect public safety, (2) enforce the law, (3) control traffic, (4) conduct criminal investigations, and (5) interpret the law. In their role as *protectors,* patrols promote and preserve the public order, resolve conflicts, and respond to requests for defensive service. Patrol *enforcement* duties include both the preservation of constitutional

Police use varied means of transportation—from bikes to Segways and even horses, as pictured here.

guarantees and the enforcement of legal statutes. The *traffic control* functions involve enforcing the motor vehicle and traffic laws and handling accidents and disasters. As *investigators,* police officers on patrol conduct preliminary examinations of complaints of criminal acts, gather physical evidence, and interview witnesses. During such investigations they may also uncover evidence, identify and apprehend suspects, and recover stolen property. Finally, patrol officers have *quasi-judicial functions,* making the first judgment as to whether a law has been violated.[53] It is here that the discretionary aspects of policing surface. In such circumstances police may choose to arrest or to take no action, or they may advise, instruct, or warn.

In part related to a study from the 1970s known as the Kansas City experiment, the value of police patrol in preventing and suppressing crime has been called into question. For purposes of the study, fifteen police beats were divided into five matched groups of similar beats. One beat in each group was randomly assigned to perform a particular level of patrol: normal, proactive, or reactive. *Normal* patrol involved a single car cruising the streets when not responding to calls; in the *proactive* patrol strategy, the number of cruising cars was doubled or tripled; and in the *reactive* patrol strategy, police entered the designated areas only in response to specific requests. At the conclusion of the study, no significant differences were found in any of the

Traffic citations offer one of the more common opportunities for officers to use discretion in deciding which offenders to hold criminally responsible for law violations.

DISCRETION MATTERS

How might intelligence-led policing interact with departmental discretion in targeting those neighborhoods requiring patrol?

beats—regardless of the level of patrol—in the amount of crime officially reported to the police or in victim surveys, observed criminal activity, citizen fear of crime, or citizen satisfaction with police.[54] In effect, the Kansas City experiment suggested that police patrol was not deterring crime or having any effect on citizens' perceptions. In the decades since then, law enforcement agencies have used directed patrol—intelligence- or evidence-led policing that uses technology to identify locations where patrol might be most effective in responding to crime.

Criminal Investigations   Although patrol units conduct preliminary investigations of criminal acts, most sustained investigations are assigned to a police department's detective force, which specializes in apprehending offenders. Detective-level policing includes the following responsibilities: (1) identification, location, and apprehension of criminal offenders; (2) collection and preservation of physical evidence; (3) location and interviewing of witnesses; and (4) recovery and return of stolen property.[55] In addition, detective duties may occasionally involve some of the law enforcement functions of patrol units, such as responding to the dispatch of a burglary in progress.

In small police departments, detective functions are often carried out by members of the patrol force, or a single detective generalist may handle all or most criminal investigations. Larger departments, however, have detective squads, as well as special investigative units for homicides, robberies, burglaries, and rape. Typically, a detective unit will investigate all crimes that occur in its geographically assigned area. However, if the nature and method of the offense suggest a link to similar crimes in other areas, or if the crime might have political repercussions, a specialized unit will become involved in the case.

Cities and metropolitan areas where crime rates are high may have numerous and sometimes exotic-sounding detective units with narrowly focused concerns. Miami,

Florida, for example, has its TOMCATS (Tactical Operations Multi-Agency Cargo Anti-Theft Squad), a team targeting cargo theft rings.[56] Special detective sections and teams may also be organized for specific crimes or investigations.

Media portrayals of detectives suggest that they spend much of their time pursuing criminal offenders and that their efforts at detection are quite successful. But in reality, this is not the case. Detectives generally receive cases in the form of reports written by patrol officers. Although detectives investigate practically all serious offenses, such crimes are extremely difficult (and often impossible) to solve. In most robberies, burglaries, and thefts—which account for the majority of the FBI Crime Index offenses—physical evidence that can be subjected to any kind of serious analysis is rarely found. Moreover, if witnesses to a crime are available, many are unwilling to cooperate, or their descriptions of the offender are so vague that they are of little value. Even victims typically are uncertain about the facts of the case. As a result, detectives often engage in a screening process when they make decisions as to which crimes to investigate.[57]

Detectives are evaluated on a variety of criteria, including their success in solving major cases, their ability to keep up with paperwork, their skill at handling special types of cases, their capacity to reflect a positive and professional image, and most important, the number of felony arrests they make during a year and the **clearance rate** for specific crimes. A crime is "cleared" when a suspect has been taken into custody, and the term *clearance rate* refers to the proportion of crimes that result in arrest. Thus, detectives may generally choose to focus on those crimes that are most likely to be cleared. It is for this reason that clearance rates for homicide, aggravated assault, and forcible rape are relatively high. A large proportion of these offenses occur as the result of personal quarrels, and the victims and offenders often are at least minimally acquainted. Thus, in these cases, victims or members of their families can provide detectives with the identity of the offender or with leads and clues that can result in a possible identification. In contrast, clearance rates for robbery and burglary are quite low.

Specialized Police Units In addition to the patrol and investigative units, many large urban police departments have juvenile, or youth, bureaus, which use proactive strategies to prevent and deter delinquent behavior. Large departments also have specialized units for enforcing vice laws or gathering information about organized crime. We discuss a few of these specialized units next.

Cybercrime Units. With the dramatic rise in computer use and the explosive growth of digital technology, Internet crime has proliferated, and new varieties of criminals now stalk their victims in cyberspace. The most common crimes include e-mail fraud, trade-secret hacking, child pornography, pedophilia, and extortion and threats via e-mail. High-profile cases of Internet hacking into government computers and threats of cyberattacks on corporate e-mail accounts have resulted in changes in security and responses from law enforcement agencies.

To address this growing threat, law enforcement agencies at the federal, state, and local levels have established Internet, or cybercrime, units. Many of these employ specialists trained in computer science. The activities of these law enforcement officials include decoy operations that attempt to root out pedophiles and purveyors of child pornography, drug smugglers and arms merchants who sell contraband over the Internet, and con artists engaging in all manner of fraud. Others specialize in hunting the elite Internet criminals—the malicious hackers and virus writers.[58]

SWAT Teams. The most controversial of the specialized approaches to crime control are elite police teams known by such names as *SWAT* (Special Weapons and Tactics), *ERT* (Emergency Response Team), or *TNT* (Tactical Neutralization Team) that use aggressive military procedures in exceptionally dangerous or potentially explosive situations. A forerunner of these groups was New York City's Tactical Patrol Force

(TPF), a fast-moving battalion made up of the very best police-academy recruits trained in mob control.[59]

SWAT teams, or police paramilitary units, which are carefully chosen and trained in the use of weapons and strategic invasion tactics, are typically used in situations involving hostages, airplane hijackings, and prison riots. These squads range in size from small two-person teams in suburban and rural areas to large 160-member teams in densely populated metropolitan regions.[60] By the late 1990s, almost every large jurisdiction had some type of SWAT team.[61]

These squads are controversial because a significant number of them are regularly engaged in everyday police work. A study by Peter Kraska and Victor Kappeler found that many agencies surveyed used tactical units for routine patrol activities on a frequent basis.[62] The deployment of these teams, with their significant show of police force and tactics, can cause concern among community members.

Sting Operations and Drug-Enforcement Units. *Sting operations* play a significant role in urban law enforcement. The typical sting involves the use of undercover methods to control large-scale crime, such as theft. Police officers pose as purchasers of stolen goods (*fences*), setting up contact points and storefronts wired for sound and videotape. When a crime is observed or recorded, police move in and arrest the suspect. In a similar vein, almost every urban locale and many rural communities have one or more specialized drug-enforcement units. These are organized to disrupt street-level drug dealing and/or cooperate with state and federal drug-enforcement groups in investigating and apprehending upper-level trafficking organizations.

Crime Analysis Units. With increasing pressure on law enforcement agencies to prevent and respond effectively to crime, many departments are using technology to track criminal offenses, identify patterns in these offenses, and effectively respond to crime in the communities they serve. To this end, many departments now employ crime analysts who track the geographic pattern of crime in the community so that the departments can deploy their resources, such as patrol, as effectively as possible (Exhibit 5.3). These crime analysts also provide immediate access to statistics and trends, which allows agencies to be more efficient in their use of resources.

Information from these analysts has been used in large and small departments all over the nation. In New York City, for example, the COMPSTAT administrative program has increased the effectiveness of policing. COMPSTAT was initiated to improve life in crime-prone neighborhoods by formalizing the exchange of information between the command staffs of the eight patrol boroughs that serve the 76 precincts of New York City.[63] COMPSTAT entails weekly meetings to disseminate information, primarily compiled using spatial analysis of crime-location data, to help the NYPD better respond to crime. This exchange has helped the NYPD develop one of the most efficient and effective methods of distributing police resources, and the managerial philosophy has been put into place in many other cities, including Washington, DC, Los Angeles, Philadelphia, San Francisco, and many others cities and towns of varying size and crime rates

Community Policing and Beyond Beginning in the 1990s, American policing saw the emergence of a new vocabulary and, to some extent, a new approach. Generally referred to as **community policing,** this approach is defined as a collaborative effort between the police and the community to identify the problems of crime and disorder and to develop solutions. At the heart of community policing is the idea that police should be more responsive and connected to the people they serve, that policing is a broad problem-solving enterprise that includes much more than reactive law enforcement, and that officers on the street should have a major role in crime prevention. This philosophy recognizes that much crime control is accomplished informally by the people within their own neighborhoods.[64]

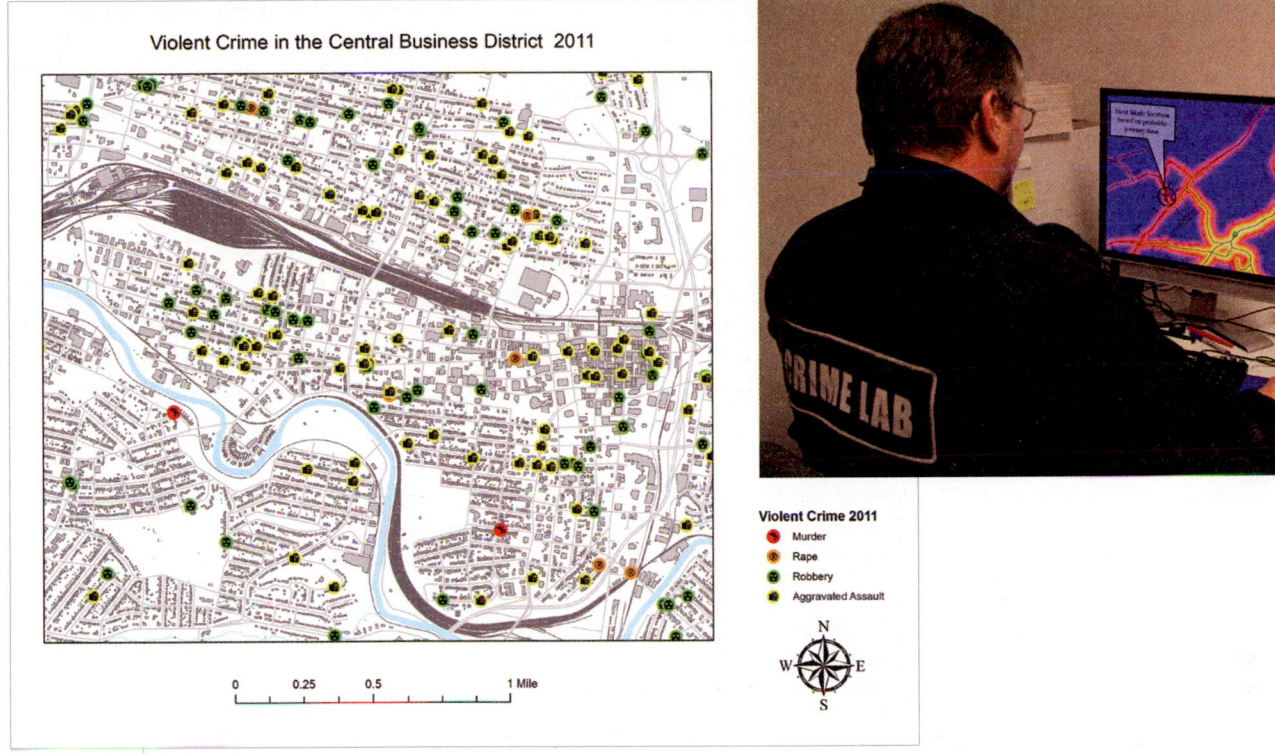

EXHIBIT 5. 3 Crime analysts use up-to-the-minute data, as reflected in this crime map. Such maps, which identify geographic locations of crime in the community, help to improve police response and ensure the efficient use of law enforcement resources.
Source: Crime map provided by Dr. Isaac Van Patten

Under community policing programs, officers are assigned to particular neighborhoods. Some are encouraged to own a home in or near that neighborhood and work out of a local substation in order to develop a personal stake in the quality of life of the area. The officers patrol, often on foot, "walking the beat" and listening to the concerns of residents. By building trust with citizens, officers make people feel safer. They also increase the likelihood that citizens will provide information to help them enforce the law more effectively.

Community policing requires officers to take a problem-oriented approach, which criminologist James Q. Wilson referred to as the theory of "broken windows."[65] Wilson argued that if the first broken window in a building is not repaired, people who like breaking windows will assume that nobody cares about the building and will break more windows. Soon the building will have no windows at all. The sense of decay in the neighborhood will increase, social disorder will flourish, and law-abiding citizens will be afraid and hide indoors. Thus, the primary task is to fix the broken window as quickly as possible and thereby influence the quality of life throughout the neighborhood.

When the concept of community policing was introduced, some police officers and administrators resisted. Undermining the implementation of this approach were officers' concerns about the additional responsibilities of working with citizens while also having to fulfill the traditional crime-fighting and peacekeeping roles.[66] However, the community policing model has been followed in many parts of the nation since the mid-1990s. Nevertheless, the events of September 11, 2001, and the threat of terrorism have altered the nature of policing. As one observer put it, "The new policing model will emphasize tactical methods, technology, and alternative service providers, such as security personnel. . . . With the threat of terrorism, [community policing] will become unsustainable."[67]

To some extent, this prediction has come true. Agencies throughout the United States have shifted scores of resources to the prevention of terrorism.[68] In most jurisdictions, attention has shifted from neighborhoods to power plants, bridges, interstate highways, international airports, convention centers, train and bus stations, tall buildings, shopping malls, amusement parks, public transit, and anywhere else that large numbers of people congregate. And because of the special vulnerability of river ports and seaports, resources have shifted to specialized forms of harbor policing. These shifts reflect the problem-oriented approach, described by Herman Goldstein, that departments have implemented over the past decade or so.[69] In problem-oriented policing, departments rely on line officers to identify problems in the communities they serve and then focus their resources in the most effective ways to combat crime and increase safety. Problem-oriented policing brings a proactive focus to law enforcement, complementing the information and problem-solving skills of line officers with research and analysis. Overall, then, the trend has been for policing agencies to develop an intelligence-led model that emphasizes the assessment and management of risk.

Studies have found female officers to be as capable as males in all areas of policing.

Women in Policing

In the majority of jurisdictions in the United States, legislation has mandated that male and female police officers have the same professional opportunities. State and local codes require that the hiring of police recruits be based on physical standards and competitive examinations that are designed to be nondiscriminatory, that all recruits receive the same training, that all officers have the same legal authority, that promotions be awarded on merit as decided by competitive procedures to determine professional knowledge and decision-making abilities, and that equal positions rate equal pay regardless of the officer's gender. However, this was not always the case, and even now gender bias in policing remains a problem. According to *Crime in the United States, 2010,* across the nation only 11.8 percent of sworn law enforcement officers are women. Breaking down the proportion by jurisdiction type, in urban areas 11.3 percent of officers are women; in metropolitan counties 13.4 percent are women; and in rural jurisdictions only 7.6 percent of officers are women.[70] These rates are higher than in years past, but they highlight how relatively small the number of female officers is in the U.S.

Opportunities for women in policing expanded with the passage of the Civil Rights Act of 1964 and the Equal Employment Opportunity Act of 1972. Title VII of the Civil Rights Act "prohibits discrimination on the basis of race, religion, creed, color, sex, or national origin with regard to hiring, compensation, terms, conditions, and privileges of employment."[71] Pursuant to the intent of Title VII, state and federal court decisions helped considerably in the movement for equal employment opportunities, not only for women in general but also for women police officers in particular. Such decisions, flowing from cases brought by women against police departments in the United States, resulted in the implementation of affirmative action policies in many police agencies. As a result, by the 1980s and continuing into the 2000s, the number of women in policing increased.[72]

Studies of women officers have examined their academy performance, capabilities for patrol work, physical training, responses in hazardous situations, and handling of violent confrontations. Virtually all this research has concluded that women do indeed have these necessary capabilities.[73] Nevertheless, women entering police work continue to encounter numerous difficulties, primarily as a result of the negative attitudes of other officers and supervisory staff.

Consequently, although women represent a significant number of the police officers in the United States, few have been fully accepted into the police subculture. Furthermore, a 2002 survey by the National Center for Women and Policing (NCWP)[74] documented that sexual harassment of women officers was common, as were instances of intimidation and discrimination. Moreover, widespread bias in police hiring, selection practices, and recruitment policies has prevented the number of women officers from expanding. In fact, in many agencies, the pace of increase in hiring women officers has stalled or is in decline.

Police Discretion and Selective Law Enforcement

Among the major tasks of policing is the enforcement of laws that protect people and property. In performing this task, police have the power to make arrests; in other words they may formally accuse individuals of law violations and initiate the criminal justice process, as you saw in the case that began this chapter. This requires that they interpret the law. On the basis of their knowledge of the criminal codes, they must make immediate judgments as to whether a law has been broken, whether to make an arrest, and whether to use force in doing so. These decisions tend to be exceedingly complex, especially because laws cannot take into account the specific circumstances surrounding every police confrontation. Moreover, not all laws can be fully enforced, and most police officers, who have minimal if any legal training, are not equipped to deal with the intricacies of law. Therefore, police must exercise a great deal of discretion in deciding what constitutes a violation of the law, which laws to enforce, and how and when to enforce them.

It is difficult to define **police discretion** in a single phrase or sentence, for the term has come to mean many things. Police behavior is often guided by community norms, departmental policies, and field standards of behavior. In the broadest sense, discretion exists whenever a police officer or agency is free to choose among alternatives—to enforce the law or to do so selectively, to use force, to deal differently with some citizens than with others, to provide or not provide certain services, to train recruits in certain ways, to discipline officers differently, and to organize and deploy resources in a variety of forms. However, most discussions of police discretion focus on officers' decisions about when and how to enforce the law.

By and large, the idea of police discretion is paradoxical, since it appears to flout legal demands. In most jurisdictions police officers are charged with the enforcement of laws—*all* laws! Yet discretion, or selective enforcement, is necessary because of limited police resources, the ambiguity and breadth of criminal statutes, the informal expectations of legislatures, and the often conflicting demands of the public. The potential for discretion exists whenever an officer is free to choose from two or more interpretations of the events reported, inferred, or otherwise observed in any police-civilian encounter. Let's look more closely at this topic.

Full versus Selective Enforcement Although police discretion is a controversial issue, the need for selective law enforcement cannot be denied. **Full enforcement** of the law would require an investigation of every disturbing event and every complaint and vigorous enforcement of every statute on the books—from homicide, robbery, and assault to spitting on the sidewalk. Full enforcement would mean arresting an elderly couple for gambling at an illegal bingo game or arresting a neighbor for not having his dog licensed.

Full enforcement, of course, is impossible and undesirable. It establishes mandates that exceed the capabilities and resources of police agencies and the criminal

DISCRETION MATTERS

What factors should determine whether specific offenses and offenders receive full enforcement of the law?

justice system as a whole. It places demands on police officers that exceed their conceptions of justice and fairness. And it goes beyond the public's conception of the judicious use of police power. Thus, police departments and officers are forced to be selective, under-enforcing some laws and not enforcing others at all, depending on the situation. However, police have few clear-cut policies to guide these choices, and therein lies the problem. Police discretion creates situations in which some think that enforcement should be initiated, *but it is not,* and others in which enforcement should not occur, *but it does.*

Factors in the Decision to Arrest   Studies of police discretion have demonstrated that the most significant factor in the decision to arrest is the seriousness of the offense committed. This is supplemented by other information, such as the offender's mental state and criminal record (when it is known to the arresting officer), the involvement (if any) of weapons, the availability of the complainant, and the amount of danger involved.[75] In addition to these seemingly objective criteria, other factors come into play as well. What many police view as "safe" arrests often involve individuals who lack the power, resources, or social position to cause trouble for the officer. In addition, a variety of studies have documented that police use their discretionary power of arrest more often when the suspect shows disrespect.

A classic study by Irving Piliavin and Scott Briar, "Police Encounters with Juveniles," provides a particularly useful perspective on these aspects of discretion and differential law enforcement.[76] The researchers found that with the exception of offenders who had committed serious crimes or who were already wanted by the authorities, the disposition of juvenile cases depended largely on how the officer evaluated the youth's character. Such evaluations and decisions were typically limited to the information gathered by police during their encounters with juveniles. Piliavin and Briar found that this had serious implications for both the accused and the justice system. When police officers believed that a youth's demeanor, race, or style of dress were good indicators of future behavior, arrests became totally discriminatory; the youths who were arrested were those who typically did not fit the officer's idea of normalcy. However, some studies suggest that displays of hostility toward police do not necessarily increase the likelihood of arrest.[77]

Command Discretion   A different level of police discretion involves departmental objectives, enforcement policies, the deployment of personnel and resources, budget expenditures, and the organizational structure of police units. Known as *command discretion,* it is implicit in the very structure and organization of a police force. It tends to be less problematic than other types of discretion since it provides at least some uniform guidelines for street-level decision-making.[78] Examples of command discretion might involve orders to "clear the streets of all prostitutes" or, conversely, to "look the other way" when observing the smoking of marijuana at rock concerts. Exactly how police discretion can be controlled is a complex question, for control must be exercised in a manner that does not destroy the basic objectives of law enforcement—effective crime control and protection of the rights of citizens.

The Police Subculture

A subculture is the normative system of a group that is smaller than and essentially different from the dominant culture. It includes learned behavior that is common to members of the group and ways of acting

Law enforcement administrators can set the tone within a department about the use of discretion.

and thinking that, together, constitute a relatively cohesive cultural system. The police are members of a subculture. Their system of shared norms, values, goals, career patterns, lifestyle, and occupational structure is essentially different from that of the wider society within which they function. Entry into the **police subculture** begins with a process of socialization through which recruits learn the values and behavior patterns characteristic of experienced officers.[79] Ultimately, many develop an occupational, or working, personality as a response to the danger of their work and their obligation to exercise authority.

The Police Personality

It is widely believed that policing attracts individuals who are predisposed toward authoritarianism and cynicism, and some research evidence supports this point of view. Yet the overwhelming majority of studies done in the past four decades have indicated that policing does *not* attract a distinctive personality type; rather, the nature of police socialization practices creates a distinctive **working personality** among many patrol officers.[80] Let's look at the elements that may contribute to this working personality.

Danger and Authority Perhaps the most definitive statement on the development of the police personality comes from Jerome H. Skolnick, who summarized the process as encompassing two principal concepts: danger and authority. These result from the pressure to appear effective in the face of potential threats in the community. The resulting state of hypervigilance isolates officers from those around them.[81]

James Skolnick includes danger and authority as key elements of the work that contribute to the police personality.

As another isolating factor, Skolnick points out that police are required to enforce unpopular laws, some of which are more morally conservative and others more morally liberal than the values of the community in which they work. Police are also charged with enforcing traffic laws and other codes that regulate the flow of public activity. In these situations police come to be viewed as adversaries. Thus, the public may become frustrated by aspects of police authority while stressing the obligation of the police to respond to danger.

Police Cynicism As numerous studies have found, an integral part of the police personality is cynicism—the notion that all people are motivated by evil and selfishness. **Police cynicism** develops through contact with the police subculture and the nature or characteristics of police work. Police officers are set apart from the rest of society because they have the power to regulate the lives of others, a role symbolized by their distinctive uniform and weapons. Moreover, their constant interactions with crime and the more troublesome aspects of social life serve to diminish their faith in humanity.

Sources of Stress in Policing

A final issue related both to the police subculture and to the police role in general is stress. Policing is a stressful occupation, and at least four sources of police stress have been identified. First, there is external stress, which results from the real dangers associated with police work—apprehending armed suspects and responding to calls involving potential conflict. Second, there is organizational stress, which is generated by the demands of the police bureaucracy—scheduling, paperwork, rules and regulations, and other requirements. Third, there is operational stress, which results from day-to-day exposure to the tragedies that police typically encounter. And fourth, there is personal stress, which is related to interpersonal relations among officers and their families and peers.[82] In addition to these sources, police stress can result from feelings of ineffectiveness in the face of forces beyond their control.

With all these stressors as part of daily life, officers face a strong likelihood of becoming ever more isolated from the rest of society, retreating behind the facade of the police personality.[83] This stress can have devastating effects on the personal lives and professional success of officers. Studies have found that law enforcement officers with higher levels of stress are more likely to divorce, participate in intimate partner violence, abuse alcohol and drugs, have cardiovascular disease, and engage in antisocial behavior.[84] Responses by agencies and the community are needed to address the serious concerns about the stressful impact of the police subculture on officers. These same issues apply to police encounters with juveniles, as you will learn from the "Juvenile Justice in Context" feature.

JUVENILE JUSTICE IN CONTEXT

Police Discretion and Juvenile Offenders

Each year, more than a million juveniles are arrested in the United States. The offenses cover all categories of crime, from the most serious violent crimes of murder, forcible rape, and robbery, to status offenses such as running away, truancy, and curfew violations. Although perhaps a third of these offenses result in release with no more than a warning, the majority are referred to the courts for official processing. However, given the less formal nature of juvenile justice combined with the dynamics of police discretion, it is likely that for each arrest of a juvenile, there are perhaps 500 potential arrest situations where officers choose an alternative to arrest.

Police officers who encounter status offenders or juveniles involved in delinquent activities have several options in responding to youth. First, the officer may simply release the youth with a reprimand. Second, the officer may take the youth to the police station, where some level of formal incident report is prepared and filed that briefly describes the incident. The parents may then be called in for a discussion, after which the youth is released.

The third option is taking the juvenile into custody. Even in this event, the police still have alternatives. Some

When police interact positively with neighborhood youth, they often have a better relationship with the community in general, which in turn helps them solve cases and reduce crime.

law enforcement agencies in large urban areas have their own diversion and de-linquency-prevention programs to which they may send a juvenile, while status offenders may be brought to social service agencies for counseling and treatment. For felony offenses, and particularly those involving violence, there is a fourth police option: referral to the juvenile court.

The working style of the officer, the circumstances of the incident, and the policies of the department typically play a role in the decision to release or detain juveniles. Studies have demonstrated, however, that numerous other factors can come into play. Among these are the attitude of the victim; the juvenile's prior record; the seriousness of the offense; the age, gender, race, and demeanor of the offender; the likelihood of adequate parental handling of the matter; the time and location of the incident; the availability of a service agency for referral; and the officer's perception of how the case will be handled by the court. Consideration of these factors by a police officer, consciously or otherwise, is more likely to result in an "on-the-street disposition" or no action at all.

CONCLUSIONS

The police, representing the largest and most visible segment of the criminal justice system, are charged with enforcing the law and keeping the peace. In the United States, the decentralized organizational structure has meant that police agencies operate independently of any national or federal oversight. Despite their autonomy, most law enforcement agencies are organized and operated in an essentially similar fashion. Today, policing can be found at many levels of the community—federal, state, local, and even international.

Police officers perform a variety of functions. In a democratic society like that of the United States, they serve as enforcers, investigators, and traffic controllers. In addition, they also serve a quasi-judicial function in that officers must determine if a crime has been committed and, if so, how to respond. What can be described as a "police personality" emerges as a result of the nature of police work—the authority and the danger—and the socialization and training processes. To combat the social isolation and stress that stem from their authoritarian role, police become part of a close-knit subculture that protects and supports its members and in which members share similar attitudes, values, understandings, and views of the world.[85]

SUMMARY AND REVIEW

- **Trace the historical development of modern policing.**
  - Modern policing has its roots in the latter part of the ninth century, with the mutual-pledge system of England's Alfred the Great. By the seventeenth century, the Crown was using thief-takers, private detectives paid on a piecework basis to apprehend highway robbers, burglars, and housebreakers.
  - The foundations for the first modern police force were established by Henry Fielding in 1748, and his

    Bow Street Runners comprised an organized investigative division that earned the standard thief-takers' rewards.
  - Sir Robert Peel's successful bill established the London Metropolitan Police and ushered in the era of modern policing.
  - In the United States, constable and nighttime watch systems were common in most colonial communities. In many cities, these early forms of policing lasted through the early nineteenth century but were

eventually replaced with more formally organized agencies, following problems with corruption and increasing crime rates.

- As settlers moved West, sheriffs emerged as active agents of law enforcement. Their duties often included apprehending criminals, conducting popular elections, collecting taxes, and assuming custody of public funds. In addition, settlers in various western communities soon established more localized police agencies.

- The nineteenth century also saw the establishment of state police agencies. In general, such agencies were created in response to the increasingly nomadic character of crime and the inability of local police agencies to coordinate their crime-fighting activities. State police agencies provided an organized means to enforce the law throughout an entire state. In addition, cities set up metropolitan police forces following the London model.

Identify the differences between federal, state, and local law enforcement agencies in terms of jurisdiction and authority.

- Federal law enforcement agencies enforce specific statutes contained in the U.S. criminal code, and their units are highly specialized. Because these agencies serve as the enforcement branches of the federal court system, their activities are confined to specific jurisdictional boundaries defined by congressional mandate.

- State police agencies generally fulfill a number of the regulatory and investigative roles of the federal enforcement groups, as well as a portion of the uniformed patrol duties of the local police. However, the majority of modern policing is provided by county and municipal authority.

Describe the functions of police.

- In a democratic society like that of the United States, police serve as enforcers, investigators, and traffic controllers.

- They also serve a quasi-judicial function in that officers must determine if a crime has been committed and, if so, what to do about it.

- In spite of conventional beliefs, the chief function of the police is not to enforce the law but to keep the peace. As demonstrated consistently in the Uniform Crime Reports and other data, serious crimes constitute only a small fraction of all arrests in any given year.

- By contrast, the daily activity of most officers involves administrative work, answering routine calls, controlling traffic, testifying in court, and providing assistance to citizens.

Explain the structure of police organizations.

- Police departments are bureaucratically structured on a military model.

- All large police organizations and many smaller ones have a fixed division of labor, chains and units of command, and rules, regulations, and discipline.

Discuss the status of women in American policing.

- State and local codes require
  - that the hiring of police recruits be based on physical standards and competitive examinations that are designed to be nondiscriminatory
  - that all recruits receive the same training and that all officers have the same legal authority
  - that promotions be awarded on merit as decided by competitive procedures to determine professional knowledge and decision-making abilities
  - that equal positions rate equal pay regardless of the officer's gender

- Regardless of these state and local codes, which were designed to provide male and female police officers with the same opportunities, gender bias in policing remains a problem due to the masculine traditions and stereotypes that permeate the field.

Define police discretion and its relationship to selective law enforcement.

- Police officers, whether detectives or those in uniform, are called on to immediately judge whether a law has been violated, whether to invoke the powers of arrest, and whether to use force in invoking that power. *Discretion* is the term used to describe these judgments.

- Police must use considerable discretion in making these judgments because departmental rules and guidelines are frequently ambiguous. An outgrowth of this discretionary power is selective law enforcement.

Identify the components of the police subculture and personality.

- Police are members of a subculture—a system of shared norms, values, goals, and lifestyle that differs from that of the wider society they are charged to protect and within which they function.

- Police undergo a process of socialization through which they learn the values and behavior patterns characteristic of experienced officers. Ultimately, many develop an occupational, or working, personality as a response to the danger of their work and their obligation to exercise authority.

KEY TERMS

clearance rate (p. 133)   patrol (p. 131)   posse comitatus (p. 117)
community policing (p. 134)   police cynicism (p. 139)   thief-takers (p. 115)
full enforcement (p. 137)   police discretion (p. 137)   vigilante (p. 125)
mutual pledge (p. 115)   police subculture (p. 139)   working personality (p. 139)

ISSUES FOR CRITICAL THINKING AND DISCUSSION

1. To what extent do the functions of federal, state, and local policing vary and overlap?

2. How might private police agencies create problems that are greater than their protection is worth?

3. Should quasi-vigilante groups be permitted to patrol the streets? Explain your answer.

4. Do you think the modern focus on terrorism affects the manner in which the various styles of policing are applied? Why or why not?

5. In what ways are police agencies similar to military organizations? If you could imagine a police department not organized along military lines, what would it be like?

6. Do the advantages of police discretion outweigh the disadvantages?

7. How, if at all, might an increase in the number of female police officers impact a community?

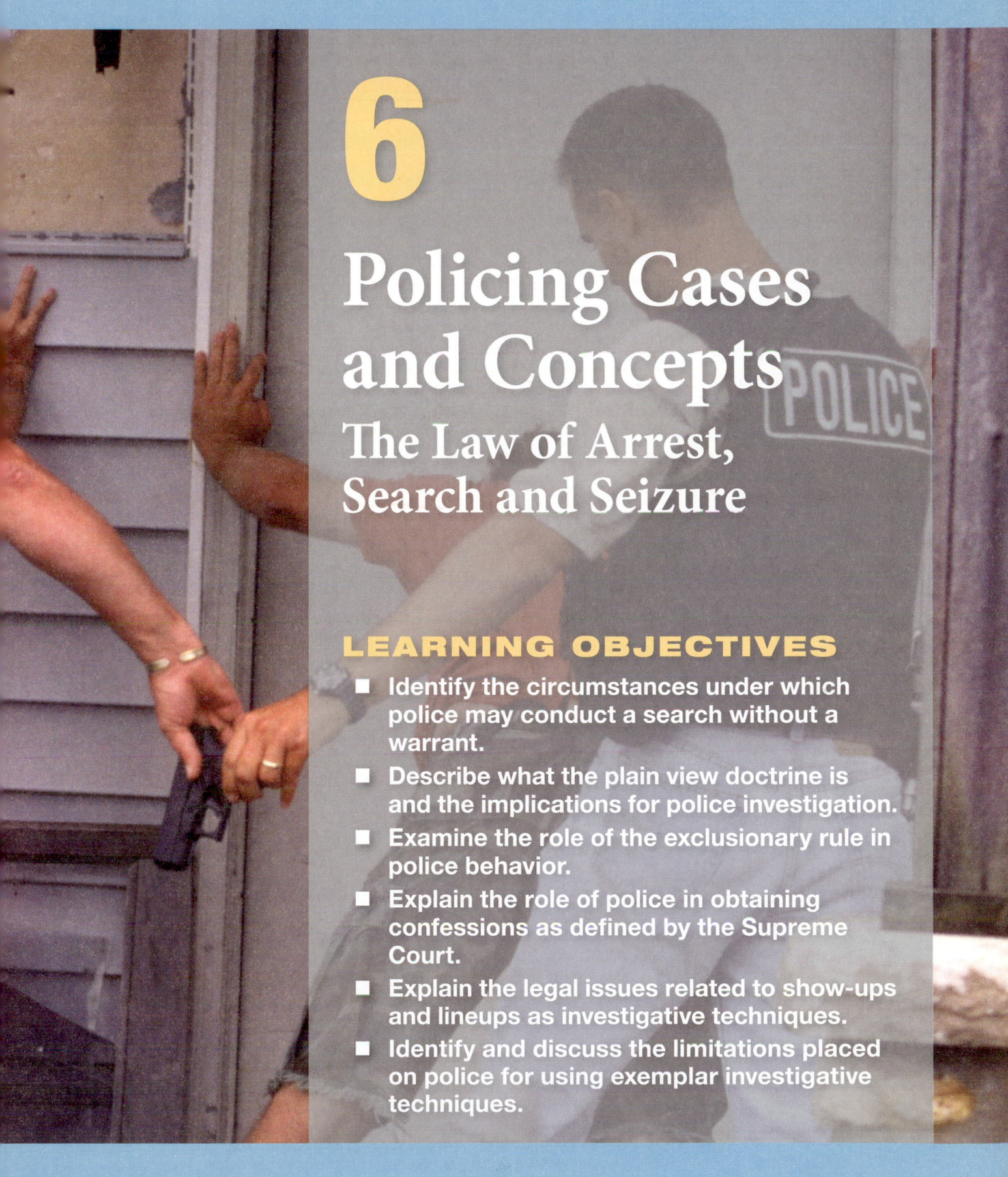

6

Policing Cases and Concepts

The Law of Arrest, Search and Seizure

LEARNING OBJECTIVES

- Identify the circumstances under which police may conduct a search without a warrant.

- Describe what the plain view doctrine is and the implications for police investigation.

- Examine the role of the exclusionary rule in police behavior.

- Explain the role of police in obtaining confessions as defined by the Supreme Court.

- Explain the legal issues related to show-ups and lineups as investigative techniques.

- Identify and discuss the limitations placed on police for using exemplar investigative techniques.

SEARCH, SEIZURE, AND THE NOT-SO-SMART THIEF

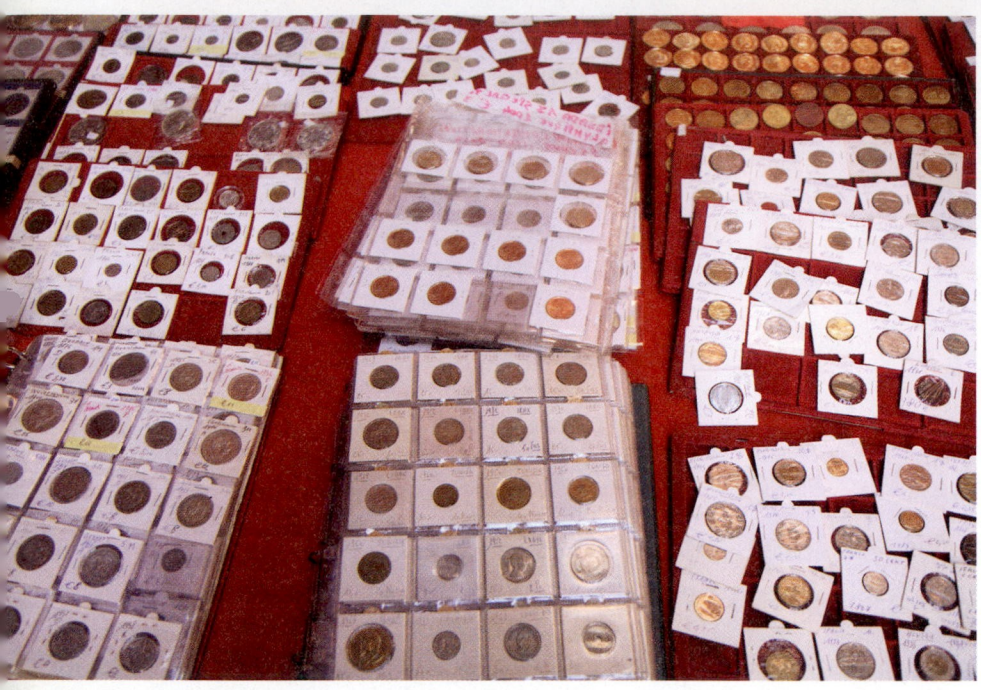

The warrantless search of Ted Steven Chimel's home never did turn up the coins police believed he had stolen.

Ted Steven Chimel was not a particularly astute thief. In 1965, before he robbed the coin store for which he was ultimately arrested and convicted, Chimel committed several incriminating blunders.[1] He approached the owner of the coin store, told him he was planning a big robbery, and questioned him about his alarm system, his insurance coverage, and the location of the most valuable coins. After the burglary, he called the owner and accused him of robbing himself. When the victim suggested to Chimel that the crime had been sloppy, Chimel argued that it had been "real professional." On the night of the burglary, Chimel told friends that he "was going to knock over a place" and that "a coin shop was all set."[2]

One afternoon shortly thereafter, three police officers arrived at Chimel's Santa Ana, California, home with a warrant authorizing his arrest for the burglary of the coin shop. The officers knocked at the door and identified themselves to Chimel's wife, who let them inside. They waited in the house until Chimel returned from work. When he arrived, the officers handed him the arrest warrant and asked if they could "look around." He objected,

but the officers said that although no search warrant had been issued, they could conduct a search on the basis of the lawful arrest.[3]

With Chimel's wife, the police officers searched the entire three-bedroom house. They requested that she open drawers in the master bedroom and sewing room and physically move their contents so that the officers might see any items that would have come from the burglary. In the process, the officers seized a variety of items, including a number of coins. At Chimel's trial on two counts of burglary, the coins were admitted into evidence against him in spite of his objections that they had been illegally seized. Chimel was convicted, and the judgment was later upheld by the California Supreme Court.[4]

On appeal to the U.S. Supreme Court, however, Chimel's conviction was reversed. The court found that when an arrest is made, it is reasonable for the arresting officer to search the person arrested to remove any weapons the person might use to resist arrest or escape. Additionally, the court found that it is reasonable for the arresting officer to search and seize any evidence held by the person being arrested in order to prevent its concealment or destruction. This includes the area into which an arrestee has access in order to grab a weapon or other evidence. A weapon located near the arrestee can be as threatening to the officer as one hidden in the individual's clothing or effects. However, the court found that the broader search of the entire Chimel home could not be justified.[5]

Under the United States Constitution, law enforcement officials are given certain powers to regulate behavior and enforce order. These powers can be divided into two general areas: investigative powers and arrest powers, both of which the police invoked in the *Chimel* case. Police *investigative powers* include, but are not necessarily limited to, the following:

- the power to stop
- the power to frisk
- the power to order someone out of a car
- the power to question
- the power to detain

Police *arrest powers* include the following:

- the power to use force
- the power to search
- the power to exercise seizure and restraint

Both kinds of powers are rooted in the ability of the government, most commonly the states, to protect citizens and provide for the general welfare of the community. At the same time, however, because the U.S. Constitution was designed to protect each citizen's rights, it placed certain restrictions on the exercise of police powers. But as you can see from the *Chimel* case, the specifics of these powers are not always clearly defined, leaving decisions regarding implementation to the discretion of individual officers who are on the scene. This chapter discusses the legal constraints on these powers and traces their evolution through Supreme Court decisions, focusing on the court's impact on law enforcement practice. We'll begin with search and seizure, two of the police arrest powers.

Officers might approach citizens for a number of reasons, including to offer assistance or to ask questions.

SEARCH AND SEIZURE

The Fourth Amendment is the primary rule guiding the investigative and arrest activities of the police. The first objective of investigation is to determine whether a crime has been committed and, if so, what type of crime it is. Police generally analyze available information to find out whether the elements that constitute violation of criminal codes are present. The next objective is to identify the offender through further intelligence-gathering activities. When these activities are successful, an arrest is made—that is, a suspect is taken into custody.

Beyond the investigation and apprehension aspects of law enforcement, police are responsible for gathering additional evidence, if necessary, and for preserving it so that the prosecution phase of the criminal justice process can be effective. Each of these aspects of police investigation and apprehension is subject to procedural rules dictated by law and constitutional rights. It is when these procedures are called into question that law enforcement practice becomes a matter for judicial review.

At the outset, evidence gathering typically depends on search—the examination or inspection of premises or persons with a view to discovering stolen or illicit property or evidence of guilt to be used in the prosecution of a criminal action. Associated with search is seizure—the taking of a person or property into custody in consequence of a violation of public law. **Search and seizure,** then, involves means for the detection and accusation of crime. It entails the search for and the taking of persons and property as evidence of crime.

The very language of the Fourth Amendment, however, prohibits "unreasonable searches and seizures."[6] Unreasonableness, in the constitutional sense, is an ambiguous term. In general, however, it refers to that which is extreme, arbitrary, capricious, and overall, not justified by the apparent facts and circumstances. In the following sections, we examine these concepts in more detail, paying particular attention to their legal and judicial interpretation as they relate to police behavior.

Search Warrants

Search warrants sanction the use of police search powers by giving them the formal authority of the law. A **search warrant** is a written order, issued by a magistrate or judge and directed to a law enforcement officer, commanding search of specified premises for stolen or unlawful goods or for suspects or fugitives and the bringing of these, if found, before a judge. We return to the subject of judges and magistrates in Chapter 8, where we cover the structure and functions of American courts.

The U.S. Supreme Court has repeatedly ruled that the Fourth Amendment indicates a preference for searches conducted pursuant to a warrant. Past Supreme Court cases have stressed the importance of maintaining an incentive for police officers to obtain search warrants whenever possible. The court has encouraged law enforcement officials to seek warrants whenever possible specifically because their issuance affords the additional scrutiny of a judge or magistrate.

P23

THE STATE OF TEXAS §

§ SEARCH WARRANT

COUNTY OF HARRIS §

TO THE SHERIFF OR ANY PEACE OFFICER OF HARRIS COUNTY, TEXAS

GREETINGS:

WHEREAS, I am a District Court Judge in and for Harris County, Texas, and WHEREAS, E.G. Chance, a peace officer employed by the Houston Police Department Narcotics Division, hereafter called Affiant, came before me this day with a sworn affidavit (which is attached hereto and is specifically incorporated by reference for all purposes along with the sworn affidavit of LAPD Officer Orlando Martinez), requesting a search warrant; and WHEREAS I have made inquiry of the basis of said beliefs of the Affiant and find that; the affidavit sets forth substantial facts establishing that probable cause does exist for the issuance of a search warrant, that the person, place or thing to be searched and seized is not one which is prohibited nor beyond the authorization of this magistrate, and that the search is requested upon proper grounds.

THEREFORE, YOU ARE COMMANDED to search a self storage unit at **2100 W. 18th Street, Unit #337, in Houston, Harris County, Texas**, and search for, seize and examine all items including but not limited to, billing records, medication orders, transport receipts, billing receipts, medical records and computerized medical records, for implements and instruments used in the commission of a crime and for property or items constituting evidence of the offense of manslaughter that tend to show that Dr. Conrad Murray committed the said criminal offense.

It is Ordered that any items recovered may be removed from Harris County, where it was seized to any county in the State of California;

HEREIN FAIL NOT, as the peace officer to whom this warrant is delivered, you shall execute it without delay and within three whole days and due return make by faithfully completing the form attached hereto designated for said purpose.

SIGNED, ENTERED and ORDERED this the 22nd day of July, 2009, at ___ o'clock _.m., to attest to which I subscribe my name.

Hon. Judge _____
District Court
Harris County, Texas

RECORDER'S MEMORANDUM
This instrument is of poor quality at the time of imaging

BY _____
CRIMINAL CUSTOMER SERVICE
2009 JUL 23 PM 2:47

Search warrants, like the one pictured here, are issued by the court to authorize the search of a person or private property. They must include specific information about the items to be seized.

Probable Cause

Warrants authorizing a search must pass the constitutional test of reasonableness. In the language of the Fourth Amendment, "no warrants shall issue, but upon probable cause."[7] **Probable cause,** as defined through the development of judicial case law on this matter, refers to facts or apparent facts that are reliable and generate a reasonable belief that a crime has been committed. In the absence of such facts, the probable cause element has not been met, and the validity of the warrant can be questioned. And, according to case law, while probable cause "means less than evidence which would justify condemnation,"[8] it does require "belief that the law was being violated on the premises to be searched; and the facts are such that a reasonably discreet and prudent man would be led to believe that there was a commission of the offense charged."[9] In the most basic terms, probable cause means there is a reasonable belief that a crime has been committed. The definition of probable cause continues to evolve as cases make their way to the Supreme Court and are reviewed in reference to constitutional issues related to police investigation and procedure.

Establishing probable cause for the issuance of a search warrant is a matter that the Supreme Court has addressed at length. As a result of *Aguilar v. Texas* in 1964 and *Spinelli v. United States* in 1969,[10] the general rule was that probable cause for search could not be based solely on hearsay information received by the police. Rather, a valid warrant had to contain a statement that the police had reasonable cause to believe that property of a certain kind might be found "in or upon a designated or described place, vehicle, or person," combined with "allegations of fact" supporting such a statement.[11] The High Court's ruling in *Illinois v. Gates* in 1983,[12] however, eliminated the *Aguilar-Spinelli* test, replacing it with a "totality of circumstances" analysis. *Gates* required magistrates to simply make a practical, commonsense decision as to whether, given all the circumstances set forth in an affidavit (a written sworn statement), there was a fair probability that contraband would be found in a particular place.

Moreover, *Gates* indicated that the provisions that determine the validity and legality of search warrants also apply to arrest warrants. In other words, if there is no warrant, the legality of an arrest can be more easily questioned. Under common law, an arrest could not be made without a warrant, but if the felony or breach of the peace occurred within the view of an officer who was authorized to make an arrest, the officer had a duty to arrest without a warrant. This common law rule of arrest is not at odds with constitutional guarantees; however, it tends to be vague, leaving much to the interpretation of the individual officer. Even in more definitive statements of this rule in criminal procedure codes, it is the officer's responsibility to determine the probable cause for, and hence the potential legality of, an arrest.

DISCRETION MATTERS

Why might vague definitions of probable cause expand the discretionary decisions that law enforcement officers make?

WARRANTLESS SEARCH

The general rule regarding the application of the Fourth Amendment is that any search or seizure undertaken without a valid search warrant is unlawful. Nevertheless, there are exceptions, provided that the arrest, search, and seizure are reasonable. The major exceptions are discussed in the sections that follow.

Search Incident to Lawful Arrest

Traditionally, police were allowed to search without a warrant if they did so in the context of a lawful arrest. Arrests often result in the search of a suspect and the seizure of evidence. In cases when police do not have an arrest warrant, search and seizure, like the arrest itself, occurs without the constitutional review of a judge or magistrate that takes place when a warrant *is* issued. Urgency, or exigent circumstances, complicates the issues. Because of concerns that suspects may dispose of or destroy evidence, the Supreme Court has carved out exceptions that allow officers to conduct

These police officers are about to enter a home to serve a warrant for an arrest and search the property for evidence of a crime. Apprehending suspects and securing evidence are key to the arrest and investigation powers of law enforcement personnel and can be risky for both the officers and suspects.

searches and seize or preserve evidence that will help identify culpable individuals without a warrant.

The crucial role of urgency was affirmed in the 2011 case *Kentucky v. King,* where the justices ruled that police can enter someone's home without a search or arrest warrant if they first knock on the door, identify themselves, and believe that evidence is being destroyed.[13] In the *King* case, officers following a suspect in an unrelated investigation smelled marijuana coming from the King home and banged loudly on the door while announcing their presence. When no one answered but they could hear movement inside, the officers broke down the door and entered without a warrant for either the search or the arrest. They arrested King, his girlfriend, and a guest in the home, but they never found the individual they had initially followed into the apartment complex.

If an arrest is determined to be "unlawful" or "false," the consequence can be significant as the case advances through the criminal justice process. First, evidence seized as an outgrowth of an unlawful arrest may be ruled inadmissible under the long-standing **fruit of the poisonous tree** doctrine. Under this rule, evidence that has been seized illegally is considered "tainted" and cannot be used against a suspect. Subsequent evidence derived from the initially tainted evidence must also be suppressed. Similarly, any resulting conviction may ultimately be overturned. Typically, however, if it is clear in the early stages of the criminal justice process that the arrest was indeed unlawful, the charges against the suspect are often dropped. Moreover, in most jurisdictions, a citizen who has been wrongly taken into custody can institute a civil suit against the officer and the police department that initiated or authorized the arrest (although these suits are seldom won).

Issues associated with wrongful arrest vary greatly from one state to another. Under Tennessee law, for example, numerous court decisions have declared that if "the officer . . . has no right to make an arrest without a warrant, or if his warrant is not valid, he is a trespasser."[14] Under such circumstances, the police officer is liable for money damages. However, where the arrest "would have been proper without a warrant, it is immaterial whether or not the warrant was good or bad."[15]

In Tennessee, Alabama, and numerous other jurisdictions, case law has dictated that every person has a right to resist an unlawful arrest and that "in preventing such illegal restraint of his liberty he may use such force as may be necessary."[16] In Idaho, by contrast, the suspect has no such right.[17] Further, in jurisdictions where resistance to wrongful arrest is lawful, the means or amount of resistance cannot be disproportionate to the effort of the police officer to make the arrest.

Finally, few states place liability for wrongful arrests on police officers if they make the arrest on the basis of a valid warrant or probable cause but a verdict of not guilty is returned. Thus, an acquittal is not tantamount to a finding of no reasonable grounds for arrest.[18] However, in 1986, the Supreme Court ruled in *Malley v. Briggs* that a police officer could be held liable for damages if he or she made an arrest without probable cause—even if he or she had obtained an arrest warrant.[19]

Stop-and-Frisk

Field interrogation, or stop-and-frisk, procedures can be a useful mechanism for police in areas where crime rates or the potential for crime is high. In fact, police commonly stop people whose behavior seems suspicious, detain them briefly by asking them for identification, and frisk (conduct a limited search by running the hands over the outer clothing) those whose answers and/or conduct suggest criminal involvement or threaten police safety.

Before the Supreme Court clarified the legal status of stop-and-frisk procedures in *Terry v. Ohio*,[20] the authority for those procedures came from individual department directives, state judicial policy, police discretionary practices, and legislative statutes. In *Terry,* which was decided in 1968, the Supreme Court held that police officers are not entitled to seize and search every person they see on the streets and every person they want to talk to. Before placing a hand on a citizen in search of anything, the officer must have constitutionally adequate, reasonable grounds for doing so. Let's examine the details of the *Terry* decision to put this in context.

At 2:30 p.m. on October 31, 1963, Cleveland police detective Martin McFadden noticed the activities of two men—Richard Chilton and John Terry—who were conversing at the intersection of two streets in the downtown area. Periodically, one man separated from the other, walked southwest along one of the streets, paused to peer into a particular store window, walked on a short distance, and then turned around and headed back to the corner, pausing once again to look into the same window. The two men then conferred briefly before the second man repeated the process. Detective McFadden saw the men repeat this ritual roughly a dozen times until a third man appeared, spoke with them briefly, and departed. Chilton and Terry resumed their pacing, peering, and conferring for another ten minutes, after which they departed together, following the path taken earlier by the third man.

The police detective was convinced that Chilton and Terry were "casing a job." He followed them, and when they stopped to converse with the third man who had met them earlier on the street corner, he decided to intervene. Detective McFadden

Field interrogations, which can include a pat down, can be useful for police officers in detecting street crime, particularly in high-crime communities. They can also be controversial and questionable in terms of officers' decisions about which individuals to approach.

approached the three men, identified himself as a police officer, and asked for their names. When the men "mumbled something" in response to his inquiries, McFadden spun Terry around so that he was facing the other two men, patted down the outside of his clothing, and felt what he believed to be a pistol. A more thorough search found that it was a .38-caliber revolver, and a frisk of the other two men revealed a revolver in Chilton's overcoat pocket. All three suspects were taken to the police station, where Chilton and Terry were formally charged with carrying concealed weapons.

In *Terry v. Ohio*, the prosecution argued that the guns had been "seized" in a "search" incident to a lawful arrest. The defense, however, maintained that Detective McFadden had no probable cause for arrest and that the guns ought to be suppressed as evidence obtained through illegal search and seizure. Not surprisingly, the court recognized that McFadden's search was *not* incident to a lawful arrest, for he had made no arrest prior to the search; rather, the court viewed it as a case of stop-and-frisk. In fact, in the court's opinion, it "would be stretching the facts beyond reasonable comprehension" to find that the officer had probable cause to arrest the three men for attempted robbery *before* he patted them down for weapons.[21] Nonetheless, the Ohio trial court did rule that Detective McFadden's method of obtaining the evidence had been lawful: He had a duty to investigate the observed suspicious activity and had an absolute right to protect himself by frisking for weapons.

Chilton and Terry were both convicted of the weapons charge, and Terry was sentenced to a term of one to three years in the state penitentiary. Two appellate courts in Ohio upheld Terry's conviction, and the U.S. Supreme Court granted *certiorari* (review) in 1967 in order to consider a number of questions concerning the constitutional validity of the stop-and-frisk practice. Showing rare solidarity, the High Court decided by an 8–1 margin to uphold a police officer's right to frisk and seize weapons under such circumstances. The court ruled that Detective McFadden had reasonable grounds to believe that the suspects were armed and dangerous, that swift measures were necessary to protect himself and others, and that his frisk was appropriately limited to a patting down of the outer clothing until he felt weapons. Nevertheless, the Supreme Court articulated a general concern over police–citizen street encounters. Delivering the opinion of the court on this issue, Chief Justice Earl Warren stated the following:

> Our first task is to establish at what point in this encounter the Fourth Amendment becomes relevant. That is, we must decide whether and when Officer McFadden "seized" Terry and whether and when he conducted a "search." There is some suggestion in the use of such terms as "stop" and "frisk" that such police conduct is outside the purview of the Fourth Amendment because neither action rises to the level of a "search" or "seizure" within the meaning of the Constitution. We emphatically reject this notion. It is quite plain that the Fourth Amendment governs "seizures" of the person which do not eventuate in a trip to the station house and prosecution for crime—"arrests" in traditional terminology. It must be recognized that whenever a police officer accosts an individual and restrains his freedom to walk away, he has "seized" that person. And it is nothing less than sheer torture of the English language to suggest that a careful exploration of the outer surfaces of a person's clothing all over his or her body in an attempt to find weapons is not a "search." Moreover, it is simply fantastic to urge that such a procedure performed in public by a policeman while the citizen stands helpless, perhaps facing a wall with his hands raised, is a "petty indignity." It is a serious intrusion upon the sanctity of the person, which may inflict great indignity and arouse strong resentment, and it is not to be undertaken lightly.[22]

With these concerns in mind, Chief Justice Warren emphasized that a frisk must be a limited search of the outer clothing in an attempt to discover weapons and that the scope of any frisk or search associated with stop-and-frisk procedures must be limited by the circumstances of the particular encounter.

According to Chief Justice Warren, five conditions—all of which must be met—justify a stop-and-frisk action:

1. Where a police officer observes unusual conduct that leads him reasonably to conclude, in light of his experience, that criminal activity may be afoot
2. Where the person with whom he is dealing may be armed and dangerous
3. Where in the course of investigating this behavior he identifies himself as a police officer
4. Where he makes reasonable inquiry
5. Where nothing in the initial stages of the encounter serves to dispel his reasonable fear for his own or others' safety[23]

Related to search and seizure issues in both *Terry* and the poisonous tree doctrine discussed earlier is the 1991 case of *California v. Hodari D.,*[24] which was precipitated to a great extent by the war on drugs. Two officers on a routine drug patrol in a high-crime Oakland neighborhood spotted a group of youths, who fled when they saw the police approaching. The officers had *not* seen anything illegal happening, yet they knew that drug sales were common in the area. One of the officers chased Hodari D., a 16-year-old, and saw him toss away a small rock that the officer believed to be crack cocaine. At that point, the officer tackled and restrained Hodari and retrieved the "rock" (which was indeed crack cocaine). The California court of appeals ruled that Hodari had been "seized" when he saw the officer running toward him and that such a seizure was unreasonable under the Fourth Amendment. As such, the crack was the *fruit* of an illegal seizure. The U.S. Supreme Court reversed this decision, however, arguing that the police chase was not a "seizure" but a "show of force" that is not limited by the Constitution.[25] The seizure did not occur until the officer tackled Hodari, but by that time the officer's observance of the discarded rock represented the necessary probable cause.

In 1993, the U.S. Supreme Court significantly expanded the power of police to seize property from a suspect undergoing a *Terry*-type frisk. The original purpose of *Terry* was to allow police to conduct pat-down searches for weapons when confronting suspicious individuals. In *Minnesota v. Dickerson,*[26] however, the officer conducting the frisk admitted that he did not feel anything resembling a weapon but did feel a "small lump" in the suspect's jacket pocket. He reached into the pocket and pulled out a small packet of cocaine. The Minnesota Supreme Court ruled that the cocaine could not be admitted as evidence, holding that although the stop-and-frisk procedure was permissible under *Terry,* the seizure of the cocaine went beyond the search for a weapon and thus violated the Fourth Amendment.

The U.S. Supreme Court agreed that the cocaine must be suppressed, but it disagreed with the narrow scope of the Minnesota court's decision. The High Court created what is now known as the "plain feel" doctrine;[27] that is, when police officers conduct *Terry*-type searches for weapons, they are free to seize items detected through their sense of touch, as long as the plain feel makes it "immediately apparent" that the item is contraband. Interestingly, however, since the officer in the *Dickerson* case conceded that he did not instantly recognize the lump as drugs, the plain feel did not apply, and the cocaine was not admissible as evidence in Dickerson's trial.

Situations similar to those in *Hodari D.* and *Dickerson* are not uncommon in contemporary police work, and those who work in the law enforcement field seem to generally agree that they have good reason to be suspicious of a person who runs away from the mere sight of a police officer. The Supreme Court addressed this issue in 2000, based on an incident that occurred in 1995 in a Chicago neighborhood where drug sales were known to occur. As four police cars on patrol approached the sidewalk where Sam Wardlow was standing, he turned and ran down an alley. Two officers pursued and apprehended Wardlow and, in a pat-down search, felt a gun in a bag he was carrying under his arm. After Wardlow's conviction for the unlawful use of a weapon by a felon, the Illinois Supreme Court held that the search violated the

DISCRETION MATTERS
Did the police have probable cause to search Hodari based solely on the fact that he ran away?

Fourth Amendment in that "flight upon the approach of a police officer may simply reflect the exercise—at top speed—of a person's constitutional right to move on."[28] However, the Supreme Court ruled in *Illinois v. Wardlow* that flight at the mere sight of a police officer could often, in the context of other factors, be suspicious enough to justify police in conducting a stop-and-frisk. The majority opinion in the case explained that Wardlow's presence in an area known for heavy narcotics trafficking, combined with the unprovoked flight, justified the *Terry* stop and search.[29]

Automobile Searches

As early as 1925, the Supreme Court ruled that because of the extreme mobility of motor vehicles, warrantless searches of vehicles can be justified in certain situations. In a 1925 case, *Carroll v. United States*,[30] George Carroll was convicted of transporting liquor for sale, in violation of the federal prohibition law and the Eighteenth Amendment. The contraband liquor that was used as evidence against him had been taken from his car by government agents acting without a search warrant. The Supreme Court sustained Carroll's conviction, despite his contention that the seizure violated his Fourth Amendment rights. The court determined that the officers had probable cause for the search.

Known as the **Carroll doctrine,** the court's decision maintained that an automobile or other vehicle may, upon probable cause, be searched without a warrant even though there might be enough time to obtain a warrant. Subsequent rulings clarified the scope of this doctrine. In 1931, the Supreme Court upheld the search of a parked car as reasonable, since the police could not know when the suspect might move the car.[31] The Carroll doctrine was reaffirmed in 1970, when the Supreme Court held that it was lawful to conduct a warrantless search of an automobile that resulted in the seizure of weapons and other evidence, even though the search was conducted at a police station many hours after the arrests of the suspects.[32]

A related issue is how *extensive* the search of an automobile may be in the absence of a warrant. In *United States v. Ross*,[33] decided in 1982, the Supreme Court held that when police have probable cause, they may search an entire vehicle, including containers and packages that may conceal the items sought. A year earlier, in *New York v. Belton,* the court examined the scope of a vehicle search incident to an arrest.[34] Two principles were established. First, after making a custodial arrest, police officers may

Searches of automobiles and other vehicles pose particular concerns for law enforcement officers because of mobility and the potential for the destruction of evidence.

search the entire passenger compartment of the vehicle in conjunction with that arrest. Second, if any containers are found during the course of the search, they may be opened and searched. In effect, this decision seemed to impose no limits on the scope of a search of a vehicle's passenger compartment. And in *California v. Acevedo*,[35] decided in 1991, the Supreme Court expanded this idea, permitting police to open and search a closed container found in a car, without a warrant, if they have probable cause to believe that the container contains contraband or evidence of a crime.

As a final point here, in 1998 the Supreme Court put a major restriction on police traffic-stop searches. In *Knowles v. Iowa*,[36] the court unanimously held that issuing a speeding ticket does not automatically give the police the authority to search the car. This point was further confirmed in a 2009 case, *Arizona v. Gant*, when the court held that the Fourth Amendment requires police officers to demonstrate an actual and continuing threat to their safety posed by the arrestee or the need to preserve evidence related to the crime in order to conduct a warrantless vehicular search incident to arrest. Once the vehicle occupants have been arrested and secured, law enforcement must justify this continued warrantless search.[37]

Related to automobile searches is the random stopping of cars, with the searches and arrests that may result. Known as *spot checks*, police have often performed random stops of automobiles to check drivers' licenses and vehicle registrations as a form of proactive police patrol. Spot checks can aid in the apprehension of criminals; however, they also entail potential dangers and can lend themselves to discriminatory enforcement procedures.

The Supreme Court has taken a strong stand against random spot checks, as indicated in the case of *Delaware v. Prouse*.[38] On November 30, 1976, a Delaware police officer stopped the automobile in which William J. Prouse was riding. The car belonged to Prouse, but he was not the driver. As the officer approached the vehicle, he smelled marijuana smoke, and when he came to the window, he observed marijuana on the floor of the automobile. Prouse was arrested and later indicted for illegal possession of the drug.[39]

At a hearing on Prouse's motion to forbid the use of the marijuana as evidence, the police officer characterized the stopping of the car as "routine," explaining that "I saw the car in the area and was not answering any complaints so I decided to pull them off." He further indicated that before stopping the vehicle he had not observed any traffic or equipment violations, nor was he acting in accordance with directives regarding spot checks of automobiles.

After the hearing, the trial court ruled that the stop and detention had been wholly capricious and therefore violated Prouse's Fourth Amendment rights. When the prosecution appealed the case, the Delaware Supreme Court ruled in favor of Prouse, and the case went to the U.S. Supreme Court. The Supreme Court agreed to hear the case in an effort to resolve the conflict between the Delaware Supreme Court's decision (along with similar decisions in five other jurisdictions) and decisions in six other jurisdictions holding that the Fourth Amendment does *not* prohibit random spot checks.

Ultimately, the Supreme Court ruled that random spot checks do violate constitutional rights. However, it did not preclude states from devising methods for spot-checking drivers' credentials in a way that does not involve police discretion, such as roadblock inspections in which all motorists are stopped. Since *Prouse*, a number of states have established roadblock-type stops, primarily for combating drunk driving. Although several state supreme courts (including Oregon and Louisiana) have held that these "sobriety checkpoints" violate their state constitutions' prohibition of unreasonable search and seizure, the Supreme Court ruling in a 1990 case, *Michigan Department of State Police v. Stiz*, upheld the procedure.[40]

In 2000, however, the Supreme Court ruled against the use of roadblocks set up to search for drugs. In *Indianapolis v. Edmond*,[41] the justices held that police checkpoints designed to catch drug traffickers or others engaged in general criminal activity infringe on the Fourth Amendment protection against illegal search and seizure. The High Court distinguished the antidrug roadblocks from the previously upheld checkpoints for illegal immigrants or drunken drivers, noting that the latter are aimed at protecting U.S. borders and reducing immediate hazards on the road. The ruling in *Edmond* would not affect such checkpoints but would quash new attempts to erect roadblocks aimed wholesale at criminal activity. Later, however, in the 2004 case of *Illinois v. Lidster,*[42] the High Court endorsed the use of police roadblocks as an investigational tool for finding witnesses to recent crimes.

While it might appear from a shallow analysis that the court has difficulties making up its mind about what does and does not constitute appropriate search and seizure, the court, in fact, is charged with evaluating case circumstances and characteristics of the incidents individually. Because each case is so very different, the court must reach a decision about the appropriateness of police action based on those specific circumstances. New decisions address these variations and attempt to clarify how police should behave in accordance with the Constitution, as well as federal and state law. In addition, as our society grows and technology develops, our perspectives and political climate change, and the court's decisions reflect such changes in turn.

Fresh Pursuit

A fourth circumstance in which warrantless arrest and search is permissible involves situations of fresh pursuit (or "hot" pursuit)—a situation in which a law enforcement officer engages in a chase for the purpose of preventing the escape or effecting the arrest of any person who is suspected of committing a crime. The pursuit cannot be delayed substantially but need not be immediate. Fresh pursuit can also refer to the pursuit of suspects in vehicles. In common law, fresh pursuit referred to the pursuit of a person for the purpose of arrest when the pursuit continued without substantial delay from the time of the commission or discovery of an offense. Thus, fresh pursuit involved following a fleeing suspect who was attempting to avoid capture.

In contemporary statutes, the notion of fresh pursuit has been broadened considerably. In Tennessee, for example, the law reads as follows:

> Fresh pursuit includes fresh pursuit as defined by the common law, and also the pursuit of a person who has committed a felony or who is reasonably

Police use of high-speed chase, particularly within populated areas, remains controversial.

suspected of having committed a felony. It also includes the pursuit of a person suspected of having committed a supposed felony, though no felony has actually been committed, if there is reasonable ground for believing that a felony has been committed. "Fresh pursuit" does not necessarily imply instant pursuit, but pursuit without unreasonable delay. [43]

Although most state statutes permit hot pursuit—or the fresh pursuit—of suspects in vehicles, the practice of high-speed automobile chases has been controversial in past years. The National Highway Traffic Safety Administration has estimated that police officers initiate more than 100,000 high-speed chases each year, 20 percent of which end in accidents, with hundreds of deaths. [44] The vast majority of those who die are fleeing the police, but some are innocent bystanders who simply get in the way. Police departments have responded with new regulations and training initiatives, and the courts and researchers are also examining the matter. Ultimately, the issue is a matter of police discretion, with individual officers having to balance the demands of enforcing the law and apprehending offenders with the risks to public safety. [45]

> **DISCRETION MATTERS**
>
> What characteristics of offenders or offenses might factor into a police officer's decision to engage in a high-speed pursuit?

Consent Searches

The fifth basis for warrantless searches occurs when the person in control of the area or object consents to the search. However, consent searches often give rise to problematic legal issues, since consent waives the person's right to the Fourth Amendment protection against unreasonable search and seizure. Thus, in a consent search, neither probable cause nor a search warrant is required, but when evidence obtained through such a search is used, the burden of proving consent becomes the responsibility of the prosecution. The issues involved are (1) who can give consent to search what, (2) what constitutes free and voluntary consent, and (3) whether there is a principle of limited consent.

Ordinarily, courts are unwilling to accept the idea that a defendant waived his or her Fourth Amendment right, and they require the state to prove that the consent was given explicitly and voluntarily. In *Wren v. United States,* [46] the U.S. court of appeals ruled that consent is indeed "voluntary" when the search is expressly agreed on or expressly invited by the person whose right is involved. The case of *United States v. Matlock* expanded the range of voluntary consent to third parties who possess joint authority with the defendant over the property or premises to be searched. [47] Another case, *Bumper v. North Carolina,* [48] addressed the issue of coercion by law enforcement officers as well as the involvement of a third party. The police had obtained the consent of the defendant's grandmother to search her house in connection with a crime the defendant was suspected of committing. But the officers had incorrectly informed her that they had a lawful search warrant, and it was on that basis that she had consented. The Supreme Court ruled that her consent was not constitutionally valid. Finally, in *Schneckloth v. Bustamonte,* [49] the Supreme Court ruled that police officers are not required to inform individuals that they do not have to give consent.

Although the rulings in *Wren, Matlock,* and *Schneckloth* give police wide discretion in carrying out consent searches, the Supreme Court has also ruled that voluntary consents are to some degree limited. For example, a search based on voluntary consent must be limited to those items connected to the crime that triggered the desire to search and to other items clearly connected to that crime. [50] By contrast, in 1991 the Supreme Court expanded the scope of consent in two cases. In *Florida v. Jimeno,* [51] the court held that a consent to search an automobile automatically includes a consent to search any closed containers found therein. In *Florida v. Bostick,* [52] the court delved further into the issues of warrantless searches, warrantless seizures, and the workings of consent. The details of this case, presented in the opening of Chapter 5, highlight these complex issues in the context of drug investigations. Cases like these and others have broadened the police powers of search and seizure and increased the use of discretion as officers attempt to reduce drug use and trafficking.

Other Warrantless Searches

In addition to lawful arrests, stop-and-frisks, automobile searches, fresh pursuit, and consent searches, the search warrant requirement has been waived in other types of situations. These include the following:

- *Private searches:* As early as 1921, the Supreme Court ruled in *Burdeau v. McDowell*[53] that the Fourth Amendment protects individuals only against searches and seizures by governmental agents, not against such actions carried out by private individuals who are not acting in concert with law enforcement authorities. An example would be a dry cleaner who finds drugs in a customer's coat and then turns them over to the police. Actions will be analyzed to see if the private person conducted the search for his or her own purposes and whether the police initiated, encouraged, or participated in the search.

- *Border searches:* Although a series of rulings in the mid-1970s made it clear that warrantless searches of persons entering the United States at its borders violate the Fourth Amendment guarantee, *United States v. Martinez-Fuerte*[54] in 1976 established that border patrol officers need not have probable cause or a warrant before stopping cars for brief questioning at fixed checkpoints.

- *Inventory searches:* In 1976, the Supreme Court established an inventory-search exception to the warrant rule. It held that when police have custody of a lawfully impounded automobile, they do not need a warrant or the owner's consent before routinely inventorying items left in plain view or in the glove compartment.[55] Also of importance is *Illinois v. Lafayette,*[56] which was decided by the Supreme Court in 1983. In this decision the court upheld a police inventory search of an arrestee's shoulder bag, which revealed illicit drugs. The court stated that such searches serve important goals—protecting the suspect's property, deterring false claims of theft, and the like—and do not require a warrant or probable cause, so long as the inventory search is part of a regular and routine police procedure.

- *Electronic eavesdropping:* In response to the 1967 case of *Katz v. United States,*[57] in which the Supreme Court ruled that conversations intercepted through warrantless electronic eavesdropping violated the Fourth Amendment, Congress passed the Omnibus Crime Control and Safe Streets Act of 1968, which included a provision involving electronic surveillance. The act authorized the federal use of wiretaps and other eavesdropping devices through the issuance of warrants that can be approved only by the attorney general of the United States or his or her designated assistant. This area of law has grown increasingly complicated in the years since, as digital communications, including e-mails, texts, and cell phone calls, have proliferated and are easily accessed by third-party individuals, including police.

- *Abandoned property:* In the 1960 case of *Abel v. United States,*[58] the Supreme Court spelled out an "abandoned property exception" to the warrant rule. A hotel manager gave an FBI agent permission to search a room that had been occupied by Abel. During the search, incriminating evidence was found in a wastepaper basket. The court held that once Abel vacated the room, the hotel had exclusive right to its possession and could freely consent to a search.

- *Expectation of privacy:* After learning from an informant that Billy Greenwood of Laguna Beach, California, might be dealing in drugs, and after observing a parade of cars making brief nocturnal stops at Greenwood's home, the police asked the local refuse collector to give them the trash bags from Greenwood's house. A search of the garbage uncovered a large amount of drug paraphernalia, including razor blades, straws containing cocaine residue, and phone bills listing calls to people with records of drug law violations. The police obtained a warrant to search the house, found hashish and cocaine inside, and arrested Greenwood. Two California courts ruled that the search of Greenwood's garbage violated the

Fourth Amendment ban against unreasonable search and seizure. However, in the case of *California v. Greenwood,*[59] decided in 1988, the Supreme Court ruled against Greenwood, stating that in this instance Greenwood could have no expectation of privacy because he had discarded the items, thus giving the police broad power to search trash.

- *Open fields:* As early as 1924, in *Hester v. United States,*[60] the Supreme Court declared that police officers may enter and search a field without a warrant. In *Oliver v. United States* (and the companion case of *Maine v. Thornton*),[61] decided in 1984, the court went further, holding that fences and No Trespassing signs provide no reasonable expectation of privacy to owners of properties large enough to include areas that extend beyond the curtilage of houses or other buildings. *Curtilage* refers to the land around a home and the expectation that the homeowner will have some degree of privacy within that boundary. As such, the decision in *Oliver* assured police that even if they enter such property beyond the curtilage by going over fences or ignoring No Trespassing signs in violation of state law, any evidence they discover on the property is nevertheless admissible at trial.

Search and seizure of evidence is vital to police investigations, apprehension of suspects, and successful prosecution of offenders—and it is an area of law that continues to pose important questions for citizens and police. While this section has focused on overt searches of private property and individuals, important legal questions also surround evidence that is out in the open. Should officers have to acquire a warrant in order to seize items they can plainly see? In the next section, we turn to this topic.

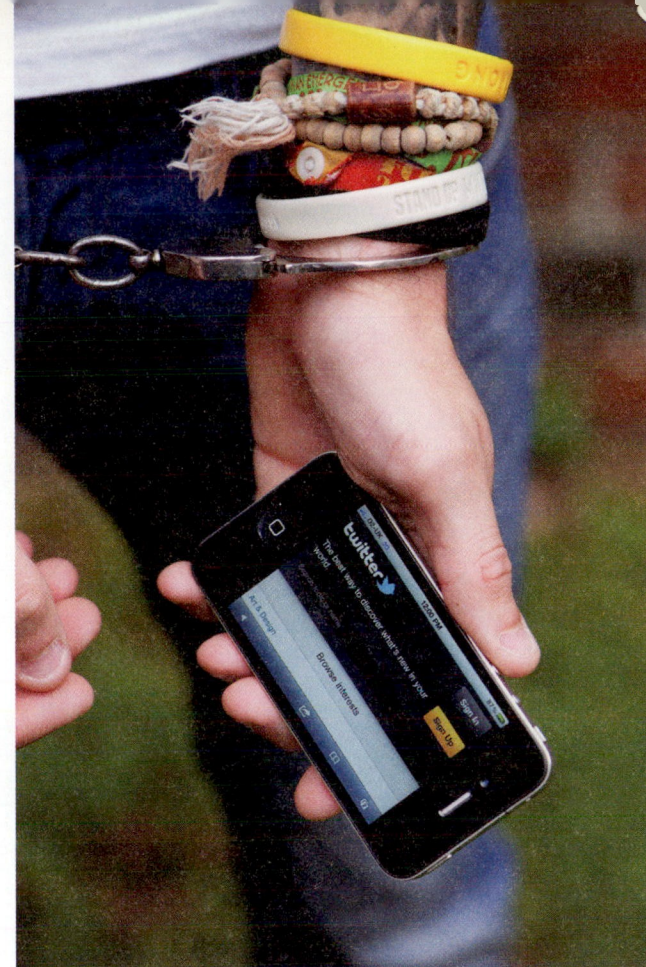

Recent state-level cases have allowed the examination of suspects' cell phones to retrieve evidence of criminal activity.

THE PLAIN VIEW DOCTRINE— THE SEARCH THAT ISN'T

Pertinent to this discussion of warrantless search and seizure is the **plain view doctrine.** Plain view typically refers to anything in the view of the police officer. In *Harris v. United States* (1968),[62] the Supreme Court established that anything a police officer sees in plain view, when the officer has a right to be where he or she is, is not the product of a search and is therefore admissible as evidence. James E. Harris's automobile had been observed leaving the scene of a robbery in Washington, DC. The vehicle was traced, and Harris was later arrested near his home as he was getting into his car. The arresting officer made a quick inspection of the car and then took the suspect to the police station. After some discussion, a decision was made to impound the car as evidence. Harris's vehicle was towed to the station house about 90 minutes after the arrest, arriving there with its doors unlocked and its windows open. Then it began to rain.

According to police procedures in the District of Columbia, the arresting officer is required to thoroughly search an impounded vehicle, remove any valuables, prepare a written inventory, and submit a report on the impounding. The officer conducted the search and tied a property tag to the steering wheel. He then began to close up and lock the auto. When he opened the front door on the passenger side so that he could roll up the window, he saw a registration card lying face up on the metal stripping over which the door closes. The card, which was in "plain view," belonged to the victim of the robbery.

Harris claimed that the registration card could not be used as evidence because it was not seized at the time of his arrest. In the Supreme Court's opinion, however, the observation of the card had not resulted from a search; rather, it stemmed from efforts to protect the vehicle while in police custody. The seizure was therefore lawful.

Anything an officer can see in plain view is open for use as evidence against the suspect. The gun in this photo is clearly visible, and the officer can therefore collect it as evidence.

Under the **protective sweep doctrine,** which has been the subject of numerous court cases, the scope of plain view has been expanded considerably. The protective sweep doctrine suggests that when law enforcement officers make an arrest on or outside private premises, they may, despite the absence of a search warrant, examine the entire premises for other persons whose presence could pose a threat either to the officers' safety or to the protection of evidence that could be removed or destroyed. Moreover, protective sweep procedures may be initiated even if police only suspect that other such persons are present on the premises, and they may lawfully seize any evidence that is in plain view during the search, or sweep.[63]

THE EXCLUSIONARY RULE: IMPORTANT CASES AND CONCEPTS

In 1914, the U.S. Supreme Court announced its well-known and highly controversial **exclusionary rule,** prohibiting the use of evidence seized by federal agents if they violated the Fourth Amendment protection against unreasonable search and seizure. The rule was an outgrowth of *Weeks v. United States,*[64] and during the many years since that case, debate has continued over whether the decision is an effective remedy against Fourth Amendment violations by police or a constitutional right with great potential costs to society. The following discussion focuses on cases that will help you understand the implications of this very important area of criminal justice and constitutional law.

Weeks v. United States

In common law proceedings, the admissibility of evidence in criminal trials was unrelated to any illegal actions the police engaged in when securing such evidence. Moreover, the courts, even at the appellate and supreme levels, were not concerned with the legality of the methods used to obtain evidence. If the police obtained the evidence of the crime illegally, they could still use it in court proceedings.

Yet attorneys had long argued on behalf of defendants that any illegally obtained evidence should not be admissible and that establishing a rule to that effect would provide the only deterrent to illegal searches and seizures. Nevertheless, even the Supreme Court adhered to the common law principle, as in *Adams v. New York* (1904),[65] when it ruled that the admissibility of evidence was not affected by the illegality of the means by which it was obtained.

In *Weeks v. United States,*[66] the defendant was arrested at his place of business. The police officer then searched Weeks's house and turned over the articles and papers found there to a U.S. marshal. The marshal, accompanied by police officers, repeated the search of Weeks's home and confiscated other documents and letters. No warrants had been obtained for the arrest or the search. Before his trial, Weeks petitioned the federal district court for the confiscated articles and papers, but the court refused and allowed the materials to be used against him at trial, resulting in his conviction.

On appeal, the Supreme Court ruled in Weeks's favor, thus initiating the exclusionary rule. Speaking for the court, Justice William R. Day explained:

> If letters and private documents can thus be seized and held and used in evidence against a citizen accused of an offense, the protection of the Fourth Amendment, declaring his right to be secure against such searches and seizures, is of no value, and, so far as those thus placed are concerned, might as well be stricken from the Constitution. The efforts of the courts and their officials to bring the guilty to punishment, praiseworthy as they are, are not to be aided by the sacrifice of these great principles established by years of endeavor and suffering which have resulted in their embodiment in the fundamental law of the land.[67]

The decision in *Weeks* quickly became the subject of much legal controversy. By denying prosecutors the use of certain evidence, the rule sometimes caused the collapse of the government's case and the freeing of a defendant against whom there was strong evidence of guilt. Thus in 1931, George W. Wickersham, chairman of the National Commission on Law Observance and Enforcement, commented that the "guarantees as to searches and seizures are often in the way of effective detection."[68] And Benjamin Cardozo (who later became a Supreme Court justice) wrote, "The criminal is to go free because the constable has blundered."[69]

But *Weeks* was only a partial victory for the Fourth Amendment. The exclusionary rule applied only to material obtained in an unconstitutional search and seizure by a *federal* agent in a *federal* case; it did not apply to *state* actions. In addition, *Weeks* made possible the silver platter doctrine, which permitted federal prosecutors to use evidence obtained by state agents through unreasonable search and seizure (handed to them on a "silver platter"), provided that the evidence was obtained without federal participation and was turned over to federal officials.[70] From there, the rule evolved in a significant case—*Mapp v. Ohio.*

Mapp v. Ohio

Nearly half a century after the Supreme Court first announced the exclusionary rule, it fully extended and applied the principle to the states in *Mapp v. Ohio.*[71] Decided in 1961, the *Mapp* case began on May 23, 1957, when three Cleveland police officers arrived at the residence of Dollree ("Dolly") Mapp. They had been informed that a suspect in a recent bombing was hiding out in her home and also that a large amount of gambling paraphernalia was being concealed at the residence. Mapp and her daughter lived on the top floor of the two-family dwelling. When they arrived, the police knocked at the door and demanded entry. After telephoning her attorney, Mapp refused to admit them without a search warrant. The officers advised their headquarters of the situation and began a surveillance of the house.

The *Mapp* case requires officers to specify places to be searched and items to be seized when seeking a warrant to search a suspect's home or business.

When at least four additional officers arrived on the scene some three hours later, the police again sought entry. When Mapp did not come to the door immediately, they forced their way in. Meanwhile, Mapp's attorney arrived, but the police barred him from either seeing his client or entering the house. From the testimony, Mapp was apparently about halfway down the stairs from the second floor when the police broke into the lower hall. She demanded to see the search warrant. One officer held up a paper that he claimed to be a warrant.

Mapp grabbed the alleged warrant and stuffed it into her bra. A struggle ensued, during which the officers removed the paper and at the same time handcuffed her because she was "belligerent" in resisting their official rescue of the warrant paper from her. They then took her forcibly to her bedroom, where they searched a dresser, a chest of drawers, a closet, and some suitcases. They also looked through a photo album and some of Mapp's personal papers. The search then spread to the remainder of the second floor, including the daughter's bedroom, the living room, the kitchen, and the dining area. They also searched the basement and a trunk they found there. They found neither the bombing suspect nor the gambling paraphernalia, but the search did turn up an unspecified amount of pornographic literature.

After the search, Mapp was arrested on a charge of possessing "lewd and lascivious books, pictures, and photographs."[72] She was convicted in an Ohio court on possession of obscene materials. At the trial, no search warrant was produced by the prosecution, nor was the failure to produce one ever explained or accounted for.

The issue in *Mapp*, of course, was the legality of the arrest, search, and seizure. The police had no search warrant and no consent to search, but one could argue, as the prosecution did, that when the police applied force and searched her apartment, Dolly Mapp was indeed under arrest; hence, it was a search incident to arrest. Yet, as the defense pointed out and the facts of the case confirmed, the police had no probable cause to arrest her. The only background the police had was "information that a fugitive was hiding in her home."[73]

It was on the basis of these facts, or rather the lack of them, that the Supreme Court reversed the decision of the Ohio court and extended the exclusionary rule to all the states. The court ruled that the Fourth Amendment is incorporated, by inference, in the due process clause of the Fourteenth Amendment. From then on, any evidence that police obtained illegally would be inadmissible in any and every courtroom in the country.

The *Mapp* decision was controversial, both within and outside the Supreme Court. The day after the decision came out, the *New York Times* referred to *Mapp* as "an historic step," and Harvard Law School dean Erwin Griswold—soon to become solicitor general of the United States—saw the case as requiring "a complete change in the outlook and practices of state and local police."[74] The decision also produced a frantic torrent of complaints from outraged police across the nation, who felt they were being deprived of their legal right to search for and obtain evidence.[75]

The Impact of *Mapp* In 1965, the Supreme Court held in *Linkletter v. Walker*[76] that the *Mapp* decision would not be retroactively applied. In other words, it would not overturn state criminal convictions that occurred before the expansion of the exclusionary rule in 1961. The court stated that the goal of *Mapp* was to deter future unlawful police conduct and thereby carry out the guarantee of the Fourth Amendment against unreasonable searches and seizures. The purpose was to deter, not to redress, the injury to former search victims, and making the rule retroactive would not have any deterrent effect. Despite this decision, for the 26 state jurisdictions that had rejected the exclusionary rule prior to that point, the *Mapp* decision was an explosive one. Not only were police required to suddenly change their search and seizure procedures, but the rule also immediately applied to all cases that were currently under court review.

DISCRETION MATTERS

How might the Supreme Court's decision in *Mapp* affect the way officers apply their discretion in the field?

The Retreat from *Mapp* Throughout the 1960s and into the following decades, dissatisfaction with the *Mapp* rule continued. Members of Congress, the Supreme Court, and the public—fearful that levels of street crime would increase and that criminals would be released into the community based on technicalities—demanded modification, if not outright abolition, of the rule.

The justices who wished to modify *Mapp* thought it had developed into a series of confusing and complicated requirements that puzzled the police more than it restrained them. The Fourth Amendment prohibited unreasonable searches, but the term *unreasonable* had never been fully defined by either the Constitution or the court. Moreover, the Fourth Amendment also required that police obtain a warrant and that a warrant be issued only when "probable cause" was shown. Yet over the years, the court had allowed numerous exceptions to this requirement.

In the spring of 1971,[77] fearing the "death of *Mapp*," and possibly of *Weeks* as well, Justices Brennan and Marshall instructed their clerks not to accept cases involving the Fourth Amendment. The message was that there would be no free shots at the Fourth Amendment; the court would hear only cases involving flagrant police violations, not those intended to "right little wrongs." Nonetheless, a series of cases during the 1970s represented a retreat from *Mapp* by defining various exceptions to the exclusionary rule. These included rulings that exempted the exclusionary rule from the presentation of illegally obtained evidence at grand jury proceedings and removed access to federal review by state prisoners convicted by means of illegal searches and seizures.[78]

A further setback for the exclusionary rule came in 1984 with the Supreme Court's statement of the "good-faith" exception in *United States v. Leon* and *Massachusetts v. Sheppard*,[79] two cases involving defective search warrants. In *Leon*, the police were issued a search warrant based on information from surveillance and an informant. When the case was appealed, the lower court found that the information was problematic and that the search warrant had been issued without probable cause. However, because the police believed the search warrant to be valid, the Supreme Court disagreed with the lower court's decision to exclude the evidence and adopted a good-faith exception to the exclusionary rule. This exception was then applied in the *Sheppard*[80] case, allowing the evidence resulting from the warrants to be admitted at trial and used against the defendants.

Following *Leon,* the Supreme Court added three good-faith exceptions to the exclusionary rule in a series of cases. First, the court made an exception for evidence obtained by police officers who carry out a search under a state law even if the search is later found to be unconstitutional.[81] Second, the court added an "independent-source" exception, holding that evidence discovered by police during a warrantless entry into a warehouse was admissible because they discovered the same evidence in a second search pursuant to a warrant based on information obtained independently of the initial, illegal search.[82] Last, the court extended an exception to situations where police are operating on information that results from errors by third parties, such as clerical errors by courthouse staff.[83] While these concepts are complex, they boil down to the court's attempt to clarify how evidence can be used if police have secondary information about a crime that leads to an additional search.

CONFESSIONS AND THE INVESTIGATION OF CRIME

Confessions, the Supreme Court stated more than a century ago in *Hopt v. Utah*,[84] are "among the most effectual proofs of the law," but they are admissible as evidence only when made voluntarily. This has long been the rule in the federal courts, where the Fifth Amendment clearly applies. A **confession,** whether written or oral (but now usually recorded), is simply a statement by a person admitting to the violation of a law. Within the legal context, confessions are connected to self-incrimination, since one way a person might incriminate himself or herself is through a confession. As such, these aspects of police investigation are examined under the Fifth Amendment. In the *Hopt* case, the court defined as involuntary, or coerced, any confession that "appears to have been made, either in consequence of inducements of a temporal nature . . . or because of a threat or promise . . . which, operating upon the fears or hopes of the accused . . . deprive him of that freedom of will or self-control essential to make his confession voluntary within the meaning of the law."[85]

In 1896, the Supreme Court restated this position, ruling that the circumstances in which a confession was made must be considered in order to determine if the confession was made voluntarily.[86] In the following sections, we examine the cases that helped identify the complex issues surrounding confessions and the impact on law enforcement behaviors used to illicit them.

DISCRETION MATTERS

Why might we be concerned about how officers obtain confessions from suspects?

Twining v. New Jersey

Before *Twining,* the Supreme Court rulings on involuntary confessions did not apply to the states. The court's decision in *Twining v. New Jersey* (1908)[87] specifically emphasized this point. The defendants, Albert C. Twining and David C. Cornell, executives of the Monmouth Safe and Trust Company, were indicted by a grand jury for having knowingly displayed a false paper to a bank examiner "with full intent to deceive him" as to the actual condition of their firm. At trial, Twining and Cornell refused to take the stand. Judge Webber A. Heisley addressed the jury as follows:

Confessions remain one of the most effective means of closing crimes.

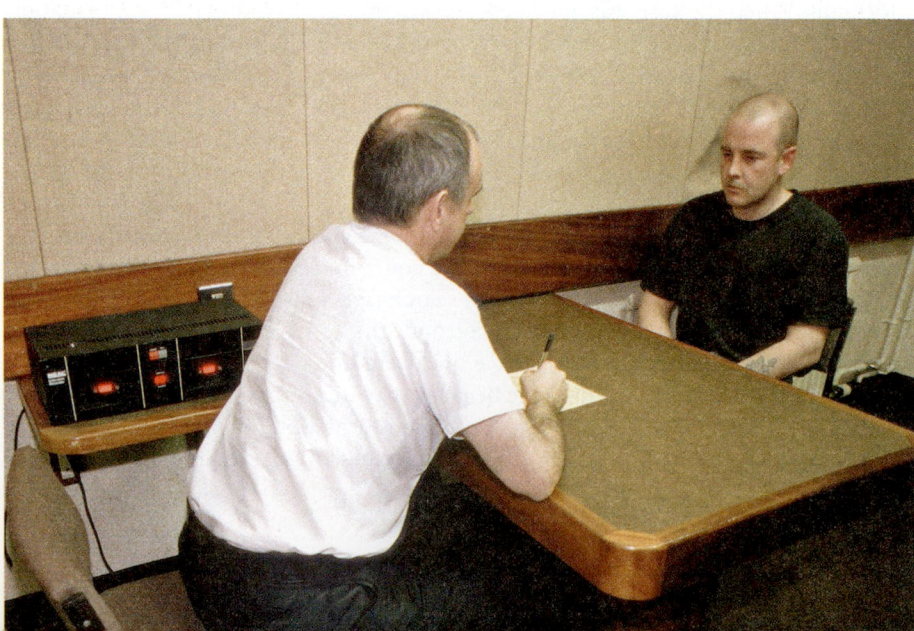

Because a man does not go upon the stand you are not necessarily justified in drawing an inference of guilt. But you have a right to consider the fact that he does not go upon the stand where a direct accusation is made against him.[88]

The jury returned a verdict of guilty, at which point Twining and Cornell appealed to the U.S. Supreme Court. They contended that the exemption from self-incrimination was one of the privileges and immunities that the Fourteenth Amendment forbade the states to abridge. They claimed that the judge's statement amounted to compulsory self-incrimination and therefore constituted a denial of due process. In an 8–1 decision, the court ruled against Twining and Cornell, stating that the privilege against self-incrimination was "not fundamental in due process of law, not an essential part of it."[89]

Twining was not a case of forced confession in the strictest sense of the term, for no confession had actually occurred. But the notion of a potentially involuntary confession was inferred through the judge's instructions to the jury, and the resulting decision was that defendants in state courts do not enjoy the Fifth Amendment privilege against compulsory self-incrimination. While *Twining* specifically withheld the Fifth Amendment privileges from use in state courts, it opened the question of how far police could go in compelling defendants to confess or incriminate themselves, the topic we turn to next.

Brown v. Mississippi

Although more than half a century passed before the Supreme Court specifically applied the Fifth Amendment privilege to the states, the court, through its unanimous decision in *Brown v. Mississippi* (1936),[90] forbade states to use coerced confessions to convict persons of crimes.

The case involved three black men who were arrested for the murder of a white man. At trial, they were convicted solely on the basis of their confessions and sentenced to death. But the police had coerced their confessions. The defendants had been tied to a tree, whipped, twice hanged by a rope, and told that the process would continue until they confessed. And although torture had clearly been used to elicit the confessions, the convictions were affirmed by the Mississippi Supreme Court.

On appeal to the U.S. Supreme Court, Mississippi defended its use of the confessions obtained through beatings and torture by citing the earlier *Twining* ruling that state court defendants do not enjoy the Fifth Amendment privilege against compulsory self-incrimination. The court agreed with *Twining* but rejected the Mississippi defense, holding that the state's right to withdraw the privilege of self-incrimination was not the issue. Speaking for the court, Chief Justice Charles Evans Hughes distinguished between "compulsion" as forbidden by the Fifth Amendment and "compulsion" as forbidden by the Fourteenth Amendment's due process clause:

> The compulsion to which the Fifth Amendment refers is that of the processes of justice by which the accused may be called as a witness and required to testify. Compulsion by torture to extort a confession is a different matter. . . .
>
> Because a state may dispense with a jury trial, it does not follow that it may substitute trial by ordeal. The rack and torture chamber may not be substituted for the witness stand. It would be difficult to conceive of methods more revolting to the sense of justice than those taken to procure the confessions of these petitioners, and the use of the confessions thus obtained as the basis for conviction and sentence was a clear denial of due process.[91]

In the years that followed, the Supreme Court reversed numerous decisions in which confessions had been compelled, examining in each case the totality of circumstances surrounding the arrest and interrogation. The court's philosophy made it clear that coercion could be psychological as well as physical. Justice Felix Frankfurter summarized the issue this way in 1961, stating that methods used to extract involuntary confessions "offend an underlying principle in the enforcement of our criminal law: that ours is an accusatorial and not an inquisitorial system—a system in which the State must establish guilt by evidence independently and freely secured."[92]

Before the 1960s, the Fifth Amendment privilege against self-incrimination and the Sixth Amendment right to counsel were not linked. The *Brown v. Mississippi* decision in 1936 had ruled on the inadmissibility of confessions obtained by physical compulsion. In the 1960s, the Supreme Court, under Chief Justice Earl Warren, issued a series of decisions that linked the provisions of the Fifth and Sixth Amendments and at the same time strengthened defendants' rights. In 1964, the court declared in *Massiah v. United States*[93] that an indicted person could not be properly questioned or otherwise persuaded to make incriminating statements in the absence of his or her attorney. Shortly thereafter, the court's decision in *Malloy v. Hogan* finally extended the privilege against self-incrimination to state defendants.[94] At the same time, it laid the groundwork for the most important decision of the court's 1964 term, *Escobedo v. Illinois*.[95]

Escobedo v. Illinois

On the night of January 19, 1960, Manuel Valtierra, the brother-in-law of 22-year-old Danny Escobedo, was fatally shot in the back. Several hours later, Escobedo was arrested without a warrant and interrogated for some 15 hours. During that period, he made no statements to the police and was released after his attorney had obtained a writ of *habeas corpus* (a court challenge of the suspect's confinement).[96] Eleven days after the shooting of Valtierra, Escobedo was arrested for a second time and again taken to a police station for questioning. Shortly thereafter, Escobedo's attorney arrived at the station, but the police would not permit him to see his client. Both the attorney and Escobedo repeatedly requested to see each other, but both were continually denied the privilege. Escobedo was told that he could not see his attorney until the police had finished their questioning. It was during this second period of interrogation that Escobedo made certain incriminating statements that would be construed as his voluntary confession to the crime.[97]

Danny Escobedo was convicted of murder and sentenced to a 22-year prison term. On appeal to the state supreme court of Illinois, Escobedo maintained that he was told "he would be permitted to go home if he gave the statement and would be granted an immunity from prosecution."[98] The statement in question referred to the complicity of his four codefendants, who had all been arrested on the murder charge. The Illinois Supreme Court reversed Escobedo's conviction, but the state petitioned for, and the court granted, a rehearing of the case. The state supreme court sustained the trial court's original conviction, and Escobedo still faced the 22-year prison term. Escobedo's counsel appealed further, and the U.S. Supreme Court granted *certiorari*.

On June 22, 1964, the Supreme Court ruled in favor of Danny Escobedo by a 5–4 decision. The court noted five pivotal facts in the interrogation that were problematic:

1. The investigation was no longer a general inquiry into an unsolved crime but had begun to focus on a particular suspect.
2. The suspect had been taken into police custody.
3. The police carried out a process of interrogations that lent itself to eliciting incriminating statements.
4. The suspect had requested and been denied an opportunity to consult with his lawyer.
5. The police had not effectively warned him of his absolute constitutional right to remain silent.[99]

Thus, the *Escobedo* decision required that an accused person be permitted to have an attorney present during interrogation. The majority view held that the adversary system of justice had traditionally been restricted to the trial stage but that the same rules should apply to earlier stages of criminal proceedings. It also contended, however, that the *Escobedo* decision need not affect the powers of the police to investigate unsolved crimes. But when "the process shifts from investigatory to accusatory," the court stated, "when its focus is on the accused and its purpose is to elicit a confession, our adversary system begins to operate, and under the circumstances here, the accused must be permitted to consult with his lawyer."[100]

The four dissenting justices were not convinced; they believed that the decision would hamper law enforcement efforts. Across the country, police and prosecutors echoed these feelings. The police practice of interrogating suspects behind closed doors in order to secure confessions was deeply entrenched and based on centuries-old custom and usage. No longer, they feared, would the "third degree" and "good guy–bad guy" interrogation routines be readily available.[101]

Miranda v. Arizona

Escobedo[102] seemed to raise more questions than it answered regarding police conduct during arrest and interrogation. In its discussion of the conditions that existed in Danny Escobedo's interrogation, was the court suggesting that *all* these conditions had to be met for a confession to be admissible as evidence? Were police required to warn suspects of their right to remain silent? If a suspect requested counsel but none was at hand, could a police interrogation continue? If a suspect did not wish counsel, what then? And most important, how were the police to determine when an investigation began to "focus" on a particular suspect?

Given these unsettled issues, by January 1966 two separate U.S. courts of appeals had interpreted *Escobedo* in opposite ways. To resolve the conflict, the U.S. Supreme Court sifted through some 170 confession-related appeals and agreed to hear four cases: *Miranda v. Arizona, Vignera v. New York, Westover v. United States,* and *California v. Stewart.*[103] Known by the leading case, *Miranda,* this set of cases brought together the appeals of four individuals who had been convicted on the basis of confessions made after extended questioning in which they had not been informed of their right to remain silent. In all four cases, the crimes for which the defendants had been convicted involved major felonies—Miranda had been convicted of kidnapping and rape, Vignera of robbery in the first degree, Westover of bank robbery, and Stewart of robbery and first-degree murder. The convictions were reversed by the Supreme Court, and from this decision came the so-called Miranda warnings, which a police officer must state to a suspect before any questioning occurs:

1. "You have a right to remain silent."
2. "Anything you say can and will be used against you in a court of law."
3. "You have a right to consult with a lawyer and to have the lawyer present during any questioning."
4. "If you cannot afford a lawyer, one will be obtained for you if you so desire."

The reactions to *Miranda,* even within the Supreme Court, were immediate. Four justices prepared a dissenting opinion, and the *New York Times* reported that Justice Harlan, his face flushed and his voice occasionally faltering with emotion, denounced the decision from the bench, terming it "dangerous experimentation" at a time of a "high crime rate that is a matter of growing concern" and a "new doctrine" without substantial precedent, reflecting "a balance in favor of the accused."[104]

Since then, lower courts and the Supreme Court have heard numerous cases examining the application of the Miranda warning. These courts have carved out exceptions and clarified the application of the ruling. For example, in the 2010 Supreme Court case *Berghuis v. Thompkins,*[105] the justices held that suspects retain the Fifth Amendment right to remain silent. However, if a suspect waives this right and then police initiate an interrogation or interview, the suspect must verbally and specifically

Ten years after the landmark Supreme Court decision that bears his name and assures a set of rights for those being questioned by police, Ernesto Miranda was killed in a bar fight in Phoenix.

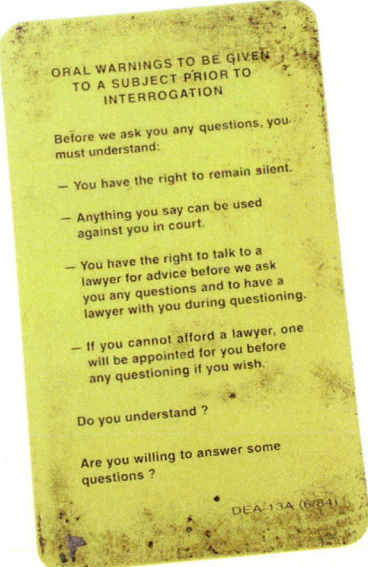

ORAL WARNINGS TO BE GIVEN TO A SUBJECT PRIOR TO INTERROGATION

Before we ask you any questions, you must understand:

— You have the right to remain silent.

— Anything you say can be used against you in court.

— You have the right to talk to a lawyer for advice before we ask you any questions and to have a lawyer with you during questioning.

— If you cannot afford a lawyer, one will be appointed for you before any questioning if you wish.

Do you understand ?

Are you willing to answer some questions ?

DEA-13A (6/84)

Police officers commonly carry a card like the one shown here that depicts the Miranda warning or a version of the Miranda warning used by their individual police departments. The court did not specify a required wording but rather the elements that must be included.

state that he or she is invoking the Fifth Amendment right and revoking the prior waiver of the Fifth Amendment rights. Constitutional requirements continue to develop as cases are brought up for appellate review.

In another 2010 case, the Supreme Court addressed the question of whether a suspect can ever be interrogated after asking for an attorney. In *Maryland v. Shatzer,*[106] the suspect was incarcerated, and police asked to question him. Shatzer declined to be interrogated without his attorney, and the interview ended. Three years later, the police opened a new investigation and again asked to question the inmate. This time Shatzer waived his right to counsel and gave incriminating statements to the police. The justices found that this evidence was admissible, as a break in custody had occurred during the three-year time span between requests for interviews.

In 2011, this issue was further clarified by the Supreme Court ruling in *J.D.B. v. North Carolina,*[107] when a seventh-grader suspected in a pair of home break-ins was questioned by a uniformed officer. The 13-year-old student was taken from his middle school classroom to a conference room, where two officers and two school administrators questioned him for 30 to 45 minutes. The child did not receive a Miranda warning and confessed. The Supreme Court held that a child's age is a relevant factor in determining whether the child is in custody for the purposes of the waiver of rights required by *Miranda v. Arizona* and that a child is more likely to feel pressed by the demands of adult authority figures.

SHOW-UPS AND LINEUPS

In addition to interrogation, law enforcement officers employ a variety of investigative techniques to detect and identify criminal offenders. Among these are show-ups, lineups, and the presentation of photographs and other forms of non-testimonial material, which the Supreme Court has allowed as admissible evidence under certain conditions.

The show-up is not consistently used by either the police or the courts; the lineup is more popular. In general, the *show-up* is a one-on-one procedure that generally takes place shortly after a crime has been committed. The victim or witness is taken to the police station, confronted with a suspect, and asked, "Is he the one?"

Here is an example of a show-up, described in the 1972 case of *Kirby v. Illinois:*[108] "After Kirby and his alleged accomplice Ralph Bean were arrested, police officers brought Willie Shard, the robbery victim, to a room in a police station where Kirby and Bean were seated at a table with two other police officers. Shard testified at trial that the officers who brought him to the room asked him if Kirby and Bean were the robbers and he indicated they were."[109] In contrast, in a *lineup,* the suspect is placed together with several other persons, live or via a photo lineup, and the victim or witness is asked to pick out the suspect from this array of individuals. Photo lineups are becoming more and more common.

The constitutional issues in the use of lineups and show-ups have generally focused on their fairness; in particular, critics point to the

Police often use photo lineups when it is not possible to conduct a traditional in-person lineup.

suggestiveness of producing someone for witnesses to identify, as well as the potential infringement of suspects' and defendants' rights to counsel during these procedures. In *Foster v. California*,[110] for example, there was only one witness to a robbery. The suspect, who was six feet tall, was first placed in a lineup with two other men who were several inches shorter. He was wearing a leather jacket similar to the one the witness had seen one of the robbers wearing. The witness thought the suspect was indeed the robber but was not absolutely sure. Several days later another lineup was held, and the suspect was the only one in the second lineup who had been in the earlier one. At this point the witness positively identified the suspect as the robber. The Supreme Court ruled against this type of identification procedure, stating that "in effect, the police repeatedly said to the witness, 'This is the man.'"[111]

United States v. Wade[112] addressed the issue of a defendant's right to counsel during a lineup. The defendant had been shown to witnesses at a post-indictment lineup, without the accused or his attorney being notified beforehand and without the attorney present. The Supreme Court ruled that under these conditions the chances of an unfair identification, whether unintentional or not, are so great that a person who is subjected to a pretrial lineup or show-up is entitled to representation by counsel at that time. Note, however, that *Wade* referred only to post-indictment lineups and not to those occurring in earlier phases of the criminal justice process.

DNA AND OTHER NON-TESTIMONIAL EXEMPLARS

The Supreme Court has used the term *exemplar* in its decisions to identify various physical representations of a suspect—DNA, voice, blood, or anything else that could identify a suspect without his or her consent or that could give the court information about a suspect without his or her knowledge. Thus, as technology has advanced and increased the ability to collect and use such exemplars, the law has struggled to keep up while also protecting citizens from unreasonable searches and seizures. How these technological advances impact the liberties afforded to citizens continues to change. In this section we examine various exemplars to illustrate the challenges they pose to modern police officers and agencies. We begin with the rapidly evolving field of DNA evidence.

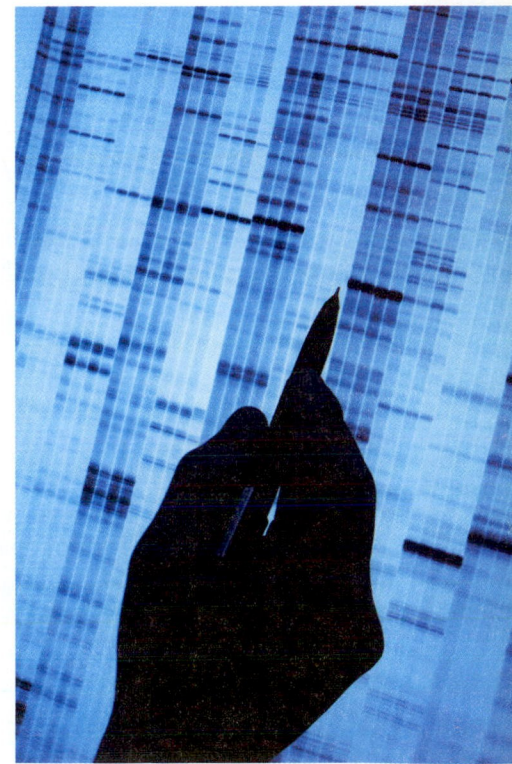

DNA is a long double-stranded molecule wound in a spiral called a helix. Each strand in the helix contains billions of subunits, and the manner in which these are arranged determines an individual's unique genetic code, or DNA profile. DNA can be extracted from an individual's blood, saliva, semen or vaginal secretions, or even a speck of skin. When forensic scientists conducting criminal investigations examine DNA, they cannot focus on all of these billions of subunits. However, they can look at certain substrands of DNA. If three of these substrands match those of a suspect, the chances are two thousand to one that the police have the right person. Nine matches boost the odds to a billion to one, and FBI procedures require no fewer than 13 matches. Quite clearly, DNA is a powerful tool in criminal investigation. DNA testing has been especially useful in rape cases, because the predator's semen is generally left behind in the victim's vagina or anus. As such, DNA evidence can either convict or exonerate suspects. In fact, in recent years, more than 280 inmates have had their convictions overturned on the basis of new DNA evidence.[113] But because the use of DNA evidence is still relatively new, the U.S. Supreme Court has yet to define the parameters of its collection and use.

With respect to other exemplars, the Supreme Court has maintained a firm position:

- In *Schmerber v. California*,[114] the court ruled that the forced extraction of a blood sample from a defendant who was accused of driving while intoxicated was admissible at trial.

DNA sequencing images, like this one, are often used for comparisons with suspects' DNA samples.

- In *United States v. Dionisio*,[115] the court held that a suspect could be forced to provide voice exemplars.
- In *United States v. Mara*,[116] the court held that a suspect could be compelled to provide a handwriting exemplar.
- In *United States v. Ash*,[117] the court held that the Sixth Amendment does not grant the right to counsel at photographic displays conducted for the purpose of allowing a witness to attempt to identify an offender.

The position of the Supreme Court in these cases has been that the Fifth Amendment privilege protects an accused only from being compelled to testify against himself or herself—that is, from evidence of a communicative nature. On the other hand, in *Winston v. Lee*[118] the court held that a suspect cannot be forced to undergo surgery to remove a bullet from his or her chest, even though probable cause exists that surgery would produce evidence of a crime. As you can see, then, the use of exemplars as investigative tools is evolving, as is the court's view of their constitutionality.

CONCLUSIONS

Investigating crime and apprehending offenders are major functions in police service to the community. These actions are guided by the Constitution and judicial case law, as well as by organizational and agency policy and procedure. Over the past 100 years, the Supreme Court has attempted to carve out constitutionally supported guidelines for police behavior, particularly related to search and seizure. As you have seen in this chapter, this area of policing and of case law continues to evolve as the court and law enforcement personnel respond to changing technology within our contemporary society. As you've also seen, a recurrent theme for the courts and the police is how to best enforce the law to promote public safety while also protecting the rights of citizens under the Constitution.

SUMMARY AND REVIEW

■ **Identify the circumstances under which police may conduct a search without a warrant.**

- search incident to arrest
- stop-and-frisk (*Terry* stop)
- automobile search
- fresh pursuit
- consent search
- search of plain view areas

■ **Describe what the plain view doctrine is and the implications for police investigation.**

- In *Harris v. United States* (1968), the Supreme Court ruled that anything a police officer sees in plain view, when the officer has a right to be where he or she is, is not the product of a search and is therefore admissible as evidence.

- In an extension of the plain view doctrine, officers are also allowed to do a protective sweep when they make an arrest on or outside private premises. They may, despite the absence of a search warrant, examine the entire premises for other persons whose presence would pose a threat either to their safety or to evidence that could be removed or destroyed.

■ **Examine the role of the exclusionary rule in police behavior.**

- The exclusionary rule is a remedy and a rule. This ruling by the Supreme Court prohibits the use of evidence seized by law enforcement officials in violation of the Fourth Amendment protection against unreasonable search and seizure.

- The rule was an outgrowth of *Weeks v. United States,* and during the many years since that case, there has been continuing debate over the result of that decision—as to whether the exclusionary rule is an effective remedy or an expensive constitutional right.

■ **Explain the role of police in obtaining confessions as defined by the Supreme Court.**

- According to the *Miranda v. Arizona* decision by the Supreme Court, police must notify suspects that they have the constitutional right to remain silent, that what they say will be used against them in a court of law, that they have the right to consult an attorney during questioning, and that an attorney will be obtained if they cannot afford one.
- Offenders must waive those rights verbally or in writing and specifically state that they are invoking the Fifth Amendment right.

■ **Explain the legal issues related to show-ups and lineups as investigative techniques.**

- Show-ups are one-on-one procedures that generally take place shortly after crimes have been committed. A victim or witness is taken to a police station and confronted with a suspect and then asked to identify the individual.

- Lineups entail placing the suspect together with several other persons, and the victim or witness is asked to pick out the suspect from this array of individuals.
- The constitutional issues in the use of lineups and show-ups have generally focused on the fairness of the procedures used (how police conduct them); in particular, critics point to the suggestiveness of producing someone for witnesses to identify, as well as the potential infringement of suspects' and defendants' rights to counsel during such procedures.

■ **Identify and discuss the limitations placed on police for using exemplar investigative techniques.**

- The term *exemplar* has been used in decisions by the Supreme Court to identify various physical representations of a suspect—DNA, voice, blood, or anything else that could identify a suspect without his or her consent or that could give the court information about a suspect without his or her knowledge.
- The Supreme Court has ruled that the following forced exemplars were all admissible at trial: extraction of a blood sample from a defendant who was accused of driving while intoxicated, voice and handwriting exemplars provided by suspects, and use of a suspect's photograph in the absence of counsel for witness identification.

KEY TERMS

Carroll doctrine (p. 154)	fruit of the poisonous tree (p. 150)	protective sweep doctrine (p. 160)
confession (p. 164)	plain view doctrine (p. 159)	search and seizure (p. 147)
exclusionary rule (p. 160)	probable cause (p. 149)	search warrant (p. 148)

ISSUES FOR CRITICAL THINKING AND DISCUSSION

1. Why must we limit the investigative powers of the police?
2. What are the rights of the accused during the investigation phases of the criminal justice process?
3. Applying the concept of probable cause, what specifically was considered unreasonable about the search and seizure in *Mapp v. Ohio*?
4. What factors must police officers take into account even when they have obtained consent for a warrantless search?

5. Do you consider the Supreme Court decisions related to how police obtain confessions reasonable? Why or why not? Should we limit what police can do to obtain information from suspects? If so, what should those limits be?
6. How might DNA databases help law enforcement officials identify and apprehend offenders? What, if any, constitutional concerns might they present?

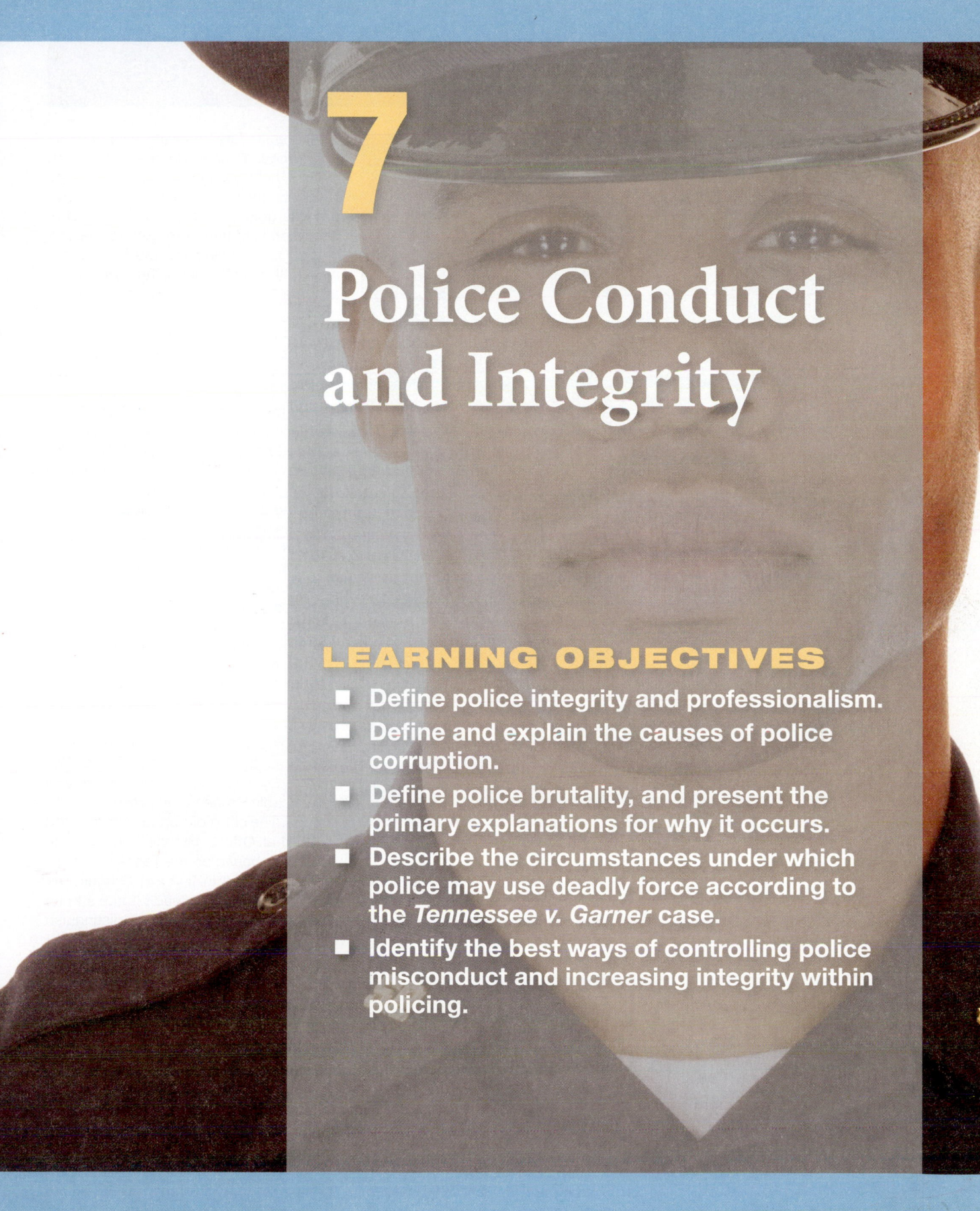

7

Police Conduct and Integrity

LEARNING OBJECTIVES

- Define police integrity and professionalism.
- Define and explain the causes of police corruption.
- Define police brutality, and present the primary explanations for why it occurs.
- Describe the circumstances under which police may use deadly force according to the *Tennessee v. Garner* case.
- Identify the best ways of controlling police misconduct and increasing integrity within policing.

DISCRETION AND POLICE USE OF DEADLY FORCE

The circumstances under which an officer can shoot a fleeing suspect are complex and were tested in the case of Edward Garner. This case set the standards for police use of deadly force across the country.

During a late-October evening, Memphis police officers Elton Hymon and Leslie Wright answered a call about a suspicious person inside a house. When they arrived, the officers saw a woman standing on her porch and gesturing toward the house next to hers, indicating that "someone" was breaking in. Officer Hymon went behind the house, heard a door slam, and saw someone run across the backyard. The suspect, Edward Garner, stopped at a chain-link fence at the edge of the yard. While shining a flashlight on Garner, Officer Hymon was able to see his face and hands. There was no sign of a weapon, and Hymon later indicated that he was "reasonably sure" that the suspect was not armed. Officer Hymon called out, "Police, halt!" At this point Garner began to climb the fence. Believing that Garner was going to get away, Hymon shot him to prevent him from getting over the fence. Garner was hit in the back of the neck with a fatal wound. Ten dollars and a purse from the house were found on his body.[1]

Tennessee statute provided that "if, after notice of intention to arrest the defendant, he either flee(s) or forcibly resist(s), the officer may use all the necessary means to effect the arrest."[2] Officer Hymon's shooting of Garner was appropriate under this statute and the departmental policy in place, which gave officers the authority to use any means, including deadly force, to stop a suspect from fleeing.[3]

Garner's father, Cleamtee Garner, filed a lawsuit in federal district court on the ground that the shooting had violated his son's constitutional rights under the Fourth, Fifth, Sixth, Eighth, and Fourteenth Amendments. Seeking damages, Garner named Hymon, the police department and its director, and the mayor and city of Memphis as defendants. The district court dismissed Garner's suit, concluding that the Tennessee statute was constitutional and that Officer Hymon had used the only "reasonable" and "practicable" means of preventing the escape. The court of appeals agreed and found that Officer Hymon had acted in good faith based on the Tennessee statute, but it ruled in favor of Garner. The court noted that the deadly-force statute was faulty since it failed to distinguish between felonies of different seriousness. The state of Tennessee, which had intervened in the case to defend the constitutionality of its statute, appealed the decision to the U.S. Supreme Court.[4]

In *Tennessee v. Garner,* the High Court ruled in favor of Cleamtee Garner, holding the Tennessee statute to be unconstitutional in that it authorized the use of deadly force against an apparently unarmed, non-dangerous suspect. The court emphasized that deadly force may not be used unless it is necessary to prevent the escape of a suspect for whom there is reasonable cause to believe a "significant threat of death or serious physical injury to the officer or others exists."[5] While the death of Garner was tragic, the officer's actions were consistent with departmental policy, training, and state law. Officers on the beat must rely on their training, agency policies and procedures, and experience in the field to determine levels of threat. How do officers make decisions in these high-pressure, split-second circumstances? Understanding the complexity of demands on police in such situations is key to understanding the challenging concepts explored in this chapter.

This chapter examines the full range of police conduct—from the highest standards of professionalism and integrity to extreme examples of misconduct, brutality, and use of deadly force. Any incident of police misconduct harms the community and its agencies while also challenging and undermining policing organizations. When high-profile cases of police brutality come to the attention of the public, they are rightfully disturbing. However, most officers and police organizations strive to serve and protect the citizens of their communities within the constraints of ethical and professional behavior—the topic we examine first.

POLICE INTEGRITY AND PROFESSIONALISM

Police integrity refers to the exercise of powers and use of discretion according to the highest standards of competence, fairness, and honesty. Historically, the administrative perspective was that police integrity depended on the moral virtues of individual police officers.[6] Working from this perspective, agencies focused on carefully screening applicants for police positions and aggressively pursuing and removing defective officers through internal policing. And while no one questions the value of these efforts, they focus on the "bad apple" theory of police misconduct, which as you will see later in the chapter, has its limits. The newer approach, thus, focuses on enhancing integrity with **police professionalism,** or the view of policing as a profession with high standards and expectations for law enforcement conduct within the community. This approach stresses the importance of (1) organizational rule-making, (2) detecting, investigating, and disciplining rule violations, and (3) circumscribing "The Code," a term we discuss later in the chapter. Let's look at each of these concepts in turn.

Organizational Rule-Making

Every police agency has rules, but because police departments in the United States are decentralized, the rules governing behavior differ from jurisdiction to jurisdiction. This is especially the case with regard to such marginally corrupt practices as accepting free meals, small gifts, discounts from merchants, and off-duty employment. Moreover, while the official agency policy may prohibit these behaviors, the unofficial policy often ignores such behaviors, provided they are limited and are done discreetly. Still, to further professionalism and integrity, the goals of organizational rule-making within a department are to create policies, make officers fully aware of them, and communicate the agency's rationale for them.

Reform based on rule-making has come in the form of state- and national-level accrediting agencies. These agencies develop consistent professional standards about all aspects of law enforcement, including the use of force, working with diverse populations, responding to victims of sexual assault, and hiring and training procedures. These accrediting organizations help law enforcement agencies develop self-assessment procedures to ensure that standards are being met, and they provide training and resources to increase the professionalism and integrity of the entire field.

The best known of such organizations is the Commission on Accreditation for Law Enforcement Agencies (CALEA). CALEA was created in 1979 with the help of four other national organizations: the International Association of Chiefs of Police (IACP), the National Organization of Black Law Enforcement Executives (NOBLE), the

Police car cameras can protect both police and the community by providing accurate details about encounters between officers and suspects.

National Sheriffs Association (NSA), and the Police Executive Research Forum (PERF). CALEA develops standards for state and local police agencies, covering every aspect of modern law enforcement—from management procedures and personnel practices to matters of service delivery, including community relations. CALEA standards help departments maintain extremely high levels of professionalism.[7] At the end of 2010, 985 agencies were enrolled in CALEA programming.

Most jurisdictions have a state-funded accrediting body that oversees training, policies, and standards for local and state policing agencies. In addition, these government-funded agencies often offer resources for smaller departments to acquire tools, training, and other resources that may be difficult to fund with local budgets. For example, the Department of Criminal Justice Services (DCJS) of Virginia provides resources, training, accreditation, and grants for local departments to ensure the highest quality service to the citizens of the commonwealth. Many of the DCJS initiatives focus on partnerships between law enforcement and the greater community to increase the effectiveness of policing agencies.[8]

Detecting, Investigating, and Disciplining Rule Violations

Police administrators should strive to develop a culture in their agencies that supports disciplining officers who violate established standards of integrity. A wide range of activities can support this goal, including inspections, internal and external reviews of officer behavior, audits, and the disciplining of offending police officers. In addition, the use of technology has helped to identify behaviors that violate departmental policies and expectations, as well as the law. Cameras mounted on police cars are relatively routine today; even smaller departments install and maintain them to protect the community and the officers, as these cameras act as objective observers and can give crucial evidence in cases of alleged police misconduct.

In addition to facing internal reprimands, suspension, and discipline, law enforcement officers can also be criminally prosecuted for their misconduct. Equally concerning to agencies and officers is the fact that both the agency and the individual officer may face civil liability, and the agency as a whole may incur enormous fees and penalties if its procedures did not prevent misconduct or punish it appropriately when identified. For these reasons, law enforcement agencies must respond appropriately to misconduct within their ranks. Despite departmental efforts, however, police misconduct surfaces in various forms and degrees of severity, the subject we turn to next.

DISCRETION MATTERS

What kinds of officer violations or misconduct might police organizations be most likely to investigate and pursue? Why?

POLICE CORRUPTION

Research on white-collar crime—combined with government inquiries concerning the internal operations of organized crime, labor unions, and various business enterprises—has demonstrated that work-related lawbreaking can be found in every profession and occupation.[9] Law enforcement agencies are no exception. Virtually every large urban police department in the United States has experienced both organized corruption and some form of scandal. Similar problems have been uncovered in small towns and rural police and sheriffs' departments across the nation, as well.[10]

Policing is rich in opportunities for corruption—more so than in many other occupations. Why is this so? The police officer stands at the front lines of the criminal justice system in a nation where crime rates are high and the demands for illegal goods and services are widespread. In addition, police officers work autonomously, without direct supervision for much of their shifts, and they spend much of their time interacting with individuals and groups involved in the world of illegal goods and services. These conditions, combined with a range of other variables, including community characteristics and the nature of crime in the jurisdiction served, create a situation in which police officers are confronted daily with opportunities for committing illegal acts, such as accepting funds for ignoring their duties or fulfilling them inconsistently.

Police corruption is best defined as misconduct in the form of illegal activities for economic gain, including accepting gratuities, favors, or payment for services that police are sworn to carry out as part of their peacekeeping role. Corruption occurs in many forms, but researchers agree that it is most evident in nine specific areas:[11] meals and services, kickbacks, opportunistic theft, planned theft and robbery, shakedowns, case fixing, protection, private security, and patronage. The rest of this section explores each of these areas.

Meals and Services

Free or discount meals are available to police officers across the United States, and some see these as a perk of the job. A number of restaurant chains have a policy of providing meals to officers on a regular basis, keeping records so that they can demonstrate their goodwill to both the department and the city. Numerous diners, coffee shops, and other small restaurants have a similar policy, but their goal is to encourage police presence in the establishment, making their places of business more secure. It is true that holdups are much less likely to occur at locations that are regularly visited by police, and if a crime or altercation does occur, police response is typically more rapid.

The free coffee, meals, gifts, and other gratuities—often referred to as "mooching"—that some officers receive from restaurants or small businesses, although a minor form of corruption, are frowned upon by police organizations. Not only are they illegal, but they can lead to major abuses. As a result, many police departments have established "no acceptance" policies, the violation of which can result in formal disciplinary procedures.[12]

Kickbacks

Police officers have numerous opportunities to profit from referring or directing individuals to specific persons or businesses for assistance. This illegal behavior is often informally referred to as **kickbacks.** For example, police might refer arrested suspects to specific bail bond agents and defense attorneys, put accident victims in contact with certain physicians and lawyers who specialize in personal injury claims, send selected tow trucks and ambulances to accident scenes, and arrange for the delivery of bodies to particular funeral homes. Such businesses can and do encourage such referrals by offering kickbacks, or police may themselves ask for such kickbacks. Some police departments explicitly prohibit these arrangements, while others take formal steps to discourage or prevent these practices.

Opportunistic Theft

Police have numerous opportunities to pilfer valuable items. Such opportunistic theft typically involves jewelry and other goods taken from the scene of a burglary or from a suspect; narcotics confiscated from drug users and dealers; merchandise taken from the scene of a fire; funds taken during a gambling raid; money and personal property removed from the bodies of drunks, crime victims, and deceased persons; and confiscated weapons. While such thefts are clearly illegal, if they are discovered and made known to the public, they are also extremely detrimental to the integrity of policing generally.

Restaurant owners often provide free meals and drinks to police officers as a way to demonstrate goodwill and encourage a police presence in the community.

DISCRETION MATTERS

Why might departments want to prevent officers from accepting meals and other gratuities?

DISCRETION MATTERS

Why would police departments limit officer discretion in making referrals to businesses in their communities?

Opportunistic theft often involves money or drugs that officers have access to in the field while conducting their job duties.

Planned Theft and Robbery

Another serious form of police corruption, planned theft and robbery occurs when police engage in predatory criminal activities, either directly or in collusion with criminals. Unlike some minor forms of corruption, such behavior is not tolerated by police departments. Although some departments might passively support free meals and small kickbacks, if a police theft or robbery becomes known to the public, all departments will react forcefully.[13]

The Shakedown

A **shakedown** is a form of extortion in which police officers demand money from citizens in exchange for not enforcing the law. The term *shakedown* has its roots in the nineteenth-century British underworld, where it referred to a temporary substitute for a bed, common in many an English prostitute's room. Hence, her quarters also became known as a shakedown. Police have been known to shake down bar and restaurant owners and shopkeepers by threatening to enforce obscure liquor laws, health regulations, and zoning violations. Moreover, as the war on drugs has escalated, there have been numerous reports of police shakedowns of drug traffickers and dealers—taking money or drugs instead of enforcing drug laws.[14]

Case Fixing

As a form of corruption, **case fixing** appears at all levels of the criminal justice process and involves not only police but bailiffs, court personnel, members of juries, prosecutors, and judges. Typically, this is a practice in which law enforcement officials illegally alter the outcome of cases. Fixing a case with a police officer, however, is the most direct method, and often the least complicated and least expensive. The most common form involves a bribe to an officer in exchange for not being arrested—a practice that is typically initiated by many street criminals, including pickpockets, prostitutes, gamblers, drug users, the parents of juvenile offenders, members of organized crime,

Former Police Chief M. Cachopa (*standing, on right,* at his arraignment) and two other officers of the Stoughton Police Department in Massachusetts were charged with intimidation and extortion following the beating of a suspect. The chief and one officer were ultimately convicted.

and sometimes burglars. Case fixing can also take the form of perjury on the witness stand, when a police officer testifies in a way that reduces the seriousness of a charge against an offender, or it can occur during an investigation, when an officer agrees not to pursue leads that might produce evidence supporting a criminal charge.

Traffic-ticket fixing is likely the most common form of case fixing, and often it does not involve any monetary payment. In some jurisdictions, a call to the police chief or simply knowing someone on the police force is all it takes to have a summons discharged. However, these practices are not publicized, nor are they limited to police officers. Connections to various court personnel, magistrates, and even correctional officials can impact the experience of particular offenders. This practice is not universal, but it is not uncommon.

Protection and Private Security

The protection of illegal activities by police has been commonplace for well over a century. Protection occurs when officers do not enforce laws related to criminal activity or when they accept drugs, money, or stolen property in exchange for overlooking these activities. Protection is often associated with illegal services such as prostitution, gambling, and sales of drugs and pornography. This form of corruption is typically well organized, meaning that officers make formal arrangements with offenders for this protection, and multiple officers within a particular unit may be involved. Unlike the acceptance of gratuities or other lesser forms of corruption, this behavior involves intent to protect criminal offenders and overt actions to carry out the protection. It is difficult to identify how extensive this practice is.

Corruption in the form of private security involves providing more police protection or presence than is required by standard operating procedures. Examples include checking the security of private premises more frequently and intensively than is usual, escorting businesspeople to make bank deposits, and providing a visible police presence in stores or establishments to keep out undesirables. In such instances, payoffs typically take the form of goods, services, and favors. Some officers hire themselves out as bodyguards, even while on duty. In contrast to protection, private security is offered to private citizens or businesses rather than to criminals. However, these are related and similar behaviors.

This discussion should not suggest that all private policing by public police is corrupt. On the contrary, "extra-duty policing," as it has come to be known, is common in many parts of the nation. In fact, in many jurisdictions there is a great demand for extra-duty uniformed officers: for traffic control and pedestrian safety at road construction and repair sites; for crowd control at major private events, such as football games and rock concerts; and for private security and protection of life and property.[15] In all these instances, employers contract directly with police departments for the services of uniformed officers, and the officers, in turn, are paid overtime wages by their departments. The presence of formal relationships clearly differentiates the legal from the illegal behavior.

Patronage

Patronage can take a variety of forms, all of which involve the use of one's official position to influence decision-making. Historically, patronage has meant making governmental appointments in such a way as to increase one's political strength, and it has always been a part of political life in one form or another.

Although ethical issues surround the practice of political patronage, it is not necessarily illegal in all its forms. However, patronage clearly becomes corruption when payments are made for political favors. Within the ranks of policing, corruption by patronage can occur when an officer pays a fee to gain a promotion or transfer. When an officer arranges for an outsider to have access to confidential department records or agrees to alter such records, this may also be construed as patronage. Another form of patronage occurs when a private citizen influences department recommendations regarding the granting of licenses.

The Rampart scandal in the late 1990s implicated 58 Los Angeles police officers in a wide range of offenses, including involvement in the 1997 death of hip-hop artist Notorious B.I.G. Scholars offer a variety of explanations for this kind of widespread corruption in a department.

Patronage can occur in other ways as well. Within a police department, for example, people have been paid to falsify attendance records, influence the choice of vacations and days off, report officers as being on duty when they are not, and provide unearned passing grades for training programs and promotion exams.

While the extent of police corruption is unknown, understanding how it occurs is an important part of preventing it, reducing it, and better responding to it as it occurs.

CAUSES OF POLICE CORRUPTION

A number of researchers and observers have offered hypotheses as to why police corruption occurs. In the following sections, we discuss the most common ideas—that corruption is caused by society at large; by influences within police departments, including the informal code of police conduct; and by a predisposition toward corruption in some individuals ("rotten apples") who become police officers.[16]

The Society-at-Large Explanation

The society-at-large explanation comes from the late O. W. Wilson and is based on his observations and experiences as Chicago's superintendent of police during the 1960s. As Wilson put it, "This force was corrupted by the citizens of Chicago. . . . It has been customary to give doormen, chauffeurs, maids, cooks and delivery men little gifts and gratuities. . . . It is felt that the level of service depends on these gratuities."[17]

According to Wilson's theory, such practices, in turn, led to small bribes made to police officers to dissuade them from enforcing traffic laws or minor city ordinances. Accepting small payoffs from drivers and business operators then extended to more serious crimes. Wilson called this progression the slippery-slope hypothesis—that is, corruption begins with apparently harmless and well-intentioned practices and eventually leads, in individual officers or in departments as a whole, to all manner of crimes for profit. This explanation focuses on the culture and characteristics of whole communities that encourage corrupt practices by the police.

Structural Explanations

As the late Arthur Niederhoffer wrote in his well-known book *Behind the Shield*, "Actual policemen seem to accept graft for other reasons than avarice. Often the first transgression is inadvertent. Or, they may be gradually indoctrinated by older policemen. Step by step they progress from a small peccadillo [trifling sin] to outright shakedown and felony."[18] The willingness of the law enforcement organization to respond to small offenses may have a significant impact on reducing instances of corruption.

Going further, Niederhoffer asserted, this step-by-step progress results from the contradictory sets of norms that police officers see both in the world at large and in their own departments. Officers, particularly those in large cities, are exposed to a steady stream of criminal behavior of varying degrees. They discover, moreover, that dishonesty and corruption are not limited to those the community views as criminals but also extend to individuals of good reputation—including fellow officers with whom they must establish mutual trust. In time, they can develop cynical attitudes, so that they view corruption as a game in which every person is out to get a share.[19] Additionally, the internal code of policing, which goes by a variety of names—the "Code of Silence," the "Blue Curtain," the "Blue Wall of Silence," or more simply, **The Code**—is the informal prohibition in the culture of policing against reporting the misconduct of other officers. The Code likely exists in every police agency, and weakening the bonds of loyalty that support its existence is difficult, but it is nevertheless possible when administrators discipline those who violate the rights and privileges of their positions. Victims of police brutality and corruption are often unwilling to come forward out of fear of retaliation by police. Victims may also be concerned that other officers will protect the officers who have harmed them.

Endeavors such as community policing and police outreach to community members can be helpful in breaking organizational silence and penetrating the Blue Wall. Community policing seeks to involve members of the community in crime prevention. Outreach activities, such as bike-registration drives and neighborhood meetings where police hear citizens' concerns, provide the community with positive police experiences. These and other kinds of positive contacts can improve the image of police and expose citizens to the difficulties of police work.

The Rotten-Apple Explanation

The "bad-apple" or "rotten-apple" view is perhaps the most popular explanation of police corruption. It suggests that in an otherwise honest department, there are a few bad officers who are operating on their own. According to this theory, corruption results from the moral failure of just a few officers that then spreads to the others. After all, as the old adage says, "One rotten apple spoils the whole barrel."

Police chiefs and commissioners frequently use the rotten-apple theory to explain misconduct in their ranks. They do so because they might otherwise feel compelled to scrutinize or condemn the very systems in which they have risen to the top. Still, the rotten-apple explanation is the most criticized, for it fails to explain why individual officers become corrupt. As one critic of the theory wrote, "If corruption is to be explained in terms of a few 'bad' people, then some departments attracted a disproportionately high number of rotten apples over long periods of time."[20]

In reality, however, no single explanation can likely account for all police corruption, and unfortunately, we have no empirical data supporting any of the explanations. The three hypotheses discussed here are the principal views, and most likely they work in conjunction with one another.

POLICE VIOLENCE

Law enforcement officers often have to use at least some minimal level of force to gain citizen compliance. This force can advance along a continuum from a verbal command to deadly force, as you saw in the chapter-opening case regarding Edward Garner. Police frequently use the lower levels of force, such as verbal commands, and infrequently resort to the most serious levels, particularly those involving weapons. Because we lack national data on this topic, there is no way to offer an accurate comparison of police use of justified versus excessive force. Although police use of force is authorized and regulated by state and federal mandates and departmental policies and national and regional accrediting bodies, incidents of police violence and brutality unfortunately do occur.

Police brutality is most often defined as unwarranted or excessive use of physical force, though it can also include verbal assaults. Police violence in the form of excessive force, unwarranted deadly force, and other mistreatment of citizens is not uncommon in American history. Documents that describe the growth and development of both the urban metropolis and the rural frontier give ample testimony to the unwarranted use of force by police. Law enforcement records west of the Mississippi provide numerous examples of the "shoot first and ask questions later" philosophy. Moreover, we have many reports in the histories of urban police systems of the brutal and sadistic application of the police officer's nightstick.

It was not until the 1960s that the issue of police misconduct in the forms of brutality and deadly force took on any public and political urgency. This change can be attributed to two phenomena: the "criminal law revolution" carried on by the Supreme Court under the leadership of Chief Justice Earl Warren and the findings of the Kerner Commission—the National Advisory Commission on Civil Disorders.

In 1936, *Brown v. Mississippi* established the Supreme Court's position on brutality, at least as far as coerced confessions were concerned.[21] It was the first time a state conviction was overturned because it relied on a confession extracted by torture. But the importance of *Brown* remained unnoticed for 25 years, until the court developed some hard-and-fast rules concerning methods for interrogating suspects while in police custody. In *Rogers v. Richmond* (1961), *Greenwald v. Wisconsin, Sims v. Georgia,* and *Brooks v. Florida* (1967), the court asserted that the Fourteenth Amendment bars confessions when "the methods used to extract them offend the underlying principle in the enforcement of our criminal law," especially those that reflect "shocking displays of barbarism."[22]

While the Supreme Court examined police violence in the context of squad room interrogations, the Kerner Commission targeted the wider issue of street justice. Known more formally as the National Advisory Commission on Civil Disorders, its purpose was to investigate the causes of the rioting and destruction that occurred in Detroit, Los Angeles, Newark, New York, and 20 other urban areas during the summer of 1967. The commission identified numerous causes, but it highlighted police practices in inner-city areas as the primary one. Aggressive preventive patrol, police brutality, unwarranted use of deadly force, harassment, verbal abuse, and discourtesy created tension between police and African Americans, and complaints of such practices were found in all the locations studied.[23] Let's now take a closer look at the specifics of police brutality and its close associate—use of deadly force.

Accrediting bodies, such as the Commission on Accreditation for Law Enforcement Agencies (CALEA), help departments develop procedures and policies that limit the discretionary use of force and prevent police violence.

Police Brutality and Use of Force

Police brutality exerts a heavy toll on society, as each year officers and citizens alike are injured or killed during violent confrontations. Such incidents can result in expensive lawsuits against agencies and generate feelings of mistrust among the public, often costing law enforcement the cooperation of those they are under oath to protect and serve. Although the Supreme Court and the Kerner Commission brought police violence to public attention during the 1960s, the subject had long been the focus of rigorous study. Findings from recent studies suggest that severe use of force continues to be a challenge for modern police agencies.[24]

Several noteworthy examples of excessive use of force have focused national attention on the issue of police brutality. Perhaps the best known are the videotaped assault of Rodney King by Los Angeles police officers in 1991, the attack on Abner Louima by New York City police officers in 1997 (featured in the "Victims and Justice" box), the videotaped beating of Thomas Jones by Philadelphia police in 2000, and the videotaped beating of Robert Davis by New Orleans police in 2005.

VICTIMS AND JUSTICE

Victim Responses to Police Misconduct

Prosecutors investigating allegations of police misconduct are aware that a code of silence exists in the majority of police departments in the United States. This code of silence holds that a police officer must not provide adverse information about fellow officers, no matter what they have been accused of. Repercussions for breaking The Code include ostracism, threats, and the fear that officers will not "back up" or protect those who break The Code.

In New York City, the assault on Haitian immigrant Abner Louima tested the limits of The Code. Louima was arrested in Brooklyn on August 9, 1997, on a charge of disorderly conduct. He claimed that he was then taken to a bathroom at the 70th Precinct, sodomized with "something" (either a toilet plunger or broken-off broom handle) by Officer Justin Volpe, and warned by Volpe that "if you tell anyone about this, I'll find you and kill you." Sometime later, Louima was taken to a local hospital for surgery, and doctors discovered that his bladder and small intestine had been punctured.

When Louima sued the city and the New York City Police Department (NYPD), the story hit the news, and the case became, among many other things, a powerful example of how police react to misconduct in their ranks. In this instance, the misconduct was so sadistic that it tested, and ultimately broke, the Blue Wall of Silence. NYPD officers testified that after the assault, Volpe pranced around the precinct house with a blood-and-feces-stained stick, inviting other officers to examine it, and boasted that "I took a man down tonight." In the face of the evidence against him, Officer Volpe eventually pleaded guilty in federal court to charges of torturing Louima. He was sentenced to a 30-year prison term.

But did the Louima/Volpe case really break the code of silence? Most observers say no, because Volpe himself refused to name all the other officers who took part in the assault, and those who testified against Volpe took weeks to come forward, and likely did so then only because of the pressure of a highly publicized investigation.

The case of Abner Louima highlights the challenges victims face when reporting police misconduct.

Although the case against Justin Volpe was the most visible and sadistic in many years, this should not suggest that the Blue Wall is limited to the NYPD or that The Code is restricted to patrol officers. In fact, more recent examples include departments large and small: the 2009 shooting death of unarmed 23-year-old Oscar Grant by Johannes Mehserle, a Bay Area Rapid Transit police officer, and the 2010 beating of Mark Ashford after he took a cell phone photo of Denver City Police Department officers involved in a traffic stop. Both incidents made national news and continue to highlight the issue of police brutality. And in both of these cases, administrators have struggled to respond appropriately to the misconduct because of the impact of The Code among fellow officers.

THINK ABOUT THIS

1. What policies or measures might police agencies implement to increase the likelihood that officers will report wrongdoing by others?
2. If you were an officer who knew about misconduct by other officers, would you come forward to testify or file a complaint against them? Why or why not?

Sources: Tom Morganthau, "Justice for Louima," *Newsweek,* June 7, 1999, 42; Helen Peterson, "Volpe Admits Louima Attack," NYDailyNews.com, May 26, 1999, http://articles.nydailynews.com/1999-05-26/news/18102173_1_police-officer-justin-volpe-abner-louima-cops; Joseph P. Fried, "Volpe Sentenced to a 30-Year Term in Louima Torture," *New York Times,* December 14, 1999; Leiloni De Gruy, "Release of Johannes Mehserle Sparks New Outrage," *Los Angeles Wave,* June 15, 2011; Jaclyn Allen, "Denver Council Approves Police Brutality Payouts," TheDenverChannel.com, June 13, 2011, http://www.thedenverchannel.com/news/28227990/detail.html.

In the past, police brutality was believed to be limited to those few sadistic officers seen as "bad apples." However, more recent commentaries suggest that police violence is the result of norms shared throughout a police department and that it is best understood as an unfortunate consequence of the police role, very similar to the structural explanations for police corruption offered by Niederhoffer earlier in the chapter.

Various national and state policing organizations, including the Commission on Accreditation for Law Enforcement Agencies (CALEA), which you read about earlier, continue to develop procedures, policies, and training for appropriate use of force in an encounter with a suspect. However, participation with these agencies varies from jurisdiction to jurisdiction, as do internal policies and directives. Moreover, some officers show characteristics of the police "working personality" (discussed in Chapter 5)—the feeling of constant pressure to perform, along with elements of authoritarianism, suspicion, racism, hostility, insecurity, and cynicism. Further, police norms that emphasize solidarity and secrecy support a structure in which fellow officers will not condemn incidents of brutality and other misconduct.

Also contributing to police brutality is the type of policing that criminologist James Q. Wilson described as the "watchman style" (see Chapter 5).[25] Watchman-style departments tend to be located in older cities with high concentrations of poor and minority citizens. In such cities, police officers act primarily as reluctant maintainers of order. They ignore many minor problems—those involving gambling, traffic violations, misdemeanors, juvenile rowdiness, and domestic disputes. Officers act tough in serious situations, but in most others, according to Wilson's view, they follow the path of least resistance. Moreover, in the past, many officers were poorly trained, and their departments rarely met even minimum standards for planning, research, and community relations. Such circumstances often led to organized corruption, discriminatory arrests, and unnecessary and destructive police violence. Much has changed since the 1970s, when Wilson's work was published, as departments now more commonly seek accreditation and increasingly focus their training and policies on ensuring professionalism.

Use of force by police officers remains a topic of controversy and public concern.

Going beyond the working personality and the watchman style as factors contributing to unnecessary police violence, sociologist Richard J. Lundman has focused on three additional issues:

1. *Police may perceive that some citizens do not accept police authority.* Because authority is essential to the police roles of enforcing the law and keeping the peace, those who question or resist that authority represent a challenge to officers, detectives, and the organizations they represent. Often police use intense verbal coercion to establish their authority quickly. Should that fail, they may use physical force to elicit compliance from citizens. Often, this exercise of police authority through physical means falls within the boundaries of appropriate police response. Other times, this force exceeds what some would see as suitable for a given situation.
2. *Police may judge certain citizens as having more social value than others.* In the view of many police officers, certain citizens—prostitutes, drunks, members of juvenile gangs, gays, sex offenders, drug users, hardened criminals—have little to contribute to society. Many officers do not consider such people worth protecting, or they protect them using norms different from those that guide their protection of other citizens. Some police even single out these people for physical abuse, due to their belief that some members of our society are more deserving of brutality than others.
3. *Police work requires officers to make quick decisions, often on the basis of fragmentary information in dangerous or threatening circumstances.* Both officers and their superiors tend to highlight the use of force as a means of rapid problem resolution within these situations.[26]

Aware that these components of the police role may increase the likelihood of brutality and illegitimate force, police organizations around the nation have sought to more clearly define policies and implement training to increase professionalism and address these issues within their departments. In the next section, we discuss the application of deadly force, the area where the most progress has been made in defining strict standards and where judicial decisions have helped form policies that benefit both police officers and the communities they serve.

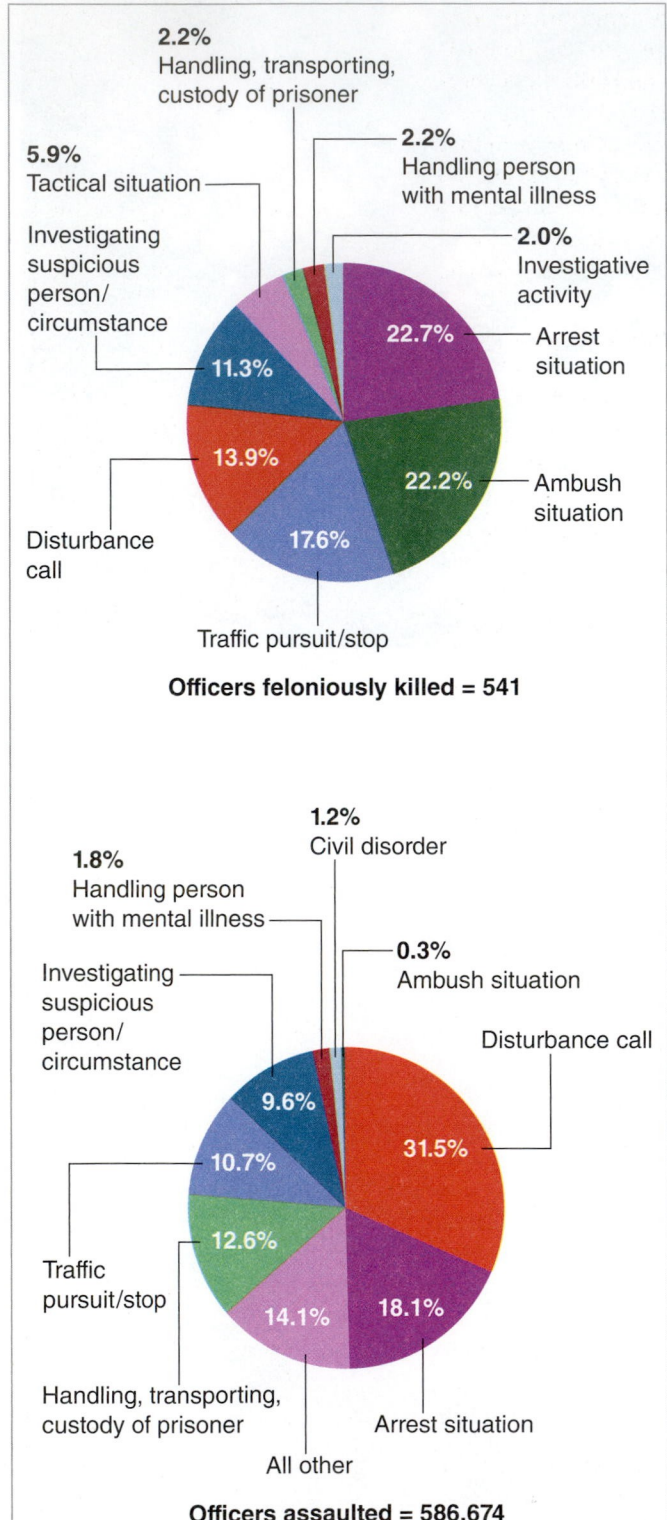

2.2%
Handling, transporting,
custody of prisoner

2.2%
Handling person
with mental illness

5.9%
Tactical situation

2.0%
Investigative
activity

Investigating
suspicious
person/
circumstance

22.7%
Arrest
situation

11.3%

13.9%

22.2%
Ambush
situation

Disturbance
call

17.6%

Traffic pursuit/stop

Officers feloniously killed = 541

1.2%
Civil disorder

1.8%
Handling person
with mental illness

0.3%
Ambush situation

Investigating
suspicious
person/
circumstance

Disturbance call

9.6%

31.5%

10.7%

12.6%

Traffic
pursuit/stop

14.1%

18.1%

Handling, transporting,
custody of prisoner

Arrest situation

All other

Officers assaulted = 586,674

EXHIBIT 7.1 Circumstances of Law Enforcement Officers' Felony Deaths and Assaults, 2001–2010

Source: FBI, *Crime in the United States, 2010*

[1]Because of rounding, the percentages may not add to 100.00.

[2]The deaths of the 72 law enforcement officers that resulted from the events of September 11, 2001, are not included in the data on officers feloniously killed.

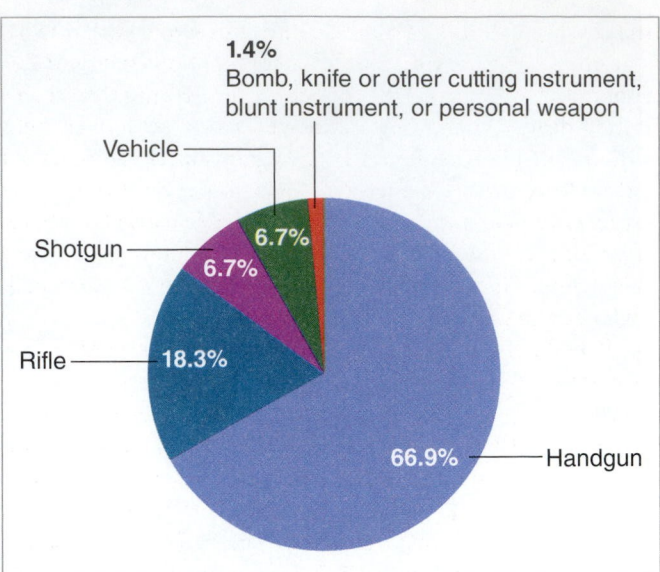

1.4%
Bomb, knife or other cutting instrument, blunt instrument, or personal weapon

Vehicle

6.7%

Shotgun

6.7%

Rifle

18.3%

66.9%
Handgun

EXHIBIT 7.2 Law Enforcement Officer Deaths by Weapon Type, 2001–2010

Source: FBI, *Crime in the United States, 2010*

[1]Because of rounding, the percentages may not add to 100.00.

[2]The deaths of the 72 law enforcement officers that resulted from the events of September 11, 2001, are not included in the data on officers feloniously killed.

Use of Deadly Force

Under common law, police were authorized to use deadly force as a last resort to apprehend a fleeing felon. The statute of use of force in place in North Carolina illustrates this point: "An officer of the law has the right to use such force as he may reasonably believe necessary in the proper discharge of his duties to effect an arrest. . . . [T]he officer is properly left with the discretion to determine the amount of force required under the circumstances as they appear to him at the time of the arrest."[27] Under existing legal requirements, deadly force may be used only when there is reasonable belief that the suspect will harm the officer or others in the community.[28] In fact, given the high number of police officers killed or assaulted in the line of duty, we know that those serving their communities do face very real dangers. As Exhibit 7.1 indicates, officers may be killed or assaulted in a wide variety of situations. In addition, they may be harmed with a variety of weapons, as shown in Exhibit 7.2. How and when officers use deadly force to prevent such harm is now our focus.

To improve procedural guidelines on the use of force against citizens, many departments have enacted general policies, as well as focusing specifically on the use of deadly force. All jurisdictions permit officers to use lethal force in their own defense, and most allow them to fire on a fleeing felon if they believe the suspect will endanger or harm others. Yet before *Tennessee v. Garner*[29] in 1985 (discussed in the chapter-opening case), the conditions under which such force could be applied to a fleeing felon were variable. Some jurisdictions required the suspect to be a "known" felon; others required that the officer be a witness to the felony; and still others permitted deadly force when the officer had a "reasonable belief" that the fleeing individual had committed the felony in question. In *Garner*, the Supreme Court held that deadly force against a fleeing felon is proper only when it is necessary to prevent the escape and when the officers have probable cause to believe that the suspect poses a significant threat of death or serious physical injury to the officer or others. Prior to this ruling, officers were left to use their own discretion about when the threat was high enough to warrant the use of deadly force.

When it comes to explaining the use of force, both lethal and nonlethal, police researcher James J. Fyfe points out that many writers on the topic fail to distinguish between (1) police violence that is clearly excessive, abusive, and unnecessary and (2) violence that results from police incompetence, meaning the inability of individual officers to deal with the situations they encounter without needlessly or too hastily resorting to force.[30] Fyfe argues that this distinction is important because the causes and motivations for the two types of violence vary greatly. The first kind involves willful and wrongful use of force by officers who knowingly exceed the bounds of their office.

Although police shootings are an inevitable part of enforcing the law and keeping the peace, ever since the Supreme Court's decision in *Garner,* virtually every police department in the United States has reexamined and expanded its policies on the use of deadly force in order to comply with state laws and constitutional standards. In addition, both new recruits and seasoned officers attend training seminars on the use of restraint and the consequences of an improper shooting. However, some police officials have expressed concern that an overemphasis on restraint has placed some officers in jeopardy.

Another phenomenon related to use of deadly force has become known as "suicide by cop." Out of the hundreds of police shootings that occur each year, a significant number are provoked by people seeking to end their own lives at the hands of police officers. Further, rather than resulting from capricious acts of mania or rage, such incidents are seen as calculated attempts to force police to act as executioners. Research conducted in Los Angeles County over a 10-year period showed that out of the 437 shootings by police officers, 11 percent were suicide-by-cop situations.[31] The impact on the involved police officers has been dramatic, typically resulting in a combination of early retirement from policing and negative psychological effects.

Concerns about the lethality of police force have led many departments and police officials to seek alternatives to deadly force. The next section examines these non- or less-than-lethal forms of force.

Nonlethal Weapons

Modern policing organizations rely on many technologies to reduce the number of fatal shootings by police. These include guns that shoot alternate projectiles, like rubber bullets, and chemical sprays that irritate the eyes and respiratory systems of offenders. One of the most common nonlethal weapons uses an electric current to temporarily immobilize suspects.[32] Called *conducted energy devices,* these weapons utilize compressed nitrogen to transmit an electronic signal to a target up to 25 feet away. When the signal makes contact with the suspect's body directly or through clothing, a 50,000-volt shock renders an immediate loss of neuromuscular control.[33] More than 16,200 law enforcement agencies nationwide have adopted the use of Tasers, a specific brand of these devices. Hundreds of police departments, including those in Phoenix, San Diego, Sacramento, Albuquerque, and Reno, have issued Tasers to every patrol officer. Federal agencies, such as the U.S. Marshals, also include the Taser in their officer training and skill development.[34]

DISCRETION MATTERS

In the long term, how do you think the availability of nonlethal weapons might affect police decisions regarding use of force?

Police officers must experience the Taser during training in order to be certified to use the weapon.

Many police forces, such as those in Seattle and San Jose, incorporated Tasers into their arsenals after controversial police shootings elicited public outcry. Advocates say Tasers reduce the number of fatal shootings by police while providing an alternative means of subduing rowdy, uncooperative, or dangerous suspects. Statistics indicate a decrease in the number of fatal shootings by several police departments after the acquisition of Tasers. In Phoenix, for example, shootings by police fell by half in the first year of their use. In Houston, civilian shootings plunged to a 25-year low, and in Aventura, Florida, injuries to suspects dropped 60 percent while injuries to police officers were down by 40 percent after the adoption of Tasers.[35]

Critics, however, maintain that the safety of the Taser has not been sufficiently proven, citing the more than 100 deaths that have occurred nationwide.[36] Although the Taser has been trumpeted as safe and effective in studies sanctioned by the manufacturer, Taser International, skeptics say the company's studies (consisting of tests on a pig in 1996 and five dogs in 1999) have not been thorough or rigorous enough.[37] Since then, however, other studies, including several by the Taser manufacturer, have been undertaken, finding various degrees of safety and allaying some concerns about the use of Tasers by police. Nevertheless, there is no federal regulation of the devices.

When Tasers were introduced, no uniform guidelines regulated their use in law enforcement agencies, prompting critics to charge some agencies with being "trigger happy." And the overall impact of Taser use is still unclear. In Orange County, Florida, for example, use of pepper spray and batons sharply declined after Tasers were acquired, but the overall use of force increased 58 percent from 2000 to 2003, which is the most up-to-date information we have. Furthermore, human rights groups have voiced concern over who is getting stunned. For example, in San Jose's first year of Taser use, 64 percent of the 174 people tasered were mentally ill or under the influence of drugs or alcohol; and Latinos, who constitute 30 percent of the city's population, accounted for 52 percent of those tasered. In just four months with Tasers, officers in Houston tasered 144 suspects, 90 percent of whom were black or Hispanic. And in Miami, the tasering of a 6-year-old boy and a 12-year-old girl prompted revisions of the police department's policy on Taser use on minors.[38]

Despite the controversies, the public appears to trust officers and agencies in the use of Tasers, even with recent controversies.[39] State and federal accrediting agencies have now developed guidelines for appropriate Taser use. As of April 30, 2010, the Taser weapon had been used nearly 1.3 million times in the field or against suspects, with less than 1 percent reporting injury.[40] Judging by its popularity among police departments and the manufacturer's tremendous financial success, the Taser and other nonlethal weapons will play an increasing role in modern policing. These weapons and other less-than-lethal options indicate a willingness of policing agencies to use technology to better respond to crime and protect the communities they serve.

CONTROLLING POLICE MISCONDUCT

Without question, policing, like many professions, is rich in opportunities for corruption, brutality, abuse of discretionary powers, violation of citizens' rights, and other forms of misconduct. Moreover, "policing the police" is difficult for a variety of reasons. Corruption generally occurs in the most covert of circumstances and involves cooperation by many. In addition, the victims of the misconduct—of the brutality, abuse of discretionary powers, and violations of due process rights—are often reluctant to report their experiences or are prevented from doing so. Further, police officers operate alone or in small teams—beyond the observation of departmental supervisors. Finally, the internal policing of certain abusive practices, combined with the elements of secrecy and solidarity that are characteristic of all police organizations, inhibit many police agencies from making instances of misconduct a matter of public record.

This is not to say that police abuses cannot be brought under greater control. Mechanisms that can affect police behavior for the better can be implemented by legislatures, the courts, communities, and police organizations themselves.

Legislative Control and Court Response

Throughout the history of the United States, criminal justice has been faced with the problem of overcriminalization (the trend in American society to use criminal law to solve any problem), as lawmakers have attempted to respond to concerns in the community about particular criminal offenses or fear of crime generally. Along these lines, laws and regulations related to alcohol consumption, drug use, prostitution, gambling, and other victimless crimes are the areas in which most police corruption occurs. Thus, if legislatures are to control police conduct, one could argue that they might begin by decriminalizing victimless crimes. In response to this argument, some legislatures have relaxed gambling laws through the establishment of state-run lotteries and off-track betting, legalized prostitution or reduced it to a minor violation, and eliminated a number of restrictions on business owners, landlords, and the building construction industry. However, much police corruption is an outgrowth of the laws controlling the possession of cocaine, crack, heroin, and numerous other drugs, which are not likely to be legalized in the near future. Calls for the end of the war on drugs and changes in restrictions on marijuana, including the legalization of medical marijuana, somewhat alter opportunities for corruption.

By contrast, some clear progress has been made in one legislative area. Section 1983 of the Civil Rights Act of 1871 authorizes lawsuits for violations of constitutional rights. Under this provision, originally enacted after the Civil War to protect newly freed slaves, an individual can hold a law enforcement agency or municipality liable for an incident of police misconduct. It has since been expanded to include any state or federal governmental official who prevents a citizen from accessing constitutionally protected rights. Legislation such as this has offered citizens and communities opportunities to respond through civil court action when police or other agents of the government abuse their power and fail to uphold the law or their mission, though many such cases are settled out of court and without much community involvement or notification.

Civilian Review Boards

The influence of citizens on police behavior may be most evident in small communities. There, one sees closer contact between the police and members of the community. Officers are typically longtime residents of the locations they patrol, police officials often depend on public support for departmental finances and tenure, and police behavior in general is more visible.[41] For all these reasons, police abuse is also less widespread. The reverse seems to be true in large urban centers, where community control over policing may be minimal due to increases in caseload and population served by the department. Historically, a number of responses have addressed this problem, including "putting the cop back on the beat," expanding community

In some communities, police misconduct allegations have led to citizen demonstrations. Such allegations and events have also prompted law enforcement agencies to implement civilian review boards that oversee police behavior and review citizens' complaints.

policing and sensitivity training for police recruits, and establishing **civilian review boards** to increase police professionalism and develop positive police and community relationships. Civilian review boards are typically appointed groups of citizens that oversee police behavior and review cases of misconduct. However, the militaristic characteristics of police organizations and the elements of the informal police culture that stress secrecy and solidarity combine to create a situation in which police appear highly resistant to outside control. The experience with civilian review boards illustrates this point well.

Before 1958, all power to discipline law enforcement personnel was in the hands of police departments, generally in the form of an internal review committee composed of one or more police officials. Concerns about this system surfaced during the late 1950s and early 1960s, when the United States Commission on Civil Rights found that many African Americans felt powerless to do anything about police malpractice. These revelations were confirmed by later studies conducted by the American Civil Liberties Union (ACLU), the National Association for the Advancement of Colored People (NAACP), and the University of California. The studies pointed to a range of objections to internal police review boards. Among other things, these studies found that the procedures in use at that time insulated police officers from being held accountable and gave the community the impression that officers were rarely, if ever, disciplined for their misconduct.[42] The ACLU also found that in an effort to protect the reputation of their departments, the internal affairs units and other special police squads that were structured for "policing the police" employed a host of tactics to discourage citizens from filing complaints against officers. In New York City, they threatened complainants with criminal libel; in Cleveland, they forced them to take lie detector tests; and in Philadelphia, Washington, DC, and Los Angeles, they took them into custody on charges of resisting arrest, disorderly conduct, or other minor offenses. Other departments intimidated witnesses, deprived complainants of access to departmental files, or otherwise acted as though the citizens were on trial.[43]

The ACLU, the NAACP, and other citizen groups urged police authorities to shift the responsibility for handling complaints to external citizen-controlled review boards. The boards were to serve several purposes:

1. They would respond to officers who engaged in brutality, harassment, and other abusive and even illegal practices.
2. By ensuring a thorough and impartial investigation of all complaints, they would protect other officers from malicious, misguided, and otherwise unfounded accusations.
3. They would offer African Americans and other minority-group members an avenue of redress, which would help restore their confidence in the police departments.
4. They would explain police procedures to citizens, review enforcement requirements with police, and initiate a genuine dialogue in place of mutual recrimination.[44]

Proposals for such civilian review boards were controversial for most police officers, and such organizations as the International Association of Chiefs of Police, the International Conference of Police Associations, and the Fraternal Order of Police bitterly fought against them. Despite opposition, however, a few cities did establish civilian review boards. The first was set up in Philadelphia on October 1, 1958, but from its inception, its potential for objective judgment was severely limited. Philadelphia's five-member Police Advisory Board had no investigatory staff and had to rely on the police department's community relations unit to investigate complaints.

In the ensuing years, civilian review boards have come and gone in a number of places; currently, at least 25 of the nation's largest cities have some form of civilian review. However, some are less effective than others. In San Francisco, for example, civilian investigators examine each complaint and present their findings to outside adjudicators. Other cities allow police personnel to investigate a complaint first and then, if the police determine it to be unfounded or unresolvable, they often turn it over to an independent review board for further consideration. In many cases, police managers, not board members, decide how to respond to the board's findings and the type of punishment to be imposed.[45] Citizens who are unhappy with the outcome of these reviews have limited options. They may file civil suits against the department or individual officers, or in some limited cases they may appeal these internal review decisions. Civilian oversight of the police agency remains controversial, and calls for reform of existing review boards have not ceased. Yet the idea of increased citizen involvement in law enforcement administration is important, particularly where the bonds between the community and the police are strained.

In order to strengthen the relationship between community members and the police and to increase citizens' knowledge about law enforcement duties, organizations, and challenges, policing agencies across the nation have developed citizen police academies. Through these opportunities, members of the community can learn about the police officer's job and some aspects of officer training. Many scholars remain unwavering in the belief that shared goals with the community will ultimately benefit all involved.[46] However, the policing organization remains the best avenue for identifying, controlling, and responding to misconduct. We discuss this in the next section.

Police Organization Control and Response

Control of police misconduct from within police departments has two forms: preventive and punitive. Preventive control involves alterations in the structure and philosophy of the police organization. One example of preventive control is the policy of internal accountability, which holds members of a law enforcement agency responsible for their own actions, as well as those of others with whom they work. Internal accountability is based on clear communication of standards regarding appropriate behavior and level of responsibility. However, internal accountability becomes workable only when police officers are under tight supervision by administrators, precinct commanders, and other control staff. Tight supervision involves direct surveillance of officers' work by field commanders, combined with daily logs documenting officer activity.

Preventive control and accountability can work to abolish corrupting procedures and increase formal training about corruption and misconduct. Every large police department and many smaller ones have numerous formal procedures that inadvertently encourage corruption. For example, some policies require levels of productivity that are all but impossible to achieve by legitimate means; others create pressures for financial contributions by officers that the officers attempt to "earn back" in corrupt ways. Vice investigators and detectives, for instance, often must "purchase" leads from informers, but funds for such purposes may be limited or unavailable in some departments. Similarly, criminal investigation work may require the use of personal autos with no provisions for expense reimbursement. Law enforcement agencies have made enormous strides in preparing new recruits for the challenges

Continued education and training help to ensure high professional standards. Such classes are typically organized to help officers keep up with changes in technology, law, and the nature of crime.

and responsibilities of the role of police officer.[47] Continued enhancement of these policies and training procedures ensures that agencies will be doing all they can to prevent misconduct.

Responsibility for punitive control lies with a policing unit known as internal affairs, or internal policing. Officers who work in such units investigate complaints against police personnel or actions involving police misconduct. Internal policing may be the responsibility of a single officer or detective, a small police unit, or an entire division or bureau, depending on the size of the department and its commitment to in-house review. Regardless of their size, however, internal affairs units are generally responsible for inquiries into the following:

1. Allegations or complaints of misconduct made by a citizen, police officer, or any other person against the department or any of its members
2. Allegations or suspicions of corruption, breaches of integrity, or cases of moral turpitude from whatever source—whether reported to or developed by internal policing
3. Situations in which officers are killed or wounded by the deliberate or willful acts of other parties
4. Situations in which citizens have been killed or injured by police officers either on or off duty
5. Situations involving the discharging of weapons by officers[48]

Internal policing began during the latter part of the nineteenth century, when headquarters personnel became responsible for making inspections on a citywide basis and investigating corruption. In New York and a number of other cities, these officers became known as "shoo-flies," a term taken from the language of the professional underworld. The shoo-fly was originally a criminal's spy who watched for police activity in order to warn the thief.[49] By 1900, detectives were also known as shoo-flies, because as nonuniformed investigators, they spied on criminals.[50] During Arthur Woods's tenure as commissioner of the New York City Police Department, which began in 1914, a confidential squad was organized to spy on the activities of police officers.[51] It was at that point that the term *shoo-fly cop* came into general use.

It was not until the mid-1900s, however, that structured bureaus for internal policing came into being. In the wake of a major scandal during the late 1940s, Los Angeles police chief William A. Worton formed the Bureau of Internal Affairs. Within a decade, Boston, Chicago, and Atlanta followed suit, and at the beginning of the 1960s New York City joined the trend when that city's police commissioner established the Inspection Service Bureau, which brought together several units that had been separately monitoring the integrity and efficiency of the police.[52]

Attempts to reduce police misconduct have not been limited to efforts by legislatures, review boards, and internal policing, as these treat only the symptoms of the problem. Reform efforts have also focused on greater professionalization of police in general. However, opinions have differed as to the definition of *professionalism*. Many police administrators have focused their professionalism efforts on more clearly defining rules and regulations, increasing central control, and implementing stricter policies regarding discipline and obedience—as you read earlier in the chapter. In other organizations, professionalism efforts have focused on granting a large measure of discretion to individuals—that is, allowing them to respond to situations on the basis of expertise gained from long training and experience rather than organizational rules and regulations. In this latter kind of law enforcement agency, professionalism is associated with better trained and educated officers, more sophisticated police resources, closer attention to the needs for community service and police-community relations, and more efficient and detailed policies regarding police behavior in contacts with citizens. These goals have been the focus of modern attempts to reform the field generally.

Properly understood, police professionalism implies that brutality and corruption are symptoms of incompetent policing. And incompetence may be judged by the following standard: While the right to use force is at the core of the police role, skill in policing is revealed by the ability to avoid its use. With respect to corruption, professionalism gives rise to norms of pride and dignity that make police intolerant of fellow officers who do not meet these standards.[53] Educating new officers about alternatives to misconduct should be paramount as agencies continue to serve an ever-changing community and respond to the evolving face of crime.

CONCLUSIONS

Attempts to control police corruption and misconduct of all varieties have emanated from the legislature, from civilian review boards, and from police agencies themselves. Perhaps the most effective method is to focus on increasing police professionalism more generally. The perspective of professionalism views brutality as incompetent policing, and it views corruption as beneath the dignity of effective law enforcement agents. A focus on encouraging professional behavior within policing agencies increases trust in the community, making law enforcement more effective and police more responsive to those they serve and protect.

SUMMARY AND REVIEW

◼ **Define police integrity and professionalism.**
  - Police integrity involves exercising powers and using discretion according to the highest standards of competence, fairness, and honesty.

- Many administrators within the police understand professionalism to mean more clearly defined rules and regulations, increased central control, strict discipline, and obedience. Others see professionalism as resulting from better trained and educated officers, more sophisticated police resources, closer attention to the needs for community service and police-community relations, and more efficient and detailed policies regarding police behavior in contacts with citizens.

■ **Define and explain the causes of police corruption.**

- Police corruption involves illegal activities for economic gain, including payment for services that police are sworn to carry out as part of their peacekeeping role.
- Examples of police corruption include meals and services, kickbacks, opportunistic theft, planned theft and robbery, shakedowns, case fixing, protection, private security, and patronage.
- Three common explanations for police corruption follow:
  - Corruption is caused by societal influences within the community.
  - Police corruption is a function of the structure and culture within the police organizations.
  - Some individuals ("rotten apples") who become police officers may be predisposed toward corruption.

■ **Define police brutality, and present the primary explanations for why it occurs.**

- Police brutality is the most commonly identified form of police violence and is most often defined as unwarranted or excessive use of physical force, though it can also include verbal assaults.
- Police brutality is often attributed to the following:
  - Police perceptions that effective policing relies on citizen acceptance of police authority

- Police judgments of the social value of certain citizens and the devaluation of other citizens
- The on-the-spot nature of police decision-making

■ **Describe the circumstances under which police may use deadly force according to the *Tennessee v. Garner* case.**

- In *Tennessee v. Garner,* the Supreme Court emphasized that deadly force may not be used unless it is necessary to prevent the escape of a suspect for whom there is reasonable cause to believe a significant threat of death or serious physical injury to the officer or others exists.
- The use of deadly force to prevent the escape of all felony suspects, whatever the circumstances, is constitutionally unreasonable, according to the Supreme Court.

■ **Identify the best ways of controlling police misconduct and increasing integrity within policing.**

- Legislative control through re-evaluation of laws that create the potential for police violations and corruption
- The use of civilian review boards to increase contact between the police and the community
- Increased and more consistent use of preventive and punitive measures within the police organization
- Efforts by law enforcement agencies to increase police integrity, including (1) organizational rule-making; (2) detecting, investigating, and disciplining rule violations; and (3) circumscribing negative impacts of police culture

KEY TERMS

case fixing (p. 179)
civilian review boards (p. 190)
kickbacks (p. 177)
patronage (p. 180)

police brutality (p. 182)
police corruption (p. 177)
police integrity (p. 175)
police professionalism (p. 175)

shakedown (p. 178)
The Code (p. 181)

ISSUES FOR CRITICAL THINKING AND DISCUSSION

1. Why might corruption be more or less widespread in policing than in other occupations and professions?
2. Do you think that providing police with gratuities, like food or drinks, contributes to corruption? Why or why not?
3. How might the war on drugs contribute to police corruption? Do you think that legalizing drugs would reduce police corruption?
4. Is the problem of police violence and brutality so much a part of the police role that it can never be routed out? Why or why not?
5. Focusing on your own community, do you think police corruption is common? What practices, policies, and activities are in place that either contribute to corruption or control it in your own community?
6. In what ways can civilian review boards become more effective in controlling police corruption and brutality?
7. Have you ever witnessed an incident of police misconduct? If so, describe what occurred. Did the incident appear to be officer-initiated or citizen-initiated?

8

The Structure and Function of American Courts

LEARNING OBJECTIVES

- Trace the evolution of the U.S. court system.
- Describe the major types of courts in the state system and the relationships between them.
- Define and identify an example of a specialty court.
- Describe the major courts in the federal system and the relationships between them.
- Describe the history and functions of the U.S. Supreme Court, including the significance of the *Marbury v. Madison* case.
- Explain the major functions of judges, prosecutors, defense attorneys, and others in the courtroom workgroup.
- Discuss the role of prosecutorial discretion, including plea bargaining and the *nolle prosequi*.

DISCRETION ON THE BENCH

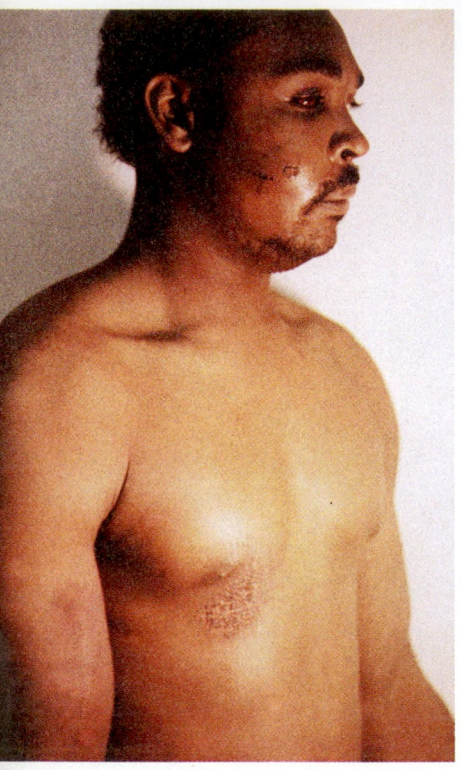

Rodney King (*left*) and Officer Stacey Koon (*right*) were two of the key parties in a dramatic illustration of the court's role in protecting individual liberty and furthering procedural due process in the criminal justice system.

On March 2, 1991, Rodney King and two friends spent several hours drinking. Then, with an intoxicated King driving, they merged onto a major freeway. California Highway Patrol (CHP) officers observed King's car traveling at an estimated speed exceeding 100 mph. The officers followed the car with lights and sirens blaring. King was ordered to pull over via loudspeaker, but he did not comply. Units of the Los Angeles Police Department (LAPD) joined the CHP officers in the pursuit. King left the freeway and, after driving about eight more miles, finally stopped the car. The officers ordered everyone to exit the car and lie on their stomachs with their legs spread and their arms behind their backs. All three exited the car, but King did not lie down.[1]

Officer Stacey Koon arrived, followed by two other officers from the LAPD. Koon was the sergeant on scene and took charge. The officers again ordered King to assume the felony prone position. King got on his hands and knees but did not lie down. Three officers tried to force him down, but he resisted, so the officers stepped away from him. Koon then fired Taser darts at King (see Chapter 7 for more on Tasers).[2]

Videotape from a citizen depicts the events that occurred next. King rises from the ground and moves toward one officer. That officer uses his baton on King, hitting him on the side of the head. King falls to the ground and then is repeatedly hit in various places on his body for the next two minutes. Finally, King submitted and was handcuffed. The police called an ambulance. One officer sent two messages by radio to the other officers that said "ooops" and "I havent [sic] beaten anyone this bad in a long time." Sergeant Koon sent a message to the police station that said, "Unit just had a big time use of force. . . . Tased and beat the suspect of CHP pursuit big time." At the hospital, King was treated for a broken leg, multiple facial fractures, and other injuries.[3]

This is a dramatic story, to be sure, but most germane to this chapter is what happened next. Koon and three other officers were initially charged with assault with a deadly weapon and excessive use of force by a police officer. They were tried in a California state court but found not guilty. The result of this trial sparked riots in Los Angeles that killed 53 people, injured more than 2,000, and resulted in nearly $1 billion worth of property damage. The four officers were later indicted by a federal grand jury and charged in federal district court under statute 18 U.S.C. § 242 with violating King's civil rights by their use of excessive force. The case was heard at the federal level because federal district courts have jurisdiction over constitutional issues, even if those issues were originally raised in state courts, as in this case. The federal court jury convicted Koon and one other officer, sentencing them to 30 months in prison, even though federal-sentencing guidelines would have set the sentence somewhere between 70 and 87 months. Ultimately, the Supreme Court heard the case.[4]

You might think that we present this case as a way to discuss police discretion in the application of force. If so, you are wrong. The question of Koon's guilt in using excessive force was never in question at the Supreme Court level. In this case, the Supreme Court was asked to examine the appropriateness of Koon's sentence.

In California, trial judges may depart from government-established sentencing guidelines for a number of reasons. However, in this case, the court had four very specific reasons for using its discretion to give Koon a lesser sentence. First, the judge noted that the widespread publicity and outrage caused by the case created a situation in which the petitioners would be targeted in prison. Next, the judge highlighted the professional impact of being sentenced. Koon and the other officer convicted would never be able to serve as police officers again. Third, the court noted the significant burden already put on the officers by being prosecuted for these offenses. Last, the court noted that neither officer was violent, dangerous, or likely to engage in future criminal conduct and therefore concluded that there was no reason to impose a sentence that reflected a need to protect the public. The Supreme Court affirmed part of the outcome of the case and rejected another portion.[5] However, this case highlights

the enormous amount of discretion in just one aspect of the court process: sentencing.

The criminal case against Koon and the other officers was first tried in a California state court, but the defendants were found not guilty. When the officers were convicted in federal district court, the trial judge determined the sentence. The prosecuting attorney appealed the sentence to the U.S. Court of Appeals for the Ninth Circuit, believing it to be an unfair departure from what was specified in the sentencing guidelines for California. Finally, Koon appealed to U.S. Supreme Court, which agreed to review the case.

In addition to the issues it raises about judicial discretion in sentencing, this case offers a good illustration of the way a case moves from one court to another, including from state to federal court. The purpose of this chapter is to explain the American court system—how state courts differ from federal courts, what their functions are, how they work together (or don't), and who does the work of the court. We begin with a brief review of the history of the U.S. court system. We then explain the organization of the state and federal courts, and finish by looking at the roles of the various court personnel.

THE EVOLUTION OF U.S. COURTS

As America evolved into a nation, the court emerged as an integral part of life in most communities. It was at the local courthouse that celebrations were held and emergencies were brought to the attention of the community. Courthouses served as mustering places during the War of Independence and the Civil War, and victories and setbacks were announced in broadsheets posted on their doors. The courthouse also served as a meeting place for religious services, dances, and town council assemblies, as well as fulfilling its primary function as a place for the dispensation of justice. In matters of law, the procedure was clear and simple. The courthouse stood at the center of town. There, the **justice of the peace** decided on all aspects of civil disputes and minor criminal transgressions. When more serious issues of crime, law, and justice arose, the procedure—at least in its outward aspects—was just as clear. Once each month, on "court day," a judge visited the community and disposed of these weightier matters.[6]

As towns became cities, the procedures became more complex. Because there were more people, and hence more problems, there were more courts. For civil matters, there were counterparts of the rural justices of the peace; for the less serious criminal affairs, there were police and magistrate's courts; and for serious problems of law and order, there was a more permanent higher court.[7]

Pictured here is an early American courthouse in Waxahachie, Texas.

As the nation grew even more populous and more complex, so too did its system of courts. By the late nineteenth century, American courts reflected a bewildering mosaic of names, types, structures, and functions. The old courthouse still stood; the rural justices of the peace and the urban magistrates still decided on certain matters of law; and the county courts, night courts, and higher courts still operated. But along with these, one could also find mayor's courts, municipal courts, probate courts, chancery courts, superior courts, and various levels of appeals and supreme courts. Some town and county courts were consolidated into circuits and districts; numerous areas had general sessions courts and special sessions courts; and legal practitioners spoke in terms of appeals courts and trial courts, higher courts and lower courts, superior courts and inferior courts. Overall, a **dual court system**—one at the state level and another at the federal level—had evolved throughout America after the signing of the Declaration of Independence. Without question, finding "the courthouse," or at least the right courthouse, had become a perplexing problem.[8]

Today, the situation is no less knotty. In fact, the court system has become even more intricate. Let's begin to unravel the intricacies by looking at the state courts.

STATE COURTS

Two key characteristics of state court systems are that no two are exactly alike and that the names of the courts in each state vary widely, regardless of their functions. For example, all states have major trial courts devoted to criminal cases. In Ohio and Pennsylvania, these are called *courts of common pleas;* in California, they are known as *superior courts;* in New York, they are *supreme courts*—a designation that is typically used elsewhere for appeals courts.[9] Moreover, while Michigan's major trial courts are called *circuit courts,* within the city of Detroit they are called *recorder's courts.*[10]

The many names, functions, and types of state court structures have resulted from the fact that each state is a sovereign government that can enact its own penal code and set up its own enforcement machinery. The term *court jurisdiction* refers to the specific practical authority to hear cases and administer justice based on law in a particular geographic region and/or hierarchy within the court system. Thus, in each of the 50 court jurisdictions, the court systems developed differently—sometimes in an unplanned, sporadic way—generally guided by different cultural traditions, demographic pressures, legal and political philosophies, and needs for justice administration. Yet despite this apparent confusion, a clear-cut structure exists within all the state court systems. State judiciaries are divided into three, four, or sometimes five tiers, each with separate functions and jurisdictions.

As shown in Exhibit 8.1, the courts of last resort are at the uppermost level, occupying the highest rung of the judicial ladder. These are the appeals courts. All states have a court of last resort, but depending on the jurisdiction, the names vary—*supreme court, supreme court of appeals,* or perhaps simply *court of appeals.* In addition, some states, including Texas and Oklahoma, have two courts of last resort, one for criminal cases and one for all others.[11]

Immediately below the courts of last resort in more than half the states are the intermediate appellate courts. Located primarily in the more populous states, these courts have been structured to relieve the caseload burden on the highest courts. Like the highest courts, they are known by various names; often the names are similar to those of the courts above them in the hierarchy (*appeals courts*), as well as below them (*superior courts*). On the next-lower rung are the major trial courts, or the courts of general jurisdiction, where felony cases are heard. Civil cases are heard here as well, but because this is a course in criminal justice, we are focused solely on the criminal aspect of the system. All states have various combinations of trial courts, and depending on the locale, they might be called *superior, circuit, district,* or some other designation. The lower courts, often referred to as *inferior, misdemeanor, minor,* or *courts of limited jurisdiction,* exist in numerous combinations in every state.

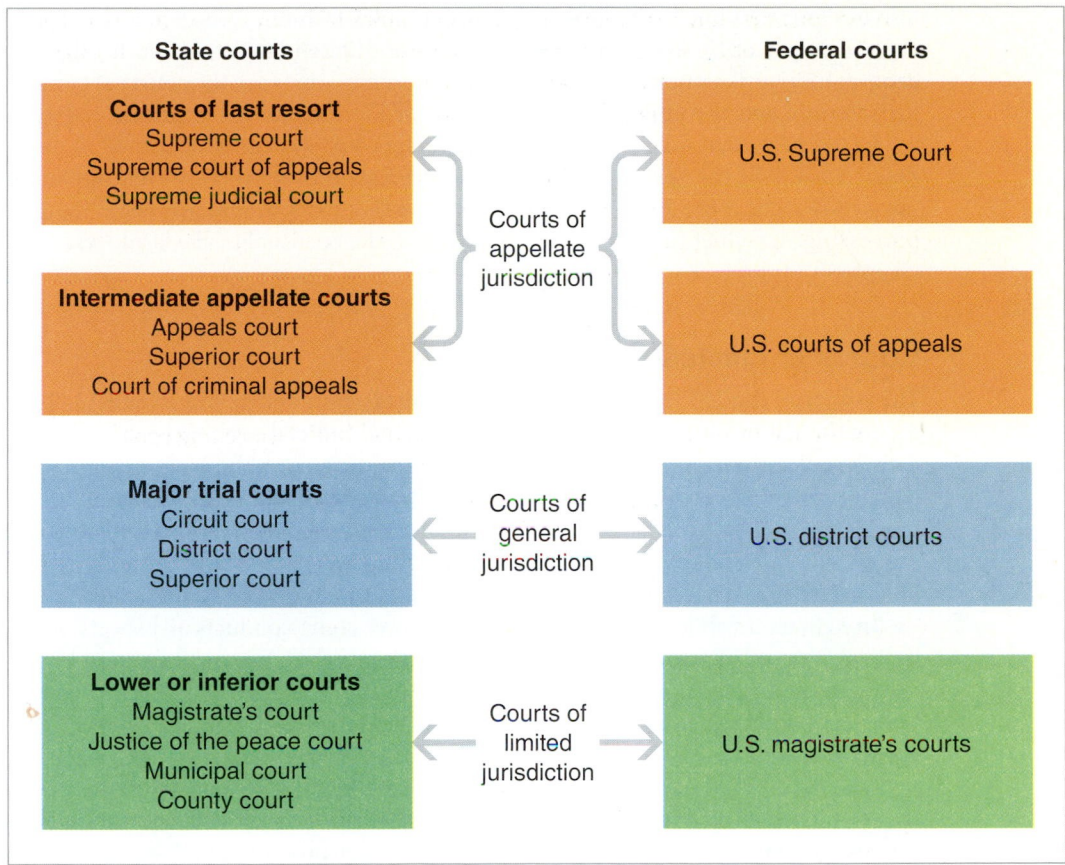

EXHIBIT 8.1 State and Federal Court Structure

Variously named *county, magistrate, police, municipal, justice of the peace,* or *justice courts,* as well as dozens of other designations, they are the entry point for most defendants and the only level at which traffic and regulatory infractions and most misdemeanors are processed.

To round out our definition, the *jurisdiction* of each court varies by geography, subject matter, and hierarchy. Thus, courts are authorized to hear and decide disputes arising within specific political boundaries—a city, borough, township, county, or group of counties. In addition, some courts are limited to specific matters—for example, misdemeanors or civil actions versus all other types of cases. There are family courts that decide on juvenile and domestic relations matters, probate courts whose jurisdiction is limited to the handling of wills and the administration of estates, and many others. Jurisdiction can also be viewed as limited, general, and appellate, as follows:

1. **Courts of limited jurisdiction,** otherwise known as the lower courts, try minor offenses, such as traffic infractions and misdemeanors.
2. **Courts of general jurisdiction,** or the major trial courts, have the power and authority to try and decide any case, including appeals from a lower court.
3. **Courts of appellate jurisdiction,** or the appeals courts, are limited in their jurisdiction to matters of appeal from lower courts and trial courts.

Court systems may be simple or complex in their organizational structure. The Florida court system has a simple four-tier structure. The county courts are the courts of limited jurisdiction, and the circuit courts have general jurisdiction. The state supreme courts and the district courts of appeal are two levels of appellate jurisdiction. This structure can be contrasted with that of the New York State court system, which also has four tiers but is organized in a more complex fashion.[12] The two lowest levels are the courts of limited jurisdiction, which are differentiated from each other by geographical jurisdiction and functions. The supreme courts are the courts of general jurisdiction, and the upper courts, like those of Florida, are the appellate courts.[13]

In the pages that follow, each level of the state court system is examined in more detail, including the specialty courts, an arena for innovation. However, our most important focus is the lower courts, for it is there that most defendants begin judicial processing. The chief function of the trial court—the criminal trial—is addressed in Chapter 9.

Courts of Limited Jurisdiction

The courts of limited jurisdiction, or lower courts—numbering more than 13,000[14] across the nation—are the entry point for criminal judicial processing. These typically handle minor criminal offenses such as prostitution, public intoxication, petty larceny, disorderly conduct, and violations of traffic laws and city and county ordinances. In addition, courts of limited jurisdiction hear most civil cases and conduct inquests. For defendants charged with felonies, the lower courts have the authority to hold initial appearances and preliminary hearings and to make bail decisions.

In matters involving minor violations, the lower court conducts all aspects of the judicial process, from initial appearance to sentencing. Given the large number of felony cases that are initially processed in this part of the state court structure, the lower courts ultimately deal in one way or another with more than 90 percent of all criminal cases.[15]

One type of lower court with limited jurisdiction, called justice of the peace courts, serves mostly rural areas—for example, in some areas of Delaware—where the justices have little if any legal training and court procedures are extremely informal. Alternatives are the county courts and their variants, which, in contrast to the justice of the peace system, involve more legal training for judges and formal proceedings. All of these courts handle minor offenses, civil issues, and the pretrial aspects of felony processing. County courts are staffed by judges, clerks, and other personnel on state or county payrolls; and judges are paid salaries rather than fees for service, which is the historical arrangement for the justice of the peace. The urban counterpart of the justice of the peace and county courts is the municipal court, also called magistrate's court. In jurisdictions where the judicial system has formally

Courts often reflect the nature and characteristics of the communities they serve. Contrast this rural courtroom from Delaware (*left*) with a courtroom in New York City (*right*).

separated the processing of criminal and civil cases, these lower courts may be known as criminal courts or police courts.

The functions of municipal courts are the same as those of county courts. Municipal courts have the added problems of large caseloads and assembly-line-like justice. In the face of heavy workloads, some magistrates exercise wide discretion—for instance, by ordering certain cases dismissed or by abbreviating the legal process. In addition, in cases involving lesser offenses, defendants are sometimes processed as a group rather than individually receiving the specific and direct attention of the court. Historically, the lower courts have been the most significant, yet typically the most neglected, of all the courts. The significance of these courts lies not only in the sheer number of defendants who pass through them but also in their jurisdiction over many of the offenses that represent the initial stage of an individual's criminal career.

In an address to the members of the New York Bar Association in 1919, Supreme Court Justice Charles Evans Hughes commented on the proper role of the lower courts:

> The Supreme Court of the United States and the Court of Appeals will take care of themselves. Look after the courts of the poor, who stand most in the need of justice. The security of the Republic will be found in the treatment of the poor and the ignorant; in indifference to their misery and helplessness lies disaster.[16]

These sentiments apply equally to the millions who pass through the lower courts each year. Unfortunately, in the decades since Justice Hughes's remarks, few changes have occurred in the lower courts.

Courts of General Jurisdiction

The major trial courts, or courts of general jurisdiction, are authorized to try all criminal and civil cases. Such courts, of which there are more than 3,000 across the nation, handle about 10 percent of the defendants originally brought before the lower courts who are charged with felonies and serious misdemeanors (the balance having been disposed of at the lower-court level).[17]

Trial courts may be called circuit, district, or superior courts, in addition to numerous other titles. However, Indiana has both circuit courts and superior courts, and in Indianapolis the court is simply called *criminal court*.[18] While many county courts may be part of a state's lower-court system, as described earlier, other county courts may actually be circuit or district courts and hence are major trial courts. Also, a given county courthouse may often serve as both a lower court and a trial court. For example, when several counties are grouped together in a **judicial circuit**—meaning an organizational assignment of several types of cases and several jurisdictions into one—it is customary for a judge to hold court in each county in turn. The judge moves from county to county within the circuit, and the local county courthouse becomes the circuit court during the judge's term there; the phrase "riding the circuit" is derived from this practice.[19]

The administration of criminal justice in major trial courts tends to be less problematic than it is in courts of limited jurisdiction. Judges are lawyers and members of the bar and hence are better equipped to deal with the complex issues of felony cases. Most are salaried, full-time justices and are not compensated by the fee-for-service payment structure. The adjudication process generally adheres to the principles of procedural criminal law and due process; and as courts of original jurisdiction, the trial courts are **courts of record,** which means that a full transcript of the proceedings is made for all cases. However, this does not mean that the trial courts are without difficulties. As we discuss in later chapters, procedural challenges associated with bail, indictment, plea negotiation, sentencing, and judicial discretion can affect the fairness of the trial court system.

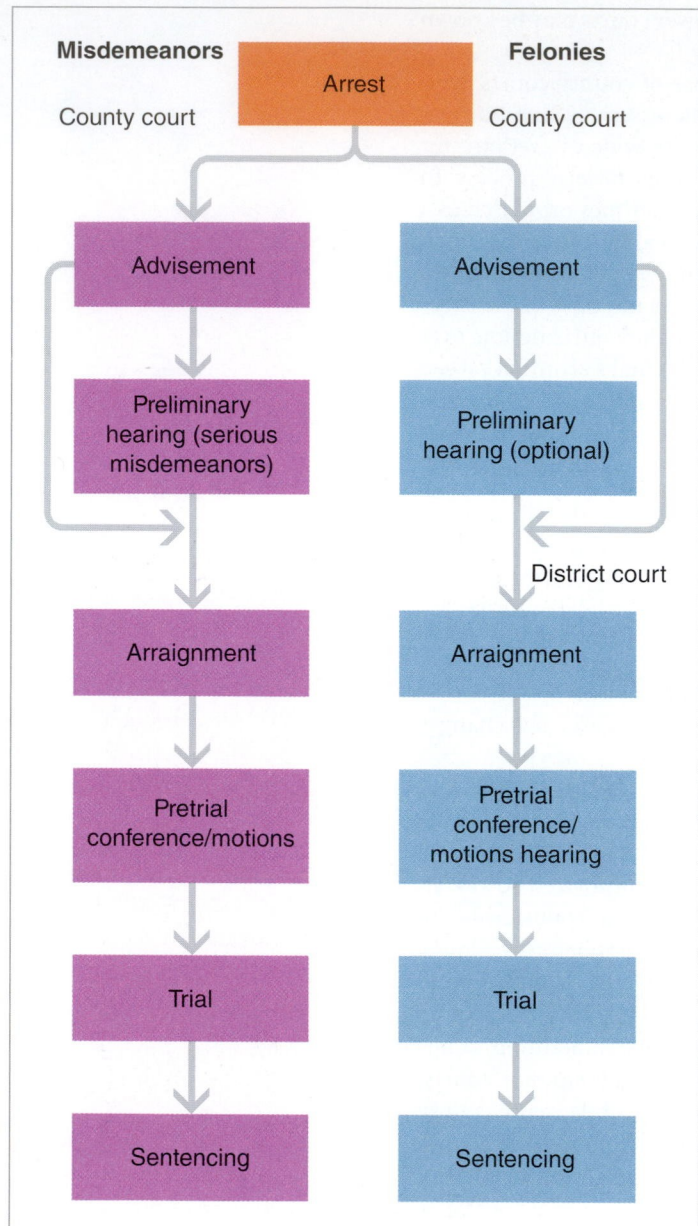

Misdemeanors   **Felonies**

County court   County court

Arrest

Advisement   Advisement

Preliminary hearing (serious misdemeanors)   Preliminary hearing (optional)

District court

Arraignment   Arraignment

Pretrial conference/motions   Pretrial conference/ motions hearing

Trial   Trial

Sentencing   Sentencing

EXHIBIT 8.2 Typical Criminal Court Process

To understand more fully the separate roles and relationships between the lower and trial courts, consider the criminal case processing in Colorado's First Judicial Circuit (Exhibit 8.2), which reflects what is typical throughout the nation. All cases involving felonies and misdemeanors begin in the lower court, called the county court in that jurisdiction. While the misdemeanor cases remain in the lower court through sentencing, felony processing shifts to the district court (the major trial court) at arraignment.[20] This contrasts to jurisdictions in which the entire felony process occurs in the trial court, or criminal court.

Courts of Appellate Jurisdiction

In law and criminal justice, the term *appeal* refers to review by a higher court of the judgment of a lower court. Thus, appellate jurisdiction is restricted to matters of appeal and review; unlike courts of general jurisdiction, appellate courts cannot try cases. However, this is not to say that the workload of these courts is light. Filings for appeal emerge not only from criminal cases but also from civil matters. And if an attorney complies with the court's rules for appealing a case, the court must review the case.[21]

As a result, more than half the states have intermediate courts of appeal. These courts relieve the state's highest court from hearing every case. An unfavorable decision from an intermediate appeals court, however, does not automatically guarantee a hearing by the state supreme court, the court of last resort in each state. The state supreme court has the power to choose which cases will be placed on its docket—a characteristic of the highest court in every jurisdiction.[22]

Reform and Unification of State Courts

The state courts have many problems. Prominent among these are organization, structure, and deployment. For most of the twentieth century and into the twenty-first, various federal, state, and city commissions and foundations have examined the state courts, and most of their recommendations for reorganization have failed to be realized through the years:

- Unify felony and misdemeanor courts.
- Create a single, unified state court system.
- Centralize administrative responsibility.
- Abolish the justice of the peace courts.
- Increase the numbers of judicial personnel.
- Improve physical facilities.[23]

Court unification and reform are more easily recommended than implemented. Some unification has occurred in Arizona, Illinois, New York, North Carolina, Oklahoma, Pennsylvania, and Washington, and each year other states consider proposals for a unified system. However, due to political, philosophical, and pragmatic obstacles, few such proposals have been adopted. Local governments wish to retain control of their

Many urban and some suburban courts struggle to respond to their assigned caseloads. Pictured here is a courtroom from one of those jurisdictions.

local courts; some judges fear that they would lose their status and discretion; political parties fear a loss of power and control; local municipalities fear the loss of revenues derived from court fines and fees; and many lawyers, judges, and prosecutors in all jurisdictions are simply resistant to change.[24]

The problem of overloaded court dockets is especially pervasive, for the costs that would be involved in expanding staff and facilities are well beyond the resources of most jurisdictions. And it seems that the overload is only getting worse, as jurisdictions across the nation struggle with a backlog in the system of justice in their own communities.

Specialty Courts

Across the nation, communities have implemented specialty courts focused on certain offenses. These are lower courts that have jurisdiction over one area of criminal activity or a particular group of offenders. Specialty courts—including drug, firearm, elder-crime, and veterans courts—are designed to respond to an identified concern within the community. The responses by the court to these special offenders or cases often involve numerous court agencies and resources, including cooperation across multiple layers of the criminal justice process.[25]

The best-known of these are drug courts. *Drug court* is actually a generic term for several kinds of initiatives designed to cope with the high number of drug cases coming to the attention of the criminal justice system. These approaches include the use of special judges, distinctive case-management systems, and pretrial diversion programs. Many of these new entities function as traditional courts by hearing evidence and adjudicating guilt, while others serve as special plea-bargaining forums. Many handle only first offenders; others have no such limitations.

In these courts, arrestees are given the opportunity to participate in a treatment program. The program's personnel closely monitor their progress through urinalysis and reports. Negative behavior can result in short periods of jail confinement, but court personnel recognize that a relapse to drug use is often part of the recovery process. Because of this focus on rehabilitation, drug court clients are given several chances to

Drug courts offer resources and incentives such as graduation ceremonies to help offenders complete their treatment programs. These incentives are coupled with the threat of increased penalties for failing to comply with the programs' requirements, such as regular drug testing.

prove themselves. Positive behaviors are rewarded with decreased reporting requirements, and successful completion may result in the charges being dropped or a lesser sentence being imposed.

Are drug courts effective? Researchers have identified a number of advantages. First, the state-paid judges, prosecutors, and public defense attorneys who are assigned to drug courtrooms become specialists and can therefore process cases more quickly and efficiently. Second, new rules for drug courtrooms—such as early and complete discovery or disclosure of evidence and firm trial dates—encourage early plea negotiation and settlement. Third, segregating drug cases can speed the processing of both drug and nondrug cases. And fourth, because drug cases tend to be relatively standardized, holding them in drug courts reduces the likelihood that defendants will seek trials, which streamlines the case preparation and investigation process for prosecutors.[26]

In short, data from a number of evaluation studies suggest that drug courts provide an effective alternative to incarceration by reducing recidivism and easing population pressures in overcrowded jails. As a result, the number of drug courts has expanded from 1 in 1989 to almost 400 by 1997 and to more than 2,400 by the beginning of 2011.[27]

FEDERAL COURT

Unlike the state court systems, the federal judiciary has a structure that is unified across the United States and its territories. It has a four-tier structure similar to that found in most of the states: the magistrate level, the district level, the appellate level, and the Supreme Court (Exhibit 8.3).[28] Although it handles fewer cases than state court systems do, the scope of the federal court system is considerably greater. It is

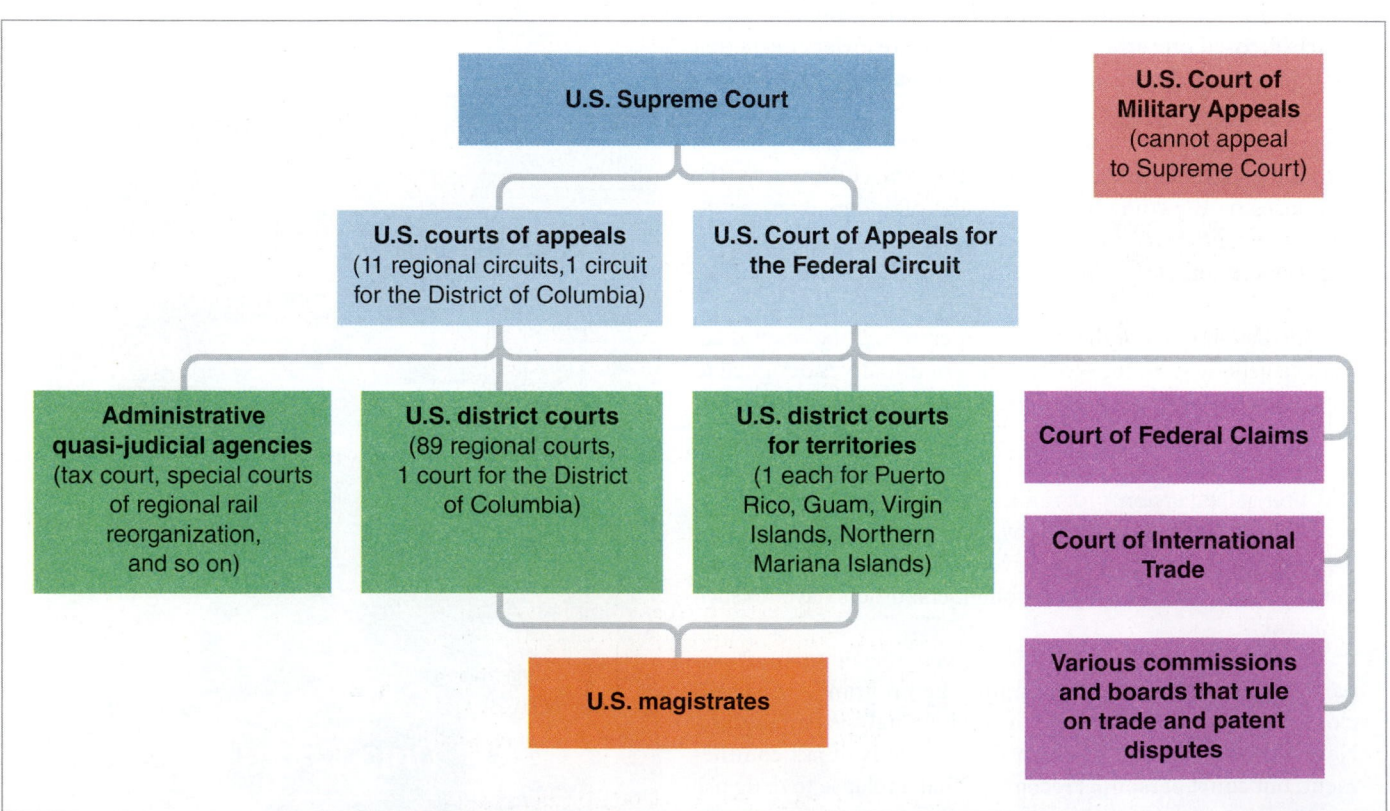

EXHIBIT 8.3   Federal Judiciary System

responsible for enforcing all federal codes (criminal, civil, and administrative) in all 50 states, U.S. territories, and the District of Columbia, and all local codes and ordinances in the territories of Puerto Rico, Guam, the Virgin Islands, and the Northern Mariana Islands. In addition, the U.S. Supreme Court has ultimate appellate jurisdiction over the federal appeals courts, the state courts of appeal, the District of Columbia Court of Appeals, and the Supreme Court of Puerto Rico.[29]

U.S. Magistrate's Courts

Congress passed the federal Magistrate's Act in 1968.[30] The act established the position of **U.S. magistrates**—lawyers whose powers are limited to trying lesser misdemeanors, setting bail in more serious cases, and assisting the district courts in various legal matters. In 1976, their authority was expanded to include the issuance of search and arrest warrants, the review of civil rights and *habeas corpus* petitions, and the conduct of pretrial conferences in both civil and criminal hearings.[31] Magistrates can be either full-time or part-time jurists, and all are appointed by the federal district court judges.

U.S. District Courts

The **U.S. district courts** were created by the federal Judiciary Act, which was passed by Congress on September 24, 1789. Originally there were 13 courts, one for each of the original states, but now there are 94—with 89 distributed throughout the 50 states, and 1 each in the District of Columbia, Puerto Rico, Guam, the Virgin Islands, and the Northern Mariana Islands.[32]

The U.S. district courts are the trial courts of the federal system and the District of Columbia—the courts of general jurisdiction. They have jurisdiction over cases involving violations of federal laws, including bank robbery, civil rights abuses, mail fraud, counterfeiting, smuggling, kidnapping, and crimes involving transportation across state lines. The district courts try cases that involve compromises of national security, such as treason, sedition, and espionage; selective service violations; copyright infringements; jurisdictional disputes; and violations of regulatory codes, such as the Securities and Exchange Act, the Endangered Species Act, the Meat and Poultry Inspection Act, and the Foreign Agents Registration Act, among many others. In addition to the 94 U.S. district courts, there are two special district courts that have nationwide jurisdiction over certain types of cases. The U.S. Court of International Trade addresses cases involving international trade and customs issues. The U.S. Court of Federal Claims has jurisdiction over most claims for monetary damages against the United States, disputes over federal contracts, unlawful "taking" of private property by the federal government, and a variety of other claims against the United States. In addition, district court caseloads include numerous civil actions and petitions filed by state and federal prisoners.[33]

Each district court has one or more judges, depending on the caseload, with a total of 677 judgeships in 2010 as authorized by law. Like Supreme Court justices and court of appeals judges, district court judges in the federal system are nominated by the president. These appointments are then confirmed by the United States Senate, as is required by the Constitution. Legislators from the president's political party often recommend nominees. The Senate Judiciary Committee typically conducts confirmation hearings for each nominee. Article III of the Constitution indicates that these judicial officers are appointed for a life term, but it includes no specific qualifications for judges. Members of Congress, who typically recommend potential nominees, and the Department of Justice, which reviews nominees' qualifications, have developed their own informal criteria.[34]

In most cases, a single judge presides over trials, and a defendant may request that a jury be present. In complex civil matters, a three-judge panel may be convened.

In addition to the U.S. magistrates discussed earlier, each court has numerous other officers: a U.S. attorney, who serves as the criminal prosecutor for the federal government; several assistant U.S. attorneys; a U.S. marshal's office; and probation officers, court reporters, clerks, and bankruptcy judges.

Since the 1980s, the district courts have had to function under near-crisis conditions. The workload has increased dramatically, from 122,624 cases in 1970 to more than 361,323 by the end of 2010. The level of criminal cases has increased in recent years to 78,428 in 2010, dealing with everything from traffic offenses to significant violations of the U.S. Criminal Code. Those cases included more than 100,000 defendants. However, the number of district court judges has not been expanded in proportion to the workload. In 1970, there were 649 judgeships with an average load of 370 cases per judge. In 2010, there were 677 judgeships but with an average load of well over 500 cases per judge.[35]

Jurisdictional conflicts between state trial courts and federal district courts have resulted in some cases being tried in both federal and state courts. More generally, the expanding federal role in criminal prosecution (especially in drug cases) means that criminal behavior, which formerly was almost exclusively the province of state courts, is now a concern of federal district courts as well. It is difficult to predict how this jurisdictional dilemma will be resolved. In 2000, however, the U.S. Supreme Court weighed in on the issue when it ruled on the constitutionality of the Violence Against Women Act (see the "Victims and Justice" feature).

VICTIMS AND JUSTICE

United States v. Morrison and the Violence Against Women Act

The issues in *United States v. Morrison*[36] date back to the fall of 1994, when Christy Brzonkala enrolled at Virginia Polytechnic Institute (Virginia Tech). Some weeks later, she met Antonio Morrison and James Crawford, both students at Virginia Tech and members of the school's varsity football team. Brzonkala claimed that within 30 minutes of meeting Morrison and Crawford at a party, they assaulted and repeatedly raped her. After the attack, Morrison allegedly told Brzonkala, "You better not have any . . . diseases." During the months that followed, Morrison allegedly announced in his dormitory's dining room that he "liked to get girls drunk and . . ." Morrison's comments, quoted verbatim in Supreme Court briefs, consisted of boasting, as well as vulgar remarks about what he would do to women.[37]

Christy Brzonkala alleged that the attack so devastated her that she became severely depressed. She sought assistance from a university psychiatrist, who prescribed antidepressant medication. Nevertheless, she stopped attending classes and withdrew from the university. She indicated that she was so despondent and humiliated by the crime that she did not go to the authorities until 1995, then filing a complaint against Morrison and Crawford under Virginia Tech's sexual assault policy. During the school's hearing on her complaint, Crawford was exonerated, but Morrison admitted to having had sexual contact with her despite the fact that she had twice told him no. Although Morrison was found guilty of sexual assault and was sentenced to immediate suspension for two semesters, he challenged his conviction. A subsequent hearing at Virginia Tech found him guilty only of "using abusive language," and his punishment was set aside by the university administration. Moreover, a local grand jury refused to indict either of the two men on any criminal charges.[38]

Christy Brzonkala (*left*) filed suit against Antonio Morrison and James Crawford under the 1994 Violence Against Women Act (VAWA). The controversy surrounding this legislation continues as Congress struggles to renew the VAWA legislation.

It was at that point that Brzonkala filed an $8.3 million suit in federal court against Morrison and Crawford under the 1994 Violence Against Women Act (VAWA). The intent of the act was to give women the alternative of filing civil lawsuits against their attackers, regardless of the status of any criminal prosecution. Brzonkala contended that the alleged rapes had violated her civil liberties and had caused her to drop out of college and, thus, suffer the economic consequence of a lesser education and diminished employment opportunities. Ultimately, the case reached the U.S. Supreme Court.[39]

When the High Court delivered its opinion in *United States v. Morrison* in 2000, the decision had little to do with rape allegations. Instead, the legal questions before the court were whether the VAWA was valid under either the interstate commerce clause of the Constitution or the Fourteenth Amendment. The commerce clause is a provision that gives Congress exclusive powers over interstate commerce. Found in Article I, Section 8, this power is the basis for a considerable amount of federal legislation and regulation. Congress frequently uses the commerce clause to outlaw activities that do social harm. The rationale for the 1964 Civil Rights Act, for example, was that discrimination hurts the economy. Title VII of the Civil Rights Act bars employment discrimination, which has clear economic consequences because it prevents people from finding work and keeping their jobs. The VAWA maintains that violence against women has an adverse impact on interstate commerce by reducing women's capacity to produce goods and services used nationwide, stymieing their travel because of safety concerns. The Fourteenth Amendment issue focused on whether the VAWA upheld Americans' right to "equal protection" under the law.[40]

Thus, at the center of the court's 5–4 ruling were the constitutional justifications Congress employed in passing the Violence Against Women Act, not the rape charge. The High Court ruled against Christy Brzonkala's attempt to sue in federal court, concluding that the VAWA improperly interfered with the sovereignty of state laws on rape. The court also rejected the equal protection argument on grounds that the purpose of the Fourteenth Amendment was to protect against governmental discrimination, not discrimination by individuals. By 2012, the controversy about the act had not diminished. The House reauthorized a version of the VAWA in May 2012, but there continued to be concerns about the lack of protections for lesbian, gay, and transsexual individuals and the handling of some victims of domestic abuse. Even if both political parties could agree on a version of the legislation, the civil rights remedy sought by Christy Brzonkala has been struck down by the *Morrison* decision.

THINK ABOUT THIS

1. The VAWA was intended to offer victims of crime alternate ways to seek justice. Should federal courts offer such alternatives? Why or why not?
2. Could these alternatives undermine the finality of state court proceedings? What might the implications be for individuals accused of crimes?
3. Why might some victims need to seek justice in federal courts?

Source: *United States v. Morrison,* 529 U.S. 598 (2000).

U.S. Courts of Appeals

Appeals from the U.S. district courts move up to the next step in the federal judicial hierarchy—that is, to the **U.S. courts of appeals.** There are 13 of these intermediate courts, with 179 authorized judgeships as of 2011.[41] Each court is located in a regional circuit—a specific judicial jurisdiction served by the court, as defined by geographical boundaries (Exhibit 8.4). There are 11 numbered circuit courts and one additional court for the District of Columbia. For example, the U.S. Court of Appeals for the First Circuit is located in Boston and serves the district courts located in Maine, Massachusetts, New Hampshire, Rhode Island, and Puerto Rico (see Exhibit 8.4). In addition to the 12 regular circuits, we have the U.S. Court of Appeals for the Federal Circuit, which has nationwide jurisdiction to hear appeals in specialized cases, such as those involving patent laws and cases decided by the U.S. Court of International Trade and the U.S. Court of Federal Claims.[42]

The 13 courts of appeals hear more than 55,000 cases each year, involving both criminal and civil matters.[43] These cases are appealed from the U.S. district courts, not from state supreme courts or appeals courts. Almost all are heard by three-judge panels; a few are heard *en banc,* or "in bank," meaning that the full bench of judges authorized for that particular court considers the appeal. In only three types of situations can a case appealed from one of the U.S. district courts bypass a U.S. court of appeals and go directly to the U.S. Supreme Court:

1. When the ruling under appeal was decided by a special three-judge district court hearing
2. When the United States is a litigant and the case involves a federal statute that was declared unconstitutional by a district court
3. When the issue under review is considered so important that it requires immediate settlement

The U.S. Supreme Court

The **U.S. Supreme Court** is the highest court in the nation. It stands at the apex of the federal judiciary and is truly the court of last resort. The Supreme Court is composed of nine justices: one chief justice and eight associate justices, who serve for life.[44] They are nominated by the president of the United States, and their appointments must be confirmed by the Senate. Over the course of U.S. history, the vast majority of these justices have been white, male, and Protestant, although currently the court has a Roman Catholic majority and no Protestants for the first time.[45] In addition, the court

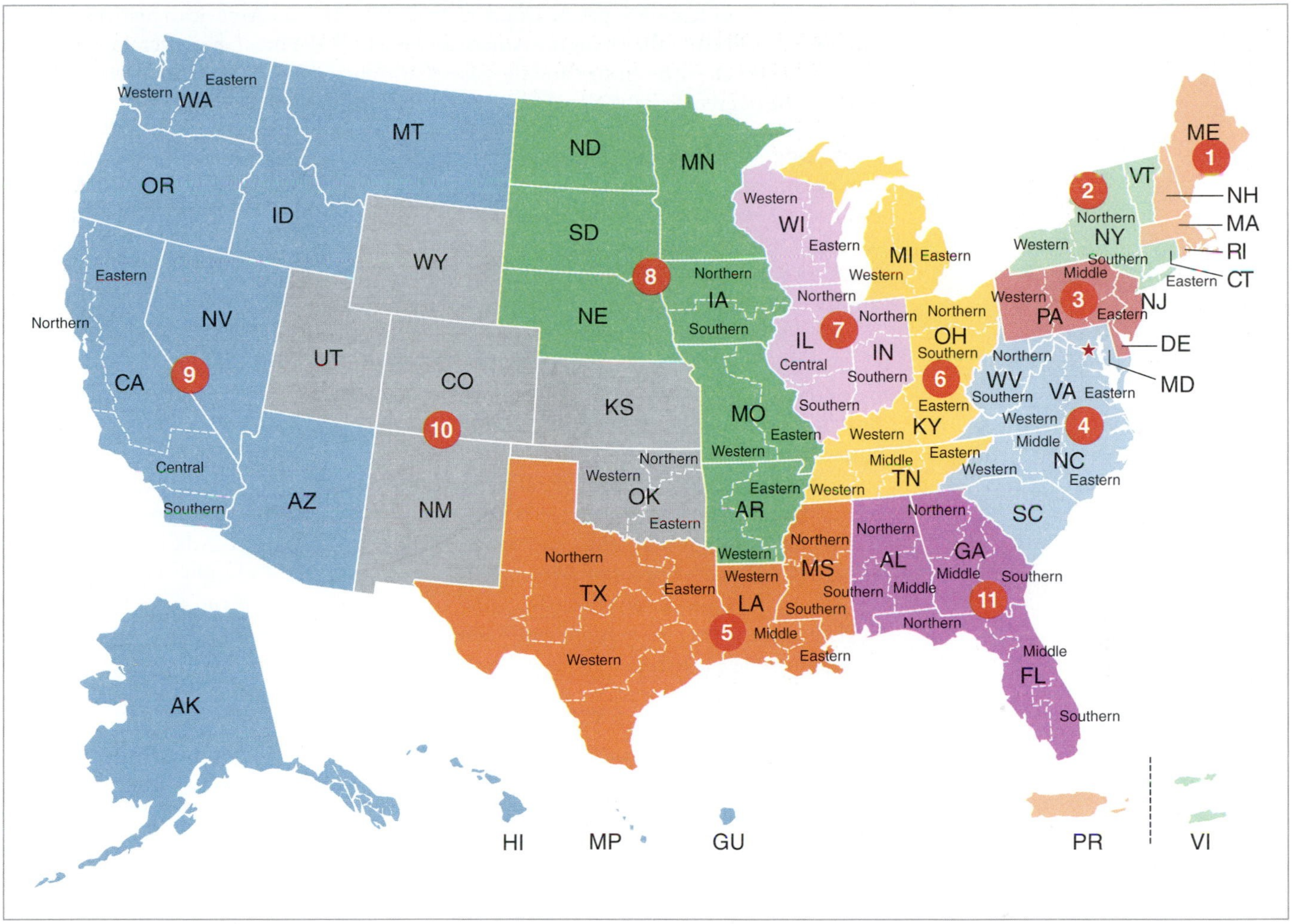

EXHIBIT 8.4   United States Federal Judicial Circuits

The Supreme Court building in Washington, DC, houses the highest court in the United States.

The nine justices of the Supreme Court, pictured here in 2012, serve as the court of last resort for American criminal justice.

has now had four female Supreme Court justices, two African American justices, and one Latina, reflecting the changing American society.[46] We must, however, look back to the early nineteenth century and the case of *Marbury v. Madison* to understand the roots of the Supreme Court's powers, the topic we turn to next.

Marbury v. Madison The role of the Supreme Court became fully established during the early decades of the nineteenth century under the leadership of John Marshall, who served as chief justice from 1801 through 1835. In 1803, just two years after Marshall assumed his post, the court announced its decision in *Marbury v. Madison*,[47] and in so doing it claimed, exercised, and justified its authority to review and nullify acts of Congress that it found to conflict with the Constitution.

Marbury v. Madison involved a dispute over presidential patronage that had escalated into a contest for authority between Congress and the Supreme Court. The case emerged from the bitter presidential election of 1800, in which Thomas Jefferson defeated Federalist John Adams. Unwilling to relinquish the power they had held since the beginning of the Union, the Federalists sought to entrench themselves in the federal judiciary. John Marshall's appointment to the Supreme Court had been part of that effort. In addition, just before Adams left office, Congress approved legislation creating 16 new district court judgeships. It also authorized Adams to appoint as many justices of the peace for the newly created District of Columbia as he deemed necessary, and it reduced the number of Supreme Court justices from six to five at the next vacancy.[48] This latter move was intended to deprive Jefferson of an opportunity to appoint a new justice.

William Marbury was one of those appointed as justice of the peace, but he did not receive his commission before Adams left office. He asked the Supreme Court to issue a writ ordering James Madison, secretary of state, to give him (Marbury) his commission. The major question was one of jurisdiction—that is, whether the Supreme Court had the authority to issue the writ. Marshall concluded that it did not, stating that Congress could not expand or contract the jurisdiction of the Supreme Court and that Congress had acted unconstitutionally, exceeding its power, when it authorized the court to issue such writs in earlier cases.[49]

Although this matter of jurisdiction absolved the Jefferson administration of responsibility for installing several of President Adams's appointees, the real significance of *Marbury v. Madison* was that it established the Supreme Court's power to review acts of Congress. Therefore, many consider the *Marbury* decision the most important ruling in Supreme Court history.[50]

The Jurisdictional Scope of the Supreme Court The Constitution— Article III, Section 2—gives the Supreme Court broad but not limitless jurisdiction. The Supreme Court has two kinds of jurisdiction over cases—general and appellate. The court's general jurisdiction usually involves suits between two states, issues that test the constitutionality of state laws, and matters relating to ambassadors. In such instances, the Supreme Court can serve as a trial court. In its appellate jurisdiction, the court resolves conflicts that raise "substantial federal questions," typically questions related to the constitutionality of some lower-court rule, decision, or procedure.[51] The court rarely exercises this power of original jurisdiction.

Selection of Cases As the final tribunal beyond which no judicial appeal is possible, the Supreme Court has the discretion to decide which cases it will review. However, the court must review cases in the following instances:

- When a federal court has held an act of Congress to be unconstitutional
- When a U.S. court of appeals has found a state statute to be unconstitutional
- When a state's highest court of appeals has ruled a federal law to be invalid
- When an individual's challenge to a state statute on federal constitutional grounds has been upheld by a state supreme court

In all other instances, as provided by the Judiciary Act of 1925, the Supreme Court decides whether it will review a particular case. The Supreme Court does not have the authority to review all decisions of state courts in either civil or criminal matters. Its jurisdiction extends only to cases in which a federal statute has been interpreted or a defendant's constitutional right has allegedly been violated. Moreover, a petitioner must exhaust all other remedies before the High Court will consider reviewing his or her case. As you can see in Exhibit 8.5, the path to review of a case by the Supreme Court requires lower-court review. That is, should a matter of "substantial federal question" emerge in a justice of the peace court, for example, the first review would not be carried out in the Supreme Court. Rather, it would be heard as a **trial de novo,** the system of new trials, in the state trial court. Following that would be an appeal to an intermediate court of appeals (in states where they exist), and then an appeal to the state's highest court. Only then would the case be eligible for review by the Supreme Court. A similar process occurs with respect to the federal court structure.

The Supreme Court's authority to decide which cases it will hear is known as its *certiorari* power and comes from the **writ of certiorari,** a writ of review issued by the Supreme Court, ordering a lower court to "forward up the record" of a case it has tried so that the Supreme Court can review it. Prior to this granting of certiorari, the potential case must pass the Rule of Four; that is, a case is accepted for review only if four or more justices feel that it merits consideration by the full court.

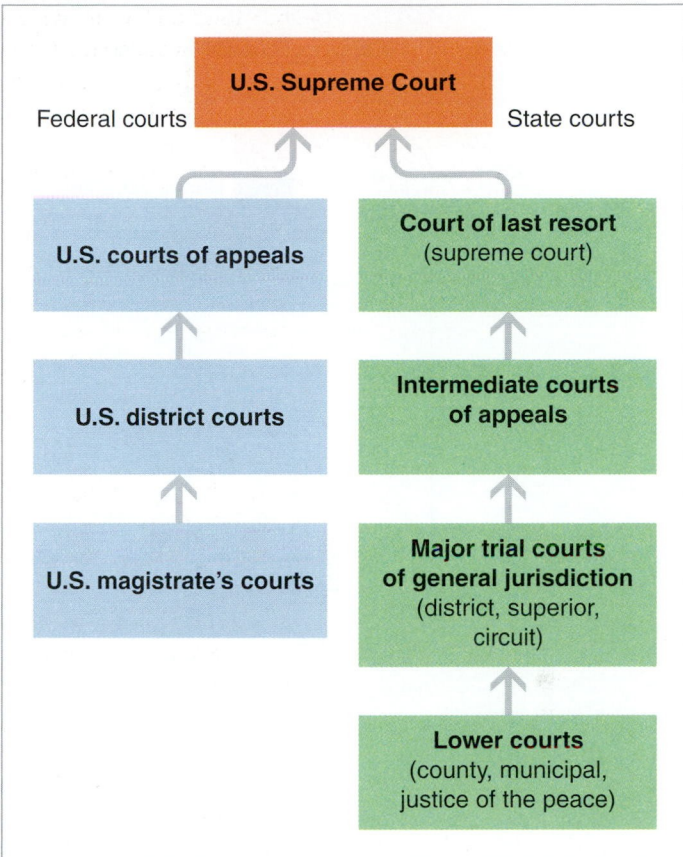

EXHIBIT 8.5   The Judicial Ladder to the Supreme Court

The Supreme Court accepts for review only cases in which its decision might make a difference to the appellant and, as stated earlier, cases involving a "substantial federal question." It does not operate as a court of last resort to correct the endless number of possible errors made by other courts. Rather, it reserves its time and energy for the most pressing matters. Currently, about 8,000 cases are filed annually for review by the Supreme Court; however, in the past few years, the court has decided fewer than 100 cases with full opinions each term.[52]

Affirming, Reversing, and Remanding   After reviewing a criminal case, the Supreme Court either affirms the lower-court ruling or reverses and remands it. When the court affirms a case, it has determined that the action or proceeding under review is free from reversible, prejudicial, or constitutional error and that the judgment of the lower court shall stand. Thus, if a conviction appealed from a lower court is affirmed, the conviction remains in force.

A Supreme Court decision that reverses, or overturns, a defendant's conviction or sentence does not necessarily free the appellant or impose a lighter penalty. Rather, it remands, or returns, the case to the court of original jurisdiction for a proper judgment. At that point the trial court has several options, depending on the nature of the case.[53] For instance, many of the criminal cases heard by the Supreme Court revolve around the constitutional issues of illegal search and seizure, illegal confessions, and other matters that might invoke the exclusionary rule. In such instances, the court of original jurisdiction can order a new trial but cannot introduce the "tainted" evidence. In many of these cases, however, the prosecution may decide that without such evidence, the state would have a weak case, and so it dismisses the charges. In other circumstances, the Supreme Court's decision may require a change of venue because

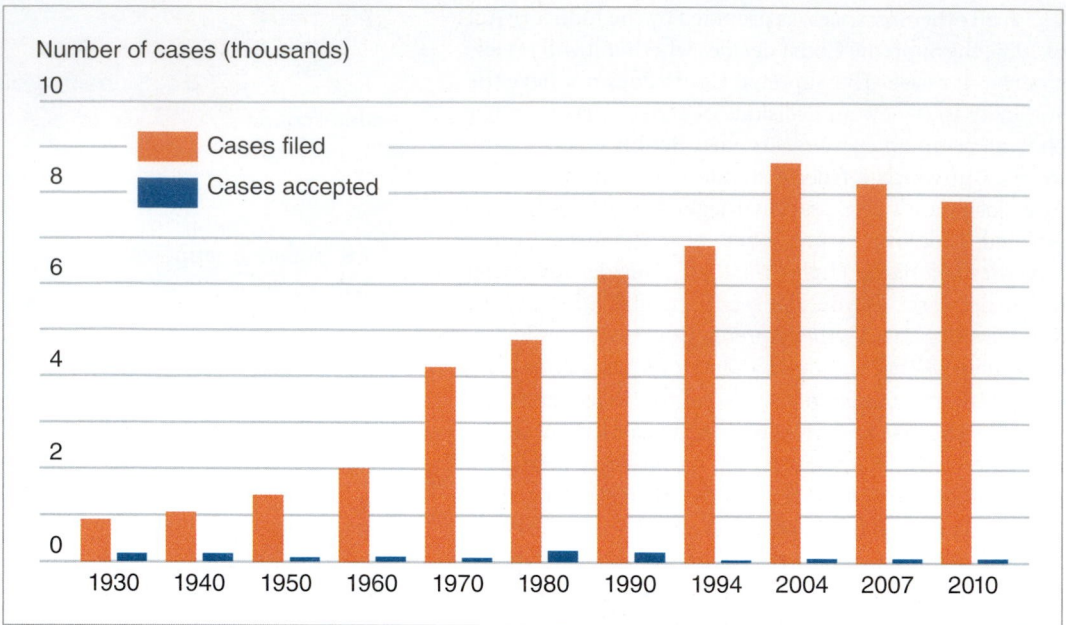

EXHIBIT 8.6 Supreme Court Caseloads, 1930–2010
Source: Supreme Court of the United States, Office of the Clerk

of pretrial publicity or community hostility that resulted in an unfair trial. Any new trial must be held in a different county or judicial district. Other Supreme Court reversals have ordered institutional authorities to remedy unconstitutional conditions of incarceration and have required trial courts to resentence certain defendants on the grounds that the original sentences constituted cruel and unusual punishment.[54]

The Supreme Court's Workload When the first Supreme Court convened in 1790, its role as guardian of the Constitution was newly conceived. At that time, the country itself was new, with 13 states and fewer than 4 million citizens. The work of the Supreme Court in those early days was simple. In its first three years it decided no cases, and during the next two years it ruled on only four matters.[55]

As the United States grew in size, complexity, and maturity, and as greater emphasis was placed on due process, human rights, and civil liberties, more and more cases began to work their way up through the appellate system (Exhibit 8.6). Although the number of justices had increased from six to nine, in the more than two centuries since the court's inception, the population the court was serving had expanded by some 270 million.[56]

As noted, during the term ending in the summer of 2011, the court received nearly 8,000 petitions. With so many appeals, the justices have been forced to rely more and more on their clerks to review cases, and a greater number of cases have been decided without written opinions. Moreover, the court has had to become more selective about cases. Or, as Erwin N. Griswold, former dean of Harvard Law School, stated many years ago, the justices have been forced into "rationing justice"—ruling in only a smattering of cases, while leaving citizens without guidance on numerous questions.[57]

> **DISCRETION MATTERS**
>
> What characteristics of a case might influence the Supreme Court to select it for review?

COURT PERSONNEL AND FUNCTION

Unquestionably, the processing of criminal cases includes dramatic moments and characters. The major participants in the drama, of course, are the judges, the prosecutors, the defense attorneys, and the accused. However, there may be many other participants, depending on the phase of the process, the type of case, and the level of court. For example, police officers and witnesses may contribute evidence of

Judges are the most visible and recognizable members of the courtroom workgroup.

innocence or guilt; grand juries and trial juries may consider the nature and importance of the evidence and render judgment; and officers of the court, such as bailiffs, clerks, and reporters, may attend to administrative matters. Finally, there are others with only quasi-judicial functions, such as coroners and medical examiners, whose testimony and judgment may be required in specific kinds of cases. Each of these participants has a specific role in criminal court processing, and without them, various phases in the judicial system would not be fully possible. The following sections examine the full spectrum of players, referred to as the *courtroom workgroup.*

Judges

No high-ranking official within the criminal justice system has the prominence and prestige of the judge, also referred to as *magistrate* or *justice.* Judges are responsible for the honest, impartial, and equitable administration of justice. To most observers, they are the ultimate arbiters and symbols of law and order. When they enter a courtroom, everyone rises; when they speak, others listen. Although at times their power to decide a case may be assigned to a jury, the judges alone have the authority to interpret the rules that govern court proceedings.[58] Like the judge in the *Koon* case, which was discussed in the chapter opener, judges generally have a great deal of power in determining the outcome of the trial process and the fate of the parties.

At the most general level, judges are both arbiters and administrators. As arbiters, they safeguard the rights of the accused, as well as the interests of the public. As administrators, they control the flow of cases through the courts and oversee such ancillary duties as the appointment and evaluation of court personnel, record-keeping, and budget requests. Generally, these roles and responsibilities apply to the justices of urban municipal courts, rural county courts, and state trial courts. Even justices of the peace have similar duties as they preside over minor offenses and civil disputes. However, there are variations depending on the size and complexity of a particular jurisdiction. County judges are more likely to have administrative duties—securing funds to operate the court, hiring personnel, purchasing supplies—than are judges on the higher rungs of the judicial ladder. Conversely, justices in urban municipal courts or state trial courts are likely to devote more of their time to managing the flow of cases through the court than are judges in less populated areas, simply because they have more defendants.

At the appellate level, the responsibilities of judges differ greatly from those of judges in the lower and felony courts. Appeals are dealt with through written briefs or oral arguments, and in the latter case the only participants are the counsels for the defense and the prosecution. The responsibilities of appeals judges include:

1. Determining whether the proper procedures were followed in the presentation of the appeal
2. Examining the written brief, the trial record, or other materials that may have been filed
3. Presiding over any oral arguments
4. Weighing the facts of the case and the nature of the appeal in order to arrive at a decision
5. Negotiating a decision through vote, persuasion, or compromise in cases in which more than one judge hears the appeal
6. Preparing a written opinion that details the logic and reasons for the decision

DISCRETION MATTERS

Why might discretion be a necessary component of the role of judges, magistrates, and other court personnel?

Beyond the general duties and responsibilities outlined above, judges also have influence over other aspects of the criminal justice process. In some jurisdictions, for example, service agencies such as probation and release-on-recognizance programs are under the administrative control of the court. In others, where these county or state agencies are separate from the court, their functioning is influenced by the attitudes and judicial policies of the local chief magistrate. Similarly, police and prosecutors are influenced by the judge, whose discretion in the acceptance of evidence and pleas and in sentencing clearly has an impact on the arrest and charging processes.

Although judges, justices, and magistrates have the highest authority in the criminal justice process, they are not always the most qualified or best trained. This situation has evolved, exposing a variety of problems regarding both the recruitment and training of judges, whether elected or appointed.

As indicated earlier, all federal judges are nominated by the president of the United States and must be confirmed by the Senate. The U.S. Constitution specifies this for Supreme Court justices, and the Judiciary Act of 1789 adopted the same procedure for other federal judgeships. Because all federal judges hold their offices for life, the appointments are extremely important, giving the president great power to shape the direction of federal judicial policy. This is unquestionably true with respect to the U.S. Supreme Court. Generally, the Senate takes the confirmation process seriously and sometimes engages in rugged battles. The nature of Supreme Court review has turned Senate confirmations into opportunities to battle over social issues, such as abortion, voting rights, immigration, and many others.

In state, county, and municipal jurisdictions where judges are elected, political connections are important. To win a judgeship, the candidate must first secure the party nomination and then campaign on the party ticket. Thus, the potential judge becomes embroiled in the same type of partisan politics seen in the election of presidents, governors, legislators, and other government officials.[59] This system generally results in the election of the most politically active, but not necessarily the most qualified, candidates.

In state jurisdictions where judges are appointed, partisan politics still can play a role, but the degree of political influence over specific selections varies by state and by level in the judicial hierarchy. In many systems, governors appear to have more freedom than the president in making selections. Generally, governors make appointments to the courts of appeals and sometimes to the major trial courts. In both instances, party connections and service in the state legislature play important roles in appointment considerations. Currently, the majority of states use merit selection, with the remainder choosing their judges through partisan (party-affiliated) or nonpartisan (non-party-affiliated) elections.[60]

At the lower levels of the judicial hierarchy, partisan politics are almost always present in the selection of judges. Mayors, county managers, or town councils typically appoint judges in municipal and justice of the peace courts, and friendship, kinship, party affiliation, and the political spoils system may play a role.

Prosecutors

The prosecutor, also known as the *district attorney (DA), county attorney, state attorney,* or *U.S. attorney*—depending on the jurisdiction of his or her office—is a government lawyer and the chief law enforcement authority of a particular community. As an elected or appointed public official, the prosecutor occupies a crucial position. The prosecutor decides how cases brought by the police will be disposed of, which cases will be pursued through the courts, and whether the original charges against an accused may be reduced to some lesser offense. In many jurisdictions, the prosecutor prepares and approves arrest and search warrants before they are formally reviewed and issued by a judge or magistrate.

At the most general level, the responsibilities of the prosecutor are threefold: (1) enforcing the law, (2) representing the government and community in matters of law, and (3) representing the government and the people in matters of legislation and criminal justice reform.[61] As such, the functions of the prosecutor are extremely broad, spanning the entire criminal justice process:

Before being appointed to the Supreme Court in 2009, Justice Sonia Sotomayor served as an assistant district attorney in New York for more than four years.

1. Investigation: Prosecutors prepare search and arrest warrants and work with police to ensure that investigation reports are complete. In some circumstances, through either citizen complaints or suspicion of alleged criminal acts, prosecutors initiate their own investigations, which may be independent of police activity.
2. Arrest: Prosecutors screen cases of those who have been arrested to determine which should be prosecuted and which should be dropped.
3. Initial appearance: During the first court appearance, prosecutors ensure that defendants are notified of the charges against them. In addition, they participate in bail decisions. Prosecutors can also discontinue a prosecution through a *nolle prosequi* (also referred to as *nol. pros.,* or simply *nolle*), a formal statement of unwillingness to proceed further in a particular case.
4. Preliminary hearing: Prosecutors have two functions at preliminary hearings—to establish probable cause and to enter a nol. pros. when appropriate. Prosecutors may also have to give formal notice of charges and participate in bail decisions.
5. Information and indictment: Prosecutors prepare the report that establishes probable cause and binds an accused person over for trial.
6. Arraignment: Prosecutors arraign felony defendants; that is, they bring the accused to the court to answer to matters charged. Prosecutors also participate in plea negotiations—that is, allowing defendants to plead guilty to a reduced charge or charges.
7. Pretrial motions: Prosecutors initiate and participate in the argument of any pretrial motions. These are formal applications or requests to the court for some action, such as an order or rule (see Chapter 9 for more on pretrial motions).
8. Trial: Prosecutors attempt to prove guilt beyond a reasonable doubt.
9. Sentencing: Prosecutors recommend either rigid or lenient sentences.
10. Appeal: Through written or oral debate, prosecutors argue that convictions were obtained properly and should not be reversed.
11. Parole: In some jurisdictions, prosecutors make recommendations for or against parole for all inmates who are up for review. In most instances, however, prosecutors typically limit themselves to opposing early parole release for serious offenders.

Of the prosecutor's many functions and roles, those with the greatest impact on criminal justice processing are the ones involving prosecutorial discretion—the decision to prosecute, to enter a nol. pros., and to plea-bargain.

Prosecutorial discretion typically begins after an arrest has been made, when police reports are forwarded to the county or state attorney for review. At that point, the prosecutor screens and evaluates the evidence and the details of the arrest and decides whether to accept or reject the case for prosecution. In this decision-making process, called *selective prosecution,* the prosecutor has, in theory, absolute and unrestricted discretion to choose who is prosecuted and who is not. The justifications

DISCRETION MATTERS

What impact might heightened discretion in one role—say, for example, that of the prosecutor—have on the cooperation among other personnel involved in the court process?

for selective prosecution are similar to those for selective enforcement of the law by police, including ambiguity in the penal codes, the seriousness of the offense, the size of the court's workload, and the need to treat defendants as individuals.

The legitimacy and necessity of the prosecutor's discretion in pressing charges has long been recognized. As the President's Commission on Law Enforcement and Administration of Justice pointed out many years ago:

> Often it becomes apparent after arrest that there is insufficient evidence to support a conviction or that a necessary witness will not cooperate or is unavailable; an arrest may be made when there is probable cause to believe that the person apprehended committed an offense, while conviction after formal charge requires proof of guilt beyond a reasonable doubt. Finally, subsequent investigation sometimes discloses the innocence of the accused.[62]

In addition, tactical matters and law enforcement needs may make it inadvisable to press particular charges against certain individuals. For example, a prosecutor may choose to conserve resources for more serious cases or to drop a charge in exchange for information about more serious crimes. Similarly, invoking the criminal process against marginal offenders may accomplish more harm than good. Attaching a criminal label to a one-time petty offender can conceivably set that person on a course toward a career in serious crime. Moreover, a large proportion of arrests are for annoying and offensive behavior—drunkenness, vagrancy, disorderly conduct—rather than dangerous crimes. Prosecuting all these cases would cause undue hardships for both the defendants and the judicial process.

In cases in which the accused person poses a serious threat to the welfare of a community—or conversely, when the offense is a minor one—the decision to prosecute or not is easy to make.[63] Often, however, the offense and its related elements fall somewhere between these extremes, and the prosecutor must decide whether the benefit to be derived from prosecution would outweigh the costs.

Nolle Prosequi Once prosecution has formally begun and the case is a matter of court record, the prosecutor can terminate any further processing through the nolle prosequi. As noted earlier, the nolle prosequi, or nol. pros., is a formal entry in the record by which the prosecutor declares that he or she "will no further prosecute" the case, either (1) as to some of the counts, (2) as to some of the defendants, or (3) altogether.

This right of the prosecutor not to prosecute further, even in the face of sufficient evidence, is one of the most powerful examples of discretionary authority in the criminal justice system. There are many reasons for entering a nol. pros. determination. The prosecutor may decide, once the judicial process has begun, that the evidence after all is not sufficient for conviction or that it is inadmissible. Alternatively, the decision may rest on aspects of the plea negotiation process or even on leniency.[64] Although this aspect of the prosecutor's discretionary powers has been heavily criticized, it has been repeatedly upheld in the appellate courts. The nol. pros. is not without problems, for it can lead to corruption, favoritism, nepotism, and discrimination. Nevertheless, some form of this discretionary process seems necessary, if only to screen out trivial cases, eliminate false accusations, and remove cases in which the accused may indeed be guilty but the prosecution is almost certain to lose—thus wasting the court's time and resources.

DISCRETION MATTERS

How might the discretionary decision not to prosecute an offender or offense, even when substantial evidence exists, benefit a community?

Plea Negotiation Usually referred to as *plea bargaining,* plea negotiation is one of the most commonly accepted practices in criminal justice processing. More than 90 percent of criminal convictions likely result from negotiated pleas of guilty.[65]

Plea bargaining takes place between the prosecutor and the defense counsel or the accused. It involves discussions aimed toward an agreement under which the defendant will plead guilty in exchange for some prosecutorial or judicial concession. These concessions are of four types:

1. The initial charges may be reduced, thus ensuring a reduction in the sentence.
2. In instances of multiple charges, the number of counts may be reduced.
3. The prosecutor may recommend leniency, thus reducing the potential sentence from incarceration to probation.
4. With charges that involve a negative label, such as child molestation, the complaint may be altered to a less repugnant one, such as assault.[66]

The widespread use of negotiated pleas is a result of overcrowded caseloads in criminal courts. Proponents of plea bargaining maintain that both the accused and the state benefit. For the accused, plea bargaining has three advantages:

1. It reduces the possibility of detention during extensive pretrial and trial processing.
2. It increases the chances of a reduced sentence.
3. It decreases the costs of legal representation.

For the state, plea bargaining also has advantages:

1. It reduces the overall financial costs of criminal prosecution.
2. It improves the efficiency of the courts by having fewer cases go to trial.
3. It enables the prosecution to devote more time and resources to more important and serious cases.

While plea negotiation is common, it is also controversial. First, it encourages the accused person to waive his or her constitutional right to trial. Second, it enables the defendant to receive a sentence that is generally less severe than the one he or she might otherwise have received; in the eyes of the public, the criminal has "beaten the system." Third, it sacrifices legislative policies (embodied in the criminal law) for the sake of tactical accommodations between the prosecution and defense. Fourth, it ignores the correctional needs of the bulk of offenders, for in many instances the accused may ultimately plead guilty to a charge that is far removed from the original crime. Fifth, it raises the danger that an innocent person, fearing a guilty verdict and harsh sentence if the case goes to trial, will plead guilty and accept conviction, hoping for lighter treatment. For example, consider the problematic case of Harry Seigler, a 30-year-old man who was tried in a Virginia court for robbery and murder. He had already been convicted of robbery three times, but having pleaded not guilty in this case, he was nervous while waiting for the jury to return a verdict. His two lawyers had disagreed on his chances of being found not guilty; he faced the possibility of being convicted of capital murder; and another man had just been executed in Virginia's electric chair. The prosecutor offered a deal: Plead guilty to first-degree murder and robbery and receive a 60-year prison term, with 20 years suspended. Seigler accepted the deal, and so did the judge. As Seigler was led away, the judge was informed that the jury had finally reached its verdict: not guilty.[67]

Despite the controversies, plea bargaining has received the blessing of the U.S. Supreme Court.[68] The court once commented that although plea bargaining may have neither a constitutional nor a statutory basis, the practice can serve the interests of both the accused and the court. In the final analysis, plea bargaining will endure because it is a great safety valve. Without this tool, every defendant charged with an offense, however serious or benign, would have to go to trial. As it is, millions of cases are processed in the courts each year. With existing resources, a person arrested today might have to wait a quarter century for his or her case to come up. Aside from expediency, however, it eliminates uncertainty for both the defense and the prosecution, and all sides generally prefer to opt for a "sure thing." For the defendant charged with

Prosecutors typically hold the power in a plea negotiation because they can determine what concessions will be offered.

The cooperative search for justice found in many local and state courtrooms across the country offers a stark contrast to the adversarial image often presented in film and on television.

murder, it can remove the possibility of a life sentence or even death; for the prosecutor, it precludes any possibility of having a serious offender escape justice because of some real or imagined weakness in the case. On the negative side, however, some innocent individuals would rather plead guilty to a negotiated offense than face the possible consequences of an adverse verdict; these are people caught in a web of circumstances that have made them appear guilty. We have no way of knowing how many innocent defendants have chosen this course and spent weeks, months, or even years in prison.

Defense Attorneys

The right of a criminal defendant to be represented by counsel is fundamental to the American system of criminal justice. The reason for this right is the need to protect individual liberties. Defendants facing criminal charges require the assistance of counsel to protect their interests at every phase of the adversarial process and to help them understand the nature and consequences of the proceedings against them. Moreover, even the best-informed defendants are ill-equipped to represent themselves tactically in the face of the complexities of criminal law and procedure. If the defendant is unable to pay for a private attorney, a publicly funded one will be provided.[69]

The defense counsel can perform many functions in the criminal process, including the following:

1. Providing advice during pretrial interrogation and procedures, in order to ensure that constitutional safeguards are not violated
2. Reviewing police reports and further investigating the details of the offense
3. Interviewing the police, the accused, and the witnesses, and seeking additional evidence and witnesses on behalf of the defendant
4. Discussing the offense with the prosecutor to gain insight into the strength of the state's case
5. Representing the accused at bail hearings and during plea negotiations
6. Preparing, filing, and arguing pretrial motions
7. Preparing the case for trial
8. Participating in jury selection
9. Representing the accused at trial
10. Providing advice and assistance at sentencing
11. Determining and pursuing the appropriate bases for appeal
12. Presenting written or oral arguments at appeal[70]

In practice, few defense attorneys participate in all of these activities. As noted earlier, a number of cases are "screened out" of the justice system through the prosecutor's decision not to prosecute, and most of the remaining cases are disposed of through guilty pleas. Thus, the defense attorney's activities are usually limited to the pretrial phases. Moreover, studies indicate that most defense lawyers have their initial contacts with their clients only after they have been placed on bail or released on recognizance.[71]

Because more and more government attorneys are prosecuting only cases in which the potential for conviction is high, the defense counsel's most intensive efforts take place at the beginning of the discretionary screening process (items 1–5 in the list above). During this period, which can last up to two weeks in urban areas where arrest rates are high, the defendant's lawyer has the opportunity to gather background material on the client and the case. If this preliminary investigation suggests that the offense was minor, that the arrest was weak or questionable, or that there were irregularities in the arresting officer's behavior (such as illegal search and seizure), the defense counsel can pressure the prosecutor to dismiss the case or can begin plea negotiations.

A second-level activity for the defense counsel involves pretrial motions (item 6 in the list above). A motion is an application made to the court or the judge, requesting an order or ruling in favor of the applicant. There are various types of motions, but the most common at pretrial proceedings are those that seek to gain information about the prosecutor's case or to suppress certain types of evidence.

The use of motions can, in part, be a bluffing game to determine how the court will react and how many rulings a judge will make.[72] Nevertheless, it tends to wear down many prosecutors. In some heavily populated jurisdictions, a prosecutor may be carrying 50 to 60 cases at any given time. With this heavy workload, the prosecutor will find it easier to negotiate a guilty plea or drop the case altogether than to continue in a time-consuming struggle to answer all of an adversary's petitions.

DISCRETION MATTERS

What impact might a defense attorney have on a prosecutor's decision to move forward with a case or to enter a nol. pros.?

Other Courtroom Regulars

In addition to the principal actors in the courtroom workgroup—judges, prosecutors, and defense attorneys—many others play a role in criminal proceedings. They include bailiffs and sheriffs, the court clerk, court reporters and stenographers, witnesses, and coroners and medical examiners.

Bailiffs and Sheriffs   Each courtroom is assigned a bailiff or sheriff, whose formal duties are to announce the arrival and departure of the judge and maintain order in the courtroom. In addition, depending on local custom, bailiffs and sheriffs serve as messengers for lawyers and other court officials; keep track of prosecutors, attorneys, and witnesses so that they are present when their cases come up; and, in some instances, provide information to defendants—advising them which court they belong in, where their attorney might be found, and if asked, what the outcome of the case might be.[73]

The Court Clerk   Every court has a clerk, whose responsibilities include "calling the calendar" (calling up the next case before the judge), updating defendants' files, managing the court's files, and ensuring that evidence in the custody of the court is secure. In the small, lower courts, a courthouse may have only one clerk. In larger jurisdictions, each courtroom may have its own court clerk, plus several courthouse file clerks who maintain the court's records, collect fines and court costs, and prepare the daily calendars.

The court clerk occupies a position of considerable importance. This is especially true of the chief clerk of a large court system. Often the clerk's post is occupied by young attorneys who use it as a stepping-stone to the prosecutor's office. Not only does it provide exposure to the routine of the courthouse, but it also offers experience in some areas of law, since many clerks are empowered to prepare formal writs and process documents issued by the court.

Court Reporters and Stenographers   A court reporter or stenographer is present at almost every judicial proceeding to report and (perhaps) transcribe matters of record. The mechanics of court reporting have changed considerably over time. In the past, most reporters were expert stenographers who used a manual shorthand system to create verbatim accounts (transcripts) of proceedings. Manual shorthand writers are almost extinct, having been replaced by machine and digital writers. Machine writers use a device that resembles a small typewriter to imprint coded letters on a tape. The tape may be translated manually, or it may be optically scanned. Alternatively, the keystrokes may be used to create a recording from which a computer is instructed to transcribe.

Enormous sums have been spent in many states on equipment for digitally and electronically recording judicial proceedings. Although the equipment is cost-effective compared to the use of live reporters—some reporters earn $500 a day or more—it has not lived up to its promise. Objectionable comments of witnesses and counsel, extraneous noises, and privileged

Bailiffs provide numerous services to the court, which include announcing the arrival and departure of the judge, escorting defendants, and maintaining order in the courtroom.

communications are regularly recorded—and not easily edited. More important, there is no court reporter present to interrupt proceedings when language is unclear, garbled, or barely audible.

To remedy this situation, reporters now monitor the digital recording of the proceedings and the transcription process. Not only are transcripts more accurate, but preparation and delivery times have been reduced. Today's court reporter, then, must be a computer-skilled writer and technician.

Witnesses Almost all criminal proceedings have witnesses, who are of three principal types: the police witness, the lay witness, and the expert witness. A police witness is generally an arresting officer who has some knowledge of the facts of the case, having been at the scene of the crime during or soon after its commission. The police witness would be called to testify if he or she observed some part of the offense or pertinent events in its aftermath—for example, observing the accused fleeing from the crime scene. Police also serve as witnesses when they present the results of an investigation that led to the arrest of a defendant.

The lay witness is a citizen bystander or victim who has some relevant personal knowledge. The lay witness is permitted to testify only on facts that he or she directly ascertained through sensory perception. Thus, the citizen cannot be a witness if his or her knowledge of the case is based on conjecture or opinion.

The expert witness is called into court to provide technical information and opinions. To qualify as an expert, the witness must have the specified qualifications and authority to offer testimony in an area in which the general public has little or no understanding. The trial judge decides whether someone qualifies as an expert witness. There are experts on fiber evidence, DNA evidence, eyewitness testimony, and so forth. A psychiatrist, for example, may testify as an expert witness regarding the accused's mental competency; an authority on ballistics may comment on whether a bullet could have been fired from a certain weapon; or a specialist in earth science may establish whether soil on the accused's clothing matches soil samples from the murder site.

The expert witness's role is a subject of debate, however. There are concerns about the evolving nature of forensic science, the merits of psychological explanations of behavior, and trustworthiness of specialists in "junk science" who are being paid to testify. This controversy has intensified since the beginning of the 1990s and has continued well into the twenty-first century, perhaps because of the wider use of DNA evidence, concerns about the use of "abuse excuse" defenses, and similar issues.[74] Surveys do suggest that judges and jurors alike find the task of evaluating scientific evidence challenging. As a safeguard, the U.S. Supreme Court concluded in *Daubert v. Merrell Dow Pharmaceuticals* that trial judges should act as gatekeepers, making preliminary evaluations of the scientific basis of such testimony before allowing the expert to testify in the presence of a jury.[75] Since *Daubert,* a number of court decisions have gone further to establish that judges must evaluate the expert evidence according to a set of criteria and make a general determination that it is sound science. As a result, the Federal Judicial Center and other judicial education programs now train judges to be "miniscientists" in addition to being judges. Moreover, experts in the field have called for national standards for the use of forensic science in determining causes of death and investigating crimes. Standards would give some consistency to the use of this information in courts of law.[76]

Coroners and Medical Examiners The coroner is an appointed or elected county official whose chief function is to investigate the cause of all deaths that have occurred in the absence of witnesses, that show evidence of violence, or that have occurred under suspicious circumstances. The office of coroner in most communities is a political position, like that of mayor or sheriff, and requires no qualifications other than eligibility to hold political office. The coroner appoints a number of deputies, a forensic pathologist—sometimes with an assistant who specializes in toxicology or ballistics—and a scattering of part-time physicians.

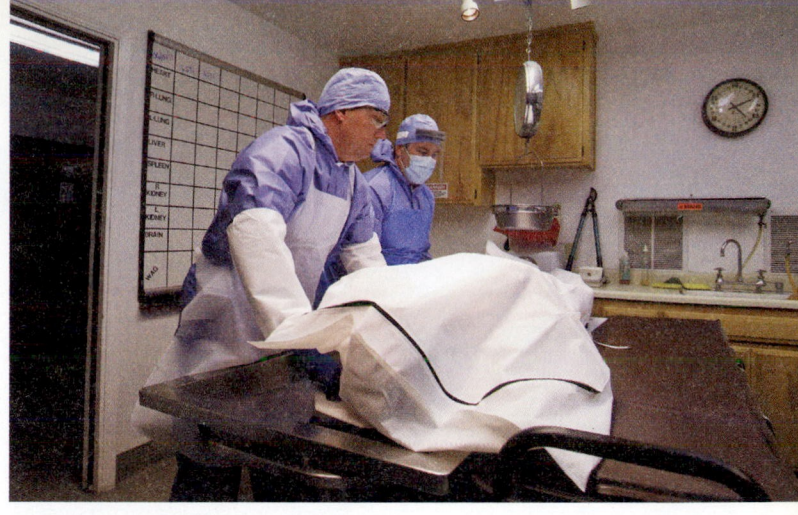

Courts rely heavily on medical examiners to help translate complex scientific information for members of the jury.

The coroner does not hold a judicial position in the strictest sense but performs certain quasi-judicial functions. The coroner is authorized, for instance, to conduct inquests, which are legal inquiries into deaths in which accident, foul play, or violence is suspected. The inquest is similar to a trial in many ways, although it is not governed by the same precise procedure. The coroner conducts the inquest, subpoenas witnesses and documents, cross-examines witnesses under oath, introduces evidence, and receives testimony—all with a jury present. Should the inquest find "just cause" to arrest a suspect, the coroner issues an arrest warrant or moves for the prosecutor to request a warrant from a magistrate.[77]

Historically, coroners were not required to have a background in either medicine or law; the physicians who work as adjuncts to the office are not necessarily required to have any medicolegal training; and if a forensic pathologist is appointed as a coroner's deputy, he or she may be a newly qualified medic with little experience.

Many jurisdictions have abolished the office of coroner and substituted it with the office of medical examiner, thus divorcing the system from political control and influence. The medical examiner is a licensed physician with training in forensic pathology who is appointed by governmental authority on a nonpartisan basis. He or she carries out only the medical aspects of any investigation, not the quasi-judicial functions, which the court handles.[78]

Auxiliary Court Personnel Depending on the jurisdiction, the size of the court, and the traditions of a given legal community, a range of additional personnel may provide support services. Both the prosecutor's and public defender's offices may have a number of secretaries, aides, translators and interpreters, and investigators who assist in the collection of evidence and the preparation of cases. In addition, court officers, police officers assigned to the court, or correctional officers may be present to maintain custody over detainees who are making court appearances. Also, because many courts have various types of pretrial diversion programs, any number of pretrial service representatives may be around. Similarly, because pretrial release often occurs, bail bond agents (discussed in Chapter 9) are also part of the court process. Finally, a number of other significant figures—probation officers, grand juries, and trial juries—will be discussed in detail in later chapters. As you can see, then, a vast array of people—from the most to the least visible—contribute to the workings of the criminal justice process. The same can be said of the juvenile court system, although the personnel, procedures, and rights that characterize the juvenile system differ in some significant ways from those of the adult system—the subject explored in the "Juvenile Justice in Context" feature.

JUVENILE JUSTICE IN CONTEXT

Juvenile Court and the System of Juvenile Justice

Much like the criminal justice process for adults, juvenile justice in America is defined by certain processes. Diagrams and flowcharts depict how the agencies and components fit together as a case moves through the system and what decisions are possible at each stage (Exhibit 8.7). Yet, as with criminal justice in general, considerable tension and dissonance exist within the juvenile justice system.

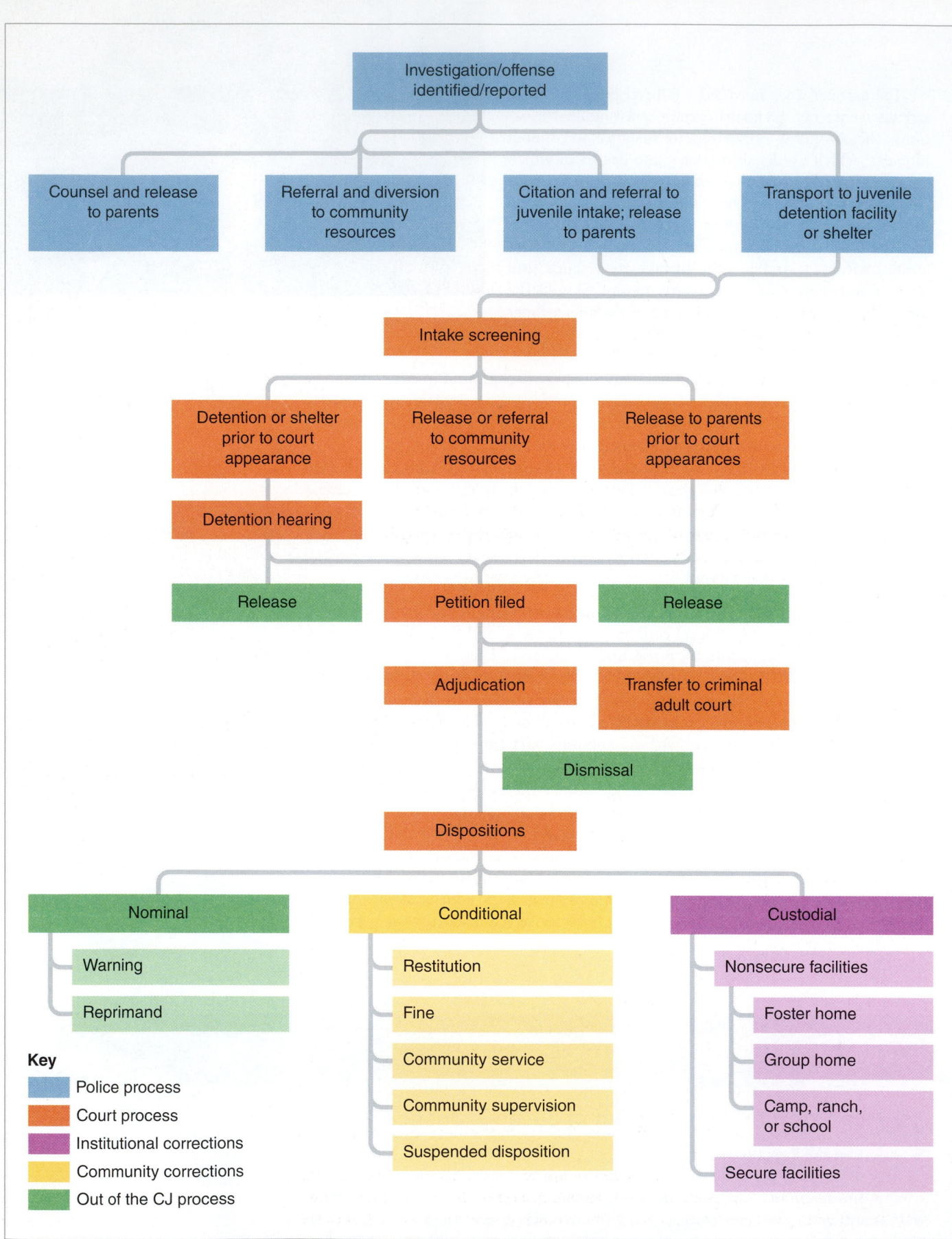

EXHIBIT 8.7 The Juvenile Justice System

Unlike the adult court process described in this chapter, the juvenile court process is not a criminal proceeding. It is not a matter of "State v. Child." There is no prosecutor acting on behalf of the state to prove the youth guilty, and there is no jury. The process is a civil one that is designed, at least in theory, to aid and protect the child. But is a youthful defendant in juvenile court protected by the Bill of Rights? Does the juvenile have the same constitutional rights as adult defendants in criminal trials? For the most part, the answer to these questions is no—and until the Supreme Court's decision in *Kent v. United States*[79] in 1966, juvenile courts seemed to accord few, if any, rights at all. In *Kent,* for the first time in its history, the Supreme Court found that youths involved in juvenile proceedings were being deprived of constitutional rights and denied the rehabilitation they were supposed to receive under juvenile court philosophy.

A year after *Kent,* the Supreme Court heard the case of *In re Gault,*[80] an appeal involving the detention of a 15-year-old in a state industrial school for allegedly making an obscene telephone call. The *Gault* decision extended to juvenile courts the requirement of notice of charges, the right to counsel, the right to confrontation and cross-examination of witnesses, the privilege against self-incrimination, and the rights to a transcript of proceedings and appellate review.

Since *Gault,* Supreme Court decisions have extended additional rights to juvenile proceedings, including the requirement of proof "beyond a reasonable doubt" to adjudicate delinquency, the Fifth Amendment protection against double jeopardy, and the Miranda protections. However, juveniles do not yet have all protections afforded adults during criminal prosecution.

Sources: *Kent v. United States,* 383 U.S. 541 (1966); *In re Gault,* 387 U.S. 1 (1967); *In re Winship,* 397 U.S. 358 (1970); *Breed v. Jones,* 421 U.S. 519 (1975); *J.D.B. v. North Carolina,* 564 U.S. ___ (2011).

Juvenile court proceedings are typically closed to protect the privacy and identity of children.

CONCLUSIONS

Over the course of its history, the American court system has evolved into a bewildering mosaic of names, structures, and functions. On the state level alone, we have justice of the peace and municipal courts, county and city courts, superior and inferior courts, and trial and appellate courts. Add to this picture the multitiered system at the federal level, which culminates with the Supreme Court. The American court system is further complicated by the fact that (1) no two state-court systems are identical, (2) the names of different states' courts vary, regardless of their function, and (3) there are various levels of jurisdictional authority related to geography and subject matter. As the chapter-opening *Koon* case illustrates, these complexities present themselves as offenders, victims, and communities seek justice, particularly as a case moves from one jurisdiction to another during the appellate process or as individuals seek remedy in alternate courts.

Judges, prosecutors, and defense attorneys are the most visible players in the courtroom workgroup, and each has considerable discretion in the conduct of their jobs, but an extensive array of court-related personnel support their work. Just as the court system has become more complex over the course of U.S. history, so too have the roles of those who work within it.

SUMMARY AND REVIEW

■ **Trace the evolution of the U.S. court system.**

- As America evolved into a nation, the court emerged as an integral part of life in most communities.

- Courthouses served as mustering places during the War of Independence and the Civil War. They also served as meeting places—for religious services, dances, and town councils—as well as fulfilling their primary function as places for the dispensation of justice.

- As towns became cities and as populations and related problems increased, legal and court procedures became more complex. For civil matters, there were counterparts of the rural justices of the peace; for the less serious criminal affairs, there were police and magistrate's courts; and for serious problems of law and order, there was a more permanent higher court.

■ **Describe the major types of courts in the state system and the relationships between them.**

- The names and organizational structures of the state courts vary greatly from one state to the next. State judiciaries are divided into two, three, four, or sometimes five tiers, each with separate functions and jurisdictions.

- State courts hear and decide disputes arising within specific political boundaries. In addition, some courts are limited to specific matters—for example, misdemeanors or civil actions versus all other types of cases.

- The jurisdictions of the state courts are designated as follows: courts of limited jurisdiction, courts of general jurisdiction, and courts of appellate jurisdiction.

■ **Define and identify an example of a specialty court.**

- Specialty courts—including drug, firearm, elder-crime, and veterans courts—are designed to respond to an identified concern within the community. The responses by specialty courts to offenders or cases often involve cooperation across multiple layers of the criminal justice process.

- Drug courts are the most common type of specialty court, with more than 2,400 operating across the United States by the beginning of 2011.

■ **Describe the major courts in the federal system and the relationships between them.**

- The federal judiciary has a complex, though unified, structure, with jurisdiction throughout the United States and its territories. It has a four-tier structure similar to that found in most of the states.

- The U.S. Supreme Court has ultimate appellate jurisdiction over the federal appeals courts, the state courts of appeal, the District of Columbia Court of Appeals, and the Supreme Court of Puerto Rico.

■ **Describe the history and functions of the U.S. Supreme Court, including the significance of the *Marbury v. Madison* case.**

- In *Marbury v. Madison,* Chief Justice Marshall stated that Congress could not expand or contract the jurisdiction of the Supreme Court and that Congress had acted unconstitutionally, exceeding its power, when it authorized the court to issue writs ordering federal officials to perform particular acts. This case established the Supreme Court's power to review acts of Congress.

- The Supreme Court has two kinds of jurisdiction: general and appellate. The general jurisdiction usually involves suits between two states, issues that test the constitutionality of state laws, and matters relating to ambassadors. In such instances, the Supreme Court can serve as a trial court. Its appellate jurisdiction resolves conflicts that raise "substantial federal questions," typically questions related to the constitutionality of some lower-court rule, decision, or procedure.

■ **Explain the major functions of judges, prosecutors, defense attorneys, and others in the courtroom workgroup.**

- Judges are both arbiters and administrators. As arbiters, they safeguard the rights of the accused as well as the interests of the public. As administrators, they control the flow of cases through the courts and oversee such ancillary duties as the appointment and evaluation of court personnel, record-keeping, and budget requests. Judges alone have the authority to interpret the rules that govern court proceedings.

- The prosecutor is a government lawyer and the chief law enforcement authority of a particular community. The responsibilities of the prosecutor are threefold: (1) enforce the law, (2) represent the government in matters of law, and (3) represent the government and the people in matters of legislation and criminal justice reform.

- Defense attorneys represent defendants throughout the criminal process—immediately after arrest, during the trial, and at sentencing. They also may determine and pursue bases for appeal and present written or oral arguments at appeal.

- The bailiff's or sheriff's formal duties are to announce the arrival and departure of the judge and to maintain order in the courtroom.

- The court clerk's responsibilities include "calling the calendar," updating defendants' files, managing the court's files, and ensuring that evidence in the custody of the court is secure.

- The court reporter or court stenographer is present at almost every judicial proceeding to report and (perhaps) transcribe matters of record.

■ Discuss the role of prosecutorial discretion, including the use of plea bargaining and the nolle prosequi.

- Prosecutorial discretion typically begins after an arrest has been made, when police reports are forwarded to the county or state attorney for review. At that point, the prosecutor screens and evaluates the evidence and the details of the arrest and decides whether to accept or reject the case for prosecution.

- Once prosecution has formally begun, the prosecutor can terminate any further processing through the nolle prosequi—a formal entry in the record by which the prosecutor declares that he or she "will no further prosecute" the case, either (1) as to some of the counts, (2) as to some of the defendants, or (3) altogether.

- Plea bargaining takes place between the prosecutor and the defense counsel or the accused and involves discussions that aim toward an agreement under which the defendant will plead guilty in exchange for some prosecutorial or judicial concession.

KEY TERMS

courts of appellate jurisdiction (p. 201)
courts of general jurisdiction (p. 201)
courts of limited jurisdiction (p. 201)
courts of record (p. 203)
dual court system (p. 200)

judicial circuit (p. 203)
justice of the peace (p. 199)
trial de novo (p. 213)
U.S. courts of appeals (p. 10)
U.S. district courts (p. 207)

U.S. magistrates (p. 207)
U.S. Supreme Court (p. 210)
writ of certiorari (p. 213)

ISSUES FOR CRITICAL THINKING AND DISCUSSION

1. What type of restructuring might help unify and simplify the state court systems?
2. What are some of the problems created by the backlog of cases in state and federal courts?
3. What kinds of "nontraditional," or specialty, courts do you think would increase the effectiveness and efficiency of the criminal court process?
4. How do you perceive the role of the modern Supreme Court? How do you think perceptions of the court have changed over time?

5. How might the relationships among the players in the courtroom workgroup affect the efficiency and effectiveness of the criminal court process?
6. How do you see the role of the prosecuting attorney in your community? How has the prosecutor's role been portrayed in the media?

9

The Business of the Court

First Appearance through Trial

LEARNING OBJECTIVES

- Identify the stages of the criminal court process.
- Explain the bail system and the challenges of pretrial release.
- Describe the main issues related to grand jury proceedings and double jeopardy.
- Define the kinds of pleas available to defendants.
- List the types of pretrial motions and explain the purposes of these.
- Explain the rights related to speedy and public trial, including jury selection.
- Outline the steps in the criminal trial and the types of evidence that can be presented.

JUSTICE FORCED AND ULTIMATELY SERVED

Much like the young man in this photo, Gary Duncan encountered racial tensions in Louisiana in the 1960s—likely contributing to the travesty of justice that prompted the Supreme Court case of *Duncan v. Louisiana.*

The setting was Plaquemines Parish, Louisiana, an oil-rich community some 50 miles northwest of New Orleans. At the time, 1966, Leander H. Perez Jr. was district attorney and a virulent segregationist. Relying on prosecutorial discretion, Perez brought charges against Gary Duncan, a 19-year-old African American youth, and Duncan was tried in the local court on a charge of simple battery—a misdemeanor punishable by a maximum of two years' imprisonment and a $300 fine. His crime had involved no more than slapping the elbow of a white youth. He was convicted, fined $150, and sentenced to 60 days in jail. Duncan had requested a trial by jury, but the court denied his request on the authority of the Louisiana Constitution, which granted jury trials only in cases in which capital punishment or imprisonment at hard labor could be imposed.[1] Duncan appealed to the U.S. Supreme Court, contending that the Sixth and Fourteenth Amendments guaranteed his right to a jury trial. In a 7–2 decision, the court ruled in favor of Duncan, thus incorporating the Sixth Amendment right to a jury into the due process clause of the Fourteenth Amendment and requiring access to protections of a jury trial for all defendants who would have been afforded that right if charged in federal court. Had Duncan been afforded access to a jury, he might have received a very different sentence or even a verdict of not guilty. In short, the jury might have acted to check the discretionary decision-making of the prosecutor.[2]

In spite of this holding, the matter was not fully resolved—not for Gary Duncan and not for thousands of defendants who would later request jury trials in state courts. The Supreme Court's reversal of the Louisiana trial court conviction of Duncan mandated either a dismissal of the simple battery charge or a new trial. However, the Louisiana court refused to comply with either alternative, thus leaving Duncan under a continuing threat of further prosecution. His situation remained unchanged for three years, until the federal courts commanded Plaquemines Parish to dispose of the case.[3]

The *Duncan* case highlights the complexities of the legal processes that determine guilt and sentences, including the complicating factors of judicial and prosecutorial discretion. For example, decisions concerning what charges to bring and against whom are subject to the discretion of prosecutors and judges. The determination that Duncan's offense was serious enough to warrant criminal prosecution was a decision the prosecutor made independent of judicial review. Additionally, the fact that at the time Louisiana law made it impossible for Duncan to have a jury trial—where he might have found some legal relief from punishment—further highlights the impact of the decision to prosecute. The trajectory of the *Duncan* case is only part of the reason why critics often refer to the organization and administration of justice as a "nonsystem" (see Chapters 1 and 4). Decisions that individual actors make—such as the one the prosecutor in *Duncan* made—may often be unrelated to the overarching goals of justice and instead reflect pressure from a community, personal bias, or prejudice. In the *Duncan* case, the prosecutor was able to file charges and proceed to seek punishment in a case where the application of due process was questionable at best. Perhaps his decision-making was related to his own bias or pressure from the community.

More generally, modern courts struggle to attend to numerous goals other than the obvious one of efficiency, particularly when it comes to low-level criminal cases. Backlogs are often colossal, workloads are always increasing, and court offices are understaffed. Moreover, some argue that the notions of due process and defendants' rights have come to dominate and that criminals are all too quickly released to continue preying on law-abiding citizens. The argument in response to that sort of claim is that millions of offenders are arrested and convicted each year, and a significant number are incarcerated. Other cases are dismissed, or those accused are exonerated, pre-sumably because the prosecutor lacks evidence—facts or information supporting one outcome or another—or the accused is innocent, but releasing individuals under such circumstances is a legitimate function of the court.

When the serious observer examines what actually happens in the criminal courts, what is remarkable is not how badly these courts seem to function but how well. Courthouse justice generally does an effective job of separating the innocent from the guilty. Although most people who are guilty of crimes are never arrested, most of those coming to the courts who should be convicted are convicted, and most of those who should be punished are punished.

The subject of this chapter—the legal process that determines guilt and sentences those found guilty—has many components and steps, including numerous hearings, pleas, juries, motions, and the trial itself. These steps are examined in detail in the following sections.

BAIL AND PRETRIAL RELEASE

Bail is a form of security, typically financial, guaranteeing that a defendant in a criminal proceeding will appear and be present in court at all required times. The amount of bail is determined by the judge or mandated by ordinance or statute and is typically determined at the time of arrest. Thus, in return for being released from jail, the accused guarantees his or her future appearance by posting funds or some other form of security, usually in the form of a cash assurance (bail) or bond (a third party guaranteeing the bail), with the court. When the defendant appears in court as required, the security is returned; if he or she fails to appear, the security is forfeited.[4]

The Right to Bail?

The Eighth Amendment to the U.S. Constitution clearly specifies that "excessive bail shall not be required," but the extent to which accused individuals have any right to bail is still a subject of debate. The Judiciary Act of 1789 established the statutory right of federal defendants to have bail set in all but capital cases.[5] Moreover, in 1895, the Supreme Court held in *Hudson v. Parker* that a presumption in favor of granting bail exists in the Bill of Rights:

> The statutes of the United States have been framed upon the theory that a person accused of crime shall not, until he has been fully adjudged guilty in the court of last resort, be absolutely compelled to undergo imprisonment or punishment, but may be admitted to bail, not only after arrest and before trial, but after conviction and pending a writ of error.[6]

But these words did not firmly guarantee release on bail for all criminal defendants. Only a year before, the Supreme Court had ruled in *McKane v. Durston* that the Eighth Amendment's bail provision placed limits only on the federal courts and did not apply to the states.[7] Since that time, the Supreme Court has decided relatively

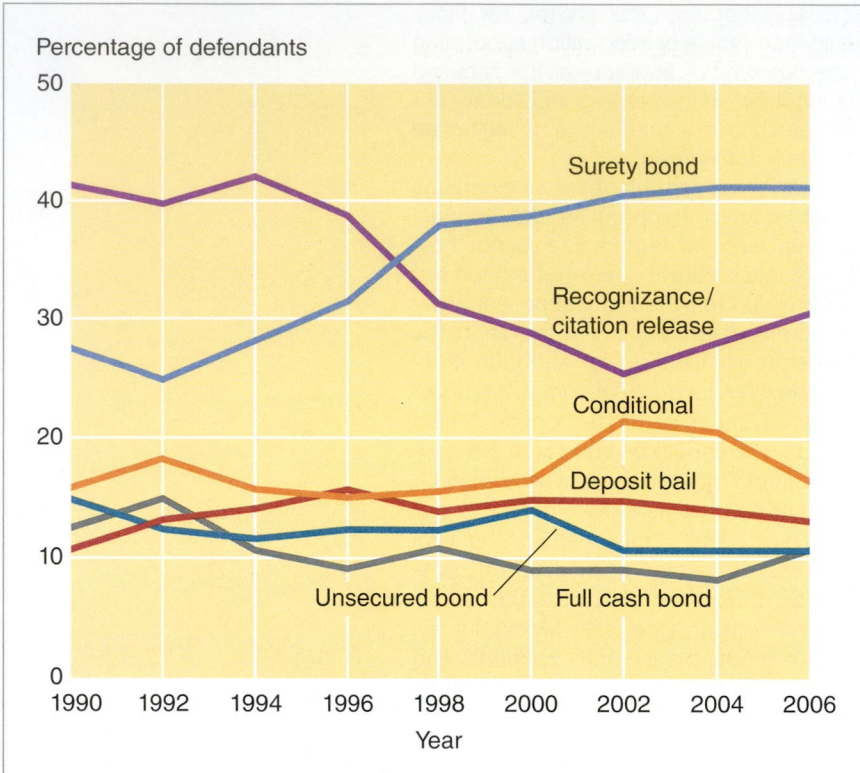

EXHIBIT 9.1   Types of Pretrial Release for Felony Defendants in the 75 Largest Counties, 1990–2006

Source: Bureau of Justice Statistics, U.S. Department of Justice, Office of Justice Programs, 2006

few cases involving bail, mainly because the issue is moot by the time a case reaches the appellate stage of the criminal process. At the state level, the vast majority of constitutions grant an absolute right to bail in noncapital cases.[8] In practice, however, a constitutional or statutory right to have bail set has never meant an absolute right to freedom before trial. In the past, judges invariably insisted on cash bail or a **surety bond,** money from a bail bond agent put up to secure a defendant's release. In modern American courts, bail takes a variety of forms (Exhibit 9.1), including any one or a combination of the following:

- A surety bond is based on an agreement by a third party to be responsible for the bail debt of the defendant. In many jurisdictions a bail bond agent provides this service. Defendants who cannot afford to pay the bail themselves contract with a bail bond agent. The defendant typically must pay the agent 10 percent of the bail amount, and the agent keeps that amount regardless of whether the defendant appears in court. The bond agency charges this fee for its service and may often require collateral outside of the 10 percent. The court in many jurisdictions, especially jurisdictions that prohibit bail bondsmen, may demand that a certain amount of the total bail (typically 10 percent) be given to the court, which unlike bail bond agents, must return the money if the defendant complies with the conditions of bail. Bail agents guarantee the court that they will pay the forfeited bond if a defendant fails to appear for the scheduled court appearances.

- Release on recognizance (ROR) is a promise to the court by the accused to attend all required judicial proceedings and to refrain from any illegal activity or other prohibited conduct as set by the court.

- Citation release is the issuing of a citation or ticket by an arresting officer, informing the arrestee that he or she must appear on an appointed court date. Citation release typically occurs immediately after arrest and requires no financial security.

- Property bond allows the accused or a person acting on his or her behalf to pledge real property that has a value at least equal to the amount of the bail. If the accused fails to appear in court, the state can foreclose on the property to recover the bail money. Often, the equity of the property must be twice the amount of the bail set. This option is available in only a few jurisdictions.

- Cash bonds are used in jurisdictions where the only form of bail the court will accept is the total amount in cash. The court holds this money until the case is concluded.

When defendants cannot afford to meet financial bail requirements, they must remain in jail awaiting trial—for days, months, and sometimes even years. Many defendants involved in serious offenses are denied bail entirely out of a concern for the safety of the community.

DISCRETION MATTERS

Judges have substantial discretion when they weigh the risks of releasing suspects into the community. Why might some offenders or offenses be more or less appropriate for release on recognizance?

In *Stack v. Boyle,*[9] the Supreme Court's principal bail ruling, it left unsettled the constitutional status of a defendant's right to bail. But the court did address the issue of "excessive bail," ruling that the amount must be based on standards relevant to ensuring the presence of the defendant at trial.

Discretionary Bail Setting

In theory, the purpose of bail is to ensure that the accused appears in court for trial. With this in mind, the magistrate is required to set bail at a level calculated to guarantee the defendant's presence at future court hearings. This view has grown out of the historical forms of bail, as well as from the premise that a person is innocent until proven guilty and therefore should not be confined while awaiting trial.[10] At the same time, however, most people believe that the protection of society is more important than bail.

In many jurisdictions, individuals arrested for minor misdemeanors can gain release almost immediately by posting bail at the police station where they are booked. In these cases, there are established bail amounts, which are relatively small. For serious misdemeanors and felonies, the amount is left to the discretion of the judge, as is the type of release. Research has demonstrated, however, that decisions regarding the amount of bail are neither random nor arbitrary.[11]

Under the law, judges in most jurisdictions must consider certain criteria in determining bail. By far the most important factor is the seriousness of the crime; it is assumed that the more serious the offense, the greater the likelihood that the accused will forfeit bail. A second factor is the defendant's prior criminal record; the rationale for this is that recidivists (repeat offenders) have a higher probability of forfeiting bond. In conjunction with these two factors is the strength of the state's case; the premise is that the greater the chance of conviction, the stronger the accused's interest will be in fleeing. Thus, if the state has a strong case against an accused person with a prior felony record, and the current offense was a dangerous crime, the amount of bail set will be high.

> **DISCRETION MATTERS**
>
> What factors should guide the judge in setting a bail amount that will guarantee the defendant's presence at future court hearings? Should this decision be left to the discretion of the judge or mandated by statute? Should different bail amounts be set for different offenders—for example, rich versus poor?

Criticisms of the Bail System

For decades, the bail system has been subjected to criticism on many grounds. First, bail tends to discriminate against the poor. When cash bail is set at a high level, it results in pretrial confinement of many low-risk defendants who do not have the funds to secure their release or retain a bond agent. Second, despite the Eighth Amendment safeguard against excessive bail, bail setting is totally discretionary on the part of judges, and many set bail at unreasonably high levels. Third, since bail is generally determined at the initial appearance, the court has little time to investigate the background of the accused and, hence, cannot adequately determine the degree of risk. Fourth, bail is often used as a mechanism for preventive detention. As a means of protecting the community against offenders who are viewed as risks to social welfare and safety, bail is set so high that the defendant can rarely meet it.[12]

As noted, the defendant forfeits bail if he or she fails to appear in court as required. In addition, a *capias,* or bench warrant, is issued by the court, authorizing the defendant's arrest. Bail jumping itself is an offense that carries criminal penalties. For example, in Maryland, which is typical of most jurisdictions, "failure to surrender after forfeiture of bail" can result in a new felony charge with penalties of five years' imprisonment with or without a $5,000 fine.[13]

Pretrial Detention

For defendants, the principal difficulty with the bail system is its relationship to financial status. Although most bail premiums paid to bond agents are 5 to 10 percent of the face amount of the bond, rates as high as 20 percent have been reported. When

Bail bond agents play a necessary role in the court process. With their assistance, defendants who may not have otherwise been able to do so can post bail. Typically, these businesses cluster in neighborhoods that are close to local or regional jail facilities.

bail is set at $1,000 or more, premiums of $100 to $500 are higher than many defendants can afford. In a study of felony defendants in the nation's 75 largest counties, for example, 30 percent failed to post bail at amounts under $5,000, 57 percent failed at amounts of $5,000 to $9,999, and 45 percent failed at amounts of $10,000 to $24,999.[14]

The result of the bail bond system, then, is the potentially arbitrary punishment of hundreds of thousands of people, many of whom may be innocent. In addition, when an accused person is detained before the trial, he or she can neither have complete access to counsel nor locate **evidence**—that is, any type of proof, including witnesses, records, documents, concrete objects, and circumstances. Detention also disrupts employment and family relations. And it coerces defendants into plea negotiations in order to settle cases rapidly. Most important, however, pretrial detainees are often confined in city and county jails, which are often overcrowded, unsanitary, and poorly equipped. Few jails have enough space for inmates to confer with counsel or visit with families.[15] Defendants awaiting trial are often mixed with convicted felons.[16] Finally, jails are filled with many violent offenders, and each year numerous detainees are attacked.[17]

Preventive Detention

The Supreme Court's decision in *Stack v. Boyle* in 1951 made it clear that the purpose of bail is "to assure the defendant's attendance in court when his presence is required."[18] At the same time, the court noted that bail is not "a means for punishing defendants nor protecting public safety."[19] Nonetheless, many magistrates use bail as a mechanism for preventive detention. In other words, for those who are considered dangerous or who are likely to commit further crimes during the pretrial period, a prohibitively high bail amount is set. In fact, despite the implication in *Stack v. Boyle,* the District of Columbia, the entire federal system, and the majority of states have laws permitting judges to consider an accused's danger to the community in setting pretrial release conditions.

THE GRAND JURY

Following the initial court proceedings, prosecution is instituted in one of three ways: by an information, indictment, or presentment. An **information** is a document filed by the prosecutor that states the formal charges, the statutes that have been violated, and the evidence supporting the charges. The information is generally filed at the preliminary hearing, and the judge then determines whether there is probable cause for further processing. An **indictment** is a formal charging document issued by a grand jury on the basis of evidence presented to it by the prosecutor. Slightly different from an indictment is a *presentment,* which is a written notice of accusation issued by a grand jury. The presentment comes not from evidence and testimony provided by the prosecution but rather from the initiative of the grand jury, based on its own knowledge and observation. In practice, however, the terms *indictment* and *presentment* are largely interchangeable.

Historically, the purposes of the grand jury were to serve as an investigatory body and to act as a buffer between the state and its citizens, to prevent the English king from unfairly invoking the criminal process against his enemies.[20] After the American Revolution, the grand jury was incorporated into the Fifth Amendment to the Constitution, which provides that "no person shall be held to answer for a capital or otherwise infamous crime, unless on a presentment or indictment of a grand jury." Despite this guarantee, however, the Supreme Court ruled more than a century ago, in *Hurtado v. California,*[21] that the grand jury was merely a form of procedure that the states could abolish at will.

The American **grand jury** has 12 to 23 jurors, and its purposes are to investigate and protect citizens from unfair accusations. Currently, about half of the states and the federal system use grand juries, whose members are generally selected from voting registers.[22] However, many of the territories west of the Mississippi that achieved statehood late in the nineteenth century did not adopt the grand jury system, choosing instead to use the prosecutor's information.[23] Many of these systems remain in place today.

Operation of the Grand Jury

There are essentially two types of grand juries: investigatory and accusatory. The investigatory grand jury looks into general allegations of unlawful activity within its jurisdiction in an effort to discover whether there is enough information to justify initiating criminal prosecutions against anyone. An investigatory grand jury may sit for as little as 1 month and as long as 18 months, and it most often examines suspicions and allegations regarding organized crime and official corruption. More common is the accusatory grand jury, a body formed for a set period—generally 3 months—that determines whether there is sufficient evidence against individuals already charged with particular crimes to warrant a criminal trial. The indictment by the accusatory grand jury parallels the prosecutor's filing of an information, and the accusatory grand jury serves as a screening body to decide whether cases in the early stages of the criminal justice process are worthy of being tried.

Since grand juries are either investigating or accusing bodies, and do not determine guilt or innocence, many of the elements of due process are absent:

- Grand jury sessions are private and secret.
- Witnesses, having been subpoenaed by the prosecutor, are sworn and heard, one by one, and excused as soon as they are finished testifying.
- Ordinarily the accused is not present, unless compelled to testify or invited to serve as a witness.
- In most jurisdictions, the defense counsel has no right to be present; if present, the defense counsel has no right to cross-examine witnesses.
- In some jurisdictions, written transcripts are not required.

When the members of a grand jury agree that an accused person should be tried for a crime, they issue a *true bill;* that is, they endorse the validity of the charge or charges specified in the prosecutor's bill, thus issuing an indictment. If they fail to find probable cause, they issue a *no bill,* and the accused is released. Since the grand jury proceeding is not a trial, only a majority vote—not a unanimous one—is required for a true bill.

Grand Juries on Trial

Historically, the grand jury was created to stand between government and the citizen as a protection against unfounded charges and unwarranted prosecutions. Critics maintain, however, that the grand jury process has now become a tool of the prosecutorial misconduct that it was intended to prevent.[24] One complaint concerns the *ex parte* nature of grand jury proceedings. An ex parte is a "one-party" proceeding, meaning that the accused person and his or her attorney are not permitted to be present.[25] Under these circumstances, the accused cannot cross-examine witnesses or object to testimony or evidence.

Critics of grand juries also suggest that they abuse their powers in granting immunity. The Fifth Amendment protects individuals against self-incrimination. Traditionally, the government could compel a witness to testify and still protect his or her Fifth Amendment privilege by providing transactional immunity. This meant that the witness was granted immunity against prosecution in return for testifying. Under a federal statute enacted in 1970, however, the government adopted a new form of immunity, called *use immunity.*[26] This is a limited immunity that prohibits the government only from using the witness's compelled testimony in a subsequent criminal proceeding. That is, if grand jury witnesses have been granted use immunity, their compelled testimony cannot be used against them as direct evidence or as an "investigatory lead" in a subsequent criminal proceeding. For example, if a grand jury witness has been given use immunity and his compelled testimony reveals that he was a participant in a bank robbery, the witness may be prosecuted for that crime if the prosecution can produce evidence at trial that is wholly independent of the witness's grand jury testimony. In the final analysis, then, use immunity is not total immunity.[27]

New York Times journalist Judith Miller, pictured here, was jailed by a federal judge for refusing to name her sources when questioned by a grand jury. The story she published resulted in the identification of CIA operative Valerie Plame.

Grand juries can also compel witnesses to provide testimony needed for criminal investigations by holding them in contempt of court. Witnesses who refuse to testify can be jailed for an indefinite period until they "purge" themselves of contempt by providing the requested information. This would seemingly result in the abridgment of certain constitutional guarantees. Nonetheless, in 1972, the Supreme Court's decision in *Branzburg v. Hayes*[28] forced journalists to testify before a grand jury when subpoenaed. Some journalists have gone to jail rather than reveal their confidential sources, because they believe that to do so would erode the freedom of the press protected by the First Amendment. Other criticisms of the grand jury are that it is really an extension of the prosecution, helping to create "plea-bargaining chips," and that it is cumbersome, expensive, and sometimes forces defendants to spend more time in jail awaiting trials.

THE PLEA

After the formal determination of charges through either the information or the indictment, the defendant is arraigned, at which time he or she is asked to make a plea. The four basic pleas are *not guilty, standing mute, guilty,* and *nolo contendere.* Finally, there is the special plea of *not guilty by reason of insanity* and those involving statutes of limitations and double jeopardy. In this section, we examine each.

When a defendant pleads **not guilty,** the most common plea, the full burden is on the state to prove the charges beyond a reasonable doubt. Under the principles of American jurisprudence, all accused individuals are morally and legally entitled to make such a plea. In the adversary system of justice, everyone charged with a crime has the right to rely on the presumption of innocence. Standing mute at arraignment by failing or refusing to make a plea is presumed to be an entry of not guilty.

The **guilty** plea, whether negotiated or not, has several consequences, as pointed out by the National Advisory Commission on Criminal Justice Standards and Goals:

> Such a plea functions not only as an admission of guilt but also as a surrender of the entire array of constitutional rights designed to protect a criminal defendant against unjustified conviction, including the right to remain silent, the right to confront witnesses against him, the right to a trial by jury, and the right to be proven guilty by proof beyond a reasonable doubt.[29]

The **nolo contendere** plea, which means "no contest," or more specifically, "I will not contest it," is essentially a guilty plea.[30] It entails the surrendering of certain constitutional rights, and conviction is immediate. However, there is one important difference between a nolo contendere plea and a guilty plea. With nolo contendere, there is technically no admission of guilt, which protects the accused in civil court should the victim subsequently sue for damages.

The nolo contendere plea is not an automatic option at arraignment. It is acceptable in the federal courts and in about half of the state courts and may be made only at the discretion of the judge and the prosecutor. Generally, this plea is entered for the benefit of the accused.[31]

The plea of **not guilty by reason of insanity** is generally not to the advantage of the accused, for it is an admission of guilt accompanied by the claim that the defendant is not culpable in the eyes of the law because of insanity at the time he or she committed the crime. More typically, a defendant makes a dual plea of not guilty and not guilty by reason of insanity. Such a plea implies that "the burden is on the government to prove that I did the act upon which the charge is based, and, even if the government proves that at trial, I still claim I am not culpable because I was legally insane at the time."[32]

Not all jurisdictions have a separate insanity plea, nor do all have the dual plea of "not guilty–not guilty by reason of insanity." However, even in jurisdictions that allow the insanity plea, the accused and his or her counsel must present an affirmative defense. In law, this defense amounts to more than a mere denial of the prosecution's allegations. Thus, while the burden of proving the guilt of the accused is on the state, the responsibility for showing insanity at the time of the commission of the offense generally rests with the defendant.

Beginning in the 1980s, many in the legal community opposed the insanity plea, much of it an outgrowth of John Hinckley Jr.'s successful plea of guilty by reason of insanity following his assassination attempt on President Ronald Reagan in 1980. The Hinckley case led to the enactment of "guilty but mentally ill" statutes in many jurisdictions. Under these regulations, defendants who are found guilty but mentally ill go to prison. If defendants require psychiatric treatment, they receive it in prison.[33]

A defendant typically enters his or her plea during the pretrial portion of the criminal justice process.

DISCRETION MATTERS

Under what circumstances might a judge encourage or allow a defendant to plead nolo contendere? How might this plea further the goals of the criminal justice process?

John W. Hinckley Jr., who attempted to assassinate President Ronald Reagan, successfully pled not guilty by reason of insanity. His case is often cited as an example of the inappropriate use of the insanity plea.

Studies suggest that the general public drastically overestimates the incidence of successful insanity pleas, primarily because insanity cases are among the most highly publicized. In reality, comparatively few defendants plead not guilty by reason of insanity. Moreover, the insanity defense rarely results in a win for the defense. Of the millions of criminal cases disposed of each year in state and federal courts, fewer than 1 percent involve insanity pleas, only one in four leads to an acquittal, and the majority of these cases involve misdemeanor charges.[34]

Another special form of plea is based on *statutes of limitations,* which bar prosecution for most crimes after a certain amount of time has passed; that is, the suspect must be accused within a reasonable period after the offense was committed. Why have such statutes? First, after the passage of time, defendants may be unable to establish their whereabouts at the time of the crime, or evidence or witnesses supporting their innocence might be lost. Similarly, after long periods, those accused of crimes may be unable to gather evidence to support their defense or mitigate their conduct.[35] Moreover, in the interim period, the offender may have become a law-abiding citizen who presents no further threat to the community, and conviction and sentencing would serve little purpose.

Statutes of limitations can be quite complex. Generally, such statutes do not apply to murder prosecutions. In addition, statutes for other offenses may be *tolled* (suspended) owing to circumstances such as the defendant's absence from the state. And finally, in most jurisdictions the plea of statute of limitations must be entered at arraignment; otherwise, the accused will be deemed to have waived that particular defense.

As another special form of plea meant to restrain the government from repeatedly prosecuting an accused person for one particular offense, the prohibition against **double jeopardy**—two trials for one offense—was included in the Constitution. The Fifth Amendment states, in part, "Nor shall any person be subject for the same offense to be twice put in jeopardy of life or limb."[36] The Supreme Court has held that this guarantee protects the accused against both multiple prosecutions for the same offense and multiple punishments for the same crime.[37]

PRETRIAL MOTIONS

All pleas of not guilty (other than those dismissed on statute of limitations or double jeopardy grounds) result in the setting of a trial date. Before the trial begins, however, and sometimes before arraignment, both the defense and the prosecution may employ a number of motions. A **motion** is a formal application or request to the court for some action, such as an order or rule. The purpose of motions is to gain some legal advantage, and most are initiated by the defense. The number and type of motions vary according to the nature and complexity of the case. Without question, the court's decisions as to whether to grant or deny motions can have a considerable impact on the outcome of a proceeding. Let's look at a few common types of motions.

The defense always benefits from knowing in advance what witnesses and kinds of evidence the prosecution plans to introduce at trial. The *motion for discovery*—a request to examine the physical evidence, evidentiary documents, and lists of witnesses that the prosecutor has—helps in this regard. Although some jurisdictions may resist such motions, discovery is a matter of constitutional law. The Supreme Court's decision in the 1963 case of *Brady v. Maryland*[38] held that a prosecutor's failure to disclose evidence favorable to the accused despite a request violates due process. However, some years later, in *Moore v. Illinois*,[39] the court ruled that there is no constitutional requirement for the prosecution to fully disclose the entire case file to the defense.

A second kind of motion, a *motion for change of venue*—from the Latin, meaning "neighborhood—is a request that the trial be moved from the county, district, or circuit in which the crime was committed to some other place. The jurisdiction does not change; the original trial court, meaning the judge and all the parties, simply moves if the motion is granted so that a different pool of jurors can be obtained. Either the defense or the prosecution can introduce such a motion. Typically, however, in sensational or highly publicized cases, the defense would make this kind of motion if it believed that the accused could not obtain a fair trial in the particular locale of the court.

Mapp v. Ohio, Escobedo v. Illinois, and *Miranda v. Arizona,* which you learned about in Chapter 6, collectively made the fourth type of motion, the *motion for suppression,* one of the most common of pretrial motions in criminal cases.[40] The motion for suppression is a request to have evidence excluded from consideration. Typically, the defense files it to bar evidence that was obtained as the result of an illegal search and seizure or wiretap or to challenge the validity of a confession.

A bill of particulars is a written statement that specifies additional facts about the charges contained in the information or indictment. Thus, when filed by the defense, a *motion for a bill of particulars* is a request for more details from the prosecution. The motion for a bill of particulars asks for details about what the prosecution claims in order to give the accused fair notice of what must be defended. For example, if a neighborhood racketeer who operates illegal lotteries and off-track-betting schemes is charged with possession of gambling paraphernalia, the defense might wish to know which of the confiscated materials (policy slips, betting cards, and so on) the prosecutor intends to use as the basis of his or her action.

The next type of motion comes up because many criminal prosecutions involve multiple charges against one defendant. The accused may have been arrested for a number of crimes resulting from a single incident—for example, an auto theft followed by destruction of property, resisting arrest, and assault on a police officer. Or

Chaos surrounding a trial, particularly the kind that surrounded the Casey Anthony trial in 2011, can provide a reason for changing the venue, or location.

the accused may be charged with multiple counts of the same offense—perhaps several sales of dangerous drugs during a given period. In both instances, and for the sake of expediency, the prosecution may consolidate these multiple charges into a single case. The defense, however, may feel that different tactics are required for dealing with each charge. Thus, the *motion for severance of charges* requests that each specific charge be tried as a separate case.

Similarly, often more than one person is charged with participation in the same crime—for example, four codefendants in a bank robbery. Sometimes the best interests of one or more of the accused are served by separate trials. Defendant Smith, for example, may wish to have a trial by jury; defendant Jones may wish to place the blame on his codefendants. Thus, the motion for severance of defendants requests that one or more of the accused be tried in separate proceedings.

Next, the *motion for continuance* requests that the trial be postponed to some future date. Either the defense or the prosecution may file such a motion on the grounds that they have not had enough time to prepare the case. For example, they may have had problems gathering evidence or locating witnesses. Some defense attorneys use this motion as a stalling tactic to enhance the accused's chances. They feel that if the case is delayed long enough, the victim's memory will fail, witnesses will lose interest, and a better plea might be negotiated.

Finally, as a matter of common practice at arraignment, defense attorneys make a *motion for dismissal of charges* on the grounds that the prosecution has failed to produce sufficient evidence to warrant further processing. Whether justified or not, most defense attorneys almost automatically file this motion. In practically all instances the judge denies it. In certain situations, however, the motion for dismissal is fully warranted and granted. For example, a previously granted motion for suppression may have weakened the state's case. Here it could be either the defense or the prosecution who files the motion. Moreover, in jurisdictions where prosecutors do not have full authority to issue a *nolle prosequi,* the dropping of charges must be sought through a judicial dismissal.

Other pretrial motions may include requests to inspect grand jury minutes, determine sanity, or discover statements made by prosecution witnesses. By far, however, the most common motions are those for suppression and dismissal. If a motion by the defense results in the dismissal of a case, the prosecution still has the legal authority to reinstate it. Charges can be filed, dismissed, and refiled, for there is no double jeopardy connected with the pretrial process. In a jury trial, jeopardy attaches when the jury is impaneled and sworn; in a bench trial, jeopardy attaches when the court begins to hear evidence.

George Zimmerman, the neighborhood watch commander accused of the 2012 killing of 17-year-old Trayvon Martin in Florida, waived his right to a speedy trial, stating that he needed additional time to prepare.

SPEEDY AND PUBLIC TRIAL

The right to a **speedy trial** appears in the Constitution of the United States.[41] Without it, individuals accused of crimes would have no protection against incarceration for an indefinite period prior to trial, but as you will see, we have no clear definition of what *speedy* means. Like all other provisions in the Bill of Rights, the guarantee of a speedy trial is to ensure the rights of individual defendants, rather than to protect the state from delays that the accused might cause.

Putting the speedy trial clause of the Sixth Amendment into practice has been difficult, for several reasons. First, since the writing of the Constitution over two centuries ago, the criminal justice system has become more complex. Many procedural steps have been added in order to guarantee a fair hearing for the accused. Second, in many jurisdictions a growing number of people are accused of violations of the law each year, making delays inevitable. In many metropolitan areas where crime rates are high, some defendants may find it difficult to receive any trial at all, let alone a speedy one. Third, criminal law has become more detailed and elaborate, causing the evidence-gathering process to become increasingly time-consuming. Fourth, the requirement of a speedy trial must be balanced against the right of both the defense and the prosecution to have enough time to prepare. Fifth, some trials are delayed by either the prosecution or the defense for the purpose of achieving their own objectives. A prosecutor, for example, may seek several continuances, hoping to put off a trial until an accused's codefendant is convinced to "strike a deal" and become a witness for the state. A defense attorney may employ the same delaying tactics, hoping that witnesses will lose interest in the case. Sixth, some delays result from little more than prosecutors' apathy or lack of concern for defendants' rights and humanity. And seventh, there is no consensus as to the meaning of *speedy trial.* Statutory time limits vary by jurisdiction and by the nature of the offense charged: In California, for example, the period between arraignment and trial must not exceed 60 days.[42] In Alabama, the time limit between arrest and trial is set at 12 months for misdemeanors and at 3 years for all felonies—except capital offenses, for which there is no time limit.[43]

The Supreme Court and Speedy Trial

The Constitution offers no clues to what its framers had in mind when they incorporated the concept of speedy trial into the Bill of Rights. As a result, the Supreme Court has attached a standard of reasonableness. This is an attempt to achieve a balance between the effects of delays and their causes and justifications. The court emphasized the need for such a balance as early as 1905, when it ruled in *Beavers v. Haubert*[44] that the right to a speedy trial is a "relative" one "consistent with delays and dependent on circumstances."

Many of the court's subsequent decisions addressed the particulars of individual cases rather than larger policy issues. At the beginning of the 1970s, however, the court's rulings in a series of cases did provide some guidelines. The first of these was *Barker v. Wingo,*[45] decided in 1972. Until that time, both federal and state courts operated under the assumption that failure to demand a speedy trial meant that the accused was not opposed to delays. In *Barker,* the Supreme Court rejected this assumption, holding that passive compliance does not amount to a waiver of the Sixth Amendment right to a speedy trial. Moreover, although the court was unwilling to announce any specific time frame for what would constitute delay, it did identify a variety of factors that trial courts should examine in determining whether the right to a speedy trial has been denied: the length of the delay, the reason for the delay, the defendant's assertion of his or her right, and prejudice to the defendant.

The following year, in *Strunk v. United States,*[46] the court unanimously held that if a defendant is denied a speedy trial, "the only possible remedy" is for the charges to be dismissed. Later in the decade, in *United States v. Lovasco,*[47] the court made clear that the Sixth Amendment right does not apply to delays before a person is accused of a crime but, rather, applies only to the interval between arrest and trial. While a speedy trial has been a constitutional guarantee at the federal level since the drafting of the Bill of Rights, it was not applied to the states until the case of *Klopfer v. North Carolina* in 1967.[48]

The Right to a Public Trial

The Sixth Amendment provides not only for a speedy trial but for a public one as well— a guarantee rooted in the heritage of English common law. The distrust of secret trials evolved from their notorious use by the Spanish Inquisition and the English court of Star Chamber, as well as the French monarchy's use of the *lettre de cachet.*[49] In the hands of despotic groups, these institutions became instruments of political and religious suppression through their ruthless disregard of the accused's right to a fair trial.

Although all jurisdictions have adopted the Sixth Amendment right to a public trial through state constitutions, statutes, or judicial decisions, there have been exceptions in the not-so-distant past. *In re Oliver,*[50] decided in 1948, was one of the very few cases in which the Supreme Court addressed the right to a public trial. The issue in *Oliver* stemmed from the actions of a Michigan judge serving in the role of a one-person grand jury. The judge's actions were described in the court's opinion as follows:

> In the case before us, the petitioner was called as a witness to testify in secret before a one-man grand jury conducting a grand jury investigation. In the midst of petitioner's testimony the proceedings abruptly changed. The investigation became a "trial," the grand jury became a judge, and the witness became an accused charged with contempt of court—all in secret.[51]

Following a charge, conviction, and sentence, the petitioner was led away to prison—still without any break in the secrecy. Even in jail, according to undenied allegations, his lawyer was denied an opportunity to see and confer with him. And that was not the end of the secrecy. His lawyer filed a *habeas corpus* proceeding in the state supreme court. Even there, the mantle of secrecy enveloped the transaction, and the state supreme court ordered the petitioner back to jail without ever having seen a record of his testimony and without knowing all that took place in the secrecy of the judge's chambers. In view of this nation's historic distrust of secret proceedings, their inherent dangers to freedom, the universal requirement of our federal and state governments that criminal trials be public, and the Fourteenth Amendment's guarantee that no one shall be deprived of his liberty without due process of law, the Supreme Court held that an accused cannot be thus sentenced to prison. The court further held that the failure to give the accused a reasonable opportunity to defend himself against the contempt charge was a denial of due process of law.[52] These practices have become even more commonplace in American criminal justice proceedings as the use of the Patriot Act has resulted in secret proceedings, detentions, and interrogations of those defined as threats to national security.

The Right to a Trial by Judge or Jury

As a criminal prosecution approaches the trial date, a pretrial hearing is held, at which point the judge hears and deals with the pretrial motions. At the same time, the court also asks whether the accused wishes a trial by judge or by jury. In a trial by judge (or judges), more commonly referred to as a *bench trial,* the presiding judge makes the decision of innocence or guilt. In some jurisdictions, state requirements may dictate the option of a trial by judge. Under Tennessee statutes, for example, the accused can waive the right to a trial by jury;[53] in Idaho, however, this waiver is permitted only in nonfelony cases.[54]

When defendants are in a position to choose, they may prefer the bench trial under several circumstances. For example, the crime may be so reprehensible or so widely publicized that it could be difficult, if not impossible, to find a neutral jury. Or the nature of the defense may be too complex or technical for jurors without legal training to fully comprehend. Also, the presiding judge may have a previous record of favorable decisions in similar cases.

The reasons for selecting a trial by jury are perhaps even more compelling. The jury serves as a safeguard against overzealous prosecutors and biased judges, and it gives the accused the benefit of commonsense judgment, as opposed to the perhaps less sympathetic reactions of a single magistrate.

The Right to Trial by Jury The trial by jury is a distinctive feature of the Anglo-American system of justice, dating back more than seven centuries. The Magna Carta, signed in 1215, contained a special provision

Jurors are seated within a separate area of the courtroom, like the one pictured here. The right to a jury trial is protected by Article III and the Sixth Amendment to the U.S. Constitution.

that no freeholder (free landowners) would be deprived of life or property except by judgment of his or her peers. This common-law principle was incorporated into the U.S. Constitution.[55] Article III contains this simple and straightforward statement: "The trial of all crimes, except in cases of impeachment, shall be by jury." Article III is reaffirmed by the Sixth Amendment, which holds that "in all criminal prosecutions, the accused shall enjoy the right to a speedy and public trial by an impartial jury."[56]

In federal cases, to which Article III applies directly, the Supreme Court has been unrelenting in its view that a jury in criminal cases must have 12 members and reach a unanimous verdict. For almost two centuries after the framing of the Constitution—despite Article III and the Sixth Amendment—the right to a trial by jury "in all criminal prosecutions" was not fully binding in state trials. This discrepancy ended with the Supreme Court's ruling in *Duncan v. Louisiana*,[57] decided in 1968 and discussed in the chapter opener.

Jury Selection   Trial juries—sometimes referred to as *petit juries* to differentiate them from grand juries—have historically consisted of 12 jurors. Twelve-member juries are required in all federal prosecutions but not in all state prosecutions. In *Williams v. Florida*,[58] decided in 1970, the Supreme Court ruled that it was proper for states to use juries composed of as few as 6 persons, at least in noncapital cases, and some eight years later it reaffirmed this decision when it rejected the use of a 5-person jury in Georgia.[59]

Jury selection involves a series of steps, illustrated in Exhibit 9.2, beginning with the preparation of a master list of eligible jurors. Eligibility requirements generally include citizenship and literacy. In addition, there are restrictions against minors and individuals with serious felony convictions. Others, such as the aged, disabled, parents with young children, and people whose employers will not allow it, may be exempted from jury service on the basis of hardship. Not too many exemptions can be allowed in preparing the master list, however, because in constitutional terms an "impartial" jury means a representative cross section of a community's citizens. This is why, in 1975, the Supreme Court struck down a Louisiana law that barred women from juries unless they specifically requested, in writing, to participate.[60]

In current practice, the local voter-registration roll is the basis of the master list in many communities. This source is considered to be representative of the population,

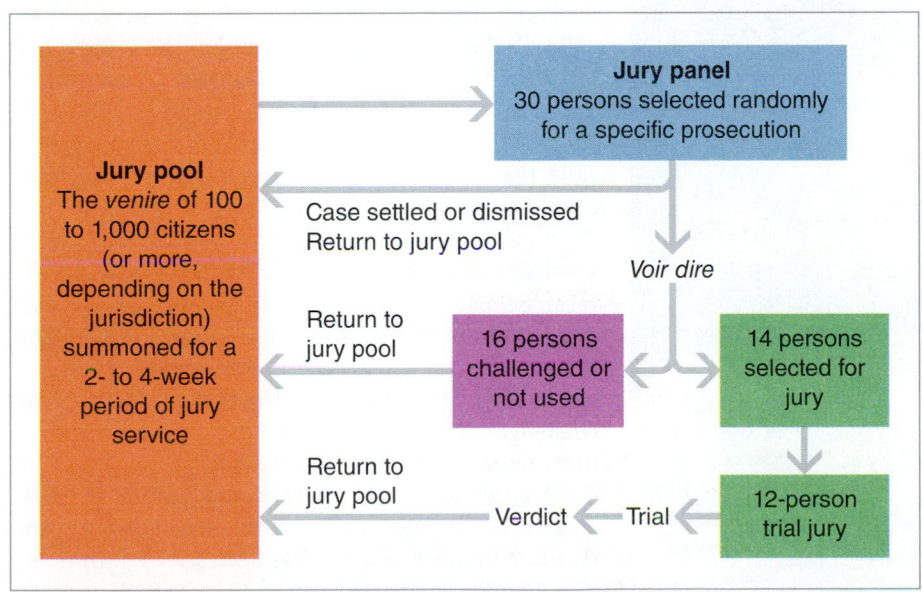

EXHIBIT 9.2   **The Selection Process for a 12-Person Jury**

at least in theory, and it is readily available. However, studies of voting behavior have demonstrated that registration lists are highly biased as sources of jury pools. From 30 to 50 percent of those eligible do not register to vote. Moreover, the registration rates for people with low incomes hover around 60 percent, compared to 85 percent for those with middle incomes or higher.[61] Similarly, members of racial minorities, young people, and the poorly educated more frequently ignore the electoral process or have been excluded from it by legal or extralegal means. To mitigate this difficulty, some communities use multiple-source lists, supplementing voter-registration lists with names drawn from rosters of licensed drivers and telephone directories.

The Venire   From the master list of eligible jurors, names are randomly selected for the **venire,** or *venire facias,* the writ that summons jurors. More commonly, however, the term refers to the list of potential jurors who are eligible for a given period of service. These summoned jurors become members of a jury pool, and they are interviewed to confirm their eligibility and availability. Those who remain in the pool are paid for their time; the current rate ranges from $15 to $50 per day. Federal jurors are paid $40 per day.[62]

The procedure through which members of the jury pool become actual trial jurors begins with the selection of a jury panel. In a felony prosecution that requires 12 jurors, as many as 30 are selected for the panel (or perhaps hundreds in some high-profile cases). Their names are drawn at random by the clerk of the court, and from there the process moves on to the *voir dire* examination.

The Voir Dire   A **voir dire,** meaning "to speak the truth," is an oath sworn by a prospective juror regarding his or her qualifications. The term generally refers to the voir dire examination, which involves questioning by the prosecutor, defense attorney, and sometimes the judge in order to determine a candidate's fitness to serve. The inquiry focuses on the person's background, familiarity with the case, associations with individuals involved in the case, attitudes about certain facts that might arise during the trial, and any other matters that may reflect on his or her willingness and ability to judge the case fairly and impartially.

A potential juror who either the prosecutor or the defense attorney deems unacceptable is eliminated through either the challenge for cause or the peremptory challenge. The *challenge for cause* means that there is a sound legal reason to remove a potential juror. Whoever makes such a challenge—either the defense attorney or the prosecutor—must explain to the judge the nature of the concern. Typically, challenges for cause allege that the prospective juror would be incapable of judging the accused fairly. Such challenges are controlled by statute, and the decision to remove a juror is vested with the court. Technically, there is no limit on the number of challenges for cause that may be made.

A *peremptory challenge* is an objection to a prospective juror for which no reason must be assigned. It can be made for any reason or no reason at all and is totally within the discretion of the attorney making it. Peremptory challenges generally reflect the biases and strategies of the defense and the prosecution.[63] These challenges are used to obtain jurors who appear more likely to be sympathetic to their side.

Regardless of the number and nature of challenges, the voir dire examination continues until the required number of jurors has been selected. In many jurisdictions where a 12-person jury is used, as many

Potential jurors fill out lengthy questionnaires to help prosecution and defense attorneys identify those most suitable for the trial.

as 14 or even more may be accepted. The additional jurors serve as alternates. They sit through the entire trial and are available to take the place of a regular jury member should he or she become ill, be forced to withdraw, or be disqualified while the trial is in progress. Potential jurors who are successfully challenged return to the jury pool, and new ones are drawn from the panel and subjected to voir dire. Those ultimately selected are sworn in and become the trial jury.

The voir dire can be brief or time-consuming. In prosecutions of misdemeanors and in felonies with little pretrial publicity and trial proceedings that are expected to be fairly routine, the parties may raise few challenges, and the voir dire may last only a few hours or even less. In other cases, the examination can continue for days, weeks, or even months. It is the challenges for cause that lengthen the proceedings. Any and every potential juror can be challenged for cause. Peremptory challenges, on the other hand, are controlled by statute. In New York, for example, the number of peremptory challenges varies with the seriousness of the offense; in serious cases such as murder, as many as twenty are allowed.[64] Peremptory challenges are also affected by case law—specifically, *Batson v. Kentucky,* in which the Supreme Court limited the use of peremptory challenges to address the elimination of jurors solely on the basis of race—a practice that violated the Equal Protection Clause of the Fourteenth Amendment.[65]

The voir dire can be a crucially important part of a criminal proceeding. Its purpose is to do more than merely choose a fair and impartial jury—as significant as this may be. Its primary functions are to instruct the citizen as to the role of the juror and to develop rapport between jurors and attorneys. Moreover, the process gives the defense and the prosecution an opportunity to influence jurors' attitudes and, perhaps, their later vote.

THE CRIMINAL TRIAL

The trial is the climax of the criminal proceeding. It begins as soon as the jury has been sworn in. The only matter that remains in doubt before commentary and testimony can begin is the judge's decision whether to sequester the jurors for the entire trial. Sequestration involves the removal of the jurors (and alternates, if any) from all possible outside influence. Sequestered jurors are housed in a hotel or motel for the duration of the trial; they are forbidden all visitors; and the newspapers they read, as well as the television programs they watch, are fully censored.[66]

Few juries are sequestered for an entire trial, because most criminal prosecutions fail to generate even a line of newspaper copy or a second of television news time. Only if continuing media coverage has the potential for influencing a juror's decision is sequestration ordered. If ordered by the judge, however, sequestration places a tremendous hardship on the jury.

The procedures used in criminal trials are, for the most part, the same nationwide. The process consists of the following steps:

- opening statements
- presentation of the state's case
- presentation of the defense's case
- rebuttal and surrebuttal
- closing arguments
- charging the jury
- deliberation and verdict

Jury members in the trial of Jerry Sandusky (pictured here) were ultimately sequestered due to the frenzy of media attention surrounding the proceedings. Typically, sequestration occurs to prevent access to the jury in order to protect both the integrity of the trial and the jury members themselves.

In bench trials, this process is altered only minimally. The steps involving the jury are eliminated, and the tactics and strategies of the defense and prosecuting attorneys are simplified, removing much of the dramatic effect.

Opening Statements

The first step in a trial proceeding is the reading of the criminal complaint by the court clerk, followed by opening statements—first by the prosecution and then by the defense. The prosecutor's statement is an attempt to give the jury an outline of the case and how the state intends to prove, beyond a reasonable doubt, that the defendant did indeed commit the crime or crimes charged in the indictment. This outline generally includes a description of the crime and the defendant's role in it and a discussion of the evidence and witnesses to be presented. In addition, the prosecutor may address the meaning of *beyond a reasonable doubt.* Reasonable doubt is fair doubt based on reason and common sense and growing out of the testimony of the case; it is doubt arising from a candid and impartial investigation of all the evidence and testimony presented. The purpose of the prosecutor's analysis here is to distinguish between reasonable doubt and vague apprehension and, at the same time, to emphasize that the state's goal is to prove guilt beyond a reasonable doubt—not beyond all doubt.

Although the prosecutor has considerable freedom as to the content of the opening statement, she or he may not refer to evidence that is known to be inadmissible or to the defendant's prior criminal record (if any exists). To make such comments would be considered a *prejudicial error*—an error of such significance that it compromises

Attorneys are key to the drama played out before the jury.

or prejudices the rights of the accused. Prejudicial errors that cannot be corrected by any action of the court are often the bases for appeals. Moreover, these can result in a **mistrial**—a discharging of the jury without a verdict. A mistrial is the equivalent of no trial at all, and it is for this reason that initiating a new trial does not constitute double jeopardy.[67]

The defense attorney's opening statement is an address to the jury that focuses on how the defense will show that the state has a poor case and that it cannot demonstrate proof of guilt beyond a reasonable doubt. Defense attorneys often stress that the accused is innocent until proven guilty and that the burden of proof rests entirely with the prosecution.

Defense attorneys and prosecutors vary their strategies for opening statements, depending on the nature of the case, the evidence, and the witnesses. One approach is to keep opening remarks short and vague, letting the particulars of the case emerge during the course of the trial. Such a tactic makes few promises to the jury, but it allows flexibility. Flexibility is often important, because it enables the attorney, during the final summation, to structure an argument that is not weakened by promises that he or she could not deliver. By contrast, a detailed opening statement, eloquently expressed and forcefully presented, predisposes the jury to accept the evidence that the attorney will ultimately deliver. This technique can be risky, but it is highly rewarding if, during the course of the trial, the attorney is able to keep the promises made in the opening.[68]

In a jury trial, the prosecutor always delivers an opening statement that explains the charges against a defendant. Without it, the jurors would have no framework within which to consider the evidence and testimony. The defense attorney, however, may choose to make no statement—out of necessity, perhaps, if the defense strategy cannot be determined until the state reveals the content of the case, or as part of the strategy, which is not to be revealed until the proper time. Opening statements are infrequently used in bench trials; these are less effective, since the judge has probably handled hundreds of similar cases.[69]

Presentation of the State's Case

To give the accused an opportunity to provide an informed defense, in the adversarial system of justice, the state presents its case first. The prosecutor begins by presenting evidence of the crime and questioning witnesses.

The Rules of Evidence Generally, evidence is any kind of proof, in the form of witnesses, records, documents, concrete objects, and circumstances. Specifically, there are four basic types:

1. *Real evidence* is physical details and objects, such as a murder weapon, stolen property, fingerprints, DNA, appearance of the victim's wounds, and appearance of the crime scene. Real evidence may be original objects or facsimile representations, such as photographs, tire tracks, or other duplicates of items that are either unavailable or unusable in their original form.
2. *Testimonial evidence* is the sworn, verbal statements of witnesses. All real evidence is accompanied by testimonial evidence, in that objects presented in evidence are explained by someone who is qualified to discuss them. Conversely, however, real evidence does not accompany all testimonial evidence.
3. *Direct evidence* is eyewitness evidence. Testimony from a witness that he or she saw a person painting a fence, for example, is direct evidence that the person painted a fence.
4. *Circumstantial evidence,* or *indirect evidence,* is evidence from which a fact can be reasonably inferred. Testimony that a person was seen with paint and a paintbrush in the vicinity of a newly painted fence is circumstantial evidence that the person painted the fence.

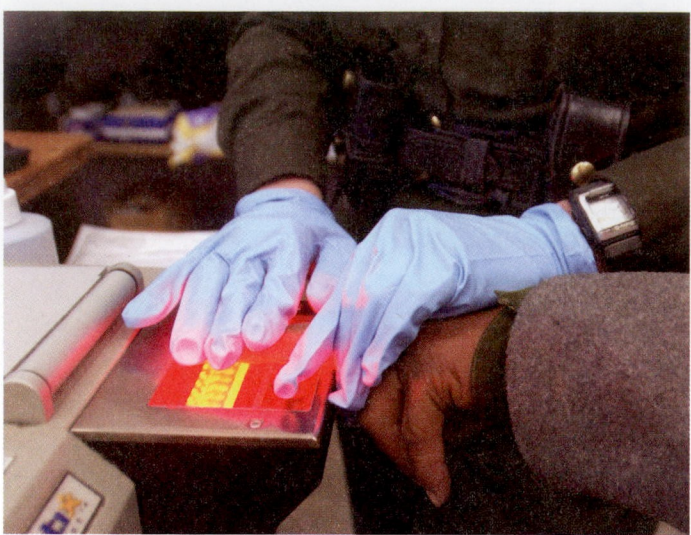

Fingerprints remain one of the most common forms of physical evidence used in criminal proceedings. Many jurisdictions now use digital equipment, as pictured here, to collect the fingerprints of individuals who have been recently arrested.

These four types of evidence necessarily overlap, since all are ultimately presented through testimony. Moreover, all evidence must be competent, material, and relevant. Evidence is *competent* when it is legally fit for admission to court. The testimony of an expert witness on a scientific matter is deemed to be competent, for example, if the court accepts his or her credentials as a reflection of proficiency in the subject area. In contrast, testimonial evidence on ballistics presented by an automobile mechanic would be considered incompetent; or an individual who has been convicted of perjury might be considered incompetent to testify.

Evidence can also be deemed incompetent if it is based on hearsay. Under most circumstances, the hearsay rule bars a witness from testifying about statements that are not within his or her personal knowledge—that is, about secondhand information. There are two exceptions to this rule. First, if the defendant makes an admission of criminal conduct to the witness, such hearsay testimony is allowed because the accused is present in court to challenge it. The second exception, called the "dying declaration," is based on something a witness has overheard or been told by a dying crime victim; it is based on the assumption that a person who is about to die will not lie.[70]

To be admissible in a court of law, evidence must also be material and relevant. There is only a slight distinction between these two requirements. Evidence is *material* when it has a legitimate bearing on the decision of the case. Evidence is *relevant* when it is applicable to the issue in question. For example, evidence of a defendant's bad character on previous occasions is immaterial (unless the defendant is submitting his or her good character in evidence). By contrast, the fact that an accused person has stolen property in the past is irrelevant to whether or not he or she has murdered someone (assuming, of course, that the accused is not being tried on multiple charges of theft and murder).

An interesting recent phenomenon has been called the "CSI effect."[71] It appears that *CSI: Crime Scene Investigation* and the *CSI* spin-offs—*Criminal Minds* and similar television dramas—foster what some say is the mistaken notion that criminal science is fast and foolproof. These programs also give the impression that the offender is always identified and apprehended. Concerns abound about the impact these popular shows have on jurors' perceptions of the criminal justice process. The disconnect between what is portrayed on television and what is possible with local and state resources may be greater than many citizens realize.[72]

For example, a local police department may not have the equipment needed to collect DNA evidence, and even when it does, its ability to study and analyze this evidence may not live up to the television depictions. Furthermore, DNA evidence is not always available, nor can it always conclusively identify a perpetrator. Thus, to counter the CSI effect, some courtroom workgroups have introduced novel procedures. In Massachusetts and a number of other states, jurors are being asked about their TV-watching habits. Other states, including Arizona, Illinois, and California, allow prosecutors to use "negative evidence witnesses," whose job is to educate jurors about the limitations and realities of criminal evidence collection and analysis.[73]

The upside of all of this is that lectures and college courses on criminal justice and forensic science are filled to capacity these days. However, as you can see in the "Victims and Justice" feature, advances in science and technology are not always paralleled by changes in the law.

VICTIMS AND JUSTICE

DNA Profiling and the Statutes of Limitations: Advancing Justice for Victims

Evidence should help crime victims seek the justice they deserve, but this is not always the case. Because of the widespread use of DNA profiling in recent years, statutes of limitations have run into a major complication in a number of jurisdictions. Rape survivors and law enforcement officials, in particular, are finding that with regard to sex crimes, science has outpaced the law and may place the finality of justice at risk. Through mandatory sampling of prisoners and other known offenders, the FBI, states, and municipalities are developing computerized databases that allow investigators to compare bits of biological evidence left at crime scenes against the DNA profiles of scores of suspects. Because these checks are quite easy and virtually infallible, they can result in breakthroughs, particularly in the great backlog of investigations of violent crimes that have essentially gone cold. DNA profiling is especially useful in rape cases, because in the majority of instances, it is possible to collect samples of the rapist's semen from the victim and then to preserve those samples for the possible identification of the perpetrator at some later date.

But a race against time is under way. Most states have statutes of limitations for rape prosecutions—often just five to seven years. What that means is that old cases might be solved but not prosecuted, because the statute of limitations has run out. And this would be so even if the names of the rapists were known and the evidence against them were overwhelming.

Florida, Nevada, Jew Jersey, and New York have already abolished the statutes of limitations on sexual assault, and other jurisdictions have extended their statutes of limitations to 10 and 15 years. Massachusetts has a 15-year statute of limitations on sexual assault. However, it has implemented another strategy to prevent offenders from escaping prosecution. In a 2010 case, *Commonwealth v. Jerry Dixon,* the Massachusetts Supreme Judicial Court ruled that a DNA profile may substitute for the name of an offender, with the result that grand juries can indict the profile and circumvent the statute of limitations. The facts of the case are these: In 1991, an offender left DNA at the scenes of multiple rapes. Another person was convicted of the crimes and served 12 years in prison. Later scientific advances in the use of DNA evidence proved that the man convicted was innocent, and he was released. A short time later, a grand jury "indicted" the unnamed owner of the DNA, just before the 15-year statute of limitations would have expired. In 2008—17 years after the rapes—this sample was matched to a DNA sample collected while Dixon was in prison on a different offense. Dixon was tried and convicted of the crimes but argued on appeal that he did not have notice of his indictment before the limitations period expired. The Massachusetts Supreme Judicial Court, however, ruled against him, stating that he was not entitled to notice.

Advances in DNA testing, including testing that takes far less time, and the increased availability of the testing, along with innovations like those in Massachusetts, promise justice for victims

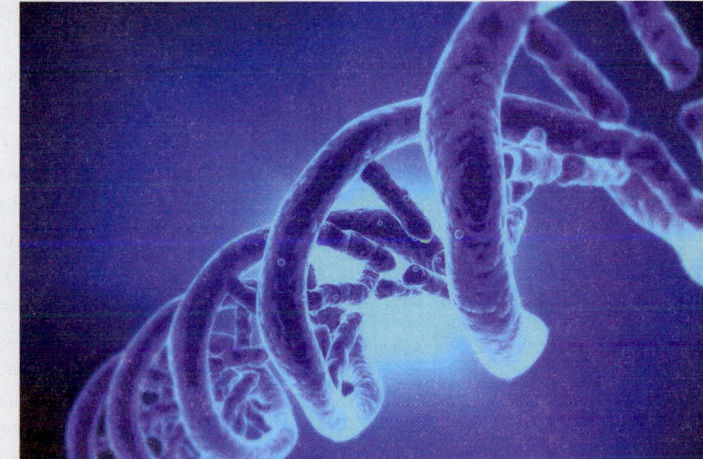

The use of DNA evidence in cases from the distant past creates challenges for the criminal justice process.

of sexual assault. However, these changes are not retroactive, and although old cases continue to expire, future cases will benefit. Other state legislatures continue to review their statutes in light of DNA profiling. But as the discussions linger, tens of thousands of cold cases are running out of time.

THINK ABOUT THIS

1. What is the purpose of a statute of limitations? Would we want to remove the limitations for violent offenses?
2. What makes DNA evidence different from other types of evidence? Why might the presence of DNA evidence call for a change in the way we think about statutes of limitations?
3. How do you think the victims of crimes would feel about the identification of their offenders 10, 20, or even 30 years after the offenses?

Sources: David H. Kaye and Edward Imwinkelried, *Forensic DNA Typing: Selected Legal Issues* (Phoenix: Arizona State University, 2000); Hans H. Chen, "DNA Indictments Push Law to the Limit," *APB Online,* March 21, 2000, http://groups.yahoo.com/group/lawpowerandjustice/message/1771; "As DNA Aids Rape Inquiries, Statutory Limits Block Cases," *New York Times,* February 9, 2000; Rape, Abuse & Incest National Network (RAINN), *The Laws in Your State,* http://www.rainn.org/public-policy/laws-in-your-state; Relief Fund for Sexual Assault Victims, *Statutes of Limitation for Prosecuting Rape and/or Sexual Assault,* data compiled by RAINN, February 2003, http://www.relieffundforsexualassaultvictims.org/resources/statutesoflimitationcrim-D.pdf; Gordon Thomas Honeywell Governmental Affairs on behalf of Applied Biosystems, *2008 Statute of Limitations DNA Legislation,* February 28, 2008, www.dnaresource.com/.../2008StatuteofLimitations Legislation.pdf. *Commonwealth v. Jerry Dixon,* 458 Mass. 446 (2010).

Examination of Witnesses The state's presentation begins with the direct examination of witnesses to elicit facts in some chronological order. The first witness called is generally one who can establish the elements of the crime. Subsequent witnesses introduce physical, direct, and indirect evidence and expert testimony.

After the prosecutor has completed his or her interrogation through direct examination, the defense is permitted (but not required) to cross-examine the witness. The purpose of cross-examination is to discredit the testimony, either by teasing out inconsistencies and contradictions or by attacking the credibility of the witness. The prosecution can ask further questions of the witness through a redirect examination, as can the defense with a re-cross-examination. This examination procedure continues until all of the state's witnesses have been called and all of the evidence has been presented.

Objections During the examination of any witness, whether by the prosecutor or the defense counsel, the opposing attorney can object to the introduction of evidence or testimony that he or she considers incompetent, immaterial, or irrelevant. Objections can also be made to *leading questions* (ones that inherently instruct or at least suggest to the witness how to answer), to eliciting a witness's opinions and conclusions, to being argumentative, and to *badgering* (abusing) a witness.

If the objection is *sustained* (consented to), the examiner is ordered to withdraw the question or cease the mode of inquiry, and the jury is instructed to disregard whatever was deemed inappropriate. If the objection is *overruled* (rejected), the examining attorney may continue with the original line of questioning.

Motion for a Directed Verdict Following the presentation of the state's case, the defense attorney may enter a *motion for a directed verdict*. With this, the defense moves that the judge enter a finding of acquittal on the grounds that the state failed to establish a clear case of guilt against the accused. If the judge so moves, he or she directs the jury to acquit the defendant. Even without a motion by the defense, the trial judge can order a directed verdict. Moreover, the judge can do so not only on the grounds that the state failed to prove its case but also on the grounds that the testimony of the prosecution witnesses was not credible or the conduct of the prosecutor was not proper. Conversely, a judge cannot direct the jury to convict the accused.

Presentation of the Defense's Case

A component of the Sixth Amendment provides that in all criminal prosecutions the accused shall enjoy the right "to have compulsory process for obtaining witnesses in his favor." *Compulsory process* refers to the subpoena power that can force a witness into court to testify. The compulsory process clause is central to the presentation of a defense case. During this presentation, the counsel for the accused calls witnesses to testify in support of the not-guilty plea. Also at this point, the counsel for the accused has the opportunity to offer evidence in chief—that is, the first, or direct, examination of a witness.

The defense attorney serves as an advocate and provides legal representation for those accused of crimes.

At the outset, the defense attorney can present many, some, or no witnesses or items of evidence on behalf of the accused. In addition, the defense must decide whether the accused will testify. The Fifth Amendment right against self-incrimination does not require it, but if the defendant chooses to testify, the prosecution has the option of cross-examination.

Once these matters have been decided, the defense's presentation follows the procedures outlined for the state's presentation: direct examination, cross-examination, redirect examination, and re-cross-examination. In addition, the rules of evidence and the right to make objections apply equally to the defense and the prosecution.

It is a common misconception that during this stage of the trial the burden of proof shifts to the defense. This is not so. The responsibility of proving guilt beyond a reasonable doubt always remains with the prosecution. What shifts to the defense is the "burden of going forward with the evidence." This means that since the prosecution has presented its suit to the jury, the defense is now responsible for offering its own argument for the jury to consider.

Rebuttal and Surrebuttal

When the defense *rests* (concludes its presentation), the prosecutor may introduce new witnesses or evidence in an effort to refute the defense's case. Known as the *prosecutor's rebuttal,* it follows the same format of examination and cross-examination, redirect and re-cross-examination. In turn, the counsel for the accused may put forth a surrebuttal, which is a rebuttal of the prosecutor's rebuttal.

Closing Arguments

The *summation,* or *closing argument,* gives each side an opportunity to recapitulate all the evidence and testimony offered during the trial. The arguments are made directly to the jury. Closing arguments are often quite eloquent and dramatic.

In most jurisdictions, the summation begins with the defense attorney, who points out any weaknesses or flaws in the prosecutor's theory and evidence. Counsel for the accused argues that proof beyond a reasonable doubt has not been established and reminds the jurors that they will have to live with their decision for the rest of their lives. Since the burden of proof rests with the state, the prosecutor is entitled to the final argument. For both the defense and the prosecution, perhaps the most vital element of the closing argument is persuasion.

There are as many ways of summing up as there are trial lawyers, and there is no one correct way to deliver a summation, or to learn how to give one. It is largely a matter of instinct and experience. Either you are able to reach out and move people with your words, or you are not, and that is all there is to it.[74]

Charging the Jury

Charging the jury involves an order by the judge that directs the jurors to retire to the jury room, consider the facts of the case and the evidence and testimony presented, and arrive at a just verdict. Regarded by many as the single most important statement made during the trial, the charge includes instructions regarding the possible verdicts, the rules of evidence, and the legal meaning of *reasonable doubt*. The instructions contained in the charge are often arrived at through consultation with the defense and the prosecution and from statutory instructions contained in the jurisdiction's code of criminal procedure.

In some states, judges are permitted to review thoroughly all the evidence that has been presented to the jury. They are free, for example, to summarize the testimony of each witness. This can be useful to jurors, especially if the trial has been long and complex. But it can also be hazardous, for a judge has opinions about innocence and guilt, and these can inadvertently influence the jury.

A difficult task for judges is to present instructions that juries can understand fully. Because the nuances of the law are so complex, it can take hours to deliver the instructions. At the end of this process, the judge instructs members of the jury that they cannot communicate with anyone except the other jurors about the facts of the case. Further sequestration might be ordered, which would place the jurors under the supervision of a court officer until they reached a verdict.

Jury Deliberations

Every jury has a foreperson who serves as the nominal leader of the group. The jurors choose the foreperson during the trial or in the jury room. In some jurisdictions, the first juror selected in the voir dire becomes the leader. Whether this person becomes the actual leader is another matter, depending on personality and the dynamics of group interaction.

Once the jury has retired, the foreperson traditionally sits at the head of the table and calls for a vote. Except in Oregon and Louisiana, the law requires unanimous verdicts.[75] If the jury reaches such a verdict, the deliberations are finished. Typically, however, things are not that simple.

Deliberations are important, because the exposure to different interpretations of the evidence prevents jurors them from relying too much on their own idiosyncratic views. In addition, jurors often correct one another's factual errors. When their collective memories are pooled, the jury as a whole recalls a substantial amount of the evidence.[76]

Jury deliberations are protected from the scrutiny of the public.

When deliberations fail to generate a unanimous decision, the dilemma is referred to as a *deadlocked, or hung, jury.* The jury is then dismissed in open court, the judge declares a mistrial, and the prosecution can either retry the case or drop the charges. Deadlocked juries result from differences of opinion over the strengths and weaknesses of evidence, varying perceptions of innocence and guilt, and the meaning of *reasonable doubt.* The deadlocked jury is not a common occurrence. Reports indicate that only 6 percent of all criminal trials end with a hung jury.[77]

Verdict and Judgment

When the jury reaches a verdict, it returns to the courtroom to announce its decision: "We, the jury, duly impaneled and sworn, find the defendant guilty [or not guilty] as charged." In cases involving multiple charges, the jury may find the accused guilty of some and not guilty of others.

An enduring issue in criminal trials is the problem of *jury nullification.* It occurs when juries do not follow the court's interpretation of the law in every instance, disregard what they have been told about the law or certain aspects of evidence, consider the application of certain laws to be unjust, refuse to convict because they consider the penalties too severe, or otherwise "nullify" or suspend the force of strict legal procedure. Though juries have the power to nullify, they do not necessarily have the right to do so. In fact, some states are taking steps to prevent jury nullification.[78] Instances of jury nullification have occurred in cases involving battered spouses who kill, political crimes, mercy killings, and perceived racial injustice.

Jury nullification can occur either inadvertently or by design. If a verdict of guilty is reached but the judge believes that it occurred from nullification and is erroneous, he or she can refuse to abide by it. The judge can direct the jury to acquit, or "arrest" the guilty verdict and enter a judgment of acquittal. However, as mentioned earlier, a trial judge does not have the authority to direct a jury to convict or enter a judgment arresting a verdict of not guilty.

Jurors can be polled at the request of the defense or the prosecution. The judge (or the bailiff) asks each juror whether the announced verdict is his or her individual verdict. Polling of jurors is done to determine whether any juror has been pressured into voting a particular way.

Many attempts have been made to reform the jury trial so as to reduce problems of comprehension and absorption of complex information, nullification, deadlocking, and related issues.[79] Changes already adopted include raising the jurors' daily payment, allowing them to ask questions and discuss evidence among themselves while the trial is going on, and allowing judges and attorneys to give further information and instruction to deadlocked jurors. In August 2005, the American Bar Association General Assembly formally adopted the Principles for Juries and Jury Trials, developed by the American Jury Project. Those nineteen principles endorse virtually all the recent American jury innovations and reforms, and they offer guidelines in many areas of controversy.[80]

Posttrial Motions

With a judgment of not guilty, the defendant is immediately released—unless other charges are still pending. With a guilty verdict, most jurisdictions allow the defense to file motions to set aside the judgment or to request a new trial.

The *motion in arrest of judgment* asks that no judgment be pronounced because of one or more defects in the record of the case. Possible defects might be that the trial court had no jurisdiction over the case, that the verdict included conviction on a charge that was not tested in the indictment or information, or that there was error *on the face of the record.* This last term refers to any faults of procedure that may have occurred during the pretrial process.

The *motion for a new trial,* which only the defense can make, can be based on numerous grounds. The defense may claim that the jury received evidence outside the courtroom, that the jury was guilty of misconduct during deliberations, that the court erred in overruling an objection or permitting the introduction of certain evidence, that the jury was improperly charged, that the prosecution was guilty of misconduct, that there is a suspicion of jury tampering (bribes or threats made to a juror to influence his or her vote), or that newly discovered evidence is available for review.

If either motion is sustained, new proceedings will be initiated. Any new trial that results, however, does not represent double jeopardy because the defendant's motion is an allegation that the earlier proceedings should be declared utterly invalid. Posttrial motions are opportunities to start over or to amend the outcome of the criminal process.

With this section on posttrial motions, we complete our discussion of the process adults follow as their cases move through the court system. This process both parallels and diverges from the process that juveniles follow. In order to compare and contrast these two systems, read the "Juvenile Justice in Context" feature.

JUVENILE JUSTICE IN CONTEXT

The Business of Modern Juvenile Courts

Every state in the United States has a juvenile court system. Currently, more than 3,000 courts across the nation hear juvenile cases. While these juvenile courts all reflect the same general underlying philosophy, their sophistication and procedures vary. Some have extensive and well-trained support staffs and large probation and treatment components. Others rely on the resources of the adult criminal courts and correctional systems.

Juvenile courts are charged with responding to status and delinquent offenders, as well as to children who are in need of social services because they have been abused or neglected.

The jurisdiction of juvenile courts is defined by the offender's age and alleged offense. Typically, the maximum age is 18, although age 16 is the upper limit in some locations, including New York.[81] Juvenile courts have authority over delinquency and status offenses. A delinquent is a juvenile offender who has been adjudicated by an officer of a juvenile court for having violated a criminal law. **Status offenses** are specific acts (truancy, running away) and general conditions (incorrigibility, uncontrollable behavior) that are unique to the status of being a juvenile. Although most cases heard by juvenile courts involve delinquents or status offenders, there is a third category: children who are deprived and/or abused. These juveniles are victims rather than offenders, and the court's intent is to provide assistance for them.

The mechanism for bringing juveniles to the attention of the courts is a petition (as opposed to an arrest warrant) filed by the police, a victim, parents, school officials, or a social worker. Like an arrest warrant, the petition specifies the offense or delinquency or deprivation and describes the circumstances of the offense or the circumstances of the victimization. Overall, the system can be represented as a funnel, as shown in Exhibit 9.3; that is, a large number of suspects may come before the court, but a far smaller number of those end up in correctional institutions.

After the petition is filed, the court conducts an *intake hearing,* or preliminary examination of the facts. The hearing officer is usually an attorney, a probation officer, a court referee with a background in social work, or someone else assigned by the juvenile court. The purpose of this hearing is to protect the interests of the child and to quickly dispose of cases that do not require formal court processing.

There are three possible outcomes of the intake hearing: dismissal of the case, in which instance the child can go home; rendering of an informal judgment, such as arbitration, restitution, or referral to a social agency; or authorization of an inquiry before the juvenile court judge. With the third outcome, most states require an *adjudication hearing* to determine whether the child should be released to a parent or guardian or retained in custody. The issues addressed might include whether the child needs protection, whether the child presents a serious threat to the community, or how likely the child is to return to court at the scheduled time. At the inquiry, which is generally closed to the public and the media, the judge or magistrate can dismiss the case, order a formal adjudication hearing, or refer the juvenile to other social service agencies.

The adjudication hearing is not a trial. It is legally classified as a civil rather than a criminal proceeding. The judge presides on behalf of the child to determine whether he or she committed the alleged offense and, if so, whether the youth's parents are providing adequate care, supervision, and discipline. In cases where the youth is being held for his or her own protection, the judge determines the circumstances that brought the youth into court custody. The judge relies on any available clinical, social, or diagnostic reports. If the judge determines that no misconduct occurred, the case is dismissed. If misconduct is apparent, a disposition hearing is scheduled.

At *disposition hearings,* juvenile court judges have extremely broad discretion. They can dismiss a case, give the juvenile a warning, impose a fine, order the payment of restitution, require the performance of community service, refer the offender to a community agency or treatment facility, or place the child on probation. They may also put the child in a foster home, enter an order against the parents for the protection of the child, or have the youth committed to a juvenile institution. In practice, the most common dispositions are probation, court-sponsored restitution programs, and institutional commitment.

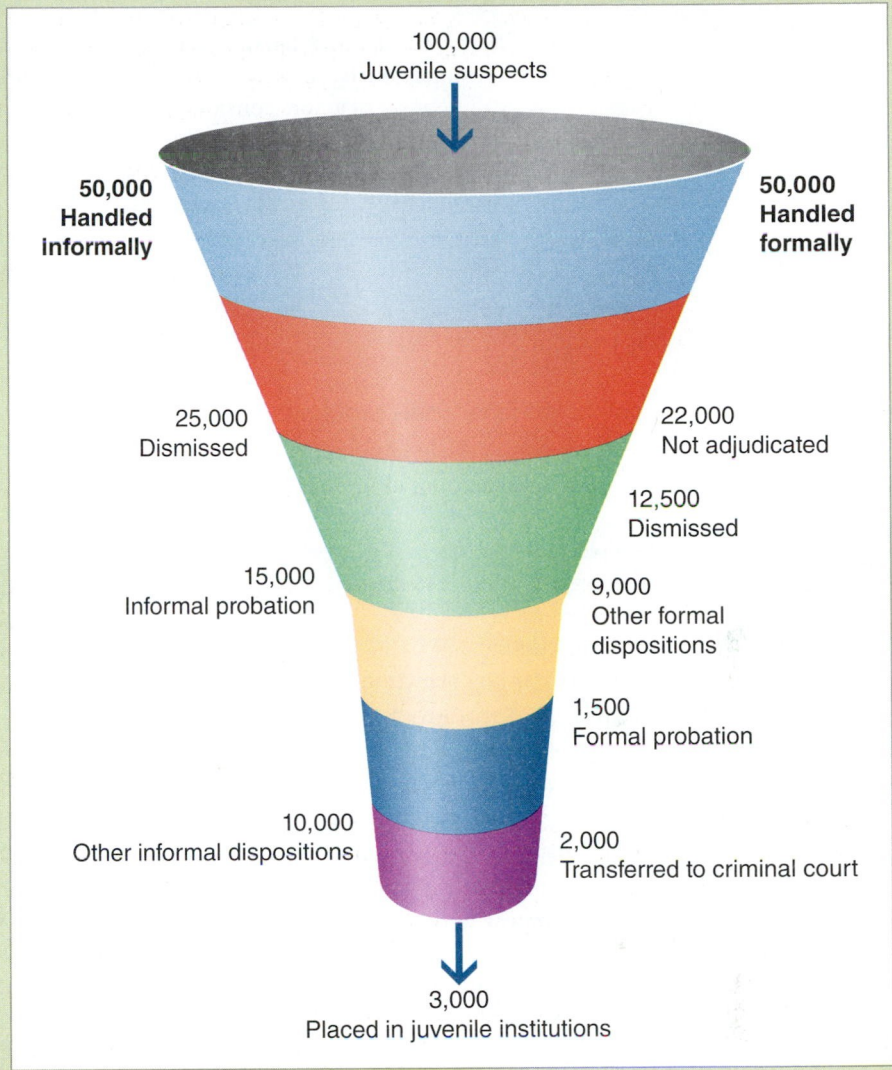

EXHIBIT 9.3 Juvenile Justice Funnel
Source: President's Commission on Law Enforcement and Administration of Justice, 1967

CONCLUSIONS

Many checks and balances characterize the movement of defendants through the criminal courts. As was illustrated by the *Duncan* case, at every stage of the process, a different set of actors considers the facts and the law and makes decisions that can affect individuals and communities, as well as set precedents for future cases or overturn existing laws. The centerpiece of the process—the criminal trial—serves to adjudicate offenders as either guilty or not and to move them through to receive appropriate punishment or allow them to leave the court without penalty if found not guilty.

SUMMARY AND REVIEW

■ **Identify the stages of the criminal court process.**

- After bail and pretrial release are determined, prosecution is instituted by an information, indictment, or presentment.
- The accused enters a plea.
- Pretrial motions are entered, and the judge rules on them.
- Jury selection begins if necessary.
- The criminal trial begins after jury selection.

■ **Explain the bail system and the challenges of pretrial release.**

- Bail and pretrial stages involve the determination of whether individuals accused of crimes will be released from jail after being arrested. Bail is the form of security guaranteeing that a defendant in a criminal proceeding will appear and be present in court as required.
- Those without economic means are often unable to raise the money needed to secure their release from jail.
- Judicial discretion may result in bail set at unreasonably high levels.
- Since bail is generally determined at the initial appearance, the court has little time to investigate the background of the accused and cannot always adequately determine the degree of risk.
- Bail is often used for preventive detention. To protect the community against offenders who are viewed as risks to social welfare and safety, bail is set so high that it can rarely be met.

■ **Describe the main issues related to grand jury proceedings and double jeopardy.**

- Grand jury proceedings have been criticized for the following reasons: their ex parte nature, abuse in granting immunity, use of the contempt power, and their cumbersome nature.
- The protection against threat of double jeopardy is included in the Fifth Amendment and prevents a person from being prosecuted repeatedly for one particular offense. The Supreme Court has held that this guarantee protects the accused against both multiple prosecutions for the same offense and multiple punishments for the same crime.

■ **Define the kinds of pleas available to defendants.**

- The four basic pleas are not guilty, standing mute, guilty, and nolo contendere. There is also the special plea of not guilty by reason of insanity, and those based on statutes of limitations and double jeopardy.
- The plea of not guilty, the most common, places the full burden on the state to prove the charges against the defendant beyond a reasonable doubt.
- The guilty plea has the effect of surrendering numerous constitutional rights, including those guaranteed under the Fifth and Sixth Amendments.
- The nolo contendere plea is essentially a guilty plea. The accused surrenders certain constitutional rights, and conviction is immediate. However, the accused makes no admission of guilt, which protects him or her in civil court should the victim subsequently sue for damages.
- The plea of not guilty by reason of insanity is an admission of guilt accompanied by the claim that the defendant is not culpable in the eyes of the law because of insanity at the time he or she committed the crime.

■ **List the types of pretrial motions and explain the purposes of these.**

- Before the trial begins, and sometimes before arraignment, both the defense and the prosecution may employ a number of motions.
- A motion is a formal application or request to the court for some action, such as an order or rule. The purpose of motions is to gain some legal advantage, and the defense initiates most of them.
- The number and type of motions vary according to the nature and complexity of the case. The court's

decisions as to whether to grant or deny motions can have a considerable impact on the outcome of a proceeding.

■ **Explain the rights related to speedy and public trial, including jury selection.**

- The Sixth Amendment guarantees the right to a speedy trial. Without it, individuals accused of crimes would have no protection against incarceration for an indefinite period prior to trial. The Constitution offers no clues as to what its framers had in mind with the concept of "speedy trial." As a result, the Supreme Court has attached a standard of reasonableness.

- The right to a public trial has been adopted in all jurisdictions through state constitutions, statutes, or judicial decisions. In view of this nation's historic distrust of secret proceedings, their inherent dangers to freedom, the universal requirement of our federal and state governments that criminal trials be public, and the Fourteenth Amendment's guarantee, the Supreme Court found that no one shall be deprived of his or her liberty without due process of law.

- Jury selection begins with the preparation of a master list of eligible jurors, which is then narrowed down to selections for the venire, or venire facias, the writ that summons jurors. Next is the voir dire examination, which involves questioning by the prosecutor, defense attorney, and sometimes the judge in order to determine a candidate's fitness to serve.

■ **Outline the steps in the criminal trial and the types of evidence that can be presented.**

- The criminal trial includes the following steps:
  - opening statements
  - presentation of the state's case
  - presentation of the defense's case
  - rebuttal and surrebuttal
  - closing arguments
  - charging the jury
  - deliberation and verdict

- Real evidence is physical details and objects, such as a murder weapon, stolen property, fingerprints, DNA, appearance of the victim's wounds, and appearance of the crime scene. Testimonial evidence is the sworn, verbal statements of witnesses. Direct evidence is eyewitness evidence, whereas circumstantial evidence, or indirect evidence, is evidence from which a fact can be reasonably inferred.

KEY TERMS

bail (p. 231)
double jeopardy (p. 238)
evidence (p. 234)
grand jury (p. 235)
guilty (p. 237)
indictment (p. 235)

information (p. 235)
mistrial (p. 247)
motion (p. 238)
nolo contendere (p. 237)
not guilty (p. 237)
not guilty by reason of insanity (p. 237)

speedy trial (p. 240)
status offenses (p. 254)
surety bond (p. 232)
venire (p. 244)
voir dire (p. 244)

ISSUES FOR CRITICAL THINKING AND DISCUSSION

1. Should the bail bond business be abolished? Why or why not?

2. Do grand juries play too large a role in criminal justice proceedings? Do prosecutors overuse them? Why or why not?

3. Given the roles of the defense and the prosecution, is their deliberate seeking of biased jurors via voir dire and their various challenges legal or ethical?

4. What are the potential consequences of a defendant's waiver of the various rights afforded during trial (right to counsel, jury trial, and so on)?

5. Are there instances when jury nullification would be more ethical than in others? Should juries nullify if they disagree with the law?

6. What impact do you think the various exemptions have on the makeup of juries?

7. What impact do you think technology will have on the use of evidence in American courts?

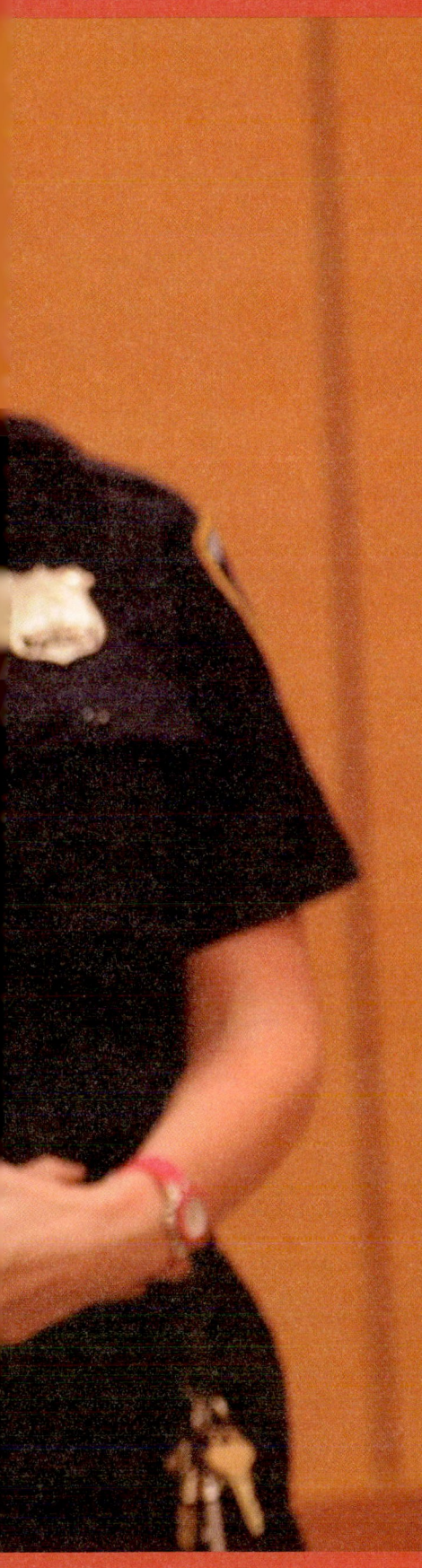

10

Sentencing, the Death Penalty, and Appeal

LEARNING OBJECTIVES

- Explain the philosophies of sentencing and punishment.
- Describe the various kinds of sentences.
- Compare the contemporary sentencing strategies for imprisonment.
- Identify the sentencing reforms developed in response to criticism of disparities in the sentencing process.
- Describe the Supreme Court interpretation of cruel and unusual punishment, including how it applies to the death penalty.
- Explain the arguments in the debate surrounding the death penalty.
- Identify the reasons a conviction can be appealed.

MANDATORY DEATH ISN'T JUSTICE

The *Woodson v. North Carolina* case involved robbery and the first-degree murder of a cashier at a convenience store, similar to the one pictured here. Woodson, one of the offenders, received a mandatory death sentence, and he appealed to the Supreme Court.

On the day in question, James Woodson had been drinking heavily. Luby Waxton and Leonard Tucker showed up at Woodson's mobile home around 9:30 p.m. The three men had been discussing the robbery of a convenience store for some time. When Woodson came outside, Waxton struck him in the face and threatened to kill him. This was intended to sober him up and coerce him to participate in the robbery. Then, the three met up with Lee Caroll, armed themselves, and set out by car to conduct their crime.[1]

When they arrived at the store, Carroll and Woodson remained in the car as lookouts while Tucker and Waxton went inside. After Tucker purchased a package of cigarettes from the female cashier, Waxton approached her. He pulled out a small gun and shot her at close range, immediately killing her. Waxton took the cash from the register and gave it to Tucker, who rushed out of the store, pushing past an entering customer. From outside, Tucker heard another gunshot. Waxton emerged, carrying more money, and the four men drove off.[2]

Eventually, the four were caught, arrested, and charged with robbery and first-degree murder. Their testimony all agreed, in large part, with this version of the robbery. However, it differed dramatically in one important respect: Waxton claimed that he never had a gun. He also stated that Tucker was the one who shot both the cashier and the customer. Tucker and Carroll were allowed to plead guilty to charges of accessory after the fact to murder and armed robbery. For the murder accessory charge, Tucker was sentenced to 10 years in prison. The armed robbery charges brought not less than 20 years nor more than 30 years, with both sentences to run concurrently. Carroll received slightly less prison time. Both men testified against Waxton and Woodson during trial. Woodson maintained his innocence throughout, arguing that Waxton had coerced him. He refused to consider pleading guilty to any of the charges.[3] In the court trial, Waxton and Woodson were found guilty on all charges levied against them, including first-degree murder and armed robbery. Most relevant to this chapter, Woodson appealed to the Supreme Court because at that time, North Carolina had imposed a mandatory death sentence for all offenders convicted of first-degree murder. This legislation was an attempt by the state to guide the discretion awarded juries in sentencing offenders to death.[4]

In the *Woodson v. North Carolina* case, the Supreme Court held that the mandatory sentence law had three distinct problems.[5] First, it departed from contemporary standards in the community concerning death sentences, including historical records that indicate the public had rejected mandatory death sentences. Second, it provided no standards to guide juries as they exercise their discretion in deciding whether murderers will be executed. Rather, it pushed back the entire impact of their discretion to the determination of guilt. Third, the statute failed to allow jurors to consider the character and record of individual defendants before inflicting the death sentence. As the court noted, these issues removed the fundamental respect for humanity required by the Eighth Amendment.[6]

As you can see from this case, after conviction, the business of the court is not yet complete. First, the defendant must be sentenced, and then, because the sentence can have such enormous consequence, the defendant may **appeal,** or ask for a review of the sentence by a higher court. What makes both sentencing and appeal significant is that in all the earlier phases of the justice process, the purpose is to establish, beyond a reasonable doubt, the criminal liability of the defendant. The adversary system of jurisprudence, grounded in due process of law, is structured on the premise that the accused is innocent until proven guilty. Once convicted, of course, the accused has been proven guilty. At sentencing, the court's obligation shifts from impartial and equitable litigation to the imposition

of sanctions. In cases of appeal, the court also deals with those who have been found guilty but who claim that errors were made in procedure or judgment. In either case, the court's position is challenging. It must mediate between the statutory authority of law, the assurances of due process, the need for correction, the burdens of a congested justice system, the urgency of political realities, the essentials of legal ethics, and demands for community protection.[7]

Sentencing is one of the most controversial aspects of criminal justice processing. Appellate review, although somewhat less visible, also generates considerable attention. Perhaps of greatest concern is the judgment of death, which prompted the appeal in the Woodson case and continues to involve passionate debate among policy makers and private citizens alike. In this chapter, we examine these final steps in the criminal justice process.

SENTENCING

What should be done with criminal offenders after they have been convicted? The answer may appear difficult for a sentencing judge, because the administration of justice often has conflicting goals: to rehabilitate offenders, discourage potential lawbreakers, isolate dangerous criminals, condemn extralegal conduct, and reinforce accepted social norms. The challenge facing the judge, and oftentimes a jury, is to choose among one or more of these various goals or to balance the multiple goals of punishing offenders who have been convicted of breaking the law. Let's examine how this works.

Sentencing and Punishment Rationales and Objectives

Throughout the history of the United States, there has been no single and clearly defined guiding principle in sentencing. The public has often alternated between revulsion at inhumane sentencing practices and prison conditions on the one hand and dissatisfaction with overly compassionate treatment on the other. The fate of convicted offenders has repeatedly shifted according to prevailing national values and perceptions of danger and fear of crime. Overall, however, sentencing objectives are based on at least five competing philosophies: retribution, vengeance, incapacitation, deterrence, and rehabilitation.

Retribution　To use a 200-year-old definition once offered by classical scholar Cesare Beccaria, **retribution** is an effort "to make the punishment as analogous as possible to the nature of the crime."[8] In more modern terminology, retribution involves an effort to ensure that an offender's punishment is commensurate not only with the crime but also with his or her moral blameworthiness and prior criminal record. Rather than the biblical "eye for an eye," the philosophy of retribution typically reflects a desire for proportionality—a sentencing structure in which the most heinous offenders receive the harshest punishments and lesser criminals receive lesser punishments.[9]

Vengeance In contrast with retribution, **vengeance** is the desire to punish criminals because society gains some measure of satisfaction from seeing or knowing that they are punished.[10] This philosophy presents an ethical dilemma: Should it be accepted as a valid rationale for punishment? The U.S. Supreme Court's decision in *Payne v. Tennessee,*[11] discussed in Chapter 4, suggests that it already has been. In *Payne,* decided in 1991, the court holding allowed for the admission of evidence and/or prosecutorial argument concerning the victim's personal characteristics, as well as evidence of the impact of the crime on the victim's family. In other words, the decision permits victim impact evidence at sentencing hearings. **Victim impact evidence** is a statement of the harm suffered by the victim or the victim's family as a result of the offender's actions. One could reasonably argue that permitting such evidence is tantamount to eliciting requests for vengeance from a sentencing judge or jury.

Incapacitation **Incapacitation** is simply the removal of dangerous persons from the community.[12] Also referred to as the *restraint,* or *isolation, philosophy,* its goal is community protection rather than revenge. By removing the offender from society through execution, imprisonment, or exile (as is the case with the deportation of foreign nationals who are convicted of certain crimes), the community is protected from further criminal activity.

As a punishment philosophy, incapacitation is problematic. If the goals are crime prevention and community protection, the sanctions would have to be quite severe to be completely effective. Regardless of the offense, execution is the only form of restraint that can guarantee the elimination of future offenses against the community.[13] Prisoners serving sentences of life-without-parole may escape from custody or commit crimes in prison against institutional staff and other inmates. The latter can be considered crimes against the community, because prison personnel are clearly part of the community;[14] and for that matter, inmates and their families are also members of the community. Temporary incarceration until the community can be reasonably assured the offender will no longer commit crimes also has unpredictable outcomes. In addition, incarceration has an enormous economic dimension. As the guiding principle of sentencing, incapacitation would require the continued construction of new prison facilities, combined with higher annual costs of supporting an expanding inmate population and increased expenses for new custodial personnel.[15]

Deterrence The most widely held justification for punishment is reducing crime. Thus, as a sentencing philosophy, **deterrence** refers to the prevention of criminal acts by making examples of individuals convicted of crimes. Deterrence can be both general and specific. General deterrence seeks to discourage would-be offenders from committing crimes; specific deterrence is designed to prevent a particular convicted offender from engaging in future criminal acts.[16]

The notion of punishment as a deterrent is best illustrated in the words of an eighteenth-century judge who reportedly told a defendant at sentencing, "You are to be hanged not because you have stolen a sheep but in order that others may not steal sheep."[17] Research supporting the efficacy of deterrence, however, is mixed. Although research on general deterrence remains inconclusive, some crimes and potential criminals are clearly more easily deterred than others. In

Confining inmates to correctional facilities may serve several punishment goals. However, it is the goal of incapacitation that is most clearly fulfilled.

addition, a number of studies reinforce the notion that punishment deters crime and, in particular, that the certainty of punishment is more important than the severity of punishment in deterring potential criminals.[18] Nevertheless, more research is needed on the various individual and social factors that may affect the relationship between certainty and severity of punishment on the one hand and crime rates on the other. By contrast, the philosophy of specific deterrence does seem to have an impact on the behavior of many white-collar criminals and first-time misdemeanor offenders, whose arrests and convictions cause them embarrassment and public disgrace and threaten their careers and family life.[19]

Rehabilitation   The last rationale for sentencing and justification for punishment concerns the prevention of future crimes by changing the offender's behavior. The **rehabilitation** philosophy rests on the premise that people who commit crimes have identifiable reasons for doing so and that these can be discovered, addressed, and altered. Its aim is to modify behavior and reintegrate the lawbreaker into the wider society as a productive citizen.[20]

The goal of rehabilitation has broad academic support, for in contrast with other sentencing philosophies, it takes a positive approach to eliminating offensive behavior.[21] Proponents argue that rehabilitation is the only humanitarian mechanism for altering criminal careers.[22]

Yet the efficacy of rehabilitation has been seriously questioned. Some suggest that since the causes of crime are not fully understood, efforts to change criminal behavior are of dubious value. Others maintain that since rehabilitative services are either minimal or nonexistent in many institutions and community-based programs, "correction" as such has only limited practical potential. Still a third group espouses a "nothing works" philosophy, arguing that rehabilitation has not demonstrated its ability to prevent or reduce crime.[23]

Statutory Sentencing Structures

Regardless of the sentencing philosophy of the presiding judge, the sentence is influenced to some degree by the statutory alternatives in the penal codes, combined with the facilities and programs available in the correctional system. Statutory sentencing guidelines, which have generally evolved over long periods and often reflect changing legislative philosophies, appear in each state's criminal code. No two state codes are quite alike; the punishments they designate for specific crimes vary, as do the methods of establishing the parameters for sentencing. Moreover, some statutes give judges wide latitude in sentencing, while others do not. In some states—Tennessee, for example—the penal code designates the range of punishments for each specific crime.[24] Other states, such as Idaho, follow the Tennessee model for some crimes but extend almost total discretion to the judge for others. And in other states, such as New York, crimes are first classified according to their severity (for example, rape in the first degree is a class B felony, while incest is a class E felony) and then are assigned punishments according to their felony or misdemeanor class.[25]

Although statutory guidelines provide a range of sentencing alternatives, in many instances judges also have discretion to deviate from the legislative norm, on the premise that sentences should be individualized. Conversely, in some situations, mandatory sentencing statutes (touched on in the chapter-opening case and discussed in more detail later in the chapter) reduce sentencing discretion used by the judge. Whatever theory of sanctions ultimately guides sentencing, the alternatives for the presiding judge include fines, probation or some other community-based program, imprisonment, or the death penalty.

Fines   Fines are monetary penalties imposed either in lieu of or in addition to incarceration or probation. They are the traditional means of dealing with most traffic-law violations and many misdemeanors, and the sentence "30 dollars or 30 days" was

---

DISCRETION MATTERS

What characteristics of offenders might influence judges or juries to apply a particular punishment philosophy? How might these characteristics affect the assignment of particularly harsh sentences to certain individuals?

DISCRETION MATTERS

Why might communities want to limit the discretion of judges on sentences for specific types of crime? Why would communities want to prevent judges from giving overly harsh or lenient sentences for particular offenses?

Fines are often included in the sentences imposed on offenders convicted of both minor and serious offenses.

often heard in courtrooms across America. Fines can also be imposed for felonies, instead of or in addition to some other sentence. They can involve many thousands of dollars and sometimes twice the amount of the defendant's gain from the commission of the crime.[26]

However, since *Williams v. Illinois* in 1970 and *Tate v. Short* the following year,[27] the use of fines has been limited. In *Williams,* the Supreme Court ruled that no jurisdiction can hold a person in jail or prison beyond the length of the maximum sentence merely to work off a fine that he or she is unable to pay—a practice that was allowed in 47 states at the time of the *Williams* and *Tate* cases. In *Tate,* the court held that the historic "30 dollars or 30 days" sentence was an unconstitutional denial of equal protection. The court's unanimous decision maintained that limiting punishment to a fine for those who could pay but expanding it to imprisonment for those who could not violated the Fourteenth Amendment.[28] In 1983, in *Bearden v. Georgia,*[29] the Supreme Court ruled that a sentencing court cannot automatically revoke a defendant's probation solely because he or she cannot pay a fine that is a condition of probation.

Imprisonment   Typically, *imprisonment* means removal of an individual from society through the use of a jail or prison sentence. In practice, there are three major types of imprisonment: indeterminate, determinate, and definite.

Indeterminate Sentences.   The **indeterminate sentence,** which is the most common, has a fixed minimum and a fixed maximum term for incarceration, rather than a definite period. The paroling authority determines the actual amount of time served. Sentences of 1 to 5 years, 7½ to 15 years, 10 to 20 years, or 15 years to life are considered indeterminate.[30]

The indeterminate sentence is based on a primarily correctional model of punishment, the underlying premise being that the sentence should meet the needs of the offender. After incarceration begins, the rehabilitation process is initiated, at least in theory, and the inmate should be confined until there is substantial evidence of "correction." At that point, the paroling authority assesses the nature and extent of such rehabilitation and releases the defendant if the evidence warrants it. Thus, the indeterminate sentence rests on the notion that length of imprisonment should be based on progress toward rehabilitation. It makes the following assumptions (all of which are disputable and not widely agreed upon in correctional and criminological circles):

1. Criminals are personally or socially disturbed or disadvantaged, and therefore their commission of crime cannot be considered a free choice. If this is the case, then setting prison terms solely commensurate with the severity of the crime is not logical.
2. Indeterminate sentences allow effective treatment to rectify psychosocial problems, which are the root of crime.
3. Readiness for release varies with the individual and can be determined only when the inmate is in the institution, not before.[31]

Indeterminate sentencing has received considerable criticism. Opponents have charged that since the causes of crime and criminal behavior are not readily understood, they cannot be dealt with under the premise of indeterminate sentencing. They have also raised doubts about the ability to rehabilitate offenders within the prison setting, regardless of the nature of the sentencing. In addition, the indeterminate sentence is used as an instrument of inmate control, put into practice through threats of disciplinary reports and, hence, extended sentences. Moreover, these sentences often vary by judge and jurisdiction, resulting in unfair and disparate terms of imprisonment, again not a focus of rehabilitation. Finally, an offender's perception of the uncertainty as to how long his or her prison term may last can lead to frustration, violence, and rioting while housed within the correctional facility.[32]

Determinate Sentences. The concerns over indeterminate sentencing have generated considerable interest in the **determinate sentence,** which is also known as the *flat, fixed,* or *straight sentence.* This sentence has no set minimum or maximum but rather a fixed period. The term of the sentence is established by the legislature, thus removing the sentencing discretion of the judge. However, under determinate sentencing guidelines, the court still has the discretion to choose prison, probation, a fine, or some other alternative. Only the length of the sentence is taken away from judicial discretion, if the judge imposes imprisonment.[33]

In some instances, the determinate sentence can, in effect, become an indeterminate sentence. Under determinate sentencing statutes, inmates may still be eligible for parole after a portion of their terms has been served. Thus, in a state where parole eligibility begins after half the term has expired, a determinate sentence of ten years really ranges from a minimum of five years to a maximum of ten.[34]

Definite Sentences. The first application of indeterminate sentencing policies in the United States appeared in 1924 at New York's House of Refuge.[35] Before then, a regular feature of incarceration was the **definite sentence**—a fixed period with no reduction by parole. This type of sentence fell out of favor, however, because advocates of rehabilitation found it to be too rigid and insensitive to defendants' individual characteristics and needs.

The diminished appeal of indeterminate sentences, combined with growing concerns over street crime and the "coddling" of criminals, led to renewed interest in definite sentences. Many states have abandoned the indeterminate sentencing system while simultaneously abolishing parole.[36] Under these sentencing laws, terms of imprisonment have become, in effect, definite sentences. Similarly, the "three strikes and you're out" (or "in") laws, which you read about in Chapter 1, calling for life imprisonment without parole upon conviction for a third felony, are a form of definite sentence.

Other Sentencing Variations. In addition to these three basic types of sentences, a number of variations and adaptations are being used across the country. Under a New York statute, for example, we find the *intermittent sentence*—a term to be served

DISCRETION MATTERS

How might reducing judicial discretion—for example, with determinate sentences—decrease or increase the effectiveness of punishment?

on certain days or periods of days specified by the court.[37] In such cases, a defendant might plead guilty to a felonious possession of marijuana charge and be sentenced to an intermittent term of 60 days, to be served on consecutive weekends, followed by five years' probation.[38] This type of sanction is used when the nature of the offense warrants incarceration but the defendant's characteristics and habits suggest that full-time imprisonment would be inappropriate. Note that a sentence of intermittent imprisonment is revocable. That is, should the offender fail to report to the institution on the days specified, he or she can be returned to court and resentenced to a more traditional term of imprisonment.

A type of determinate sentence known as the **mandatory sentence** has been a subject of extensive discussion, and in fact, you read about one such case in the chapter-opening story. Mandatory sentences limit judicial and jury discretion; they are penal code provisions that require the judge or jury to sentence individuals convicted of certain crimes to prison terms of a specified length. Under these statutes—which are intended to guarantee that recidivists, violent offenders, and other serious criminals face strict, certain punishment—neither probation nor alternative sentences are permitted.

As part of the nation's war on drugs, the mandatory minimum sentence has appeared in many jurisdictions. Numerous states have mandatory minimum sentences of three years or five years for possession of even small amounts of illegal drugs. However, research has demonstrated that the mandatory sentences are not working well. Primarily, this is because the sentences do not achieve certainty and predictability, as officials sometimes circumvent them by altering initial charges. Often these sentences are arbitrary for minor cases and occasionally result in an unduly harsh punishment for a marginal offender.[39]

Judges across the country have imposed unique variations in sentencing—not all of which include imprisonment—in an effort to "let the punishment fit the crime." Here are some examples:

- In Rogers, Arkansas, a woman who pleaded guilty to driving without strapping her 3-year-old daughter into a safety seat was ordered to write the toddler's obituary—even though the youngster is alive.[40]
- A judge in a Cincinnati suburb ordered a chronic drunk driver to move within walking distance of a liquor store so that he wouldn't have to drive to get his alcohol. He was also sentenced to spend the first week of each of the following five years in jail.[41]

Often these creative sentences strike a positive chord with the public and evoke an emotional response that speaks to the depth of concerns about justice and, in some cases, retribution. However, the use of these unique sentences is rare and arbitrary, thus making them potentially far less effective in terms of deterring or reducing crime in general.

Disparities in Sentencing

Sentencing disparities have long been a major problem in criminal justice processing. The basis of the difficulty is threefold:

1. the structure of indeterminate sentencing guidelines
2. the discretionary powers of sentencing judges
3. the mechanics of plea bargaining

The statutory minimum and maximum terms of imprisonment, combined with fines, probation, or other alternatives to incarceration, create a number of sentencing possibilities for a specific crime. With judicial discretion in sentencing, sanctions can vary widely according to the jurisdiction, the community, and the punishment

Sanctions for particular crimes can vary widely across jurisdictions, with some states imposing much harsher and longer sentences than others. The consequences of such disparities—prison overcrowding being one of them—can be significant, not only for the convicted person but also for the court, community, and correctional system.

philosophy of a particular judge. And the dynamics of plea bargaining enable various defendants accused of the same crime to be convicted and sentenced differently. These problems exist, moreover, both within an individual court and across jurisdictions.

In Delaware, for example, the sentence imposed for first-degree burglary can range from a fine to 20 years' imprisonment.[42] Minimum prison terms extend from a low of 1 year in Idaho to a high of 10 years in Alabama.[43] And the maximum term allowable can range from 10 years (West Virginia), to 25 years (New York), to perhaps even life (Alabama).[44]

The consequences of disparities in sentencing can be significant, not only for the convicted person but also for the court and correctional systems and the entire administration of justice. First, the wide variations impede an evenhanded administration of the criminal law, thus calling into question the very philosophy of justice in America. Second, disparities have a rebound effect on plea bargaining and court scheduling; that is, defendants may opt for a negotiated plea rather than face trial before a judge who is known to be severe. Last, prisoners compare their sentences, and an inmate who believes that he or she received an unfair sentence or was a victim of judicial prejudice may become hostile, resistant to correctional treatment and discipline, and even prone to rioting.

Sentencing Reform

Measures have been proposed or adopted in various jurisdictions to remedy the problem of sentencing disparities, such as removing that key phrase "not more than" from the penal laws, thereby reducing judicial discretion.[45] Mandatory sentencing statutes also clearly decrease the court's discretion. Such statutes, however, are not a panacea for either crime control or sentencing disparities, for they can easily increase prosecutorial discretion, court delays, and overcrowded prison conditions. In addition, they almost totally eliminate the rehabilitative goals of individualized justice.

A less extreme model for eliminating discretion is the *presumptive fixed sentence.* The objectives of presumptive sentencing are to (1) limit judicial discretion without totally eliminating it and (2) increase community protection by imposing a sentence that the offender is required to serve. More stringent than the indeterminate sentence but less rigid than the determinate sentence, the presumptive fixed sentence is a good combination of the two. A state legislature sets minimum and maximum terms, with a limited range, for a particular crime. The judge imposes a fixed, or determinate, sentence within that range, basing the decision on mitigating circumstances and the offender's characteristics. This sentencing scheme also eliminates the need for parole.[46]

For example, a presumptive sentence for burglary in the first degree might have a lower legislative limit of three years and an upper limit of ten, with a fixed sentence of five years as set by the judge. Through this model, imprisonment becomes mandatory, a defined range of terms is established by statute, and a degree of judicial discretion remains.

Other efforts to alter and guide judicial discretion exist in sentencing institutes, councils, and guidelines. Sentencing institutes are designed to generate interest in formulating policies and criteria for uniform sentencing. Periodically convened at the state level in the form of one- and two-day workshops, they typically involve mock sentencing experiments followed by discussions of observed disparities. Sentencing councils also work to reduce disparities. The councils typically consist of three judges who examine cases awaiting sentence and make recommendations to the sentencing judge.

Sentencing guidelines are based on the sentencing behavior of judges. Statistical tables are constructed that reflect the average sentences imposed by judges in a specific jurisdiction, broken down by the seriousness of the crime and legally relevant characteristics of the offender, including number of prior offenses. These tables make it possible for a judge to know what sentences his or her peers have imposed in similar cases. Such tables are intended to curb disparities by basing discretion on the judges' common experience.

The United States Sentencing Commission, which was created by the Sentencing Reform Act of 1984, established federal sentencing guidelines for all offenders convicted of felonies and serious misdemeanors in the U.S. federal courts system.[47] Sentencing of less serious misdemeanors is not affected by the guidelines.[48] In general, the behavior involved in the offense and the prior criminal history of the offender are used to identify the sentence, but judges can adjust sentences, known as *departures,* based on specific characteristics of the offender or offense. These adjustments can reduce or increase sentences.[49] The sentences were challenged in 2005 because the guidelines allowed judges to assign the sentences based on key facts about offenses and offenders but without the scrutiny of a jury. The Supreme Court found that this violated the Sixth Amendment guarantee of a trial by jury, because defendants were never allowed the opportunity to have a jury hear evidence about the facts used in determining the sentence.[50] This area of law continues to develop as states and the federal government respond to concerns about the nature of sentencing and the changing patterns of crime.

The Sentencing Process

Sentencing is generally a collective decision-making process that involves recommendations by the prosecutor, the defense attorney, the judge, and sometimes the presentence investigator. In jurisdictions where sentence bargaining is part of the plea negotiation process, the judge almost invariably imposes what the prosecution and the defense have agreed on.

In the federal system and the majority of state jurisdictions, the court's probation agency or presentence office may conduct a **presentence investigation.** The resulting report is a summary of the defendant's present offense, previous criminal record, family situation, neighborhood environment, school and educational history, employment record, physical and mental health, habits, associates, and group memberships. The report may also contain comments on the defendant's remorse and recommendations for sentencing by the victim, the prosecutor, and the officer who conducted the investigation.

Presentence reports vary in detail and length, depending on the resources and practices of the jurisdiction. Although presentence investigations are not mandatory in all jurisdictions, most officials agree that their value goes well beyond their use in determining appropriate sentences.[51] They also aid probation and parole officers in their supervision of offenders; assist correctional personnel in their classification, treatment, and release programs; and give parole boards useful information for release decision-making.

After the presentence report has been submitted to the judge, a sentencing hearing is held. In common law, and in most jurisdictions, a convicted offender has the right to address the court personally before the sentence is imposed. Known as **allocution,** this practice allows the court to identify the defendant as the person judged guilty, and the defendant can plead for mercy or a pardon, move for an arrest of judgment, or indicate why judgment ought not be pronounced. A defendant cannot, however, reopen the question of guilt.[52]

Following this stage, the presiding judge imposes the sentence. As noted, the most typical sanctions include fines, imprisonment, probation, some combination thereof, or death. If the defendant receives multiple sentences for several crimes, the judge may order that terms of imprisonment be served concurrently or consecutively. For example, if the defendant is convicted of both burglary and assault and is given two terms of five years' imprisonment to be served concurrently, both terms are satisfied after five years. Consecutive sentences are successive—one after another.

As noted earlier, a defendant may come before a judge for sentencing after having already spent weeks, months, and sometimes even years in a local jail or detention facility awaiting trial. This period of detention, referred to as *jail time,* is generally deducted from the length of the prison sentence. When the conviction is for a misdemeanor or minor felony and the period of pretrial detention closely matches the probable term of imprisonment, the judge may impose a sentence of *time served;* that is, the accumulated jail time represents the sentence, and the defendant is released. When the jail time spent awaiting trial is not counted as part of the final sentence, it is commonly referred to as *dead time.*

Here, the convicted DC sniper, John Allen Muhammad, participates in an allocution as he addresses the court in 2002. He was later found guilty of murder in Virginia in 2003.

THE DEATH PENALTY

For most of the nation's history, the death penalty was used as a punishment, with little thought given to its legitimacy or justification. When the framers of the Constitution created the Eighth Amendment ban against cruel and unusual punishment, the death penalty itself apparently was not an issue, given the protections in the Fifth Amendment: "No person shall be held to answer for a capital, or otherwise infamous crime, unless on a presentment or indictment of a Grand Jury, except in cases arising in the land or naval forces, or in the militia, when in actual service in time of war or public danger; nor be deprived of life, liberty, or property, without due process of law."[53] This reference in the amendment seems to attest to the acceptability of capital punishment at the time. From the earliest days of the colonial period, capital punishment was considered neither cruel nor unusual. For example, under the criminal codes for the New Haven colony, enacted in 1642 and 1650, a total of 11 offenses—some of which do not appear even as misdemeanors in contemporary

EXHIBIT 10.1 Executions under State Authority, 1850s–1960s

Decade	Executions	Percentage of Total
1850–1860s	12	0.2
1870s	18	0.3
1880s	26	0.5
1890s	154	2.7
1900s	275	4.8
1910s	625	11.0
1920s	1,030	18.0
1930s	1,520	26.6
1940s	1,174	20.6
1950s	682	12.0
1960s	191	3.3
Total	5,707	100.0

Source: Negley K. Teeters and Charles J. Zibulka, "Executions under State Authority: 1864–1967," in *Executions in America,* ed. William J. Bowers (Lexington, MA: Heath, 1974), 200–401.

statutes—called for the death sentence. These included murder but also bestiality, child rape, invasion of towns or forts, and challenges to the rule of the Crown.[54] Within such a context, execution upon conviction for numerous crimes was indeed quite usual.

What the framers of the Constitution probably had in mind when they spoke of "cruel and unusual" punishments were the many more grisly and torturous forms of execution that have periodically appeared throughout human history.[55] Through the ages, criminals have been burned at the stake, crucified, boiled in flaming oil, impaled, and flayed, to name only a few examples.[56] In short, the imposition of the death penalty generally was seen as neither cruel nor unusual. In the following sections, we examine this controversial topic from various perspectives—patterns of executions over the past century and a half, key Supreme Court rulings, methods of execution, and the debates that continue to arise in the public sector.

Capital Punishment and Discrimination

On January 20, 1864, William Barnet and Sandy Kavanagh were executed in the Vermont State Prison for the crime of murder. Over the next 100 or so years, through 1967, a total of 5,707 state-imposed death sentences were carried out across the country.[57] Few of these executions (less than 1 percent) occurred before 1890, but after that, the number grew rapidly. The imposition of the death penalty reached its peak during the 1930s, with more than 1,500 executions in that decade alone. The numbers then began to decline, from 1,174 during the 1940s to fewer than 200 by the 1960s (Exhibit 10.1).

In 1967, the President's Commission on Law Enforcement and Administration of Justice commented that the death penalty "is most frequently imposed and carried out on the poor, the Negro, and the members of unpopular groups."[58] This observation was no surprise to those who had watched the pattern of capital punishment over the years. Nor was it a surprise to many African Americans, especially in the South. In Virginia during the 1830s, for example, there were 5 capital crimes for whites but at least 70 for blacks.[59] In 1848, the Virginia legislature required the death penalty for any offense committed by a black, while for a white, a sentence of three or more years' imprisonment might be imposed.[60] And from 1882 through 1903, at least 1,985 African Americans were hanged or burned alive by the Ku Klux Klan and other southern lynch mobs—often when there was no offense at all or the mere suspicion of one.[61]

Even the most superficial analysis of executions under civil authority reveals a clear overrepresentation of blacks. In 1965, for example, sociologist Marvin E. Wolfgang and law professor Anthony Amsterdam researched the relationship between ethnicity and sentencing for rape in 11 southern and border states where rape was a capital offense. Their findings supported the notion that blacks were treated with undue severity:

> Among the 823 blacks convicted of rape, 110, or 13 percent, were sentenced to death; among the 442 whites convicted of rape, only 9, or 2 percent, were sentenced to death. The statistical probability that such a disproportionate number of blacks could be sentenced to death by chance alone is less than one out of a thousand.[62]

From 1930 through 1967, 3,859 prisoners were executed under civil authority in the United States. When these cases are studied, it becomes even more evident that capital punishment was used in a discriminatory fashion. During this period, 55 percent of those executed for all crimes were either black or members of some other minority group. Of the 455 people executed for rape alone, 90 percent were nonwhite.

This research from the 1960s became the basis for a series of challenges to the use of the death penalty in the United States, the subject we turn to in the next section. By mid-year 2012, 44 percent of all defendants executed were nonwhite, and 57 percent of individuals sitting on death row across the country are nonwhite.[63]

Cruel and Unusual Punishment

As noted, the Supreme Court's position on the death penalty has historically been grounded in the broader issue of cruel and unusual punishment as prohibited by the Eighth Amendment. The framers of the Constitution likely intended to outlaw punishments that were outside both the mainstream of penalties typically imposed in the new nation and the moral judgments of the people. Thus, the purpose of the amendment may have been to prevent a return to the thumbscrew and the rack, rather than to outlaw any sanctions that were in common use at the time. But this is only conjecture, as the Supreme Court, for more than a century, offered little interpretation of the nature and scope of the ban.

In 1892, three justices supported the notion that punishment could be cruel and unusual. The case was *O'Neil v. Vermont*,[64] in which the petitioner stood to serve 19,915 days (almost 55 years) in jail for 307 separate illegal sales of liquor. The court found that since the Eighth Amendment did not limit the states, no federal question was involved, and it upheld the sentence imposed by the Vermont court. However, in a strong dissenting opinion, Justice Stephen J. Field argued that punishment would necessarily be cruel and unusual when it did not fit the crime to which it was attached.

After *O'Neil,* the issue remained dormant for almost two decades until *Weems v. United States*,[65] decided in 1910. The case was significant for the Eighth Amendment ban, for in its ruling the court struck down a sentence involving a heavy fine, 15 years at hard labor, the wearing of chains, the lifelong loss of certain rights, plus several other sanctions—all for the offense of making false entries in official records. The Supreme Court found the sentence disproportionate to the offense; thus, *Weems* was the first case in which the court invalidated a criminal punishment on Eighth Amendment grounds. By 1958, the court had agreed that the constitutional prohibition could have no fixed and unchanging meaning. Rather, any challenges brought to the court must necessarily be viewed in terms of "evolving standards of decency."[66]

The Death Penalty and the Supreme Court

On the issue of capital punishment per se, the Supreme Court's interpretation of the Eighth Amendment has remained controversial. Nevertheless, the death penalty has been ultimately challenged on a variety of legal grounds that we discuss in the upcoming sections. And on June 3, 1967, the impending execution of more than 500 condemned prisoners throughout the country came to a halt while courts and governors waited to see what the Supreme Court would decide in the key cases. The first of these decisions—*Witherspoon v. Illinois*[67] in 1968—indicated that the death penalty might be in trouble. An Illinois court had permitted a verdict of guilty and a sentence of death from a jury, but the state had systematically excluded all prospective jurors who had any scruples against capital punishment. The Supreme Court upheld Witherspoon's challenge, ruling that the "death-qualified jury" was indeed unconstitutional.

Although *Witherspoon* had not been a total victory for those opposed to capital punishment, they remained firmly optimistic, and the moratorium on executions continued as other challenges were prepared for Supreme Court review. However, the abolition movement was thwarted by the ruling in *McGautha v. California*,[68] which upheld the idea that a jury could have total discretion in choosing between life imprisonment and death—without violating the due process clause of the Fourteenth Amendment.

DISCRETION MATTERS

How might jury discretion impact who receives the death penalty and for which types of murder?

McGautha seemed to be a fatal blow to the movement dedicated to abolishing capital punishment, and many observers thought it would be the Supreme Court's final word on the death penalty. With no new cases pending on the issue, and with jury discretion in imposing the death sentence firmly guaranteed, any argument based on the Eighth Amendment would not be likely to prevail. However, as the states began preparations for executing the more than 600 prisoners on death row, the court suddenly announced that it would hear a group of cases involving the Eighth Amendment ban on cruel and unusual punishment. The two most important, perhaps, were *Furman* and *Gregg*.

Furman v. Georgia   William Furman received the death sentence for a murder that had occurred during the course of a burglary attempt. The decision as to whether Furman's sentence should be life-without-parole or death had been left to the jury, and all of the Georgia courts had affirmed his conviction and sentence. In the fall of 1971, *Furman v. Georgia* was brought before the Supreme Court on the grounds that the death sentence ordered was "cruel and unusual" because of the arbitrary and discriminatory manner in which the sanction had been imposed in the past for the crimes of murder and rape.[69]

The Supreme Court's 1972 decision was complex and contained nine separate concurring or dissenting opinions. Only Justices Brennan and Marshall held that capital punishment was unconstitutional per se. Justices Douglas, Stewart, and White adopted a narrower view, arguing that the state statutes in question were unconstitutional because they offered judges and juries no standards or guidelines for deciding between life and death. As Justice Stewart put it, the result was that the punishment of death was tantamount to being "struck by lightning." In other words, all state and federal death penalty statutes were deemed too arbitrary, capricious, and discriminatory to withstand Eighth Amendment scrutiny. The position taken by Justices Douglas, Stewart, and White represented the common ground of agreement with Justices Brennan and Marshall, thus producing a five-justice majority.[70]

The *Furman* decision was neither a statement against capital punishment nor an argument against a jury's authority to decide on the death sentence. Rather, it was an attack on state statutes that allowed a jury to find an accused person guilty and then, in the absence of any guidance or direction, decide whether that person should live or die.[71]

Gregg v. Georgia   By effectively invalidating all existing state death penalty statutes, *Furman* removed more than 600 persons from death row. At the same time, however, the *Furman* decision provided two avenues by which states could enact new capital punishment laws. First, states could establish a two-stage procedure consisting of a trial at which the question of culpability could be determined, followed by an additional proceeding for those found guilty, during which evidence might be presented to make the death penalty decision better informed and more procedurally sound. Second, states could remove discretion from the jury by making death the mandatory punishment for certain crimes.[72]

In the wake of *Furman,* 35 states passed new capital punishment statutes. Ten chose the mandatory route, while 25 selected the two-stage procedure. By 1976, both approaches were brought before the Supreme Court. The issue in *Gregg v. Georgia* was Georgia's new bifurcated trial structure.[73] Following a conviction of guilt in first-degree murder cases, the nature of punishment was decided in a separate proceeding. The Georgia statute required the judge or jury to consider any aggravating or mitigating circumstances, including the following:

- The defendant had a prior conviction for a capital felony or a substantial history of serious assaultive criminal convictions.
- The murder was committed during the course of a rape, an armed robbery, a kidnapping, a burglary, or arson.

The execution of Troy Davis in Georgia in 2011 did not end the controversy surrounding his murder conviction. Questions remain about his guilt and, as in many death penalty cases, about the nature of justice as it relates to capital punishment.

- The defendant created a grave risk of death to more than one person.
- The defendant killed for profit.
- The victim was a judicial officer or a prosecutor killed during or because of the exercise of official duty.
- The victim was a police officer, correctional employee, or firefighter who was engaged in the performance of his or her duties.
- The defendant directed another person to kill as his or her agent.
- The murder was committed in a wantonly vile, horrible, or inhumane manner because it involved torture, depravity of mind, or aggravated battery.
- The defendant was a prison escapee.
- The murder was committed in an attempt to avoid arrest.[74]

The decision in *Gregg* upheld the Georgia law because by permitting aggravating and mitigating circumstances, the statute required juries to focus on the characteristics of the crime and the individual defendant that are legally relevant to the sentencing process.

In two companion cases, the Supreme Court upheld similar procedures adopted by Florida and Texas (and presumably 22 additional states), thus declaring capital punishment laws constitutional, as long as they gave judges and juries clear and fair criteria for deciding whether to sentence an offender to death.[75] However, in *Woodson v. North Carolina*,[76] the case you read about at the beginning of the chapter, which was decided on the same day as *Gregg*, the court struck down state laws that made death the mandatory penalty for first-degree murder. The court's position was that mandatory death penalty statutes "simply papered over the problem of unguided and unchecked jury discretion"[77] and failed to allow for differences in individual defendants and crimes. During the years after *Gregg*, the Supreme Court continued in its refusal to hold that the death penalty per se constitutes cruel and unusual punishment.

As noted, capital punishment was suspended in 1967, and for a full decade it ceased to exist in the United States. With the decision in *Gregg*, however, made on the eve of the nation's 200th birthday, the Supreme Court upheld the constitutionality of capital punishment. By 1977, more than 400 persons were on death row, with the first execution occurring early in that year.[78]

The prisoner was Gary Mark Gilmore, a convicted murderer who had been sentenced to death by a Utah court. The Gilmore case attracted national headlines, not only because it was the first execution in a decade but also because of the many bizarre events associated with it. The initial sensation came late in 1976, when Gilmore fired his attorneys, abandoned his appeal, and requested that his execution be carried out at the earliest possible date. He even appeared before the U.S. Supreme Court to argue that he had a "right to die."[79] Since reinstatement of the death penalty in 1976, 1,298 inmates have been executed. The state of Texas has executed 482 inmates, the most during that period. Virginia, with the next highest number, has executed 109 inmates as of June 2012.[80]

Methods of Execution

Paralleling the debate over the constitutionality of the death penalty has been the controversy over the constitutionality and humaneness of particular methods of execution. For inmates sentenced to death under federal statutes, the law of the state in which the punishment is to be carried out governs the method of execution. In a series of decisions, the Supreme Court has upheld as constitutional various methods of execution, including hanging, shooting, electrocution, and the use of lethal gas and injection.[81] As of mid-2012, 33 states had a death penalty in force; several have more than one method available should the primary method become unavailable either because it is determined to be unconstitutional or it becomes inaccessible for some other reason.[82] Inmates in some jurisdictions must choose the method by which they will be executed if multiple methods are available. Many states—Alabama, for example—select a primary method but also allow inmates to choose from an alternate if they wish. In the case of Alabama, inmates are executed by lethal injection, unless they choose electrocution. Other states—South Carolina, for example—require inmates to choose from two methods with no default primary method. In South Carolina, the two options are lethal injection and electrocution.[83]

Only two states—New Hampshire and Washington—still offer execution by hanging, but only if the primary method of lethal injection is not available or, in the case of Washington, if the inmate chooses hanging.[84] The most recent instance of hanging as a method of execution occurred in January of 1996, when Delaware hung William Bailey. Shortly thereafter in July of 2003, Delaware removed hanging as a method of execution available to inmates and dismantled its gallows. Two states, Oklahoma and Utah, still offer the use of a firing squad as a method of execution if lethal injection (Utah only) and electrocution are determined to be unconstitutional. Ronnie Lee Gardner was the most recent inmate executed by firing squad, on June 18, 2010, in Utah. Utah no longer offers this as a method of execution (see Exhibit 10.2, on the distribution of various methods of execution in the United States).[85]

Electrocution is generally instantaneous, though only nine states use this method and offer it only as an alternate method. Although the Supreme Court has upheld the constitutionality of electrocution, death in the electric chair appears to be a rather grim process. The most recent electrocution occurred when convicted murderer Paul Powell was executed in Virginia on March 18, 2010.[86] More than 80 years ago, Warden Lewis E. Lawes of Sing Sing Prison described the process this way:

> The condemned prisoner undergoing electrocution at Sing Sing Prison is given one shock of . . . approximately 2,000 volts. This voltage is immediately reduced at the end of three seconds to the neighborhood of 500 volts where it is held for an additional period of 57 seconds. . . .
>
> This initial force sends a startling current of 8 to 10 amperes through the human body, which causes instantaneous death and unconsciousness by its paralysis and destruction to the brain. The current is then cut down under the lower voltages to from 3 to 4 amperes in order to avoid burning the body and at the same time to hold paralysis of the heart, respiratory organs, and brain at a standstill for the remaining period of execution. This insures complete destruction of all life.
>
> As the switch is thrown into its socket there is a sputtering drone, and the body leaps as if to break the strong leather straps that hold it. Sometimes a thin gray wisp of smoke pushes itself out from under the helmet that holds

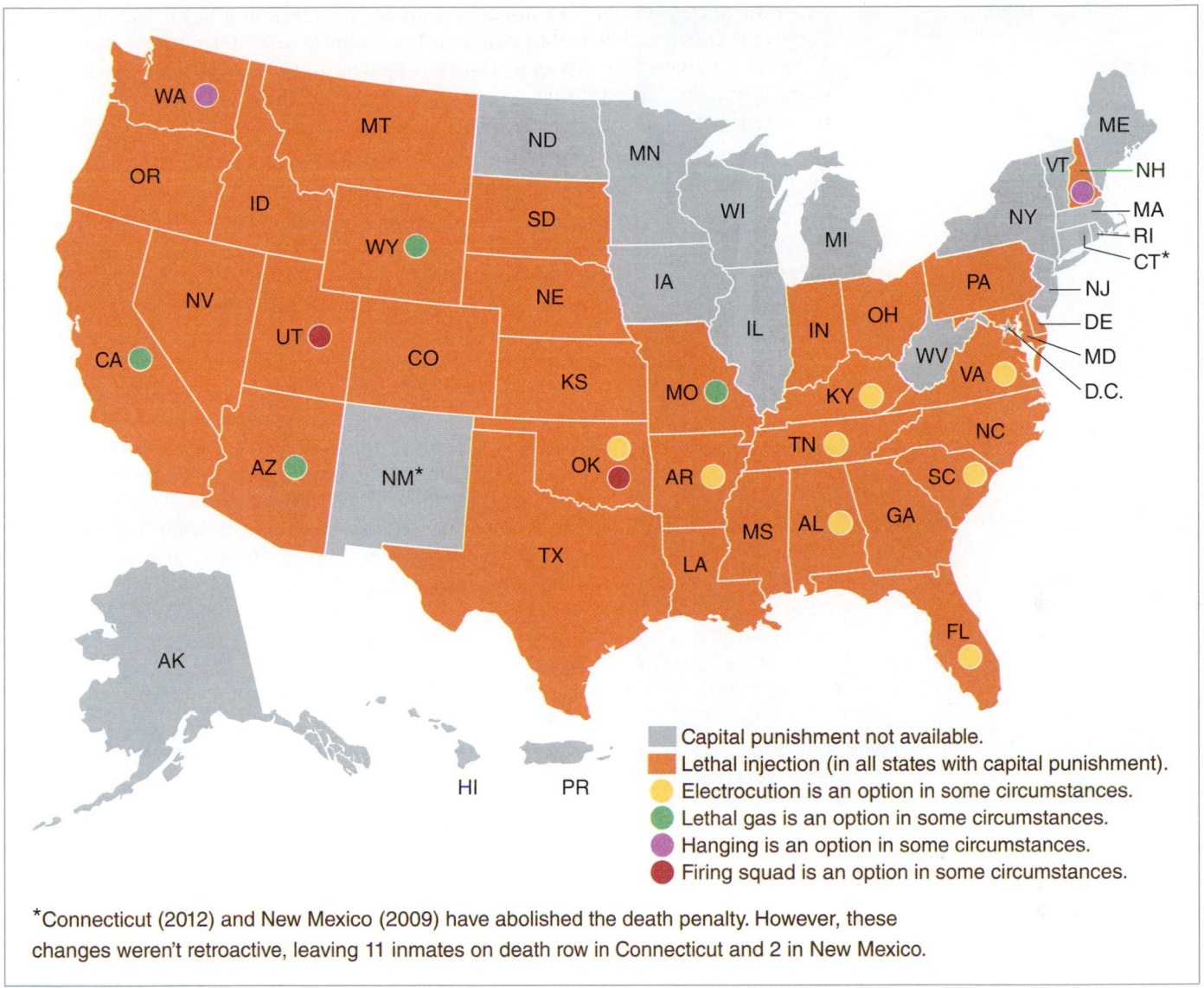

🔲	Capital punishment not available.
🟧	Lethal injection (in all states with capital punishment).
🟡	Electrocution is an option in some circumstances.
🟢	Lethal gas is an option in some circumstances.
🟣	Hanging is an option in some circumstances.
🔴	Firing squad is an option in some circumstances.

*Connecticut (2012) and New Mexico (2009) have abolished the death penalty. However, these changes weren't retroactive, leaving 11 inmates on death row in Connecticut and 2 in New Mexico.

EXHIBIT 10.2 Execution Methods Used in the United States

Lethal injection is currently used in all of the 33 states that have a death penalty, but other methods still exist and are authorized should lethal injection not be available.
Source: Death Penalty Information Center

the head electrode, followed by the faint odor of burning flesh. The hands turn red, then white, and the cords of the neck stand out like steel bands. . . .

Although it would be absolutely impossible to revive any person after electrocution in Sing Sing's death chair, an autopsy is immediately performed as provided by law.[87]

Many in the past considered the use of cyanide gas to be a more humane form of execution than electrocution, and four states still offer it. This well-known "gas chamber," however, also is grim. An eyewitness described the 1967 execution of Luis José Monge:

According to the official execution log unconsciousness came more than five minutes after the cyanide splashed down into the sulfuric acid. Even after unconsciousness is declared officially, the prisoner's body continues to fight for life. He coughs and groans. The lips make little pouting motions resembling

Gas chamber, Maryland State Penitentiary, Baltimore. Only inmates sentenced before 1994 can choose the gas chamber as a method of execution.

the motions made by a goldfish in a bowl. The head strains back and then slowly sinks down to the chest. And in Monge's case, the arms, though tightly bound to the chair, strained through the straps and the hands clawed torturously as if the prisoner were struggling for air.[88]

Interestingly, in 1994 a federal district court declared execution by lethal gas to violate the Eighth Amendment ban against cruel and unusual punishment. In making the decision, presiding Judge Marilyn Hall Patel stated that California's gas chamber at San Quentin Prison, where almost 200 prisoners had been executed since 1938, was a "brutal relic with no place in civilized society and must be immediately shut down."[89] Rejecting the state's assertion that cyanide gas causes virtually instant unconsciousness, Judge Patel cited doctors' reports and witnesses' accounts of numerous past executions as evidence that dying inmates remain conscious for up to a minute or longer. In that time, she said, the inmate is likely to suffer intense physical pain, mainly an "air hunger" similar to that experienced during strangulation or drowning. The ruling prescribed lethal injection for all future executions in California. This ruling was not applicable to Arizona, where the last use of a gas chamber occurred in 1999, when Walter LaGrand was executed.

In 1977, a number of states enacted statutes that retired their electric chairs, gas chambers, and gallows. In their place was death by lethal injection, referred to by many death row inmates as "the ultimate high." Lethal injection is the most common method used today by all 33 states that allow the death penalty.[90] Proponents of lethal injection argued that it would be a more palatable way of killing; it would be instantaneous, and the prisoner would simply fall asleep.[91] Opponents countered that sticking a needle into a vein can be tricky, with the prospect of repeated attempts on a struggling prisoner, and that the drugs themselves posed "a substantial threat of torturous pain."[92] The American Medical Association also took a stand on the matter, instructing its members not to take part in such executions and arguing that the role of the physician is to protect lives, not take them.[93]

Despite the arguments, the new method of execution went forward. On December 7, 1982, Charles Brooks Jr. was put to death in Huntsville, Texas, becoming the first person to die by a state-sanctioned lethal injection. First a catheter was placed into the vein of his left arm; through it flowed a saline solution—a sterile saltwater routinely used as a medium for drug injections. Brooks was then given intravenous doses of barbiturates and potassium chloride, which paralyzed him, stopped his breathing, and caused his death.[94]

The drug cocktail used in lethal injection procedures has been controversial from the beginning. Traditionally, a three-drug cocktail was used that included an anesthetic (usually pentobarbital), followed by pancuronium bromide to paralyze the inmate and potassium chloride to stop the inmate's heart.[95] Challenges arose after the major manufacturer of one of the anesthetics refused to sell directly to U.S. prisons for use in executions. Several prisons across the country began importing drugs from foreign pharmaceutical companies. Others switched to a one-drug protocol using a lethal dose of an anesthetic alone.[96] In 2008, in the case of *Baze v. Rees,*[97] the U.S. Supreme Court ruled that lethal injection as a method of execution did not violate the Eighth Amendment ban against cruel and unusual punishment. Writing for the majority, Chief Justice Roberts said the following: "This Court has upheld capital punishment as constitutional. Because some risk of pain is inherent in even the most humane execution method, if only from the prospect of error in following the required procedure, the Constitution does not demand the avoidance of all risk of pain."[98] Although the Supreme Court has taken a clear position on the constitutionality of the death penalty, including the use of lethal injections, this does not mean that the controversies surrounding capital punishment have been settled. The American public continues to debate the questions that surround this ultimate form of sentencing. We examine the controversy in the upcoming sections.

The Death Penalty Debate

Historically, the arguments for or against capital punishment have revolved around eight central themes: economics, retribution, public opinion, community protection, deterrence, irreversibility, discrimination, and cruel and unusual punishment. As you read about the pros and cons of each argument below, consider your own thoughts on this important issue.

The Economic Argument The economic argument for capital punishment holds that execution is far less expensive than maintaining a prisoner behind bars for the rest of his or her natural life. However, death sentences are invariably appealed, and the appeals can be costly. In fact, every available quantitative study of this argument demonstrates that because of all the additional appeals and other procedural safeguards that are constitutionally required in capital cases, the death penalty costs taxpayers substantially more than life imprisonment.[99] The extensive appellate process, in particular, is costly, but it is also necessary as a means for ensuring that the sentence is appropriate and that guilt has been determined accurately.

The Retribution Argument The retribution argument asserts that kidnappers, murderers, and rapists are vile and despicable human beings who deserve to die. This is simply a matter of individual opinion, and differences in philosophy appear even within the Supreme Court. In *Furman*, Justice Thurgood Marshall spoke against this position. At the same time, however, the court stated that while retribution was no longer a dominant objective, "neither is it a forbidden objective nor one inconsistent with our respect for the dignity of men."[100]

The Public Opinion Argument Public opinion has been a motivating factor in the enactment of death penalty statutes. In a 2010 Gallup poll, 64 percent of Americans indicated support for the death penalty for the crime of murder.[101] In the years since the *Furman* decision, throughout the United States, every poll on the matter has consistently found that the majority of Americans favor the death penalty for offenders convicted of murder.[102] However, polls have also found growing support for alternatives to the death penalty, including life in prison without the possibility of parole. Concerns about innocence, related to the argument about the irreversibility of the death sentence (discussed below), may be fueling these sentiments. The lengthy and costly appeals process, discussed earlier in this section, has also complicated the public view of the death penalty. The economic costs of the death penalty create additional burdens for state budgets already stretched to their limits.

The Community Protection Argument The community protection argument made by supporters of the death penalty maintains that such a "final remedy" is necessary to keep the murderer from further ravaging society. Counter to this position is the claim that life imprisonment could achieve the same goal. Yet, as a number of studies have pointed out, paroled murderers have lower rates of recidivism than other classes of offenders.[103]

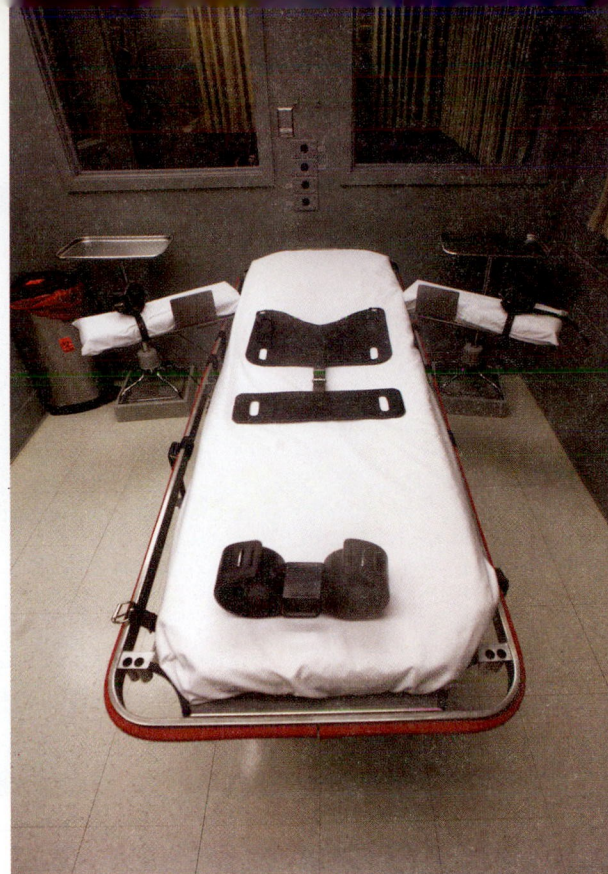

The lethal injection gurney is the most common method of execution authorized by the states.

The imposition of the death penalty continues to create controversy.

The Deterrence Argument   Related to community protection is the deterrence argument, which holds that capital punishment not only prevents the offender from committing additional crimes but deters others as well. A number of studies have been done specifically on the deterrent effects of capital punishment. One research strategy for such studies has been to compare the homicide rates in states that have death penalty provisions with homicide rates in states that do not. Another has been to examine murder rates in given areas both before and after an execution. And still a third approach has been to analyze crime rates in general, as well as murder rates in particular, in jurisdictions before and after the abolition of capital punishment. Regardless of the nature and logic of the inquiry applied, the studies have consistently produced no evidence that the death penalty deters homicide.[104]

The Irreversibility Argument   The irreversibility argument put forth by those opposed to the death penalty contends that there is always the possibility that an innocent person might be put to death. As of 2012, 140 people in 25 states have been released from death row with evidence of their innocence, which means that approximately one person has been exonerated for every eight people executed.[105] Some are released because of procedural errors, but for others, DNA evidence has demonstrated their innocence.[106] In one of the most exhaustive studies of capital punishment ever, a team of Columbia University researchers found that when capital cases were sent back for a new trial, 7 percent of the defendants were found not guilty, and less than 20 percent of those who were convicted received another death sentence. In 2001, the Center on Wrongful Convictions at Northwestern Law School analyzed the cases of 86 death row defendants who had been exonerated. The researchers found a number of reasons why innocent people are wrongly convicted in capital cases:

- eyewitness error from confusion or faulty memory
- government misconduct by both the police and the prosecution
- junk science, meaning mishandled evidence or the use of unqualified "experts"
- snitch testimony, meaning testimony given in exchange for a reduction in sentence
- false confessions resulting from mental illness or retardation, as well as from police torture
- others, including hearsay and questionable circumstantial evidence[107]

Research by Michael Radelet and Hugo Bedau uncovered compelling evidence that, since 1900, at least 23 innocent defendants have gone to their deaths. Others have criticized the study's conclusions,[108] but considering the many discretionary and potentially discriminatory aspects of the criminal justice system, a number of observers feel certain that innocents have been executed over the years—especially given the many individuals who have been released from death row and exonerated of their crimes.

The Discrimination Argument   The discrimination argument contends that the death penalty is a lottery system, with the odds stacked heavily against those who are less capable of defending themselves. As Justice Thurgood Marshall wrote in his concurring opinion in *Furman v. Georgia:*

> It also is evident that the burden of capital punishment falls upon the poor, the ignorant, and the underprivileged members of society. It is the poor, and the members of minority groups who are least able to voice their complaints against capital punishment. Their impotence leaves them victims of a sanction which the wealthier, better-represented, just-as-guilty person can escape. So long as the capital sanction is used only against the forlorn, easily forgotten members of society, legislators are content to maintain the status quo, because change would draw attention to the problem and concern might develop. Ignorance is perpetuated and apathy soon becomes its mate, and we have today's situation.[109]

Analyses of the social characteristics of death row inmates suggest that the death penalty continues to be employed in a selective and discriminatory manner. Studies indicate that a disproportionate number of individuals sentenced to death are members of minority groups, and nearly all inmates on death row across the United States are indigents—too poor to afford private counsel—who had to rely on a state-supplied attorney.[110] Further complicating this issue, defendants who kill white victims have also been found more likely to be sentenced to death than defendants who kill victims of color. Further details about this distribution are shown in Exhibit 10.3.[111]

The Cruel and Unusual Punishment Argument   The final argument we review is one we have touched on earlier in the chapter. The cruel and unusual punishment argument maintains that the death penalty is a violation of the constitutional right guaranteed by the Eighth Amendment. Supporters and opponents of capital punishment differ, however, in their interpretations of the cruel and unusual punishment clause. The former hold that capital punishment is cruel and unusual in all circumstances. The latter insist that the Eighth Amendment forbids a sentence of death only when it is a disproportionate punishment for the crime committed. These conflicting views were the bases for the Supreme Court's rulings in *Furman, Gregg,* and *Baze,* all of which you read about earlier.

Capital Punishment in Contemporary America

During the first six years after the reinstatement of capital punishment in 1976, only 6 executions occurred. After that there were 5 in 1983, 21 in 1984, 88 from 1985 to 1989, and a grand total of 1,298 through mid-2012.[112] In many ways, the machinery of the death penalty has continued unchanged for more than 35 years. However, legal developments related to capital punishment have altered the path to execution for inmates in the United States. First, the Supreme Court rulings have limited the avenues of appeal for inmates convicted of capital crimes. In *Barefoot v. Estelle,*[113] the Supreme Court limited the lengthy appeals process, stating, in effect, that federal appeals courts may compress the time they take to consider appeals, as long as all the issues are covered adequately and on their merits. While the ruling in *Barefoot* mandated nothing,

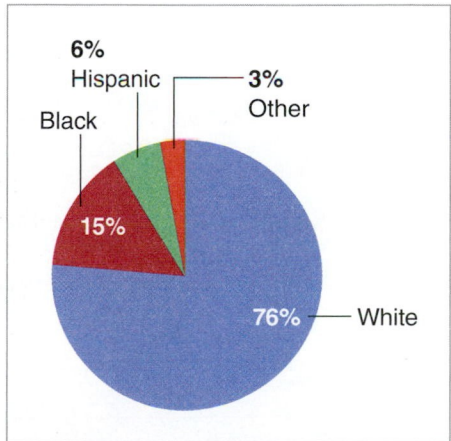

EXHIBIT 10.3   **Race of Victims in Death Penalty Cases**

Source: Death Penalty Information Center

it noted that stays of execution were not automatic upon the filing of petitions of certiorari. Additionally, *Pulley v. Harris*,[114] decided in 1984, curtailed one avenue of appeal. Specifically, petitioner Robert Alton Harris claimed that California's capital punishment statute was invalid under the Constitution because it failed to require the California Supreme Court to compare his sentence with others in similar capital cases and thereby determine whether they were proportionate. The U.S. Supreme Court held that Harris's claim was without merit, ruling that the Eighth Amendment prohibition of cruel and unusual punishment does not require, as an invariable rule in every case, a comparative proportionality review of capital sentences by an appellate court. Along those lines, many states have also streamlined the state appellate reviews available to offenders convicted of capital crimes, including the addition of automatic reviews that occur at the state level. And finally, over the past decades a number of Supreme Court decisions have reaffirmed that capital punishment would remain a visible part of American justice in the twenty-first century:

- In *Lockhart v. McCree*,[115] decided in 1986, the court asserted that even if juries that support the death penalty are "conviction prone," this in itself does not violate any constitutional provisions.
- In *McCleskey v. Kemp*,[116] decided in 1987, the court held that statistical evidence of racial discrimination in death sentencing cannot, in and of itself, establish a violation of the Eighth and/or Fourteenth Amendments. The court further held that to obtain relief, a defendant must prove either (1) that decision-makers in his or her case acted with discriminatory purpose or (2) that the legislature enacted or maintained the death penalty statute because of an anticipated racially discriminatory effect.
- In perhaps the most controversial ruling, *Herrera v. Collins*,[117] decided in 1993, the court ruled that death row inmates in all but the most extraordinary cases will not be entitled to bring a federal habeas corpus petition claiming "actual innocence" based on newly discovered evidence.
- In the case of *Atkins v. Virginia*,[118] decided in 2002, the court held that the execution of a person with "mental retardation" violates the Eighth Amendment protections against cruel and unusual punishment.
- In 2005, in the *Roper v. Simmons*[119] case, the court held that the Constitution prohibits the execution of individuals who were under 18 at the time of the offense.
- In the 2008 *Kennedy v. Louisiana*[120] case, the U.S. Supreme Court struck down as unconstitutional a Louisiana statute that allowed the death penalty for the rape of a child where the victim did not die.
- In 2011, the U.S. Supreme Court held in *Skinner v. Switzer*[121] that Hank Skinner, a Texas death row inmate who came within an hour of execution in 2010, could challenge the state's refusal to test crucial DNA evidence from his case in federal court. Skinner has always maintained his innocence of the 1993 murders of his girlfriend and her two sons and requested that Texas perform DNA testing on key pieces of evidence that might point to another suspect.

These decisions in no way indicate that the Supreme Court had made up its mind on the death penalty. Quite the contrary.

THE APPEALS PROCESS

At its core, an appeal is a complaint to a superior court of an injustice done or error committed by a lower court, whose judgment or decision the higher court is called on to correct or reverse. However, after conviction, appeals are not automatic. Specific procedural steps must be followed. First, within a specified period (from 30 to 90 days) subsequent to conviction, the petitioner must file a notice of appeal with the court. Second, and again within a specified period, the petitioner must submit an affidavit of errors, setting forth the alleged errors or defects in the trial (or pretrial)

Typically, for appellate cases at the state and federal levels, panels of three judges work together to review the case materials, called briefs. Defendants may appeal convictions, but prosecutors may not appeal acquittals.

proceedings that are the subjects of the appeal. If these requirements are followed, the higher court must review the case.[122] Appeals are argued on the basis of the affidavit of errors and sometimes through oral argument. In either case, the subject matter of the appeal must be limited to the contents of the original proceeding. Thus, no new evidence or testimony can be presented, for an appeal is not a trial. However, if new evidence is discovered that was unknown or unknowable to the defense at the time of the trial, it can be the basis of an appeal. Let's look at the way this process works, from the perspective of both the defense and the prosecution.

The Defendant's Right to Appeal

At the appellate stage, the presumption of innocence has evaporated, and the defendant is obliged to show why a conviction should be overturned. Thus, the nature of the adversary system changes, with the burden of proof shifting from the prosecution to the defense. All jurisdictions have procedural rules requiring that the defense make objections to the admission (or exclusion) of evidence, or to some other procedure, either at a pretrial hearing or at the time that evidence or other procedure becomes an issue at trial. Failure to make a timely objection results in automatic forfeiture of the claim for appeal purposes. The *timely-objection requirement* has been instituted so that trial judges can make rules and develop facts that will appear in the record and thus enable the appeals court to conduct an adequate review.

A notable exception to the timely-objection requirement is the *plain error rule*, which is included in the Federal Rules of Criminal Procedure and the procedural rules of all state jurisdictions. Under this rule, "plain errors or defects affecting substantial rights" of defendants become subject to appellate review, even though the defense may not have properly raised them at trial or during some prior appeal.[123] For example, denial of the right to counsel at trial, the admission of an involuntary confession, and the negation of some other constitutional guarantee are considered "plain errors" and are hence appealable.

On numerous occasions, the Supreme Court has held that certain constitutional errors are of such magnitude that they require automatic reversal of a conviction:

hence, the *automatic reversal rule.* The Fourteenth Amendment's due process clause, for example, guarantees a fair trial before an impartial judge. Pursuant to this guarantee, in 1927 the Supreme Court ruled in *Tumey v. Ohio*[124] that an accused person is denied due process when tried before a judge who has a direct, personal, or pecuniary interest in ruling against him or her. At issue in *Tumey* was the fact that the petitioner had been tried in a city court whose judge was the mayor and from which fines were deposited in the city treasury. The Supreme Court found the lower court's error to be so significant that it mandated an automatic reversal of Tumey's conviction. Similarly, the court considers convictions to be automatically reversible if certain plain errors were made, such as the use of an involuntary confession at trial and the denial of counsel at trial, in violation of its holding in *Gideon v. Wainwright* as we discussed in Chapter 4.[125]

In contrast, in *Chapman v. California,*[126] decided in 1967, the Supreme Court established the *harmless error rule,* holding that at times, a denial of a federal constitutional right can be of insufficient magnitude to require reversal of a conviction on appeal. Known also as the Chapman rule, the harmless error doctrine has been applied by the Supreme Court and other appellate courts in numerous areas related to constitutional review. These include, but are not limited to, areas we have discussed, such as evidence seized in violation of the Fourth Amendment, denial of counsel at a preliminary hearing, and a confession obtained from a defendant after indictment without expressly informing the defendant of his right to counsel.[127] When a court considers an error to be harmless, it is indicating that the mistake was not prejudicial to the rights of the accused and therefore made no difference in the subsequent conviction or sentence.

Finally, although uncommon, in certain instances during the course of a proceeding the defense requests the court to make a ruling that is actually erroneous, and the court does so. Under the *invited error rule,* the defense cannot make an appeal based on that error if they requested the ruling in the first place.[128]

The Prosecution's Right to Appeal

Neither the federal government nor the states may appeal the acquittal of a defendant. Nor can the prosecution appeal the conviction on some lesser offense (say, murder in the second degree or manslaughter) when the original indictment was for a greater one (murder in the first degree). Such actions are barred by the double jeopardy clause of the Fifth Amendment.

However, the prosecution may initiate appellate review in two situations. First, if a defendant successfully appeals and his or her conviction is reversed on some matter of law, the prosecution may contest the correctness of that legal ruling to the next higher court or even to the U.S. Supreme Court. Such was the case in *Delaware v. Prouse,*[129] which involved a seizure of marijuana following a random spot check of the defendant's driver's license and vehicle registration. Upon conviction, the defendant appealed to the Delaware Supreme Court, which overturned the lower court's ruling on the basis of illegal search and seizure. The prosecution then appealed to the U.S. Supreme Court to argue the constitutionality of the state's random license check practices. Alternatively, some jurisdictions permit the prosecution to initiate appeals from both convictions and acquittals, solely to correct any legal errors that may have occurred during trial.

Appellate Review of Sentences

Although appeals are commonly filed in order to review either real or imagined errors in court procedure, sentences, for the most part, cannot be appealed. This is so because each jurisdiction has statutes that mandate a range of penalties for each specific crime. Although a convicted offender might consider the sentence imposed to be unfair, as long as it falls within statutory guidelines, it is legal.

However, in a number of circumstances, sanctions can be appealed and reversed, including the following: (1) if the sentence is not authorized by statute and thus is illegal; (2) if the sentence is based on gender, ethnicity, or socioeconomic status and is, therefore, a violation of due process; (3) if the sentence has no relationship to the purposes of criminal sanctions; or (4) if the sentence is cruel and unusual.[130] Note that in these four instances, the bases for appeal are not simply issues of sentencing "excess" but rather straightforward matters of constitutional rights.

For many decades, critics have argued that all sentences should be subject to some form of appeal. The fact that sentences are discretionary within a jurisdiction's statutory guidelines and, as such, are lawful should not automatically suggest that they cannot be appealed. Discretion, after all, can be abused. Currently, about half of all states have appellate bodies that review sentences, though state appeals courts are generally reluctant to review sentences.[131] Not wishing to second-guess the sentencing judge, these higher courts feel that the magistrate who presided at the trial and pronounced the sentence had the most information available and was in the best position to determine the penalty.

Finally, although the U.S. Supreme Court has reviewed many sentences when the issue at stake was of constitutional magnitude, only once did it require a sentencing judge to explain the basis of the penalty imposed. The case was *North Carolina v. Pearce*,[132] in which the defendant, whose original conviction had been reversed, was then retried by the same judge—only to be reconvicted and sentenced more severely in the second trial. The High Court ruled that in such circumstances, the reasons for the more severe sentence must be placed in the record, the logic being that the due process clause of the Fourteenth Amendment forbids the imposition of a harsher sentence for the purpose of discouraging defendants from exercising their rights of appeal.

The sentencing of juvenile offenders differs considerably from the sentencing of adults, as you learned in Chapter 9 ("Juvenile Justice in Context"). Sentences for juveniles are far more often developed to help offenders than to punish them. However, as serious juvenile crime has found its way into the forefront of community concerns, the increased use of incarceration has become an important issue for criminal justice professionals and academics. Increasingly, juveniles are receiving our most serious punishments, including transfer to adult court and sentences of life without parole—the topic of this chapter's "Juvenile Justice in Context" feature.

JUVENILE JUSTICE IN CONTEXT

The Transfer of Juveniles to Adult Court and Life without Parole

The process of transferring a case from a juvenile court to an adult criminal court has become known as **waiver of jurisdiction.** The effect of such a transfer is to deny the youth the protection and treatment afforded by the juvenile process. Although state and federal statutes specify the age at which the criminal courts gain jurisdiction over young offenders (generally 17 or 18), they also provide for waivers of jurisdiction. The scope of such waivers varies widely, however. In addition, some states have statutes that require that juveniles committing serious crimes be waived automatically to adult court for processing.[133]

Policy-makers have looked on the transfer of juvenile offenders to adult court with increasing favor in recent years. The rationale has been that "getting tough" with juveniles will deliver the message that their offenses have "real"

The transfer of juveniles to adult courts highlights many questions about how we respond to crime generally, but it invariably brings attention to the complexity of processing a younger individual through a system designed for adults.

consequences and that they will face more severe sanctions, such as longer sentences and "hard time" in more demanding and less forgiving institutions if they continue to offend. Hence, the theory goes, transfers to adult criminal courts will have a deterrent effect on future crime. Recent research suggests, however, that this may not necessarily be the case.

In a study of all Texas youths waived to adult court over a 12-year period and sentenced to prison, their sentences were longer than those typically assigned in juvenile court. However, the youths rarely served sentences longer than those that might have been given to them in the juvenile court. On average, in fact, the youths served only 27 percent of their sentences.[134] Furthermore, a study of almost 3,000 Florida youths transferred to adult courts compared their recidivism with that of a matched sample of delinquents who were retained in juvenile court. Recidivism was examined in terms of rates of reoffending, seriousness of reoffending, and time to reoffending. By every measure, reoffending was greater among the transfers than among those retained in juvenile court.[135]

Often, juveniles are transferred to adult court for the most serious offenses. For such offenses, juveniles can receive extremely harsh and lengthy sentences, including life without parole. In 2009, more than 2,500 youth were serving life without parole sentences in the United States.[136]

Are these individuals "super-predators" with long records of vicious crimes? In fact, the majority are not. Some 59 percent received the sentence for their first-ever criminal conviction. Sixteen percent were between 13 and 15 years old when they committed their crimes. While the vast majority were convicted of murder, an estimated 26 percent were convicted of felony murder, in which the teen participated in a robbery or burglary during which a co-participant committed the homicide without the knowledge or intent of the teen. Moreover, racial disparities are marked, in that nationwide the estimated rate at which black youths receive life-without-parole sentences (6.6 per 10,000) is 10 times greater than the rate for white youths (0.6 per 10,000).[137] In 2012, the Supreme Court ruled that life without the possibility of parole for juvenile offenders constituted cruel and unusual punishment. Both of the cases before the court, *Miller v. Alabama* and *Jackson v. Hobbs,*[138] involved young men convicted of murder when they were only 14 years old.

Understandably, the fear of crime has played a role in giving many violent youths these long sentences, but does the trend fit with the philosophy of juvenile justice? Will the trend be reversed in the coming years, and if so, what will become of the young people already serving these harsh sentences? Thus far, we see no national movement in reversing this trend.

CONCLUSIONS

After the verdict is rendered, the business of the court is not complete. The judge, the jury, and the defendant still face the matter of sentencing. Throughout American history, there has been no single, clearly defined rationale to guide sentencing decisions. This absence of guidelines contributes to the discretionary nature of sentencing offenders in our country. Still, methods and philosophies for determining the most appropriate punishments for those who violate the law have evolved over time. Characteristics of offenders and offenses, impact on victims, and changes in the patterns of crime all weigh heavily on how our society reacts to individuals who are convicted of crimes. These same kinds of factors also influence judges and juries as they react to those who have been convicted of criminal offenses. And as you saw in the opening case of *Woodson,* one of the most controversial forms of sentencing is the death penalty, and our national debate continues on the use of this ultimate form of punishment.

SUMMARY AND REVIEW

- **Explain the philosophies of sentencing and punishment.**

  - *Retribution* involves creating an equal or proportionate relationship between the offense and the punishment—an effort to ensure that an offender's punishment is commensurate not only with the crime but also with his or her moral blameworthiness and prior criminal record.

  - *Vengeance* is the desire to punish criminals because society gains some measure of satisfaction from seeing or knowing that they are punished.

  - *Incapacitation* is simply the removal of dangerous persons from the community.

  - *Deterrence* refers to the prevention of criminal acts by making examples of individuals convicted of crimes. General deterrence seeks to discourage would-be offenders from committing crimes; specific deterrence is designed to prevent a particular convicted offender from engaging in future criminal acts.

  - *Rehabilitation* rests on the premise that people who commit crimes have identifiable reasons for doing so and that these can be discovered, addressed, and altered. Its aim is to modify behavior and reintegrate the lawbreaker into the wider society as a productive citizen.

- **Describe the various kinds of sentences.**

  - *Fines* are monetary penalties imposed either in lieu of or in addition to incarceration or probation. They are the traditional means of dealing with most traffic-law violations and many misdemeanors. Fines can also be imposed for felonies, instead of or in addition to some other sentence.

  - *Imprisonment* is the removal of an individual from society through the use of a jail or prison sentence. There are different types of sentences: indeterminate; determinate, or flat, fixed or straight; definite; intermittent; and mandatory, in addition to others.

  - The *death sentence* is the execution, or taking of the life, of an individual convicted of a crime, most typically murder.

- **Compare the contemporary sentencing strategies for imprisonment.**

  - The most common type of sentence, the indeterminate sentence, has a fixed minimum and a fixed maximum term for incarceration, rather than a definite period. The paroling authority determines the actual amount of time served. This strategy is controversial because the indeterminate sentence can vary by judge and by jurisdiction, resulting in unfair and disparate terms of imprisonment. Other criticisms of this strategy include the perceptions of uncertainty of inmates, inconsistency with the goals of punishment, and failure to respond to the causes of crime.

  - Determinate and definite sentences, which specify incarceration terms, have also been criticized. In some cases, they fail to allow discretion in the sentencing process to make the punishments fit the crime or respond to community needs.

- **Identify the sentencing reforms developed in response to criticism of disparities in the sentencing process.**

  - Mandatory sentencing statutes stipulate fixed imprisonment penalties, increase community protection, and decrease the court's discretion. However, they can also increase prosecutorial discretion, court delays, and overcrowded prison conditions. In addition, they almost totally eliminate the rehabilitative goals of individualized justice.

  - The presumptive fixed sentence is another attempt to respond to disparity and is used in several jurisdictions. The objectives of presumptive sentencing are to (1) limit judicial discretion without totally eliminating it and (2) increase community protection by imposing a sentence that the offender is required to serve.

- **Describe the Supreme Court interpretation of cruel and unusual punishment, including how it applies to the death penalty.**

  - The Eighth Amendment of the United States Constitution prohibits cruel and unusual punishment. The framers of the Constitution likely intended to outlaw punishments that were outside both the mainstream of penalties and the moral judgment of the community.

- In *Weems v. United States,* the Supreme Court found the sentence disproportionate to the offense; thus, *Weems* was the first case in which the court invalidated a criminal punishment on Eighth Amendment grounds. By 1958, the court had agreed that the constitutional prohibition could have no fixed and unchanging meaning. Rather, any challenges brought to the court must necessarily be viewed in terms of "evolving standards of decency."

- In reviewing the appropriateness of the death penalty, the court has found that the death penalty can be an appropriate punishment for offenses of murder, as long as judicial and jury discretion are structured and the process is responsive to evolving standards of decency.

Explain the arguments in the debate surrounding the death penalty.

- The economic argument for capital punishment holds that execution is far less expensive than maintaining a prisoner behind bars for the rest of his or her natural life.

- The retribution argument asserts that kidnappers, murderers, and rapists are vile and despicable human beings who deserve to die.

- The public opinion argument rests on the continued public support for capital punishment as a response to murder.

- The community protection argument maintains that this "final remedy" is necessary to keep the murderer from further harming society.

- Related to community protection is the deterrence argument, which holds that capital punishment not only prevents the offender from committing additional crimes but deters others as well.

- The irreversibility argument put forth by those opposed to the death penalty contends that an innocent person might be put to death.

- The discrimination argument contends that the death penalty is a lottery system, with the odds stacked heavily against those who are less capable of defending themselves.

- Finally, the cruel and unusual punishment argument maintains that the death penalty is a violation of the constitutional right guaranteed by the Eighth Amendment.

Identify the reasons a conviction can be appealed.

- Defendants can appeal for the following reasons:
  - Plain errors or defects affecting substantial rights of defendants become subject to appellate review, even though they may not have been properly raised at trial or during some prior appeal; such errors include denial of the right to counsel at trial, the admission of an involuntary confession, or the negation of some other constitutional guarantee.
  - The Supreme Court has held that certain constitutional errors are of such magnitude that they require automatic reversal of a conviction: hence, the automatic reversal rule, which includes, but is not limited to, use of an involuntary confession at trial and the denial of counsel at trial.

- Prosecutors can initiate appellate review in two situations. First, if a defendant successfully appeals and his or her conviction is reversed on some matter of law, the prosecution may contest that legal ruling. Alternatively, some jurisdictions permit the prosecution to initiate appeals to correct any legal errors that may have occurred during trial.

KEY TERMS

allocution (p. 269)

appeal (p. 261)

definite sentence (p. 265)

determinate sentence (p. 265)

deterrence (p. 262)

incapacitation (p. 262)

indeterminate sentence (p. 264)

mandatory sentence (p. 266)

presentence investigation (p. 268)

rehabilitation (p. 263)

retribution (p. 261)

vengeance (p. 262)

victim impact evidence (p. 262)

waiver of jurisdiction (p. 283)

ISSUES FOR CRITICAL THINKING AND DISCUSSION

1. Is vengeance a sound rationale for punishment?
2. How might mandatory sentencing statutes lead to increased prosecutorial discretion and court delays?
3. Would mandatory sentencing statutes increase the certainty of punishment for offenders? Would such sentences affect the crime problem?
4. Should victim impact evidence be permitted in death penalty cases?
5. Which method of execution is the most humane? Explain your answer.
6. Which argument in favor of capital punishment seems most valid? Which argument against it seems most valid? Do you think it will be abolished?
7. Should limits be placed on the number of appeals available to defendants or the amount of time they have to appeal their cases?
8. Would mandatory punishment for violations of campus plagiarism policies increase the effectiveness of these policies? As in the criminal justice system, how might the use of discretion in the application of punishment increase or decrease these policies' effectiveness?

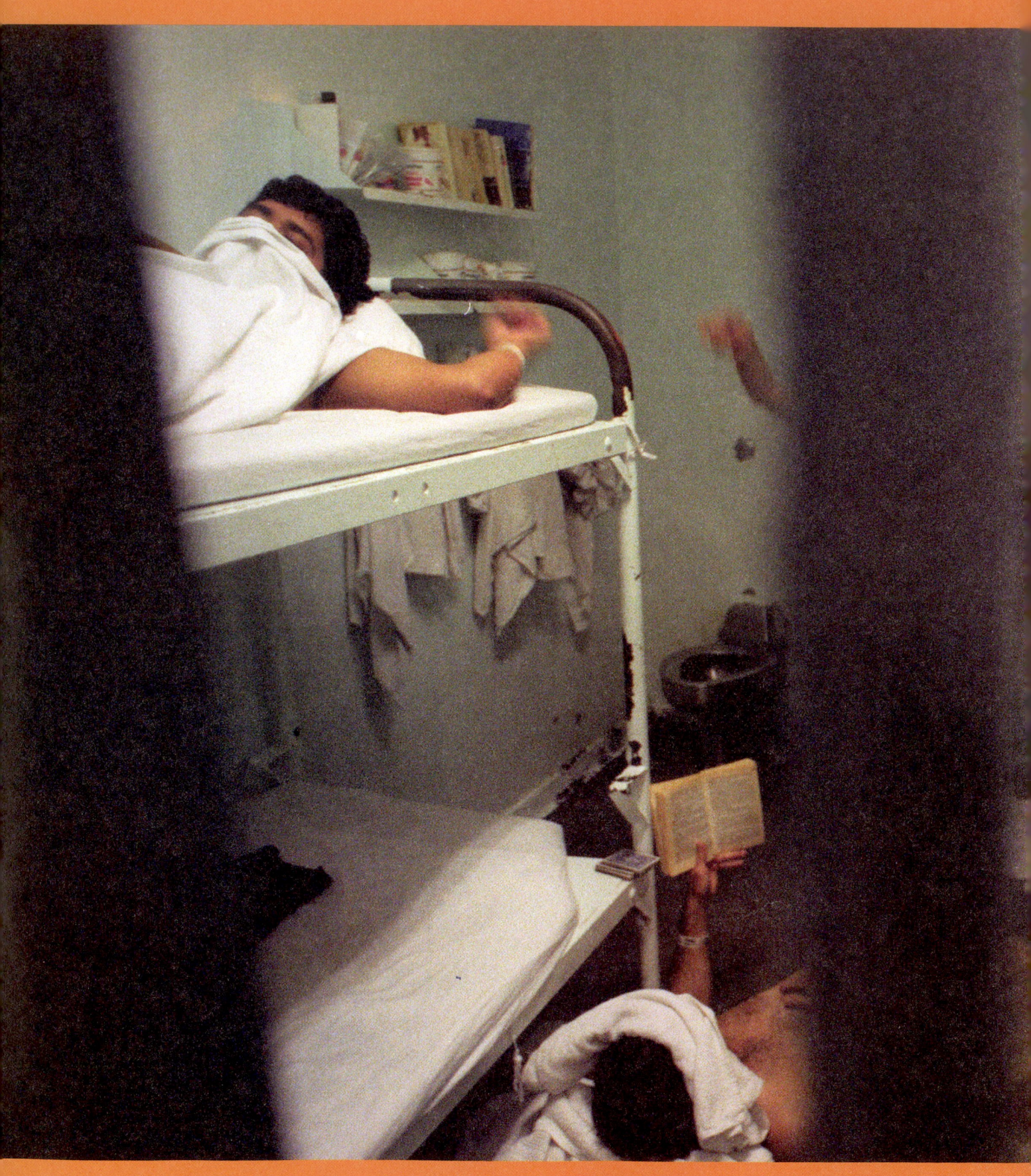

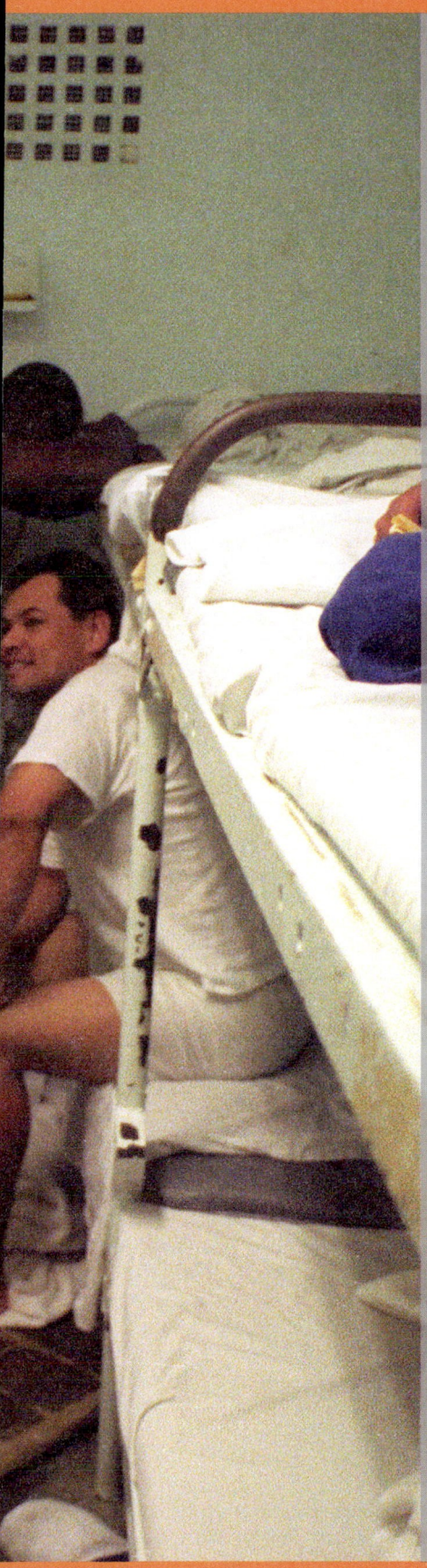

11

The Structure and Function of American Corrections

LEARNING OBJECTIVES

- Identify the key themes in the history of punishment, including the contributions of the classical school of criminology.
- Describe the structure of corrections in the United States.
- Compare and contrast the types of correctional institutions operating in modern America.
- Describe the typical administrative features of correctional institutions.
- List and describe the types of programs that commonly operate in correctional facilities.

PUNISHING THOSE WHO PUNISH

The case of Larry Hope focused on the use of a hitching post (similar to the ones pictured here) in a correctional setting and on whether correctional officers could be held responsible for their disciplinary actions.

On two separate occasions in 1995, Larry Hope, an inmate within the Alabama prison system, was handcuffed to a "hitching post" as a punishment for disruptive behavior. A hitching post is a "horizontal bar made of sturdy, nonflexible material placed between 45 and 57 inches from the ground. Inmates are handcuffed to the hitching post in a standing position," usually with their hands relatively close together, at face level. The most common complaint from inmates relates to the strain on their muscles. "In addition to their exposure to sunburn, dehydration, and muscle aches, the inmates are also placed in substantial pain when the sun heats the handcuffs that shackle them to the hitching post, or heats the hitching post itself."[1]

Larry Hope's first hitching-post incident resulted from an argument he had with a fellow inmate while they worked on a chain gang. Both men were handcuffed to the hitching post, but Hope was released two hours later when a correctional officer determined that he had not caused the incident. The second incident, about one month later, began when Hope moved too slowly in response to a guard's order. Hope and the guard exchanged ugly remarks, and the situation escalated to a wrestling

match. Four other guards intervened, and Hope was subdued, handcuffed, put in leg irons, and transported back to the prison. Once there, he was ordered to take off his shirt, and he remained exposed to the sun for seven hours while handcuffed to the hitching post. He was offered water only once or twice, was not given bathroom breaks, and was taunted by a guard about his thirst. Hope sued three correctional officers who were involved in this incident.[2]

The issue the Supreme Court faced in *Hope v. Pelzer* was whether the officers were entitled to qualified immunity, which shields public officials from liability for civil damages unless their actions clearly violated "established statutory or Constitutional rights of which a reasonable person would have known."[3] Thus, the first step was to determine whether use of the hitching post did, in fact, violate the Eighth Amendment ban against cruel and unusual punishment. The court determined that "as the facts are alleged by Hope, the Eighth Amendment violation is obvious."[4] In addition, the court ruled against immunity for the officers. The decision was supported by several factors: (1) at the time of the incidents, federal appeals courts had decided that handcuffing inmates to fences or in their cells for long periods violated the Eighth Amendment, (2) the U.S. Circuit Court of Appeals that covered Alabama had warned prisons against denying any inmate drinking water as a form of punishment, and (3) the Alabama Department of Corrections had regulations regarding the use of the hitching post, including details about drinking water and bathroom breaks. Because the correctional officers had not followed those rules, they were not entitled to qualified immunity.[5]

Compared to certain historical punishments, the hitching post is mild. Nevertheless, this case highlights the discretionary use of corporal punishment, as well as the legal issues that surround it, as corrections personnel manage and monitor the masses of inmates confined within the walls and cells of institutions across the country. To help you put this case in context, this chapter begins by tracing historical developments in the philosophy of punishment. It then explains the structure of the U.S. correctional system—that is, how the system is organized and what types of facilities it encompasses. Larry Hope was incarcerated in an Alabama state prison, but multiple other types of facilities exist, on both the federal and state levels. The final section of the chapter discusses the administrative features of correctional facilities—who runs them, what programs they provide for inmates, and how they classify and discipline inmates.

PUNISHMENT IN HUMAN HISTORY

Historically and cross-culturally, the range of punishments imposed by societies has been vast. Over the centuries, the sanctions for even minor crimes have been exceedingly harsh, and the litany of punishments down through the ages has often been referred to as the story of "man's inhumanity to man."[6] **Corporal punishment,** in the form of mutilation, branding, whipping, and torture, has been commonplace. And in attempts to "let the punishment fit the crime," thieves and robbers have lost hands, perjurers and blasphemers have had their tongues cut out or pierced with hot irons, and rapists have been castrated. Banishment and transportation to a penal colony were alternatives to capital punishment. Other punishments have included forced labor, sterilization, excommunication, loss of property and inheritance rights, disfigurement, and imprisonment. Modern punishment relies heavily on incarceration in jails and prisons.[7] **Jails** typically house inmates who are awaiting trial or who have been given short sentences, while **prisons** hold inmates serving sentences longer than one year. To understand the application of these punishments, this chapter examines the goals of punishment throughout history.

Punishment versus Reformation

While many severe punishments were common during the colonial period, not everyone agreed that these were appropriate responses to lawbreaking. In fact, throughout English and American history, scholars and kings, philosophers and reformers, and legislators and politicians have argued the merits of punishment versus reformation in the management and control of criminal offenders.[8]

Before the eighteenth century, correctional ideas and practices across Europe and America may have varied, but they all shared similar goals—punishing offenders, reducing crime, and protecting society. Criminal sanctions focused on retribution, banishment, isolation, and death and were based on the reasoning that offenders were enemies of society who deserved punishment and that severe approaches would eliminate their potential for future crime. This punishment ideology has endured.

Corporal punishments, such as the 1958 flogging dramatized here, were fairly common into the nineteenth century.

During the eighteenth century—the Age of Enlightenment—a new ideology emerged. It was a reform movement that stressed the dignity and imperfections of the human condition; it recognized the harshness of criminal law and procedure; and it fought against the cruelty of many punishments and conditions of confinement. Among the leading European thinkers in the reform movement were Charles Montesquieu, François Voltaire, and Denis Diderot in France; Cesare Beccaria in Italy; and Jeremy Bentham, John Howard, Sir Samuel Romilly, and Sir Robert Peel in England.[9]

The Classical School of Criminology

The reformist principles of Montesquieu, Voltaire, and other Enlightenment philosophers merged during the middle of the eighteenth century into what has become known as the **classical school of criminology and criminal law.** It has been called "classical" because of its historical significance as the first body of ideas before modern times that was coherently formulated to bring about changes in criminal law and procedure. At the heart of the classical tradition are the ideas that a person is a self-determining being, acting on reason and intelligence, and therefore is responsible for his or her behavior.[10]

The classical school began as an outgrowth of the acquaintanceship between **Cesare Beccaria,** an economist and jurist, and Alessandro Verri, a prison official in Milan. Beccaria's numerous visits with Verri exposed him to existing criminal justice procedures. He observed that judges applied capricious and purely personal justice, that criminal sanctions were almost totally discretionary, that many magistrates exercised their power to add to the punishments prescribed by law, and that criminals were treated brutally: branded, torn limb from limb, fed to animals, starved, scalded, burned, hanged, enslaved, crucified, and stoned or pressed to death.[11]

Outraged by what he saw, Beccaria began writing what became one of the most significant books of his time. Two years later, in 1764, his *Dei delitti e delle pene (On Crimes and Punishments)* was published. It outlined a doctrine of criminal law and procedure that (1) focused on preventing crime rather than imposing punishment, (2) limited the severity of punishment, (3) required that punishment be proportionate to the crime, and (4) assured speed and certainty in the delivery of punishment. Because the criminal law placed restrictions on individual freedom, Beccaria believed the scope of the law should be limited.[12]

Beccaria's reformist views were highly praised. His arguments were incorporated into both English and French criminal codes, and among those inspired by Beccaria's work were the framers of the U.S. Constitution. In England, classicists such as Jeremy Bentham, Samuel Romilly, and John Howard sought to reform the infamous Bloody Code—a system of laws that permitted execution for such crimes as pickpocketing, cutting down trees on government parklands, setting fire to a cornfield, escaping from jail, and shooting a rabbit.[13]

However, classical thinking also had its flaws. Classicists, for example, guided by the doctrine of free will, argued that all behavior is based on hedonism, the pleasure-pain principle. People choose the courses of action that give them the most pleasure and avoid those that bring pain. Thus, behavior is purposive—and punishment, they reasoned, should result in only enough pain to outweigh the pleasure received from the forbidden act and, thus, to prevent future criminal behavior.[14] This view applied equally to all citizens, with no allowances for aggravating or mitigating circumstances. Nevertheless, the classical school was instrumental in making the law impartial, reducing the harshness of penalties, and replacing the arbitrary powers of judges with a specified range of criminal sanctions. In addition, it increased interest in the use of imprisonment as a form of punishment that might reform the offender. The correctional system that emerged in the United States as a result is the topic we turn to next.

The writing of Cesare Beccaria influenced modern thinking about how society punishes criminal offenders.

STRUCTURE OF AMERICAN CORRECTIONS

American correctional facilities follow an organizational pattern similar to that of law enforcement and court jurisdictions as discussed in previous chapters—with a system of federal agencies that are similar in various ways to the state and local agencies. Both federal and state systems have institutions with varying levels of security, and both include specific institutions for the intake and detention of offenders and their reentry into society. The Federal Bureau of Prisons organizes and manages the federal system, while each state runs its own correctional agencies, including a system of prisons, work-release units, and other facilities and organizations. In addition to the state and federal systems, many counties, cities, and other municipalities maintain jails and detention facilities that house offenders who are awaiting trial, who have been sentenced to short periods of incarceration, or who are awaiting release back into the community. We begin our discussion of the structure of corrections in America by exploring the federal system.

The Federal Corrections System

The federal prison system, the most complex correctional organization in the United States, is designed to house those convicted of federal criminal law violations. The first federal penitentiaries were authorized by Congress in 1891, and by 1905 institutions had been opened in Atlanta, Georgia, and in Leavenworth, Kansas. In 1919, McNeil Island in Puget Sound, off the coast of Washington State, was designated as a federal facility; in 1924, a women's reformatory was constructed at Alderson, West Virginia, and in the following year, a men's reformatory was authorized at the military reservation at Chillicothe, Ohio.[15]

Established in 1930 within the Department of Justice, the Federal Bureau of Prisons gradually evolved into a leader in American correctional practice.[16] The bureau established a graded system of institutions that included maximum-security penitentiaries for the close custody of the most serious felons, medium-security facilities for those who were better prospects for rehabilitation, reformatories for young and inexperienced offenders, minimum-security open camps for offenders requiring little custodial control, detention centers for those awaiting trial and disposition, and a variety of halfway houses, work-release programs, and community treatment centers. These facilities were once designed to keep the offenders segregated from society. Today, the varying levels of custody also serve to segregate the worst offenders from each other and from less serious offenders.

By the middle of 2012, the bureau was operating an integrated system of more than 100 adult and juvenile correctional facilities, housing more than 210,000 inmates,

Leavenworth, Kansas, had one of the earliest federal penitentiaries.

DISCRETION MATTERS

Which characteristics might officials focus on when deciding whether to include rehabilitation as part of an offender's correctional experience?

including those within private facilities.[17] It currently consists of 117 institutions, 6 regional offices, a central office (headquarters), 2 staff training centers, and 22 community corrections offices.[18] As you can see from Exhibit 11.1, the prison population has continued to rise every year. In addition, the pie charts in Exhibit 11.2 give data on the makeup of the prison population—revealing that it is primarily male, disparately black, and minimally educated. Half of all inmates are between the ages of 18 and 34.

State Correctional Facilities

Each of the fifty states has its own correctional system of prisons, detention facilities, community correctional units, and facilities designed for reentry of offenders into society. These systems are similar in structure to those at the federal level and are designed to incarcerate offenders charged with (in the case of those individuals awaiting trial in jails) and convicted of state offenses. However, some do house federal inmates released to the state system. Each state system is unique, having developed its own policies and procedures for operating its correctional agencies and facilities.

The number of state correctional facilities has grown to nearly 2,000; however, the number within individual states varies dramatically. In Texas, 114 individual facilities were operating in 2012, while Rhode Island had just 8.[19] As of January 2010, over 1.4 million individuals were housed in state prison facilities.[20] This was a slight drop from the year before—attributed to programs that divert low-level offenders and probation and parole violators from prison, strengthen community supervision and reentry, and accelerate the release of low-risk inmates.[21]

Although the federal and state prison systems grew dramatically during the twentieth century, and although many aspects of correctional practice have changed over the years, large numbers of offenders never enter prisons, or do so only after a substantial period of detention in jail. Because jails house such large numbers of inmates and jail conditions are a subject of growing concern, the next section examines jails and detention centers in some detail.

DISCRETION MATTERS

Which characteristics might a judge focus on when deciding whether to incarcerate an offender?

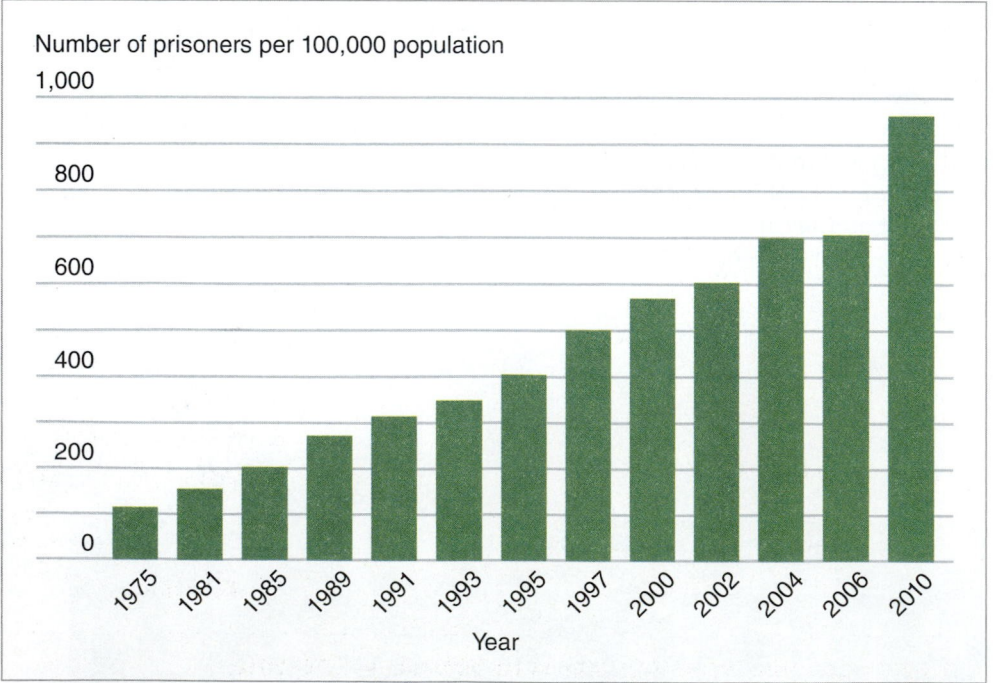

EXHIBIT 11.1   Inmates in U.S. State and Federal Prisons, 1975–2010
Source: Bureau of Justice Statistics

"The Walls," a penitentiary operated by the Texas Department of Criminal Justice, is located near downtown Huntsville, Texas.

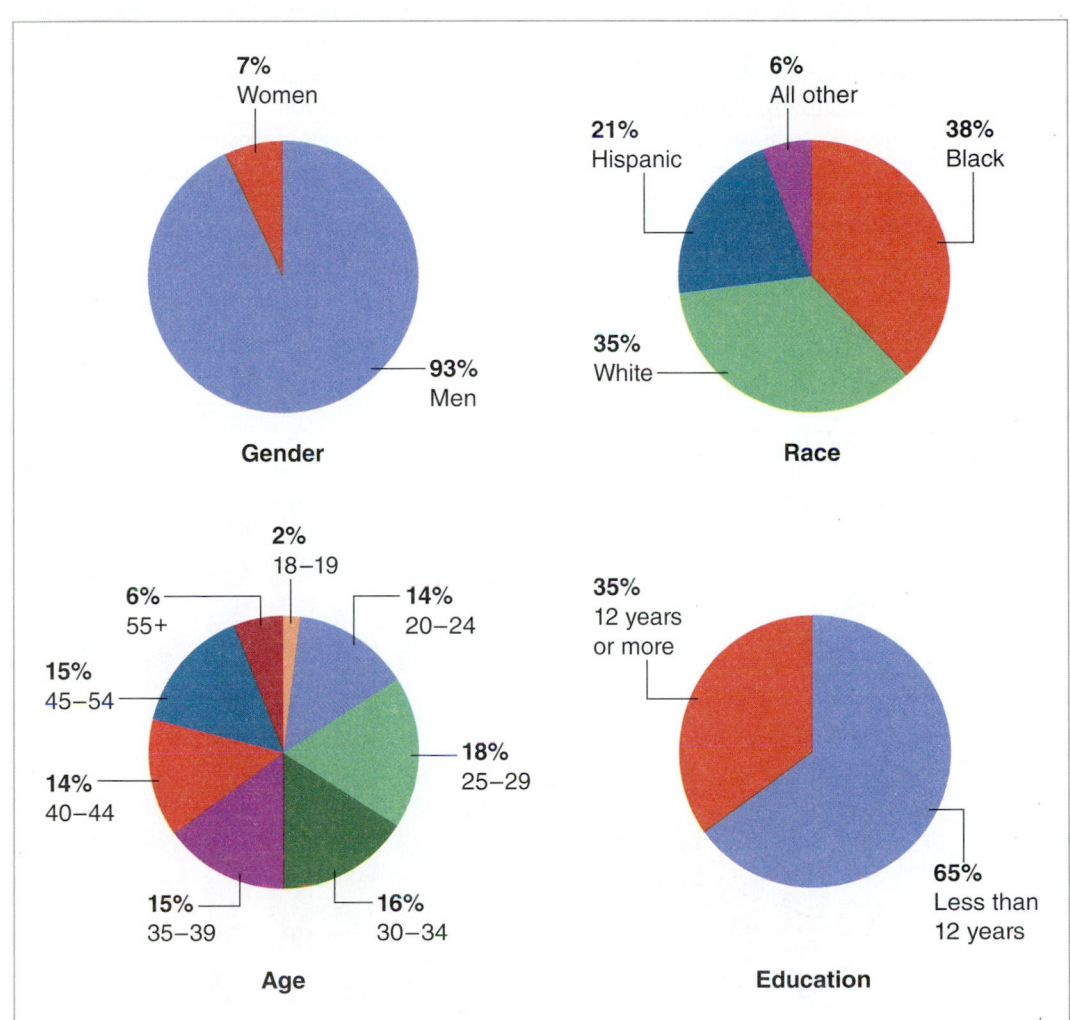

EXHIBIT 11.2 U.S. Prison Population Characteristics, 1975–2010: Gender, Race, Age, Education

Source: Bureau of Justice Statistics

Jails and Detention Centers

As noted earlier, the difference between a prison and a jail is an important one. Prisons are correctional institutions maintained by the federal and state governments for the confinement of convicted felons. Jails are typically local facilities for the temporary detention of (1) defendants awaiting trial or disposition on federal or state charges and (2) convicted offenders with short sentences for minor crimes. Historically, however, jails have been somewhat more than this; they have been used for holding many types of outcasts, suspects, and offenders.[22]

A variety of facilities and structures are referred to as *jails*. Depending on the jurisdiction and locale, they might be also called *lockups, detention centers,* or *town, city,* and *county jails.* Regardless of the terminology, however, all are used for temporary or short-term detention. Some are small and can hold only a few inmates; others can house many hundreds, even thousands, of prisoners. Jail systems vary widely in organization and jurisdictional authority. There are county jails, which are under the jurisdiction of the local sheriff, and city jails, which are under the authority of the chief of police. There are also independent correctional facilities, not tied to any jail "system" as such. In many urban areas, for example, each police precinct has its own lockup, which holds suspects during the questioning and booking stages of processing. In this phase, the jailing authority is in the hands of the precinct captain and the city police commissioner.[23] Prisoners are then shifted to one of many city or county jails or detention centers. In some states—Alaska, Connecticut, Delaware, Rhode Island, and Vermont, for example—all jails fall under the authority of a single state agency. Finally, the federal system has numerous detention centers throughout the United States under the jurisdiction of the Federal Bureau of Prisons.

The jail, then, is often the entrance to the criminal justice correctional system. Except for defendants who post bail while still in initial police custody, most arrestees are placed in jail, even if only for a short period. In 2011, the nation had more than 3,500 local jails, holding an estimated total of 735,601 inmates.[24] As you can see from Exhibit 11.3, the average daily population in American jails has dropped in recent years.

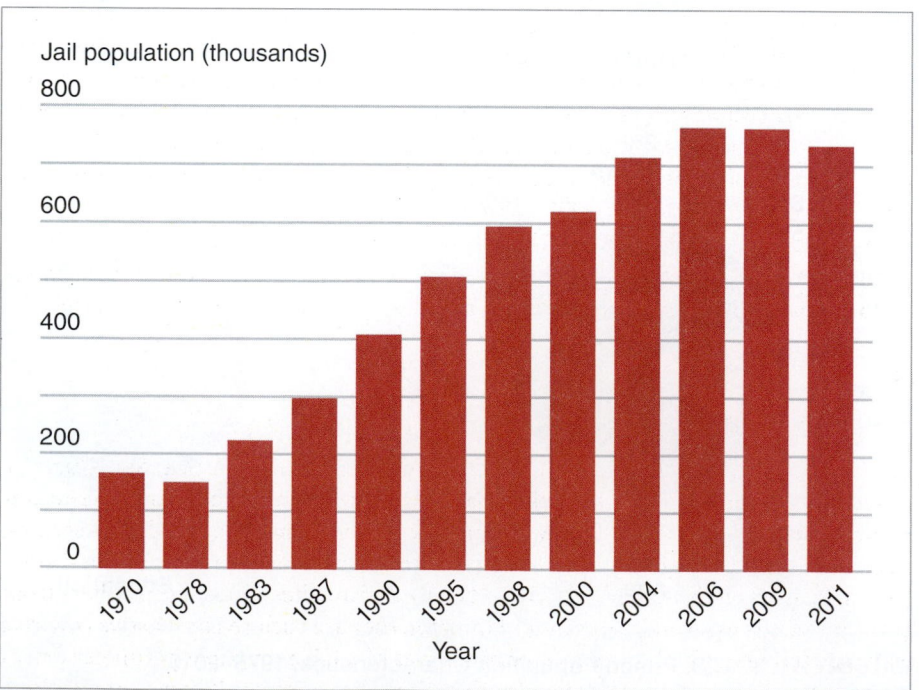

EXHIBIT 11.3   Average Daily Jail Population, 1970–2011
Source: Bureau of Justice Statistics

Adults represented 99 percent of all jail inmates in 2010, with males accounting for 87.7 percent. At midyear 2011, whites represented 45 percent of all jail inmates, blacks represented 38 percent, and Hispanics represented 15 percent. In contrast, the 2010 Census found that the distribution of race across the general population was 72 percent white, 12.6 percent black, and 16.3 percent Hispanic.[25] These distributions have remained nearly stable since the midyear statistics of 2000.

In addition to offering this kind of snapshot of the jail population, survey data reflect the traditional, twofold function of the jail: (1) as a place for the temporary detention for those awaiting trial and (2) as a confinement facility where many people who have been convicted of crimes, primarily misdemeanors, serve their sentences. As of 2010, 61 percent of all jail inmates were unconvicted, either not arraigned or arraigned and awaiting trial. The balance comprised either sentenced offenders or convicted offenders awaiting sentencing.[26]

An inmate, Noah Pope, once contended, "jail is for the poor, the street is for the rich."[27] This is borne out by contemporary survey data. The median annual income of jail inmates is below the poverty level; most have less than a high school education and are under age 30. As such, the U.S. jail population consists primarily of poor inmates who are both young and uneducated.[28]

TYPES OF CORRECTIONAL INSTITUTIONS

In discussing prisons and what happens within their walls, we begin with the concept of a **total institution**—a place that erects barriers to social interchange with the world at large.[29] In total institutions, large groups of people live together, day and night, in a fixed area and under a tightly scheduled sequence of activities imposed by a central authority.

Correctional institutions are total institutions organized to protect the community against what are viewed as dangers in the form of criminal offenders. Correctional institutions may be called *penitentiaries* or *reformatories,* but they also comprise many kinds of training schools, ranches, farms, and camps. In the United States, residential correctional institutions have traditionally been divided into three major categories, according to their construction and the measures used to maintain control. This produces three levels of custody or security: maximum, medium, and minimum. Many institutions house inmates at multiple levels of security. Larry Hope, the inmate discussed in the chapter-opening case, was housed at Limestone Correctional Facility in Alabama, a minimum- to medium-security facility. A fourth category—the open institution—differs dramatically from the other three.[30]

The nature of an offender's prior criminal history and characteristics of the current offense determine the security level of the confinement. Many state correctional agencies have clear policies about the transfer of inmates between security levels, including ways for offenders to earn lower levels of security if they cooperate with the institutional policies. We examine the types of institutions in more detail in the next sections.

DISCRETION MATTERS

What characteristics of the offender or the offense might correctional staff take into consideration when determining what level of security and type of facility is appropriate for the inmate?

Maximum-Security and Supermax Facilities

The most famous prisons in the United States are Sing Sing, Attica, San Quentin, Leavenworth, and the now-closed Joliet and Alcatraz prisons. These are **maximum-security prisons**—walled fortresses of concrete and steel that house the most serious, aggressive, and incorrigible offenders. Most maximum-security prisons have a similar design, focused on the secure custody and control of inmates. Housing anywhere from many hundreds to several thousands of inmates, they are enclosed by massive concrete walls, sometimes as high as 30 feet, or by a series of double- or triple-perimeter fences often electrically charged and topped with barbed wire or razor ribbon. Located along the outer-perimeter walls are well-protected guard towers, strategically placed to provide correctional officers with a vantage to easily observe prison yards and the areas

The outside wall of the infamous Green Haven Correctional Facility in Stormville, New York.

surrounding the prison. New York's Green Haven Correctional Facility is typical, if not an exaggeration, of this high-control design.[31] Built during World War II, leased to the military, and acquired by New York in 1949, Green Haven was designed to be an escape-proof institution. The mile-long wall of reinforced concrete around the perimeter is 30 feet high and almost 3 feet thick and is said to go 30 feet below the ground. Twelve towers, reaching 40 feet above the ground, are evenly positioned along it. Tower officers armed with shotguns, rifles, and teargas guns have a sweeping view of both sides of the wall. The towers also provide focused surveillance of no-man's-land, a 100-foot-wide stretch of open space between the inner and outer walls of the prison, across which nothing and no one can pass unobserved. No one has ever managed to successfully escape over the wall at Green Haven.[32]

A characteristic feature of the maximum-security prison is the inside cell block. Inside cells are constructed back-to-back, with corridors running along the outside shell of the cell house. In contrast to outside cells, which are affixed to the outside walls of the cell house, inside cells are considered more secure. Whereas escape through the window or wall of an outside cell would place an inmate in the prison yard, escape from an inside cell would leave the prisoner still within the cell block. Each tier of cells is called a cell block, and the cell house may contain as many as ten such blocks. The cell blocks are self-contained security enclosures, often partitioned off from one another by a series of gates and pens. This creates a complex of miniature prisons within the penitentiary, increasing overall security. Such a pattern is doubly effective because each cell house is similarly separated from all others.[33]

The emphasis on preventing escape from these institutions also includes tool-proof steel construction, multiple lock devices, frequent shakedowns (searches) and inmate counts, infrared sensing devices, and digital cameras monitoring the population. In the construction of modern maximum-security prisons, however, the trend is to move away from the double and triple security patterns—particularly the massive outside walls—because of their prohibitive cost. Instead, more prisons are using technologically sophisticated security devices. As prison administrators attempt to reduce expenses associated with managing the prisons, many turn to new and more cost-effective monitoring devices. Advanced, network-enabled cameras have been installed in many facilities, including Indiana's U.S. Penitentiary at Terre Haute. These monitoring devices digitally and continuously record the facility using 360-degree cameras.[34]

One type of high-security facilities is the *supermax prison*. Often referred to as a *secured* or *special housing unit*, a *maximum-control facility*, or just a *maxi-maxi*, the supermax prison is a highly restrictive, high-custody housing unit within a secure institution (or an entire secure penitentiary) that isolates inmates from the general prison population and from each other, due to the especially serious nature of inmates' crimes, repetitive assaultive or violent institutional behavior, the threat of (or actual) escape from a high-custody facility, or the threat of (or actual) inciting of disturbances in a correctional institution.[35]

Medium-Security Prisons

While medium-security facilities reproduce the basic pattern of the maximum-security prison, they have fewer internal fortifications. These prisons are rarely fortresslike structures with high stone walls. Rather, the perimeters are marked by a series of fences and enclosures with fewer guard towers. Outside cells are characteristic,

Offenders housed in medium-security prisons, like the one pictured here, often live in large dormitories and sleep on bunk beds, with their private things stored in foot lockers.

and in the newer structures, banks of dormitories and other types of shared living quarters are becoming common.

The inmates placed in medium-security institutions are considered less danger-ous and less escape-prone than those in the more security-oriented institutions. Their movements within the facility are less controlled, and surveillance is less vigilant. However, these prisons generally do have a maximum-security unit that can be used to house inmates who become custodial problems or threats to the safety of other prisoners.[36]

Minimum-Security Prisons

Minimum-security institutions typically operate without armed guards, without walls, and sometimes even without perimeter fences. The inmates of these facilities are considered to be low security risks—the most trustworthy and least violent offend-ers, those with short sentences, and white-collar criminals. A great deal of personal freedom is allowed, dormitory living is common, educational release is encouraged, and the level of surveillance is low. Placement in minimum- and medium-security facilities may also be earned as inmates in higher-security facilities show rehabilitative patterns of behavior, including successful fulfillment of treatment and/or educational programs, ability to follow the rules of the institution, and a general intent to change their pattern of past criminality.

Some of the newest minimum-security prisons have a villagelike atmosphere. One such facility in Vienna, Illinois, for example, does not look like a penal institution at all. Buildings resembling garden apartments are built around a "town square," com-plete with churches, school, shops, and a library. Paths lead to "neighborhoods," where "homes" provide private rooms in small clusters. Extensive provisions have been made for both outdoor and indoor recreation, and academic, commercial, and vocational education facilities equal or surpass those of many technical high schools.[37]

Minimum-security facilities like this one and others that house white-collar criminals—built on what has become known as the "cottage plan"—have often been criticized as being more like country clubs than prisons. Yet despite the attractiveness of their physical layout and resources, they nonetheless serve as effective barriers to the outside world.

DISCRETION MATTERS

Why might correctional officials need the discretion to transfer inmates between units and institutions?

Open Institutions

As a departure from the traditional maximum-, medium-, and minimum-security prisons, which are essentially closed institutions, some minimum-security facilities serve as "prisons without walls." These prison farms, camps, ranches, vocational training centers, and forestry settlements are innovations designed to decrease the cost of incarceration while providing low levels of security for the community. The modern counterparts of the nineteenth-century reformatories for youthful offenders and young adult felons, they provide instructive work for inmates within an environment conducive to behavioral change.[38]

These **open institutions** have numerous advantages over more traditional correctional facilities. They relieve the problem of overcrowding in other types of institutions; they are less costly to construct and maintain; and they enable various types of prisoners to be separated, thus reducing opportunities for contamination of attitudes. Moreover, they have economic and community service advantages. Prisoners in open camps produce crops and dairy products for use in the state correctional system and other government facilities. Ranches employ inmates in cattle raising and horse breeding. Forestry camps are used to maintain state parks, fight forest fires, and aid in reforestation. Finally, these camps and farms avoid many of the negative aspects of the traditional total institutions. Regulation and regimentation is more relaxed, and greater freedom of movement is possible.[39]

CORRECTIONAL ADMINISTRATION

Until the beginning of the twentieth century, correctional facilities were most commonly administered by individual wardens or by commissions or boards of control made up of prominent citizens.[40] Historically and generally, then, most facilities operated independently, without consistent policies or procedures across an entire system of corrections. Few jurisdictions had a state department of corrections. Governors appointed individual wardens through the system of political patronage, and institutional staff members held their positions by virtue of their political connections. While governors made hiring and budgetary decisions, the leadership roles and the administrative procedures of individual institutions were under the absolute control of the wardens. Today, every state has some form of centralized department of corrections that establishes policy for all institutions within its jurisdiction.

The two most common forms of correctional systems are subdivisions of a larger state department, such as justice or welfare, and independent structures. The U.S. Bureau of Prisons, for example, is a division of the U.S. Department of Justice; and in Virginia, the Department of Corrections is a segment of the Office of Public Safety. In contrast, California, Arkansas, Texas, Florida, and numerous other states have independent departments of corrections with lines of authority running directly to the governors' offices.[41] Additionally, there are numerous local-level correctional institutions that have the same structure and function as the larger, more complex facilities.

In the following sections, we examine typical administrative features of correctional facilities, including their personnel, their systems for classifying inmates, their programs for inmates, and their approach to discipline. While these features differ across the various state and federal systems, they also have many similarities.

Corrections Personnel

At the top of the administrative hierarchy of any department of corrections is the commissioner of corrections. This executive works directly under the governor to establish policy, shape institutional procedures, negotiate annual budgetary allotments for the various institutions, and make major personnel decisions. In local facilities, the organizational administrator will typically report to some other locally elected official, such as a mayor.

The head of each prison, generally appointed by the commissioner of corrections, is called a *warden, director,* or *superintendent,* depending on the state. In the past, the position of warden was one of great power, but also of questionable reputation because of its association with the political "spoils system." Although such arrangements persist in a few jurisdictions, most wardens and superintendents today are civil service employees who have earned their positions on a seniority or merit basis and receive no more fringe benefits than other state employees.

The job of the warden or superintendent is to manage the institution. In large institutions, the warden may be assisted by one or more associates: a deputy warden in charge of discipline, security, inmate movement and control, and prison routine; a second deputy in charge of prison programs, records, library services, mail and visitation, recreation, and release procedures; an industries manager in charge of correctional industries, farms, production, and supplies; and a medical supervisor in charge of prison health services and sanitation. Overall, the management of a prison is a major task, rivaling that of many large businesses and industries in its complexity. And interestingly, wardens rank exceptionally high in job satisfaction—well above most other professions.[42]

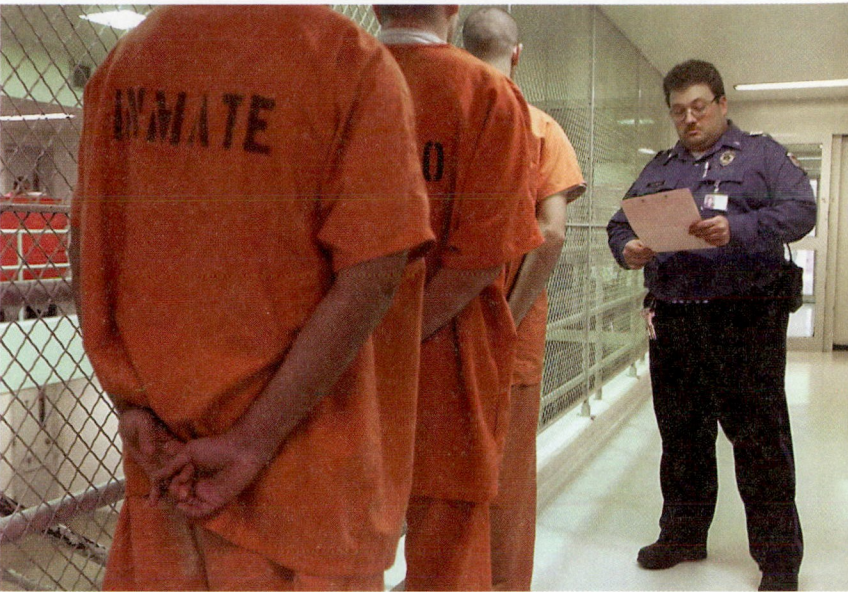

The job of corrections personnel is to ensure the safety of the community by providing proper care and supervision of inmates housed within an institution.

In addition to wardens, their deputies, and other administrators, prison personnel include both professional and custodial staff. Making up the professional staff are the counselors, physicians, nurses, dentists, chaplains, psychiatrists, psychologists, clerks and secretaries, teachers, counselors, and dietitians who deal with the institutional paperwork and serve the medical, spiritual, and treatment needs of the inmates. The size of the professional staff varies, depending on the institution and its orientation (custody versus rehabilitation). In large prisons, professionals constitute about one-third of the workforce. The custodial staff is made up of the corrections officers and their supervisors, whose basic functions fall into three areas: inmate security, movement, and discipline. Invariably, however, their roles go considerably further.

Guards are today referred to as *correction, correctional,* or *custodial officers.* Guarding is an often maligned profession, because people are repelled by the surveillance and control that are characteristic of prison life. The media are largely responsible for creating and sustaining this image. Film and television dramas portray the correctional officer as evil and savage. Without question, there are some corrupt and brutal custodial officers. However, the vast majority of correctional staff are professional and sincere as they go about their work maintaining the security of the institution.[43] In fact, if the popular image of the correctional officer were accurate, most prisons would not be able to function.

Correctional officers have difficult duties, which they perform under the most unpleasant circumstances. These men and women are responsible for the day-to-day care and operation of the correctional facilities. They supervise inmates, and they ensure that inmates have their basic needs met and participate in appropriate programs within the institution. Correctional officers are also ultimately responsible for the security of a correctional institution and, therefore, the larger community. Their careers entail being locked up in unattractive and often depressing environments, surrounded by hostile, restless, and sometimes desperate and violent inmates. They must always be watchful and always appear vigilant, alert, strong, competent, and self-confident. Burnout and stress are common problems for correctional officers.[44]

Classification of Inmates

An important function of prison administration is to determine the needs of inmates, a process referred to as **classification,** which occurs during the intake process. Theoretically, classification is the system by which a correctional agency matches the treatment and security programs of the institution with the requirements of the individual; the goal is to reduce the risk the inmate poses to the institutional operation and to meet the needs of the inmate.[45]

Classification goes beyond the mere separation of offenders on the basis of age, gender, custodial risk, or some other factor. It is based on diagnostic evaluation and treatment planning, followed by placement in the recommended institutional program or type of correctional facility.[46] The methods for classification tend to vary, however, not only from state to state but also among institutions within the same jurisdiction. Moreover, classification may occur within a variety of organizational structures. These include classification committees, reception and orientation units, and reception-diagnostic centers. The centers and units also provide orientation programs for new prisoners, giving them an overview of institutional life, routines, rules and regulations, and custodial and correctional expectations.

At a **reception center**, newly sentenced inmates are studied intensively for 20 to perhaps 90 days. These centers are generally staffed by psychologists, social workers, and other professionals. The staff members carry out a series of diagnostic studies and make recommendations to institutional authorities regarding the custodial, medical, vocational, and treatment needs of each incoming inmate. The classification report may also recommend an appropriate correctional facility for the inmate.[47]

The diagnostic procedure may range from a physical examination and a single interview to an extensive series of psychiatric and psychological tests, academic and vocational evaluations, orientation sessions, medical and dental checkups, and numerous personal interviews. Some classification programs also include analyses of athletic abilities and recreational interests, as well as contacts with religious advisers. Three factors generally combine to dictate how intensive the classification process will be: (1) available personnel, (2) inmate population size, and (3) type of classification system—that is, whether the classification is conducted in a reception and orientation unit of a prison facility, through an integrated classification committee, or at a separate reception-diagnostic center.[48]

When the testing and interviews have been completed, reports are prepared and placed in the inmate's case file. Summaries of the prisoner's social and family background, work history, criminal record, prior institutionalization (if any), current offense, and any other relevant background data are included. The classification board or committee may then evaluate the case file and makes recommendations. This board can range from a single counselor or social worker to as many as 15 members, including wardens, teachers, psychologists, physicians, researchers, members of the administrative and custodial staffs, chaplains, and experts from numerous other fields. The board discusses the various data and plans the inmate's correctional career. It is also responsible for reclassification, should the inmate's needs or situation change.[49]

The benefit of classification committees is that they bring multiple perspectives to the intake process. Their decisions are binding on the administration, and their approval is required before any changes can be made in the recommended program.[50] The integrated committee is the most widely used classification system in contemporary institutions. It permits professional and administrative staffs to work together in determining inmate needs, and at the same time it allows each group of personnel to gain some understanding of the problems the other group faces.

Correctional Programs

Institutional programs include a variety of activities, all of which can have an impact, either directly or indirectly, on the rehabilitation of offenders and their successful reintegration into the community after release. Research generally finds that

DISCRETION MATTERS

How might societal goals regarding corrections affect the discretionary decisions of staff when they classify inmates and determine their programming?

DISCRETION MATTERS

Which factors might influence the recommendations of classification committees regarding inmate placement or programming?

effective offender treatment and educational programs can reduce recidivism and increase offender employment after release.[51] Academic and vocational programs attempt to provide inmates with the skills necessary for adequate employment after release. Work programs serve many of the rehabilitative needs of the offender and, at the same time, contribute to the successful economic functioning of the institution. Some programs attempt to treat problems in an inmate's socialization and psychological development that may be responsible for the lawbreaking behaviors. Drug- and alcohol-abuse treatment programs try to help inmates overcome the spiral of addiction and substance abuse. Recreational programs have medical, social-psychological, and custodial motives; they are structured to ease the pressures of confinement, making inmates more receptive to rehabilitation and less depressed, hostile, and antisocial. And finally, medical programs and religious programs have implications for institutional management and the reintegration of the offender into the community.

Education Programs Most Americans have confidence in education as a mechanism for upgrading skills and understanding, shaping attitudes, and promoting social adjustment. Moreover, estimates place the average reading level of adult inmates at or below the fifth-grade level; more than half of all inmates have not finished high school; and even those who completed portions of formal education lag two or three grade levels behind what they completed in school.[52] It is not surprising, then, that academic education and vocational training are regarded as the primary rehabilitative programs in correctional institutions. In academic programs, the emphasis is on basic knowledge and communication skills. Most institutions have some sort of prison school, and in most state correctional systems, education for inmates is mandated by law. Courses of instruction vary from one institution to the next, ranging from literacy programs to high school equivalency studies to college-level curricula.

Correctional educational programs, however, are beset with difficulties. Many institutions are short on classroom facilities, useful teaching aids, and qualified instructors. Many inmates lack motivation, and teachers may be pressured to lower standards and complete false reports on inmate progress so that these programs will continue to receive funding and support from correctional administrators. The realities of prison security also can interfere with courses of instruction or curtail enrollments.[53]

Vocational programs focus on preparing inmates for meaningful employment after release. Most of the larger institutions and many small ones have a number of such programs, which provide training in automobile repair and maintenance, welding, sheet metal work, carpentry and cabinetmaking, plumbing and electricity, and radio and television repair. Like the academic programs, these too have some problems. Many facilities are poorly equipped and lack the appropriate technical staff; in others, the machinery and fittings are outmoded; and in some, the training is in fields in which jobs are not available in the outside world. Moreover, inmates who have acquired skills in such areas as plumbing, electrical work, carpentry, and masonry are often barred from joining unions upon release because of their criminal records. Although almost one-fourth of inmates in U.S. prisons participate in academic and vocational programs each year, at least half of all state prisons have made significant cuts in their educational programs. Generally, cutbacks appear to be motivated by shrinking state budgets and the costs associated with increases in the inmate population. Nevertheless, limiting funds for education programs may prove to be a costly choice in the long run. Studies demonstrate that inmates who participate in academic and vocational programs have lower recidivism rates than those who do not.[54]

Despite the many difficulties, the prospects for academic and vocational programs in contemporary corrections are not entirely bleak. Administrators of many institutions have encouraged community volunteers and local school districts to aid in tutoring more-motivated inmates; prison routines have been made more flexible for those who wish to attend classes; federal funds have been allocated for upgrading many prison schools; self-taught computer courses in elementary and secondary

Inmate participation in work and school is mandatory in many states.

school subjects have become more available; and a growing number of prison systems are introducing college-degree programs. Moreover, the need for more relevant vocational education has also been recognized.

Correctional Labor and Industry   Closely related to vocational training in correctional institutions are work and industrial programs. These can provide numerous opportunities for inmates to earn wages and develop regular work habits while serving their terms. They can also gain experience in machine operation, manufacturing, computer technology, and other specialized skills. In addition, such programs ease the boredom of institutional confinement.

In the past, the major industrial jobs included printing and the production of auto tags, road signs, clothing, and similar articles; nonindustrial jobs have included such tasks such as janitorial work, laundry work, and simple maintenance work.[55] As a historical note, before 1979 the chief outlet for prison-made products was the state, because both state and federal legislation barred prison industrial production from competing with private enterprise. However, Congress passed legislation in 1979 that lifted the ban on the interstate transportation and sale of prison-made goods, resulting in an increase in the number of inmates employed in prison industries.[56] Currently, prison industries are involved in the production of data-entry and telephone-answering equipment, optical ware, mattresses, flags, furniture, and cleaning equipment and supplies. In addition, inmates are employed in meatpacking, vehicle repair, picture framing, Braille translation, silk screening, fruit and vegetable production, and many other types of work.[57]

In spite of this progress, however, prison industries in many correctional institutions continue to suffer from the problems of years past. Only a minority of inmates are employed in meaningful jobs, because prison industrial plants are costly to construct, equip, maintain, and keep up to date. Moreover, because housing an inmate in a correctional institution is prohibitively expensive—costs range from $10,000 per inmate per year in some jurisdictions to more than $45,000 in others—inmates' wages are kept low, with most of the profits going into state treasuries. Consequently, inmates have little motivation to work hard and make prison industries successful. Nonetheless, many do work very hard and contribute to the success of the programs.

Clinical Treatment Programs   Academic and vocational programs are often viewed as the primary rehabilitative tools that correctional institutions offer. If inmates can learn the necessary skills to obtain and keep a job after release, the thinking goes, then they will be less likely to return to careers in crime. In this sense, academic and vocational programs can be viewed as treatment programs, for correctional treatment has generally meant explicit activities designed to alter or remove conditions that may lead to criminal behavior.[58] In a clinical sense, however, institutional treatment programs are specifically oriented toward resolving personal, emotional, and psychological problems that are related to lawbreaking behavior.

Counseling, social casework, psychological and psychiatric services, and group therapy are at the core of clinical treatment programs in correctional facilities. In this context, *counseling* refers to a relationship in which the therapist attempts to understand the prisoner-client's problems and help him or her solve them through discussion rather than advice or admonition.[59] *Social casework* is a process that (1) develops the prisoner-client's case history, (2) deals with immediate problems involving personal and familial relationships, (3) explores long-range issues of social adjustment, and (4) provides supportive guidance for any anticipated plans or activities.

Psychological and psychiatric services provide more intensive diagnosis and treatment aimed at (1) discovering the underlying causes of individual maladjustments, (2) applying psychiatric techniques to improve behavior, and (3) providing consultation to other staff members. These three modes of treatment involve direct interaction between a clinician and a prisoner-patient on an individual, one-to-one basis. Treatment in a group setting includes one or more clinicians plus several inmate-patients. The most common treatment format in the correctional setting is group therapy. Such programs have been variously referred to as *group psychotherapy, group therapy, group-guided interaction, group counseling,* and numerous other interchangeable terms.

Correctional institutions use these four models of clinical treatment—counseling, casework, psychological and psychiatric services, and group therapy—to deal with general issues associated with criminality and bring about behavioral change. They are also used to address the problems of specific kinds of offenders, such as sexual deviates and substance abusers. However, these clinical treatment services are not available in most institutions, and only a modest number of prisons have a resident psychiatrist. And although reception centers have significant numbers of psychologists, social workers, and other clinicians, the primary activity of these professionals is diagnosis rather than treatment. More common in contemporary correctional facilities are counselors; however, they generally deal with inmates' confrontations with the day-to-day pressures of institutional life rather than with any long-term treatment goals. Moreover, counselors rarely have any clinical training or experience. The position of correctional counselor is often an entry point to a criminal justice career, and for most counselors, it is their first job after graduating with an undergraduate degree.[60]

Drug-Abuse Treatment Today, much of the increased activity and backlog in the criminal justice system is an outgrowth of the nation's war on drugs. This is particularly apparent in correctional agencies and facilities (Exhibit 11.4). In fact, nationally, perhaps three-fourths of all inmates have histories of substance abuse.[61]

One approach to this upsurge in drug-abusing offenders has been to increase the capacity of correctional facilities. Another has been to expand drug-abuse

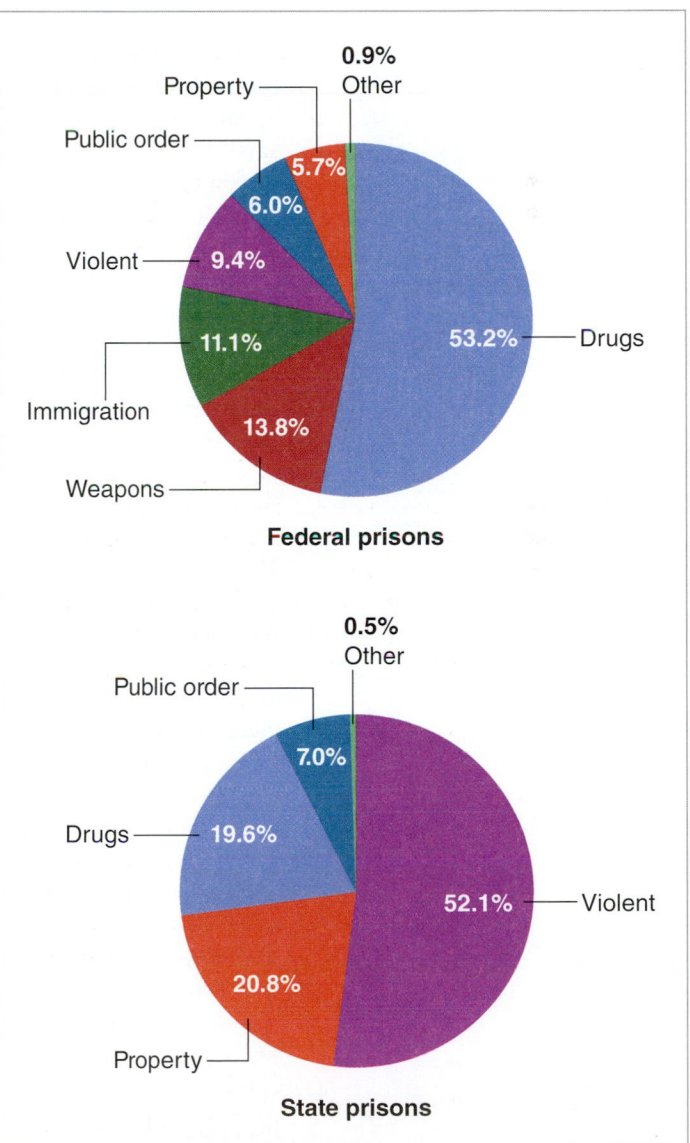

EXHIBIT 11.4 Reasons for Incarceration: Federal and State Prisons

Source: Department of Justice

treatment services. All of the states and the federal system have some sort of drug-treatment services for inmates. In addition to the four models of clinical treatment described earlier, institution-based drug-rehabilitation strategies often include the therapeutic community. More commonly referred to as a *TC*, the *therapeutic community* is a total treatment environment established in a separate residential unit of a prison.[62] TC participants are kept separate from other inmates and assigned to separate work, school, and recreational programs. The purpose of the TC is to create a partnership between prisoners and clinicians. The work supervisors, teachers, counselors, correctional officers, and other staff members involved with TC inmates become part of the treatment regimen and are regarded as agents of behavioral change.[63] Group therapy is the primary treatment method, but the peer-pressure characteristic of group therapy appears in other daily routines as well.

Health and Medical Services The number and types of programs and services available to inmates vary widely by both jurisdiction and institution. Every prison has some form of a health and medical program, although some institutions provide only the most basic medical care. All reception centers have comprehensive medical facilities with separate hospital units, some of which have well-equipped operating rooms. Similar facilities are also found in the larger institutions.

Smaller institutions use a range of medical and health alternatives. Some have small hospital units with a full-time physician or nurse and paraprofessionals who are on hand for the day-to-day care of minor illnesses and injuries. If there is no physician on the institutional staff, a physician from the local community visits on a regular basis. All but the largest prisons and reception centers contract out for the services of dentists and opticians.

The importance of adequate medical care cannot be overstated. Poor diet, alcoholism and drug abuse, and histories of inadequate medical attention are disproportionately evident among prison inmates.[64] Moreover, the communicability of even the most minor illnesses is high within a population that is confined in such close quarters. The prison medical unit is also responsible for monitoring sanitary conditions and inmate dietary needs, for these, too, are directly related to the well-being of the institution as a whole.

Religious Programs The availability of spiritual services for prison inmates has a long history in American corrections. Almost two centuries ago, solitary meditation was the theoretical basis of reform in the first American penitentiary, Philadelphia's Walnut Street Jail. Penitence was encouraged by frequent visits from missionaries and local clerics. Over the years, various Christian denominations and other religious organizations have devoted their time to the spiritual needs of inmates and have provided ongoing programs of religious instruction.[65]

Opinions as to the usefulness of religious programs in prisons are decidedly mixed. Such programs have been praised by wardens as anchors of law and order, by chaplains as powerful treatment forces, and by some inmates as sources of inspiration and cushions against despair. At the same time, however, they have been heavily criticized. Many prison administrators view religious counseling as useless and as a source of trouble and dissension; inasmuch as some jurisdictions prohibit the searching or questioning of clergy, chaplains have also been viewed as potential security risks.

Prison Discipline

When they entered Connecticut State Prison in 1830, inmates were presented with a list of six rules and regulations:

1. Every convict shall be industrious, submissive, and obedient, and shall labor diligently and in silence.

2. No convict shall secrete, hide, or carry about his person any instrument or thing with intent to make his escape.

3. No convict shall write or receive a letter to or from any person whatsoever, nor have intercourse with persons within the prison, except by leave of the warden.

4. No convict shall burn, waste, injure, or destroy any raw materials or article of public property, nor deface or injure the prison building.

5. Convicts shall always conduct themselves toward officers with deference and respect; and cleanliness in their persons, dress, and bedding is required. When they go to their meals or labor, they shall proceed in regular order and in silence, marching in the lockstep.

6. No convict shall converse with another prisoner, or leave his work without permission of an officer. He shall not speak to, or look at visitors, nor leave the hospital when ordered there, nor shall he make any unnecessary noise in his labor, or do anything either in the shops or cells, which is subversive of the good order of the institution.[66]

Over the years, lists of inmate rules have grown longer, reaching into every aspect of inmate life. Regulations in most prisons number well into the hundreds. Some rules are general, pertaining to the orderly operation and safety of the institution:

> Orders shall be obeyed promptly.
>
> Fighting is prohibited.
>
> Locking devices will not be tampered with.

Others are of questionable value:

> Long-sleeved sweatshirts will not be worn under a short-sleeved shirt.
>
> Only one cribbage board per man.[67]

New York's Attica Correctional Facility even has a regulation governing the number of times an inmate may kiss a visitor. Although one may consider the number of rules extreme and their content trivial, they all found their way into inmate handbooks for very specific reasons. Some were designed to prevent disturbances, violence, and escapes; others were meant to ensure the health and safety of both inmates and staff; still others were imposed to maintain the orderly movement of prisoners and the flow of institutional life. Many regulations, however, are strictly punitive or, as in the military, deemed necessary to provide regimentation, preserve order, and define the boundaries of inmate status. Conversely, a variety of regulations have evolved with the goal of creating a self-respecting prison community and instilling standards that will contribute to successful adjustment after release.

A major issue in inmate regulation is prison contraband. **Contraband** is officially defined as any item that can be used to break a rule of the institution or assist in escape. Such articles as drugs, alcohol, knives, guns, bombs, and vaulting poles are contraband. One of the most significant challenges in modern institutions is the smuggling of cell phones. Permitting access to the outside world, these can pose a serious risk to community safety. In practice, however, contraband becomes anything that the custodial staff designates as undesirable, and the banning power is unrestricted.[68]

Contraband is uncovered by means of periodic searches of prisoners and their cells or dormitories, and rule-breaking is either observed or discovered directly by a custodial officer or indirectly through inmate informers. In many instances, the violations are more or less ignored; sometimes the correctional officer will simply give the inmate a warning and, if minor contraband is involved, confiscate it. In more serious cases, there are formal disciplinary proceedings with many due process safeguards.

The major violations in prisons—at least those that result in disciplinary hearings—involve gambling, sex, fighting, stealing, refusing to work, and contraband. Most inmates are fairly sophisticated when it comes to hiding serious contraband items such as

DISCRETION MATTERS

Why might correctional officers sometimes ignore the minor infractions of inmates?

drugs or weapons. Penalties for violations include solitary confinement, temporary loss of privileges, temporary lockdown (being kept in the cell during recreation periods), or loss of "good time" (time off for good behavior). Corporal punishment also occurs, but when it does, it is not part of official correctional policy. Numerous disciplinary violations can also affect an inmate's parole date, since institutional conduct is taken into account in parole release decisions.

Throughout this chapter, the focus has been the correctional system as it applies to adults. Juveniles are also subject to corrections as part of the process they go through as offenders. For insight into the system of corrections as it applies to young people, and how it conforms to and differs from the system for adult offenders, read the "Juvenile Justice in Context" feature.

JUVENILE JUSTICE IN CONTEXT

Juvenile Corrections

O nce a youth is adjudicated through the juvenile justice process, he or she will be sentenced. In the most severe cases, offenders will be given a sentence that includes placement in a juvenile correctional institution. However, like an adult offender, a juvenile may also be held in detention after arrest or while the offense for which he or she is being held is processed. In 2008, slightly more than 81,000 juvenile offenders were being held in residential correctional facilities around the country.[69] These institutions are of two main types. The first, referred to as *campus* or *cottage facilities,* are similar to facilities historically used to house female offenders. They are typically organized in campus-type environments, with dormitory rooms rather than cells, and they usually house offenders adjudicated for less serious offenses. The second type of institutions, often referred to as *detention facilities,* are usually reserved for serious juvenile offenders and often resemble medium-security institutions for adults. These are secure detention, training, and industrial facilities. In addition to these secure-type facilities, juvenile correctional institutions also include shelters; diagnostic centers for determining the needs of offenders and youth in need of services; group homes and halfway houses; boot, ranch, and wilderness camps; and residential treatment facilities.

As of 2010, nearly 80 percent of juveniles held in residential facilities were there for the commission of delinquency offenses or for behaviors that would have violated the criminal law if the offenders had been adults.[70] Less than 4 percent were being held for status offenses. Nineteen percent were being held for neither status nor delinquent

Inmates prepare to enter a dormitory at the Marlin Orientation and Assessment Unit, a Texas Youth Commission facility. As in adult correctional facilities, inmate movement in juvenile correctional facilities is strictly controlled.

offenses. They may have been referred for detention because they were victims of abuse or neglect or because they were emotionally disturbed or mentally handicapped. These offenders may have also been placed in the facilities by a parental referral.[71]

As of 2010, 35 percent of juvenile offenders were being held in correctional institutions for offenses against people (rather than property), 25 percent of those involving violent offenses.[72] Sixty-five percent of juvenile offenders in residential facilities were minority youth. Nationally, residential placement was highest for black youth. Female offenders accounted for just 13 percent of youths placed in juvenile residential facilities. More than one-third of females were held in private facilities.[73]

Juvenile facilities can be either public or private. Public facilities are operated by state or local governments, receive public funding, and are overseen by state or local government entities to ensure quality care of the youth in custody. Private facilities are operated by private nonprofit or for-profit corporations or organizations. Private facilities tend to be smaller than public institutions.[74] As of 2010, less than half of all juvenile facilities were publicly operated; however, these facilities held 69 percent of all juvenile offenders.[75]

Nearly all juvenile correctional facilities have a variety of treatment programs—counseling on an individual or group basis, vocational and educational training, recreational and religious programs, and medical and dental facilities. A number of institutions also provide legal services for juveniles, as well as substance-abuse treatment programs. Many of these programs have been found to decrease recidivism and aid rehabilitation.[76]

CONCLUSIONS

The American correctional system encompasses a complex network of local, state, and federal facilities and a diverse array of personnel. These institutions and the individuals who work in them are responsible for the incarceration of millions of offenders every year. The purposes of these facilities are to house and supervise offenders who are either awaiting trial or serving sentences and to protect the public and apply the punishment determined by courts across the nation. As the chapter-opening case involving Larry Hope demonstrates, multiple legal issues surround the confinement of offenders. A key issue centers on the use of discretion in responding to inmates' disruptive behavior.

SUMMARY AND REVIEW

■ **Identify key themes in the history of punishment, including the contributions of the classical school of criminology.**

- In the American colonial period, the most common forms of punishment were corporal.
- Prior to the eighteenth century, correctional ideas and practices across Europe and America varied, but they shared similar goals—taking vengeance, reducing crime, and protecting self and society.

- Criminal sanctions focused on retribution, banishment, isolation, and death; they were based on the reasoning that offenders were enemies of society who deserved punishment and that severe approaches would eliminate their potential for future crime. This punishment ideology has endured.
- The classical school of criminology, initially built on the writings of Cesare Beccaria, assumed that a person is a self-determining being, acting on reason

and intelligence, and therefore is responsible for his or her behavior. This perspective was instrumental in making the law impartial, reducing the harshness of penalties, and replacing the arbitrary powers of judges with a specified range of criminal sanctions. The shift in correctional philosophy stemming from the writings of the classical school led to the use of less severe forms of corporal punishment and a focus on imprisonment as a way to punish offenders.

■ **Describe the structure of corrections in the United States.**

- The federal corrections system is the most diversified prison system in the United States and is designed to house those convicted of federal criminal law violations. The first federal penitentiaries were authorized by Congress in 1891, and by 1905 institutions had been opened in Atlanta, Georgia, and Leavenworth, Kansas.
- The Bureau of Federal Prisons includes a graded system of institutions: maximum-security penitentiaries for the close custody of the most serious felons, medium-security facilities for those who are better prospects for rehabilitation, reformatories for young and inexperienced offenders, minimum-security prisons for federal offenders requiring little custodial control, detention centers for those awaiting trial and disposition, and a variety of halfway houses, work-release programs, and community treatment centers.
- By the middle of 2012, the Federal Bureau of Prisons was operating an integrated system of more than 100 adult and juvenile correctional facilities, housing more than 210,000 inmates, including those housed in private facilities.
- Each state has its own correctional system for offenders convicted of violating state criminal law. These vary dramatically in size and, to some extent, in philosophy, but each state system includes prisons, detention facilities, community correctional units, and facilities designed for reentry of the offender into society.
- The number of state facilities has grown to nearly 2,000; however, the number within individual states varies dramatically. In Texas, 114 individual facilities were operating in 2012, while Rhode Island had only 8. As of January 2010, more than 1.4 million individuals were housed in state prison facilities.

■ **Compare and contrast the types of correctional institutions operating in modern America.**

- Jails and detention centers are local facilities for the temporary detention of (1) defendants awaiting trial or disposition on federal or state charges and (2) convicted offenders who have been sentenced to short-term imprisonment for minor crimes.
- Maximum-security prisons house the most serious, aggressive, and incorrigible offenders and have the highest level of security and custody.
- The supermax prison is a highly restrictive, high-custody housing unit within a secure institution (or an entire secure penitentiary) that isolates inmates from the general prison population and from each other due to the especially serious nature of their crimes, repetitive assaultive or violent institutional behavior, the threat of (or actual) escape from a high-custody facility, or the threat of (or actual) inciting of disturbances in a correctional institution.
- Medium-security facilities reproduce the basic pattern of the maximum-security prison, but with somewhat less emphasis on internal fortification. The inmates placed in medium-security institutions are considered less dangerous and less escape-prone than those in the more security-oriented institutions. Their movements within the facility are less controlled.
- Minimum-security correctional institutions typically operate without armed guards, without walls, and sometimes even without perimeter fences. The inmates of these facilities are considered to be low security risks. A great deal of personal freedom is allowed, dormitory living is common, educational release is encouraged, and the level of surveillance is generally low.
- Open institutions are characterized as prisons without walls. These are the prison farms, camps, ranches, vocational training centers, and forestry settlements where regulation and regimentation is more relaxed, and greater freedom of movement is possible.

■ **Describe the typical administrative features of correctional institutions.**

- The Federal Bureau of Prisons and all state corrections systems are organized with a centralized department of corrections that establishes policy for every institution within its jurisdiction.

- The two most common forms of correctional systems are (1) those that are subdivisions of some larger state department, such as justice or welfare, and (2) those that are independent structures.
- At the top of the administrative hierarchy of any department of corrections is the commissioner of corrections. This executive works directly under the governor to establish policy, shape institutional procedures, negotiate annual budgetary allotments for the various institutions, and make major personnel decisions.
- The head of each prison, generally appointed by the commissioner of corrections, is a warden, director, or superintendent, depending on the state.
- In addition to wardens, their deputies, and other administrators, prison personnel include physicians, nurses, dentists, dietitians, chaplains, psychiatrists, psychologists, clerks and secretaries, teachers, counselors, custodial staff, and correctional officers. These people deal with the institutional paperwork and serve the medical, spiritual, and treatment needs of the inmates.

■ **List and describe the types of programs that commonly operate in correctional facilities.**

- Institutional programs include a variety of activities, all of which can have an impact, either directly or indirectly, on the rehabilitation of offenders and their successful reintegration into the community after release.
- Academic and vocational programs attempt to provide inmates with the skills necessary for adequate employment after release.
- Work programs serve many of the rehabilitative needs of the offender yet also contribute to the successful economic functioning of the institution.
- Treatment programs attempt to remove alleged "defects" in an inmate's socialization and psychological development that are responsible for some lawbreaking behaviors.
- Drug- and alcohol-abuse treatment programs try to help inmates overcome the spiral of addiction and substance abuse.
- Recreational programs have medical, social-psychological, and custodial motives; they are structured to ease the pressures of confinement, making inmates more receptive to rehabilitation and less depressed, hostile, and antisocial.
- Finally, medical and religious programs have implications for institutional management and reintegration of the offender into the community.

KEY TERMS

Cesare Beccaria (p. 292)
classical school of criminology and criminal law (p. 292)
classification (p. 302)

contraband (p. 307)
corporal punishment (p. 291)
jails (p. 291)
maximum-security prisons (p. 297)

open institutions (p. 300)
prisons (p. 291)
reception center (p. 302)
total institution (p. 297)

ISSUES FOR CRITICAL THINKING AND DISCUSSION

1. Which of Beccaria's ideas of punishment are reflected in current conceptions of corrections?
2. What changes could be made to better structure the corrections staff's use of discretion in their interactions with inmates?
3. In what ways is life in prison similar to that in the military or on the college campus?
4. What steps could be taken to change prisons into environments more suitable for rehabilitation and reform? Should we take these steps?
5. Should drug-abuse treatment be expanded within correctional institutions? Why or why not?

12

Life on the Inside: Institutional Conditions and Inmate Rights

LEARNING OBJECTIVES

- Describe the inmate experience, including the unique situation of women in prison.

- Explain the legal principles that allow inmates to challenge conditions of confinement.

- Describe the rights of inmates regarding religion, mail, rehabilitation, medical treatment, and institutional discipline.

- Describe the contemporary trends in confinement, including the privatization of prisons.

CHAOS BEHIND BARS

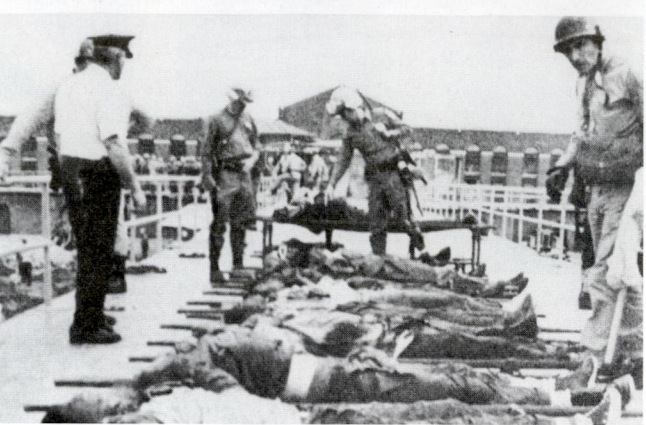

In the aftermath of the 1971 Attica prison riot, many questions were left unanswered about the conditions that lead to prison unrest, the need for correctional administrators to respond to inmate complaints, and the rights, if any, of prisoners.

For prisoners in Attica Correctional Facility in late 1971, correction meant little more than daily degradation and humiliation. They were locked in cells for 14 to 16 hours each day and worked for wages that averaged 30 cents a day. The jobs that were available held little or no vocational value, and prisoners had to follow hundreds of seemingly insignificant rules for which violation resulted in harsh punishment. In addition, inmates believed the prison routinely violated their privacy by reading and censoring their mail as well as screening and censoring radio programs and reading materials. Prisoners' movements outside their cells were tightly regulated. Patrolling officers observed while they used bathroom facilities, and visits with family and friends took place through a mesh screen, preceded and followed by invasive strip searches.[1]

The sources of inmate frustration and discontent did not end there. Prison meals were unpalatable, often devoid of any real nutrition. Inmates wore ill-fitting, old, and often inadequate clothing. Showers were allowed only once a week. Because they were not issued sufficient clothing, toiletries, or other items, prisoners had to make purchases from a commissary where prices did not reflect their low wages. To get along in the prison economy, inmates often resorted to criminal behavior. Medical care was only adequate to meet acute health needs and was often delivered in a callous and indifferent manner by doctors who feared and despised most of the offenders they treated. Moreover, inmates were often sexually victimized, and even the ticket to freedom for most

inmates—parole—was handled inequitably by correctional officials.[2]

For officers, a job in corrections meant a steady but monotonous 40-hour work week, with a pension after 25 years of service. Officers maintained custody and control over an ethnically diverse inmate population primarily from low-income inner-city neighborhoods—men whom the officers could not understand and were not trained to deal with. Many inmates responded to the officers and the overall conditions with aggressive confrontations. Thus, being a corrections officer boiled down to keeping inmates in line, seeing that everything ran smoothly, and enforcing the rules. It did not mean, for most officers, helping inmates solve their problems or preparing them to return to society. Always outnumbered by inmates, correctional officers felt a legitimate concern about security, but the institutional policies and conditions created a level of tension that was far more dangerous than the security risks they were intended to avert.[3]

Two incidents that occurred early in September sparked the 1971 prisoner uprising in Attica.[4] The first was a confrontation between inmates and officers in the prison yard; the second was the beating of two inmates by several officers. Then, on the morning of September 9, the inmates' anger coalesced, and because of a defective weld on a gate at a central point in the institution, the inmates quickly spread throughout the prison, attacking officers, taking hostages, and destroying property. By afternoon, the New York State Police had regained control of part of the prison, but most of the inmates had assembled in one of the exercise yards along with their 39 hostages, threatening to kill them if their demands were not met.[5]

Negotiations went on for days. Governor Nelson Rockefeller was asked to visit Attica to help with the negotiations and prevent a bloodbath, but he refused. On the morning of September 13, 1971, the commander of a local state police troop led an assault to retake the prison. Within 15 minutes, the uprising was over. However, 29 inmates and 10 hostages had been killed while many more were left wounded.[6]

According to the Supreme Court's ruling in *Ruffin v. Commonwealth* in 1871, "A convicted felon has, as a consequence of his crime, not only forfeited his liberty, but all of his personal rights except those which the law in its humanity accords him. He is for the time being a slave of the state."[7] Until the 1960s and into the 1970s, the opinion expressed in *Ruffin,* which maintained that prisoners have no legal rights, accurately reflected the judicial attitude toward correctional affairs. The conditions of incarceration and every aspect of institutional life were left to the discretion of the prison administration. Because prisoners were "slaves" of the state, privileges were matters of custodial benevolence, which wardens and correctional staff could alter at any time and without explanation. The courts maintained a steadfast **hands-off doctrine** regarding correctional matters until the 1960s, thus allowing correctional personnel and administrators to determine for themselves what was appropriate behavior in their treatment of inmates.

Several years after the Attica riot, in an unrelated case, *United States ex rel. Gereau v. Henderson,*[8] the U.S. Court of Appeals for the Fifth Circuit found that "prisoners are not stripped of their constitutional rights, including the right to due process." Thus, the hands-off doctrine began to lose its vitality, and during that

decade and the years that followed, prisoners were given the right to be heard in court regarding such matters as the widespread violence that threatened their lives and security, the problems of overcrowding, the nature of disciplinary proceedings, conditions affecting health and safety, regulations governing visitation and correspondence, and limitations on religious observance, education, work, and recreation. When the prisoners' rights movement began more than four decades ago, higher courts became the instruments of change in correctional policy.

After 28 years of litigation, the Supreme Court established that guards killed the hostages during the riot, and New York State was finally ordered to pay $8 million to the inmates who had been brutalized in the Attica riot.[9] The inmate uprising at New York's Attica Correctional Facility continues to be a case study of the conditions that bring about prison unrest—even now as American corrections moves through the twenty-first century. Even though reforms have been made throughout the system, correctional administrators and personnel have an enormous amount of discretion in how they treat inmates. For example, in a move toward more professionalism, national accrediting agencies, such as the American Correctional Association, have developed procedures and policies to guide the treatment of offenders. Still, the closed nature of correctional facilities keeps many of the decisions that officials make out of the public spotlight. This means that the experiences of many inmates are never scrutinized in the same way as are other aspects of the criminal justice system.

This chapter focuses on the experience of inmates within correctional institutions across America—and the balancing act that occurs between institutional discretion and constitutional principles such as due process and adherence to the law. We begin by examining the nature and conditions of confinement.

THE INMATE EXPERIENCE

Prisons and other correctional facilities are designed to separate inmates from the rest of society and provide punishment, by means of confinement, for their illegal behavior within our communities. The experience varies from one facility to the next and even from one prisoner to another. Nevertheless, some characteristics apply generally. In this section we explore those experiences, as well as the unique experience of women prisoners.

Conditions of Confinement

The primary task of correctional institutions is custody of inmates. The internal order of the institution is maintained by strictly controlling the inmates and regimenting every aspect of their lives. Thus, in addition to losing their freedom and basic liberties, goods and services, heterosexual relationships, and autonomy, inmates are deprived of their personal identities. When they enter a facility, they are stripped of their clothing and most of their personal possessions. They are also examined, inspected, weighed, documented, and given a number. The experience is intended to be uncomfortable both physically and psychologically. The modern intake process is also intended to transition the offender from street to institution, to identify the needs of the individual, and to provide appropriate programs, resources, and activities. Much of the inmate's experience in the institution will be focused on the plan developed by counselors and program staff, and it will hopefully reduce the likelihood that he or she will return to a criminal lifestyle upon release.

The rigors and frustrations of confinement leave only a few outlets for inmates. They can bind themselves to their fellow captives in ties of mutual aid and loyalty, typically in opposition to prison officials. They can wage a war against all, seeking their own advantage without regard for the needs and claims of others. Or they can simply withdraw into themselves. Most inmates combine characteristics of the first two. Affiliations with street gangs can help acclimate offenders to institutional life. Inmates who associated with gangs on the outside often find and associate with members on the inside in order to survive the institutional experience.

Exposure to the social system of the prison community is almost immediate, for all new inmates become quickly aware of the norms and values that their fellow inmates share. Within moments of arriving, they begin to internalize the rules and regulations of the institution, as well as the informal rules, values, customs, and general culture. The physical proximity in which inmates must live destroys much, if not all, of their privacy; prison regulations and routines push them toward conformity; and their physical isolation from the outside world limits their range of experience. Moreover, institutional life fosters a monotonous egalitarianism among inmates. Prisoners occupy similar cells; they wear the same clothes and eat the same food; and they do the same things at the same time and according to the same rules, regulations, and potential for disciplinary punishment. And all of this happens under the same

The intake process serves to identify medical, psychological, nutritional, and other needs of offenders. However, the body search can be one of the most invasive experiences of an inmate's life.

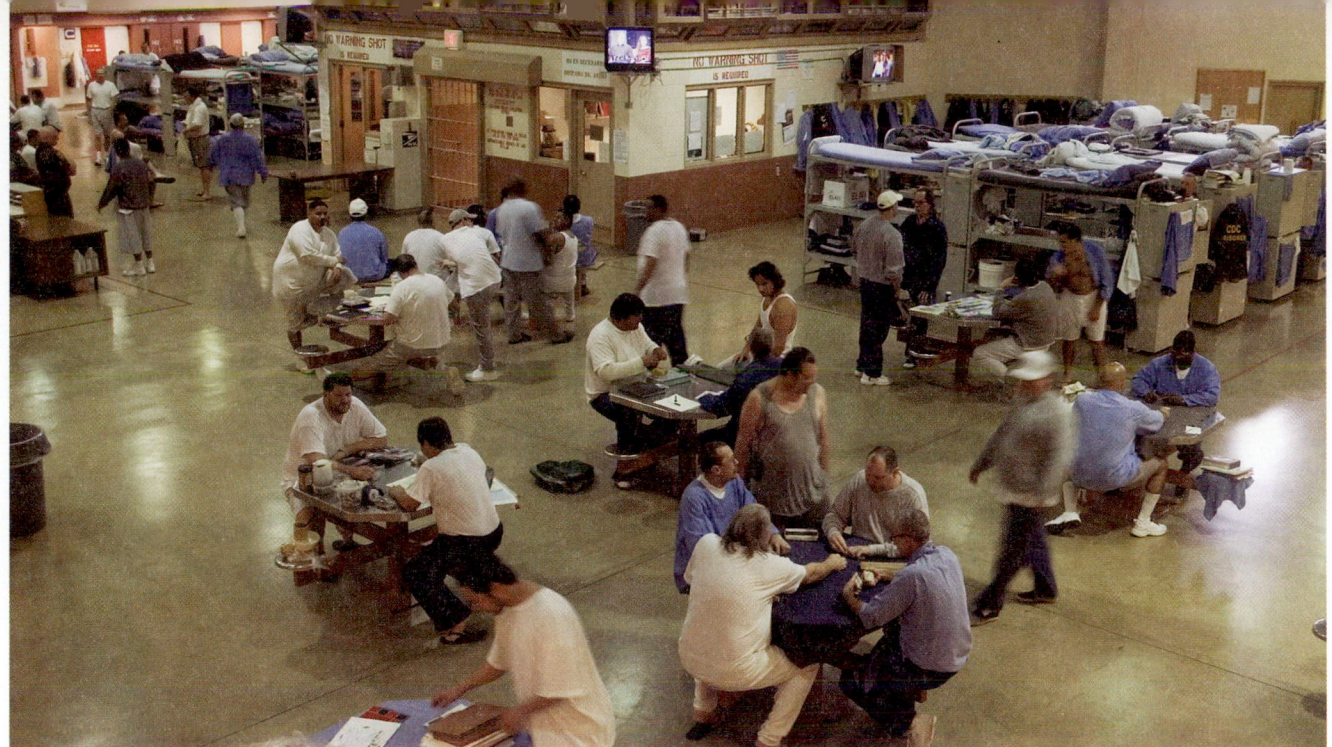
For inmates entering the correctional institution, interactions with other offenders can be a source of support—and conflict.

structure of authority—one that is direct, immediate, inescapable, and at times brutal. Almost everything prisoners have, or fail to have, can be traced to the structure and function of the institution.

In addition, every correctional institution has a subculture with its system of norms that influence prisoners' behavior, typically to a greater extent than the institution's formally prescribed rules. These subcultural norms are unwritten rules, but their violation can evoke sanctions from fellow inmates ranging from ostracism to physical violence or even death. The informal rules are referred to as the **inmate code.**[10]

Although the inmate code is violated regularly, many prisoners adhere to its major directives. They do so, however, not because it represents a "code of honor" but because it has a more serious implication—as a means of surviving the prison experience. Changes in the offender population, primarily related to the focus on drug offenses, have altered the inmate code. Inmates today are more likely to value the same toughness, respect, and authority they knew on the street or in their own communities, rather than the traditional codes of the correctional institution.[11]

Women in Prison

Before the twentieth century, women accounted for less than 1 percent of the adult felon prison population. However, from the 1970s through 2010, the proportion of women in state and federal correctional institutions increased from 2.9 percent to nearly 7 percent (Exhibit 12.1).[12] Despite the increase, these relatively low percentages have resulted in a series of rather disjointed and arbitrary policies for the incarceration of female offenders. Not until 1873, in Indianapolis, Indiana, was the first separate prison for women opened in the United States. Before that time, women were confined with men or held in isolation within small sections of men's penitentiaries and supervised by male wardens.[13] During the past 50 years, and especially over the past three decades, there has been a dramatic increase not only in the number of correctional facilities for women but also in the number of incarcerated women (Exhibit 12.2). Today, women are confined in separate prisons, in isolated wings of men's facilities, in coeducational facilities, and in open institutions.

The increasing number of women behind bars in many ways reflects tougher drug laws and mandatory sentencing policies. A survey of women inmates found that the

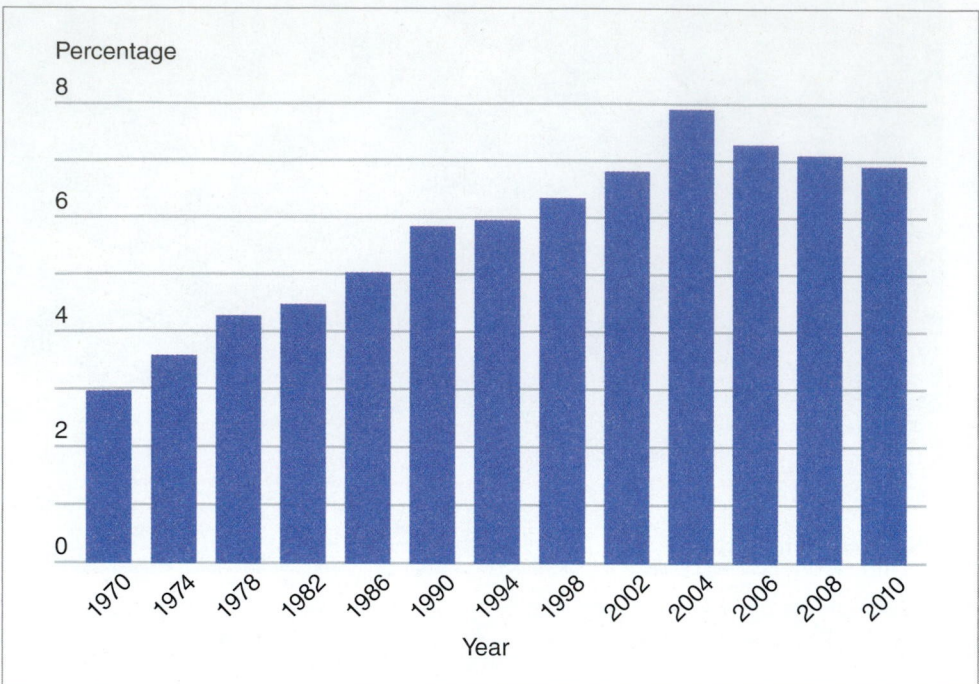

EXHIBIT 12.1   Proportion of Female Inmates in State and Federal Correctional Institutions, 1970–2010

Source: Bureau of Justice Statistics

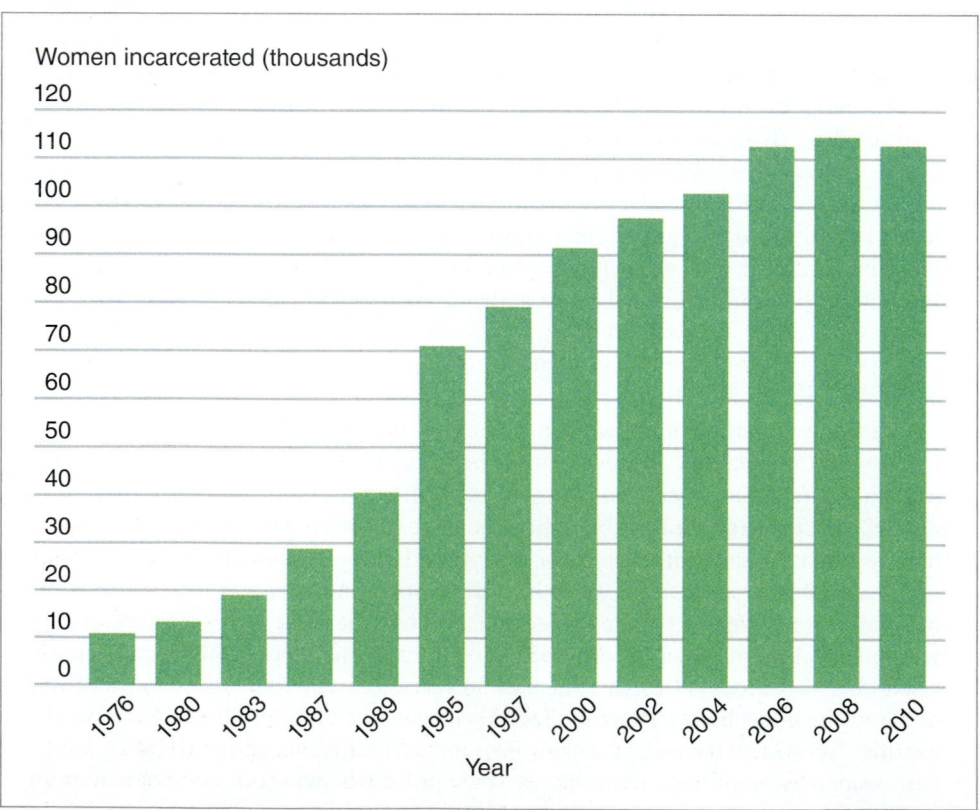

EXHIBIT 12.2   Female Inmates in State and Federal Institutions, 1976–2010

Source: Bureau of Justice Statistics

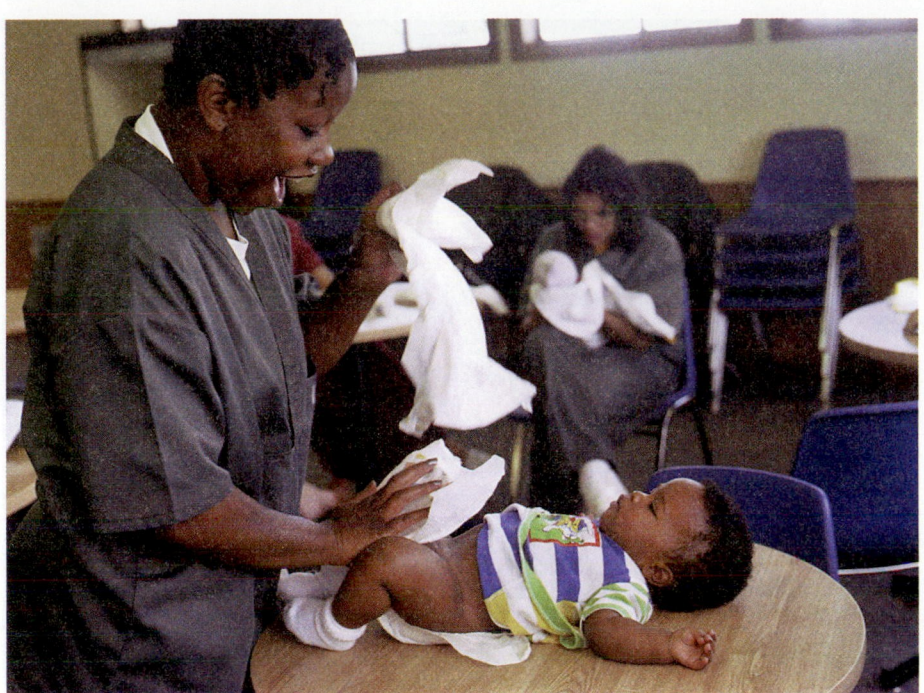

A mother changes the diaper of her son while another mother visits with her newborn baby in the visitor's center of the Colorado Women's Correctional Facility. The two incarcerated mothers get to visit with their children for three hours each week through a program run by the New Horizons Ministries, a Mennonite prison ministry that cares for the children of inmates and reconnects them with their parents following release.

majority were serving time for drug or drug-related and property charges, and less than a third were classified as violent offenders.[14] Despite the growing numbers of incarcerated women, many states have not adequately reformed their policies and programs for female offenders, though they have made definite advances. For example, many state institutions for women do not provide the range of educational and vocational opportunities and privileges available at most institutions for men. Research has found that a disproportionate number of female inmates are still involved in cleaning, kitchen, and manufacturing work, while male inmates participate in a far wider range of work initiatives.[15] The gender-typed nature of much vocational programming for women, such as food and cleaning services, is particularly problematic, since these types of jobs on the outside are notorious for their lack of benefits and low wages, making it difficult for women inmates (the great majority of whom are single parents) to achieve economic independence after release.[16]

An additional challenge posed by the growing incarceration of women centers on their children. In response, many correctional systems have developed structured arrangements whereby female inmates can have meaningful visits with family members in general and with their children in particular. At Bedford Hills Correctional Facility in New York, infants may remain with their mothers for up to 18 months, in nursery areas segregated from general housing. At the Nebraska Correctional Center for Women, among the rewards for good behavior are visits of up to five days a month by children between the ages of 12 months and 9 years. Other prisons have similar arrangements.[17] And at the Key Village, a drug-treatment program in a separate housing unit at the Baylor Women's Correctional Institution in New Castle, Delaware, two cells have been decorated as nurseries. Each weekend, two women have the opportunity to care for their infants from Friday afternoon to Sunday evening.[18] Female inmates who have these kinds of contacts with their children appear to adjust better not only to prison confinement but also to life in the community after release.[19]

Visits with children and family keep inmates connected to those on the outside. These connections also increase the effectiveness of rehabilitation programs on the inside.

Most studies of prison communities and inmate social systems have been carried out in men's institutions, and the findings are not fully applicable to women's prisons.[20] Perhaps this is because fewer women are convicted of crimes, and a greater proportion of those who are found guilty are placed on probation. However, we do have some data on the women's prison populations. First, those who do receive terms of imprisonment have typically been convicted of aggravated assault, check forgery, shoplifting, and violations of drug laws, with few serving time for burglary and robbery.[21] Second, women are far more likely than men to have committed a violent offense against someone they know.[22] Third, many women's prisons have an even greater proportion of minority group members than do institutions for men, but fewer of these women have had prior prison experiences. And although few female inmates in women's prisons are confined in cells, the more "open" nature of the women's institution often requires more frequent security checks and, hence, closer custodial supervision. As noted earlier, the great majority of female prisoners are mothers of young children, and in a growing number of institutions, children are living with their mothers for varying periods of time. All of these factors combine to affect the social order of female correctional institutions.[23]

The social system in women's prisons bears some resemblance to that in all-male facilities. For example, in both one finds particular social roles, an inmate code, and norms for interacting with correctional staff. Moreover, the social system of women inmates is defined in the same way as that of male inmates, for women belong to a micro-society potentially made up of four main groups. There are the "squares" from conventional society, who are having their first experience with custodial life. Many of these are members of the middle class. They see themselves as respectable people and view prison as a place where only "criminals" go. Most of them have been convicted of embezzlement or situational homicides. A second group can be labeled the "professionals," career criminals who view incarceration as an occupational hazard. Expert shoplifters fall into this group. They adopt a "cool" approach to prison life that involves taking maximum advantage of institutional amenities without endangering their chances for parole or early release. The third group, and perhaps the largest, is made up of repeat offenders who have had numerous experiences with the criminal justice system since their teenage years. Some are prostitutes who have assaulted and robbed their clients; many are thieves; and others are chronic drug users and sellers. For them, institutional life provides social status, often not found on the outside, and familial-type attachments that make institutional life more bearable. Finally, the culture includes the correctional staff, whose values and attributes are similar to those of staff in men's institutions.[24] Even as the rate of female incarceration has increased in some areas, the unique culture of female institutions persists.

Despite the institutional pressure toward conformity and relinquishment of individual identity, each inmate, whether male or female, has a unique experience, depending on the nature of the confinement and the offender's characteristics and personality. Moreover, the inmate experience is significantly affected by the laws surrounding the conditions of confinement, the subject we turn to next.

INMATE ACCESS TO THE COURTS

Over the past fifty years, conditions of confinement for inmates have changed dramatically. And some of that change is attributable to the uprising at Attica Correctional Facility, described in the chapter-opening case. Courts have provided the primary means of challenging the nature of inmate confinement and changing the policies and procedures used in both federal and state correctional facilities. In the following sections, we examine the key areas of law that apply.

The Writ of Habeas Corpus

One means of challenging prison conditions is via the **writ of habeas corpus.** The right to mount such a claim is guaranteed by Article I, Section 9, of the U.S. Constitution, which states that the "privilege of the writ of habeas corpus shall not be suspended."[25] Thus, whenever an individual is being confined in an institution under state or federal authority, he or she is entitled to seek habeas corpus relief. Habeas corpus relief also has statutory bases in the federal Habeas Corpus Act and in state habeas corpus laws.[26]

By applying for a writ of habeas corpus, the person seeking relief challenges the lawfulness of his or her confinement. *Habeas corpus* is a Latin term meaning "you should have the body." In practice, habeas corpus relief involves a writ, issued by a court, commanding the person who holds another in captivity to produce the prisoner in court so that the legality of the prisoner's confinement can be adjudicated.[27]

Traditionally, the writ was limited to contesting the legality of confinement itself. However, in *Coffin v. Reichard*,[28] decided in 1944, the Sixth Circuit U.S. Court of Appeals held that suits challenging conditions of confinement could be brought under the federal habeas corpus statute. The court reasoned as follows:

> A prisoner is entitled to the writ of habeas corpus when, though lawfully in custody, he is deprived of some right to which he is lawfully entitled even in his confinement, the deprivation of which serves to make his imprisonment more burdensome than the law allows or curtails his liberty to a greater extent than the law permits.[29]

Although the U.S. Supreme Court has never fully resolved the question of whether the writ of habeas corpus can be applied specifically in seeking relief from allegedly unconstitutional conditions of confinement, most federal courts have followed the logic of *Coffin*.[30] From the prisoner's perspective, however, the difficulties of bringing a habeas petition to a federal court are almost insurmountable. This is because existing law requires that inmates of state institutions exhaust all state judicial and administrative remedies before they apply for the federal writ of habeas corpus. Victorious habeas petitioners can, however, win **injunctive relief**—a court order directing prison officials to improve conditions or to stop enforcing unlawful policies.

DISCRETION MATTERS

How might the decision in *Coffin* affect correctional officials' discretion to determine conditions in a facility?

Besides the writ of habeas corpus, the second major means for prisoners to address institutional conditions arose with the civil rights movement of the late 1950s and early 1960s. At that time, the climate became more conducive to a serious reexamination of the legal rights of prisoners and even to the view that prisoners themselves could be victims, the topic explored in the "Victims and Justice" feature.

VICTIMS AND JUSTICE

The Victimization of Inmates: The Arkansas Prison Scandal

In 1966, Winthrop Rockefeller, grandson of industrialist and philanthropist John D. Rockefeller, was elected governor of Arkansas. As a candidate, he had pledged to eliminate corruption in state government and to hire a professional penologist to reform the state prison system. The following year, Thomas O. Murton, a professor of criminology from Southern Illinois University, was put in charge of the Arkansas prisons. What Murton found was a prison system that had been operating on fear for more than a century.[31] The traditional methods of instilling inmate compliance included beatings, needles under the fingernails, starvation, and floggings with the "hide," a leather strap five inches wide and five feet long. In 1968, custodial officers at Tucker Prison Farm used a contraption known as the "Tucker telephone" to punish inmates and extract information. Designed by prison superintendent Jim Bruton, this device consisted of an electric generator taken from a crank-type telephone and wired with two dry-cell batteries. When the device was in use, a nude inmate was strapped to the treatment table at Tucker Hospital, and electrodes were attached to his big toe and his penis. The crank was then turned, sending an electrical charge into his body. In "long distance calls," several charges were inflicted—of a duration designed to stop just short of the inmate's fainting. Sometimes the "telephone operator" was poorly skilled, and the sustained current not only caused the inmate to lose consciousness but also resulted in irreparable damage to his body.[32]

For more than 50 years, many boasted that the Arkansas prison system was a symbol of efficiency, for no state appropriations were needed to support the convicts. Murton found that this was so only because of the exploitation of inmate labor. Moreover, control of inmates, work assignments, promotions, food rations, bed assignments, visiting privileges, commissary privileges, laundry and clothing procedures, and the very survival of the inmate had been delegated to a few powerful convicts who ran the prison. To make such a system operable, these "trusties" had been granted many privileges, including freedom to sell alcohol and narcotics, gamble and lend money, live in squatter shacks outside the prison, spend nights with female companions, and profit from illegal trafficking in prison produce. Thus, the institutions had no traditional custodial officers. Rather, they were run by a powerful structure of convict guards who used bribery and torture to maintain the status quo and profit from inmate slavery. In Arkansas's Cummins Prison Farm (Cummins Unit), it was alleged that inmates had been routinely murdered as punishment for disciplinary infractions

The Tucker Prison Farm (Tucker Unit) was a working agricultural facility, like the one pictured here.

and then buried in a remote cow pasture. The number killed was estimated at more than 100.[33]

The barbaric conditions in the Arkansas prisons came to national attention in January 1968 as a result of Murton's discoveries and efforts at reform. However, fearing that Murton was damaging the image of Arkansas, on March 2, 1968, Governor Rockefeller fired him and placed him under house arrest. At a press conference the following day, the governor explained that Murton had been a "poor prison administrator." In the years following Murton's departure, the Arkansas prisons were in constant turmoil. On several occasions, prison officials shot at inmates protesting prison conditions.[34] Explanations for the continuing difficulties focused on racial conflicts and efforts at integration.

When the courts finally listened to the Arkansas prisoners, the savage discipline and inhumane conditions were more fully acknowledged. In 1970, in *Holt v. Sarver*,[35] a federal court declared the entire Arkansas prison system to be in violation of the Eighth Amendment ban on cruel and unusual punishment. After long and careful consideration, the court came to the conclusion that the Fourteenth Amendment prohibits confinement under the conditions that had been described and that the Arkansas penitentiary system as it existed, particularly at Cummins, was unconstitutional. The court found the confinement to be inherently dangerous.[36]

The ability of incarcerated offenders to seek help from the criminal justice system is limited. The public is often unsympathetic or unwilling to believe that inmates are being abused. However, the historical example of the Arkansas prison scandal highlights the potential victimization that can occur when correctional staff and the administration allow abuse to become part of the culture of an institution. Fortunately, such abuses today seem to be rare, primarily due to the professionalization of the corrections industry, increased and improved training, and intervention by courts across the nation.

THINK ABOUT THIS

1. What attitude do you think most Americans have about the abuse and victimization of prisoners?
2. Do you think the closed nature of institutional life contributes to the lack of sympathy for victimized inmates? Why or why not?
3. Why do you think we hear so little about the treatment of incarcerated offenders?

The vehicle that opened federal courts to inmates confined in state institutions was **Section 1983** of the Civil Rights Act of 1871.[37] The long-dormant Section 1983 was resurrected in *Monroe v. Pape*,[38] which was decided by the Supreme Court in 1961. In that case, the court held that citizens could bring Section 1983 suits against state officials in federal courts without first exhausting state judicial remedies. Three years later, in *Cooper v. Pate*,[39] the court made it clear that the earlier *Pape* holding applied to state prisoners who could articulate clear and easily identifiable constitutional claims against state prison officials or employees. However, in *Preiser v. Rodriguez*,[40] decided in 1973, the court held that although a Section 1983 suit is a proper vehicle for a constitutional challenge to the conditions of prison life, it cannot be used to challenge the fact or length of custody.

The major advantages of a Section 1983 suit, as opposed to a habeas corpus petition, are: (1) a Section 1983 suit does not require the plaintiff to exhaust available state remedies before the federal district courts will have jurisdiction, and (2) an award of monetary damages is possible. However, the remedy of release from imprisonment is

Overcrowding has been found to increase violence and aggression within correctional institutions. This poses a risk to both inmates and staff.

not available under a Section 1983 suit. As the High Court stated in *Preiser*, only the writ of habeas corpus could secure such release.[41]

Despite the importance of Section 1983 of the Civil Rights Act of 1871, actions by the U.S. Supreme Court beginning in the 1980s and continuing today have weakened it as a vehicle by which state prisoners can go to the federal courts to sue prison officials. To cite but one example, in *Will v. Michigan Department of State Police*,[42] the High Court ruled that states are not "persons" who can be sued under a Section 1983 suit. As such, a prisoner cannot sue a state official for monetary damages for acting in his or her "official capacity" as a state employee. Instead, the prisoner must make it clear in his or her Section 1983 suit that the cause of action identifies a state official who allegedly was acting in his or her individual capacity. In addition, more recently the 1996 Prison Litigation Reform Act severely limited the ability of prisoners to file civil lawsuits alleging unconstitutional conditions of confinement and inhibited the power of courts to intervene on their behalf. In May of 2011, this act was tested, as the Supreme Court ruled in the case of *Brown v. Plata*[43] that conditions in California prisons were so overcrowded as to be unconstitutional and ordered California to reduce the prison population. Without access to the courts, the ruling asserted, conditions such as those identified in California would remain. Nevertheless, many prisoners must begin the process of filing Section 1983 cases on their own, particularly if they have few economic resources. This problem raises questions about access to legal services from inside an institution, the topic we explore next.

Legal Services Inside

The case of *Ex parte Hull*[44] involved a state prison regulation that required inmates to submit all legal documents in their court proceedings to an institutional official for examination and censorship before they could file them with the court. These policies allowed prison officials to intervene in inmate attempts to access the courts and to potentially respond retributively if inmates challenged the nature of their confinement. The Supreme Court found this and similar prison regulations invalid, holding that whether a petition to the court is properly drawn and what allegations it must contain are issues for the court, not the prison authorities, to decide.

In spite of the rule established by *Hull*, an inmate's right of access to the courts often proved to be more theoretical than actual. In many prison systems, disciplinary actions against inmates pursuing legal remedies, or wholesale confiscation of a prisoner's legal documents, were quite common. Moreover, court access was either curtailed or totally inhibited because most prison officials withheld any services related to inmates' legal needs. In most instances, inmates were provided with a few outdated law books and the occasional services of a notary public. Since most prisoners were indigent and could not hire an attorney, the courts were essentially closed to them. Many correctional institutions had "jailhouse lawyers"—inmates who claimed to have legal expertise and provided advice and counsel to their fellow prisoners, with or without compensation. Yet even this aid was severely restricted by prison officials, thus further denying inmates their basic constitutional right of access.

In 1969, the Supreme Court acknowledged and resolved a number of these problems in *Johnson v. Avery*.[45] The case involved a challenge to the constitutionality of a Tennessee prison regulation with the following provision:

> No inmate will advise, assist or otherwise contract to aid another, either with or without a fee, to prepare writs or other legal matters. . . . Inmates are forbidden to set themselves up as practitioners for the purpose of promoting a business of writing writs.[46]

The petitioner was a jailhouse lawyer serving a life sentence who had spent almost a year in solitary confinement for repeatedly violating the rule against writ writing.

In its analysis of the Tennessee rule, the Supreme Court addressed the fact that many prisoners are illiterate and frequently unable to obtain legal help from sources beyond the prison walls. Thus, the justices held that unless the state could provide some reasonable alternative type of legal assistance, a jailhouse lawyer must be permitted to aid inmates in filing habeas corpus petitions.[47] Although the decision in *Johnson* was significant, it did not go into detail on exactly how inmates could obtain legal services. In the years that followed, the U.S. Supreme Court addressed this vagueness and made a number of decisions on the specifics of access to legal services for inmates.

The prison regulations that forbade inmates from assisting or receiving counsel from fellow inmates in the preparation of legal documents were an outgrowth of several factors. Initially, the rule reflected the general custodial attitude toward prison inmates. That is, the inmate was considered a ward of the state who possessed no civil rights, and the privilege of obtaining legal help from other inmates was simply unthinkable. In addition, a number of security issues were involved. "Writ writers," as they were often called, were seen as potential troublemakers. Officials felt that the jailhouse lawyer, in advising inmates of their legal rights, might create dissatisfactions that could lead to belligerence and revolt. Moreover, some interpreted inmates' conferring about legal matters as plotting against administrative authority. Finally, some

A well-equipped law library gives inmates the means to access the courts, thus protecting their due process rights.

feared that jailhouse lawyers would give their clients inferior representation and false hopes while flooding the courts with spurious claims.

Most of these administrative and custodial concerns have had some basis in fact, but in general the problems that jailhouse lawyers have caused in correctional institutions have been more often ones of inconvenience to the staff than of discipline and security. For example, jailhouse attorneys do help prisoners challenge aspects of custody, which often does create additional paperwork for the staff. However, since *Johnson* and numerous other state and federal court decisions, the activities of jailhouse lawyers in many jurisdictions have been relatively unrestricted. Much of their work centers on the loss of civil rights by offenders within an institution. We examine those constitutional rights in the next section.

CONSTITUTIONAL RIGHTS OF INMATES

Historically, individuals convicted of serious crimes could lose much more than their liberty or their lives. Under early English common law, they lost all their civil rights and forfeited their property to the Crown. Their families were also declared corrupt, which made them unworthy to inherit their convicted relative's property. The U.S. Constitution forbids such practices,[48] and similar prohibitions are found in the constitutions and statutes of the states. Yet in spite of these laws, every state has enacted **civil disability laws** that affect convicted offenders. These laws remove rights from individuals convicted of criminal offenses. Depending on the jurisdiction, civil disability laws may include the loss of the right to vote, hold public office, sit on a jury, be bonded, collect insurance or pension benefits, sue, hold or inherit property, receive worker's compensation, make a will, marry and have children, or even remain married. The most severe disability is the loss of all civil rights, or civil death. Depending on the jurisdiction, civil disability may apply only while the offender is incarcerated or for a specified time period following his or her imprisonment. Here is the current Idaho statute, for example:

> A sentence of custody to the Idaho state board of correction suspends all the civil rights of the person so sentenced including the right to refuse treatment authorized by the sentencing court, and forfeits all public offices and all private trusts, authority or power during such imprisonment.[49]

Once offenders have completed their probations or parole sentences in Idaho, their voting rights are automatically restored. They must simply register to vote. However, other states—Virginia, for example—require ex-offenders to petition the court to restore their voting rights.

Technically, a civil right is a right that belongs to a person by virtue of his or her citizenship. Since civil rights include constitutional rights, state statutes and provisions placing civil disabilities on convicted and imprisoned offenders seem to directly conflict with the Constitution. However, the Supreme Court has interpreted these statutes not as complete denials of prisoners' civil rights but as restrictions and conditions on expression of these rights. Nevertheless, the court has removed a number of these restrictions. We examine a few of these basic rights in more detail in the following sections.

DISCRETION MATTERS

Under what circumstances might correctional officials want to limit the ability of inmates to practice their religion?

Religion

The First Amendment to the Constitution provides that "Congress shall make no law respecting an establishment of religion, or prohibiting the free exercise thereof."[50] Historically, freedom of religion was rarely a problem in correctional institutions. In fact, participation in religious instruction and worship services was encouraged. Infringements on this right began only when the increasing number of non-Christian inmates demanded to have the same rights as inmates of Judeo-Christian faiths.

The leading cases involving religious expression occurred with the growing influence of the Black Muslim movement during the 1960s. Black Muslim inmates raised issues such as the right to attend services, obtain literature, and wear religious medals, because unlike Protestant or Catholic inmates, they had been denied the right to engage in such practices. The core question was the recognition of the Black Muslim faith as a religion. This was answered by a federal court in 1962 in *Fulwood v. Clemmer*,[51] and in subsequent cases,[52] with the assertion that Black Muslims are entitled to the same constitutional protections as members of other recognized religions. However, although these cases established the Black Muslims' right to hold religious services, the courts have refused to extend that right in some specific circumstances. In some institutions and at certain times, for instance, custodial authorities have considered assemblies of Black Muslims to be revolutionary in character and to represent "clear and present dangers" to security. In several decisions, the courts ruled that although Black Muslims had the right to worship, their right to hold religious services could be withheld if they represented potential breaches of security.[53] In *O'Lone v. Estate of Shabazz*,[54] decided in 1987, the Supreme Court ruled that prison policies depriving Muslim inmates of the opportunity to attend *Jumu'ah*—a weekly congregational service—did not violate the free exercise clause of the First Amendment. The court held that (1) the policies were reasonably related to legitimate penological interests and (2) there were other reasonable alternative methods for accommodating the Muslims' religious rights.[55]

Other cases involving religious freedom in prisons dealt with inmates' access to clergy, special diets, and the right to wear religious medals.[56] In 1972, the U.S. Supreme Court addressed these issues in *Cruz v. Beto*.[57] Cruz, a Buddhist, had been barred from using the chapel in a Texas prison and was placed in solitary confinement for sharing his religious materials with other inmates. The court ruled that the Texas action was "palpable discrimination" in violation of the equal protection clause of the Fourteenth Amendment. On the other hand, the federal courts have held that placing limits on the practice of Satanism is not a violation of prisoners' First Amendment rights, particularly if the correctional facility believes the religious practice is being used to cover up criminal acts.[58] Nonetheless, the courts have been clear that correctional officials cannot deny religious practice rights as long as the beliefs are sincerely held.[59]

The number of Muslim inmates is growing in correctional facilities across the United States. Officials must make reasonable accommodations for all inmates to practice their religions within the walls of an institution.

Mail

Prison officials in the United States have traditionally placed certain restrictions on inmates' use of mail services. These restrictions generally include limiting the number of people with whom inmates may correspond, opening and reading incoming and outgoing mail, deleting sections from incoming and outgoing mail, and refusing to mail for an inmate or forward to an inmate certain types of correspondence. The reasons for these restrictions have to do with security and budgetary requirements. Contraband must be intercepted, escape plans must be detected, and material that might incite the inmate population in some way must be excluded. Moreover, correctional budgets do not allow for unlimited use of the mail services, as paper, writing utensils, and postage are typically provided at the expense of the facility. Prisons have also used the goal of rehabilitation to justify certain restrictions on inmate correspondence, including limiting access to mail from other known offenders, limiting access to certain inflammatory materials that might incite inmates, or removing access to pornography or other materials that are perceived as contributing to negative behaviors. The courts have generally accepted these justifications for mail censorship and limitation and in the past have rarely intervened in prison mail regulations.

Correctional officials must be on guard for the many ways inmates can obtain contraband, including the prohibited items hidden within other items that come in the mail.

The Supreme Court ruled in *Wolff v. McDonnell*[60] that officials are permitted to open a communication from an inmate's attorney to check for contraband, but it must be done in the presence of the inmate, and the contents must not be read. *Procunier v. Martinez*[61] dealt with the broader issue of censorship of nonlegal correspondence. In that case, the Supreme Court held that prison-mail censorship is constitutional only when two criteria are met: (1) The practice must promote substantial government interests such as security, order, or rehabilitation; and (2) the restrictions must not be greater than necessary to satisfy the particular government interest involved. In 2006, this issue was further explored in *Beard v. Banks,* when the court found that denying access to all books, magazines, and newspapers violates the First Amendment and was not shown to serve a legitimate penological interest.[62]

Correctional facilities in states such as Iowa and Ohio, as well as those within the Federal Bureau of Prisons, are coming into the age of technology. With shrinking correctional budgets, many are turning to digital communication to reduce the expense of postal services. The CorrLinks system, for example, operates via the Trust Fund Limited Inmate Computer System (TRULINCS) used by the Federal Bureau of Prisons. This is an easy, secure Internet message system that charges a fee to the inmate and the individual receiving the message but allows for faster communication between the inmate and the outside world. Corrections staff monitor all messages to ensure safety and security of the public and the facility. Officials believe these communications will increase the connection inmates have with the outside world, particularly their families, and ultimately make their reentry into the community more successful, reducing recidivism.[63]

Rehabilitative and Medical Services

Many clinicians, legislators, and members of the general public agree that in addition to confinement, rehabilitation is an important purpose of imprisonment. Moreover, in the constitutions and statutes of many states, the rehabilitation of prison inmates is implied, if not stated outright, as a purpose.[64] The courts, however, while supporting the rehabilitative ideal, have not defined rehabilitative treatment as a constitutional right. Nevertheless, they have taken a strong stand against several "rehabilitative" practices of questionable moral and legal status, including electroshock therapy for sex offenders.[65] The courts have supported some prison requirements that mandate enrollment in certain institutional programs (such as class attendance by illiterate convicts) and disciplinary measures for those who refuse to participate. Many states

Inmates may be required to complete a general education degree as part of their treatment plan.

and the Federal Bureau of Prisons now require inmates to participate in educational classes and seek general education degrees, particularly if they wish to be awarded good time for progress on their rehabilitative efforts.[66]

Similarly, in *Washington v. Harper*,[67] decided in 1990, the Supreme Court held that the due process clause of the Fourteenth Amendment permits a state to treat a prison inmate who has a serious mental illness with antipsychotic medication against his will if the inmate is dangerous to himself or others and the treatment is in his or her medical interests. In *Brown v. Plata*,[68] mentioned earlier, the court found that overcrowding in California institutions prevented access to adequate medical care and mental health treatment, violating inmates' federal rights to this care. Suicidal and mentally ill inmates were being held in telephone-booth-sized cages because prison officials had nowhere else to put them. The court found that these conditions violated basic standards of care for inmates and constituted cruel and unusual punishment. Thus the court, in a drastic move, ordered the immediate release of inmates.

In principle, inmates have a right to "adequate" and "proper" medical care on several grounds. The right is protected by common law and state statutes, the Civil Rights Act of 1964, the due process clauses of the Fifth and Fourteenth Amendments, and the Eighth Amendment ban on cruel and unusual punishment. Nevertheless, prisoners have made claims regarding improper and inadequate medical care and total denial of medical and health services.

In 1976, in *Estelle v. Gamble*,[69] the Supreme Court enunciated its position on the medical rights of inmates:

> Deliberate indifference to serious medical needs of prisoners constitutes the "unnecessary and wanton infliction of pain" proscribed by the Eighth Amendment. This is true whether the indifference is manifested by prison doctors in their response to the prisoner's needs or by prison guards in intentionally denying or delaying access to medical care or intentionally interfering with the treatment once prescribed.[70]

Beyond this statement, the court has generally left the specifics of medical rights to the lower courts. The federal judiciary has taken the position that determining what amount of medical aid is "adequate" largely depends on the facts of each case.[71] Thus, no uniform definition of "adequate" health care has been specified. Moreover, in *Priest v. Cupp*,[72] an Oregon court made it clear that the constitutional prohibition against cruel and unusual punishment does not guarantee that an inmate will be free from or cured of all real or imagined medical problems while in custody. Thus, although prison officials cannot deny medical aid, inmates cannot expect perfect medical services. In the *Brown v. Plata* case, the Supreme Court noted that in one California prison, up to 50 sick inmates were sometimes held together in a 12-by-20-foot cage for up to five hours awaiting treatment. The majority opinion also cited an example of the death of a prisoner with severe abdominal pain who died after a five-week delay in referral to a specialist. These and other examples were cited as reasons for finding the overcrowded confinement of California inmates unconstitutional.[73]

Another issue related to medical care is the rise in incarceration rates and the lengthening of average prison sentences that have resulted in an increasingly aging prison population.[74] With shrinking budgets across the country, many facilities are struggling to provide adequate care to elderly inmates. Recent innovations include allowing hospice care for dying inmates and creating fellowships for medical students to provide basic care to inmates while studying geriatric medicine in corrections facilities. Other states are expanding programs to allow the release of elderly offenders who are no longer threats to society. Doing so can relieve the economic burden on the state and allow these offenders an opportunity to return to their families and communities.[75]

Overcrowding can cause prison officials to use extreme measures to manage and respond to the inmate population. These cage-like units were used to hold mentally ill inmates awaiting psychological services. In part, this practice led to the *Brown v. Plata* decision.

Discipline

Modern correctional staffs utilize a variety of discipline procedures to ensure inmate compliance with rules and regulations. The vast majority of these procedures involve a reduction in privileges (such as access to programs, visitations, or the commissary) or short-term isolation in segregated housing units. Transfers to more-secure and more-restrictive institutions can also be used to ensure that inmates behave appropriately within the institution.

Solitary confinement is variously referred to as *isolation* or *segregation in the hole* or *in a strip cell*. It involves the total separation of an inmate from the general prison population in a small, uncomfortable cell, combined with the revocation of all privileges within the institution. Placement in solitary generally occurs as a punishment for serious violations of prison regulations, such as escape attempts, forced sexual advances, assaults on correctional officers or other inmates, or refusals to obey institutional rules and procedures. The use of solitary confinement in the United States is as old as the nation's prison system, and its application is acknowledged in many state statutes.

Despite an unwillingness to ban solitary confinement on constitutional grounds, the courts have taken a stand on how it can be imposed and administered. Using standards established by the Supreme Court for interpreting what constitutes cruel and unusual punishment,[76] the federal courts have examined the duration of an inmate's confinement, the physical conditions of the cell, the hygienic conditions of the inmate, the exercise allowed, the diet provided, and the nature of the infraction that resulted in punitive isolation.[77] These cases have typically found that prison officials can restrict inmate behavior or privileges as long as they have a justifiable reason for the restrictions. For example, in 2009, the U.S. Court of Appeals for the Second Circuit found that an inmate's right to exercise could be limited if there was a legitimate safety concern. The inmate in question, Timothy Dumpson, challenged the use of restraints during his one hour of exercise per day. Correctional officials argued that the use of the restraints was appropriate given his disciplinary history.[78] And in a 2001 case, the U.S. Court of Appeals for the Tenth Circuit found that 28 days of solitary confinement did not rise to the level of cruel and unusual punishment prohibited by the Eighth Amendment.[79]

Throughout the history of corrections, disciplinary actions against prison inmates have often been arbitrary administrative operations controlled solely by wardens, their deputies, or other custodial personnel. Without a formal hearing, and at the discretion of an institutional officer, inmates could be placed in solitary confinement, lose some or all of their privileges, or be deprived of good-time credits. Even in correctional settings in which disciplinary hearing committees were convened to review serious infractions of prison regulations, decisions could be made entirely on the basis of a custodial officer's testimony. Outside evidence was generally not required, prisoners were rarely permitted to speak on their own behalf, and the rules of due process were typically ignored. When the prisoners' rights movement first brought these practices to the attention of the federal courts during the 1960s, the due process clauses of the Fifth and Fourteenth Amendments were applied sparingly and only in specific circumstances. The position of the courts seemed to be that due process should prevent only "capricious" or "arbitrary" actions by prison administrators.

During the 1970s, however, the courts began to focus on the specific procedures used in prison disciplinary proceedings, seeking to resolve the wider issue of due process requirements.[80] The principal case was *Wolff v. McDonnell*,[81] decided by the Supreme Court in 1974. The court held as follows:

1. An inmate must be given written notice of the charges at least 24 hours prior to his or her appearance before the prison hearing committee.
2. There must be a written statement by the fact finders as to the evidence and the reasons for the disciplinary action.

DISCRETION MATTERS

What factors should guide the application of discretion in disciplining offenders housed within correctional institutions?

Segregation, or solitary confinement, is used to isolate inmates who are a threat to or are threatened by the general correctional population.

3. The prisoner should be allowed to call witnesses and present documentary evidence, provided that such actions would cause no undue hazards to institutional safety or correctional goals.

4. The inmate must be permitted representation by a counsel substitute (a fellow inmate or staff member) when the prisoner is illiterate or when the complexity of the case goes beyond the capabilities of the person being charged.

5. The hearing committee must be impartial (suggesting that those involved in any of the events leading up to the hearing—such as the charging or investigating parties—may not serve as members of the committee).[82]

In establishing these requirements, the court made it clear that neither retained or appointed counsel nor the right to confrontation and cross-examination were constitutionally required. The decision stressed some additional points. First, the ruling did not apply retroactively. Second, in writing the court's opinion, Justice Byron White emphasized that the limitations on due process imposed by the decision were "not graven in stone"; future changes in circumstances could require further "consideration and reflection" by the court. Third, the due process requirements set forth in the decision applied only to proceedings that could result in solitary confinement and the loss of good-time credits.[83]

Since that time, the Supreme Court has not gone much beyond *Wolff* in protecting inmates' rights in prison disciplinary proceedings. A case in point is *Superintendent, Massachusetts Correctional Institute at Walpole v. Hill,*[84] decided in 1985. As noted earlier, *Wolff* set forth certain safeguards that must be provided when a disciplinary hearing may result in the loss of good-time credits, but that ruling did not require either judicial review or a specific level of evidence to support a disciplinary board's decision. The matter of evidence was addressed in *Hill,* and here the court ruled that only "some evidence" was necessary. In the *Hill* case, the evidence consisted of a correctional officer's report that he had heard a commotion, discovered an inmate who had apparently been assaulted, observed three other inmates (including those in this case) fleeing down an enclosed walkway, and noticed no other inmates in the area. In delivering the court's opinion, Justice Sandra Day O'Connor emphasized that although the evidence presented in the disciplinary proceeding was "meager," it was sufficient to meet due process requirements. Specifically, she added the following broad guideline: "The relevant question is whether there is any evidence in the record that could support the conclusion reached by the disciplinary board."[85]

THE EVOLUTION OF PRISONERS' RIGHTS

While the 1960s ushered in the era of prisoners' rights and the 1970s witnessed agitation for prison reform, the 1980s and 1990s encountered calls for "law and order" that brought into focus a dilemma that had been evolving for decades. Initially, civil libertarians agitated for the rights of prison inmates. The federal courts responded by strengthening the mechanisms available to inmates in their attempts to file lawsuits against their keepers. Prisoners were no longer complete slaves of the state. They slowly won significant victories with respect to legal and medical services, religious expression, access to the media, and their general treatment inside penitentiary walls. Moreover, the courts began to take a more balanced look at the conditions of incarceration. The result was that conditions in correctional systems in many jurisdictions were declared unconstitutional and ordered to reform. At the same time, however, a slow erosion of the rights of the accused, combined with calls for strict and certain punishment of criminal offenders, led to an unprecedented escalation in the growth of prison populations. The ultimate consequence was a corrections system that, while in the throes of reform, was still deteriorating rapidly. We can trace this pattern of deterioration if we look back to the 1970s and into the twenty-first century.

In 1979, for example, in *Bell v. Wolfish*,[86] the Supreme Court upheld the constitutionality of "double-celling," broad search powers, frequent body-cavity searches, and other restrictions imposed on federal pretrial detainees, on the grounds that such restrictions are rational responses to legitimate security concerns. Writing for the majority, Justice William Rehnquist commented that he did not see "some sort of one man, one cell principle lurking in the Due Process Clause of the Fifth Amendment."[87] The court upheld the double-celling, in part, on the grounds that pretrial detainees rarely remain incarcerated for more than 60 days.

Then there was *Rhodes v. Chapman*,[88] which was decided by the Supreme Court in 1981. The suit was filed in 1975 by Kelly Chapman, an armed robber being held at the Southern Ohio Correctional Facility in Lucasville. Chapman argued that the one-man cell he shared with another prisoner gave him only 32 square feet of personal living space, an area about 4 feet wide and 8 feet long. That was less, he contended, than Ohio law required for five-week-old calves in feedlots. The district court agreed that double-celling violated the Eighth Amendment, and ordered Lucasville to reduce its inmate population. Governor James Rhodes of Ohio filed an appeal for the state, but the U.S. court of appeals affirmed the lower court's decision.

Nevertheless, in an 8–1 decision, the U.S. Supreme Court reversed the lower court's ruling, upholding the policy of double-celling at the Ohio prison. The court did not claim that double-celling was itself constitutional but rather that—given the nature of other services and conditions at the institution—the cell overcrowding was neither "cruel or unusual" nor the cause of physical or mental injury. Thus, as Justice William Brennan pointed out, the court had used the "totality of circumstances" test and found the double-celling to be constitutional. *Rhodes* has resulted in a reduction—but not a drastic reduction—in the number of cases in which prisoners successfully challenge overcrowding on Eighth Amendment grounds.

In 1984, in *Hudson v. Palmer*,[89] the Supreme Court made clear that prison inmates have few, if any, privacy rights. On September 16, 1981, Ted S. Hudson, an officer at the Bland Correctional Center at Bland, Virginia, along with a fellow officer, conducted a shakedown search of inmate Russel Palmer's prison locker and cell. Looking for contraband, the officers discovered a ripped pillowcase in a trash can near Palmer's cell bunk. Palmer was charged with destroying state property and ordered to reimburse the state for the material destroyed.

In petitioning the U.S. district court, Palmer asserted that Hudson had intentionally destroyed letters from his wife, pictures of his children, legal papers, and other noncontraband items. He also claimed that the search of his cell and the destruction of the noncontraband items were violations of his Fourth Amendment rights. The Supreme Court ruled that a prisoner has no reasonable expectation of privacy in his prison cell entitling him to the protection of the Fourth Amendment against unreasonable searches. Moreover, the court noted that prison personnel could not possibly prevent the importation of weapons, drugs, and other contraband if inmates retained a right of privacy in their cells. Imprisonment, the court emphasized, carries with it the loss of many rights as necessary to meet the institutional needs and objectives of prison facilities, particularly internal security and safety. Moreover, the court held that since the state of Virginia provided an adequate mechanism through which Palmer could bring suit for any losses he suffered from the destruction of his personal property, he was not entitled to bring a civil rights suit against Hudson in federal court.

The examination, and in some cases erosion, of the rights of prisoners continued through the 1990s. A key case was *Wilson v. Seiter*,[90] decided in 1991. The Supreme Court ruled that prisoners filing lawsuits about inhumane living conditions must show not only that conditions are so deplorable as to violate the Constitution but also that prison officials have acted with "deliberate indifference" to basic human needs. This standard of "deliberate indifference" previously applied only in medical care cases, as ordered by *Estelle v. Gamble* in 1976 (discussed earlier). The *Seiter* decision made it considerably more difficult for prisoners to prevail in Eighth Amendment lawsuits. Cases that followed over the next two decades resulted in very narrow definitions of what conditions constitute cruel and unusual punishment.[91]

As has been previously discussed, however, this progression of cases was halted in 2011, when the Supreme Court found California's overcrowded prison conditions unconstitutional and ordered a reduction in the population size. The community reaction has been swift. Fears about inmates released into the community and increases in crime rates are most often cited.

THE FUTURE OF CONFINEMENT

Throughout the 1990s and into the twenty-first century, conditions in many prisons have remained unconstitutional and in a constant state of chaos.[92] In the aftermath of the 1971 riot at Attica Correctional Facility, a number of reforms were proposed and implemented. But as the years passed, conditions there deteriorated again. By the early 1980s, Attica had become overcrowded; it had absorbed inmates from two state hospitals for the criminally insane; most of the inmates were violent offenders; and the number of assaults on correctional officers was increasing steadily. In September 1981, just a few days before the tenth anniversary of the riot, one officer who had been on duty during the 1971 rebellion commented that tensions in Attica once again were reaching the boiling point. "We have all the ingredients for a disaster here," he remarked. Another officer said, "This place could go right now."[93] Throughout the 1990s, the same comments were being heard, not only at Attica but elsewhere. Think about the conditions cited in California prisons as late as 2011. While Attica has not exploded again, as have other correctional institutions, it has undergone a series of what might be called "prison riots in slow motion."

Since 2000, scores of prison disturbances have occurred every year in federal and state penitentiaries throughout the nation.[94] At the same time, a number of institutions have experienced lengthy **lockdowns,** situations in which inmates are confined to their cells

Lockdown is used to maintain control over an institution experiencing unrest or conflict between inmate groups. Inmates are typically confined to their cells for the duration of the lockdown.

around the clock—denied exercise, work, recreation, and visits. Lockdown status typically results from inmate violence and is intended to separate prisoners to prevent further violence.

The reasons for the numerous riots, protests, hunger strikes, and other disturbances are twofold. First, federal courts have found prisons in almost half the states unfit. The deplorable conditions of confinement—combined with the very fact of confinement—produce anger, frustration, and emotions that are difficult to control. Second, penitentiaries are very dangerous places. Prisoners assault and kill one another. They assault each other sexually, and racial and ethnic tensions are common. The strong prey upon the weak, and rivalries and jealousies are common. Seeking protection and status, many inmates join gangs. But the presence of gangs within prison walls means additional violence resulting from struggles over power, turf, and contraband. While many inmates simply try to do their time and survive incarceration, smaller groups within the facilities challenge that very notion of survival.

It is difficult to predict how correctional systems will deal with such problematic conditions of incarceration. Some jurisdictions have instituted procedures for early parole, while others have placed some of their excess prisoners in local jails. However, early paroling of convicted offenders is unpopular with the public; placement of prison inmates in local facilities further strains the already excessive jail populations; and neither approach addresses the basic need for better institutional conditions. A number of states and the federal system have allocated funds for new prison construction. However, correctional facilities are costly to build, equip, and properly staff; the prison population continues to expand; and the funding for new institutions must come from increased taxation. Although citizens continue to ask for swifter and more certain punishment for criminal offenders, they tend to be unwilling to bear the financial and social costs of new prison construction. As both taxpayers and the victims of crime, they feel that they would be paying twice for the misdeeds of lawbreakers.

One new approach to the problem is the **privatization of corrections**—the construction, staffing, and operation of prisons by private companies for profit. Such an approach was believed to be highly cost-effective, but as some research indicates, those claims were overly inflated, and strong opposition to privatization has been expressed in some jurisdictions.[95] Opponents raise a variety of moral, legal, and ethical questions: Is it appropriate for the state to hand over incarceration to a profit-making organization? How will liability and disciplinary issues be handled? And will private firms end up lobbying for more and longer prison sentences instead of alternatives to incarceration? Privatization, which began in 1982 in Florida, has become a growth industry as states look for more cost-effective ways to house their increasing numbers of inmates. Private prisons are currently operating in 26 states, with many other states leasing beds in their own facilities to jurisdictions or states that are experiencing overcrowding.

As a final point here, prisoners file tens of thousands of lawsuits each year. Many of them are legitimate—seeking relief for constitutional violations of the conditions of incarceration. At the other end of the continuum, however, are far too many frivolous suits. Inmates have filed petitions in federal courts over broken cookies, chunky rather than smooth peanut butter, a lack of X-rated films in prison libraries, and quilted rather than flat toilet paper. A California inmate once claimed that prison officials had planted an electronic device in his brain, and an Idaho prisoner filed suit after correctional officers refused to "tidy up" his cell after a search. There have been waves of frivolous lawsuits on religious grounds as well, over practices ranging from masturbation to reggae music to serving expensive cuts of beef as part of religious freedom. A potential solution to the problem lies in the Prison Litigation Reform Act, which restricts inmate lawsuits and discourages "abusive" filers from bringing suits against their keepers. And as Supreme Court Justice Antonin Scalia has pointed out,

DISCRETION MATTERS

What impact could privatization of prisons have on decisions about offender care, programming, and so on?

Though often cost-effective for communities, privatization of corrections brings controversy and challenges, as profit becomes the focus when responding to offenders.

"The constitution does not guarantee inmates the wherewithal to transform themselves into litigating engines capable of filing everything from shareholder derivative actions to slip-and-fall claims."[96]

As our society confines more and more of its citizens in jails and prisons across the country, we will struggle with the nature and conditions of their confinement. Their access to remedies that allow for a reduction in abuse and an increase in effective programming remains one of the biggest challenges facing the criminal justice system today.

CONCLUSIONS

For the better part of U.S. history, prisoners were considered slaves of the state. When they were convicted, defendants experienced "civil death." Their lives and living conditions were left entirely to the discretion of correctional personnel, which sometimes led to negative outcomes, as illustrated by the Attica prison riot you read about at the opening of this chapter. The conditions in prison were generally brutal, and inmates had no recourse. The Supreme Court, furthermore, maintained a "hands-off" doctrine regarding correctional matters, refusing even to consider inmates' complaints. However, the Constitution guarantees that all individuals have the right to file habeas corpus petitions, including those confined to correctional institutions. It follows, then, that inmates have the right to challenge the lawfulness of the conditions of their confinement. Through a number of federal and Supreme Court cases, inmates have secured favorable decisions regarding such conditions.

Still, the conditions of confinement within institutions of all kinds across the United States present challenges for corrections officials—and they are not easily dealt with. The persistent problems include overcrowding, inadequate programming, and a general lack of inmate safety. Additionally, programs to prepare offenders for reentry into the community have proven insufficient.

SUMMARY AND REVIEW

◼ **Describe the inmate experience, including the unique situation of women in prison.**

- Inmates begin to internalize the formal rules and regulations of the institution—as well as its informal rules, values, customs, and general culture—within moments of arriving at the institution.
- The inmate subculture is organized around a set of informal rules that include the following: Don't interfere with the interests of other inmates. Keep out of quarrels or feuds with fellow inmates. Don't exploit other inmates. Withstand frustration or threat without complaint. Don't give respect or prestige to the correctional staff or to the world they represent.
- While violated regularly, these rules help inmates to survive the prison experience.
- Historically and comparatively, there have been few female prisoners. Currently, women make up nearly 7 percent of the state and federal correctional population, the majority of them serving time for drug or drug-related and property crimes. Less than a third are classified as violent offenders.
- Research has found that a disproportionate number of female inmates are still involved in cleaning, kitchen, and manufacturing work, while male inmates participate in a far wider range of work initiatives. Vocational training programs also focus on "traditional" women's work.
- Fueled by the growing number of incarcerated women over the past two decades, many correctional systems have developed structured arrangements whereby female inmates can have meaningful visits with their family members, especially children.
- The social system in women's prisons is similar to that in the all-male facilities, with particular roles, an inmate code, and norms for interactions between inmate and correctional staff.

◼ **Explain the legal principles that allow inmates to challenge conditions of confinement.**

- Whenever an individual is being confined in an institution under state or federal authority, he or she

is entitled to seek habeas corpus relief as protected by the Constitution and federal statutes. By applying for a writ of habeas corpus, the person seeking relief is challenging the lawfulness of his or her confinement.
- In *Coffin v. Reichard* (1944) the Sixth Circuit U.S. Court of Appeals held that suits challenging conditions of confinement could be brought under the federal habeas corpus statute.
- The specific vehicle that opened federal courts to inmates confined in state institutions was Section 1983 of the Civil Rights Act of 1871. Section 1983 cannot be used to challenge the length of confinement, only the conditions.
- The major advantages of a Section 1983 suit, as opposed to a habeas corpus petition, are: (1) a plaintiff does not need to exhaust state remedies before the federal district courts will have jurisdiction, and (2) an award of monetary damages is possible.
- The Supreme Court held in *Johnson v. Avery* that a jailhouse lawyer must be permitted to aid inmates in filing habeas corpus petitions unless the state can provide some reasonable alternative for legal assistance. Few inmates have the resources for outside legal assistance.

◼ **Describe the rights of inmates regarding religion, mail, rehabilitation, medical treatment, and institutional discipline.**

- First Amendment protections of religious freedom have been upheld for prisoners. In cases where the institution limited these rights, the Supreme Court has held that (1) the policies were reasonably related to legitimate penological interests and (2) there were other reasonable alternative methods for accommodating the religious rights.
- Prison officials in the United States have traditionally limited the number of people with whom inmates may correspond, as well as the rights of correctional officers to open and read incoming and outgoing mail, delete sections from incoming and outgoing

mail, and refuse to mail for an inmate or forward to an inmate certain types of correspondence.

- Although inmates cannot be subjected to immoral or illegal rehabilitative practices, such as electro-shock therapy for sex offenders, they do not have a right to rehabilitative treatment. Conditions of confinement, such as overcrowding, may reduce the effectiveness of mental health and medical treatment and therefore violate the Constitution's protection against cruel and unusual punishment.
- Inmates have a right to "adequate" and "proper" medical care on several grounds. The right is protected by common law and state statutes, the Civil Rights Act of 1964, the due process clauses of the Fifth and Fourteenth Amendments, and the Eighth Amendment ban on cruel and unusual punishment.
- Discipline procedures in most correctional facilities involve a reduction in privileges (such as access to programs, visitations, and the commissary) or short-term isolation in segregated housing units. Transfer to more-secure and more-restrictive

institutions can also be used to ensure that inmates behave appropriately within the institution.

- *Wolff v. McDonnell* (1974) held that inmates must be afforded some protection during disciplinary proceedings. Prisoners should also be able to call witnesses and present documentary evidence, provided that such actions cause no undue hazards to institutional safety or correctional goals.

■ **Describe the contemporary trends in confinement, including the privatization of prisons.**

- The future of confinement lies in reform and rehabilitation rather than the "law and order" focus of the past few decades. This includes an emphasis on the successful reentry of inmates into society.
- Privatization of corrections includes the construction, staffing, and operation of prisons by private companies for profit. This approach may be highly cost-effective, but there is strong opposition to privatization, including concerns about the ethical and legal concerns of turning prisons into profit centers.

KEY TERMS

civil disability laws (p. 326)
hands-off doctrine (p. 315)
injunctive relief (p. 321)

inmate code (p. 317)
lockdown (p. 333)
privatization of corrections (p. 334)

Section 1983 (p. 323)
solitary confinement (p. 330)
writ of habeas corpus (p. 321)

ISSUES FOR CRITICAL THINKING AND DISCUSSION

1. What do you think about the conditions at Attica as described in the opening of the chapter?
2. What would you consider the most difficult part of acclimating to an incarcerated environment?
3. What principles should guide the confinement of inmates in American prisons and jails? In particular, what principles, if any, should guide the enormous amount of discretion of correctional staff and administrators?

4. Why are inmates' rights to proper and adequate medical care protected by the Constitution?
5. What impact do you think solitary confinement or segregated housing has on inmates within the prison? Why might courts examine this practice closely?
6. What issues make privatization of prisons controversial? Given current economic issues, does privatization seem like the way to handle the cost of incarceration?

13

Community-Based Corrections

LEARNING OBJECTIVES

- Describe the philosophy of community-based corrections.
- Explain criminal justice diversion and the reasons it is used.
- Define and give examples of intermediate sanctions.
- Explain probation and the services associated with it.
- Describe parole and the controversy surrounding its use.
- Identify the issues related to reentry of offenders into society.

KEEPING CORRECTIONS IN THE COMMUNITY

Innovative sentences, like the one Shawn Gementera received for stealing mail, have taken many forms, including requiring offenders to publicly proclaim their guilt, as the young man above is doing.

On May 21, 2001, a police officer noticed two men who appeared to be stealing letters from residential mailboxes. One man, later determined to be Shawn Gementera, was keeping watch while the other, Andrew Choi, was stuffing the letters into his jacket. The officer immediately detained both men, and they were ultimately indicted. After the indictment, under a plea agreement, Gementera pled guilty to mail theft. A second count of receiving a stolen U.S. Treasury check, which was part of the stolen mail, was dismissed. This was not Gementera's first offense. Although only 24 years old at the time, Gementera had a lengthy criminal history, and his offenses were growing more serious. At 19 he had been convicted of misdemeanor criminal mischief, and by 20 he had been convicted twice of driving with a suspended license. Other arrests and citations included driving with a suspended license, failing to provide proof of financial responsibility, misdemeanor battery, possession of drug paraphernalia, additional driving offenses, and, before turning 25, taking a vehicle without the owner's consent.[1]

Nearly two years after the mail-theft offense, Judge Vaughn Walker of the U.S. District Court for the Northern District of California sentenced Gementera for that crime. According to the U.S. Sentencing Guidelines, the range was two to eight months' incarceration. Judge Walker sentenced Gementera to the lower end of the range, imposing two months' incarceration, along with three years of supervised

release. In an unusual move, he also imposed additional conditions. For example, Gementera was required to "perform 100 hours of community service," to consist of "standing in front of a postal facility in the city and county of San Francisco with a sandwich board which in large letters declares: 'I stole mail. This is my punishment.'"[2]

Gementera later challenged the sentence and asked that the sandwich board condition be removed. In response, Judge Walker invited both parties to present "an alternative form or forms of public service that would better comport with the aims of the court."[3] Instead of the 100-hour signboard stipulation, the district court imposed a four-part special condition. The new terms, proposed jointly by counsel, mandated that the defendant observe postal patrons visiting the "lost or missing mail" window, write letters of apology to any identifiable victims of his crime, and deliver several lectures at a local school.[4] He was also required to spend "8 total hours of community service . . . either (i) wear[ing] a two-sided sandwich board-style sign or (ii) carry[ing] a large two-sided sign stating, 'I stole mail; this is my punishment,' in front of a San Francisco postal facility identified by the probation officer."[5]

Gementera appealed to the U.S. Court of Appeals for the Ninth Circuit, arguing that the sandwich-board/sign portion of the sentence violated the Sentencing Reform Act.[6] This U.S. federal statute was intended to increase consistency in federal sentencing outcomes while also giving district courts broad discretion in formulating appropriate conditions of supervised release. The act mandates that such conditions should serve legitimate objectives.[7] Gementera argued that there were no legitimate reasons to sentence him to wear or display a sign stating his crime. In fact, he argued that the only reason the court assigned that punishment was to humiliate him. Unfortunately for Gementera, the justices of the ninth circuit disagreed and upheld the sentence.[8] Gementera appealed to the U.S. Supreme Court, but the High Court denied his request to review his case.

While the primary nature and length of sentences are determined by state and federal statutes, judges have some discretion to alter or add to these punishments. Courts and specific judges across the nation are adding unique punishments to standard community correction sentences, including requiring offenders to wear bracelets and T-shirts that identify them as offenders or to use special license plates if they've been convicted of a DUI (driving under the influence) offense. The state courts have been mixed in their analyses of these sentences. Some—for example, in Minnesota—have found that the sentences are inconsistent with state constitutions or statutes because they humiliate offenders or subject them to public ridicule. Other state courts have upheld the sentences, finding that they meet the goals of justice.[9] The point is that many of these alternative sentences are served out in the community and involve an enormous amount of court and judicial discretion. This chapter examines the policies, strategies, and responses to offenders that occur within the community rather than within an institution.

THE GOALS OF COMMUNITY CORRECTIONS

The principle of community-based corrections rests on the fundamental fact that some offenders are incarcerated while others are not. Logically, therefore, **community-based corrections** refer to all correctional strategies that take place within the community rather than inside the institutions that traditionally incarcerate offenders. Accordingly, many types of court-determined sentences could be viewed as community-based corrections. Some sanctions of the colonial era—such as the stocks, the pillory, the ducking stool, and the scarlet letter—were certainly community-based. The same might be said of fines. However, saying so would be an oversimplification of the community-based correctional philosophy. To be more precise, then, community-based corrections include activities and programs within the community that have effective ties to the local environment. These are generally rehabilitative rather than punitive and can include arrangements with employment, educational, social, and clinical service-delivery systems and resources. Many also involve supervision by a community and/or governmental agency.[10]

Typical forms of community-based correctional services include pretrial diversion projects; probation and parole; education and work-release activities; and furlough, restitution, and halfway house programs—all of which are discussed in this chapter. Certain types of community-based correctional services, including work-release programs and probation, are referred to as **intermediate sanctions**—sanctions falling between the extremes of fines and imprisonment. All these strategies offer ways for the criminal justice system to find appropriate responses to those who have violated the laws of our society.

Community-based correctional strategies rest on the following range of rehabilitative, fiscal, and pragmatic philosophical perspectives. First, incarceration may be unnecessary for some offenders, particularly low-level and first-time offenders. Second, from an economic point of view, it generally costs far less to supervise criminals in the community than to maintain them in institutions. Third, many reformers hold that the unfavorable consequences of imprisonment—loss of liberty and self-esteem, placement in physical jeopardy, and the fact that prisons can be "schools of crime"—impede successful rehabilitation and community reintegration. Moreover, families of

In community correction service programs, offenders can repay some of the harm of their crimes through work. Here, for example, inmates from a sheriff's community service program clean Bourbon Street in the French Quarter of New Orleans the day after Mardi Gras.

inmates often become financial burdens to the state. Fourth, many community-based correctional strategies help offenders play productive roles in their neighborhoods and communities, as opposed to being burdened with the more negative implications of imprisonment. Fifth, given the current trends in prison overcrowding, reducing or altogether eliminating an offender's period of confinement can be viewed as a more pragmatic approach to managing and controlling the less seriously involved criminal offenders. And sixth, a "last resort" philosophy has developed in corrections. In this view, the traditional avenues of punishment and correction have not been working, and new, more innovative approaches must be tested.[11] To understand these points more fully, let's look at the ways in which community corrections programs are being implemented.

DIVERSION AND INTERMEDIATE SANCTIONS

Community corrections programs come in various forms, with varying levels of restriction and supervision. In this section we examine some of the most common—diversion programs, community service programs, and home confinement. Probation and parole, which are also forms of community corrections, will be covered in the sections that follow.

Diversion Programs

Diversion refers to the removal of offenders from the criminal law at any stage of the police and court processes, from arrest to incarceration.[12] This means that traditional proceedings against individuals who have violated criminal statutes are formally halted or suspended in favor of some noncriminal disposition or process. Thus, diversion often occurs before adjudication but can also occur during or following adjudication. While many offenders are diverted before sentencing, they may also be supervised by community correctional agencies and organizations while completing their sentences.

Diversion is not a new practice. It has existed in an informal fashion for thousands of years, ever since the inception of organized law enforcement and social control. In both ancient and modern societies, informal diversion has occurred in many ways: A police officer removes a public drunk from the street to a shelter; a prosecutor decides to enter a nolle prosequi for a petty theft; a magistrate releases with a lecture an individual who assaulted a neighbor during the course of an argument. These are generally discretionary decisions, seemingly made at random and sometimes off the record, and they tend to be personalized and inconsistent. Each is determined on a case-by-case basis. They are also often problematic, in that they may reflect individual, class, or social prejudices. Moreover, in the past and even today in some jurisdictions, these serve only to remove offenders from the application of criminal penalties; there is no attempt to provide appropriate alternatives. Although these haphazard and unsystematic practices will continue, more formal diversion programs place offenders into community social or therapeutic programs in lieu of conviction and punishment.

As criminal justice diversion has evolved, the arguments in its favor have increased. At their introduction, these programs were believed to reduce court backlog, provide early intervention before the development of full-fledged criminal careers, ensure some consistency in selective law enforcement, reduce the costs of criminal processing, and enhance an offender's chances for successful community reintegration. More important, however, many social scientists and penal reformers concluded that the criminal justice process, which was designed to protect society from criminals, often contributed to the very behavior it was trying to eliminate.[13]

The overall value and impact of the national diversion effort is difficult to assess. Many programs have never been evaluated, and estimations of their effectiveness

DISCRETION MATTERS

What goals might motivate criminal justice professionals to use their discretionary powers and divert offenders out of the criminal justice process?

have ranged from promising to mixed.[14] As jail and prison populations continue to grow beyond capacity, diversion programs remain popular, because they permit judges to impose intermediate-level sanctions yet avoid incarcerating offenders.

Community Service Programs

Community service programs are often linked to diversion. In many jurisdictions, defendants charged with petty offenses perform community service in lieu of prosecution or instead of incarceration once convicted. Offenders placed in community service programs generally have been found guilty of lesser crimes such as shoplifting, soliciting prostitution, and low-level drug offenses. Community service programs have been used across the United States in communities large and small. Under the "broken windows" theory discussed in Chapter 5, individuals arrested for panhandling, loitering, and similar "quality of life" crimes are sentenced to community cleanups and other public works initiatives to help reduce crime through their own efforts.[15]

Home Confinement and Electronic Monitoring

Another intermediate sanction used to keep offenders out of institutional correctional settings or to allow them to leave facilities and reenter the community is home confinement. This is often coupled with some type of electronic or digital monitoring. Although home incarceration or confinement, also known as *house arrest,* has likely existed in one form or another for quite some time, its use as an official sanction for criminal behavior did not begin in the United States until 1984, when the first sentence of electronic monitoring was used.[16] It quickly became popular for two reasons: increased crowding of correctional facilities and the development of electronic and digital monitoring technology. In the 1980s, when electronic monitors became small enough to be wearable and reliable enough to be used for home incarceration purposes, both the number of programs and the number of equipment manufacturers increased rapidly.[17] The use of the internet and GPS technology has led to more accurate

Alternative sanctions, like the electronic monitoring seen here, allow offenders to maintain positive ties to the community, including employment and schooling.

DISCRETION MATTERS

Why might court officials want to identify offenders who appear to be suffering disproportionately while incarcerated?

tracking and location of offenders. The technology and use of this sanction not only allow offenders to remain in the community, even working and going to school, but also provide some measure of control and response from the criminal justice system. Currently, these programs exist in all states and the District of Columbia. Research has found home incarceration to be a safe and effective community sanction for low-level offenders who might suffer disproportionately from even short-term incarceration.[18]

PROBATION

The concept of *probation* arose in the United States in 1841, when a Boston shoemaker, John Augustus, began the practice of posting bail for an offender after conviction and then providing him with friendship and support in family matters as well as job assistance. When the defendant was later brought to court for sentencing, Augustus would report on his progress toward reformation and request that the judge order a small fine and court costs instead of a jail sentence.[19] As such, Augustus could be considered the first probation officer. By 1858, he had bailed almost 2,000 defendants. His efforts led to the first probation statute, passed in Massachusetts in 1878. By 1900, four other states had enacted similar legislation, and probation became an established alternative to incarceration.

The Nature of Probation

Probation is a sentence of conditional release to the community. More specifically, as defined by the American Bar Association, probation is a sentence not involving confinement that imposes conditions and retains authority in the sentencing court to modify the conditions of the sentence or to resentence the offender if he or she violates the conditions.[20]

In addition to being a disposition, the word *probation* has also been used to refer to a status, a system, and a process.[21] As a status, probation reflects the unique character of the probationer: He or she is neither a free citizen nor a confined prisoner. As a system, probation is a component in the administration of justice, as embodied by the agency or organization that administers the probation process. As a process, probation refers to the functions, activities, and services that characterize the system. This process includes preparing reports for the courts, supervising probationers, and obtaining and providing services for them.

Probation is administered by hundreds of independent state and federal government agencies, each jurisdiction operating under different laws and many with widely varying philosophies. In some jurisdictions, such as those of Hawaii and Delaware, a single state authority provides services for all probationers. In other jurisdictions, probation is administered by the lower courts. In some areas, such as South Carolina, probation and parole departments are combined into a single state unit. In the federal system, probation is administered as an arm of the federal district courts.

The premise behind the use of probation is that many offenders are not dangerous; they represent little menace to society; and once institutionalized, they shift their focus to the prison community—that is, they are forced into contact with hardened criminals, the prison experience generates bitterness and hostility, and the "ex-con" label becomes a stigma that encourages recidivism. Probation provides a more therapeutic alternative. The term comes from the Latin *probare,* meaning "to test or prove"; the probationer is given the opportunity to demonstrate that if given a second chance, he or she will engage in more socially acceptable behavior. The probation philosophy also includes elements of community protection and offender rehabilitation. Probationers are supervised by agents of the court or probation authority. These are trained personnel with dual roles. They ensure that the conditions of probation are fulfilled and provide counseling and assistance in community reintegration.

While these are the philosophical underpinnings of probation, several more pragmatic issues have entered into its use as an alternative to imprisonment. First, as noted, correctional institutions throughout the nation have been extremely overcrowded. In view of the almost prohibitive costs of new prison construction, many see probation as a more economically viable correctional alternative. Second, and also as a matter of simple economics, the probation process is considerably cheaper than the prison process. In 2010, the average state costs of maintaining an inmate in prison were estimated at $31,307 and ranged from $14,603 in Kentucky to $60,076 in New York per year.[22] Probation costs tend to be less than one-tenth of that amount. In 2011, Georgia reported that it cost $51.19 per day to keep an inmate in the state's prison system; however, it cost only $1.68 per day for an offender supervised on probation.[23] Third, within some sectors of the criminal justice community, imprisonment is being viewed more and more as cruel punishment, particularly for low-level or nonviolent offenders. Inmates are often physically, sexually, and emotionally victimized. Probation is considered a more humane form of correctional intervention.

Most states have statutory restrictions on the granting of probation. In some jurisdictions, defendants who have been convicted of such crimes as murder, kidnapping, and rape are ineligible for probation, as are second- and third-felony offenders. Other states tend to be less specific, but they structure their penal codes in such a manner as to preclude a sentence of probation for most serious offenders. Thus, in most jurisdictions, probation is a statutory alternative to imprisonment for many offenses, including some felony convictions. Judges differ, however, in their approaches to granting it. Both plea bargaining and information contained in the presentence report enter into the decision. Other factors are the prosecutor's recommendation, anticipated community reaction, political considerations, the court's backlog, the availability of space in the prison system, and the judge's estimation of the utility of probation for the particular offense or offender.[24]

Suspended Sentences and Conditional Release

A variety of terms are used interchangeably with probation but represent quite different concepts. The best known of these is the **suspended sentence,** a disposition that implies supervision of the offender but often defers punishment with a set of specified criteria and goals. The suspended sentence is a form of quasi-freedom that can be revoked at the pleasure of the court. Suspended sentences are of two types: *suspension of imposition of sentence* and *suspension of execution of sentence*. If imposition is suspended (which is not common in all jurisdictions), there may be a verdict or plea, but no sentence is pronounced. The presiding judge or magistrate releases the defendant on the general condition that he or she stay out of trouble and make **restitution** or reparations for the losses suffered by the victims of the crime. When execution is suspended, the sentence is prescribed but is postponed or not carried out. In a number of jurisdictions, a suspension of execution of sentence is followed by an order for probation.

Alternatively, the laws of several states provide for sentences of *conditional discharge* and *unconditional discharge*. The sentence of conditional discharge is similar to a suspended sentence, in that the court may decide that (1) neither the public interest nor the interests of justice would be served by a sentence of imprisonment and (2) probation supervision is not appropriate. In New York, for example, the period of conditional discharge is one year for a misdemeanor and three years for a felony, and the conditions generally involve making restitution.[25] The sentence of unconditional discharge goes one step further: The defendant is released without imprisonment, fine, probation, or any conditions whatsoever. Such a sentence is used when the court decides that no proper purpose is served by the imposition of conditions. However, such a discharge is still considered a final judgment of conviction.[26]

The Presentence Investigation

The *presentence investigation*, also sometimes called a *probation investigation*, is one of the basic services the probation or community corrections agency provides. Almost all presentence investigation reports are conducted by the probation authority. However, some are done privately, commissioned by the accused's defense attorney.[27] The idea is that since probation officers are overworked, a privately commissioned report can be more thorough and comprehensive. The private report may also include elements that the defendant and his or her counsel believe are important for the court to consider. These may or may not be items identified by probation officers.

The goal of presentence investigation reports is to compile information about the background and characteristics of defendants in order to develop the most appropriate sentence. Reports vary widely in depth, content, and usefulness. In some regional offices in South Carolina, for example, reports may be less than a page long and contain only the basic facts of the defendant's criminal history and current offense, followed by a brief statement of the offender's prognosis and the probation agent's recommendation for sentencing. In contrast, some presentence investigations conducted in Kings County (Brooklyn), New York, take up more than 30 single-spaced legal-size pages and recount numerous aspects of the defendant's life, including whether he or she had a normal birth experience. The typical report is somewhere between these two extremes, however, and outlines the characteristics of the offender, the circumstances of his or her offense, an evaluative summary, and a recommendation regarding the sentence itself and the conditions of supervision.

Conditions of Probation

As part of their probation agreement, defendants are required to abide by a variety of regulations and conditions. These are fairly standard from state to state. The probationer must live a law-abiding and productive life, including obtaining work, supporting his or her dependents, maintaining contact with the supervising probation officer, and remaining within the jurisdiction of the court. Special conditions of probation, like those imposed in the *Gementera* case, which you read about at the beginning of the chapter, may also be imposed, by either the sentencing judge or the supervising probation agency. Many of these conditions have been challenged, but state appellate courts have upheld most of them. Courts have affirmed the appropriateness of special requirements such as undergoing treatment for drug abuse,[28] abstaining from the use of alcohol,[29] serving a short jail sentence prior to release on probation with no credit for prior confinement,[30] refraining from operating a motor vehicle during the period of probation,[31] submitting to a search by the supervising probation officer,[32] and making a payment of restitution.[33]

Since the 1980s, a new condition of probation has become common: In more than half the states, probation clients are being assessed a fee for services. Supervision services typically range from $30 to $75 per month, with presentence investigation costs running from $100 to $500.[34] Although there are waivers for the indigent, nonpayment brings sanctions from the court or probation agency. Texas is among the most successful states in collecting fees from probationers. Officials estimate that probation departments in Texas collect fees from at least 90 percent of all misdemeanor probationers and 65 percent of all felony offenders on probation.

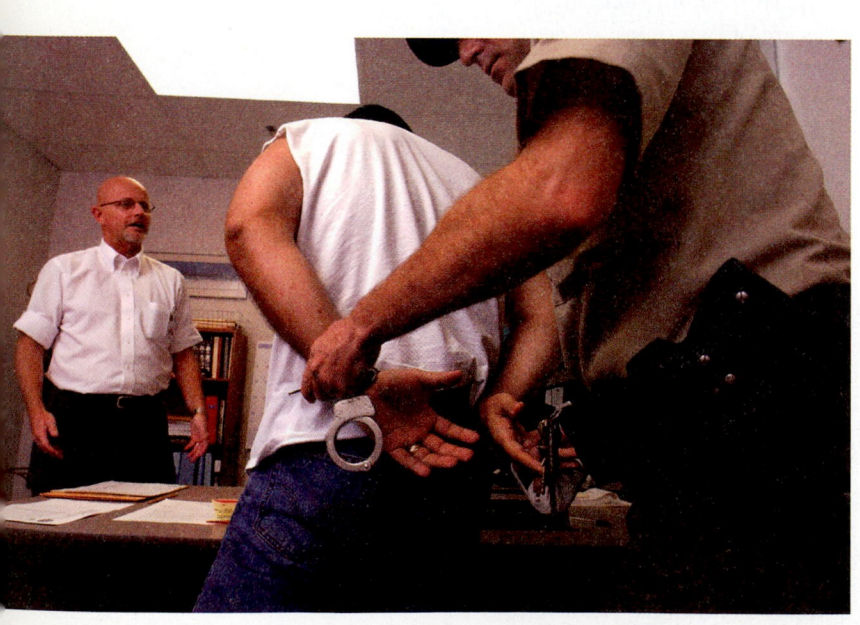

Offenders must meet with their probation officers within days of release into the community. Failure to do so can result in arrest and incarceration.

Collected fees pay for more than the cost of basic supervision. In 2004, for example, for every $1 the state invested, it collected $1.13 in offender fees for supervision, victim restitution, court costs, and fines.[35]

Generally, conditions of probation are considered constitutional and proper unless they bear no reasonable relationship to the crime committed or the defendant's probationary status. Thus, placement in a drug-treatment program becomes an appropriate condition of probation only when the offense is considered to be a consequence of a drug-abuse problem. Conversely, staying away from places where children congregate would be an improper condition for probationers who had never been convicted of child molestation. Among the more widely endorsed conditions of probation is restitution: requiring offenders to compensate their victims for damages or stolen property (monetary restitution) or to donate their time to community service (community service restitution).

There are numerous rationales for restitution. First, while fines go into court or government treasuries, monetary restitution often goes directly to the victims of crime, compensating them for injuries, time lost from work, and other losses. Second, restitution forces the offender to take personal responsibility for his or her crime and the impact it had on victims. Restitution also has the potential for reconciling victims and offenders and can be incorporated into a probation program without the need for additional programs and expenditures. Last, restitution provides a vehicle for including the victim in the administration of justice.[36]

Despite these apparent virtues, restitution has its critics. Some view it as a punitive sanction rather than a rehabilitative one, since it places an additional burden on offenders. More important, restitution might nullify any deterrent effects of punishment by allowing criminals to "write a check" and "pay a fee" for their offenses. Finally, restitution may serve the interests of only the people who can afford it. Although in many ways this last argument is true, a number of alternatives make restitution available to offenders at all levels of the socioeconomic ladder. For example, juvenile vandals can make restitution by repairing the damage they have caused; drunk drivers can work in alcohol detoxification centers; and other offenders can work in hospitals, nursing homes, or juvenile counseling programs.[37]

In cases of white-collar crime, judges typically attach heavy restitution payments to offenders' sentences—money to compensate victims for their losses. These assessments, often announced with considerable media attention, take on even greater importance, given that most prison sentences imposed on white-collar criminals tend to be short, if imposed at all. However, despite the fanfare, many of these restitution orders are never enforced. A study by the U.S. Government Accountability Office found that the amount of criminal debt owed in federal cases, but uncollected, increased from $5.6 billion in 1995 to $13 billion in 1999, to $16.2 billion by 2002, and to $25 billion in 2006.[38]

Probation Services

At least in theory, probation services incorporate the casework approach. During an initial interview, the probation officer evaluates the probationer to determine what type of treatment supervision is most appropriate. On the basis of information contained in the presentence investigation report and on his or her skills in counseling and problem solving, the officer designs a treatment schedule to allow the probationer to make a reasonable community adjustment. He or she examines the probationer's peer relationships, family problems, work skills and history, educational status, and involvement with drug or alcohol abuse. Treatment may be limited to one-to-one counseling, or it may involve referral to community service agencies for drug-abuse treatment, vocational skill enhancement, or job assistance. Some probation agencies have special supervision units with officers specifically trained in these areas. Others provide psychiatric services or structured group counseling.

Because probationers are convicted criminal offenders, one of the officer's roles involves community protection. Thus, a second function of the intake interview is to determine what level of community supervision appears necessary. Such supervision can involve regular visits to the probationer's home and place of employment and can require him or her to report to the probation office on a weekly, semimonthly, or monthly basis. Although many probation agencies do operate in the manner outlined, in practice many offenders receive little treatment, contact, and supervision. Large caseloads and lack of resources in many jurisdictions, coupled with increasing use of probation for more serious offenders, pose challenges to the delivery of services.[39]

Shock Probation and Split Sentences

In 1965, the Ohio state legislature passed the first **shock probation** law in the United States, allowing judges to incarcerate an offender for a brief part of the sentence, suspend the remainder, and place him or her on probation.[40] Many states followed suit, going even further by developing shock incarceration sentences that focused on enhancing the incarceration portion of the sentence. Such programs, known as *boot camps,* have been implemented for adults and juvenile offenders.[41] More than half the states allow for some sort of incarceration followed by probation for various classes of offenders. These split sentences typically utilize a specified length of incarceration with some post-incarceration supervision.

Opinions regarding the suitability of shock probation as a rehabilitative tool are mixed. From a positive standpoint, it represents a way for the courts to (1) impress offenders with the seriousness of their actions without imposing a long prison sentence, (2) arrive at a just compromise between punishment and leniency in appropriate cases, and (3) provide community-based treatment for offenders who can be rehabilitated, while still imposing deterrent sentences where public policy demands it.[42] In addition, because the imprisonment is only short-term, the offender is less likely to be absorbed into the institutional inmate culture. Moreover, the costs of shock probation are significantly lower than those of a full-term incarceration.

Opponents of shock probation view it as counterproductive as a rehabilitative tool. First, its deterrent effect is limited or totally negated by the job loss and broken community ties associated with incarceration, however brief. Second, the purpose of probation is to avoid incarceration, not supplement it. Even a short period of incarceration can expose offenders to hardened criminals and the hostilities and resentment of prison life, and it can stigmatize offenders for having been in jail or prison, potentially damaging their self-concept. Third, prison and probation are at opposite

When an offender receives a split sentence, she may be released after a short-term incarceration but still face heavy supervision.

ends of the punishment-rehabilitation continuum; they are mutually exclusive, the theory goes, and therefore should not be mixed.[43]

Perhaps most important, we have no evidence demonstrating that it reduces recidivism. Several empirical studies have examined the shock probation experience, but the findings remain inconclusive.[44] In the opinion of the National Institute of Justice, shock probation and split sentences do not reduce repeat offending.[45] Going further, some research correlates shock probation with higher rearrest rates, particularly for violent offenders and DUI cases.[46] Because of such findings, many states have decreased or eliminated their use of shock probation.[47]

Intensive Probation Supervision

Intensive probation supervision (IPS) is a program that places a probationer under tighter control than he or she might experience under regular probation. It offers a potential solution to the growth of prison populations and the associated costs by controlling selected offenders in the community and satisfying at least a part of society's demand that offenders be punished for their crimes.[48]

The degree of surveillance under IPS varies considerably from one jurisdiction to another and is dependent on numerous factors about the offense or offender. In general, caseloads are small, and the probationer and probation officer have frequent contact in the home, on the job, and at the probation office. Typical standards include the following:

- five face-to-face contacts per week
- mandatory community service
- mandatory employment
- mandatory curfew
- weekly checks of local arrest records
- routine alcohol and drug testing

As for the effectiveness of IPS, research data suggest somewhat mixed and ambiguous results. For example, in a comprehensive study of fourteen such programs in nine states, no clear relationship was found between frequency of contact and recidivism.[49] Offenders under intensive probation supervision were just as likely as those on regular probation to commit a crime. Nor was there any indication that probationers under IPS were rearrested for less serious crimes than their counterparts. IPS did, however, succeed in altering offenders' perceptions about crime. Those in intensive programs believed that their chances of getting caught for a crime while on probation were high, particularly if the crime involved drug use. They also believed that, if caught, they would be treated more harshly than offenders on regular probation. Finally, the study found that while IPS is not necessarily more cost-effective than regular probation, it is considerably cheaper than housing offenders in prison.[50]

Probation Violation and Revocation

Because probation is a conditional release, it does not guarantee absolute freedom and actually restricts the rights of individuals serving these types of sentences. Arrests for new crimes or violations of the conditions of probation can result in revocation of probation and imprisonment. As noted earlier, the conditions of probation are established by statute, and the sentencing court can impose special conditions. A new arrest can often constitute a violation of probation for the offender and can result in a return to prison or jail. Moreover, the appellate courts have given the lower courts considerable latitude in imposing conditions of probation. Thus, such technical violations as nonpayment of a fine, failure to pay off a civil judgment for fraud for an individual who is able to pay, failure to make child support payments, failure to report to one's probation officer, and driving while intoxicated, to name only a

DISCRETION MATTERS

What factors might prompt a criminal justice professional to place an offender under intensive probation supervision? What factors might affect the intensity and/or success of the supervision?

few types of violations, have been grounds for revocation. Absconding from probation supervision—that is, failing to report and concealing oneself from the probation authorities—represents another serious violation.

The issue of probation violation underscores the tremendous discretionary authority of the probation officer. Technical violations generally come to the attention of only the supervising officer. If the defendant fails to report, reverts to using drugs, consorts with known criminals, refuses to remain gainfully employed, or fails to live up to other conditions of the probation contract, the officer has several options. He or she can cite the probationer for violation, can engage in more intensive counseling and supervision, or can simply choose not to respond. Thus, the probation officer initiates violation proceedings, and these generally begin only when revocation is the goal. However, although the probation officer or department can recommend revocation, only the court has the authority to revoke probation.

In the event of a new arrest, a warrant may be lodged against the probationer in order to prevent his or her release on bail. If the violation is only technical, a warrant may also be issued, and either the police or probation authorities may take the violator into custody. Some jurisdictions issue such warrants as a matter of course; others do so only when they have evidence that the probationer might abscond if left in the community pending a revocation hearing. Once the probation authorities decide to seek revocation, the offender is given notice of the decision, the probation officer prepares a violation report, and a formal court hearing is scheduled. In the past five decades, both state and federal courts have made a number of significant decisions regarding revocation proceedings. These decisions often stress the rehabilitative nature of probation and clarify the practices associated with revoking probation.[51]

The Effectiveness of Probation

Probation is by far the most widely used criminal sanction. At the end of 2010, for example, nearly 4.9 million offenders were under probation supervision in the United States.[52] Half (51 percent) had been convicted of a felony, 47 percent had been convicted of a misdemeanor, and 2 percent had been convicted of other infractions. Twenty-six percent of the offenders on probations were there for drug offense convictions.[53]

There are reasons for this widespread use of probation, most stemming from economic and rehabilitative considerations. In addition, some observers believe that probation is the most effective phase of the criminal justice process. However, one of the more comprehensive studies of probation effectiveness, conducted by the RAND Corporation, found that most felony offenders placed on probation were still a considerable threat to the community.[54] The RAND study found that 65 percent of those placed on probation were rearrested. Almost 80 percent of these, or 51 percent of the entire sample, were convicted of new crimes. Of the sample, 18 percent were reconvicted of serious violent crimes, and 34 percent were reincarcerated.[55] The RAND study, however, described only the population of California. In 1986, researchers conducted a similar study for the state of Missouri and found considerably lower rearrest rates.[56] Another analysis of probation by the Department of Justice in 2000 came to the same conclusion, with later studies confirming these findings.[57] The mixed nature of the findings suggests that the effectiveness of probation varies from one jurisdiction to the next and that individual studies of probation effectiveness may not be representative of felony probation in general. More recent studies suggest that probation can have a positive impact when it occurs in conjunction with treatment, particularly for drug abuse.[58]

PAROLE

Like probation, **parole** is given to offenders who have been adjudicated. However, unlike probation, parole applies after the offender has served some portion of his or her prison sentence; it allows the offender to serve the final portion of the sentence in the community (see Exhibit 13.1 for some basic characteristics of this population). Parole is a condition of release, not a sentence like probation. Parole, a term that comes from the same word in French, meaning "word of honor," was first used in 1846 by the Boston penal reformer Samuel G. Howe.[59] Parole actually comprises two operations: (1) *parole release,* the procedures used to establish the periods of confinement that prisoners serve, and (2) *parole supervision,* the conditions and provisions that regulate parolees' lives outside prison until the final discharge from their sentences. In theory, parole ensures that incarceration is tailored to the needs of the inmate, reducing the harshness of long sentences and hastening the offender's reintegration into the community when it appears that he or she is able to function as a law-abiding citizen. In addition, it has had the goals of alleviating the overcrowded conditions of correctional institutions and maintaining social control within prisons through the threat of denial of parole as punishment for misbehavior.

Parole Administration

The terms *parole* and *probation* have often been used interchangeably—but as is already apparent, the two differ in many ways. Probation involves a sentence to community supervision in lieu of imprisonment; parole is a conditional release from a correctional institution after a period of imprisonment. Beyond this distinction, there are administrative differences. First, the authority to both grant and revoke probation falls within the realm of the lower courts. In contrast, the authority to grant and revoke parole is held by an administrative board that can be (1) an independent state agency, (2) a unit within some larger state department, or (3) the body that regulates the state's correctional institutions. Second, responsibility for the supervision of probationers can rest with a single court, a county agency (at times the same agency that supervises probationers), a state department or division, or some combination thereof in any given jurisdiction. Parole supervision services, however, are under the authority of a single state agency in all instances.[60] The functions of parole boards are essentially fourfold: (1) to select and place prisoners on parole, (2) to provide continuing control over parolees in the community, (3) to discharge parolees from supervision when they complete their sentences, and (4) to review parole violations and determine whether revocation and return to prison are appropriate.[61]

Since parole boards make decisions on parole release and revocation, as well as create policy regarding planning and supervision services, it seems logical that the efficiency and viability of the entire parole system depend on the qualifications, skills, and experiences of the members of the board. The American Correctional Association recommends that parole board members command respect and public confidence; be appointed without reference to creed, color, or political affiliation; possess academic training that would qualify them for their professional practice; and have intimate knowledge of the situations and problems confronting offenders.[62]

Eligibility for Parole

Numerous statutes restrict the granting of parole. As a result, inmates are not automatically paroled as a matter of right. Parole eligibility refers to the earliest date that an inmate can be considered for parole. However, because of the nature of their offenses and sentences, some prisoners can never be paroled. Eligibility for parole is defined by legal statutes within the particular jurisdiction the offense was committed.

A key factor in the determination of parole eligibility is the specific statute in each jurisdiction regarding "good time." **Good time** refers to the number of days deducted from a sentence for good behavior, meritorious service, particular kinds of work, or

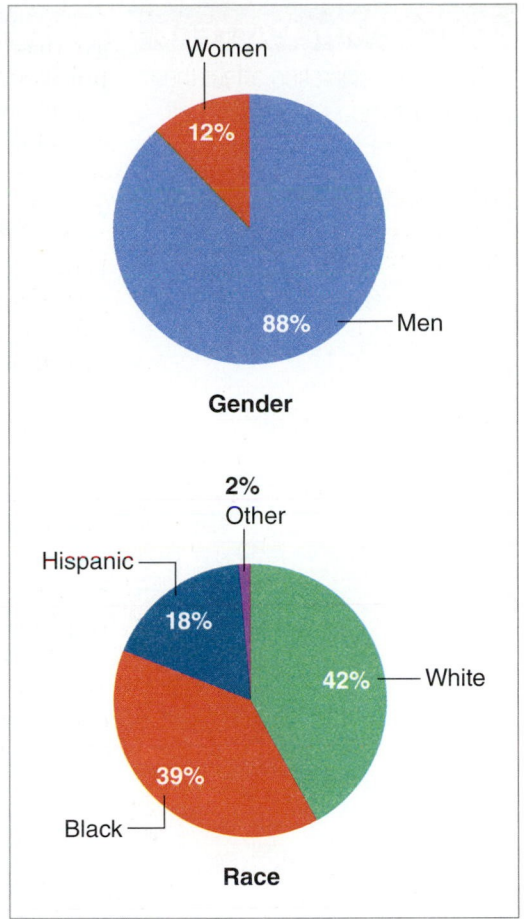

EXHIBIT 13.1 Offenders on Parole, 2010
Source: Bureau of Justice Statistics

DISCRETION MATTERS

How might discretion affect the amount of good time awarded to particular offenders in correctional facilities?

other considerations. Some states have a fixed formula for allocating good time, such as two or three days for each month served. In others it is left to the discretion of the prison authorities but cannot exceed a certain portion of the term imposed by the court. Good-time credits must be earned, and as noted in the discussion of prison disciplinary proceedings in Chapter 12, they can be forfeited for poor behavior.[63]

The Parole Hearing

Parole hearings are generally private and are attended only by the inmate, the board, a representative of the institution in which the inmate is incarcerated, and an individual charged with recording the proceedings. The board reviews the inmate's case, as well as any institutional reports that may have been submitted, and questions the inmate regarding his or her adjustment, plans if released, and the circumstances of the offense. The inmate often makes a statement on his or her own behalf. The inmate is then dismissed, and the board discusses the case and makes its decision.

Parole boards vary in their specific procedures. Some meet as a group for every case; others break up into groups to hold hearings in different parts of the jurisdiction. Since the mid-1970s, the U.S. Parole Commission and many of the larger states have used hearing examiners, who make recommendations on which the board acts. Regardless of the particular procedure, parole authorities have been given wide discretion as to how they conduct hearings. This discretion has been supported by the courts. In *Menechino v. Oswald*,[64] decided by the U.S. Court of Appeals for the Second Circuit, the petitioner argued that the manner in which his parole hearing had been conducted violated his due process rights. He claimed that the Constitution required that he be given the following:

1. notice
2. fair hearing with right to counsel, cross-examination, and presentation of witnesses
3. specification of the reasons for the parole board's decision

The court, however, ruled that the due process clause did not apply to parole hearings, since inmates, who are already imprisoned, do not have "present private interests"

Parole hearings provide the criminal justice system and victims the opportunity to make decisions about the supervised release of offenders into the community.

that require protection. The following year, though, the court did hold that written reasons must be given for denial of parole.[65] However, in 1979, the U.S. Supreme Court in *Greenholtz v. Inmates of Nebraska Penal and Correctional Complex*[66] affirmed previous decisions that parole hearings need not have all the elements of due process that are required at criminal trials. And in 1998, in *Pennsylvania Board of Probation and Parole v. Scott*,[67] the U.S. Supreme Court ruled that the exclusionary rule does not apply in parole revocation hearings, thus giving parole and police agencies a powerful weapon in investigating parole violations and criminal activity.

Parole Selection

An overview of contemporary parole practice suggests that many release decisions reflect variable and sometimes arbitrary standards. A variety of legislative mandates, for example, express the vague policy that a prisoner should be paroled only when such action is compatible with the welfare of the community.[68] More specific criteria have included such factors as the offender's prior criminal record, personality and physical condition, social history, employment record, intelligence, family status, institutional conduct, parole plan, prior probation or parole history, and stated intentions for the future.

Parole release decisions can also be affected by politics and policy. The recommendations of a sentencing judge or a prosecuting attorney or the media depictions of justice invariably affect the parole process. This is the reason that very similar offenders or offenses may not have identical parole processes. Moreover, in some state and federal release hearings, victims of crime are permitted to testify against the offenders—a practice with a probable impact on parole decision-making.

In recommending an offender for parole, the members of a paroling board may have to guess, or follow their instincts, on the basis of the limited information submitted to them; they may observe a potential candidate and make a prediction based on insight, intuition, and inductive assumption; or they may examine various types of more or less scientific data to arrive at a decision. Further confounding this process is the tendency to base decisions on a majority rule or, in some jurisdictions, a unanimous verdict.

Predictions of human behavior are especially problematic when the individuals under review have already demonstrated a reduced capacity to function in a socially approved manner. Parole boards have been known to release only prisoners who are seen to be good risks while denying parole to the remainder.[69]

Risk-assessment tools can aid in the determination of which offenders are most amenable to parole. Statistical programs that analyze the characteristics of offenders and past offenses attempt to calculate the likelihood of recidivism. These programs have been used with mixed results, though some modest success has been noted.[70] In some cases, especially notorious ones, an inmate will repeatedly be denied parole despite his or her eligibility for conditional release. This may occur for several reasons. First, depending on the nature of the case, the prosecutor's parole recommendation can influence the board's decision. Second, the police, the news media, the victims of the crime, and the general public may oppose an inmate's parole. For example, Sirhan Sirhan, the assassin of Robert F. Kennedy, and mass murderer Charles Manson are not likely to ever be paroled, even if they are virtually incapable of committing future offenses.

In cases in which inmates are serving indeterminate sentences and parole is repeatedly denied, or in certain types of determinate ("flat") sentences, another factor comes into play—good-time credits. As noted earlier, good time refers to the number of days deducted from a sentence for good behavior, meritorious service, particular kinds of work, or other considerations. Almost all jurisdictions provide for some type of automatic good time, ranging from 4.5 days per month in the federal system to 30 days per month in Alabama.[71] Although the maximum number of good-time days is fixed by statute, in some jurisdictions "earned-time" credits, which can total

These inmates are cleaning up an oil spill. By doing so, they can earn good time applied toward their parole dates.

as many as 30 days per month, are applied beyond this upper limit. The accumulation of good-time days may ultimately result in **mandatory release**—release as a matter of law. Mandatory release refers to the release from prison required by statute when an inmate has been confined for a time period equal to his or her full prison sentence minus any statutory good time. Many states have eliminated good-time legislation altogether so that sentences determined by the court are in fact the sentences served by the offender. This focus on so-called truth in sentencing has led to changes in the ways offenders are sentenced, released, and managed within corrections.

Conditions of Parole

As with probation, parole involves release under a series of conditions, whose violation can result in revocation and a return to prison. Parole conditions are fairly uniform from state to state and can be grouped into two general areas: *reform conditions,* which urge parolees toward a noncriminal way of life, and *control conditions,* which enable the parole agency to keep track of parolees. These conditions are determined by the paroling body (an agency or parole board). The most common reform conditions are:

- Comply with the laws.
- Maintain employment or education and support dependents.
- Refrain from use of drugs and alcohol.

The most common control conditions are:

- Report to the parole officer upon release and periodically thereafter.
- Cooperate with the parole officer.
- Get permission (or notify the parole officer of plans) to change employment or residence.

As with probationers, parolees may be assigned additional conditions geared to their particular treatment and control needs. Parole boards have an enormous amount of discretion in determining the conditions of parole.

Parole Supervision and Services

Like probation officers, parole officers are responsible for supervising, aiding, and controlling the clients assigned to them. As counselors, parole officers ease parolees' reentry into society and help them overcome obstacles to adjustment. They may also help in the development of employment plans and job readiness, work with families to resolve problems, and refer parolees to community agencies that can help with certain persistent difficulties. Some parole agencies have special units that focus on alcoholism, drug use, unemployment, and the needs of mentally ill or mentally impaired offenders. In some jurisdictions, parole and probation are housed within the same agency or organization.

In addition to counseling and assisting their clients, parole officers have the duty to police the behavior of those under their supervision. In many states, parole officers are armed peace officers. Although quasi–law enforcement responsibilities are apparent in probation supervision, they are considerably more pronounced with respect to parole, given the nature of the post-incarceration supervision.

Parole Violation and Revocation

The violation and revocation process in parole is very similar to that described earlier for probation. After a new arrest or serious technical violation, a warrant is issued and the parolee is taken into custody. Pursuant to the Supreme Court's decision in *Morrissey v. Brewer*,[72] the delinquent parolee is given a measure of due process during his or her preliminary and revocation hearings, and the parole board can make one of two decisions: "restore to supervision" or "return to prison." If parole is revoked, the next issue is exactly how much time the parolee must serve in prison. The parole board makes this decision either at the revocation hearing or during the next board meeting at the institution.

Parole Discharge

Individuals can be discharged from parole in a number of ways. First, they can reach their maximum expiration date—the date on which their full sentence formally terminates. Second, in many of the states and the federal system, parolees can be discharged by the parole board before their maximum expiration date. In this instance, however, a number of jurisdictions require that some minimum parole period be served. In Ohio, for example, discharge can occur after one year of satisfactory supervision, except in the case of a life sentence, when discharge can occur after five years of satisfactory supervision.[73] Under New York's executive clemency statute, if the time remaining on the maximum sentence at the time of parole is more than five years, the board can issue a discharge after five consecutive years of satisfactory supervision.[74] Discharge can also occur through commutation of a sentence or a pardon by the governor.

The State of Parole in the United States

The institution of parole in the United States has undergone significant changes in the past several decades. For example, some states and the federal government have eliminated parole altogether or diminished the authority of parole boards, while others have retained it as a significant function of prisoner reentry. By the end of 2010, about 1 in 48 adults in the United States were under community supervision; 840,700 individual offenders were being supervised using parole. The number of offenders on parole increased by 0.3 percent from 2009, when America saw the first small decline in parole population since the Bureau of Justice Statistics had begun collecting data. The general reduction was primarily due to the removal of parole as a community sanction in some states.[75] For example, due to budget constraints, many states are attempting to reduce their correctional populations. Washington and California both developed legislation that attempts to limit their community corrections populations, specifically reserving parole and probation supervision for the most serious offenders while often diverting less serious offenders to other programs.[76]

The first major component of parole—deciding whether and when to release an offender—has also shifted over time. Discretionary decisions have been the traditional function of the parole board, while mandatory release is a matter of law. The criminal justice system has moved away from the practice of indeterminate sentencing, which in turn granted parole boards considerable flexibility in deciding the length of an offender's sentence. Increasingly, however, the legislative branch of government is dictating the release of offenders by establishing mandatory sentencing and release laws.

Parole failures can be classified as either technical violations (i.e., violating a term or condition of release) or new-crime violations (i.e., being arrested, charged, and convicted of new and unrelated charges). Between 1998 and 2009, the number of parole violators sent back to prison remained relatively stable.[77] More than a third of incoming prisoners are incarcerated for parole violations.

We have no national standard for measuring the success rate of parole. The Bureau of Justice Statistics defines success as the completion of the terms of supervision without the parolee's returning to prison or jail or absconding. Using this standard, 52 percent of parolees were successful in 2010, a measurement that had remained relatively constant since the 1990s, when success rates ranged from 41 percent to 49 percent.[78] However, policies and level of enforcement vary by state and contribute to widespread differences in success rates. Differences also exist among first-release and re-release parolees, the latter having already returned to prison at least once for violation of parole. Moreover, a study by the Urban Institute in Washington, DC, found that in the two years following release, 62 percent of inmates released with no parole supervision were rearrested at least once.[79] While examining these trends provides some insight into the current state of parole, continued research into what does and doesn't work among states is needed to better direct future public policy initiatives.

PRISONER REENTRY

Prisoner reentry is one of the most pressing issues in the U.S. criminal justice system. Hundreds of thousands of offenders are released every year, and recidivism rates are high. The challenge lies in developing innovative ways to ensure the successful reintegration of ex-offenders into the community. However, few comprehensive research efforts or policy directives have been aimed at prisoner reentry, and budgets for these programs have been reduced. Those in the criminal justice field who are involved in reentry initiatives advocate programs that favor treatment and accountability measures over surveillance and enforcement. For example, a National Institute of Justice analysis of 53,614 individuals found that adding a treatment component to a release program resulted in a 10 percent reduction in recidivism.[80]

Nonetheless, without sufficient preparation in terms of housing, employment, social support, and counseling, ex-offenders are more likely to fail in their attempts to reintegrate into the community. While funding for prison construction and operating costs have been increasing dramatically, funding for rehabilitative programs has not kept pace with the needs of the ex-offender population. Resources, including job skills training and counseling for substance abuse and mental health issues, are important for individuals coping with reintegration into the community. Given the high relapse rates of addiction and the connection between drug use and criminal activity, treatment options deserve increased attention. Likewise, studies have found that a substantial number of inmates have serious mental health problems and that their greater involvement in the criminal justice system is due partially to their mental health needs going unmet.[81]

The Sentencing Project in Washington, DC, calls the restrictions and obstacles facing newly released offenders a form of "invisible punishment."[82] For example, a lack of job skills and stigmatization by potential employers who do not want to hire individuals with criminal backgrounds can hinder ex-offenders' chances of avoiding crime and rearrest. The denial of federal benefits and services because of a criminal record puts ex-offenders at a further disadvantage. Programs that aim to reduce these barriers are essential to the success of prisoner reentry and need to be funded with greater urgency.[83]

The needs of ex-offenders are varied and many; they require assistance in their transition to the community after they have paid their debt to society. However, ex-offenders must also develop accountability for their actions in order to achieve long-term results. Accountability and responsibility have become the focus of many community programs, particularly those steeped in the philosophy of **restorative justice.** The impact of these programs is examined in more detail in the "Victims and Justice" feature.

The diminishing authority of parole boards in many states in favor of mandatory sentencing, as discussed earlier in the chapter, is one area that experts say must be more closely evaluated. Diminishing the power of the parole board in release decisions may actually be removing a crucial gatekeeping mechanism that prevents incarcerated offenders from reentering society when they are deemed unfit to do so. And when prisoners are released, integrating offender accountability measures into parole supervision may play an important function in their reintegration.

Reentry courts represent an initiative that provides services while placing a high value on accountability. Reentry courts are based on the drug-court model and use judges to closely monitor released offenders and to sanction or reward them as necessary for changing their behavior. Initial results have proved promising. Although the sheer number of ex-offenders released from prison has forced attention on the topic of prisoner reentry, our understanding of what makes the transition successful remains limited. Continued development of innovative programs, funding of services, and increased research evaluations are needed to strengthen reentry initiatives. To increase the success of offenders, some states have authorized the use of furlough and temporary release programs, the topic we turn to next.

VICTIMS AND JUSTICE

Restoring Justice for Victims, Communities, and Offenders

Criminal justice has been criticized for focusing on retribution while ignoring high recidivism and incarceration rates. In addition, the role of victims is minimal in the traditional criminal justice process. In response, restorative justice programs—also known as *reparative justice* and *victim-offender reconciliation*—emphasize repairing the harm done by the criminal offense.[84] Broadly, restorative justice focuses on more than punishing those who break the law; it allows the victim, offender, and community to become involved in the criminal justice process in the hopes of reducing the overall harm of crime and the likelihood of future criminal events (Exhibit 13.2).[85]

The focus on responding to the needs of victims, as well as offenders and the community, makes restorative justice particularly useful for reducing crime and repairing the harm it causes.

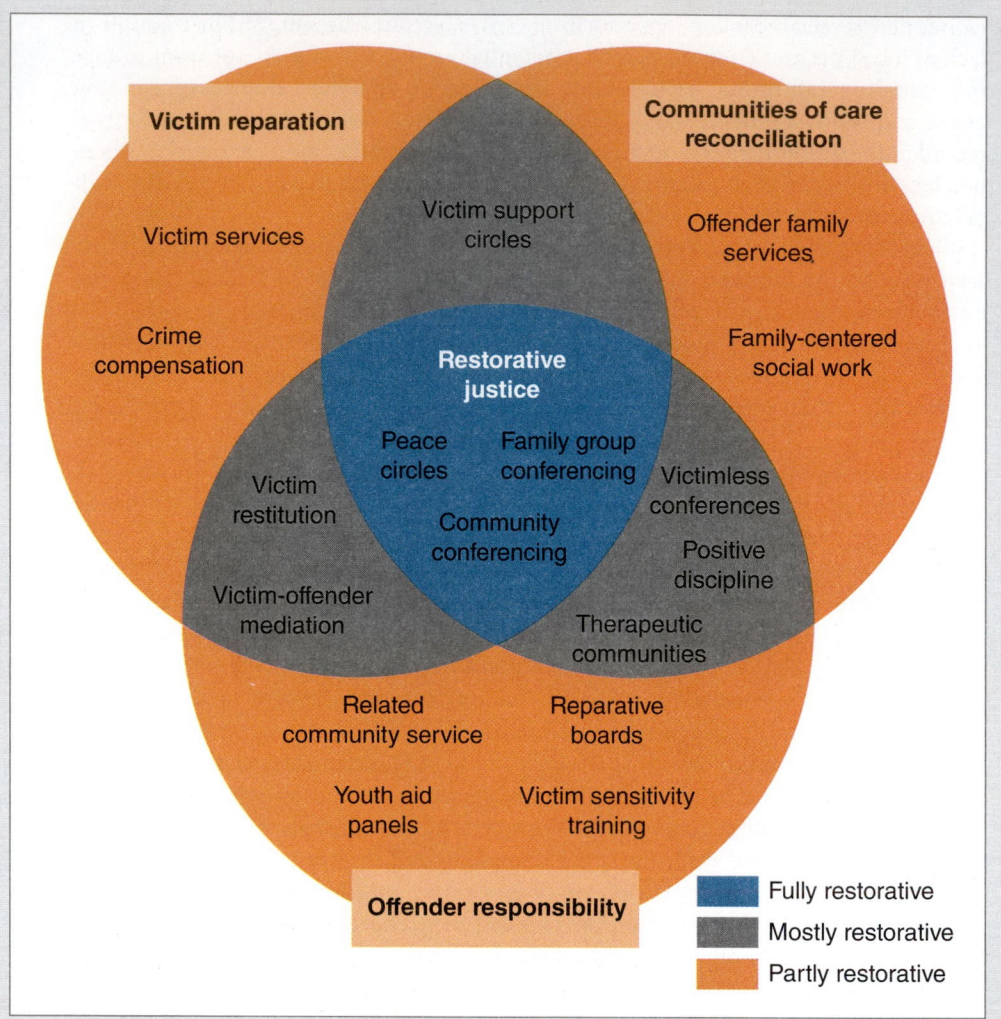

EXHIBIT 13.2   Restorative justice programs focus on reducing crime and its impact by integrating community, victims, and offenders.

Source: International Institute for Restorative Practices

Consider, for example, the account of the Paintball Case, as described by Professor Tom Cavanaugh. A young man shot into a group of teenagers with a paintball gun, and a girl in the crowd was permanently blinded in one eye. The offender was charged with second-degree assault with a deadly weapon in juvenile court. He agreed to plead guilty and to serve a community probation sentence with conditions set out by the court. These conditions included a conference between the families of the victim and the offender. During the four-hour conference, the offender heard from the victim and also expressed his own remorse and concern. In addition, the offender agreed to take financial responsibility for the costs the victim's family had incurred as a result of the shooting. Because of that meeting, the victim agreed to help the offender find a job with an acquaintance, to enable him to pay the restitution.[86] This case illustrates the tenets of restorative justice—that bringing all parties together can create a positive result for the larger community, the victim, and the offender.

In many ways, restorative justice is a process that criminal justice officials facilitate rather than lead.[87] Police, courts, and correctional personnel help individuals work out their own solutions for both holding offenders accountable and repairing, as far as possible, the damage to victims and communities. Programs vary across the country. Many of these involve some combination of victim and offender mediation, victim assistance (counseling and victim rights advocacy), restitution, community service, and ex-offender assistance (to repair the offender and ultimately reduce recidivism).[88] Restorative justice programs are found at all stages of the criminal justice process, from arrest through release from jail or prison.[89] Officials within community correctional agencies generally facilitate these experiences. The tenets of restorative justice guide many reentry programs for adults and diversion programs for juveniles.[90]

THINK ABOUT THIS

1. What role might discretion play in the use of restorative justice programs? Should all offenders or offenses be eligible for participation?
2. How might meeting with offenders help victims recover from their experiences with crime?
3. In the context of restorative justice, do you think it is appropriate to diminish the role of criminal justice professionals and instead focus on victims and the community?

Furlough and Temporary Release

A **furlough** is an authorized, unescorted absence from a correctional institution for a specified period. It is granted for the purpose of enabling inmates to reestablish community contacts and family ties on a gradual basis. Under furlough programs, eligible inmates are given the opportunity to leave the institution so they can seek employment, maintain family ties, solve family problems, seek post-release housing, or attend short-term educational or vocational training courses. Eligibility criteria vary, however. In some states, it is a statutory matter and applies only to inmates who are within one year of parole eligibility or conditional release and have not been convicted of escape, absconding, or violent offenses. In others, eligibility is a matter of legislative, judicial, or correctional policy, with the criteria ranging from highly specific to hopelessly vague.[91] In the following sections, we discuss two types of furlough—home furlough and work release.

Home Furlough A home furlough is a short leave of absence, often taken on weekends and lasting anywhere from half an hour to as long as 180 days.[92] The home furlough serves a number of rehabilitative and pragmatic purposes. First, inmates can begin to normalize family relationships, reestablish contacts with the community, and prepare for eventual release. In addition, prison administrators view the furlough as an instrument of institutional management, asserting that the promise of a home visit for good behavior fosters greater compliance with custodial regulations. In settings where conjugal visitations or private visits with spouses or significant others are either impractical or not permitted, the furlough also has the benefit of reducing sexual frustration.

Work Release Similar in concept and purpose to the home furlough, work release is an alternative to total incarceration, whereby inmates are permitted to work for pay in the community but must spend their nonworking hours in an institution, usually a jail or detention facility. Work release is not a recent innovation; it was initiated in 1913 in Wisconsin.[93] However, the idea has been accepted only slowly, and it was not until the early 1970s that work release became a widespread correctional practice for felony offenders.[94] Eligibility criteria are similar to those for home furloughs, restricting release to inmates nearing parole or conditional release who do not represent a significant risk to the community.

In addition to the advantages of furloughs in general, work release has the potential to reshape an offender's self-image and promote the process of decarceration. Moreover, offenders can assume some financial responsibilities by paying for transportation to and from the institution, contributing to the costs of their room and board, supplementing any welfare benefits given to their families, and paying any court-ordered restitution. Thus, work release can also serve the interests of the taxpaying public.

In spite of incidents in which released offenders have caused harm or further victimization, the concept of temporary release continues to hold promise as a bridge between prison and free society—and as another treatment mechanism in the spectrum of community-based correctional services. Perhaps many of the difficulties in existing programs might be eliminated, or at least minimized, with better screening of candidates and monitoring of offenders. However, militating against its use as a correctional tool is the public outrage that arises when even a few isolated violent crimes are committed by people who are supposed to be behind bars. This, combined with many unresolved questions as to whether temporary release reduces recidivism—and the political realities associated with it—have led to reductions in the use of furloughs and their outright removal as an option in many jurisdictions.

Transitions into the Community

Halfway houses and prerelease centers provide a strong contrast to furloughs. Designed for inmates who are just a few months away from their parole dates, these residential facilities in urban locations provide individual counseling, vocational guidance, and job placement. Residents are required to abide by minimum-security regulations, attend counseling and therapy sessions, and actively seek employment when ready.[95]

Whether halfway houses are effective at reintegrating offenders into the community is open to question. Studies have found conflicting outcomes. Concerns about significant levels of escape, recidivism, and return to prison for disciplinary violations have led some to question the practice.[96] However, since recidivism seemed to be no higher among prerelease-center residents than among other newly released inmates, it has been recommended that the halfway house concept be expanded. This is not likely to occur, however, not only for political reasons but also because of broad community opposition to "placing convicts in our backyards."

Young people who have become entangled in the juvenile justice system also may be subject to community corrections, including halfway houses. To see how the juvenile system compares and contrasts with the adult system, read the "Juvenile Justice in Context" feature.

JUVENILE JUSTICE IN CONTEXT

Community Corrections and Diversion for Juvenile Offenders

The juvenile due process requirements, combined with the rising costs of operating correctional institutions, have resulted in wider use of community-based treatment for adjudicated juveniles. Many young offenders are diverted out of the formal criminal justice process through programs that provide resources and social services in order to decrease their likelihood of committing future offenses. These programs and services often involve remedial education and drug-abuse treatment programs, foster homes, and counseling services. Probation is by far the primary form of community treatment in the juvenile justice system, and the probation process for youths is essentially the same as that for adults.

Community corrections programs began to emerge within the juvenile justice system during the early part of the twentieth century. Among the first was the Chicago Boys' Court, founded in 1914 as an extralegal form of probation. As explained many years ago by Chicago municipal court judge Jacob Braude, the rationale of the Boys' Court was to process and treat young offenders without branding them as criminals.[97] The Boys' Court system of supervision placed a young defendant under the authority of community agencies. After a time, the court requested a report of the defendant's activities and adjustment, and if it was favorable, the child was officially discharged from the court with no criminal record.

Over the years, scores of juvenile diversion programs have emerged. One of these is the Arbitration Intervention Worker initiative. Designed for first offenders, it provides intensive case management services for juveniles charged with relatively minor offenses. Accompanied by their parents, youths assigned to the program meet with a counselor who outlines sanctions that they must complete in order to satisfy the diversion requirements. Common categories of sanctions include restitution, as well as participation in psycho-educational groups, substance-abuse monitoring and/or treatment, and violence prevention.[98]

Diversion and community programs attempt to keep youths out of trouble by involving them in activities that contribute positively to their neighborhoods.

CONCLUSIONS

By the end of 2010, nearly 4.9 million people were under supervision in the community, as either probationers or parolees.[99] Factors related to this significant number include the overcrowding of prisons, the pressures on states to remedy the unconstitutional conditions in many of them, the trend toward mandatory prison sentences for serious and violent offenders, and budget constraints at both the state and federal levels. Over the next decade, then, correctional facilities will increasingly become places for holding the most serious offenders, at least for a time, and community corrections will increasingly become the solution for other types of offenders. Thus, the numbers in probation, diversion, and other forms of community-based supervision and service will continue to be significant. Moreover, corrections will increasingly focus on reentry for those offenders deemed fit for release into the community.

How the system determines which offenders to release and how to treat them will reflect the concerns about crime and justice in communities across the country. As courts and communities use their discretion in developing innovative responses to crime and offenders, creative sanctions such as those you read about in the chapter-opening case of Shawn Gementera may become more common.

SUMMARY AND REVIEW

◾ **Describe the philosophy of community-based corrections.**

- The basic principle of community-based corrections rests on the fundamental fact that offenders are either incarcerated or not.
- Community-based corrections comprise activities and programs that have effective ties to the local environment.
- Generally, these criminal justice responses are rehabilitative rather than punitive and can include arrangements with employment, educational, social, and clinical service-delivery systems and resources. Many also involve supervision by a community and/or governmental agency.

◾ **Explain criminal justice diversion and the reasons it is used.**

- Diversion refers to the removal of offenders from the application of criminal law at any stage of the police and court processes, from arrest to incarceration.
- At their introduction, these programs were believed to reduce court backlog, provide early intervention before the development of full-fledged criminal careers, ensure some consistency in selective law enforcement, reduce the costs of criminal processing, and enhance an offender's chances for successful community reintegration.

◾ **Define and give examples of intermediate sanctions.**

- Intermediate sanctions fall between the extremes of fines and imprisonment.
- Examples include community service, home confinement, electronic monitoring, and numerous treatment and rehabilitative programs.

◾ **Explain probation and the services associated with it.**

- Probation refers to a sentence of conditional release to the community. It does not involve confinement, but it does impose conditions. The sentencing court retains authority to modify the conditions of the sentence or to resentence the offender if he or she violates the conditions.
- As a status, probation reflects the unique character of the probationer: He or she is neither a free citizen nor a confined prisoner.
- As a system, probation is a component in the administration of justice, as embodied by the agency or organization that administers the probation process.
- As a process, probation refers to the functions, activities, and services that characterize the system's transactions with the courts, the offender, and the community.

◾ **Describe parole and the controversy surrounding its use.**

- Parole is the practice of allowing offenders to serve the final portion of a prison sentence in the community. It includes two operations: (1) parole release, the procedures used to establish the periods of confinement that prisoners serve, and (2) parole supervision, the conditions and provisions that regulate parolees' lives outside of prison until the final discharge from their sentences.
- Criticism of parole centers on concerns that convicted offenders will commit offenses once released. The determination of the point at which offenders can be released is especially controversial.

◾ **Identify the issues related to reentry of offenders into society.**

- One of the most pressing issues in modern criminal justice is the return of offenders released from correctional facilities to the community.
- Without sufficient preparation in terms of housing, employment, social support, and counseling, ex-offenders are less likely to reintegrate into the community.
- Reentry programs attempt to balance treatment and the reduction of recidivism with accountability measures for ex-offenders. Ex-offenders' future success in the community is balanced against concerns about recidivism and security.

KEY TERMS

community-based corrections (p. 341)

diversion (p. 342)

furlough (p. 359)

good time (p. 351)

intensive probation supervision (IPS) (p. 349)

intermediate sanctions (p. 341)

mandatory release (p. 354)

parole (p. 350)

probation (p. 344)

restitution (p. 345)

restorative justice (p. 357)

shock probation (p. 348)

suspended sentence (p. 345)

ISSUES FOR CRITICAL THINKING AND DISCUSSION

1. What is your opinion of creative sentences like those mentioned in the chapter-opening case of Shawn Gementera? Should judges and/or juries be allowed to craft such specialized responses to criminal offenders?

2. What goals might be met by the use of community correctional sanctions?

3. What is your view of community-based corrections? Are these responses helpful for nonviolent offenders? Why or why not?

4. Should parole be abolished? Why or why not?

5. What is your opinion of shock probation programs? Why do you think they might or might not be effective?

6. Is house arrest a rehabilitative or punitive option for offenders?

Endnotes

Chapter 1

1. Florida v. J.L., 529 U.S. 266 (2000).
2. Ibid.
3. Ibid.
4. For discussions of the social values and dissent of the 1960s, see Roderick Aya and Norman Miller, eds., *The New American Revolution* (New York: Free Press, 1971); and Godfrey Hodgson, *America in Our Time: From WWII to Nixon—What Happened and Why* (New York: Vintage Books, 1995). Many of the violent episodes of the 1960s are described at length in H. D. Graham and T. R. Gurr, eds., *Violence in America: Historical and Comparative Perspectives* (New York: Bantam, 1970); and Richard Hofstadter and Michael Wallace, eds., *American Violence: A Documentary History* (New York: Random House, 1970).
5. See Peter Joseph, *Good Times: An Oral History of America in the Nineteen Sixties* (New York: Morrow, 1974).
6. Henry J. Abraham, *Freedom and the Court: Civil Rights and Liberties in the United States* (New York: Oxford, 1977), 33–105.
7. President's Commission on Law Enforcement and Administration of Justice, *The Challenge of Crime in a Free Society* (Washington, DC: U.S. Government Printing Office, 1967).
8. Lyndon B. Johnson, "Message to the Congress," March 9, 1966.
9. President's Commission, *The Challenge of Crime.*
10. President's Commission, *The Challenge of Crime,* vi.
11. President's Commission, *The Challenge of Crime.*
12. Edwin H. Sutherland and Donald R. Cressey, *Principles of Criminology* (Philadelphia: Lippincott, 1966), 95, 241, 265.
13. James Q. Wilson, *Thinking About Crime* (New York: Basic Books, 1975), 3.
14. President's Commission, *The Challenge of Crime,* 7.
15. J. Edgar Hoover, *Crime in the United States, 1968* (Washington, DC: U.S. Government Printing Office, 1969).

16. See Leon Gibson Hunt and Carl D. Chambers, *The Heroin Epidemics* (New York: Spectrum, 1976).
17. Richard Harris, *The Fear of Crime* (New York: Praeger, 1968), 15–16.
18. Nigel D. Walker, "Lost Causes in Criminology," in *Crime, Criminology, and Public Policy,* ed. Roger Hood (New York: Free Press, 1974), 47–62.
19. The Omnibus Crime Control and Safe Streets Act, 18 U.S.C. § 2518 (1968).
20. Twentieth Century Fund Task Force on the Law Enforcement Assistance Administration, *Law Enforcement: The Federal Role* (New York: McGraw-Hill, 1976), 4.
21. Jeff Gerth, "The Americanization of 1984," *Sundance Magazine,* April/May 1972, 58–65.
22. See, for example, Philip Parsons, *Crime and the Criminal: An Introduction to Criminology* (New York: Knopf, 1926); Harry Elmer Barnes, *The Repression of Crime* (New York: Doran, 1926); Marcus Kavanagh, *The Criminal and His Allies* (Indianapolis: Bobbs-Merrill, 1928); Fred E. Haynes, *Criminology* (New York: McGraw-Hill, 1930); Harry Best, *Crime and the Criminal Law in the United States* (New York: Macmillan, 1930); Nathaniel F. Cantor, *Crime, Criminals, and Criminal Justice* (New York: Holt, 1932); Edwin H. Sutherland, *Principles of Criminology* (Philadelphia: Lippincott, 1924, 1939, 1947); Harry Elmer Barnes and Negley K. Teeters, *New Horizons in Criminology* (Englewood Cliffs, NJ: Prentice-Hall, 1959).
23. Paul W. Tappan, *Crime, Justice, and Correction* (New York: McGraw-Hill, 1960).
24. Herbert Packer, *The Limits of Criminal Sanction* (Stanford, CA: Stanford University Press, 1968), 154–73.
25. Bernard Schwartz, *The Warren Court: A Retrospective* (New York: Oxford University Press, 1996).
26. Bernard Schwartz, ed., *The Burger Court: Counter-Revolution or Confirmation?* (New York: Oxford University Press, 1998).
27. Samuel Walker, *Sense and Nonsense About Crime, Drugs, and Communities* (Belmont, CA: Wadsworth, 2010).

28. Samuel Walker, *Sense and Nonsense About Crime and Drugs* (Belmont, CA: Wadsworth, 2006), citing President's Commission on Law Enforcement and Administration of Justice, *Task Force Report: Science and Technology* (Washington, DC: Government Printing Office, 1967), 61.
29. National Center on Addiction and Substance Abuse, *Shoveling Up: The Impact of Substance Abuse on State Budgets* (New York: Columbia University Press, 2001).
30. Substance Abuse and Mental Health Services Administration and Office of Applied Studies, *The DASIS Report: Substance Abuse Treatment Admissions Referred by the Criminal Justice System: 2006,* July 30, 2007, http://www.samhsa.gov/data/factsDASIS.htm.
31. Jill K. Doerner and Stephen Demuth, "The Independent and Joint Effects of Race/Ethnicity, Gender, and Age on Sentencing Outcomes in U.S. Federal Courts," *Justice Quarterly* 27, no. 1 (2010).
32. Darrell Steffensmeier and Emilie Allen, "Gender and Crime: Toward a Gendered Theory of Female Offending," *Annual Review of Sociology* 22 (1996): 459–87.
33. "Prisoners in 2003," *Bureau of Justice Statistics Bulletin* (November 2004); "Prisoners in 2010," *Bureau of Justice Statistics Bulletin* (December 2011).
34. Katherine Stuart van Wormer and Clemens F. Bartollas, *Women and the Criminal Justice System* (Upper Saddle River, NJ: Prentice Hall, 2010).
35. American Bar Association, *New Perspectives on Urban Crime* (Washington, DC: U.S. Government Printing Office, 1969).
36. Jerome Skolnick, *Justice Without Trial: Law Enforcement in Democratic Society,* 3rd ed. (New York: Macmillan, 1993).
37. From U.S. Code Title 22, Chapter 38, Section 2656f(d).
38. David Cole and James X. Dempsey, *Terrorism and the Constitution: Sacrificing Civil Liberties in the Name of National Security* (New York: New Press, 2002); Bruce Hoffman, "Rethinking Terrorism and Counterterrorism Since 9/11," *Studies in Conflict and Terrorism* 25 (2003): 303–316.

39. Adapted from an essay by James A. Inciardi.

40. This discussion of critical thinking is based, in part, on Margaret W. Matlin, *Psychology*, 3rd ed. (Fort Worth, TX: Harcourt Brace, 1999), 19–25.

41. Paul Takagi, "A Garrison State in a Democratic Society," *Crime and Social Justice* 1 (Spring/Summer 1974): 27–33.

42. Ryan Gabrielson, accessed 2012, "'Three Strikes' Ballot Initiative Could Save California $100 Million, Claim Authors," http://www.huffingtonpost.com/2012/01/11/three-strikes-ballot-initiative_n_1199585.html.

Chapter 2

1. Robinson v. California, 370 U.S. 660 (1962).

2. Ibid.

3. Ibid.

4. Sir Henry Sumner Maine, *Ancient Law: Its Connection to the History of Early Society*, available online: http://www.gutenberg.org/files/22910/22910-h/22910-h.htm.

5. Edward Adamson Hoebel, *The Law of Primitive Man: A Study in Comparative Legal Dynamics* (Cambridge, MA: Harvard University Press, 2006).

6. Tamera Bryant, *The Life and Times of Hammurabi* (Hockessin, DE: Mitchell Lane, 2005).

7. For additional information see John Curra, *The Relativity of Deviance* (Newark, NJ: Sage, 2010); and Nicole Rafter, "The Social Construction of Crime and Criminal Justice," *Journal of Research in Crime and Delinquency*, 27, no. 4 (1990): 376–89.

8. Kai T. Erikson, *Wayward Puritans: A Study in the Sociology of Deviance* (New York: Wiley, 1966), 6.

9. Howard S. Becker, *Outsiders* (New York: Simon and Schuster, 1997), 147–63.

10. Pew Research Center, *A Portrait of Generation Next: How Young People View Their Lives, Futures and Politics*, January 9, 2007, http://www.people-press.org/2007/01/09/a-portrait-of-generation-next/.

11. Jerome Michael and Mortimer J. Adler, *Crime, Law and Social Science* (New York: Harcourt Brace, 1933), 2.

12. Edwin H. Sutherland, *White Collar Crime* (New York: Dryden, 1949), 31.

13. Henry Campbell Black, *Black's Law Dictionary*, 4th ed. (St. Paul, MN: West, 1968), 444.

14. Dean J. Champion, *The Roxbury Dictionary of Criminal Justice* (Los Angeles: Roxbury, 1997), 33.

15. Paul W. Tappan, *Crime, Justice, and Correction* (New York: McGraw-Hill, 1960), 10.

16. See Nathan F. Leopold, *Life Plus Ninety-Nine Years* (New York: Doubleday, 1958).

17. Richard Harris, *The Fear of Crime* (New York: Praeger, 1968), 15–16; People v. Beardsley, 150 Mich. 206, 113 N.W. 1128 (1907).

18. Twentieth Century Fund Task Force on the Law Enforcement Assistance Administration, *Law Enforcement: The Federal Role* (New York: McGraw-Hill, 1976), 4.

19. Robinson v. California, 370 U.S. 660 (1962).

20. Ibid.

21. Black, *Black's Law Dictionary*, 1101.

22. Durham v. United States, 214 F.2d 862 (1954).

23. United States v. Brawner, 471 F.2d 969 (1972).

24. R. D. Mackay, B. J. Mitchell, and L. Howe, "Yet More Facts about the Insanity Defence," *Criminal Law Review* (2006): 399–411; Scott O. Lilienfeld and Hal Arkowitz, "Facts and Fictions in Mental Health: The Insanity Verdict on Trial," *Scientific American*, January/February 2011, 2; L. A. Callahan, H. J. Steadman, M. A. McGreevy, and P. C. Robbins, "The Volume and Characteristics of Insanity Defense Pleas: An Eight-State Study," *The Bulletin of the American Academy of Psychiatry and the Law* 19, no. 4 (1991): 331–38.

25. Lambert v. California, 355 U.S. 225 (1957).

26. The Supreme Court affirmed the Lambert ruling most recently in Ratzlaf v. United States, 510 U.S. 135 (1994).

27. Hampton v. United States, 425 U.S. 484 (1976).

28. United States v. Vue, 38 F.3d 973 (1995).

29. "Robert Randall, 53; Sued for Marijuana," *New York Times*, June 8, 2001, http://www.nytimes.com/2001/06/08/us/robert-randall-53-sued-for-marijuana.html.

30. U.S. v. Oakland Cannabis Buyers' Cooperative, 532 U.S. 483 (2001).

31. Pam Belluck, "Judge Spares Shopping Addict from Prison," *New York Times*, May 25, 2001; Paul Gray and Leslie Whitaker, "Her Lucky Day," *Time*, June 4, 2001, 56.

32. L. L. Downs, "PMS, Psychosis and Culpability: Sound or Misguided Defense?" *Journal of Forensic Sciences* 47 (2002): 1083–89.

33. "Not Guilty Verdict for Andrea Yates; Missing Girl's Body Found in Utah" *Nancy Grace*, aired on CNN, July 26, 2006.

34. Sir James Fitzjames Stephen, *History of the Criminal Law of England*, vol. 2 (New York: Macmillan, 1883), 75.

35. John H. Wigmore, *A Panorama of the World's Legal Systems* (Washington, DC: Washington Law Book, 1936), 4.

36. F. A. Inderwick, *The King's Peace* (London: Swan Sonnenschein, 1895), 3.

37. Lawrence M. Friedman, *A History of American Law* (New York: Simon & Schuster, 1973), 17.

38. See Richard A. Posner, *Overcoming Law* (Cambridge: Harvard University Press, 1995).

39. Harry Elmer Barnes, *The Repression of Crime: Studies in Historical Penology* (New York: Doran, 1926), 44–45.

40. This quotation from Lombroso's opening speech at the Sixth Congress of Criminal Anthropology at Turin, Italy, in 1906 appears in Leon Radzinowicz, *Ideology of Crime* (New York: Columbia University Press, 1966), 29.

41. Gina Lombroso Ferrero, *Criminal Man According to the Classification of Cesare Lombroso* (New York: Putnam's, 1911), 10–24.

42. Cesare Lombroso and William Ferrero, *The Female Offender* (New York: Appleton, 1895), 101.

43. See also Arthur H. Estabrook, *The Jukes in 1915* (Washington, DC: Carnegie Institution, 1916); Arthur H. Estabrook and Charles P. Davenport, *The Nam Family* (Cold Spring Harbor, NY: Eugenics Record Office, 1912); and Henry H. Goddard, *The Kallikak Family* (New York: Macmillan, 1912).

44. Earnest A. Hooton, *Crime and the Man* (Cambridge, MA: Harvard University Press, 1939).

45. Nicole Rafter, "Earnest A. Hooton and the Biological Tradition in American Criminology," *Criminology* 42 (2004): 735–71.

46. William H. Sheldon, S. S. Stevens, and W. B. Tucker, *The Varieties of Human Physique* (New York: Harper, 1940).

47. R. G. Fox, "The XYY Offender: A Modern Myth?" *Journal of Criminal Law, Criminology, and Police Science* 62 (March 1971): 59–73. See also Donald J. West, ed., *Criminological Implications of Chromosome Abnormalities* (Cambridge: University of Cambridge, Institute of Criminology, 1969); and "The XYY Chromosome: A Challenge to Our System of Criminal Responsibility," *New York Law Forum* 16 (Spring 1970): 232.

48. James Q. Wilson and Richard J. Herrnstein, *Crime and Human Nature* (New York: Simon & Schuster, 1985).

49. Robert E. Park, Ernest W. Burgess, and Roderick D. McKenzie, *The City* (Chicago: University of Chicago Press, 1925).

50. Ibid.

51. Clifford R. Shaw and Associates, *Delinquency Areas* (Chicago: University of Chicago Press, 1929).

52. Clifford R. Shaw, *Brothers in Crime* (Chicago: University of Chicago Press, 1938); Clifford R. Shaw, *The Jack Roller* (Chicago: University of Chicago Press, 1930).

53. Emile Durkheim, *Suicide: A Study in Sociology* (New York: Free Press, 1951).

54. Robert K. Merton, "Social Structure and Anomie," *American Sociological Review* 3 (1938): 672–82.

55. Robert Agnew, "Foundation for a General Strain Theory," *Criminology* 30 (1992): 47–87.

56. Robert Agnew, "Building on the Foundation of General Strain Theory: Specifying the Types of Strain Most Likely to Lead to Crime and Delinquency," *Journal of Research in Crime and Delinquency* 38 (2001): 319–61; Robert Agnew, "A General Strain Theory of Community Differences in Crime Rates," *Journal of Research in Crime and Delinquency* 36 (1999): 123–55.

57. Michael and Adler, *Crime, Law and Social Science*, 5.

58. Thorsten Sellin, *Culture Conflict and Crime* (New York: Social Science Research Council, 1938), 21.

59. Albert K. Cohen, *Delinquent Boys: The Culture of the Gang* (Glencoe, IL: Free Press, 1955).

60. Richard Cloward and Lloyd Ohlin, *Delinquency and Opportunity* (New York: Free Press, 1960).

61. Walter B. Miller, "Lower Class Culture as a Generating Milieu for Gang Delinquency," *Journal of Social Issues* 14 (1958): 5–19.

62. Edwin H. Sutherland, *The Professional Thief* (Chicago: University of Chicago Press, 1937).

63. Edwin H. Sutherland and Donald Cress, *Principles of Criminology* (Philadelphia: Lippincott, 1947), 6–7.

64. Robert Burgess and Ronald Akers, "A Differential Association-Reinforcement Theory of Criminal Behavior," *Social Problems* 14 (1968): 28–47.

65. Travis Hirschi, *Causes of Delinquency* (Berkeley: University of California Press, 1969).

66. Edwin M. Lemert, *Social Pathology* (New York: McGraw-Hill, 1951), 75–76.

Chapter 3

1. Wisconsin v. Mitchell, 508 U.S. 476 (1993).

2. Ibid.

3. Ibid.

4. Ibid.

5. Ibid.

6. New York State Penal Law, Section 10.00(3).

7. For additional information, see the FBI's Uniform Crime Report's Web site: http://www.fbi.gov/about-us/cjis/ucr/ucr.

8. United States v. Timothy James McVeigh and Terry Lynn Nichols, CR-95-110-A (W.D. Okla. 1995).

9. See criminal codes of Florida, Minnesota, and Wisconsin.

10. Jerome Hall, "Analytic Philosophy and Jurisprudence," *Ethics* 77 (October 1966): 14–28.

11. John Gramlich "Should Murder Accomplices Face Execution?" *Stateline,* August 13, 2008, http://www.stateline.org/live/details/story?contentId=333117.

12. Karl Vick, "Intoxicated N.C. Driver Handed Life Sentence," *Washington Post,* May 7, 1997.

13. John F. Boudreau, Quon Y. Kwan, William E. Faragher, and Genevieve C. Denault, *Arson and Arson Investigation: Survey and Assessment* (Washington, DC: U.S. Government Printing Office, 1977), 1.

14. See, for example, Delaware Code, Title 11, Sections 824, 825, 826.

15. Louisiana Criminal Code, Title 14, Section 67.

16. Delaware Code, Title 11, Section 840.

17. Ohio Code, Section 2913.02.

18. Wayne Logan, Lindsay S. Stellwagen, and Patrick A. Langan, *Felony Laws of the 50 States and the District of Columbia* (Washington, DC: Bureau of Justice Statistics, 1987).

19. Western Regional Popular Cultural Association Convention, Las Vegas, Nevada, February 12, 1976.

20. Lawrence v. Texas, 539 U.S. 558 (2003).

21. Henry F. Fradella and Kegan Brown, "Withdrawal of Consent Post-Penetration: Redefining the Law of Rape," *Criminal Law Bulletin* 41, no. 1 (2005): 3–23; Sue Titus Reid, *Criminal Law* (Boston: McGraw-Hill, 1998), 211.

22. See Ian O'Donnell, "Prison Rape in Context," *British Journal of Criminology* 44, no. 2 (2004): 241–55; Robert W. Dumond, "Confronting America's Most Ignored Crime Problem: The Prison Rape Elimination Act of 2003," *Journal of the American Academy of Psychiatry and the Law* 31, no. 3 (2003): 356–60; and Christine A. Saum, Hilary L. Surratt, James A. Inciardi, and Rachael E. Bennett, "Sex in Prison: Myths and Realities," *The Prison Journal* 75 (1995): 413–30.

23. Michael M. v. Superior Court of Sonoma County, 458 U.S. 747 (1981).

24. Erin Van Bronkhorst, "Teacher Has Baby by One of Her Sixth-Grade Pupils," Associated Press Wire Services, October 29, 1997.

25. Letourneau marries Fualaau amid media circus," *Seattle Post-Intelligencer,* May 21, 2005, http://www.seattlepi.com/local/article/Letourneau-marries-Fualaau-amid-media-circus-1174066.php.

26. James P. Gray, *Why Our Drug Laws Have Failed and What We Can Do about It: A Judicial Indictment of the War on Drugs* (Philadelphia, PA: Temple University Press, 2001).

27. Ibid.

28. Madison Gray, "New York's Rockefeller Drug Laws," *Time,* April 2, 2009, http://www.time.com/time/nation/article/0,8599,1888864,00.html.

29. P. A. Manscuso, "Resentencing after the "Fall" of Rockefeller: The Failure of the Drug Law Reform Acts of 2004 and 2005 to Remedy the Injustices of New York's Rockefeller Drug Laws and the Compromise of 2009," *Albany Law Review* 73 (2010): 1535.

30. *A Guide to State-Controlled Substances Acts,* rev. ed. (Washington, DC: Bureau of Justice Assistance and the National Criminal Justice Association, 1999).

31. Federal Bureau of Investigation (FBI), *Crime in the United States, 2010,* http://www.fbi.gov/about-us/cjis/ucr/crime-in-the-u.s/2010/crime-in-the-u.s.-2010/tables/10shrtbl10.xls.

32. For some of the classic studies, see Marvin Wolfgang, *Patterns in Criminal Homicide* (Philadelphia: University of Pennsylvania Press, 1958); David J. Pittman and William Handy, "Patterns in Criminal Aggravated Assault," *Journal of Criminal Law, Criminology and Police Science* 55 (December 1964): 462–70; Duncan Chappell, Robley Geis, and Gilbert Geis, eds., *Forcible Rape: The Crime, the Victim, and the Offender* (New York: Columbia University Press, 1977); Edwin M. Lemert, "An Isolation and Closure Theory of Naive Check Forgery," *Journal of Criminal Law, Criminology, and Police Science*

44 (1953): 296–307; Mary Owen Cameron, *The Booster and the Snitch* (New York: Free Press of Glencoe, 1964); Werner J. Einstadter, "The Social Organization of Armed Robbery," *Social Problems* 17 (Summer 1969): 64–83; Gilbert Geis, "From Deuteronomy to Deniability: A Historical Perlustration of White-Collar Crime," *Justice Quarterly* 5 (March 1988): 7–32; Joseph L. Albini, *The American Mafia: Genesis of a Legend* (New York: Appleton-Century-Crofts, 1971); Daniel Bell, *The End of Ideology: On the Exhaustion of Political Ideas in the Fifties* (New York: Free Press, 1962), 127–50; Norval Morris and Gordon Hawkins, *The Honest Politician's Guide to Crime Control* (Chicago: University of Chicago Press, 1970), 202–35; Edwin H. Sutherland, *The Professional Thief* (Chicago: University of Chicago Press, 1937); James A. Inciardi, *Careers in Crime* (Chicago: Rand McNally, 1975), 5–82.

33. FBI, *Crime in the United States, 2010.*

34. See Carla Smith Stover, "Domestic Violence Research: What Have We Learned and Where Do We Go from Here?" *Journal of Interpersonal Violence* 20, no. 4 (2005): 448–54; Rashmi Goel, "Restorative Justice, Domestic Violence, and South Asian Culture," *Violence Against Women* 11, no. 5 (2005): 639–65; Jeanette Zanipatin, Stacy Shaw Welch, Jean Yi, and Patty Bardina, "Immigrant Women and Domestic Violence," in *Race, Culture, Psychology, and Law,* ed. Kimberly Holt Barrett and William H. George (Thousand Oaks, CA: Sage, 2005), 375–89; and Cliff Mariani, *Domestic Violence Survival Guide* (Flushing, NY: Looseleaf, 1996).

35. See Neil B. Guterman, "Advancing Prevention Research on Child Abuse, Youth Violence, and Domestic Violence: Emerging Strategies and Issues," *Journal of Interpersonal Violence* 19, no. 3 (2004): 299–321; Gail Erlick Robinson, "Current Concepts in Domestic Violence," *Primary Psychiatry* 10, no. 12 (2003): 48–52; and Eve S. Buzawa and Carl G. Buzawa, *Domestic Violence: The Criminal Justice Response* (Thousand Oaks, CA: Sage, 1996).

36. See Kris Henning and Lynette Feder, "A Comparison of Men and Women Arrested for Domestic Violence: Who Presents the Greater Threat?" *Journal of Family Violence* 19, no. 2 (2004): 69–80; Cindy L. Seamans, "A Qualitative Study of Women Perpetrators of Domestic Violence: Comparison with Literature on Men Perpetrators of Domestic Violence," *Dissertation Abstracts International: Section B, The Sciences and Engineering* 64, 3-B (2003): 1506; Coramae Richey Mann, *Women Who Kill* (Albany: SUNY Press, 1996); and Richard B. Felson, "Big People Hit Little People: Sex Differences in Physical Power and Interpersonal Violence," *Criminology* 34, no. 3 (1996): 433–52.

37. Bureau of Justice Assistance, *A Policymaker's Guide to Hate Crimes* (Washington, DC: Office of Justice Programs, 1997).

38. FBI, *Hate Crime Statistics, 2010,* http://www.fbi.gov/news/pressrel/press-releases/fbi-releases-2010-hate-crime-statistics.

39. Ibid.

40. Jacksonville FBI, "White-Collar Crime," http://www.fbi.gov/about-us/investigate/white_collar.

41. FBI, *Crime in the United States, 2006* (Washington, DC: Department of Justice, 2006).

42. Jay S. Albanese, Dilip K. Das, and Arvind Verma, *Organized Crime: World Perspectives* (Upper Saddle River, NJ: Prentice Hall, 2003); Adam Edwards and Peter Gills, eds., *Transnational Organized Crime: Perspectives on Global Security* (London: Routledge, 2003); William Kleinknecht, *The New Ethnic Mobs: The Changing Face of Organized Crime in America* (New York: Free Press, 1996).

43. See, for example, United States Code, Title 22, Section 2656f(d)(2).

44. *National Counterterrorism Council 2010 Report,* http://www.nctc.gov/witsbanner/docs/2010_report_on_terrorism.pdf.

45. FBI, *Crime in the United States, 2010.*

46. Ibid.

47. Ibid.

48. FBI, *Crime in the United States, 2010, Crime Clock,* http://www.fbi.gov/about-us/cjis/ucr/crime-in-the-u.s/2010/crime-in-the-u.s.-2010/offenses-known-to-law-enforcement/crime-clock.

49. FBI, *Crime in the United States, 2010.*

50. Ibid.

51. See Clayton J. Mosher, Terance D. Miethe, and Timothy C. Hart, *The Mismeasure of Crime* (Thousand Oaks, CA: Sage, 2010); James A. Inciardi, "The Uniform Crime Reports: Some Considerations on Their Shortcomings and Utility," *Public Data Use* 6 (November 1978): 3–16.

52. Benjamin Bowling, "The Rise and Fall of New York Murder," *British Journal of Criminology* 39, no. 4 (Autumn 1999).

53. Danny Monteverde, "Audit Finds No Intentional Manipulation of Crime Data during Serpas' Tenure with Nashville Police," *Times Picayune,* June 28, 2011, http://www.nola.com/crime/index.ssf/2011/06/audit_finds_some_errors_in_cri.html.

54. Ernie Suggs, "Pennington's Way," *Atlanta Journal-Constitution,* April 24, 2003.

55. Donna Leinwand, "Campus Crime Underreported: Colleges Have Been Caught Misreporting Violence Statistics" *USA Today,* October 4, 2000.

56. FBI, *Structure and Implementation Plan for the Enhanced UCR Program* (Washington, DC: Federal Bureau of Investigation, 1989).

57. Bureau of Justice Statistics, *UCR and NIBRS Participation,* November 17, 2004, http://www2.fbi.gov/ucr/faqs.htm.

58. President's Commission on Law Enforcement and Administration of Justice, *Crime and Its Impact: An Assessment* (Washington, DC: U.S. Government Printing Office, 1967), 17.

59. Law Enforcement Assistance Administration, *Criminal Victimization in the United States—1977* (Washington, DC: U.S. Government Printing Office, 1979).

60. Bureau of Justice Statistics, *Criminal Victimization—2010* (Washington, DC: Office of Justice Programs, 2011), http://www.bjs.gov/content/pub/pdf/cv10.pdf.

61. Thorsten Sellin, *Research Memorandum on Crime in the Depression* (New York: Social Science Research Council, 1937).

62. James S. Wallerstein and Clement J. Wyle, "Our Law-Abiding Law-Breakers," *Probation* 35 (April 1947): 107–18.

63. J. Andenaes, N. Christie, and S. Skirbekk, "A Study in Self-Reported Crime," in *Scandinavian Studies in Criminology,* Scandinavian Research Council on Criminology (Oslo: Universitels-forloget, 1965), 87–88.

Chapter 4

1. District of Columbia v. Heller, 554 U.S. 570 (2008).

2. Ibid.

3. Luke Owen Pike, *A History of Crime in England,* vol. 1 (London: Smith, Elder, 1873–1876), 52–55; Christopher Hibbert, *The Roots of Evil* (Boston: Little, Brown, 1963), 5–8.

4. Ashford v. Thornton (1818) 106 ER 149.

5. Ibid.

6. Ibid.; Charles Rembar, *Law of the Land* (New York: Simon and Schuster, 1980).

7. Henry M. Christman, ed., *The Public Papers of Chief Justice Earl Warren* (New York: Simon & Schuster, 1959), 70.

8. See Randy E. Barnett, ed., *The Rights Retained by the People: The History and Meaning of the Ninth Amendment* (Fairfax, VA: George Mason University Press, 1989).

9. Cited in Irving Brant, *The Bill of Rights* (Indianapolis: Bobbs-Merrill, 1965), 49–50.

10. Barron v. Baltimore, 32 U.S. (7 Pet.) 243 (1833).

11. Ibid.

12. United States Constitution, Fourteenth Amendment, Section 1.

13. See Richard C. Cortner, *The Supreme Court and the Second Bill of Rights* (Madison: University of Wisconsin Press, 1981), 3–11; Henry J. Abraham, *Freedom and the Court: Civil Rights and Liberties in the United States,* 4th ed. (New York: Oxford University Press, 1982), 30–48.

14. Hurtado v. California, 110 U.S. 516 (1884).

15. See Maxwell v. Dow, 176 U.S. 581 (1900); Twining v. New Jersey, 211 U.S. 78 (1908).

16. Maxwell v. Dow, 176 U.S. 581 (1900).

17. Gitlow v. New York, 268 U.S. 652 (1925).

18. Ibid.

19. Fiske v. Kansas, 274 U.S. 380 (1927).

20. Near v. Minnesota, 283 U.S. 697 (1931).

21. Powell v. Alabama, 287 U.S. 45 (1932).

22. Ira Rosenwaike, *Population History of New York City* (Syracuse, NY: Syracuse University Press, 1972), 18–36.

23. *Commercial Advisor,* August 20, 1840, cited in James F. Richardson, *The New York Police: Colonial Times to 1901* (New York: Oxford University Press, 1970), 26.

24. Palko v. Connecticut, 302 U.S. 319 (1937).

25. Ibid.

26. Ibid.

27. Ibid.

28. Ibid.

29. Ibid.

30. Ibid.

31. Everson v. Board of Education, 330 U.S. 1 (1947).

32. In re Oliver, 333 U.S. 257 (1948).

33. Trop v. Dulles, 356 U.S. 86 (1958).

34. Mapp v. Ohio, 367 U.S. 643 (1961).

35. Robinson v. California, 370 U.S. 660 (1962).

36. Gideon v. Wainwright, 372 U.S. 335 (1963).

37. Malloy v. Hogan, 378 U.S. 1 (1964).

38. Pointer v. Texas, 380 U.S. 400 (1965).

39. Parker v. Gladden, 385 U.S. 363 (1966).

40. Klopfer v. North Carolina, 386 U.S. 213 (1967).

41. Washington v. Texas, 388 U.S. 14 (1967).

42. Duncan v. Louisiana, 391 U.S. 145 (1968).

43. Benton v. Maryland, 395 U.S. 784 (1969).

44. Ibid.

45. Griswold v. Connecticut, 381 U.S. 479 (1965).

46. Roe v. Wade, 410 U.S. 113 (1973).

47. Bowers v. Hardwick, 106 S. Ct. 2841 (1986).

48. Lawrence v. Texas, 539 U.S. 558 (2003).

49. Dartmouth College v. Woodward, 17 U.S. (4 Wheat.) 519 (1819).

50. Coates v. City of Cincinnati, 402 U.S. 611 (1971).

51. Smith v. Goguen, 415 U.S. 566 (1974).

52. Cox v. Louisiana, 379 U.S. 536 (1965).

53. Buck v. Bell, 274 U.S. 200 (1927).

54. Cited in H. J. Abraham, *Freedom and the Court* (New York: Oxford University Press, 1972): 111–14.

55. Skinner v. Oklahoma, 316 U.S. 535 (1942).

56. United States v. Valdovinos-Valdovinos, 743 F.2d 1436 (1984).

57. Ibid.

58. Ibid.

59. Brinegar v. United States, 338 U.S. 160 (1949).

60. New York State Penal Law, Article 40; Section 80.05.

61. Booth v. Maryland, 482 U.S. 496 (1987).

62. Payne v. Tennessee, 501 U.S. 808 (1991).

63. President's Commission on Law Enforcement and Administration of Justice, *The Challenge of Crime in a Free Society* (Washington, DC: U.S. Government Printing Office, 1967), 7.

64. See James A. Inciardi, *Reflections on Crime* (New York: Holt, Rinehart and Winston, 1978), 160.

65. President's Commission on Law Enforcement and Administration of Justice, *Task Force Report: Juvenile Delinquency and Youth Crime* (Washington, DC: U.S. Government Printing Office, 1967), 2–3.

66. Evelina Beldon, "Courts in the United States Hearing Children's Cases," *Children's Bureau Publication* 65 (Washington, DC: U.S. Department of Labor, 1918), 8.

67. Illinois Juvenile Court Act, Illinois Statutes, 1899, Section 131.

Chapter 5

1. Florida v. Bostick, 501 U.S. 429 (1991).

2. Ibid.

3. Ibid.

4. Luke Owen Pike, *A History of Crime in England,* vol. 2 (London: Smith, Elder, 1873–1876), 457–62.

5. Ibid., 218.

6. See Patrick Pringle, *Hue and Cry: The Story of Henry and John Fielding and Their Bow Street Runners* (New York: Morrow, 1965), 29–58.

7. Patrick Colquhoun, *A Treatise on the Police of the Metropolis* (London: Mawman, 1806).

8. Ibid.

9. Carl Bridenbaugh, *Cities in the Wilderness: Urban Life in America, 1625–1742* (New York: Capricorn, 1964), 63–64.

10. Bruce Smith, *Rural Crime Control* (New York: Columbia University Institute of Public Administration, 1933), 61–63.

11. Walter Prescott Webb, *The Texas Rangers: A Century of Frontier Defense* (Boston: Houghton Mifflin, 1935).

12. Bruce Smith, *Police Systems in the United States* (New York: Harper & Brothers, 1949), 168.

13. Frank R. Prassel, *The Western Peace Officer: A Legacy of Law and Order* (Norman: University of Oklahoma Press, 1972).

14. Ira Rosenwaike, *Population History of New York City* (Syracuse, NY: Syracuse University Press, 1972), 18–36.

15. Smith, *Police Systems in the United States,* 168.

16. Ibid.

17. Edward R. Maguire, Jeffrey B. Snipes, Craig D. Uchida, Margaret Townsend, "Counting Cops: Estimating the Number of Police Departments and Police Officers in the USA," *Policing: an International Journal of Police Strategies and Management* 21, no. 1 (1998): 97–120.

18. See www.fbi.gov for additional information and resources.

19. See www.atf.gov for additional information and resources.

20. See www.justice.gov/dea/ for additional information and resources.

21. See www.usmarshals.gov for additional information and resources.

22. See www.dhs.gov/index.shtm for additional information and resources.

23. See www.irs.gov for additional information and resources.

24. See www.fws.gov for additional information and resources.

25. U.S. Government Accountability Office, *Federal Law Enforcement:*

Investigative Authority and Personnel at 32 Organizations (Washington, DC: U.S. Government Printing Office, 1997). Also see the GAO Web site: www.gao.gov.

26. Chris Hawley, "Air Marshals Likely to Step Up Presence," *Miami Herald,* September 16, 2001; Sally B. Donnelly, "My Life as an Air Cop," *Time,* June 28, 2004, 42–43; Samantha Levine, "The Marshals' Cloudy Skies," *U.S. News & World Report,* November 29, 2004, 28–29.

27. Jean-Germain Gros, "Trouble in Paradise: Crime and Collapsed States in the Age of Globalization," *British Journal of Criminology* 43 (2003): 63–80; Michael Fooner, *Interpol: Issues in World Crime and International Criminal Justice* (New York: Plenum, 1989); National Institute of Justice, *A Guide to Interpol: The International Criminal Police Organization in the United States* (Boulder, CO: Paladin Press, 1991).

28. See Advisory Commission on Intergovernmental Relations, *State-Local Relations in the Criminal Justice System* (Washington, DC: U.S. Government Printing Office, 1971).

29. Katherine Mayo, *Justice to All: The Story of the Pennsylvania State Police* (New York: Putnam, 1917).

30. Law Enforcement-Private Security Consortium, *Operation Partnership: Trends and Practices in Law Enforcement and Private Security Collaborations.* Report to the U.S. Department of Justice, Office of Community Oriented Policing Services, July 2009, http://www.ilj.org/publications/docs /Operation_Partnership_Private _Security.pdf.

31. Tim Newburn, "The Commodification of Policing: Security Networks in the Late Modern City," *Urban Studies* 38, nos. 5–6 (2001): 829–48; Deanna Hodgin, "Private Crime Fighting for a Profit," *Insight,* January 21, 1991, 44–45; see also the Wackenhut Corporation Web site: http://www.g4s.com.

32. Ibid.

33. Samuel Walker, *Popular Justice: A History of American Criminal Justice,* 2nd ed. (New York: Oxford University Press, 1998).

34. Lawrence M. Friedman, *Crime and Punishment in American History* (New York: Harper Collins, 1993).

35. Ibid.

36. Walker, *Popular Justice.*

37. For a more detailed discussion of police tasks, see National Research Council, *Fairness and Effectiveness in Policing* (Washington, DC: National Academy Press, 2000); David

Weisburd and John E. Eck, "What Can Police Do to Reduce Crime, Disorder, and Fear?" *The Annals* 593 (May 2004): 42–65; Egon Bittner, *The Functions of Police in Modern Society* (New York: Aronson, 1975); Jonathan Rubinstein, *City Police* (New York: Farrar, Straus & Giroux, 1973); and Herman Goldstein, *Policing a Free Society* (Cambridge, MA: Ballinger, 1977).

38. Federal Bureau of Investigation (FBI), *Crime in the United States, 2010,* http://www.fbi.gov/about-us/cjis/ucr /crime-in-the-u.s/2010/crime-in-the -u.s.-2010/tables/10shrtbl10.xls.

39. FBI, *Law Enforcement Officers Killed and Assaulted 2010,* http://www.fbi .gov/about-us/cjis/ucr/leoka/leoka-2010.

40. James Q. Wilson, *Varieties of Police Behavior: The Management of Law and Order in Eight Communities* (Cambridge, MA: Harvard University Press, 1968); Albert J. Reiss Jr., *The Police and the Public* (New Haven, CT: Yale University Press, 1971); Richard J. Lundman, "Police Patrol Work: A Comparative Perspective," in *Police Behavior: A Sociological Perspective,* ed. Richard J. Lundman (New York: Oxford University Press, 1980), 52–65.

41. Wilson, *Varieties of Police Behavior.*

42. David L. Carter and Jeremy G. Carter, "Intelligence-Led Policing: Conceptual and Functional Considerations for Public Policy," *Criminal Justice Policy Review* 20, no. 3 (2009): 310–25.

43. Mark L. Dantzker, *Understanding Today's Police* (Upper Saddle River, NJ: Prentice Hall, 2000); O. W. Wilson and Ray C. McLaren, *Police Organization* (New York: McGraw-Hill, 1977).

44. NYPD, Office of Public Relations, 2008.

45. Arthur Niederhoffer, *Behind the Shield* (Garden City, NY: Doubleday, 1967), 41–42.

46. FBI, *Crime in the United States, 2010.*

47. Patricia Tjaden and Nancy Thoennes, *Extent, Nature, and Consequences of Intimate Partner Violence* (Washington, DC: National Institute of Justice and the Centers for Disease Control and Prevention, 2000); Karen Scott Collins, Cathy Schoen, Susan Joseph, et al., *Health Concerns Across a Woman's Lifespan: The Commonwealth Fund 1998 Survey of Women's Health,* http://www.commonwealthfund.org /Publications/Fund-Reports/1999/May /Health-Concerns-Across-a-Womans -Lifespan--The-Commonwealth-Fund -1998-Survey-of-Womens-Health.aspx.

48. M. C. Black, K. C. Basile, M. J. Breiding, et al., *The National Intimate Partner and Sexual Violence Survey (NISVS): 2010 Summary Report* (Atlanta, GA: National Center for Injury Prevention and Control and the Centers for Disease Control and Prevention, 2011).

49. Henry Ansgar Kelly, "Rule of Thumb and the Folklaw of the Husband's Stick," *Journal of Legal Education* 44, no. 3 (September 1994): 341–65.

50. *Bradley v. State,* 1 Miss. 156 (1824).

51. T. K. Logan, Lisa Shannon, and Robert Walker, "Police Attitudes Toward Domestic Violence Offenders," *Journal of Interpersonal Violence* 21, no. 10 (2006): 1365–374.

52. David Hirschel, Charles Dean, and Richard Lumb, "The Relative Contribution of Domestic Violence to Assault and Injury of Police Officers," *Justice Quarterly* 11 (1994): 99–117.

53. Richard v. Ericson, *Reproducing Order: A Study of Police Work* (Toronto: University of Toronto Press, 1984).

54. George L. Kelling, *The Kansas City Preventive Patrol Experiment: A Summary Report* (Washington, DC: Police Foundation, 1974).

55. W. B. Sanders, *Detective Work: A Study of Criminal Investigations* (New York: Free Press 1977).

56. For more information see the Miami-Dade County Police Web site: http://www.miamidade.gov/mdpd /BureausDivisions/bureau_Robbery .asp.

57. David A. Schroeder and Michael D. White, "Exploring the Use of DNA Evidence in Homicide Investigations: Implications for Detective Work and Case Clearance," *Police Quarterly* 12, no. 3 (2009): 319–42; F. Horvath and R. Meesig, "Criminal Investigation Process and the Role of Forensic Evidence: A Review of Empirical Findings," *Journal of Forensic Science* 41, no. 6 (1996): 963–69; J. L. Peterson, S. Mihajlovic, and M. Gililand, *Forensic Evidence and the Police—The Effects of Scientific Evidence on Criminal Investigations* (Washington, DC: National Institute of Justice, 1984).

58. S. Hindjua and J. A. Schafer, "Cybercrime Units on the Worldwide Web: A Content Analysis," *Policing: An International Journal of Police Strategies and Management* 32 (2009): 278–96.

59. Charles Whited, *The Decoy Man* (New York: Playboy Press, 1973), 12.

60. See David A. Klinger and Jeff Rojek, *A Multi-Method Study of Special Weapons and Tactics Teams,* National Institute of Justice Document

Number 223855, https://www.ncjrs
.gov/pdffiles1/nij/grants/223855.pdf.

61. Peter B. Kraska and Victor E. Kappeler, "Militarizing the American Police: The Rise and Normalization of Paramilitary Units," *Social Problems* 44 (February 1997): 1–18.

62. Kraska and Kappeler, "Militarizing the American Police"; Peter B. Kraska and Victor E. Kappeler, "Police: The Rise and Normalization of Paramilitary Units," *Social Problems* 44, no. 1 (February 1997): 1–18; Peter Kraska, "Militarization and Policing—Its Relevance to 21st Century Police," *Policing* 1, no. 4 (2007): 501–13, doi: 10.1093/police/pam065.

63. David Weisburd, Stephen D. Mastrofski, Ann Marie McNally, et al., "Reforming To Preserve: COMPSTAT and Strategic Problem Solving in American Policing," *Criminology and Public Policy* 2, no. 3 (2003): 421–56.

64. Ralph A. Weisheit, L. Edward Wells, and David N. Falcone, "Community Policing in Small Town and Rural America," *Crime and Delinquency* 4 (October 1994): 549–67.

65. James Q. Wilson and George Kelling, "The Police and Neighborhood Safety," *Atlantic Monthly,* March 1982, 29–38.

66. See Malcolm K. Sparrow, Mark H. Moore, and David M. Kennedy, *Beyond 911: A New Era for Policing* (New York: Basic Books, 1990).

67. James F. Pastor, "Terrorism and Public Safety Policing," *Crime and Justice International* (March/April 2005): 4–8.

68. Edward R. Maguire and William R. King, "Trends in the Policing Industry," *The Annals* 593 (May 2004): 15–41.

69. Herman Goldstein, "Improving Policing: A Problem-Oriented Approach," *Crime & Delinquency* (April 1979): 236–43.

70. FBI, *Crime in the United States, 2010,* tab. 74.

71. Title VII of the Civil Rights Act of 1964, 42 U.S.C., § 2000e et seq. (1964).

72. Susan L. Miller, *Gender and Community Policing: Walking the Talk* (Boston: Northeastern University Press, 1999).

73. Barbara Raffel Price, *Female Police Officers in the United States,* National Criminal Justice Reference Service, 1996, http://www.ncjrs.org/policing/fem635.htm.

74. National Center for Women and Policing, *Equality Denied: The Status of Women in Policing* (Arlington, VA: Feminist Majority Foundation, 2002).

75. Stephen D. Mastrofski, "Controlling Street-Level Discretion," *The Annals* 593 (May 2004): 100–118.

76. Irving Piliavin and Scott Briar, "Police Encounters with Juveniles," *American Journal of Sociology* 70 (September 1964): 206–214.

77. See David A. Klinger, "Demeanor or Crime: Why 'Hostile' Citizens Are More Likely to Be Arrested," *Criminology* 32 (1994): 475–93; and Richard J. Lundman, "Demeanor or Crime: The Midwest City Police-Citizen Encounters Study," *Criminology* 32 (1994): 631–56.

78. Paul M. Whisenand and R. Fred Ferguson, *The Managing of Police Organizations* (Upper Saddle River, NJ: Prentice Hall, 1973), 199–201.

79. For example, see Richard Bennett and Theodore Greenstein, "The Police Personality: A Test of the Predispositional Model," *Journal of Police Science and Administration* 3 (1975): 439–45; and Larry L. Tifft, "The 'Cop Personality' Reconsidered," *Journal of Police Science and Administration* 2, no. 3 (September 1974): 266–78.

80. Terry Eisenberg, "Successful Police Chief Mentoring: Implications from the Subculture," *Public Management* (December 2005): 21–25.

81. Jerome H. Skolnick, *Justice Without Trial: Law Enforcement in Democratic Society* (New York: Wiley, 1966).

82. Joseph Victor, "Police Stress: Is Anybody Out There Listening?" *New York Law Enforcement Journal* (June 1986): 19–20.

83. For a discussion of the complexity of culture as it relates to policing, see Steve Herbert, "Police Subculture Revisited," *Criminology* 36 (1998): 343–69.

84. J. Brown, C. Cooper, and B. Kirkcaldy, "Occupational Stress among Police Officers." *British Journal of Psychology* 17, no. 6 (1996): 491–505.

85. George T. Patterson, "Examining the Effects of Coping and Social Support on Work and Life Stress among Police Officers," *Journal of Criminal Justice* 31, no. 3 (May–June 2003): 215–26.

Chapter 6

1. Chimel v. California, 395 U.S. 752 (1969).

2. Ibid.

3. Ibid.

4. Ibid.

5. Ibid.

6. United States Constitution, Fourth Amendment.

7. Ibid.

8. Locke v. United States, 11 U.S. (7 Cranch) 339 (1813).

9. Dumbra v. United States, 268 U.S. 435 (1925).

10. Aguilar v. Texas, 378 U.S. 108 (1964); Spinelli v. United States, 393 U.S. 410 (1969).

11. Ibid.

12. Illinois v. Gates, 462 U.S. 213 (1983).

13. Kentucky v. King, 131 S. Ct. 1849 (2011).

14. McQueen v. Heck, 41 Tenn. 212 (1860); Shelton v. State, 460 S.W.2d 869 (1970).

15. Harris v. State, 206 Tenn. 276, 332 S.W.2d 675 (1960).

16. Lowery v. State, 39 Ala. App. 659, 107 So.2d 366 (1958).

17. State v. Autheman, 47 Idaho 328, 274 P. 805, 62 A.L.R. 195 (1929); Appleton v. State, 61 Ark. 590, 33 S.W. 1066 (1896).

18. For example, Neal v. Joyner, 89 N.C. 287 (1883).

19. Malley v. Briggs, 475 U.S. 335 (1986).

20. Terry v. Ohio, 392 U.S. 1 (1968).

21. Ibid.

22. Ibid.

23. Ibid.

24. California v. Hodari D., 499 U.S. 621 (1991).

25. Ibid.

26. Minnesota v. Dickerson, 508 U.S. 366 (1993).

27. Ibid.

28. Illinois v. Wardlow, 528 U.S. 119 (2000).

29. Ibid.

30. Carroll v. United States, 267 U.S. 132 (1925).

31. Husty v. United States, 282 U.S. 694 (1931).

32. Chambers v. Maroney, 399 U.S. 42 (1970).

33. United States v. Ross, 456 U.S. 798 (1982).

34. New York v. Belton, 453 U.S. 454 (1981).

35. California v. Acevedo, 500 U.S. 565 (1991).

36. Knowles v. Iowa, 525 U.S. 113 (1998).

37. Arizona v. Gant, 556 U.S. 332 (2009).

38. Delaware v. Prouse, 440 U.S. 648 (1979).

39. Ibid.

40. Michigan Department of State Police v. Stiz, 496 U.S. 444 (1990).

41. Indianapolis v. Edmond, 531 U.S. 32 (2000).

42. Illinois v. Lidster, 540 U.S. 419 (2004).

43. Tennessee Code Annotated, Section 40-7-202.

44. John Hill, "High-Speed Police Pursuits: Dangers, Dynamics, and Risk Reduction," *Crime and Justice International* 20 (May/June 2004): 27–34.

45. Geoffrey P. Alpert, Dennis Jay Kenney, and Roger Dunham, "Police Pursuits and the Use of Force: Recognizing and Managing 'The Pucker Factor'—A Research Note," *Justice Quarterly* 14 (June 1997): 371–85; Geoffrey P. Alpert and Lorie A. Fridell, *Police Vehicles and Firearms* (Prospect Heights, IL: Waveland Press, 1992); Geoffrey P. Alpert, "Analyzing Police Pursuit," *Criminal Law Bulletin* 27 (July/August 1991): 358–67.

46. Wren v. United States, 352 F.2d 617 (1965).

47. United States v. Matlock, 415 U.S. 164 (1974).

48. Bumper v. North Carolina, 391 U.S. 543 (1968).

49. Schneckloth v. Bustamonte, 412 U.S. 218 (1973).

50. United States v. Dichiarinte, 445 F.2d 126 (1971).

51. Florida v. Jimeno, 500 U.S. 248 (1991).

52. Florida v. Bostick, 501 U.S. 429 (1991).

53. Burdeau v. McDowell, 256 U.S. 465 (1921).

54. United States v. Martinez-Fuerte, 428 U.S. 543 (1976).

55. South Dakota v. Opperman, 428 U.S. 364 (1976).

56. Illinois v. Lafayette, 462 U.S. 640 (1983).

57. Katz v. United States, 389 U.S. 347 (1967).

58. Abel v. United States, 362 U.S. 217 (1960).

59. California v. Greenwood, 486 U.S. 35 (1988).

60. Hester v. United States, 265 U.S. 57 (1924).

61. Oliver v. United States, 466 U.S. 170 (1984); Maine v. Thornton, 466 U.S. 170 (1984).

62. Harris v. United States, 390 U.S. 234 (1968).

63. Gary Kelder and Alan J. Statman, "The Protective Sweep Doctrine: Recurrent Questions Regarding the Propriety of Searches Conducted Contemporaneously with an Arrest on or near Private Premises," *Syracuse Law Review* 30 (1979): 973–1092.

64. Weeks v. United States, 232 U.S. 383 (1914).

65. Adams v. New York, 192 U.S. 585 (1904).

66. Weeks v. United States, 232 U.S. 383 (1914).

67. Ibid.

68. National Commission on Law Observance and Enforcement, *Report on Prosecution* (Washington, DC: U.S. Government Printing Office, 1931), 24.

69. People v. Defore, 242 N.Y. 13 (1926).

70. Elder Witt, ed., *Guide to the U.S. Supreme Court* (Washington, DC: Congressional Quarterly, 1979), 549.

71. Mapp v. Ohio, 367 U.S. 643 (1961).

72. Ibid.

73. Ibid.

74. "High Court Bars Evidence States Seized Illegally," *New York Times,* June 20, 1961.

75. Arthur Niederhoffer, *Behind the Shield* (Garden City, NY: Doubleday, 1967), 159.

76. Linkletter v. Walker, 381 U.S. 618 (1965).

77. See Bob Woodward and Scott Armstrong, *The Brethren: Inside the Supreme Court* (New York: Simon & Schuster, 1979), 112–19.

78. United States v. Calandra, 414 U.S. 338 (1974) and Stone v. Powell, 428 U.S. 465 (1976).

79. United States v. Leon, 468 U.S. 897 (1984); Massachusetts v. Sheppard, 468 U.S. 981 (1984).

80. Illinois v. Krull, 480 U.S. 340 (1987).

81. Murray v. United States, 487 U.S. 533 (1988).

82. Arizona v. Evans, 514 U.S. 1 (1995); Herring v. United States, 555 U.S. 135 (2009).

83. Hopt v. Utah, 110 U.S. 574 (1884).

84. Ibid.

85. Wilson v. United States, 162 U.S. 613 (1896).

86. Twining v. New Jersey, 211 U.S. 78 (1908).

87. Cited in Henry J. Abraham, *Freedom and the Court: Civil Rights and Liberties in the United States* (New York: Oxford University Press, 1977), 59.

88. Twining v. New Jersey, 211 U.S. 78 (1908).

89. Brown v. Mississippi, 297 U.S. 278 (1936).

90. Ibid.

91. Rogers v. Richmond, 365 U.S. 534 (1961).

92. Massiah v. United States, 377 U.S. 201 (1964).

93. Malloy v. Hogan, 378 U.S. 1 (1964).

94. Escobedo v. Illinois, 378 U.S. 478 (1964).

95. Ibid.

96. Ibid.

97. Ibid.

98. Ibid.

99. Ibid.

100. Ibid.

101. Ibid.

102. Miranda v. Arizona, Vignera v. New York, Westover v. United States, California v. Stewart—all 384 U.S. 436 (1966).

103. "High Court Puts New Curb on Powers of the Police to Interrogate Suspects," *New York Times,* June 14, 1966.

104. Berghuis v. Thompkins, 130 S. Ct. 2250 (2010).

105. Maryland v. Shatzer, 130 S. Ct. 1213 (2010).

106. J.D.B. v. North Carolina, 131 S. Ct. 2394 (2011).

107. Kirby v. Illinois, 406 U.S. 682 (1972).

108. Ibid.

109. Foster v. California, 394 U.S. 440 (1969).

110. Ibid.

111. United States v. Wade, 388 U.S. 218 (1967).

112. *The Innocence Project Fact Sheet,* accessed December 26, 2011, http://www.innocenceproject.org/Content/Facts_on_PostConviction_DNA_Exonerations.php.

113. Schmerber v. California, 384 U.S. 757 (1966).

114. United States v. Dionisio, 410 U.S. 1 (1973).

115. United States v. Mara, 410 U.S. 19 (1973).

116. United States v. Ash, 413 U.S. 300 (1973).

117. Winston v. Lee, 470 U.S. 753 (1985).

Chapter 7

1. Tennessee v. Garner, 471 U.S. 1 (1985).

2. Ibid.

3. Ibid.

4. Ibid.

5. Ibid.

6. Carl B. Klockars, Sanja Kutnjak, and Maria Haberfeld, *Enhancing Police Integrity* (Dordrecht, Netherlands: Springer, 2006).

7. For additional information, see the CALEA Web site at www.calea.org.

8. For additional information, see the Virginia DCJS Web site at www.dcjs.virginia.gov.

9. Michael Benson and Sally Simpson, *White Collar Crime: An Opportunity Perspective* (Boca Raton, FL: Taylor & Francis, 2009).

10. Lawrence W. Sherman, *Scandal and Reform* (Berkeley: University of California Press, 1978), xxii.

11. See, for example, Kenneth J. Peak, *Policing America* (Upper Saddle River, NJ: Prentice Hall, 2000), 254; Richard J. Lundman, *Police and Policing* (New York: Holt, Rinehart and Winston, 1980), 142–48; Herman Goldstein, *Policing a Free Society* (Cambridge, MA: Ballinger, 1977), 194–95; Thomas Barker and Julian Roebuck, *An Empirical Typology of Police Corruption: A Study in Organizational Deviance* (Springfield, IL: Thomas, 1973); and Jonathan Rubinstein, *City Police* (New York: Ballantine, 1973).

12. Mark L. Dantzker, *Understanding Today's Police* (Upper Saddle River, NJ: Prentice Hall, 2000), 179–80.

13. Lundman, *Police and Policing*, 148; Barker and Roebuck, *An Empirical Typology of Police Corruption*, 36.

14. See James A. Inciardi, *The War on Drugs IV: The Continuing Saga of the Mysteries and Miseries of Intoxication, Addiction, Crime, and Public Policy* (Boston: Allyn and Bacon, 2008).

15. Albert J. Reiss Jr., *Private Employment of Public Police* (Washington, DC: National Institute of Justice, 1988).

16. Edwin J. Delattre, *Character and Cops: Ethics in Policing* (Washington, DC: American Enterprise Institute for Public Policy Research, 1989), 71–78; National Research Council, *Fairness and Effectiveness in Policing* (Washington, DC: National Academy Press, 2004), 271–75.

17. Cited in Ralph Lee Smith, *The Tarnished Badge* (New York: Arno Press, 1974), 191–92.

18. Arthur Niederhoffer, *Behind the Shield: The Police in Urban Society* (Garden City, NY: Doubleday, 1969), 70.

19. Goldstein, *Policing a Free Society*, 199.

20. Samuel Walker, *The Police in America* (New York: McGraw-Hill, 1983), 180–81.

21. Brown v. Mississippi, 297 U.S. 278 (1936).

22. Rogers v. Richmond, 365 U.S. 534 (1961); Greenwald v. Wisconsin, 390 U.S. 519 (1968); Sims v. Georgia, 385 U.S. 538 (1968); Brooks v. Florida, 389 U.S. 413 (1967).

23. U.S. Riot Commission, *Report of the National Advisory Commission on Civil Disorders* (New York: Dutton, 1968).

24. Eugene A. Paoline III and William Terrill, "Police Use of Force: Varying Perspectives," *Journal of Crime and Justice* 34, no. 3 (2011): 159–62, doi: 10.1080/0735648X.2011.613157; H. R. Hutson, D. Anglin, P. Rice, et al., "Excessive Use of Force by Police: A Survey of Academic Emergency Physicians," *Emergency Medicine Journal* 26 (2009): 20–22, doi:10.1136/emj.2007.053348; J. Garner, J. Buchanan, T. Schade, and J. Hepburn, *Understanding the Use of Force by and Against the Police: National Institute of Justice Research Brief* (Washington, DC: U.S. Department of Justice, Office of Justice Programs, National Institute of Justice, 1996).

25. James Q. Wilson, *Varieties of Police Behavior* (New York: Atheneum, 1975), 140–71.

26. Lundman, *Police and Policing*, 161–64.

27. Livingston v. Browder, 285 So.2d 923 (1973); State v. Anderson, 253 S.E.2d 48, 50 (1979); North Carolina General Statutes, Section 15A-401(d)(1).

28. Tennessee v. Garner, 471 U.S. 1 (1985).

29. Ibid.

30. James J. Fyfe, "The Split-Second Syndrome and Other Determinants of Police Violence," in *Violent Transactions,* ed. Anne Campbell and John Gibbs (New York: Basil Blackwell, 1986).

31. "Ten Percent of Shootings Found to be 'Suicide by Cop,'" *Criminal Justice Newsletter,* September 1, 1998, 1–2; Alan Feuer, "Desperadoes; Drawing a Bead on a Baffling Endgame: Suicide by Cop," *New York Times,* June 21, 1998; H. R. Hutson, D. Anglin, J. Yarbrough, et al., "Suicide by Cop," *Annals of Emergency Medicine* 32, no. 6 (1998): 655–69.

32. Michael R. Smith, Robert J. Kaminski, Geoffrey P. Alpert, et al., *Multi-Method Evaluation of Police Use of Force Outcomes, Executive Summary,* https://www.ncjrs.gov/App/Publications/abstract.aspx?ID=253226.

33. A Joint Project of PERF and COPS, *2011 Electronic Control Weapon Guidelines,* cops.usdoj.gov/Publications/e021111339-PERF-ECWGb.pdf.

34. Ibid.

35. Lise Olsen and Roma Khanna, "Harris County Credits Crackdown and Taser Guns for a 25-Year Low," *Houston Chronicle,* December 26, 2004; Charisse Jones, "Police Say Taser Shocks Are Replacing Deadly Shots," *USA Today,* July 14, 2004; Carli Teproff, "A Stunning Lesson," *Miami Herald,* March 27, 2005.

36. Alan Gathright, "Police Should Quit Using Stun Guns, Group Says; Officers Seen as Too Quick to Use Tasers—Safety Questioned," *San Francisco Chronicle,* May 10, 2005.

37. Alex Berenson, "As Police Use of Tasers Soars, Questions over Safety Emerge," *New York Times,* July 18, 2004.

38. Roma Khanna, Officers' Rate of Taser Use Troubles Activists: Critics Complain Some Use Devices Too Often; HPD Says Each Instance Is Being Scrutinized, *Houston Chronicle,* April 1, 2005; "Deputy Uses Taser On 12-Year-Old Girl Skipping School," Monday, Nov. 15, 2004, http://www.wftv.com/news/news/deputy-uses-taser-on-12-year-old-girl-skipping-sch/nJdyQ/; Berenson, "As Police Use of Tasers Soars, Questions Over Safety Emerge"; Kris Axtman, "Police

Stun Guns Pack Volts—and Debate," *Christian Science Monitor,* July 15, 2004.

39. Yung-Lien Lai and Jihong Solomon Zhao, "The Impact of Race/Ethnicity, Neighborhood Context, and Police/Citizen Interaction on Residents' Attitudes Toward the Police," *Journal of Criminal Justice,* 38, no. 4 (2010): 685–92.

40. W. P. Bozeman, W. E. Hauda II, J. J. Heck, et al., "Safety and Injury Profile of Conducted Electrical Weapons Used by Law Enforcement Officers Against Criminal Suspects," *Annals of Emergency Medicine,* 53, no. 4 (April 2009): 480–89.

41. Ralph A. Weisheit, L. Edward Wells, and David N. Falcone, "Community Policing in Small Town and Rural America," *Crime and Delinquency* 40, no. 4 (October 1994): 549–67, doi: 10.1177/0011128794040004005; David N. Falcone, L. Edward Wells, Ralph A. Weisheit, "The Small-Town Police Department," *Policing: An International Journal of Police Strategies & Management* 25, no. 2 (2002): 371–84.

42. Paul Chevigny, *Police Power: Police Abuses in New York City* (New York: Vintage, 1969), 260; David H. Bayley and Harold Mendelsohn, *Minorities and the Police: Confrontation in America* (New York: Free Press, 1971), 127–35.

43. Robert M. Fogelson, *Big City Police* (Cambridge, MA: Harvard University Press, 1977), 283–84.

44. Ibid., 284.

45. See Jerome H. Skolnick and James J. Fyfe, *Above the Law: Police and the Excessive Use of Force* (New York: Free Press, 1993); National Research Council, *Fairness and Effectiveness in Policing,* 288–89; Suzanne Smalley, "O'Toole to Create Police Review Board; Citizen Panel Will Probe Complaints," *Boston Globe,* January 1, 2005; Jake Wagman, "St. Louis Mayoral Election Ushers in Crucial Time for City: Next Years Are Vital to Turnaround," *St. Louis Post-Dispatch,* March 6, 2005; and Maxine Bernstein, "Portland Police Study Role of Civilian Review," *Oregonian,* August 15, 2003.

46. Tim Prenzler, *Police Corruption: Preventing Misconduct and Maintaining Integrity* (Boca Raton, FL: CRC Press, Taylor and Francis Press, 2009).

47. Christopher Stone and Jeremy Travis, *New Perspectives in Policing: Toward a New Professionalism in Policing,* https://www.ncjrs.gov/pdffiles1/nij/232359.pdf.

48. George D. Eastman, ed., *Municipal Police Administration* (Washington, DC: International City Management Association, 1969), 203–204.

49. Langdon W. Moore, *His Own Story of His Eventful Life* (Boston: Moore, 1893), 287–89.

50. Hutchins Hapgood, *The Autobiography of a Thief* (New York: Fox, Duffield, 1903), 265.

51. Thomas A. Reppetto, *The Blue Parade* (New York: Free Press, 1978), 162.

52. Prenzler, *Police Corruption.*

53. Egon Bittner, *The Functions of Police in Modern Society* (New York: Aronson, 1975).

Chapter 8

1. Koon v. United States, 518 U.S. 81 (1996).

2. Ibid.

3. Ibid.

4. Ibid.

5. Ibid.

6. Samuel Walker, *Popular Justice: A History of American Criminal Justice,* 2nd ed. (New York: Oxford University Press, 1997).

7. For a retrospective overview of the charm of the early American courthouse, see Richard Pare, ed., *Court House* (New York: Horizon Press, 1978).

8. Walker, *Popular Justice.*

9. See specific state court Web sites for detailed explanations: Ohio, http://www.sconet.state.oh.us; Pennsylvania, http://www.pacourts.us; California, http://www.courts.ca.gov; and New York, http://www.courts.state.ny.us/courts/structure.shtml.

10. See the Michigan state court Web site for detailed information: http://www.courts.michigan.gov.

11. See state court Web sites for detailed explanations: Texas, http://www.courts.state.tx.us/; and Oklahoma, http://www.oscn.net/applications/oscn/start.asp?viewType=COURTS.

12. New York state courts Web site: http://www.courts.state.ny.us/courts/structure.shtml.

13. Florida state courts Web site: http://www.flcourts.org/.

14. For more information about the structure and function of courts in the United States, see: http://www.uscourts.gov.

15. *Judicial Business of the United States Courts: 2011 Annual Report of the Director,* http://www.uscourts.gov/uscourts/Statistics/JudicialBusiness/2011/JudicialBusiness2011.pdf.

16. Proceedings of the 42nd Annual Meeting of the New York State Bar Association, 1919, 240–41, as quoted in the President's Commission on Law Enforcement and Administration of Justice, *Task Force Report: The Courts* (Washington, DC: U.S. Government Printing Office, 1967), 29.

17. Caseload statistics from *Judicial Business of the United States Courts: 2011 Annual Report of the Director.*

18. Indiana state courts Web site: http://www.in.gov/judiciary/.

19. Murray S. Stedman, *State and Local Governments* (Cambridge, MA: Winthrop, 1984), 156.

20. See additional details about the Colorado court system at: http://www.courts.state.co.us.

21. Chad M. Oldfather and Michael M. O'Hear, "Criminal Appeals: Past, Present, and Future," *Marquette Law Review* 93, no. 2 (Winter 2009): 339–48.

22. For examples see the following state court Web sites: Hawaii, www.courts.state.hi.us/courts/appeals/intermediate_court_of_appeals.html; and Virginia, www.courts.state.va.us/courts/cav/cavinfo.pdf.

23. See, for example, *Final Report, West Virginia Independent Commission on Judicial Reform,* November 15, 2009, http://www.scribd.com/doc/22604435/West-Virginia-Independent-Commission-on-Judicial-Reform-Final-Report; *Justice Most Local: The Future of Town and Village Courts in New York State, A Report by the Special Commission on the Future of New York State Courts,* September 2008, www.nyslocalgov.org/pdf/Justice_Most_Local.pdf; *A Court System for the Future: The Promise of Court Restructuring in New York State, A Report by the Special Commission on the Future of the New York State Courts,* February 2007, www.courts.state.ny.us/reports/courtsys-4future_2007.pdf.

24. See Victor Flango, "Court Unification and the Quality of State Courts," *Justice System Journal* 16 (1994): 33–56; Harry Stumpf and John Culver, *The Politics of State Courts* (White Plains, NY: Longman, 1992); David W. Neubauer, *America's Courts and the Criminal Justice System* (New York: Wadsworth, 2005); U.S. Department of Health and Human Services, *The National Evaluation of the Court Improvement Program,* http://www.pal-tech.com/cip/index.cfm; The New York State Bar Association, Judicial Salaries, Court Reform, Selection of Judges, *Access to Justice for the Poor, Medicaid Reform, Equal Rights for Same-Sex Couples Among 2008 Legislative Priorities for State Bar Association,* January 2, 2008, http://www.nysba.org/AM/Template.cfm?Section=News_Center&template=/CM/ContentDisplay.cfm&ContentID=54276; Bureau of Justice Statistics, *Special Report: State Court Organization, 1987–2004,* October 2007, www.bjs.gov/content/pub/pdf/sco8704.pdf.

25. JoAnn Miller and Donald C. Johnson, *Problem Solving Courts: New Approaches to Criminal Justice* (Lanham, MD: Rowman & Littlefield, 2009).

26. See the following for discussions of the effectiveness of drug courts: Shelli B. Rossman, John K. Roman, Janine M. Zweig, et al., eds., "The Multi-Site Adult Drug Court Evaluation: The Impact of Drug Courts," http://www.urban.org/uploadedpdf/412357-MADCE-The-Impact-of-Drug-Courts.pdf.

27. West Huddleston and Douglas B. Marlowe, *Painting the Current Picture: A National Report on Drug Courts and Other Problem-Solving Court Programs in the United States,* July 2011, pcp_report_final_and_official_july_2011.pdf.

28. See the federal courts Web site for additional details: http://www.uscourts.gov.

29. For additional details see the Supreme Court Web site: www.supremecourt.gov.

30. *Landmark Judicial Legislation,* via the Federal Judiciary Center Web site: http://www.fjc.gov/history/home.nsf/page/landmark_19.html.

31. See United States v. Ford, 824 F.2d 1430 (1987).

32. Administrative Office of the United States Courts Web site: http://www.uscourts.gov/FederalCourts/UnderstandingtheFederalCourts/AdministrativeOffice.aspx.

33. Ibid.

34. Ibid.

35. Ibid.

36. United States v. Morrison, 529 U.S. 598 (2000).

37. Ibid.

38. Ibid.

39. Ibid.

40. Ibid.

41. United States Courts Web site: http://www.uscourts.gov/.

42. Ibid.

43. Ibid.

44. Supreme Court of the United States, *A Brief Overview of the Supreme Court,* http://www.supremecourt.gov/about/briefoverview.aspx.

45. Robert G. McCloskey and Sanford Levinson, *The American Supreme Court* (Chicago: University of Chicago Press, 2010).

46. Supreme Court of the United States Web site: http://www.supremecourt.gov/.

47. Marbury v. Madison, 5 U.S. (1 Cranch) 137 (1803).

48. Ibid.

49. Ibid.

50. McCloskey and Levinson, *The American Supreme Court.*

51. Supreme Court of the United States, *A Brief Overview of the Supreme Court.*

52. Jonathan Kastellec and Jeffrey R. Lax, "Case Selection and the Study of Judicial Politics," *Journal of Empirical Legal Studies* 5, no. 3 (2008): 407–46.

53. McCloskey and Levinson, *The American Supreme Court.*

54. For examples see Johnson v. California, 543 U.S. 499 (2005); Skilling v. United States, 561 U.S. ___ (2010); Brown v. Plata, 563 U.S. ___ (2011).

55. McCloskey and Levinson, *The American Supreme Court.*

56. Supreme Court of the United States, *A Brief Overview of the Supreme Court.*

57. Erwin Griswold, "Rationing Justice: The Supreme Court's Case Load and What the Court Does Not Do," *Cornell Law Review* 60, no. 3 (March 1975): 335–54.

58. Neubauer, *America's Courts and Criminal Justice System.*

59. Ibid.

60. Joanna Sheperd, "The Influence of Retention Politics on Judges' Voting," *Journal of Legal Studies* 38, no. 1 (2009); Mark Hansen, "A Run for the Bench," *ABA Journal* 84 (October 1998): 68–72; Robert L. Brown, "From Whence Cometh Our State Appellate Judges: Popular Election versus the Missouri Plan," *University of Arkansas at Little Rock Law Journal* 20 (1998): 313; D. Y. Joseph, M. D. Zimmerman, C. E. Ares, and K. K. Stuart, "Evaluating the Performance of Judges Standing for Retention," *Judicature* 79 (January/February 1996): 190–97.

61. Earl J. Silbert, "The Role of the Prosecutor in the Process of Criminal Justice," *ABA Journal* 63 (1977): 1717; President's Commission on Law Enforcement and Administration of Justice, *Task Force Report,* 5.

62. Ibid.

63. Kenneth Adams and Charles R. Cutshall, "Refusing to Prosecute Minor Offenses: The Relative Influence of Legal and Extralegal Factors," *Justice Quarterly* 4 (1987): 595.

64. See Joan E. Jacoby, *The Prosecutor's Charging Decision: A Policy Perspective* (Washington, DC: U.S. Department of Justice, 1977).

65. U.S. Department of Justice and Bureau of Justice Statistics, *The Prosecution of Felony Arrests* (Washington, DC: U.S. Government Printing Office, 1998).

66. See Candace McCoy, *Politics and Plea Bargaining: Victims' Rights in California* (Philadelphia: University of Pennsylvania Press, 1993); Arthur Rosett and Donald R. Cressey, *Justice by Consent: Plea Bargains in the American Courthouse* (Philadelphia: Lippincott, 1976); and Pamela A. MacLean, "Mixed Signals on Plea Bargains," *National Law Journal* (December 17, 2007).

67. "Plea No Bargain," *Time,* August 30, 1982, 22.

68. See Brady v. United States, 397 U.S. 742 (1970); Santobello v. New York, 404 U.S. 257 (1971); and North Carolina v. Alford, 400 U.S. 25 (1970).

69. See also Neubauer, *America's Courts and Criminal Justice System.*

70. See also Dean Champion, Richard D. Hartley, and Gary A. Rabe, *Criminal Courts: Structure, Process, and Issues,* 3rd ed. (New York: Prentice Hall, 2011); Roy Flemming, Peter Nardulli, and James Eisenstein, *The Craft of Justice* (Philadelphia: University of Pennsylvania Press, 1992); and Paul W. Wice, *Criminal Lawyers: An Endangered Species* (Beverly Hills, CA: Sage, 1978).

71. Caroline Wolf Harlow, *Defense Counsel in Criminal Cases: Bureau of Justice Statistics Special Report,* November 2000, www.bjs.gov/content/pub/pdf/dccc.pdf; Douglas L. Colbert, "Thirty-Five Years after Gideon: The Illusory Right to Counsel at Bail Proceedings," *University Illinois Law Review* 1 (1998).

72. Anthony C. Friloux, "Motion Strategy—The Defense Attack," speech before the National College of Criminal Defense Lawyers, Houston, 1975, cited in Wice, *Criminal Lawyers,* 148.

73. See David W. Neubauer and Henry F. Fradella, *America's Courts and the Criminal Justice System* (New York: Wadsworth, 2010).

74. J. Sanders, "Science, Law, and the Expert Witness," *Law and Contemporary Problems* (2009): 63–90.

75. Daubert v. Merrell Dow Pharmaceuticals, 509 U.S. 579 (1993).

76. Committee on Identifying the Needs of the Forensic Science Community, Committee on Science, Technology, and Law Policy and Global Affairs, Committee on Applied and Theoretical Statistics Division on Engineering and Physical Sciences, National Research Council of the National Academies, *Strengthening Forensic Science in the United States: A Path Forward* (Washington, DC: National Academies Press, 2009), available online at www.ncjrs.gov/pdffiles1/nij/grants/228091.pdf.

77. Julie Jonas, "True Independence for Medical Examiners Equals Due Process for Criminal Defendants and More Efficiencies in the Criminal Justice System," *William Mitchell Law Review* 37, no. 2 (2011): 698.

78. Ibid.

79. Kent v. United States, 383 U.S. 541 (1966).

80. In re Gault, 387 U.S. 1 (1967).

Chapter 9

1. Duncan v. Louisiana, 391 U.S. 145 (1968).

2. Ibid.

3. Perez v. Duncan, 404 U.S. 1071, certiorari denied (1971).

4. See David W. Neubauer and Henry F. Fradella, *America's Courts and the Criminal Justice System* (New York: Wadsworth, 2010).

5. Judiciary Act of 1789 (ch. 20, 1 Stat. 73).

6. Hudson v. Parker, 156 U.S. 277, (1895).

7. McKane v. Durston, 153 U.S. 684 (1894).

8. For additional information, see Ariana Lindermayer, "What the Right Hand Gives: Prohibitive Interpretations of the State Constitutional Right to Bail," *Fordham Law Review* (2009–2010): 267.

9. Stack v. Boyle, 342 U.S. 1 (1951).

10. For additional historical discussion, see Samuel Walker, *Popular Justice: A History of American Criminal Justice,* 2nd ed. (New York; Oxford University Press, 1997).

11. See Ilene H. Nagal, "The Legal/Extra-Legal Controversy: Judicial Decisions in Pretrial Release," *Law and Society Review* 17 (1983): 481–515; and David Abrams and Chris Rohlfs, "Optimal Bail and the Value of Freedom: Evidence from the Philadelphia Bail Experiment," *Economic Inquiry* 49, no. 3 (2010): 750–70.

12. See James G. Carr, "Bailbondsmen and the Federal Courts," *Federal Probation* 57 (March 1993): 9–13; and K. B. Turner, "The Effect of Legal Representation on Bail Bond Decisions," *Criminal Law Bulletin* 39 (July/August 2003): 426–44.

13. U.S. Department of Justice, *Pretrial Release of Felony Defendants* (Washington, DC: Bureau of Justice Statistics, 2007).

14. Ibid.

15. For additional information, see Vera Institute of Justice, *Los Angeles County Jail Overcrowding Reduction Project Final Report: Revised,* September 2011, LA%20County%20Jail%20 Overcrowding%20Reduction%20 Report.pdf; G. B. Palermo, "Jail and Prison Overcrowding and Rehabilitative Justice Programs," *Internal Journal of Offender Therapy and Comparative Criminology* 55, no. 6 (2011): 843–45.

16. President's Commission on Law Enforcement and Administration of Justice, *Task Force Report: The Courts* (Washington, DC: U.S. Government Printing Office, 1967), 38.

17. Nancy G. La Vigne, Sara Debus-Sherrill, Diana Brazzell, and P. Mitchell Downey, "Preventing Violence and Sexual Assault in Jail: A Situational Crime Prevention Approach," *Urban Institute,* December 6, 2011, http:// www.urban.org/UploadedPDF /412458-Preventing-Violence-and -Sexual-Assault-in-Jail.pdf.

18. Stack v. Boyle, 342 U.S. 1 (1951).

19. Ibid.

20. For additional details about the historical development of the court, see Walker, *Popular Justice.*

21. Hurtado v. California, 110 U.S. 516 (1884).

22. Max Bolstad, "The Grand Jury: Eight Centuries of Myth and Reality," *Criminal Law Bulletin* 36 (July/August 2000): 281–315.

23. Ibid.

24. See, for example, Ex parte Milligan, 71 U.S. (4 Wall.) 2 (1866), among many others.

25. Bolstad, "The Grand Jury."

26. Ibid.

27. Ibid.

28. Branzburg v. Hayes, 408 U.S. 665 (1972).

29. National Advisory Commission on Criminal Justice Standards and Goals, *Courts: Report of the National Advisory Commission on Criminal Justice Standards and Goals, 1973* (Washington, DC: U.S. Government Printing Office, 1973), 13.

30. Thomas C. Marks and J. Tim Reilly, *Constitutional Criminal Procedure* (North Scituate, MA: Duxbury, 1979), 136.

31. Ibid.

32. Rita J. Simon and David E. Aaronson, *The Insanity Defense: A Critical Assessment of Law in the Post-Hinckley Era* (Westport, CT: Greenwood, 1988).

33. See Eric Silver, Carmen Cirincione, and Henry J. Steadman, "Demythologizing Inaccurate Perceptions of the Insanity Defense," *Law and Human Behavior* 18 (1994): 63–70; Henry J. Steadman, Margaret A. McGreevy, Joseph P. Morrissey, et al., *Before and After Hinckley: Evaluating Insanity Defense Reform* (New York: Guilford, 1993); and James Hooper and Alix McLearen, "Does the Insanity Defense Have a Legitimate Role?" *Psychiatric Times* 19 (April 2002).

34. Ibid.

35. Kyle Graham, "The Continuing Violations Doctrine," *Gonzaga Law Review* 43, no. 2 (2008): 272–326.

36. United States Constitution, Fifth Amendment.

37. For examples, see Blockburger v. United States, 284 U.S. 299 (1932); Fong Foo v. United States, 369 U.S. 141 (1962); and United States vs. Felix, 503 U.S. 378 (1992).

38. Brady v. Maryland, 373 U.S. 83 (1963).

39. Moore v. Illinois, 408 U.S. 786 (1972).

40. Mapp v. Ohio, 367 U.S. 643 (1961); Escobedo v. Illinois, 368 U.S. 478 (1964); Miranda v. Arizona, 384 U.S. 436 (1966).

41. United States Constitution, Sixth Amendment.

42. California Penal Code, Section 1382(1).

43. Code of Alabama, Section 15-3-1.

44. Beavers v. Haubert, 198 U.S. 77 (1905).

45. Barker v. Wingo, 407 U.S. 514 (1972).

46. Strunk v. United States, 412 U.S. 434 (1973).

47. United States v. Lovasco, 431 U.S. 783 (1977).

48. Klopfer v. North Carolina, 386 U.S. 213 (1967).

49. Norman F. Cantor, *The Civilization of the Middle Ages* (New York: Harper Collins, 1993).

50. In re Oliver, 333 U.S. 257 (1948).

51. Ibid.

52. Ibid.

53. Tennessee Code Annotated, Section 40-2504.

54. Idaho Code, Section 19-1902.

55. Frederic Jesup Stimson, *The Law of the Federal and State Constitutions of the United States; Book One, Origin and Growth of the American Constitutions* (Boston: Lawbook Exchange, The Boston Book Exchange, 2004).

56. United States Constitution, Article III.

57. Duncan v. Louisiana, 391 U.S. 145 (1968).

58. Williams v. Florida, 399 U.S. 78 (1970).

59. Ballew v. Georgia, 435 U.S. 223 (1978).

60. Taylor v. Louisiana, 419 U.S. 522 (1975).

61. See Hiroshi Fukurai, Edgar Butter, and Richard Krooth, *Race and the Jury* (New York: Plenum, 1993); Laura Rose Handman, "Underrepresentation of Economic Groups in Federal Juries," *Boston University Law Review* 57 (January 1977): 198–224; W. C. Smith, "Challenges of Jury Selection," *ABA Journal* 88 (April 2002): 34–39; Hiroshi Fukurai and Richard Krooth, *Race in the Jury Box: Affirmative Action in Jury Selection* (Albany: State University of New York Press, 2003); and Ronald Randall, James A. Woods, and Robert G. Martin, "Racial Representatives of Juries: An Analysis of Source List and Administrative Effects of the Jury Pool," *Justice System Journal* 29 (2008): 71.

62. Federal Court Web site: http:// www.uscourts.gov/FederalCourts /JuryService/JurorPay.aspx.

63. Michael I. Norton and Samuel R. Sommers, "Bias in Jury Selection: Justifying Prohibited Peremptory Challenges," *Journal of Behavioral Decision Making* 20, no. 5 (2007): 467–79.

64. New York Criminal Procedure Law, Section 270.25.

65. Batson v. Kentucky, 476 U.S. 79 (1986).

66. James P. Levine, "The Impact of Sequestration on Juries," *Judicature* 79 (1995–1996): 266.

67. David S. Rudstein, "A Brief History of the Fifth Amendment Guarantee against Double Jeopardy," *William & Mary Bill of Rights Journal* 14 (2005–2006): 193.

68. See G. Thomas Munsterman, Paula Hannaford, and Marc G. Whitehead, eds., *Jury Trial Innovations* (Williamsburg, VA: National Center for State Courts, 1997); American Bar Association and American Jury Project, *Principles for Juries and Jury Trials,* 2005, http://www.abanet.org /juryprojectstandards/principles.pdf; and Jury Trial Project, *Jury Trial Innovations in New York State,* April 2009, www.nyjuryinnovations.org /materials/JTI%20booklet05.pdf.

69. L. Timothy Perrin, "From O.J. to McVeigh: The Use of Argument in the Opening Statement," *Emory Law Journal* 107 (1999).

70. David A. Jones, *The Law of Criminal Procedure* (Boston: Little, Brown, 1981), 475.

71. See also Young S. Kim, Gregg Barak, and Donald E. Shelton, "Examining

the 'CSI-effect' in the Cases of Circumstantial Evidence and Eyewitness Testimony: Multivariate and Path Analyses," *Journal of Criminal Justice* 37 no. 5 (2009): 22; and Kit R. Roane, "The CSI Effect," *US News & World Report,* April 17, 2005.

72. N. J. Schweitzer and Michael J. Saks, "CSI Effect: Popular Fiction about Forensic Science Affects the Public's Expectations about Real Forensic Science," *Jurimetrics* 47 (2006–2007): 357.

73. Richard Willing, "'CSI Effect' Has Juries Wanting More Evidence," *USAToday,* August 5, 2004.

74. Steven J. Phillips, *No Heroes, No Villains* (New York: Random House, 1978), 196–97.

75. State v. Logan, Court of Appeals for the State of Oregon (2011), http://www.publications.ojd.state.or.us/Publications/A137661.htm.

76. Phoebe Ellsworth, "Are Twelve Heads Better than One?" *Law and Contemporary Problems* 52 (1989): 205–24.

77. Valerie P. Hans, Paula L. Hannaford-Agor, Nicole L. Mott and G. Thomas Munsterman, "The Hung Jury: The American Jury's Insights and Contemporary Understanding," *Criminal Law Bulletin* 39 (2003); and Nicole L. Waters and Valerie P. Hans, "A Jury of One: Opinion Formation, Conformity, and Dissent on Juries," *Journal of Empirical Legal Studies* 6, no. 3 (September 2009): 513–40.

78. Nancy S. Marder, "Jury Reform: The Impossible Dream?" *Tennessee Journal of Law and Policy* 5 (2008–2009): 149.

79. See Munsterman, Hannaford, and Whitehead, *Jury Trial Innovations;* American Bar Association and American Jury Project, *Principles for Juries and Jury Trials;* and Jury Trial Project, *Jury Trial Innovations in New York State.*

80. American Bar Association and American Jury Project, *Principles for Juries and Jury Trials.*

81. Juvenile Justice and Juvenile Delinquency Prevention Act of 1974, Pub. L. No. 93–415, 88 Stat. 1109 (1974).

Chapter 10

1. Woodson et al. v. North Carolina, 428 U.S. 280 (1976).
2. Ibid.
3. Ibid.
4. David C. Baldus, George Woodworth, and Charles A. Pulaski, *Equal Justice and the Death Penalty: A Legal and Empirical Analysis* (Boston: Northeastern University Press, 1990).

5. Woodson et al. v. North Carolina, 428 U.S. 280 (1976).
6. Ibid.
7. Federal Judicial Center, http://www.fjc.gov/.
8. Cesare Beccaria, *An Essay on Crimes and Punishments with The Commentary by Voltaire* (London: E. Hodson, 1801), 75.
9. See Beccaria. *An Essay on Crimes and Punishments with The Commentary by Voltaire, 75;* and Andrew von Hirsch, *Doing Justice: The Choice of Punishments* (Boston: Northeastern University Press, 1985).
10. Kenneth C. Haas, "The Triumph of Vengeance over Retribution: The United States Supreme Court and the Death Penalty," *Crime, Law and Social Change: An International Journal* 21 (1994): 127–54.
11. Payne v. Tennessee, 501 U.S. 808 (1991).
12. Paul W. Tappan, *Crime, Justice and Correction* (New York: McGraw-Hill, 1960), 255.
13. Raymond Paternoster, Robert Brame, and Sarah Bacon, *The Death Penalty: America's Experience with Capital Punishment* (New York: Oxford University Press, 2008).
14. Jon R. Sorenson, Mark D. Cunningham, Mark P. Vigen, and S. O. Woods, "Serious Assaults on Prison Staff: A Descriptive Analysis," *Journal of Criminal Justice* 39, no. 2 (2011): 143–50.
15. John Schmitt, Kris Warner, and Sarika Gupta, *The High Budgetary Cost of Incarceration,* June 2010, www.cepr.net/documents/publications/incarceration-2010-06.pdf.
16. See Andrew von Hirsch, *Doing Justice: The Choice of Punishments* (Boston: Northeastern University Press, 1985).
17. Quoted in Sanford H. Kadish and Monrad G. Paulsen, *Criminal Law and Its Processes* (Boston: Little, Brown, 1969), 85.
18. D. M. Kennedy, *Deterrence and Crime Prevention: Reconsidering the Prospect of Sanction* (New York: Routledge, 2008); Henry N. Pontell, *A Capacity to Punish: The Ecology of Crime and Punishment* (Bloomington: Indiana University Press, 1984); Franklin E. Zimring and Gordon J. Hawkins, *Deterrence* (Chicago: University of Chicago Press, 1973).
19. Katherine Coleman, "Controlling Corporate Crime: An Analysis of Deterrence versus Compliance," *Northwestern Interdisciplinary Law Review* 2 (2009): 185; Ronald J. Allen and Alexia Brunet Marks, "To Tow or

Not to Tow: The Deterrent Effect of a Municipal Ordinance," *Criminal Law Bulletin* 47, no. 3 (2011).
20. See von Hirsch, *Doing Justice.*
21. D. A. Andrews and James Bonta, "Rehabilitating Criminal Justice Policy and Practice," *Psychology, Public Policy, and Law* 16, no. 1 (2010): 39–55.
22. Frank Cullen, "It's Time to Affirm Rehabilitation," *Criminology and Public Policy* 5, no. 4 (2006): 665–72.
23. David Farabee, "Reexamining Martinson's Critique: A Cautionary Note for Evaluators," *Crime & Delinquency* 48, no. 1 (January 2002): 189–92; R. Martinson, "What Works?—Questions and Answers about Prison Reform," *Public Interest* 35 (1974): 22–54.
24. Tennessee Code Annotated, Section 40-35-111.
25. New York State Penal Law, Article 130.00.
26. David Levinson, *Encyclopedia of Crime and Punishment* (Thousand Oaks, CA: Sage, 2002).
27. Williams v. Illinois, 399 U.S. 235 (1970); Tate v. Short, 401 U.S. 395 (1971).
28. Ibid.
29. Bearden v. Georgia, 461 U.S. 660 (1983).
30. Levinson, *Encyclopedia of Crime and Punishment.*
31. Michael Tonry, "The Fragmentation of Sentencing and Corrections in America," *Sentencing & Corrections: Issues for the 21st Century,* no. 1 (September 1999), www.ncjrs.gov/pdffiles1/nij/175721.pdf.
32. See Michael Tonry, "Reconsidering Indeterminate and Structured Sentencing," *Sentencing & Corrections: Issues for the 21st Century,* no. 2 (September 1999), www.ncjrs.gov/pdffiles1/nij/175722.pdf; Marvin E. Frankel, *Criminal Sentences: Law without Order* (New York: Hill and Wang, 1973); Karl Menninger, *The Crime of Punishment* (New York: Viking, 1968); von Hirsch, *Doing Justice;* Nigel Walker, *Sentencing in a Rational Society* (London: Penguin, 1972); and William L. Gillespie, "State Sentencing Policy: Review and Illustration," *Justice System Journal* 24, no. 2 (2003): 205–10.
33. Levinson, *Encyclopedia of Crime and Punishment.*
34. For more information, see Dhammika Dharmapala, Nuno Garoupa, and Joanna M. Shepherd, "Legislatures, Judges, and Parole Boards: The Allocation of Discretion Under

Determinate Sentencing," *Florida Law Review* 62 (September 2009): 1037.

35. Harry Elmer Barnes, *The Repression of Crime* (New York: Doran, 1926), 220.

36. Tonry, "Reconsidering Indeterminate and Structured Sentencing."

37. New York State Penal Law, Section 85.10.

38. People v. Warren, 79 Misc.2d 777, 360 N.Y.S.2d 961 (1974).

39. See General Accounting Office, *Mandatory Minimum Sentences,* November 4, 1993, www.legistorm.com/showFile/...==/ful23761.pdf; Jonathan P. Caulkins, C. Peter Rydell, William L. Schwabe, and James Chiesa, *Mandatory Drug Sentences: Throwing Away the Key or the Taxpayers' Money?* (Santa Monica, CA: Rand, 1997); and Marc Maur, Ryan S. King, and Malcolm C. Young, "The Meaning of 'Life': Long Prison Sentences in Context," May 2004, www.sentencingproject.org/doc/publications/inc_meaningoflife.pdf.

40. Ryan Kellus Turner, "Shame-Based Sentencing: Thinking 'Outside of the Box' or 'Out of Bounds'?" *Municipal Court Recorder,* 11, no. 7 (August 2002): 12, http://www.tmcec.com/public/files/File/.../2002/Aug02recorderNo2.pdf.

41. "National News Briefs; Drunken Driver Is Given Ultimatum on Housing," *New York Times,* January 3, 1998.

42. Delaware Code, Title 11, Section 826; and Section 4204(5).

43. Idaho Code, Sections 18-1403, 19-2601; Code of Alabama, Sections 13-2-40, 15-22-50.

44. New York State Penal Law, Articles 70.00, 80.00; West Virginia Code, Sections 61-3-11, 62-12-2.

45. Albert W. Alschuler, "The Changing Purposes of Criminal Punishment: A Retrospective on the Past Century and Some Thoughts About the Next," *University of Chicago Law Review* 70, no. 1 (Winter 2003).

46. Bureau of Justice Statistics, *National Assessment of Structured Sentencing* (Washington, DC: U.S. Department of Justice, 1996).

47. United States Sentencing Commission, "Introduction to the Sentencing Reform Act," www.ussc.gov/Research/Research_Projects/.../15_Year.../chap1.pdf.

48. United States Sentencing Commission (USSC), *2011 Federal Sentencing Guidelines Manual,* Section 1B1.9, http://www.ussc.gov/Guidelines/2011_Guidelines/Manual_HTML/1b1_9.htm.

49. United States Sentencing Commission, Office of Legislative and Public Affairs, *An Overview of the United States Sentencing Commission,* http://www.ussc.gov/About_the_Commission/Overview_of_the_USSC/USSC_Overview.pdf.

50. United States v. Booker, 543 U.S. 220 (2005).

51. Gary M. Maveal, "Federal Presentence Reports: Multi-Tasking at Sentencing," *Seton Hall Law Review* 26, no. 2 (1996): 544–96.

52. Kimberly A. Thomas, "Beyond Mitigation: Towards a Theory of Allocution," *Fordham Law Review* 75 (2007): 2641.

53. United States Constitution, Fifth Amendment.

54. H. E. Barnes, *The Repression of Crime: Studies in Historical Penology* (Montclair, NJ: P. Smith, 1969), 44–45.

55. Wilkerson v. Utah, 99 U.S. 130 (1878).

56. Lawrence Friedman, *A History of American Law* (New York: Simon & Schuster, 2005).

57. Negley K. Teeters and Charles J. Zibulka, "Executions Under State Authority: 1864–1967," in *Executions in America,* ed. William J. Bowers (Lexington, MA: Heath, 1974), 200–401.

58. President's Commission on Law Enforcement and Administration of Justice, *Task Force Report: The Courts* (Washington, DC: U.S. Government Printing Office, 1967), 28.

59. C. Spear, *Essays on the Punishment of Death* (London: Green, 1844), 227–31.

60. David A. Jones, *The Law of Criminal Procedure* (Boston: Little, Brown, 1981), 543.

61. Gennaro F. Vito, Jeffrey R. Maahs, and Ronald M. Holmes, *Criminology: Theory, Research, and Policy* (Boston: Jones & Bartlett, 2006).

62. Marvin E. Wolfgang and Marc Riedel, "Race, Judicial Discretion, and the Death Penalty," *Annals of the American Academy of Political and Social Science* 407 (May 1973): 129.

63. Death Penalty Information Center, *Facts about the Death Penalty,* updated June 18, 2012, http://www.deathpenaltyinfo.org/documents/FactSheet.pdf.

64. O'Neil v. Vermont, 114 U.S. 323 (1892).

65. Weems v. United States, 217 U.S. 349 (1910).

66. Trop v. Dulles, 356 U.S. 86 (1958).

67. Witherspoon v. Illinois, 391 U.S. 510 (1968).

68. McGautha v. California, 402 U.S. 183 (1971).

69. Furman v. Georgia, Jackson v. Georgia, Branch v. Texas, 408 U.S. 238 (1972).

70. Ibid.

71. Ibid.

72. Gregg v. Georgia, 428 U.S. 153 (1976).

73. Ibid.

74. Code of Georgia Annotated, Sections 26-1101, 26-1311, 26-1902, 26-2201, 26-3301 (1972).

75. Profitt v. Florida, 428 U.S. 242 (1976); Jurek v. Texas, 428 U.S. 262 (1976).

76. Woodson et al. v. North Carolina, 428 U.S. 280 (1976).

77. Ibid.

78. Death Penalty Information Center, *Facts about the Death Penalty.*

79. Summary of execution via http://www.clarkprosecutor.org/html/death/US/gilmore001.htm.

80. Death Penalty Information Center, *Facts about the Death Penalty.*

81. Wilkerson v. Utah, 99 U.S. 130 (1878), In re Kemmler, 136 U.S. at 447 (1890), Louisiana ex rel. Francis v. Resweber, 329 U.S. 459 (1947), Baze v. Rees, 128 S. Ct. 1520 (2008).

82. Death Penalty Information Center, *Methods of Execution,* http://www.deathpenaltyinfo.org/methods-execution.

83. Ibid.

84. Ibid.

85. Ibid.

86. Ibid.

87. Lewis E. Lawes, *Life and Death in Sing Sing* (Garden City, NY: Garden City Publishing, 1928), 170–71, 188–90.

88. Quoted in Austin Sarat and Neil Vidmar, "Public Opinion, the Death Penalty, and the Eighth Amendment: Testing the Marshall Hypothesis," *Wisconsin Law Review* (1976): 206.

89. Fierro v. Gomez, 865 F.Supp. 1387 (1994).

90. Death Penalty Information Center, *Facts about the Death Penalty.*

91. Teresa A. Zimmers, Jonathan Sheldon, David A. Lubarsky, et al., "Lethal Injection for Execution: Chemical Asphyxiation?" *PLoS Medicine* (April 2007), http://www.plosmedicine.org/article/info:doi/10.1371/journal.pmed.0040156.

92. Heckler v. Chaney, 470 U.S. 821 (1985).

93. American Medical Association, *Opinion 2.06—Capital Punishment,* http://www.ama-assn.org/ama/pub/physician-resources/medical-ethics/code-medical-ethics/opinion206.page.

94. "Death Dealing Syringes," *Time,* December 20, 1982, 28–29. See also "Charlie Brooks' Last Words," *Texas*

Monthly, February 1983, 100–105, 170–176, 182.

95. Death Penalty Information Center, http://www.deathpenaltyinfo .org/lethal-injection-moratorium -executions-ends-after-supreme -court-decision.

96. Kevin Sack, "Executions in Doubt in Fallout Over Drug," *New York Times,* March 16, 2011.

97. Baze et al. v. N. Rees, 128 S. Ct. 1520 (2008).

98. Ibid.

99. See M. Garey, "The Cost of Taking a Life," *University of California–Davis Law Review* 18 (1985): 1221–70; Dale O. Cloninger and Roberto Marchesini, "Execution and Deterrence: A Quasi-Controlled Group Experiment," *Applied Economics* 33 (2001): 569–76; and Death Penalty Information Center, *Costs of the Death Penalty,* http://www.deathpenaltyinfo .org/costs-death-penalty.

100. Furman v. Georgia, Jackson v. Georgia, Branch v. Texas, 408 U.S. 238 (1972).

101. Gallup, *Death Penalty,* http://www .gallup.com/poll/1606/death-penalty .aspx.

102. James O. Finckenauer, "Public Support for the Death Penalty: Retribution as Just Deserts or Retribution as Revenge?" *Justice Quarterly* 5 (March 1988): 81–100; Scott Vollum, Dennis R. Longmire, and Jacqueline Buffington-Vollum, "Confidence in the Death Penalty and Supporting Its Use: Exploring the Value-Expressive Dimension of Death Penalty Attitudes," *Justice Quarterly* 21, no. 3 (2004): 521–45. See also Jeffrey M. Jones, *Americans' Views of Death Penalty More Positive This Year; Nearly Three in Four Favor It as a Penalty for Convicted Murderers,* May 19, 2005, http://www.gallup.com /poll/16393/Americans-Views-Death -Penalty-More-Positive-Year.aspx.

103. James W. Marquart and Jonathan R. Sorensen, "A National Study of the Furman-Committed Inmates," *Loyola of Los Angeles Law Review* 23 (1989): 5–28; Texas Defender Service, *Deadly Speculation: Misleading Texas Capital Juries with False Predictions of Future Dangerousness* (Houston, TX: Texas Defender Service, 2004).

104. See Thorsten Sellin, ed., *Capital Punishment* (New York: Harper & Row, 1967); Karl F. Schuessler, "The Deterrent Influence of the Death Penalty," *Annals of the American Academy of Political and Social Science* 284 (November 1952): 54–62; Hugo Adam Bedau and Chester M. Pierce, eds.,

Capital Punishment in the United States (New York: AMS Press, 1976), 299–416; Hashem Dezhbakhsh, Paul H. Rubin, and Joanna M. Shepherd, "Does Capital Punishment Have a Deterrent Effect? New Evidence from Postmoratorium Panel Data," *American Law and Economics Review* 5, no. 2 (2003): 344–76; Helmut Kury, Theodore N. Ferdinand, and Joachim Obergfell-Fuchs, "Does Severe Punishment Mean Less Criminality?" *International Criminal Justice Review* 13 (2003): 110–48; and Jongmook Choe, "Another Look at the Deterrent Effect of Death Penalty," *Journal of Advanced Research in Law and Economics* 1, no. 1 (2010): 12–15.

105. Death Penalty Information Center, *Innocence: List of Those Freed from Death Row,* http://www .deathpenaltyinfo.org/innocence -list-those-freed-death-row.

106. Ibid.

107. Death Penalty Information Center, *Innocence and the Crisis in the American Death Penalty* (Washington, DC: Death Penalty Information Center, 2004).

108. Michael L. Radelet and Hugo Adam Bedau, "Fallibility and Finality: Type II Errors and Capital Punishment," in *Challenging Capital Punishment: Legal and Social Science Approaches,* ed. Kenneth C. Haas and James A. Inciardi (Newbury Park, CA: Sage, 1988), 91–112; Stephen J. Markman and Paul G. Cassell, "Protecting the Innocent: A Response to the Bedau-Radelet Study," *Stanford Law Review* 41, no. 1 (1990): 121–60.

109. Furman v. Georgia, Jackson v. Georgia, Branch v. Texas, 408 U.S. 238 (1972).

110. William J. Bowers and Glenn L. Pierce, "Arbitrariness and Discrimination Under Post-Furman Capital Statutes," *Crime & Delinquency* 26 (October 1980): 563–635; Kenneth C. Haas, "Reaffirming the Value of Life: Arguments Against the Death Penalty," *Delaware Lawyer* 3 (Summer 1984): 12–20; Raymond Bonner and Marc Lacey, "Pervasive Disparities Found in the Federal Death Penalty," *New York Times,* September 12, 2000; Marvin D. Free, "Race and Presentencing Decisions in the United States: A Summary and Critique of the Research," *Criminal Justice Review* 27, no. 2 (2002): 203–32; Jon Hurwitza and Mark Peffley, "And Justice for Some: Race, Crime, and Punishment in the U.S. Criminal Justice System," *Canadian Journal of Political Science* 43 (2002): 457–79.

111. D. Baldus et al., "Race Discrimination and the Death Penalty in the Post *Furman* Era: An Empirical and Legal Overview, with Preliminary Findings from Philadelphia," *Cornell Law Review* 83 (1998).

112. Death Penalty Information Center, *Facts about the Death Penalty.*

113. Barefoot v. Estelle, 463 U.S. 880 (1983).

114. Pulley v. Harris, 465 U.S. 37 (1984).

115. Lockhart v. McCree, 476 U.S. 162 (1986).

116. McCleskey v. Kemp, 481 U.S. 279 (1987).

117. Herrera v. Collins, 506 U.S. 390 (1993).

118. Atkins v. Virginia, 536 U.S. 304 (2002).

119. Roper v. Simmons, 543 U.S. 551 (2005).

120. Kennedy v. Louisiana, 554 U.S. 407 (2008).

121. Skinner v. Switzer, 131 S. Ct. 1289 (2011).

122. Paul Marcus and Melanie D. Wilson, *Gilbert Law Summaries on Criminal Procedure,* 18th ed. (New York: Thomson, 2011).

123. Federal Rules of Criminal Procedure, Rule 52(b), http://www.law.cornell .edu/rules/frcrmp/rule_52.

124. Tumey v. Ohio, 273 U.S. 510 (1927).

125. Gideon v. Wainwright, 372 U.S. 335 (1963).

126. Chapman v. California, 386 U.S. 18 (1967).

127. Gideon v. Wainwright, 372 U.S. 335 (1963), Brewer v. Williams, 430 U.S. 387 (1977).

128. Chapman v. California, 386 U.S. 18 (1967); Gresham v. Harcourt, 93 Tex. 149, 53 S.W. 1019 (1899).

129. Delaware v. Prouse, 440 U.S. 648 (1979).

130. Robert A. Carp, Ronald Stidham, and Kenneth L. Manning, *Judicial Process in America* (Washington, DC: CQ Press, 2010).

131. Ibid.

132. North Carolina v. Pearce, 395 U.S. 711 (1969).

133. Joshua T. Rose, "Innocence Lost: The Detrimental Effect of Automatic Waiver Statutes on Juvenile Justice," *Brandeis Law Journal* 41 (2002–2003): 977.

134. Eric J. Fritsch, Tory J. Caeti, and Craig Hemmens, "Spare the Needle but Not the Punishment: The Incarceration of Waived Youth in Texas Prisons," *Crime & Delinquency* 42 (October 1996): 593–609.

135. Donna M. Bishop, Charles E. Frazer, Lonn Lanza-Kaduce, and Lawrence Winner, "The Transfer of Juveniles

to Criminal Court: Does It Make a Difference?" *Crime & Delinquency* 46 (April 1996): 171–91.

136. Human Rights Watch, *State Distribution of Youth Offenders Serving Juvenile Life Without Parole (JLWOP)* October 2, 2009, http://www.hrw.org/news/2009/10/02/state-distribution-juvenile-offenders-serving-juvenile-life-without-parole.

137. Human Rights Watch and Amnesty International, *The Rest of Their Lives: Life without Parole for Child Offenders in the United States,* October 2005, http://www.amnesty.org/en/library/asset/AMR51/162/2005/en/209dd2da-d4a1-11dd-8a23-d58a49c0d652/amr511622005en.pdf.

138. Miller v. Alabama 567 U.S. ___ (2012); Jackson v. Hobbs, 132 S. Ct. 281 (2011).

Chapter 11

1. Hope v. Pelzer, 536 U.S. 730 (2002).
2. Ibid.
3. Ibid.
4. Ibid.
5. Ibid.
6. Harry Elmer Barnes, *The Story of Punishment: A Record of Man's Inhumanity to Man* (Montclair, NJ: Patterson Smith, 1972).
7. Samuel Walker, *Popular Justice: A History of American Criminal Justice,* 2nd ed. (New York; Oxford University Press, 1997).
8. Luke Owen Pike, *A History of Crime in England,* vol. 2 (Montclair, NJ: Patterson Smith, 1968), 87–88.
9. Ibid.
10. G. Bernard Vold and J. Snipes, *Theoretical Criminology* (Oxford, UK: Oxford University Press, 1998).
11. Norma Landau, *Law, Crime, and English Society, 1660–1830* (Cambridge, UK: Cambridge University Press, 2002), 118.
12. Vold and Snipes, *Theoretical Criminology.*
13. Ibid.
14. Ibid.
15. Lawrence Friedman, *Crime and Punishment in American History* (New York: Basic Books, 1994).
16. Norman A. Carlson, "The Federal Prison System: Forty-Five Years of Change," *Federal Probation* 39, no. 2 (June 1975): 37–42.
17. Federal Bureau of Prisons, *Bureau of Prisons Inmate Report,* June 21, 2012, http://www.bop.gov/locations/weekly_report.jsp.
18. Federal Bureau of Prisons, *About the Bureau of Prisons,* http://www.bop.gov/about/index.jsp.

19. For additional information, see the Texas Department of Criminal Justice Web site, http://www.tdcj.state.tx.us/, and the Rhode Island Department of Corrections Web site, http://www.doc.ri.gov/index.php.
20. Pew Center on the States, *Prison Count 2010,* April 1, 2010, http://www.pewstates.org/research/reports/prison-count-2010-85899372907.
21. Ibid.
22. Walker, *Popular Justice.*
23. Peter M. Carlson and Judith Simon, *Prison and Jail Administration: Practice and Theory* (Burlington, MA: Jones and Bartlett, 1999).
24. Todd D. Minton, *Jail Inmates at Midyear 2011,* April 2012, http://bjs.ojp.usdoj.gov/content/pub/pdf/jim11st.pdf.
25. Karen R. Humes, Nicholas A. Jones, and Roberto R. Ramirez, *Overview of Race and Hispanic Origin: 2010, Census Briefs,* March 2011, www.census.gov/prod/cen2010/briefs/c2010br-02.pdf; Minton, *Jail Inmates at Midyear 2011.*
26. Minton, *Jail Inmates at Midyear 2011.*
27. Cited in Ronald Goldfarb, *Jails: The Ultimate Ghetto of the Criminal Justice System* (Garden City, NY: Anchor, 1976), 3.
28. Caroline Wolf Harlow, *Education and Correctional Populations,* January 1, 2003, bjs.ojp.usdoj.gov/content/pub/pdf/ecp.pdf.
29. Erving Goffman, *Asylums* (Garden City, NY: Anchor, 1961), 1–8.
30. Gresham M. Sykes and Bruce Western, *The Society of Captives: A Study of a Maximum Security Prison* (Princeton, NJ: Princeton University Press, 2007).
31. Town of Beekman, *Green Haven Prison,* http://www.beekmanhistory.com/id57.html.
32. Ibid.
33. Gresham M. Sykes, *The Society of Captives: A Study of a Maximum Security Prison* (Princeton, NJ: Princeton University Press, 2007).
34. Ibid.
35. Erik Sofge, "High-Tech Lockup: Inside 4 Next-Gen Prison Security Systems," *Popular Mechanics,* October 1, 2009.
36. Hans Toch, "The Contemporary Relevance of Early Experiments with Supermax Reform," *Prison Journal* 83 (June 2003): 221–28.
37. Todd R. Clear, George F. Cole, and Michael D. Reisig, *American Corrections* (Independence, KY: Wadsworth, 2010).
38. Ibid.

39. Ibid.
40. Blake McKelvey, *American Prisons: A History of Good Intentions* (Montclair, NJ: Patterson Smith, 1977), 150–96.
41. For more information, see the Federal Bureau of Prisons Web site, http://www.bop.gov/, and the Florida Department of Corrections Web site, http://www.dc.state.fl.us/.
42. Timothy J. Flanagan, W. Wesley Johnson, and Katherine Bennett, "Job Satisfaction Among Correctional Executives: A Contemporary Portrait of Wardens of State Prisons for Adults," *Prison Journal* 76 (December 1996): 385–97.
43. Gerald Melnic, Wendy R. Ulaszek, Hsiu-Ju Lin, and Harry Wexler, "When Goals Diverge: Staff Consensus and the Organizational Climate," *Drug and Alcohol Dependence* 103, supp. 1 (2009): S17–S22; Eric G. Lambert, Nancy L. Hogan, Shannon M. Barton, and O. Oko Elechi, "The Impact of Job Stress, Job Involvement, Job Satisfaction, and Organizational Commitment on Correctional Staff Support for Rehabilitation and Punishment," *Criminal Justice Studies* 22, no. 2 (2009).
44. Marie L. Griffin, Nancy L. Hogan, Eric G. Lambert, et al., "Job Involvement, Job Stress, Job Satisfaction, and Organizational Commitment and the Burnout of Correctional Staff," *Criminal Justice and Behavior* 37, no. 2 (February 2010): 239–55; Joseph R. Carlson, Richard H. Anson, and Greg Thomas, "Correctional Officer Burnout and Stress: Does Gender Matter?" *Prison Journal* 83 (September 2003): 277–88; Mary Ann Farkas, "A Typology of Correctional Officers," *International Journal of Offender Therapy and Comparative Criminology* 44 (2000): 431–49; Robert Johnson, *Hard Time: Understanding and Reforming the Prison* (Belmont, CA: Wadsworth, 1996); K. Kauffman, *Prison Officers and Their World* (Cambridge, MA: Harvard University Press, 1988).
45. Virginia Hutchinson, Kristin Keller, and Thomas Reid, *Inmate Behavior Management: The Key to a Safe and Secure Jail,* August 2009, static.nicic.gov/Library/023882.pdf; Beverly D. Rivera, Ernest L. Cowles, and Laura G. Dorman, "An Exploratory Study of Institutional Personal Control and Environmental Satisfaction in a Gang-Free Prison," *Prison Journal* 83, no. 2 (2003): 149–70; James E. Robertson, "Foreword: 'Separate but Equal' in Prison: *Johnson v. California* and Common Sense Racism," *Journal of*

Criminal Law and Criminology 96, no. 3 (Spring 2006): 795–848.

46. Sarah Lawrence, Daniel P. Mears, Glenn Dubin, and Jeremy Travis, "The Practice and Promise of Prison Programming," *Urban Institute,* May 2002, www.urban.org/uploadedpdf /410493_PrisonProgramming.pdf.

47. Richard A. Berk, Heather Ladd, Heidi Graziano, and Jong-Ho Baek, "A Randomized Experiment Testing Inmate Classification Systems," *Criminology and Public Policy* 2, no. 2 (2003): 215–42; Kathryn Ann Farr, "Classification for Female Inmates: Moving Forward," *Crime & Delinquency* 46 (January 2000): 3–17.

48. Jeffrey L. Metzer, "Monitoring a Correctional Mental Health System," in *Handbook of Correctional Mental Health,* ed. Charles L. Scott (Arlington, VA: American Psychiatric, 2010).

49. Berk, Ladd, Graziano, and Baek, "A Randomized Experiment Testing Inmate Classification Systems"; Farr, "Classification for Female Inmates: Moving Forward."

50. Metzer, "Monitoring a Correctional Mental Health System."

51. Rosa M. Cho and John H. Tyler, "Does Prison-Based Adult Basic Education Improve Postrelease Outcomes for Male Prisoners in Florida?" *Crime & Delinquency,* November 30, 2010, http://cad.sagepub.com/content /early/2010/11/30/0011128710389588 .full.pdf+html; Gennaro F. Vito and Richard Tewksbury, "Improving the Educational Skills of Inmates," *Corrections Compendium* 24 (October 1999): 1–4, 16–17.

52. Gail Spangenberg, "Current Issues in Correctional Education: A Compilation and Discussion," February 2004, www.caalusa.org/correct_ed_paper .pdf.

53. J. Lillis, "Prison Education Programs Reduced," *Corrections Compendium* 19, no. 3 (March 1994): 1–11; Charles B. A. Ubah, "A Grounded Look at the Debate over Prison-Based Education: Optimistic Theory versus Pessimistic Worldview," *Prison Journal* 83 (June 2003): 115–29; Harlow, *Education and Correctional Populations;* Gail Coulter and Eric Brookens, "Corrective Reading: A Systemwide Program to Improve Reading Performance for Incarcerated Adult Basic Education Students," *Corrections Compendium* 28 (October 2003); 1–4, 28–30.

54. Ibid.

55. G. Wees, "Prison Industries 1997: Outside Federal System, Inmate-Employees Remain an Elite Group,"

Corrections Compendium 22, no. 6 (June 1997): 10–21.

56. Ibid.

57. Noah Zatz, "Working at the Boundaries of Markets: Prison Labor and the Economic Dimension of Employment Relationships," *Vanderbilt Law Review* 61 (2008): 857–958; Congressional Research Service, *Federal Prison Industries,* July 13, 2007, www .fas.org/sgp/crs/misc/RL32380.pdf; "Prison Industries," *Corrections Compendium* 27, no. 9 (September 2002): 8–9; "Prison Industries," *Corrections Compendium* 25, no. 3 (March 2000): 8–22.

58. Don C. Gibbons, *Changing the Lawbreaker: The Treatment of Delinquents and Criminals* (Englewood Cliffs, NJ: Prentice Hall, 1965), 136.

59. American Correctional Association, *Manual of Correctional Standards* (Washington, DC: American Correctional Association, 2011).

60. Brett E. Garland, William P. Mccarty, and Ruohui Zhao, "Job Satisfaction and Organizational Commitment in Prisons: An Examination of Psychological Staff, Teachers, and Unit Management Staff," *Criminal Justice and Behavior* 36 (2009): 163.

61. Bureau of Justice Statistics, *Sourcebook of Criminal Justice Statistics* (Washington, DC: Bureau of Justice Statistics, 2007).

62. National Institute on Drug Abuse, *Research Report: Therapeutic Communities,* August 2002, http://www .drugabuse.gov/publications/research -reports/therapeutic-community.

63. Wayne N. Welsh, "A Multisite Evaluation of Prison-Based Therapeutic Community Drug Treatment," *Criminal Justice and Behavior* 34, no. 11 (November 2007): 1481–98.

64. Barbara A. Nadel, "Correctional Health Care: Challenges and Opportunities for the Future," *Corrections Compendium* (October 1996): 1–5; Jill A. McCorkel, Clifford A. Butzin, Steven S. Martin, and James A. Inciardi, "Utilization of Health Care Services in a Sample of Drug-Involved Offenders: A Comparison with National Norms," *American Behavioral Scientist* 41 (Spring 1998): 1079–1089; Kamala Mallik-Kane and Christy A. Visher, "Health and Prisoner Reentry: How Physical, Mental, and Substance Abuse Conditions Shape the Process of Reintegration," *Urban Institute,* February 2008, www.urban .org/UploadedPDF/411617_health _prisoner_reentry.pdf.

65. Jim Thomas and Barbara H. Zaitzow, "Conning or Conversion? The Role

of Religion in Prison Coping," *Prison Journal* 86, no. 2 (June 2006): 242–59.

66. Leonard Orland, *Justice, Punishment, Treatment* (New York: Free Press, 1973), 263–69.

67. David Lovell and Ron Jemelka, "When Inmates Misbehave: The Costs of Discipline," *Prison Journal* 76 (June 1996): 165–79.

68. Ibid.

69. Sarah Hockenberry, Melissa Sickmund, and Anthony Sladky, "Juvenile Residential Facility Census, 2008: Selected Findings," *Juvenile Offenders and Victims: National Report Series,* July 2011, www.ncjrs.gov/pdffiles1 /ojjdp/231683.pdf.

70. M. Sickmund, T. J. Sladky, W. Kang, and C. Puzzanchera, "Easy Access to the Census on Juveniles in Residential Placement," updated December 16, 2011, http://www.ojjdp.gov /ojstatbb/ezacjrp/.

71. Ibid.

72. Ibid.

73. Ibid.

74. Hockenberry, Sickmund, and Sladky, "Juvenile Residential Facility Census, 2008: Selected Findings."

75. Sickmund, Sladky, Kang, and Puzzanchera, "Easy Access to the Census of Juveniles in Residential Placement."

76. Peter Greenwood and Susan Turner, "Overview of Prevention and Intervention Programs for Juvenile Offenders," *Victims & Offenders* 4 no. 4 (October 2009): 365–74; Sickmund, Sladky, Kang, and Puzzanchera, "Easy Access to the Census of Juveniles in Residential Placement."

Chapter 12

1. "People & Events: Attica Prison Riot—September 9–13, 1971," *American Experience—The Rockefellers,* Public Broadcasting Service.

2. "Attica Prison Riot: Memories Strong after 40 Years," *Democrat andChronicle.com,* 2012, http:// www.democratandchronicle.com /section/ATTICA01/Attica-Prison -Riot-Before-the-riot.

3. Ibid.

4. Ibid.

5. Ibid.

6. *Attica: The Official Report of the New York State Special Commission on Attica* (New York: Bantam, 1972), 3–15.

7. Ruffin v. Commonwealth, 62 Va. (21 Gratt.) 790, 796 (1871).

8. United States ex rel. Gereau v. Henderson, 526 F.2d 889 (1976). For a history of the "hands-off" doctrine, see Kenneth C. Haas, "Judicial

Politics and Correctional Reform: An Analysis of the Decline of the Hands-Off Doctrine," *Detroit College of Law Review* (Winter 1977–1978): 795–831.

9. Joseph P. Fried, "To Victim of Attica, Settlement Is Apology," *New York Times,* May 22, 2005.

10. Gresham M. Sykes and Sheldon L. Messenger, "The Inmate Social System," in *Theoretical Studies in the Social Organization of the Prison,* ed. Richard Cloward, Donald R. Cressey, George H. Grosser, et al. (New York: Social Science Research Council, 1960), 6–8; Mark Fleisher, *Warehousing Violence* (Beverly Hills, CA: Sage, 1989).

11. T. L. Winfree, G. Newbold, and S. H. Tubb, "Prisoner Perspectives on Inmate Culture in New Mexico and New Zealand: A Descriptive Case Study," *Prison Journal* 82, no. 2 (2002): 213–33; B. Crewe, "Prisoner Society in the Era of Hard Drugs," *Punishment and Society* 7, no. 4 (2005): 457–81; B. Crewe, "Codes and Conventions: The Terms and Conditions of Contemporary Inmate Values," in *The Effects of Imprisonment,* ed. A. Liebling and S. Maruna (Portland, OR: Willan, 2005), 177–208.

12. Paul Guerrino, Paige M. Harrison, and William J. Sabol, *Prisoners in 2010,* revised February 9, 2010, bjs.ojp .usdoj.gov/content/pub/pdf/p10.pdf.

13. Paul W. Tappan, *Crime, Justice, and Correction* (New York: McGraw-Hill, 1960), 653.

14. Lawrence A. Greenfield and Tracy L. Snell, *Women Offenders,* revised October 3, 2000, www.bjs.gov/content /pub/pdf/wo.pdf.

15. Merry Morash, Robin Haar, and Lila Rucker, "A Comparison of Programming for Women and Men in U.S. Prisons in the 1980s," *Crime & Delinquency* 40 (1994): 197–221; Robert Ross and Elizabeth Fabiano, *Female Offenders: Correctional Afterthoughts* (Jefferson, NC: McFarland, 1986).

16. Jennifer E. Cobbina, "Reintegration Success and Failure: Factors Impacting Reintegration Among Incarcerated and Formerly Incarcerated Women," *Journal of Offender Rehabilitation* 49, no. 3 (2010): 210–32; Barbara A. Nadel, "Designing for Women: Doing Time Differently," *Corrections Compendium* (November 1996): 1–5.

17. George Kiser, "Female Inmates and Their Families," *Federal Probation* 55 (1991): 56–63; Peter Breen, "Bridging the Barriers," *Corrections Today* 57 (1995): 98–99; Sasha Nyary, "When Mom Can't Come Home," *Life,* October 1997, 84–90; Fox Butterfield, "As Inmate Population Grows, So Does a Focus on Children," *New York Times,* April 7, 1999.

18. Center for Drug and Alcohol Studies, *Annual Report* (Newark: University of Delaware, 2003).

19. Janet I. Warren, Susan Hurt, Ann Booker Loper, and Preeti Chauhan, "Exploring Prison Adjustment among Female Inmates: Issues of Measurement and Prediction," *Criminal Justice and Behavior* 31, no. 5 (October 2004): 624–45; Liebling and Maruna, *The Effects of Imprisonment.*

20. For descriptive material on women's prisons, see Kathryn W. Burkhart, *Women in Prison* (New York: Doubleday, 1973); Jocelyn Pollock-Bryne, *Women, Prison, and Crime* (Pacific Grove, CA: Brooks/Cole, 1990); James A. Gondles, *Female Offenders: Meeting the Needs of a Neglected Population* (Lanham, MD: American Correctional Association, 1992); Kathryn Watterson, *Women in Prison: Inside the Concrete Womb* (Boston: Northeastern University Press, 1996); Cynthia Blinn, ed., *Maternal Ties: A Selection of Programs for Female Offenders* (Lanham, MD: American Correctional Association, 1997); and Andi Rierden, *The Farm: Life Inside a Women's Prison* (Amherst: University of Massachusetts Press, 1997).

21. Howard N. Snyder, *Arrest in the United States, 1980–2009,* September 2011, www.bjs.gov/content/pub/pdf /aus8009.pdf; Greenfield and Snell, *Women Offenders;* Allen J. Beck, *Prisoners in 1999,* August 2000, bjs .ojp.usdoj.gov/content/pub/pdf/p99 .pdf; Allen J. Beck, *Prisoners in 2000,* August 2001, www.bjs.gov/content /pub/pdf/p00.pdf.

22. Stephanie S. Covington and Barbara E. Bloom, "Gendered Justice: Women in the Criminal Justice System," in *Gendered Justice: Addressing Female Offenders,* ed. Barbara E. Bloom (Durham, NC: Carolina Academic Press, 2003).

23. For descriptive material on women's prisons, see Burkhart, *Women in Prison;* Pollock-Bryne, *Women, Prison, and Crime;* Gondles, *Female Offenders;* Watterson, *Women in Prison;* Blinn, *Maternal Ties;* Rierden, *The Farm;* and David Ward and Gene Kassebaum, *Women's Prison: Sex and Social Structure* (Piscataway, NJ: Aldine Transaction, 2007).

24. Ibid.

25. United States Constitution, Article I, Section 9.

26. Federal Habeas Corpus Act, 28 U.S.C. § 2254 (1897).

27. David A. Jones, *The Law of Criminal Procedure* (Boston: Little, Brown, 1981), 574.

28. Coffin v. Reichard, 143 F.2d 443 (1944).

29. Ibid.

30. See Kenneth C. Haas, "The Comparative Study of State and Federal Judicial Behavior Revisited," *Journal of Politics* 44 (August 1982): 729–39.

31. Tom Murton, "Too Good for Arkansas," *Nation,* January 12, 1970, 12–17.

32. Tom Murton and Joe Hyams, *Accomplices to Crime: The Arkansas Prison Scandal* (New York: Grove, 1969), 7.

33. Bruce Jackson, *Killing Time: Life in the Arkansas Penitentiary* (Ithaca, NY: Cornell University Press, 1977).

34. Thomas O. Murton, *The Dilemma of Prison Reform* (New York: Holt, Rinehart and Winston, 1976), 35–38.

35. Holt v. Sarver, 309 F.Supp. 362 (1970).

36. Ibid.

37. Civil Rights Act of 1871, 42 U.S.C. § 1983.

38. Monroe v. Pape, 365 U.S. 167 (1961).

39. Cooper v. Pate, 378 U.S. 546 (1964).

40. Preiser v. Rodriguez, 411 U.S. 475 (1973).

41. Ibid.

42. Will v. Michigan Department of State Police, 491 U.S. 58 (1989).

43. Brown v. Plata, 131 S. Ct. 1910 (2011).

44. Ex parte Hull, 312 U.S. 546 (1941).

45. Johnson v. Avery, 393 U.S. 483 (1969).

46. Cited by Kenneth C. Haas and Anthony Champagne, "The Impact of *Johnson v. Avery* on Prison Administration," *Tennessee Law Review* 43 (Winter 1976–1977): 275.

47. Johnson v. Avery, 393 U.S. 483 (1969).

48. See the United States Constitution, Article I, Section 9.

49. Idaho Statutes, Section 18-310.

50. United States Constitution, First Amendment.

51. Fulwood v. Clemmer, 206 F.Supp. 370 (1962).

52. Howard v. Smyth, 365 F.2d 28 (1966); State v. Cubbage, 210 A.2d 555 (1965); Jones v. Willingham, 248 F.Supp. 791 (1965); Cooke v. Tramburg, 43 N.J. 514, 205 A.2d 889 (1964).

53. Ibid.

54. O'Lone v. Estate of Shabazz, 482 U.S. 342 (1987).

55. Ibid.

56. Williams v. Morton, 343 F.3d 212 (2003): Cutter v. Wilkinson, 544 U.S. 709 (2005).

57. Cruz v. Beto, 405 U.S. 319 (1972).

58. Cutter v. Wilkinson, 544 U.S. 709 (2005).

59. Kay v. Bemis, 500 F.3d 1214 (2007); Singson v. Norris, 553 F.3d 660 (2009).

60. Wolff v. McDonnell, 418 U.S. 539 (1974).

61. Procunier v. Martinez, 416 U.S. 396 (1974).

62. Beard v. Banks, 548 U.S. 521 (2006).

63. Vanessa Miller, "Jail Mail: Iowa Prison Correspondence Goes Electronic for Inmates," (Iowa) *Gazette*, August 5, 2011; Federal Bureau of Prisons, *TRULINCS FAQs*, http://www.bop.gov/inmate_programs/trulincs_faq.jsp.

64. Francis T. Cullen, "Make Rehabilitation Corrections' Guiding Paradigm," *Criminology & Public Policy* 6, no. 4 (November 2007): 717–27.

65. Rutherford v. Hutto, 377 F.Supp. 268 (1974); Jackson v. McLemore, 523 F.2d 838 (1975).

66. See Federal Bureau of Prisons, *Program Statement: Literacy Program (GED Standard),* December 1, 2003, http://www.bop.gov/policy/progstat/5350_028.pdf; Lance Lochner and Enrico Moretti, "The Effect of Education on Crime: Evidence from Prison Inmates, Arrests, and Self-Reports," *American Economic Review* 94 (March 2004): 155–89; Robert J. Di Vito, "Survey of Mandatory Education Policies in State Penal Institutions," *Journal of Correctional Education* 42, no. 3 (1994): 126–32.

67. Washington v. Harper, 494 U.S. 210 (1990).

68. Brown v. Plata, 131 S. Ct. 1910 (2011).

69. Estelle v. Gamble, 429 U.S. 97 (1976).

70. Ibid.

71. For example, see Gates v. Collier, 390 F.Supp. 482 (1975).

72. Priest v. Cupp, 545 P.2d 917 (1976).

73. Brown v. Plata, 131 S. Ct. 1910 (2011).

74. Joann B. Morton, "Implications for Corrections of an Aging Prison Population," *Corrections Management Quarterly* 5, no. 1 (2001): 78–88; Ashley Nellis and Ryan S. King, "No Exit: The Expanding Use of Life Sentences in America," July 2009, www.sentencingproject.org/doc/.../inc_noexitseptember2009.pdf; Timothy Curtin, "The Continuing Problem of America's Aging Prison Population and the Search for a Cost-Effective and Socially Acceptable Means of Addressing It," *Elder Law Journal* 15 (2007): 473.

75. Tina Chiu, *It's About Time: Aging Prisoners, Increasing Costs, and Geriatric Release,* April 2010, http://www.vera.org/download?file=2973/Its-about-time-aging-prisoners-increasing-costs-and-geriatric

-release.pdf; Mike Mitka, "Aging Prisoners Stressing Healthcare System," *Journal of the American Medical Association* 292, no. 4 (2004): 423.

76. Wilkerson v. Utah, 99 U.S. 130 (1878); Weems v. United States, 217 U.S. 349 (1910); Trop v. Dulles, 356 U.S. 86 (1958); Robinson v. California, 370 U.S. 660 (1962).

77. Jordan v. Fitzharris, 257 F.Supp. 674 (1966); Bauer v. Sielaff, 372 F.Supp. 1104 (1974); Landman v. Royster, 333 F.Supp. 621 (1971); Novak v. Beto, 453 F.2d 661 (1971); Novak v. Beto, 456 F.2d 1303 (1972).

78. Dumpson v. McGinnis, 2009 U.S. App. LEXIS 22453 (2009).

79. Parker v. James, 15 Fed. Appx. 670 (2001).

80. Wilkerson v. Utah, 99 U.S. 130 (1878); Weems v. United States, 217 U.S. 349 (1910); Trop v. Dulles, 356 U.S. 86 (1958); Robinson v. California, 370 U.S. 660 (1962).

81. Wolff v. McDonnell, 418 U.S. 539 (1974).

82. Ibid.

83. Ibid.

84. Superintendent, Massachusetts Correctional Institute at Walpole v. Hill, 472 U.S. 445 (1985).

85. Ibid.

86. Bell v. Wolfish, 441 U.S. 520 (1979).

87. Ibid.

88. Rhodes v. Chapman, 452 U.S. 337 (1981).

89. Hudson v. Palmer, 468 U.S. 517 (1984).

90. Wilson v. Seiter, 501 U.S. 294 (1991).

91. *AELE Law Library of Case Summaries: Corrections Law for Jails, Prisons and Detention Facilities; Prison and Jail Conditions: General,* http://www.aele.org/law/Digests/jail88.html.

92. For example, see Jens Erik Gould, "As California Fights Prison Overcrowding, Some See a Golden Opportunity," *Time,* September 29, 2011.

93. Noam S. Cohen, "Attica Town Struggles to Forget 1971," *New York Times,* September 1, 1991.

94. Jon R. Sorensen, Mark D. Cunningham, Mark P. Vigen, and S. O. Woods, "Serious Assaults on Prison Staff: A Descriptive Analysis," *Journal of Criminal Justice* 39, no. 2 (March–April 2011): 143–50.

95. Lucas Anderson, *Kicking the National Habit: The Legal and Policy Arguments for Abolishing Private Prison Contracts,* January 10, 2010, available at http://ssrn.com/abstract=1534372.

96. Ira P. Robbins, "Privatization of Corrections: Defining the Issues," *Judicature* 69 (April/May 1986): 325–31; United States General Accounting

Office, *Private Prisons: Cost Savings and Bureau of Prisons' Statutory Authority Need to Be Resolved,* February 7, 1991, archive.gao.gov/d21t9/143337.pdf; Christine Bowditch and Ronald S. Everett, "Private Prisons: Problems within the Solution," *Justice Quarterly* 4 (September 1987): 441; Jeff Gerth and Stephen Labaton, "The Pitfalls of Private Penitentiaries," *New York Times,* November 24, 1995; Pam Belluck, "As More Prisons Go Private, States Seek Tighter Controls," *New York Times,* April 15, 1999.

Chapter 13

1. United States v. Gementera, 379 F.3d 596 (2004).

2. Ibid.

3. Ibid.

4. Ibid.

5. Ibid.

6. Ibid.

7. United States Sentencing Commission, *An Overview of the United States Sentencing Commission,* http://www.ussc.gov/About_the_Commission/Overview_of_the_USSC/USSC_Overview.pdf.

8. United States v. Gementera, 379 F.3d 596 (2004).

9. Aaron S. Book, "Shame On You: An Analysis of Modern Shame Punishment as an Alternative to Incarceration," *William and Mary Law Review* 40, no. 2 (1999): 653–86.

10. Mark A. Kleiman, "Community Corrections as the Front Line in Crime Control," *UCLA Law Review* 46 (1998–1999): 1909.

11. See also Karen Dunlap, *Community Justice: Concepts and Strategies* (Lexington, KY: American Probation and Parole Association, 1998); Samuel Walker, *Sense and Nonsense About Crime and Drugs,* 7th ed. (Belmont, CA: Wadsworth, 2010); and John Irwin and James Austin, *It's About Time: America's Imprisonment Binge,* 2nd ed. (Belmont, CA: Wadsworth, 1996).

12. Shannon Langea, Jürgen Rehm, and Svetlana Popova, "The Effectiveness of Criminal Justice Diversion Initiatives in North America: A Systematic Literature Review," *International Journal of Forensic Mental Health* 10, no. 3 (2011): 200–14; Duane C. McBride, "Criminal Justice Diversion," in *Crime and the Criminal Justice Process,* ed. James A. Inciardi and Kenneth C. Haas (Dubuque, IA: Kendall/Hunt, 1978), 246.

13. McBride, "Criminal Justice Diversion," 250.

14. See Hung-En Sung, "From Diversion to Reentry: Recidivism Risks Among Graduates of an Alternative to Incarceration Program," *Criminal Justice Policy Review* 22 (2011): 219.

15. For additional information about this topic, see George L. Kelling and Catherine M. Coles, *Fixing Broken Windows: Restoring Order and Reducing Crime in Our Communities* (New York: Free Press, 1996).

16. Juliet Lapidos, "You're Grounded! How Do You Qualify for House Arrest?" *Slate Magazine,* January 28, 2009.

17. Richard A. Ball and J. Robert Lilly, "A Theoretical Examination of Home Incarceration," *Federal Probation* 50 (March 1986): 17–24; Patricia K. Loveless, "Home Incarceration with Electronic Monitoring: Myths and Realities," *American Jails* (January/February 1994): 2–3.

18. Brian K. Payne and Randy R. Gainey, "The Electronic Monitoring of Offenders Released from Jail or Prisons: Safety, Control, and Comparisons to the Incarceration Experience," *Prison Journal* 84 (2004): 413–23.

19. See John Augustus, *A Report of the Labors of John Augustus, for the Last Ten Years, in Aid of the Unfortunate* (Boston: Wright & Hasty, 1852), reprinted as *John Augustus, First Probation Officer* (New York: National Probation Association, 1939).

20. American Bar Association Project on Standards for Criminal Justice, *Standards Relating to Probation* (New York: Institute for Judicial Administration, 1970), 9.

21. National Advisory Commission on Criminal Justice Standards and Goals, *Corrections—Report of the National Advisory Commission on Criminal Justice Standards and Goals, 1973* (Washington, DC: U.S. Government Printing Office, 1973), 312.

22. Christian Henrichson and Ruth Delaney, *The Price of Prisons, What Incarceration Costs Taxpayers,* updated March 20, 2012, http://www.pewstates.org/uploadedFiles/PCS_Assets/2012/http.www.vera.org_download_file=3495_the-price-of-prisons-updated.pdf.

23. Georgia Department of Corrections, *FY2011 Allocation of Cost to Inmates, Probationers, Etc.,* February 28, 2012, http://www.dcor.state.ga.us/pdf/CorrectionsCosts.pdf.

24. Denise Leifker and Lisa L. Sample, "Do Judges Follow Sentencing Recommendations, Or Do Recommendations Simply Reflect What Judges Want to Hear? An Examination of One State Court," *Journal of Crime and Justice* 33, no. 2 (2010): 127–51; James A. Inciardi, "The Impact of Presentence Investigations on Subsequent Sentencing Practices," paper presented at the Annual Meeting of the American Sociological Association, New York City, August 1976; Robert M. Carter and Leslie T. Wilkins, "Some Factors in Sentencing Policy," *Journal of Criminal Law, Criminology, and Police Science* 58 (December 1967): 503–14.

25. Mary T. Phillips, *Estimating Jail Displacement for Alternative-to-Incarceration Programs in New York City, Final Report,* August 2002, http://www.cjareports.org/reports/ati.pdf; New York State Penal Law, Section 65.05.

26. New York State Penal Law, Section 65.20.

27. Thomas Gitchoff and George Rush, "The Criminological Case Evaluation and Sentencing Recommendation: An Idea Whose Time Has Come," *International Journal of Offender Therapy and Comparative Criminology* 33 (1989): 77–83.

28. Cox v. The State, 159 Ga. App. 488, 283 S.E.2d 716 (1981).

29. People v. Mitchell, 125 Cal. App.3d 715 [178 Cal. Rptr. 188] (1981).

30. State v. Behrens, 285 N.W.2d 513 (1979).

31. State v. Wilson, 604 P.2d 739 (1979).

32. Wood v. State, 378 So.2d 110 (1980).

33. State v. Alexander, 267 S. E. 2d 396 (1980).

34. Denny C. Langston, "Probation and Parole: No More Free Rides," *Corrections Today* (August 1988): 90–93; Texas Department of Criminal Justice, *Strengthening Community Supervision,* http://www.tdcj.state.tx.us/documents/cjad/CJAD_Strengthening_Community_Supervision.pdf. See also specific states, such as Idaho Code, Section 20-225.

35. Texas Department of Criminal Justice, *Strengthening Community Supervision.*

36. See Roy Sudipto, "Juvenile Restitution and Recidivism in a Midwestern County," *Federal Probation* 59 (1995): 55–62; Gilbert Geis, "Restitution by Criminal Offenders: A Summary and Overview," in *Restitution in Criminal Justice,* ed. Joe Hudson and Burt Galaway (Lexington, MA: Lexington, 1977), 246–64.

37. Richard Lawrence, "Restitution Programs Pay Back the Victim and Society," *Corrections Today* (February 1990): 96–98; Michael Courlander, "Restitution Programs: Problems and Solutions," *Corrections Today* (July 1988): 165–67; Barbara Sims, "Victim Restitution: A Review of the Literature," *Justice Professional* 13, no. 3 (2000): 247–69; R. Barry Ruback, Jennifer N. Shaffer, and Melissa A. Logue, "The Imposition and Effects of Restitution in Four Pennsylvania Counties: Effects of Size of County and Specialized Collection Units," *Crime & Delinquency* 50, no. 3 (2004): 168–88; R. Barry Ruback, *Restitution in Pennsylvania: A Multimethod Investigation* (Erie, PA: Pennsylvania Commission on Crime and Delinquency, 2002); Albert W. Dzur and Alan Wertheimer, "Forgiveness and Public Deliberation: The Practice of Restorative Justice," *Criminal Justice Ethics* 21, no. 1 (2002): 3–20.

38. U.S. Government Accountability Office, *Criminal Debt: Oversight and Actions Needed to Address Deficiencies in Collection Processes,* July 16, 2001, http://www.gao.gov/new.items/d01664.pdf; Matthew Dickman, "Should Crime Pay? A Critical Assessment of the Mandatory Victims Restitution Act of 1996," *California Law Review* 97 (2009): 1687.

39. Matthew DeMichele and Brian K. Payne, "Probation and Parole Officers Speak Out—Caseload and Workload Allocation," *Federal Probation* 71, no. 3 (2007); Joan Petersilia, "Probation in the United States," *Perspectives* (Summer 1998).

40. "The Law: Shock Probation," *Time,* May 7, 1973.

41. D. L. MacKenzie, L. A. Gould, L. M. Riechers, and J. W. Shaw, "Shock Incarceration: Rehabilitation or Retribution?" *Journal of Offender Counseling Services and Rehabilitation* 14 (1989): 25–40; James B. Wells, Kevin I. Minor, Earl Angel, and Kelli D. Stearman, "A Quasi-Experimental Evaluation of a Shock Incarceration and Aftercare Program for Juvenile Offenders," *Youth Violence and Juvenile Justice* 4, no. 3 (July 2006): 219–33.

42. Doris Layton MacKenzie, "Evidence-Based Corrections: Identifying What Works," *Crime & Delinquency* 46, no. 4 (October 2000): 457–71.

43. Paul C. Friday and David M. Petersen, "Shock of Imprisonment: Comparative Analysis of Short-Term Incarceration as a Treatment Technique," paper presented at the Inter-American Congress of the American Society of Criminology and the Inter-American Association of Criminology, Caracas, Venezuela, November 1972.

44. See David M. Petersen and Paul C. Friday, "Early Release from Incarceration: Race as a Factor in the Use of 'Shock Probation,'" *Journal of Criminal Law and Criminology* 66 (March 1975): 79–87; Joseph A. Waldron and Henry R. Angelino, "Shock Probation: A Natural Experiment on the Effect of a Short Period of Incarceration," *Prison Journal* 57 (Spring/Summer 1977): 52; Gennaro Vito, "Developments in Shock Probation: A Review of Research Findings and Policy Implications," *Federal Probation* 50 (1985): 22–27; Michael S. Vaughn, "Listening to the Experts: A National Study of Correctional Administrators' Responses to Prison Overcrowding," *Criminal Justice Review* 18, no. 1 (1993): 12–25; South Carolina State Reorganization Commission, *An Evaluation of the Omnibus Criminal Justice Improvements Act of 1986,* sect. 3, 4, and 5, Second Year Report (Columbia, SC: South Carolina State Reorganization Commission, 1990); David Diroll, *The Use of Community Corrections and the Impact of Prison and Jail Crowding on Sentencing* (Columbus, OH: Governor's Office of Criminal Justice Services, 1989); Susette M. Talarico and Martha A. Myers, "Split Sentencing in Georgia: A Test of Two Empirical Assumptions," *Justice Quarterly* 4, no. 4 (1987): 611–29.

45. Lawrence W. Sherman, Denise C. Gottfredson, Doris L. MacKenzie, et al., "Preventing Crime: What Works, What Doesn't, and What's Promising," *National Institute of Justice: Research in Brief,* July 1998, www .ncjrs.gov/pdffiles/171676.pdf.

46. Jason Riley, "Many on Shock Probation in Jefferson Rearrested," *Louisville Courier-Journal,* December 23, 2007.

47. Edward J. Latessa and Paula Smith, *Corrections in the Community* (Burlington, MA: Anderson, 2011).

48. Billie S. Erwin and Lawrence A. Bennett, *New Dimensions in Probation: Georgia's Experience with Intensive Probation Supervision* (Washington, DC: U.S. Department of Justice, National Institute of Justice, 1987).

49. Joan Petersilia and Susan Turner, *Evaluating Intensive Supervision Probation/Parole: Results of a Nationwide Experiment* (Washington, DC: U.S. Department of Justice, Office of Justice Programs, National Institute of Justice, 1993), 1–10.

50. See also Kelly L. Brown, "Effects of Supervision Philosophy on Intensive Probations," *Justice Policy Journal* 4 (Spring 2007).

51. Joan Petersilia, Susan Turner, James Kahan, and Joyce Peterson, *Granting Felons Probation: Public Risk and Alternatives* (Santa Monica, CA: Rand, 1985).

52. Lauren E. Glaze and Thomas B. Bonczar, *Probation and Parole in the United States, 2010,* November 2011, www.bjs.gov/content/pub/pdf /ppus10.pdf.

53. Ibid.

54. Johnny McGaha, Michael Fichter, and Peter Hirschburg, "Felony Probation: A Re-examination of Public Risk," *American Journal of Criminal Justice* 11 (1987): 1–9.

55. Joan Petersilia, "Probation in the United States: Practices and Challenges," *National Institute of Justice Journal* (September 1997): 2–8.

56. For example, see Kirk M. Broome, Kevin Knight, Matthew L. Hiller, and D. Dwayne Simpson, "Drug Treatment Process Indicators for Probationers and Prediction of Recidivism," *Journal of Substance Abuse Treatment* 13 (1996): 487–91; Shelley Johnson Listwan, Francis T. Cullen, and Edward J. Latessa, "How to Prevent Prisoner Re-entry Programs from Failing: Insights from Evidence-Based Corrections," *Federal Probation* 70, no. 3 (December 2006); and John L. Worrall, Pamela Schram, Eric Hays, and Matthew Newman, "An Analysis of the Relationship Between Probation Caseloads and Property Crime Rates in California Counties," *Journal of Criminal Justice* 32 (2004).

57. Vincent O'Leary and Kathleen J. Hanrahan, *Parole Systems in the United States* (Hackensack, NJ: National Council on Crime and Delinquency, 1976). For more updated results, see also Joan Petersilia, *When Prisoners Come Home: Parole and Prisoner Reentry (Studies in Crime and Public Policy)* (Cary, NC: Oxford University Press, 2003); and William Parker, *Parole: Origins, Development, Current Practices and Statutes* (College Park, MD: American Correctional Association, 1975).

58. Ibid.

59. G. I. Giardini, *The Parole Process* (Springfield, IL: Thomas, 1959), 9.

60. National Advisory Commission on Criminal Justice Standards and Goals, *Corrections: Report of the National Advisory Commission on Criminal Justice Standards and Goals, 1973* (Washington, DC: U.S. Government Printing Office, 1973), 399.

61. Petersilia, *When Prisoners Come Home;* Parker, *Parole: Origins, Development, Current Practices and Statutes;* O'Leary and Hanrahan, *Parole Systems in the United States.*

62. National Advisory Commission on Criminal Justice Standards and Goals, *Corrections,* 399.

63. Petersilia, *When Prisoners Come Home;* Parker, *Parole: Origins, Development, Current Practices and Statutes;* O'Leary and Hanrahan, *Parole Systems in the United States.*

64. Menechino v. Oswald, 430 F.2d 403 (1970).

65. United States ex rel. Johnson v. Chairman, New York State Board of Parole, 500 F.2d 925 (1974).

66. Greenholtz v. Inmates of Nebraska Penal and Correctional Complex, 422 U.S. 1 (1979).

67. Pennsylvania Board of Probation and Parole v. Scott, 524 U.S. 357 (1998).

68. See, for example, Tennessee Code Annotated, Section 40-3614.

69. James A. Inciardi and Duane C. McBride, "The Parole Prediction Myth," *International Journal of Criminology and Penology* 5 (August 1977): 235–44; Peter P. Lejins, "Parole Prediction: An Introductory Statement," *Crime & Delinquency* 8 (July 1962): 209–14.

70. Stephen D. Gottfredson and Laura J. Moriarty, "Statistical Risk Assessment: Old Problems and New Applications," *Crime & Delinquency* 52 (January 2006): 178–200; U.S. General Accounting Office, *Federal Offenders: Trends in Community Supervision* (Washington, DC: U.S. Government Printing Office, 1997); Peter B. Hoffman, "Twenty Years of Operational Use of a Risk Prediction Instrument," *Journal of Criminal Justice* 22 (1994): 447–94. See also John S. Carroll and Pamela A. Burke, "Evaluation and Prediction in Expert Parole Decisions," Criminal Justice and Behavior 17, no. 3 (September 1990); and J. Stephen Wormith, Hugh E. Stevenson, Mark E. Olver, and Lina Girard, "The Long-Term Prediction of Offender Recidivism Using Diagnostic, Personality, and Risk/Need Approaches to Offender Assessment," *Psychological Services* 4, no. 4 (2007).

71. "Good Time," *Corrections Compendium* (July 1997): 4–15.

72. Morrissey v. Brewer, 408 U.S. 471 (1972).

73. Ohio Administrative Code, Section 5120:1-1-13.

74. Sobell v. Reed, 327 F. Supp. 1294 (1971).

75. Glaze and Bonczar, *Probation and Parole in the United States, 2010.*

76. Ibid.

77. Ibid.

78. Glaze and Bonczar, *Probation and Parole in the United States, 2010.*

79. Jeremy Travis and Sarah Lawrence, *Beyond the Prison Gates: The State of Parole in America* (Washington, DC: Urban Institute, 2002); Glaze and Bonczar, *Probation and Parole in the United States, 2010.*

80. See J. M. Byrne and F. Taxman *Emerging Roles and Responsibilities in the Reentry Partnership Initiative: New Ways of Doing Business,* September 16, 2002, http://www.ncjrs.gov/pdffiles1/nij/grants/196441.pdf; and J. Travis, A. Solomon, and M. Waul, *From Prison to Home: The Dimensions and Consequences of Prisoner Reentry,* June 2001, http://www.urban.org/pdfs/from_prison_to_home.pdf.

81. Richard P. Seiter and Karen R. Kadela, "Prisoner Reentry: What Works, What Does Not, and What Is Promising," *Crime & Delinquency* 49 (July 2003): 360–88.

82. Marc Mauer, *Invisible Punishment: Block Housing, Education, Voting,* May/June 2003, http://www.sentencingproject.org/doc/publications/cc_mauer-focus.pdf.

83. Joan Petersilia, "Prisoner Reentry: Public Safety and Reintegration Challenges," *Prison Journal* 81 (2001): 360–75.

84. Suffolk University, College of Arts & Sciences, Center for Restorative Justice, *What Is Restorative Justice?*

http://www.suffolk.edu/research/6953.html.

85. Ibid.

86. Tom Cavanaugh, *The Paintball Case: A Restorative Justice Case Study,* http://cms.skidmore.edu/campusrj/upload/CaseStudyPaintball.pdf.

87. Susan Miller, *After the Crime: The Power of Restorative Justice Dialogues between Victims and Violent Offenders* (New York: New York University Press, 2001).

88. Gerry Johnstone and Daniel Van Ness, *Handbook of Restorative Justice* (Portland, OR: Willan, 2011).

89. Ibid.

90. Lawrence W. Sherman and Heather Strang, *Restorative Justice: The Evidence,* http://www.sas.upenn.edu/jerrylee/RJ_full_report.pdf.

91. Seiter and Kadela, "Prisoner Reentry," 360–88.

92. Richard P. Seiter, *Halfway Houses: National Evaluation Program* (Washington, DC: U.S. Government Printing Office, 1977).

93. Andrew von Hirsch and Kathleen J. Hanrahan, *Abolish Parole?* (Washington, DC: U.S. Government Printing Office, 1978), 1. See also Amy L. Solomon, Vera Kachnowski, and Avinash Bhati, "Does Parole Work? Analyzing the Impact of Postprison Supervision on Rearrest Outcomes," March 2005, http://www.urban.org/UploadedPDF/311156_Does_Parole_Work.pdf.

94. John J. Dilulio, "Reinventing Parole and Probation," *Brookings Review* (Spring 1997): 1–3; Peggy Burke, *Abolishing Parole: Why the Emperor Has No Clothes* (Philadelphia: Center

for Effective Public Policy, 1995); Belinda Rodgers McCarthy, Bernard J. McCarthy Jr., and Matthew C. Leone, *Community Corrections,* 4th ed. (Independence, KY: Wadsworth, 2001); Elmer H. Johnson and Kenneth E. Kotch, "Two Factors in Development of Work Release: Size and Location of Prisons," *Journal of Criminal Justice* 1 (March 1973): 44–45.

95. Petersilia, "Prisoner Reentry, 360–75.

96. Carol Van Ryswyk, Margaret Churchill, Joan Velasquez, and Richard McGuire, "Effectiveness of Halfway House Placement for Alcohol and Drug Abusers," *American Journal of Drug and Alcohol Abuse* 8, no. 4 (1981): 499–512; Josh Sweigart, "Study: Halfway House Ineffective," March 20, 2010, http://www.journal-news.com/news/hamilton-news/study-halfway-house-ineffective-611025.html; Seiter, *Halfway Houses.*

97. Daniel Glaser, James A. Inciardi, and Dean V. Babst, "Later Heroin Use by Marijuana-Using, Heroin-Using, and Non-Drug-Using Adolescent Offenders in New York City," *International Journal of the Addictions* 4 (June 1969): 145–55. See also *Journal of Offender Rehabilitation* 43, 4 (2008): 1–131; and Melissa Sickmund, *Juveniles in Corrections,* June 2004, http://www.ncjrs.gov/pdffiles1/ojjdp/202885.pdf.

98. Lauren E. Glaze, *Correctional Populations in the United States, 2009,* December 2010, http://bjs.ojp.usdoj.gov/content/pub/pdf/cpus09.pdf.

99. Glaze and Bonczar, *Probation and Parole in the United States, 2010.*

Glossary

abettor A person who, with the requisite criminal intent, encourages, promotes, instigates, or stands ready to assist the perpetrator of a crime.

accessory after the fact A person who, knowing that a felony has been committed, receives, believes, comforts, or assists the felon to hinder apprehension or conviction.

accessory before the fact A person who abets a crime but is not present when the crime was committed.

administrative law A branch of public law that deals with the powers and duties of government agencies.

adversarial system A system of justice in which the accused is presumed innocent and the burden of proof is placed on the court or state.

allocution A procedure that allows (1) the court to identify the defendant as the person judged guilty and (2) the defendant to plead for mercy or a pardon, move for an arrest of judgment, or indicate why judgment ought not be pronounced.

appeal A party's request for review of a sentence by a higher court.

arrest The action of taking a person into custody for the purpose of charging him or her with a crime.

arson The willful or malicious burning or attempt to burn, with or without intent to defraud, any dwelling, other building, vehicle, or personal property.

assault An intentional attempt or threat to physically injure another person.

assault and battery An assault that inflicts some violence on the victim.

bail A form of security, typically financial, set by the court to guarantee that a defendant in a criminal proceeding will appear and be present in court at all required times.

Bill of Rights The first ten amendments to the Constitution of the United States.

booking The administrative steps and procedures carried out by the police in order to record an arrest properly and officially.

breaking and entering The forcible entry into a building or structure with the intent to commit a felony.

Burger Court The Supreme Court under the leadership of Chief Justice Warren Burger, from 1969 to 1986.

Carroll doctrine The ruling, from the Supreme Court's decision in *Carroll v. United States,* that warrantless searches of vehicles are permissible where reasonable suspicion of illegal actions exists.

case fixing An illegal practice in which law enforcement officials alter the outcome of cases by, for example, reducing or dismissing charges or exchanging release for information.

case law Law that results from court interpretations of statutory law or from court decisions regarding rules that have not been fully codified or have been found to be vague or in error.

Cesare Beccaria The founder of the classical school of criminology and criminal law.

civil disability laws Laws that remove rights from individuals convicted of criminal offenses.

civilian review boards Appointed groups of citizens that oversee police behavior and review cases of misconduct.

civil law The body of principles that determines private rights and liabilities.

classical school of criminology and criminal law A body of ideals from Enlightenment philosophers and reformers for transforming criminal law and procedure.

classification The process through which the educational, vocational, treatment, and custodial needs of the offender are determined.

clearance rate The proportion of crimes that result in arrest.

common law Customs, traditions, judicial decisions, and other materials that guide courts in decision-making but that have not been enacted by the legislatures into statutes or are embodied in the Constitution.

community-based corrections Rehabilitative activities and programs for criminal offenders that are delivered within the community.

community policing A collaborative effort between the police and the community to identify the problems of crime and disorder and to develop solutions.

confession A statement by a person admitting to the violation of a law.

conspiracy Concert (collaboration) in criminal purpose that involves two or more people.

constitutional law The law set forth in the Constitution of the United States and in the constitutions of the various states.

contraband Any item that can be used to break a rule of the institution or assist in escape.

corporal punishment Punishment applied to the body, such as whipping or branding.

courts of appellate jurisdiction Courts that are limited in their jurisdiction to matters of appeal and review from lower courts and trial courts; also known as *appeals courts.*

courts of general jurisdiction The major trial courts that have the power and authority to try and decide any case, including appeals from a lower court.

courts of limited jurisdiction Courts that try minor offenses, such as traffic infractions and misdemeanors; also known as *lower courts.*

courts of record Courts in which a full transcript of the proceedings is made for all cases.

crime An intentional act or omission in violation of criminal law committed without defense or justification and sanctioned by the state as a felony or misdemeanor.

crime control model The model of the criminal justice system that views the repression of criminal conduct as its most important function.

crime rate A number determined by taking the total number of crime incidents in a given area, dividing that number by the total population, and multiplying that number by 100,000.

criminal intent A person's awareness of what is right and wrong under the law combined with the intention to violate the law; also known as *mens rea*.

criminal justice The structure, functions, and decision processes of those agencies that deal with the responses to crime and criminals—the police, the courts, and corrections.

criminal justice process All the agencies and procedures set up to manage both crime and those accused of violating the criminal law.

criminal law The branch of jurisprudence that deals with offenses committed against the safety and order of the state.

criminal procedure The series of orderly steps and actions, authorized by law or the courts, used to determine whether a person accused of a crime is guilty or not guilty.

criminology The scientific study of the nature and causes of crime, rates of crime, the punishment and rehabilitation of offenders, and the prevention of crime.

defense Any number of situations that excuse or mitigate guilt in a criminal offense.

definite sentence A fixed period of time to be served with no reduction by parole.

deliberation Full and conscious knowledge of the purpose of killing, suggesting that the offender has considered the motives for the act and its consequences.

determinate sentence A sentence with no set minimum or maximum but rather a fixed period; also known as a *flat, fixed,* or *straight sentence.*

deterrence The prevention of criminal acts by making examples of individuals convicted of crimes.

deviance Conduct that the people of a group consider so dangerous, embarrassing, or irritating that they bring special sanctions to bear against the persons who exhibit it.

diversion The removal of offenders from the criminal justice process at any stage of the police or court processes.

domestic violence A form of violent personal crime; activities of a physically aggressive nature occurring as a result of conflicts between members of a family, current or former spouses or lovers, or others in close relationships.

double jeopardy The repeated prosecution of an accused person for one particular offense; prohibited by the Fifth Amendment of the Constitution.

dual court system A system like that in the United States, with courts at both the state and federal levels.

due process model The model of the criminal justice system that stresses the possibility of error in the stages leading to trial; emphasizes procedural rights over system efficiency.

due process of law A concept that asserts fundamental principles of justice and implies the administration of laws that do not violate the sacredness of private rights.

duress Refers to any unlawful constraints exercised on an individual that force him or her to consent to committing some act that he or she would not otherwise have done.

Durham Rule The legal standard by which an accused is not held criminally responsible if he or she suffers from a diseased or defective mental condition at the time the unlawful act is committed.

entrapment The inducement of an individual to commit a crime that he or she did not previously contemplate, undertaken for the sole purpose of instituting a criminal prosecution against the person.

evidence Any type of proof, including witnesses, records, documents, concrete objects, and circumstances.

exclusionary rule A remedy and rule established by the Supreme Court that prohibits the use of evidence seized by law enforcement officials in violation of the Fourth Amendment protection against unreasonable search and seizure.

felony A crime punishable by death or imprisonment in a federal or state prison.

felony-murder doctrine The principle that any death resulting from the commission of, or attempt to commit, the crimes of arson, burglary, larceny, rape, or robbery is to be considered murder.

fruit of the poisonous tree A doctrine establishing that evidence seized as an

outgrowth of an unlawful arrest may be ruled inadmissible.

full enforcement The goal of investigating every disturbing event and every complaint and vigorously enforcing every statute.

funnel model A model based on findings from the President's Crime Commission that showed that despite the fact that many offenses were reported to the police, few offenders are ultimately incarcerated.

furlough An authorized, unescorted absence from a correctional institution for a specified period.

good time The number of days deducted from a sentence for good behavior, meritorious service, particular kinds of work, or other considerations.

grand jury A jury that consists of 12 to 23 jurors, whose purposes are to investigate crimes and protect citizens from unfair accusations.

guilty A plea that serves as an admission of guilt and a surrender of constitutional rights, including the right to remain silent.

hands-off doctrine The refusal of the courts to hear inmate complaints about the conditions of incarceration and the constitutional deprivations of institutional correctional life.

hate crime An offense motivated by hatred against a victim because of his or her race, ethnicity, religion, sexual orientation, handicap, national origin, or tribal membership.

homicide The killing of one human being by another.

incapacitation A sentencing philosophy seeking to remove the offender from society.

indeterminate sentence A sentence with a fixed minimum and a fixed maximum term for incarceration rather than a definite period.

indictment A formal charging document issued by a grand jury on the basis of evidence presented to it by the prosecutor.

information A document filed by the prosecutor that states the formal charges, the statutes that have been violated, and the evidence supporting the charges.

injunctive relief A court order, emanating from a habeas corpus action, directing prison officials to improve conditions or to stop enforcing unlawful policies.

inmate code The unwritten rules of the prison subculture, which, if violated, can result in sanctions ranging from ostracism to death.

inquiry system A system of justice in which all the participants—judge, prosecutor, defense attorney, defendant, and witnesses—are obliged to cooperate with the court in its inquiry into a crime.

inquisitorial system A system in which the accused person was considered guilty until proven innocent; only divine intervention or an admission of guilt could spare the accused from pain, suffering, or death, usually after torture or other forms of corporal punishment.

insanity A legal concept, not a medical one; a condition in which any unsoundness of mind, madness, mental alienation, or want of reason, memory, or intelligence prevents an individual from comprehending the nature and consequences of his or her acts or from distinguishing between right and wrong conduct.

intensive probation supervision (IPS) A program of close surveillance and exhaustive services that places a probationer under tighter control than he or she might experience under regular probation.

intermediate sanctions Penalties falling between the extremes of fines and imprisonment.

jails Local facilities for temporary detention.

judicial circuit A specific jurisdiction served by a judge or court, as defined by given geographical boundaries.

justice of the peace The judge in many lower courts in rural areas; typically not a lawyer and typically appointed rather than elected.

justification Any just cause or excuse for the commission of an act that would otherwise be a crime.

kickbacks The profits that police officers gain by referring or directing individuals to persons or businesses for assistance.

law and order A political ideology and slogan that sought a return to the morality and values of earlier times and rejected the growing permissiveness in government and social affairs.

Law Enforcement Assistance Administration (LEAA) A federal bureaucracy created to involve the national government in local crime control by supplying funds to the states for training and upgrading criminal justice agencies.

lockdown A situation in which inmates are confined to their cells around the clock and denied exercise, work, recreation, and visits.

malice aforethought The intent to cause death or serious harm or to commit any felony whatsoever.

mandatory release A release from prison required by statute when an inmate has been confined for a time period equal to his or her full prison sentence minus statutory "good time," if any.

mandatory sentence A sentence based on penal code provisions that require the judge or jury to apply prison terms of a specified length to individuals convicted of certain crimes.

manslaughter A category of criminal homicide, typically charged when a killing occurs under circumstances that are not severe enough to constitute murder yet are beyond the defenses of justifiable or excusable homicide.

maximum-security prisons Correctional institutions designed to hold the most aggressive and incorrigible offenders.

misdemeanor A crime punishable by no more than a $1,000 fine and/or one year of imprisonment, typically in a local correctional institution.

mistrial The discharge of a jury without a verdict.

M'Naghten Rule The "right-or-wrong" test of criminal responsibility used by some states for determining criminal liability of offenders; based on whether offenders understood the nature and quality of their actions.

motion A formal application or request to the court for some action, such as an order or rule.

murder The felonious killing of another human being with malice aforethought.

mutual pledge Alfred the Great's system of organizing the country around family groupings that assumed responsibility for the acts of their members.

natural law General principles that determine what is right and wrong according to some higher power.

nolo contendere A plea that means literally "no contest," or more specifically, "I will not contest it"; essentially a guilty plea.

not guilty The most common plea; places the full burden on the state to prove the charges beyond a reasonable doubt.

not guilty by reason of insanity An admission of guilt accompanied by the claim that the defendant is not culpable in the eyes of the law because of insanity at the time he or she committed the crime.

omission Failure to perform an act that is legally required.

open institutions Minimum-security correctional camps, farms, ranches, vocational training centers, and forestry settlements; also known as *prisons without walls.*

organized crime Business activities directed toward economic gain through unlawful means.

parole A condition of release from a correctional institution in which one has served a part of his or her maximum sentence, requiring the offender to maintain good behavior and remain in the custody and under the guidance of the institution or some other agency approved by the state until a final discharge is granted.

patrol A means of deploying police officers that gives them responsibility for a defined area and that usually requires them to make regular circuits of that area.

patronage A system of making governmental appointments in such a way as to increase one's political strength.

plain view doctrine The doctrine that when a police officer has a right to be where he or she is, anything he or she sees in plain view is admissible as evidence.

police brutality Unwarranted or excessive use of physical force and verbal assaults by a police officer.

police corruption Misconduct in the form of illegal activities for economic gain, including accepting gratuities, favors, or payment for services that police are sworn to carry out as part of their peacekeeping role.

police cynicism The notion held by some officers that all people are motivated by evil and selfishness.

police discretion Decision-making that is guided by departmental policies, as well as laws, norms, and standards in the field of criminal justice, and that is responsive to the diverse circumstances that officers and agencies encounter.

police integrity The exercise of powers and use of discretion according to the highest standards of competence, fairness, and honesty.

police professionalism The notion that policing is a profession in which individuals adhere to high standards for law enforcement conduct within the community.

police subculture The values and behavior patterns characteristic of experienced police officers.

posse comitatus Latin: meaning "power of the country"; a historical law enforcement concept in which all the able-bodied men in a county were at the absolute disposal of a sheriff and required to respond when called on to do so.

premeditation A design or plan to do something; a conscious decision to commit an offense.

presentence investigation An investigation into the background and character of a defendant that assists the court in determining the most appropriate sentence.

President's Commission on Law Enforcement and Administration of Justice A series of task forces appointed by President Lyndon B. Johnson to study crime and justice in the United States and to make recommendations for change.

prisons Correctional institutions maintained by federal and state governments for the confinement of convicted felons.

privatization of corrections The construction, staffing, and operation of prisons by private industry for profit.

probable cause Facts or apparent facts that are reliable and generate a reasonable belief that a crime has been committed.

probation A sentence not involving confinement that imposes conditions and retains authority in the sentencing court to modify the conditions of the sentence or to resentence the offender if he or she violates the conditions.

procedural due process Processes for ensuring the fundamental principles of justice and administering laws that protect individual rights.

protective sweep doctrine Allows law enforcement officers making an arrest on or outside private premises, despite the absence of a search warrant, to examine the entire premises for other persons whose presence would pose a threat either to the officers' safety or to the protection of evidence that could be removed or destroyed.

public order crimes A large collection of offenses, mostly misdemeanors, that disturb public order and safety.

reception center A central receiving institution where all felony offenders sentenced to a term of imprisonment are committed for orientation and classification.

rehabilitation A sentencing philosophy based on reintegrating the offender into society.

restitution A condition of probation requiring offenders to compensate their victims for damages or to donate their time in service to the community.

restorative justice Community correctional programs that emphasize repairing the harm done by the criminal offense; also known as *reparative justice* and *victim-offender reconciliation*.

retribution A sentencing philosophy based on creating an equal or proportionate relationship between the offense and the punishment.

robbery The felonious taking of money or goods from a victim's person, or in a victim's presence, and against his or her will, through the use or threat of force and violence.

search and seizure The detection and accusation of crime; includes the search for and the taking of persons and property as evidence of crime.

search warrant A written order, issued by a magistrate or judge and directed to a law enforcement officer, commanding the search of specified premises for stolen or unlawful goods or for suspects or fugitives and the bringing of these, if found, before a judge.

Section 1983 The section of the Civil Rights Act of 1871 used by state prisoners as a vehicle for gaining access to the federal courts to litigate inmate rights.

selective incorporation The individual application of most, but not all, of the provisions of the Bill of Rights as binding on the states.

self-reported crime Crime statistics compiled on the basis of self-reports by offenders.

sexual assault Any sexual contact with another person that occurs without the consent of the victim or is offensive to the victim.

shakedown A form of extortion in which police officers demand money from citizens in exchange for not enforcing the law.

shock probation Brief incarceration followed by suspension of sentence and probation.

solitary confinement The total separation of an inmate from the general prison population in a small, uncomfortable cell, combined with the revocation of all privileges within the institution.

speedy trial The Sixth Amendment guarantee that protects an accused from indefinite incarceration prior to trial.

status offenses Specific acts (truancy, running away) and general conditions (incorrigibility, uncontrollable behavior) that are unique to the status of being a juvenile.

statutory law The set of laws and statutes enacted by legislatures.

substantive due process A concept related to the content or subject matter of a law; protects people against unreasonable, arbitrary, or capricious laws or acts of government.

surety bond Money from a bail bond agent put up to secure a defendant's release.

suspended sentence A court disposition that allows a convicted person to defer or postpone (potentially indefinitely) a correctional sentence.

The Code The informal prohibition in the culture of policing against reporting the misconduct of other officers.

theft The broadest of terms relating to property offenses; the unlawful taking, possession, or use of another person's property without the use or threat of force and with the intent to deprive permanently.

thief-takers Private detectives who were paid by the Crown on a piecework basis.

total institution A place that erects barriers to social interchange with the world at large.

trial de novo A new trial, on appeal from a lower court to a court of general jurisdiction.

Uniform Crime Reports (UCR) Crime data compiled and published by the FBI using standardized forms completed by police departments.

U.S. courts of appeals The federal courts of appellate jurisdiction.

U.S. district courts The trial courts of the federal judiciary.

U.S. magistrates Federal lower-court officials whose powers are limited to trying lesser misdemeanors, setting bail, and assisting district courts in various legal matters.

U.S. Supreme Court The highest court in the nation and the court of last resort.

vengeance A sentencing philosophy based on seeking satisfaction from knowing or seeing that offenders are punished.

venire The writ that summons jurors; also referred to as *venire facias*.

vicarious liability Legal liability imposed on an employer for certain illegal acts committed by employees during the course and scope of their employment.

victim impact evidence A statement of the harm suffered by the victim or the victim's family as a result of the offender's action.

victimization surveys Surveys of the victims of crime based on interviews with representative samples of the household population.

vigilante An individual who takes the law into his or her own hands.

voir dire Meaning "to speak the truth"; the oath sworn by a prospective juror regarding his or her qualifications.

waiver of jurisdiction The process by which the juvenile court relinquishes its jurisdiction over a child and transfers the case to a court of criminal jurisdiction for prosecution as an adult.

Warren Court The Supreme Court under the leadership of Chief Justice Earl Warren, from 1953 to 1969.

wedding cake model A model demonstrating that very few of the cases that pass through the criminal justice system have characteristics of the celebrated ones portrayed in the media.

white-collar crime Offenses committed by persons acting in their legitimate occupational roles; also known as *corporate crime*.

working personality A personality attributed to police and characterized by authoritarianism, cynicism, and suspicion, developed in response to danger and the obligation to exercise authority.

writ of certiorari A writ issued by the Supreme Court ordering a lower court to "forward up the record" of a case it has tried so the High Court can review it.

writ of habeas corpus A formal written order that directs the person holding a prisoner to bring him or her before a judicial officer to determine the lawfulness of imprisonment.

Credits

Photo

Chapter 1 Opener: © Royalty-Free/Corbis; p. 4: © Hemis/Alamy; p. 5 (left): © CBS Photographer Lorenzo Aguis; p. 5 (right): © Bruce Glikas/FilmMagic/Getty Images; p. 7 (top): © Bettmann/Corbis; p. 7 (bottom): AP Photo/Bill Hudson; p. 8: © S. Meltzer/PhotoLink/Getty Images; p. 10: © Aaron Roeth Photography; p. 11: © Bettmann/Corbis; p. 14: © Design Pics/Steve Nagy; p. 15: © Brand X Pictures; p. 18 (left): © Monty a/CBS via Getty Images; p. 18 (right): © Mike Karlsson/Arresting Images; p. 19 (a): © Aaron Roeth Photography; p. 19 (b): © Jupiter Images/Brand X/Alamy; p. 19 (c): © The Star-Ledger/Ed Murray/The Image Works; p. 19 (d): © ZUMA Press/Newscom; p. 19 (e): © Andrea Morini/Digital Vision/Getty Images.

Chapter 2 Opener: © Tetra Images/Tetra Images/Corbis; p. 26: © Steven Senne/AP/Corbis; p. 28: © DeAgostini/Getty Images; p. 29: Agencia Estado via AP Images; p. 30: © Topical Press Agency/Getty Images; p. 31: © Aaron Roeth Photography; p. 32: © Alain Le Bot/Photononstop/Getty Images; p. 34: © Susan Wright/Alamy; p. 36: © Andy Holzman/La Daily News/ZUMA Press/Newscom; p. 37: © Dave Moyer; p. 38: AP Photo/Steve Ueckert; p. 40: © Dieter Spears/Getty Images; p. 41: © Mary Evans Picture Library/Alamy; p. 45: © Ingram Publishing; p. 47: © Royalty-Free/Corbis; p. 48: © Charley Gallay/Stringer/Getty Images; p. 49: © Mary Evans Picture Library/Alamy; p. 50: © Larry Kolvoord/The Image Works.

Chapter 3 Opener: © Monalyn Gracia/Corbis; p. 56: © John Larkin/Alamy; p. 59: AP Photo/Tampa Tribune, Stephen McKnight; p. 61: AP Photo/Nick Ut; p. 62: © Patrick Strattner/fstop/Corbis; p. 65: © Reuters/Corbis; p. 66: © Travelib India/Alamy; p. 67: © Mikael Karlsson/Arresting Images; p. 69: © Robin Nelson/PhotoEdit; p. 71: © Underwood & Underwood/Corbis; p. 72: © Lynsey Addario/VII Network/Corbis; p. 76: © Prince James/Photo Researchers, Inc.; p. 77: © Bob Daemmrich/

The Image Works; p. 78: AP Photo/The Daily Sentinel, Andrew D. Brosig; p. 79: © Scott Olson/Getty Images.

Chapter 4 Opener: © Image Source/Corbis; p. 86 (top): © Brendan Smialowski/Bloomberg via Getty Images; p. 86 (bottom): © Daniel Grill/Tetra Images/Corbis; p. 87: © SuperStock; p. 90: © Robin Nelson/ZUMA Press/Newscom; p. 93: © Bettmann/Corbis; p. 94: © Barton Silverman/NYT Picture Service/Redux Pictures; p. 96: © Richard Whelan/Demotix/Demotix/Corbis; p. 97: © Comstock Images/Getty Images; p. 98: © Alan Thornton/Getty Images; p. 102: © Bob Daemmrich/The Image Works; p. 103: © PNC/Getty Images; p. 105: © Mike Karlsson/Arresting Images; p. 107: AP Photo/Kelley McCall; p. 108: Courtesy of the New York State Library.

Chapter 5 Opener: © Don Farrall/Photodisc/Getty; p. 114: © Mario Tama/Getty Images; p. 115: © UpperCut Images/Getty Images; p. 116, p. 117: Culver Pictures; p. 119: AP Photo/Kingsport Times-News, Erica Yoon; p. 120: AP Photo/Susan Sterner; p. 121: © Mike Shipman/Alamy; p. 123: © Bruce Chambers/ZUMA Press/Corbis; p. 124: © J. Emilio Flores/Corbis; p. 126: © Richard Eaton/Demotix/Demotix/Corbis; p. 130: © Scott Olson/Getty Images; p. 131: © Lars A. Niki; p. 132: © Aaron Roeth Photography; p. 135 (left): © Dr. Isaac Van Patten, Radford University; p. 135 (right): © David R. Frazier Photolibrary, Inc.; p. 135 (computer screen): © Louise Murray/Visuals Unlimited, Inc.; p. 136: © Radius Images/Alamy; p. 138: AP Photo/Chuck Burton; p. 139: © Hill Street Studios/Blend Images/Getty Images; p. 140: © Janine Wiedel Photolibrary/Alamy.

Chapter 6 Opener: © Mikael Karlsson/Arresting Images; p. 146: © Wilmar/AGE Fotostock; p. 147: © Masterfile; p. 148: © HO/Reuters/Corbis; p. 150: © Mikael Karlsson; p. 151: © David R. Frazier Photolibrary, Inc.; p. 154: FEMA; p. 156: © Charlie Nye/Rapport Press/Newscom; p. 159: © Tim Gainey/Alamy; p. 160:

© Jeremy Woodhouse/Blend Images/Getty Images; p. 162: © Mario Villafuerte/Getty Images; p. 164: © Shout/Alamy; p. 167 (top): AP Photo; p. 167 (bottom): © Tony Cenicola/NYT Picture Service/Redux Pictures; p. 168: © Mikael Karlsson/Alamy; p. 169: © Don Farrall/Photographer's Choice/Getty Images.

Chapter 7 Opener (left): © Blend Images/Getty Images; Opener (right): © Ryan McGinnis/Alamy; p. 174: © Marla Rutherford/Corbis; p. 176: AP Photo/Birmingham Alabama Police Department; p. 177: © Sean Murphy/Photodisc/Getty Images; p. 178: © ZUMA Wire Service/Alamy; p. 179: AP Photo/Michael Dwyer; p. 180: © Des Willie/Redferns/Getty Images; p. 182: Courtesy of Commission on Accreditation for Law Enforcement Agencies (CALEA); p. 183: © Spencer Platt/Getty Images; p. 185: © Andrew Burton/Getty Images; p. 188: © ZUMA Wire Service/Alamy; p. 190: © Jim West/Alamy; p. 192: © Mario Tama/Getty Images.

Chapter 8 Opener: © Greg Lovett-Pool/Getty Images; p. 198 (left): AP Photo/Pool; p. 198 (right): © Vince Bucci/AFP/Getty Images; p. 199: © Lindsay Hebberd/Corbis; p. 202 (left): © Izzy Schwartz/Photodisc/Getty Images; p. 202 (right): © Guy Cali/Corbis; p. 205 (top): © Press-Register/Mike Kittrell; p. 205 (bottom): © Aaron Roeth Photography; p. 209 (left): AP Photo; p. 209 (right): © STR/AFP/Getty Images; p. 211 (left): © The McGraw-Hill Companies, Inc./Jill Braaten, photographer; p. 211 (right): © Jim Lo Scalzo/epa/Corbis; p. 215: © Royalty-Free/Corbis; p. 217: © Alliance Images/Alamy; p. 219: © Michael Newman/PhotoEdit; p. 220: © Brand X Pictures; p. 221, p. 223: © ZUMA Wire Service/Alamy; p. 225: AP Photo/Akron Beacon Journal, Ed Suba Jr.

Chapter 9 Opener: © David R. Frazier Photolibrary, Inc.; p. 230: AP Photo/Hinton; p. 234: © Ilene MacDonald/Alamy; p. 236: © Andrew Ross/AFP/Getty Images; p. 237: © Mikael Karlsson/Alamy; p. 238: © Everett Collection Inc/Alamy;

Text

Exhibit 2.2, p 29 Proportions of U.S. Population Reporting Crime or Poverty as the Most Important Problem Facing the Nation (percentages). Reproduced by permission of The McGraw-Hill Companies, Inc.

Ch. 2, p 33 M'Naghten Rule—the "right-or-wrong" test of criminal responsibility: Black, *Black's Law Dictionary*, 1101. Reproduced by permission of Thomson Reuters.

Ch. 3, p 80 J. Andenaes, N. Christie, and S. Skirbekk, "A Study in Self-Reported Crime," in *Scandinavian Studies in Criminology*, Scandinavian Research Council on Criminology (Oslo: Universitetsforlaget, 1965), 87–88. Reproduced by permission of Universitetsforlaget AS.

Exhibit 4.1, p 89 Reproduced by permission of Professor Ken Dautrich.

Exhibit 5.3, p 135 Reproduced by permission of Issac T. Van Patten.

Exhibit 8.1, p 199 State and Federal Court Structure. Inciardi, *Criminal Justice,* 9e, 266. Reproduced by permission of The McGraw-Hill Companies, Inc.

Exhibit 8.2, p 202 Typical Criminal Court Process. Inciardi, *Criminal Justice,* 9e, 274. Reproduced by permission of The McGraw-Hill Companies, Inc.

Exhibit 8.3, p 204 Federal Judiciary System, Inciardi, *Criminal Justice,* 9e, 276. Reproduced by permission of The McGraw-Hill Companies, Inc.

Exhibit 8.5, p 211 The Judicial Ladder to the Supreme Court, Inciardi, *Criminal Justice,* 9e, 283. Reproduced by permission of The McGraw-Hill Companies, Inc.

Exhibit 8.7, p 222 The Juvenile Justice System, Inciardi, *Criminal Justice,* 9e, 561. Reproduced by permission of The McGraw-Hill Companies, Inc.

Exhibit 9.2, p 241 The Selection Process for a 12-Person Jury, Inciardi, *Criminal Justice,* 9e, 353. Reproduced by permission of The McGraw-Hill Companies, Inc.

Exhibit 10.1, p 268 Executions Under State Authority, 1850s–1960s. Negley K. Teeters and Charles J. Zibulka, "Executions Under State Authority: 1864–1967," in *Executions in America,* edited by William J. Bowers (Lexington, MA: Heath, 1974). Reproduced by permission of William J. Bowers.

Exhibit 10.2, p 272 Reproduced by permission of the Death Penalty Information Center.

Exhibit 10.3, p 277 Reproduced by permission of the Death Penalty Information Center.

Exhibit 13.2, p 354 Reproduced by permission of the International Institute for Restorative Practices, www.iirp.edu.

Subject Index

Name Index

Case Index

What Can I Do With a Criminal Justice Major?

Areas of Employment	Potential Employers
Law Enforcement	
Patrol Investigations Forensics Probation and Parole Security Crime analysis	Local Government Organizations Police departments Correctional facilities County sheriff departments Liquor Control Commission State Government Organizations State troopers Crime labs Penitentiaries Federal Government Organizations U.S. Customs and Border Protection Federal Bureau of Investigations (FBI) Internal Revenue Service (IRS) Drug Enforcement Agency (DEA) Central Intelligence Agency (CIA) Department of Homeland Security Postal Service Federal Marshals Wildlife, Fisheries, and Parks United States Department of Agriculture National Parks Service Crime laboratories Colleges and university police departments
Business	
Private Security Consulting Investigations System Investigation Private Investigation Internet Security Loss and Prevention	Insurance companies Banks Private security companies Software companies Hotels and resorts Health care facilities Transportation services Nuclear power plants Manufacturers Online companies
Social Services	
Corrections Counseling Juvenile Justice Casework Administration Probations & Parole Victim Advocacy	State and federal correctional facilities County jails Law enforcement organizations Probation/parole organizations Correctional facilities Halfway houses and pre-release programs Re-entry and reintegration programs Juvenile detention centers and group homes Women's and family shelters Domestic violence agencies Immigration and naturalization services
Judiciary and Law	
Court Reporting Legal Assistance Legal Research Administration Attorney Court Administrator	Local, state, and federal courts Law firms Corporate legal departments Public interest law organizations